FORTEAN TIMES 37-41
HEAVEN'S REPRIMANDS

How rats steal eggs. An engraving by Gustave Doré for *Fables of La Fontaine*. See FT40:5.

PREFACE

The five issues of *Fortean Times* in this book are reproduced facsimile, except for new running heads. Our thanks go to Steve Moore for compiling the contents lists. As before, these have been made as detailed as possible as compensation for the lack of a full index.

The book includes a major interview with the biologist Rupert Sheldrake about his book *A New Science of Life* and his idea of formative causation – that nature is habit-forming rather than rule-bound. As we prepare this volume for the printer, the controversy over Sheldrake's visionary ideas continues a decade later, stoked by his latest provocative book *Seven Experiments that could Change the World*.

In this period, we were still producing *Fortean Times* as an unpaid hobby (Bob and I were working as layout artists on the revised British Library Catalogue). We continued to receive invaluable help from the other members of the informal Gang of Fort – Richard Adams, Hunt Emerson, Ion Will and Steve Moore – who were joined by Mike Dash in the summer of 1983. The magazine was becoming better known and more established, and we were able to call upon a widening variety of talent – both academic and oddball – as these issues demonstrate.

Contributors included George Andrews, Larry Arnold, Janet and Colin Bord, Peter Christie, Jerome Clark, Loren Coleman, Peter Costello, Hilary Evans, David Fideler, Di Francis, Rex Gilroy, Bernard Heuvelmans, Michael Hoffman, Robert Barbour Johnson, Peter Jordan, John Keel, Kevin McClure, John Michell, Nigel Pennick, Michael Persinger, Paul Pinn, Don Robbins, Mike Rowe, Leslie Shepard, Doc Shiels, Bob Tarte, Nigel Watson, Ron Westrum and Robert Anton Wilson.

A word about this volume's title, 'Heaven's Reprimands'. For the ancient Chinese, unusual events were seen as portents with a moralistic purpose. If the emperor's reign was peaceful and thriving, the portents would be good; if not, Heaven would first send warnings, then reprimands. Alas, a good many of the Fortean phenomena chronicled here seem more like reprimands than portents of peace.

Paul Sieveking
March 1994

FORTEAN TIMES 37-41 (1982-1983)

CONTENTS

FORTEAN TIMES 37 - Spring 1982

Whetnall) - *The Unfathomed Mind* (Corliss) - *The Natural History of the Mind* (Taylor)
- *Search for the Tasmanian Tiger* (Beresford & Bailey) - *The Tasmanian Tiger* (Smith) -
Savage Shadow (O'Reilly) - *Mythical Monsters* (Gould) - *The Subterranean Kingdom*
(Pennick) - *The Lost World of Agharti* (Maclellan) - *Hollow Earth Mysteries* (Benton) -
Hitler's Secret Sciences (Pennick) - *Megalithomania* (Michell) - *Earth Rites* (Bord &
Bord) - *Velikovsky's Sources* (Forrest) - *Trance and Subjectivity + Jazz* (Reissig) - *An
Investigative Report into the Alleged Alien Body Photos* (Ohio UFO Investigators
League).

FORTEAN TIMES 38 - Autumn 1982

FORTEAN TIMES 39 - Spring 1983

FORTEAN TIMES 40 - Summer 1983

FORTEAN TIMES 41 - Winter 1983

TENTH ANNIVERSARY ISSUE

Fortean Times

ISSUE No. 37 | The Journal of Strange Phenomena. | PRICE: £1·25 $3·00

Rupert Sheldrake

A New Science of Life

A NEW SCIENCE OF LIFE

Dr. RUPERT SHELDRAKE ON EVOLUTION/MUTATION/MEMORY/LAMARCKIAN INHERITANCE/SOUL/POMPOUS PROFS/REINCARNATION/TELEPATHY/ANGELS/ MONSTERS/POLTERGEISTS/CASTANEDA/THOUGHTFORMS/SYNCHRONICITY/ KARMA/PSYCHOKINESIS/& GOD.

Fortean Times

BM-Fortean Times
London WC1N 3XX.

The Journal of Strange Phenomena.

Spring 1982
ISSN 0308.5899

EDITORIAL TEAM

Editor Robert J.M. Rickard
David Fideler
Steve Moore
Paul R.A. deG Sieveking
Art Dir. Richard Adams
ComixEd. Hunt Emerson

SPECIAL CORRESPONDENTS

Australia Greg Axford (Vic)
Paul Cropper (NSW)
Rex Gilroy (NSW)
Tony Healy (ACT)
Richard King (Vic)
Belgium Henri Premont
Canada Dwight Whalen (Ont)
Mister X (Ont)
England Richard Cotton
Peter Christie
Peter Hope Evans
Alan Gardiner
Chris Hall
Valerie Martin
John Michell
Nigel Pennick
Paul Screeton
Anthony Smith
David Sutton
Andy Townsend
Paul R. Thomas
Finland Tuuri Heporauta
France Dr Bernard Heuvelmans
Ireland Doc Shiels
Japan Jun-Ichi Takanashi
Malaysia Ahmad Jamaludin
Dr C.H. Yeang
Roving Ion A Will
Scotland Roland Watson
Jake Williams
S. Africa Chris J. Holtzhausen
Sweden Ake Franzen
Anders Liljegren
Sven Rosen
USA Larry E. Arnold (PA)
Tom Adams (TX)
Loren Coleman (MA)
Richard T Crowe (IL)
Ron Dobbins (AZ)
Mark A Hall (MN)
Steve Hicks (KS)
Michael Hoffman (NY)
Phil Ledger (CN)
Kurt Lothmann (TX)
Gary S Mangiacopra (CN)
Joseph Swatek (NB)
Paul Willis (MD)
Joseph W Zarzynski (NY)
Wales Janet & Colin Bord
Yugoslavia Milos Krmelj

Represetting Mostly by Cecelia Boggis:
11 Ashburnham Rd, Bedford.
Photosetting Wordsmiths: 19 West End,
Street, Somerset.
Printed by Golden Valley Publications
Piccadilly Mill Lower St.,
Stroud, Glos.

Overseas Overseas Postal Services Ltd,
Mailing 2-8 Hornsey St,
London N7 8HF
Sub Labels Anagram
316A Richmond Rd,
Twickenham TW1 2PD

Cover art by
Richard Adams

ARTICLES

COMIX

USUAL STUFF

TICK
TICKA TICKA
TACK TOCK
TACKA

NEW PRICES – NEW DEAL

Some readers, fed up with our regular carping about our financial insecurity, begged us to consider putting up the issue price. We have resisted the idea for a long time because: a) as a legacy of the time we explored the idea of a commercial newsstand version of FT we were led to believe that there was a ceiling price (£1) beyond which readers would be driven away; and b) we felt somewhat guilty about asking people for more. Our last price rise was in summer 1980 (FT32), and since then events have overtaken us. We can no longer absorb all the increases in the cost of labour, materials and services. It was quite unfair to entrust FT's future solely to the good will of donors (God bless 'em), while our own altruism was beginning to endanger that future. So we took a realistic look at our costings in the knowledge that subscriptions might hover around the 1000 mark for some time yet. The result is that **from this issue FT will cost £1.25, (i.e. £5.00 for four issues) or $3.00 per issue**, and the subscriptions pro-rata depending on how many you want.

We changed our minds about the magic ceiling of £1 because it was based on commercial distribution and could not be applied strictly to the world of small subscription-based periodicals. Besides, the reknowned *FSR* broke the barrier some time ago, and is now £1.15 an issue. Another reason is that FT is unique, and to judge from your supportive letters, much valued, and therefore worth its price. We felt that the great majority of our readers would not baulk at this slight increase if it meant the continuance of FT to the standard we have achieved and worked hard for.

We at FT wanted to offset this increase with some practical benefit to our faithful readers, to sugar the pill, if you like. Firstly, we've increased our regular pagination from 56 to 60 pages – more value than ever compared to most other publications at the same price.

Secondly, we have found a way to get FT to most countries in the world in about two weeks, instead of up to eight or more by the old method. The slight price rise apart, the new service will cost our foreign readers NOTHING. That's right, we can now offer airmail service at surface postal rates. But because this special deal only applies to bulk mailing of

FT, the cost of individual issues or special packets (like gift subs or backissue orders) will have to remain at the old rates. The slight difference between the UK and US prices, allows for a variable exchange rate, a banking commission on foreign cheques, and surface post rates (which are higher than domestic rates).

THIS ISSUE & NEXT

The usual limit for an article in FT is about 5-6 pages, but our lead feature – an expanded interview with botantist/philosopher Rupert Sheldrake – well exceeds this. The interview with him was long enough and explores the genesis and implications of his radical new ideas on the origins of forms in nature, and the interesting, almost Fortean, conclusion that the so-called 'laws' of nature behave more like habits (or acquired patterns of behaviour) on a cosmic scale than fixed or eternal patterns. We have supplemented this with an introduction and examples, and feel the importance of this new theory warranted the extra space.

However this expansion is not without casualties. Our apologies go to Peter Jordan – whose paper on psychometric research into cattle mutilation has been deferred twice and which will now have pride of place next issue – and the authors of other delayed contributions.

Other features of this issue are: a report on giant monitor lizards (the first of many reports from Australian Fortean Rex Gilroy, whose interests range from cryptozoology to the Earth Mysteries of Oz; FT associate editor Steve Moore wondering aloud if the stories of encounters between ancient Greeks and their gods have any relevance for today's CE4 re-
Cont on p 65

FORTEAN TIMES is an occasional journal, intended to be quarterly, of news, notes, reviews and references on all manner of strange phenomena and related subjects and philosophies, continuing the work of Charles Fort (1874-1932). The views of contributors are not necessarily those of FT and vice versa. Published from BM–FORTEAN TIMES, LONDON WC1N 3XX, ENGLAND. **SUBSCRIPTION INFO:** see index for page. **RIGHTS:** all articles and art are the copyright of the authors and artists – everything else in this issue is copyrighted throughout the universe by FT. Uncredited material is by the editors. **SUBMISSION** is invited of articles, art, cartoons and news clippings. FT assumes no responsibility for submissions, but all reasonable care will be taken while in FT's possession. **ADVERTISING** and **SALES:** enquiries to the above address, or ring the editor on 01 552 5466.

Letters of comment, personal experience or information, related to the contents and interests of FT, are invited and should not be more than 500 words. If replies are required, please include an SAE or reply coupon. We regret we cannot guarantee to reply, or reply promptly.

CLOUD OF MYSTERY

Whether or not your readers believe there is any substance to the 'Philadelphia Experiment', they will surely find food for thought and possibly for their belief or disbelief, in a curious parallel with an event which occurred in July 1904, reprinted in *Fate* for July 1963 [reprinted below], well before the Carlos Allende legend had begun to take its place in the mythology of our time. Was this incident the basis for the Allende incident, or is it a separate case which thereby lends substance to Allende's claims?

Hilary Evans
London.

PARALYZED BY A MAGNETIC CLOUD
By Jeanne Booth Johnson

AN INTERESTING "Fortean" item was reported in "Shipping News," a chatty column which appeared around the turn of the century in *The Maui News*, published on the island of Maui, Hawaii. The item, originating in Philadelphia, apparently reached the islands by cable, and was not identified with any newspaper or other Philadelphia source. It appeared in the August 13, 1904, issue of *The Maui News*.

"PHILADELPHIA, July 31— When the British steamship Mohican, Captain Urquhart, from Ibraila, Roumania, which was in this port today, was making for Delaware Breakwater, it had a most remarkable experience which terrorized the crew, played havoc with the ship's compass, and brought the vessel to a standstill for a half-hour.

"For that length of time the Mohican was enshrouded in a strange vapor, which glowed like phosphorous. The entire vessel looked as if it were on fire and the sailors flitted about the deck like glowing phantoms. The cloud had a strange magnetic effect on the vessel, for the needle of the compass revolved with the speed of an electric motor and the sailors were unable to raise pieces of steel from the magnetized decks. The captain says:

"'The seamen were in terror. Their hair stood straight on end, not from fright so much as from the magnetic power of the cloud. They rushed about the deck in consternation and the more they rushed about the more excited they became. I tried to calm them, but the situation was beyond me.

"'For a half-hour we were enveloped in that mysterious vapor. Suddenly the cloud began to lift. The phosphorescent glow of the ship began to fade. It gradually died away and in a few minutes the cloud passed and we saw it moving off to sea.'"

MORE WHALE TUMOURS

Having read Colin Bord's letter in FT33 about 'Whale Tumour' stories, and Rodney Dale's article in *Curious Facts Monthly* No.2, I am now quite sure that an article in *Strange Stories: Amazing Facts* (Readers Digest, 1975) is a WTS.

It concerns an eminent 19th century American doctor who, on a winter's evening opens the front door to a bedraggled young lady in a raggy shawl. She explains to him that her mother is desperately ill and in urgent need of help. The doctor agrees to come and follows her home.

He recognizes the lady in bed as a former servant of his, examines her, and commends her dutiful daughter. At this the lady gives him a long stare, then says quietly: "My daughter died a month ago. Her shoes and shawl are in that cupboard." The doctor looks and lo!, there is the shawl, dry and folded. He looks for the girl, but of course she is nowhere to be found. If that ain't a WTS, I'll eat my hat!

Steven Thompson (14)
Whitley Bay, Tyne & Wear.
[This will be recognized as one of the many variants of the 'phantom hitchhiker' motif— see 'On the road again' by Mike Goss, FT34p14-16.—a perennial theme of folklore all over the world. Part of our interest in WTSs is that they are a dynamic, contemporary

Cont on p62

A New Science of Life.

Last year a 'new theory of life' was published, which at one stroke extended the boundaries of conventional science to include many of the subjects now considered to be anomalous or paranormal. The new paradigm not only organizes these areas with a radically new field theory, but also provides for scientific predicton and practical experiments. Reaction from scientists has been mixed, ranging from enthusiastic endorsement to primitive rage. The author of this philosophical break-through is **Dr Rupert Sheldrake** , and FT editor **Bob Rickard** interviewed him at the home of **John Michell**.

Richard Adams

Part One.
A Candidate for Burning.

It was Thomas Kuhn[1] who showed clearly, once and for all, that scientific progress is continuous warfare between the proponents of old and new ideas, and, contrary to the propaganda, very rarely is it an orderly and dignified progression from enigma to law, through observation, theory and experiment. According to Kuhn progress is a succession of 'paradigm shifts' or revolutions in the way scientists structure the world. Briefly—there comes a time when a generally accepted theory of the way a particular part of the universe works is first hampered, then seriously threatened by an accumulation of anomalies. Champions of the ailing paradigm—or 'Old Dominant', to use Fort's phrase—become increasingly entrenched and defensive and resist ever more desperately (even to the extent of ungentlemanly and unscholarly behaviour) both the embarassing data and the appearance of new, apparently more workable, theories. At this stage the sniping breaks into open and often vicious warfare—the new contenders jousting for supremacy as the old view collapses impotently. It ends only when a satisfying model emerges which harmonizes the old knowledge and the anomalies (or most of them) into a more or less unified model. But for the New Dominent there is only an uncertain reign, until it too is challenged by the evidence it fails to explain or suppress.

We were recently treated to a classical example of the hostility accorded by the orthodox to the new idea. In this case it was the publication of a new theory about how forms arise in nature and are repeated—a fundamental question which ramifies into almost every cranny of the known sciences, and for our interest has implications for many areas of anomalous and unexplained phenomena. It is a complex new idea, a new way of thinking about science, which unites mystical elements with the hardest science into a theory which, if not a new paradigm itself, points the way to one. Its author, Dr Rupert Sheldrake, calls it a hypothesis of 'formative causation' and explains it in his book *A New Science of Life* [2]. The importance of Sheldrake's ideas was recognized immediately by *New Scientist*, which gave them an enthusiastic endorsement when his article, introducing his ideas and book, appeared in their 18 June 1981 issue[3]. Sheldrake suggests that what scientists mistake for immutable laws may be simply 'habit', patterns of form and behaviour created by the repetition of events over time. If Sheldrake's theory is substantiated, wrote *New Scientist*, then "Western science has sadly misconstrued the world and all the creatures therein."

FORMATIVE CAUSATION

Embryologists and developmental biologists, despite their increasing knowledge of the biophysical elements and forces, have never been able to solve a fundamental mystery—how do similar forms arise in nature, and how, as the fertilized seeds or eggs grow, is their growth, structure and form organized according to the pattern of the species, etc? For more than 50 years scientists in these areas have used the vague but useful concept of 'morphogenetic fields' (Greek: morphe = form, genesis = coming-into-being) to represent these mysterious structuring factors that enable living organisms, plants or animals, to develop into their characteristic forms. Modern genetic theory *assumes* such information is somehow 'programmed' into the DNA, but all that is known with any degree of certainty is that DNA simply codes sequences of amino acids. It is quite a different thing to suggest that DNA somehow regulates the form and structure of cells, tissue, organs and whole organisms [See 'The TV Analogy' box]. Nevertheless the need was felt for an entity—the morphogenetic field —which both served as the model and the source of regulation for the coming into being of forms on these levels of complexity, despite the fact that such entities could not be explained or tested experimentally in terms of the current paradigms. Even the late eminent biologist, CH Waddington, found the concept useful, but referred to it merely as a "descriptive convenience" because it was basically untestable. Sheldrake's breakthrough provides a fairly comprehensive theory and description of these formative fields and their manner of working in such a way that the effects can be determined experimentally—he even suggests several experiments in the book.

When a seed or egg is fertilized, it becomes what Sheldrake calls a 'morphogenetic germ'—a starting point for the development which immediately begins to unfold. This development is influenced by "previous systems of which structures similar to these morphogenetic germs were a part. [It] thus becomes surrounded by, or embedded within, the morphogenetic field of the higher-level system [eg. the cell is influenced by the tissue-field, the tissue by the organ-field, etc], which then shapes or moulds the process of development towards the characteristic form."[3]

The influence of one morphogenetic field upon another is termed 'morphic resonance'. It involves a new kind of 'action-at-a-distance' of a type not yet recognized by physics because it acts independently of the usual limitations imposed by space and time. Consequently all the

Rupert Sheldrake.

Rupert Sheldrake was born in 1942. He studied at Clare College, Cambridge, where he became a fellow and a director of studies in biochemistry and cell biology until 1973, during which time he was awarded a Rosenheim Research Fellowship of the Royal Society. In 1974 he was set for a professorship at the university of his choice, but decided instead to study growing plants in fields. Until 1978 he was a member of the staff of the International Crops Research Institute for the Semi-Arid Tropics, in Hyderabad, India, and is now a consultant to the Institute.

In the preface to his book Sheldrake acknowledges his debt to the Epiphany philosophers, a group of scientists and philosophers, mainly Christians, at Cambridge University, with whom Sheldrake was associated from 1966. The group was formed in the 1950s to explore the area between science, philosophy and mysticism, and from 1966 to 1981 published the quarterly journal *Theoria to Theory*. It was in the group's meetings and seminars that Sheldrake found considerable encouragement for his early ideas. The fully-fledged hypothesis was eventually written up during a long stay at a Christian ashram in South India.

In introducing Sheldrake and his work, *New Scientist* [3] gave three reasons for taking him seriously: "The first is that he is an excellent scientist; the proper, imaginative kind that in an earlier age discovered continents and mirrored the world in sonnets...The second is...that the science in his ideas is good...The third reason for taking Sheldrake seriously is that other people do...The scientists who take him most seriously and sit up at nights working through the implications are the ones who ought to be most affronted: the physicists."

past fields of a given type are available instantly to, and indeed, coexistent with, subsequent similar systems. Such effects, says Sheldrake, are cumulative.

Without such formative fields the development of the morphogenetic germs would be out of control—each time it replicated its genetic material the probabilities multiplying exponentially and randomly. Morphogenetic fields exclude such genetic chaos probably because they restrict developmental permutations to the general limits for that form. Individuality within these limits—eg. even though they share the same symmetry no two roses, kidneys or human faces are quite the same—is explained as the product of local variations in the composite field [See 'The Composite Analogy' box]. Despite their undiscovered physical nature, Sheldrake maintains that the formative fields are not themselves energetic. "They act by patterning probabilistic events...[and] are themselves probabilistic in nature."[3]

Sheldrake distinguishes between two major types of formative fields: the morphogenetic fields proper which order the repetition of form and structure; and motor fields which order action and behaviour. There may be others—for example a field which structures perception. Behaviour is structured in much the same way as form—that is a hierarchy of behavioural patterns is given directly to a young organism by morphic resonance from previous organisms of the same species. On a basic level we have a non-chemical mechanism for the transmission of instincts; on a sophisticated level we would have something akin to psi phenomena (telepathy, collective experiences, etc) It could also explain how C.G.Jung's archetypes propagate their influence from the Collective Unconscious to the individual mind.

Morphogenetic fields act also to regenerate parts of an organism after loss or damage, and the motor fields would restore behaviour to characteristic or given patterns. For example: while instinct drives the potter wasp to make its distinctive nest, its behaviour, in promptly re-sealing a hole poked in its pot-nest, is more akin to thinking than to instinct (Sheldrake likens instinct to *habits* acquired, not by individuals, but by a species as a whole.). It is a motor field, says Sheldrake, which not only gives an organism a behavioural pattern, but also drives the organism to complete it to the best of its ability under the circumstances. This regulation of behaviour is most likely accomplished directly, "by bringing order to the randomness of synaptic firings in the central nervous system."[3]

ACROSS TIME AND SPACE

Because morphic resonance acts across time present forms and behaviour are affected by those from the past, and a similar influence is exerted across space so that an individual or colony may be affected by whatever happens to other individuals or colonies of the same species elsewhere in the world. An example of groups of rats in Scotland and Australia developing the same behaviour pattern as rats in the USA in a series of scientific experiments which have remained puzzling, is now cited by Sheldrake as both accountable and predictable in the light of formative causation.

In 1920, William McDougall, at Harvard University, found that successive generations of rats put through the same spcially designed water maze learned to escape from it sooner and with less mistakes than their parents. McDougall concluded that the rats were passing on to their offspring their new behaviour, which would confirm the long disregarded theory of the inheritance of acquired characteristics formulated by Jean-Baptiste Lamarck in 1809. Each generation of these rats had been bred from pairs of maze-runners chosen at random, but McDougall anticipated the criticism that he had selected the most successful rats to be parents. So he repeated the experiment breeding only from the slowest-learners in each generation. According to conventional theory the rate of success in the maze should decrease because the rats were being bred for poor performance, but as in the first series each generation mastered the maze a bit better and faster than their parents. This unexpected result attracted much attention and the experiment was duplicated exactly by researchers in Edinburgh and Melbourne. The experimenters were even more astonished to find their first generation rats learning the maze faster than McDougall's early generations. At Edinburgh some of the first rats completed the maze without error on their first run.

To test the Lamarckian-like results obtained by McDougall, the experimenters at Melbourne compared them with the performance of a control line—and these too showed a steadily improved learning rate. Because the parents of each generation in the control line had never run the maze there was no possiblity the results could be explained by the genetic inheritance of acquired abilities. "Thus McDougall's *conclusions* were refuted, [while] his *results* were confirmed," writes Sheldrake, "and to this day [they] have not been satisfactorily accounted for in conventional terms."[3] Sheldrake's hypothesis, however, predicts that the motor field created by the success of the first rat, reinforced by subsequent successes, became available to ratkind in general and maze-runners in particular, even though they were separated by time and space.

FIELDS AND FORERUNNERS

Field theories, accounting for the mystery of the origins of form are, in themselves, nothing new. The archetypal Forms of Ideas of Plato spring to mind. According to Plato the objects, creatures and ideas of this world were but imperfect reflections of 'ideal' forms—but, says Sheldrake, Plato's theory "failed to explain how the eternal forms were related to the changing world of phenomena."[2] More recently a number of scientists have attempted an explanation for morphogenesis.

One such, not mentioned by Sheldrake, is Dr Gustaf Stromberg, an astronomer at Mount Wilson Observatory, who, in the 1940s, developed an almost mystical philosophy out of his dissatisfaction with materialistic science. He eventually conlcuded that there existed some kind of organizing force, independent of genetics, which acted as an "immaterial" mould for its physical counterpart, whether this be a whole organism or an organ or cell etc. He believed these fields—or *genii* as he termed them (Latin: genius = spirit) were electromagnetic and had no mass. The genie of the human body was the equivalent of the idea of a soul, and the genie of the universe was the equivalent of the idea of God[4]. This cosmic aspect led him to believe that the fields were immortal and indestructable, rather like Platonic Forms, and therefore, in Sheldrake's terms, failed to explain individuality, creativity and the problem of the origins of form.

In 1972, Harold S. Burr, a professor of biology at Yale University, published his own ideas based on years of embryological research. Like Stromberg, Burr throught his 'life fields' [5] were electrodynamic in nature. In referring to Burr's ideas, Sheldrake argues that the identification of morphogenetic fields generally with electromagnetic fields has in fact created much confusion and obstructed any progress in clarifying the situation. According to Sheldrake's theory, the difference between them is simple: EM fields depend upon the *actual* state of the system and are energetic by nature, whereas the formative fields depend only on the *potential* of a system while remaining largely independent of its actual form and are non-energetic.

Aristotle also developed a theory of 'eternal forms', but his differed from Plato's in that he believed they were not only inherent in the forms of which they were the model, but somehow *caused* the characteristic form to develop. This concept was picked up in the late 19th century by a German embryologist, Hans Driesch, who called the non-physical factor which forms, regulates and regenerates a living organism *entelechy* (Greek: en-telos = something which bears its end or goal in itself). Driesch identified several important characteristics of entelechy—the fields are natural (ie. arose from natural, not metaphysical, processes); they acted independently of space; and they were non-energetic, probably affecting the timing of microphysical processes, he thought. These ideas proved a valuable springboard for Sheldrake's own thinking.

PSYCHIC RELEVANCE

Curtis Fuller, in his report on Sheldrake's theory for *Fate*[6], alluded to the appeal of field theories to parapyschologists, occultists and mystics. "Many persons involved in psychical studies come to a concensus that somehow all minds and perhaps all events are linked in some mysterious way.

It is a curious fact that a small number of respected scientists have arrived at a belief in some sort of field theory, not through their science, but through their interest in paranormal phenomena. Sheldrake cites [2] Walter Carington, the psychical researcher, and the biologist Sir Alister Hardy. Carington thought that instincts might be some kind of collective memory; that individuals of a species were "linked up into a larger system (or common subconscious if you prefer it) in which all the... experience of the species is stored up."[7] –and Hardy believed that the transmission of the morphogenetic information formed "two parallel streams", one the known genetic system, and the other a "psychic stream of shared experience...the subconscious species 'blueprint'..."[8].

As Fuller points out William McDougall, the Lamarckian rat-man, also had a keen interest in psychic research. Later, when at Duke University, he encouraged his young colleague, J.B.Rhine, to set up the now-famous parapsychology lab there. McDougall could have formulated a field theory based on the data available to him in the 1920s to explain the mystery of the maze-rats' learning curves–but he didn't. It was Sheldrake who made the quantum leap to a new paradigm.

Part Two: Interview.
The Habit-forming Universe.

☐ **FT**: A good place to start would be to ask you to define for us exactly what you mean by 'formative causation' and 'morphogenetic fields'.

☐ **SHELDRAKE**: Formative causation is responsible for giving order and pattern to material systems, such as atoms, molecules, crystals, cells, organs and organisms. Its patterning activity is expressed through morphogenetic fields, which are responsible for form, and motor fields, which are responsible for behaviour. These fields derive their structure by morphic resonance from the form and behaviour of previous similar systems. Morphogenetic fields are responsible for the coming-into-being and the maintenance of the form of organized systems. They are hierarchically organized, and act by restricting the inherent indeterminism of the lower-level systems under their control.

☐ **FT**: How did your philosophy–the idea of your theory– develop? At the end of *A New Science of Life* you show how several of the conventional positions are quite compatible with the new theory, and are in fact enriched by it. You arrange them in a hierarchy of complexity–or as your critics might say, preposterousness–concluding with a passionately religious statement. It doesn't take much to realize you are in fact saying that an ultimate creative agency, God, is the source of all formative fields, and that you are a theist. Did religious sentiment inform the development of your hypothesis?

☐ **SHELDRAKE**: In fact it's the other way around. When I was at Cambridge I spent 10 years working along mechanistic lines. I was a materialist then and believed in mechanistic explanations. I didn't really like them but I felt there was no real alternative. I got interested in Transcendental Meditation, but I had no particular religious faith. Mainly through taking dope–acid a few times–I became interested in meditation and mental phenomena, and through that I got interested in Hindu philosophy. Then I assosiated with a group of people at Cambridge interested in psychical research, who kept drawing my attention to the evidence of things like telepathy. I just refused to read it. It was far too disconcerting. I couldn't handle it because it just didn't fit in.

I read a lot on the philosophy of biology– the organismic type view of Koestler and people like that–but the trouble is that they didn't seem to have anything positive to offer. The real break came for me when I read books by vitalists. In all the standard textbooks on biology they ritually denounce the leading members of the Vitalist school, Hans Driesch and Henri Bergson, as absurd people whose ideas have been swept aside by the tide of rational progress. I had thought the mechanistic view was shallow and inadequate, and the alternatives seemed waffly–eg. Gregory Bateson and Koestler, who I thought were the best of these people–with their talk of vague holistic perspectives; but when it came to the crunch they really weren't saying anything.

So I read Bergson, because he was suggested to me by a friend of mine who studied French literature. I'd read Proust, so it was from a literary interest that I read Bergson first. I read *Creative Evolution*[9] and thought it tremendous stuff–a new vision. He has the most vigorous critique of the meachanistic Darwinian view. He shows how evolution can only be understood properly in terms of creative forces at work in nature. He deals with well known problems like the eye, and with similar types of animals cropping up in unrelated groups (convergent evolution) which cannot be explained in a mechanistic manner. Then I read Driesch's *Science and Philosophy of the Organism* [10] and found his vitalist view, based on Aristotle's concepts of entelechy and formal causation, extremely persuasive, very profound; but utterly out of fashion. When I got the book from a zoological library reserve stack it was covered in dust, quite unread. People like Crick, who denounce Bergson and Driesch, have clearly never read them. They set up straw men, imagining they know what the vitalists thought, but what they really thought was quite different. I try to rehabilitate Driesch in my work to show that far from being an absurd obscurantist he was a thoroughly well-informed and original thinker.

But the book that caused the scales to drop from my eyes, about the mechanistic theory of life, was Bergson's *Matter and Memory* [11], an extraordinarily original book. He was a thorough-going dualist, and asked the question what does the soul do that is different from the body? What is it about the psychic that is different from the material? He concluded that the primary distinction lay in the power of memory. Matter was bound to the present and had no past, as it were, whereas the psychic, as we know from our own experience of memory, can transcend time. Aritistotle and others had the idea that the memory was like a series of impressions in sealing wax, that somehow inside the body were impressions on 'sealing wax' —an early form of the physical 'trace' theory of memory, of which the hologram analogy is an updated version. Modern theories of memory

The Composite Analogy.

Reproduced by courtesy of the John Innes Institute.

Because space and time are no barriers to morphic resonance, argues Sheldrake, the influence of all systems of a similar type, whether they be in the past or elsewhere spatially, are immediately available to the developing system in the present. "As these systems are similar rather than identical, when a subsequent system comes under their collective influence by morphic resonance, its morphogenetic field will not be sharply defined. This process can be thought of by analogy with composite photography, in which 'average' pictures are produced by superimposing a number of similar images."

Accompanying this statement in his article [3] was this illustration, being a composite of 30 female (left) and 45 male (right) members of the John Innes Institute, Norwich. In Sheldrake's book [2]. however, the same point is additionally illustrated by examples of the work of the pioneering scientific philosopher Sir Francis Galton, who invented the composite technique in the hope that he could identify the fundamental common facial characteristics of groups of people (eg. Family 'resemblance', or criminal types).

are nothing more than updated versions of the 'sealing wax' idea, and with no more evidence in their favour than the 'sealing wax' theory.

Descartes had a memory trace theory. He thought in terms of fluids playing around the brain and valves getting opened and closed and pores getting more or less distended through the flows of liquids....a version of the synaptic multiplication theory of memory. Plotinus criticized the 'sealing wax' theory of memory and said that memory is a function of the soul, not of matter. The soul is non-material and therefore there is no reason why memory should have physical traces. Bergson developed this, saying the memory is not stored inside the brain, and all the phenomena of memory needn't depend on brain-traces. He analysed all the evidence that existed then, which is much the same as what exists now—loss of memory through brain lesions, etc—and showed that none of this necessarily shows that the memory is inside the brain. All it shows is that the brain lost the ability to respond to memory. Bergson and Driesch thought the brain was an instrument of action, through which the soul worked on the body to bring about action. The brain was like a keyboard on which the pianist (soul) plays. The TV analogy [see box] is a better one than the pianist.

Bergson's case for the memory not being inside the brain is totally persuasive. But Driesch thought in terms of entelechy as something which controlled embryology and instinct in animals. He wasn't concerned much with conscious phenomena, which Bergson dealt with in *Matter and Memory*. Driesch didn't say where entelechy came from, as a non-physical factor controlling form. He assumed, almost, that it was eternally given. Bergson had the idea that memory wasn't material, and by coupling up these two ideas—that entelechy depends upon past influences, which needn't be material, in controlling forms—you get something like the view I develop in my book.

For several years I adopted this vitalist view, and assumed that these phenomena only occurred in life; that the mechanistic view of physical nature, up to and including crystals, was more or less all right, but that in life there was a new set of problems requiring new casual factors. That's what vitalism is all about—that life is radically different from non-life. Whereas the organismic view is that there is something funny about life, and non-life as well.

☐ **FT:** You have attracted attention to a fundamental mystery about crystals—how newly synthesized compounds, which have never before been crystallized, are very hard to crystallize for the first time, but once done, subsequent crystallizations become consistently easier. You say the conventional explanation is that seeds of the first or subsequent crystals are transmitted around the world on the wind or in the clothing of migrant scientists. But your

theory suggests a quite different explanation: that the very first crystal formed—by chance or design, you don't actually say—a morphogenetic field, or was formed by a totally new field, and this field then made all subsequent crystallizations easier.

☐ **SHELDRAKE:** Every time I read mechanistic books they compared morphogenesis to crystallization. If crystallization can occur by physical forces from the chaos of a solution, then morphogensis is more complicated but is only a difference of degree. I kept stumbling over this persuasive argument, until I read more about crystallization and the chemical literature —Linus Pauling on the chemical bond, etc—and discovered that no one actually knew how crystals formed. The whole thing was a jungle of assumptions. Most assume that crystallization is fully understood, but even Pauling admits you can't actually predict the structure of crystals. Then I read of the difficulties in getting a new compound to crystallize, and that it gets easier as time goes on. Such problems made me realize that my line of thinking could be extended to the non-living as well, in an all-embracing new physical view of things in terms of these influences across time.

I was stuck on this crystal problem for four years. I thought it must be right because it was so universally accepted. I'm a biochemist by training—then I read the literature and talked to crystallographers. Then, in this group I belong to—the Epiphany Philosophers—I talked to quantum physicists interested in new kinds of physics; they thought it was very interesting.

I leave it quite open whether there are prior forms or the product of a first accident.

Another possibility is pre-existing crystals of the same kind on other planets. But that raises the question of whether these fields really do operate independently of space.

☐ **FT:** In Damon Knight's biography of Fort [12] he mentions a belief common among American chemical engineers that the processes described in chemical patents are generally impossible to duplicate or start up first time, despite setting up rigs identical to the original research rig, and despite rigorous checks, until they bring in someone who has worked on the original set-up. Then suddenly the apparatus and process work as advertized. It is said to be a well known effect, that certain people can get chemical reactions where others can't in the same situation—the chemical equivalent of the gardener's 'green thumb'—and no one knows why. To me, there is an analogy here with the human agency aspect of poltergeist phenomena. To what extent do you think the experimenter influences the outcome of his own experiment?

☐ **SHELDRAKE:** I agree it raises that issue. No chemists have yet denounced my suggestions. On the contrary, they've all admitted this is indeed a problem—about how you get the first crystals. Chemists have described this to me as the 'occult' side of chemistry. I've heard stories, told in pubs, about how scientists stroke their beards and get seeds of crystals off. One of the most successful chemists in getting crystallizations was a chap called Perkins, who was bearded. The early beard anecdotes are all about Perkins, the great synthetic chemist, whose beard was said to be loaded with seeds of hundreds of different crystals.

The difficulties of getting new compounds to crystallize are not well documented. It is part of chemists' gossip, part of the folklore of chemistry. Crystallography doesn't deal with it. X-ray crystallography only begins when they have got crystals to analyse... How you get the crystals has remained a folklore area∴the artisan or alchemical side of chemistry.

☐ **FT**: What have been the reactions to the book?

☐ **SHELDRAKE**: You know there's a great variety of opinion among scientists. They don't all think the same at all. Within a single department some openly say it's very stimulating; others say it is pseudoscience. They simply define science in a way that excludes it, because they don't recognize it as potentially being within the sphere of science. These are people who, on the whole, are unsophisticated in terms of the philosophy of science. This reaction conforms to Kuhn's theories about the nature of scientific revolutions, the paradigm model of scientific change. Because they have a

mechanistic paradigm that defines the kinds of problems they can tackle, they don't recognize that anything outside that could be considered science.

☐ **FT**: What Fort called Exclusionism...

☐ **SHELDRAKE**: Yes. The *Nature* editorial [13 - see also 'Two Views' box] makes this quite clear. When the article came out in *New Scientist*[3] and in the *Brain/Mind Bulletin* [14], I got a lot of letters from scientists who said they found it terribly interesting where it implies this or that, or where it would fit such-and-such into metaphysical theory. Then I got a few saying it isn't really science—but not many. Some correspondents wrote, in *New Scientist*[15], that it was "arrant nonsense", and others wrote in the following week to ask why it was that whenever any new idea appeared that some pompous prof wrote in to say it was arrant nonsense?

☐ **FT**: Well your ideas would seem threatening to exclusionist science...

☐ **SHELDRAKE**: The most interesting question in the history of science is how you get from one view of the world to a completely different view in periods of scientific revolution, and what is the nature of the change? If you have a new paradigm, you simply enlarge or change the area of what's considered to lie within the scope of science.

Sir Karl Popper suggests that you can distinguish a scientific theory from a metaphysical

The TV Set Analogy.

To help explain the nature and action of 'morphic resonance'— the way in which previous morphogenetic fields may influence a present form or behaviour—Sheldrake offered the following analogy[2]:

"Imagine an intelligent and curious person who knows nothing about electricity or electromagnetic radiation. He is shown a television set for the first time. He might at first suppose that the set actually contained little people, whose images he saw on the screen. But when he looked inside and found only wires, condensers, transistors, etc, he might adopt the more sophisticated hypothesis that the images somehow arose from complicated interactions among the components of the set. This hypothesis would seem particularly plausible when he found that the images

became distorted or disappeared when components were removed, and that the images were restored to normal when these components were put back."

If the suggestion was put to him that the images in fact depended on invisible influences entering the set from far away, he might reject it on the grounds that it was unnecessary and obscurantist. His opinion that nothing came into the set from outside would be reinforced by the discovery that the set weighed the same switched on and switched off. While admitting that he could not explain in detail how the images were produced from complicated interactions within the set, and nothing more, he might well claim that such an explanation was possible in principle, and that it would in fact eventually be achieved after a great deal of

further research."

"This point of view may resemble the conventional approach to biology. By contrast, in terms of this analogy the hypothesis of formative causation does not involve a denial of the importance of the wire, transistors, etc (corresponding to DNA, protein molecules, etc); but it recognises in addition the role of influences transmitted from outside the system, the "transmitters" being past organisms of the same species. Genetic changes can affect the inheritace of form or instinct by altering the "tuning", or by introducing distortions into the "reception". But genetic factors cannot by themselves fully account for the inheritance of form and instinct, any more than the particular pictures on the screen of a TV set can be explained in terms of its wiring diagram alone.

one by the ability to test it by experiment, and that's what gives you a criterion of science, not the established orthodoxy of the theory. If you had the latter you'd never have science breaking out of established orthodoxies, and the most interesting changes in science are precisely those breaks with orthodoxy: Copernicus, Newton, Darwin, Einstein and the quantum theory. Any view which said science could work with the established rules would exclude scientific revolutions. What Popper calls the "criteria of demarcation" between science and metaphysics is that a scientific hypothesis 1) starts from the problem, is an attempt to deal with a problem within science, or potentially within science, facts or phenomena which don't fit into the established view, or which fit in badly, or which could be looked at in a different way; 2) it should be universal (ie. not an *ad-hoc* hypothesis to explain a few or particular cases but should have a wider application); and 3) it should be testable by experiment. This view is generally accepted by philosophers of science and on these criteria my proposals *are* scientific, and this is pointed out in the *New Scientist* introduction. But if you take the orthodox exclusionist view, then my proposals aren't scientific. That's where this difference comes.

□ **MICHELL**: This is a bit like the Marxists, who have a framework to explain everything and who won't go outside it.

□ **SHELDRAKE**: Yes, but on the whole Marxists aren't as bad as other exclusionists. Since their view is based on a more or less Hegelian view of the dialectical evolution of science, more sophisticated Marxists are prepared to admit that science can change and proceed by this method. They believe that science is a progressive developing system rather than a static fixated one. Modern versions of the philosophy of science in the Soviet Union have this dialectical view of the development of scientific ideas, eg in relation to biology. They are not all reductionists because they believe that through dialectics you get new higher-level syntheses—in fact a sort of Marxist holism.

□ **MICHELL**: On the other hand they take a more firm line behind Darwinian materialism than other people do now.

□ **SHELDRAKE**: Darwinism in itself is slightly ambiguous. Darwin admitted the inheritance of acquired characteristics, and the Soviet Union has that long tradition of Lysenko's biology which is highly heterodox. Although it is no longer the orthodoxy in the Soviet Union, you can't have two generations of biologists reared on that orthodoxy and change it overnight. There must be an awful lot of residual Lysenkoism around in the Soviet Union.

□ **MICHELL**: It's amazing though, how quickly scientists and historians will switch according to a political orthodoxy.

□ **SHELDRAKE**: Yes, but in the Soviet Union all these Lysenko doctrines—eg. on the inheritance of acquired characteristics—were

A New Science of Life–Two Views.

The editors of *Nature* launched an amazing attack on Sheldrake and his book in their editorial pages. It was in fact a sarcastic review of the book and appeared anonymously under the title 'A book for burning?'[13]. Here are a few extracts...

• "*What is to be made of Dr Rupert Sheldrake's book...This infuriating tract has been widely hailed by the newspapers and popular science magazines as the "answer" to materialistic science, and is now well on its way to being a point of reference for the motley crew of creationists, anti-reductionists, neo-Lamarckians and the rest. The author, by training a biochemist and by demonstration a knowledgeable man, is, however, misguided. His book is the best candidate for burning there has been for many years.*

In reality, Sheldrake's argument is in no sense a scientific argument but is an exercise in pseudo-science. Preposterously, he claims that his hypothesis can be tested—that it is falsifiable in Popper's sense—and indeed the text includes half a dozen proposals for experiments that might be carried out to verify that the forms of aggregations of matter are indeed moulded by the hypothetical morphogenetic fields that are supposed to pervade everything. These experiments have in common the attributes of being time-consuming, inconclusive in the sense that it will always be possible to postulate yet another morphogenetic field to account for some awkwardly inconclusive result, and impractical in the sense that no self-respecting grant-making agency will take the proposals seriously...Many readers will be left with the impression that Sheldrake has succeeded in finding a place for magic within scientific discussion—and, this, indeed, may have been a part of the objective of writing this book.

His book should not be burned (nor even confined to closed shelves in libraries) but, rather, put firmly in its place among the literature of intellectual aberrations."

A few issues later, *Nature*[13] published a few letters of criticism of this "emotional outburst", as one called it, and significantly no letters of support for their comments. Robert Hughes, of Oxford University, thought that perhaps the book should be burned after all, "For seeing the disastrous effect Sheldrake's book has wrought taught up until 1964, and although some of it has been shown to be false, there is no reason to think that all Lysenko's work, and that of hundreds of other scientists who followed him and who claimed to have examples of the inheritance of acquired characteristics, are false. C.H.Waddington's experiments with the 'bithorax types of fruitflies in fact showed that the inheritance of acquired characteristics is possible.

Lamarckian theory was based on the idea of actual material transformation of the germ plasm. He didn't actually use the word 'genes', because they weren't discovered until much later. But the late 19th C Lamarckians, and 20th C ones did: for example, R.Semon, in his book *The Mneme*[16]. He was a German biologist who believed in the inheritance of acquired characteristics and saw inheritance as a kind of memory. Hence the title. He thought that memories were somehow coded in chemical changes in bodily protoplasm, and were passed on materially in germ cells. Most Lamarckian theorizing, including Lysenko's, assumed that the transmission of acquired characteristics must be due to material changes in the germ cells, and as the DNA theory got more influential, that meant it ought to depend on changes in the genes. But there was no way in which this could be shown to happen. In fact there were ways in which it could be shown it didn't happen, and that is what really refuted Lysenko—the fact that the mechanism they proposed wasn't correct.

One of the fascinating new lights on the subject comes from Dr Mae-Wan Ho, an anti-neo-Darwinist at the Open University, who has repeated Waddington's 'bithorax' experiments, exposing the eggs of fruitflies to ether. The halteres on the 3rd thoracic segment turn into a pair of wings—making, in fact, a copy of the 2nd thoracic segment—forming a 4-winged fly

Waddington found a minority of such bithorax files in the first generation. He selected those and bred from them, exposing their eggs to ether, and so on. The 2nd generation contained more bithorax flies, and so on, up to about 80% of the population in the 20th generation.

Waddington explained his discovery as "genetic assimilation—a seemingly Lamarckian kind of inheritance that could be fully explained in terms of orthodox Mendelism." But he never identified all the alleged genes responsible for the bithorax effect because he assumed it was due to a large number of genes, each with small individual effects, but collectively bringing about this effect. You can only identify small numbers of genes by standard tests—so it was an untestable theory really. But it is generally accepted and in textbooks you often see a statement to the effect that Waddington has shown that seemingly Lamarckian inheritance can be explained in terms of 'genetic assimilation'.

Mae-Wan Ho repeated the experiment, but

---

upon the detachment, not to say the common sense, of one with the responsibilities of the editorship of *Nature*, I shudder to contemplate the effect upon the ordinary man." Well, Mr Hedges—here we all are, cheering from the sidelines at the spectacle of outraged authority. Hedges goes on to suggest that the editors of *Nature* were in the grip of temptation, having succumbed to "the influence of a pulpit from which to denounce scientific heresies..." The matter was put into a fairer perspective by Nobel laureate physicist, Prof Brian Josephson, of Cambridge University, who virtually accused the editors of this, one of the world's most pretigious science journals, of actually obstructing scientific progress. This is what he had to say...

● "*You reject Dr Sheldrake's morphogenetic fields as*

"*pseudo science*" *on the grounds that he does not prescribe their nature or origin, or discuss how their laws of propagation might be discovered. But the properties of heat, light and sound were investigated long before there was any understanding of their true nature, and electricity and magnetism originally had exactly the status that you criticized in the hypothetical water-divining example. Were such investigations pseudoscience?*

You claim that hypotheses can be dignified as theories only if all aspects of them can be tested. Such a criterion would bar general relativity, the black hole and many other concepts of modern science from being regarded as legitimate scientific theories.

The discussion of Dr Sheldrake's proposed experi-

ments and their falsifiability is rendered void since it assumes a priori that the experiments will fail...

By referring to "self-respecting grant-making agencies" you show a concern not for scientific validity but for respectability. The fundamental weakness is a failure to admit even the possibility that genuine physical facts may exist which lie outside the scope of current scientific descriptions. Indeed, a new kind of understanding of nature is now emerging, with concepts like implicate order and subject-dependent reality (and now, perhaps formative causation). These developments have not yet penetrated to the leading journals. One can only hope that the editors will soon cease to obstruct this avenue of progress, and instead encourage reviews of the field."

without the genetic selection. Her first generation had about 2% bithorax types; the 2nd about 4-5%, up to 50% in ten generations. There is a natural selection *against* the bithorax characteristic because the 4-winged flies tend to get stuck in the goo and the bottom of test-tubes, and are not very good at mating. But still you get the same effect that Waddington observed in increasing proportions, in the absence of genetic selection.

She then took some control flies, from the same stock, bred in parallel but without the ether treatment, and exposed *their* eggsto ether. The first generation produced 9% bithorax types; and the 2nd 19%. A very much quicker effect of the ether in flies which had no selection at all. Now I predicted this kind of effect—that the control flies would be affected by the morphogenetic fields of the ones already transformed.

☐ **FT:** In FT35[17] we printed a reference to spreading immunity among isolated colonies of bacteria, for which the researchers postulated a 'common mind' to explain the effect.

☐ **MICHELL:** I read a news story of rats becoming immune to something and that immunity spreading to rats not in contact with them, but damn me I didn't clip it.

☐ **SHELDRAKE:** I wish you had. I've heard about this effect but I haven't been able to get any references. I know about spreading immunity in rats, and that certain types of traps cease to work effectively after a while...

☐ **MICHELL:** Do you mean here the telepathic spread of information?

☐ **SHELDRAKE:** Yes, but there's a thin dividing line between telepathy and morphic resonance.

☐ **FT:** Occultists and spiritualists will find some comfort in the morphogenetic idea because it provides an analogy to whatever it is that they believe survives the dissolution of the physical body at death. Spiritualists could derive from it a field of resonance between the morphogenetic fields of the medium and the deceased for the transfer of information. And the idea of a memory field outside time and space could have implications for reincarnation.

☐ **SHELDRAKE:** When I was in India I got interested in reincarnation and read Stevensen's work[18], and that evidence seems to me to be quite good—that there are memories of past life, however you explain them. This reinforced what I got from Bergson—memory not being inside the brain, because if it's not then matters like telepathy and reincarnation become much more easy to understand.

My theory expands the scope of physical explanation for these phenomena, in terms of tuning into memories of people who are dead without postulating the continuation of an individualized soul. But it also makes the interactionist view more plausible. It is easier to think of a ghost among the motor fields than a ghost in the machine. My theory throws up the problem of where you get these motor fields from. One can think of consciousness as somehow involved with choices among fields of possible actions, and with the development of new ones. If consciousness is the creative factor which is not reducible to the physical, then the question is, can you have consciousness surviving as a sort of core around which these fields cluster? You could actually have something like the soul theory of survival. Both physicalist and interactionist explanations are possible—the one you take depending on your metaphysical view.

☐ **FT:** It seems to me that the phenomena attributed to reincarnation needn't necessarily imply personal survival of death. Given morphic resonance across time and space one might be tapping into the memories or life of someone while they actually lived in another time and place.

☐ **SHELDRAKE:** But it doesn't rule out survival across death. Both are possible.

☐ **FT:** The notion of non-physical entities which regulate growth, regeneration and reproduction seems like a scientific expression of the Theosophical idea of nature spirits, fairies and devas as entities which preside over all the processes of the natural world. This is clearly stated in Gardner's introduction to that curious and delightful book of fairy observations by Geoffrey Hodson[19] : "In the development of the earlier forms, mineral, vegetable, animal, the Nature spirits...or elementals lead the way. Their work is the evolution of beautiful and responsive forms." He calls them "tiny workers ...whose magnetic bodies act as the matrix in which miracles of growth and colour become possible." Theosophists think of a complex hierarchy of nature spirits, from microscopic to planet-sized entities, as a parallel stream of evolution to man. But despite this important difference to your theories of fields, I find it interesting that they see these deva-entities as non-conscious, non-physical organizing forces for the regulation of natural form and order.

☐ **SHELDRAKE:** The theory I've put forward is strictly one of repetition. Deva's don't naturally come out of a theory of repetition, although you could have them as a sort of bonus extra.

☐ **MICHELL:** Changes, anachronisms, throwbacks, recurrence of eternal ideas. This is a cast of mind so completely different from what we've become used to in so-called scientific literature. We quote you in our latest book, *Living Wonders*[20], in relation to our theory of the return or revivals of species long presumed extinct. Monsters seem to be traditionalists, and are always seen or described in terms of ancient forms or types. They often appear about the time that fossil remains of similar creatures are discovered.

☐ **SHELDRAKE:** The Loch Ness monster

could be a kind of haunting—a sort of thought-form. I don't try to involve human thought-forms because there's been an awful lot of evolution before humans came along. In the book I don't deal with thoughtforms in so far as they are conscious processes. I see conscious-ness as an autonomous process... and in that final chapter I try to smooth the way for physicalists to accept the theory, showing them that they can still be physicalists and accept it, having an enriched, enhanced, physicalism, without having to accept these other things, like paranormal phenomena.

☐ **FT:** Many people believe that the human body and its parts have subtle counterparts on a non-physical plane of existence—an astral, etheric or subtle body, or whatever term they use. If these turn out to be morphogenetic fields and interact with motor fields it would help understand the successes of faith-healing and other phenomena of the magical type. An example that springs to mind is Max Freedom Long's explanation of how Hawaiian kahunas could set broken bones by rematerializing them using an 'astral' replica of the healthy part as a sort of 'mould'[21]

☐ **SHELDRAKE:** It depends on how auton-omous thoughtforms are. If they're things which have only been in thought and haven't been realized, then the theory of morphic resonance as a physical theory wouldn't explain purely mental phenomena. But I think mental phenomena operate according to analogous laws.

☐ **FT:** Do you mean there is resonance between mental phenomena in the same way as similar forms resonate?

☐ **SHELDRAKE:** Yes, I think there is—but that's because I have an interactionist view. It's not part of the morphogenetic theory. I'm very interested in Castaneda's books. They imply an autonomous realm of thoughtforms of the kind you get in dreams, built up by all the dreams people have had, and which we can all tune into. You might have an autonomous realm of thoughtforms which have never actually been physically realized. Loch Ness Monsters, Yetis and so on, raise the question of how real are these things that people see? Are they like ghosts which have a reality as thought-forms but not a physical reality? Are they thought projections?

☐ **FT:** Many Fortean researchers have observed that phenomena are getting more and more paradoxical, having the characteristics of both physical things and of ghosts—John Keel is a particular advocate of this feeling—but they have never been able to suggest a satisfying mechanism or explanation to back this up.

☐ **SHELDRAKE:** The thing about ghosts is that there are different categories. The spectre, which could be merely a hallucination or an apparition is one kind, but there are haunting poltergeists. Are the footprints of Yetis and

chicken huts smashed by Bigfoot really any different from poltergeist-type phenomena? If poltergeists can move heavy objects like chests of drawers, you don't need to assume something is physically real. We reach a point where we can say, if they're like ghosts but they also have poltergeist-like manifestations, then you come up against the problem of what really is real. Is there a real dividing-line between a ghost which has poltergeist-like manifestations and a monster which can leave footprints and smash chicken huts, and are these separate kinds of things from real physical things? This is a whole new vista of idealist philosophy—how much of reality, even physical reality, is a thoughtform?

☐ **FT:** ...the concensus reality...

☐ **SHELDRAKE:** Yes.

☐ **FT:** If a morphogenetic field is repeated often enough does it become, to use Fort's phrase, "more nearly real"?

☐ **SHELDRAKE:** You mean, the more often a thoughtform is repeated the more it approxi-mates to physical reality?

☐ **FT:** Yes. I'm thinking of your example of the composite portraits [see 'The Composite Analogy'], of which you could say the features which are repeated most in the same position become more defined, focussed, more solid, while those with more variation in their positions remain vague. The repeated thing seems more identifiable. The stable thing more real...

☐ **SHELDRAKE:** Well it doesn't necessarily follow from my theory, the way I put it...I don't open up the question "Is physical reality really real?" I take the naive realist view because that's the point at which most people start. One addresses oneself to the current view and tries to move on from there. Since I'm a theist, a Christian in fact, I think that divine creation involves the ultimate source of all forms and reality. Creation is a mental act of an essentially spiritual nature. A theist believes that God is spirit rather than matter, and if you have a view that the physical world is created from the spiritual, or from the non-material, then all reality has to be a solidified thoughtform in a sense. It is just a question of how far you go.

The possibility that Yetis could become more and more material through being re-seen is a tiny tip of the iceberg. If the whole of reality, and the creation of reality through the divine mind, the divine act, is a solidification of thought, then that would be just one aspect of a much wider process. One can start from the physical world as the primary reality. Then one thinks that there is also thought—a limited interactionist view: thought merges into human consciousness—then maybe through human thoughtforms things can become increasingly real. One can go back and say "Why couldn't this be a model for the creation of the whole reality through a divine act?" That's the kind of view I have myself. Once one admits this progressive solidification of thoughtforms through the action of human consciousness one would have a hybrid philosophy of the real physical world with funny phenomena cropping up...

☐ **FT:** Your book ends with an encouraging picture of the whole universe as one organism, perhaps a sentient one, and perhaps one of many in the cosmos. Charles Fort too had this conception of the total collectivity of existence behaving like a living organism, its reactions and processes being the phenomena we observe.

☐ **SHELDRAKE:** In other words the universe is indeed a uni-verse—one created thing...

☐ **FT:** Yes, but with hierarchical structures within it.

☐ **SHELDRAKE:** Yes, I certainly have that sort of view...

☐ **FT:** Because things exist, they exist in relationship to each other. Fort's 'organism' is like your field idea, and the relationship acts like your resonance... Your model also works for Jung's theory of the Collective Unconscious, which must exist also as a hierarchical structure, from the personal unconsious, to that of the family, tribe, nation, race, species, biosphere, and so on up to the psychic entity that represents the existence of all things.

☐ **SHELDRAKE:** That's the view I hint at in my penultimate section. I talk about 'immanent creativity' and hierarchies within that. I think it ties in, also, with pre-Jung views—the idea of the *anima mundi* for example, and the 'soul of the universe' of Plotinus and the more limited versions like the 'soul of the earth'—and the traditional views about angelic hierarchies. In Aquinus you get the idea of the planet being ruled by angels as the 'intelligences' of the planets, actually a classical Greek idea.

☐ **FT:** This is a fundamental image. It occurs to me that in the literature of demonology you get the picture of demons ranked in principalities and levels, which is a mirroring of the hierarchies in heaven; the angels, cherubim, seraphim, thrones, archangels, etc. It also occurs in the rituals of the Golden Dawn and other 'modern' magical cosmologies based on a system of gods, demons and psychic agencies which are invoked ritually as the 'intelligences' of things.

☐ **SHELDRAKE:** But there are two ideas of angels which get very confused. There is the more limited Biblical idea of angels as messengers. And there is the idea of them as hierarchical conscious ordering principles governing different aspects of nature. The notion of angels as creative forces is held by a lot of people.

One person who had it was none other than Alfred Russell Wallace, the co-discoverer of the theory of evolution by natural selection. He wrote a book called *The Wonder of Life* towards the end of his life. Wallace and Darwin

went in completely opposite directions, starting from the same belief in evolution. Wallace ended the book with the idea of hierarchies of creative agencies, exactly of the kind we are talking about. He then says the traditional name for these agencies is 'angels'. At the end of the book he has this extraordinary view of the creation of life and evolution under the guidance of hierarchies of angels. It's a wonderful passage. And Wallace is normally considered a founder of the materialist theory of evolution —a joint apotheosis with St Charles Darwin.

☐ **FT:** Your theory seems to offer a model for the means by which archetypes order or affect patterns of human experience. As far as I know there have been no satisfying ideas of how influences or patterns are transmitted from the Collective Unconscious to the personal unconscious or to personal experience. But morphic resonance between mental phenomena is a real possibility in your theory. Do you accept the equivalences, already being pointed out, between hierarchies of formative fields and hierarchies of Jungian-type archetypes?

☐ **SHELDRAKE:** Yes—but Jung is primarily concerned with dreams, myths and human conscious phenomena. He didn't extend the archetype idea [to material forms], say, for a frog which actually causes a tadpole to develop...

☐ **FT:** But out of his ideas, one of his main disciples, Marie-Louise von Franz[22] has developed the notion that inanimate matter and primitive organisms are ordered in the same way as human consciousness by archetypes of number and time. When things exist in groups, the group has a property or 'field' which orders its constituents...

☐ **MICHELL:** That's the old Platonic idea that number preceded creation; that is, the original thought was a numerical code, and the ancient idea of 'the canon' was an attempt to recreate the creative formula. The image of the world has the structure of number...

☐ **SHELDRAKE:** I've never been particularly interested in numbers myself. I think they've been overrated. There is such a strong neo-Pythagorean streak in modern science, especially in physics—the idea that we only really understand nature when we've got it in equation.

☐ **MICHELL:** With Platonic ideals, the 'moulds' as it were, the archetypes are pre-existant. But with Rupert's idea the archetypes come into being and are confirmed all the time by averaging, becoming more real... The more specimens there are of a certain type, the more nearly it approaches the ideal.

☐ **SHELDRAKE:** Yes, but I still leave open the question of where the new fields come from.

I think they come from creative agencies and ultimately derive from a divine source, the One.

If one thinks that archetypes are invented by higher consciousness, or come in through higher consciousness, then it is a theological question to what extent the consciousness of God, or the divine or delegated creative consciousness, is completely free, or to what extent it is constrained by necessities of a mathematical kind. I myself take a non-numerical view. I don't think God *calculates* forms. It is perfectly possible for forms to be primary and numbers to be secondary. Pythagoras wanted numbers to be primary. Plato had a composite view in which both number and form were primary.

☐ **MICHELL**: Number can't evolve from anything because it is a whole system, no part of which can exist without any other part. The ancient image of the universe was a codification of key numbers which somehow represented the whole. I always see the priority of number as different from original thought, being a whole primary thing in itself.

☐ **SHELDRAKE**: I agree that number as such has laws of its own, and in the number of petals on a flower and in other natural phenomena we see these numbers—triangles, 6-petalled flowers, 5-fold symmetry and so on. One can recognize the reality of number in patterns in nature and in symmetrical structures without saying every aspect of its form has to be numerical.

☐ **FT**: The idea of the cumulative effect of repetitions of forms and the influence of fields across time is very interesting. In psychological theory there is no sense of time in the unconscious world, unlike that of the conscious world, so that to every new experience our memory adds the accumulated experience of past perceptions and traumas. An event may occur by chance but your reactions to it are two-fold; firstly the conscious reaction involves a degree of creativity or innovation; secondly, memory, both conscious and unconscious, imposes some limitations, being the accumulation of past experiences of a similar nature. This might be a good analogy for the way your fields accumulate an influence...

☐ **SHELDRAKE**: I take a somewhat pessimistic view... In a sense you could say it's a generalized view of karma. When I first thought of this book I planned to write a book called *Samsara*. I thought of writing it as a philosophical book before I saw that I could actually write it as a scientific book. The notion of karma is usually interpreted to mean individual transmigration, but you can take it in the sense it is implied in the early *Upanishads,* as a universal system of causation, and even in the way Theosophists interpret it. Theosophists think when animals die their experiences are returned to the pooled soul of the species. They have a karmic view of inheritance, but with humans it is highly individualized. I'm missing out the individual aspects of this view and applying the 'pool' theory everywhere. It certainly means that habits of thought, habits of reaction, that have been built up in any part of the human race

☐ **FT**: The universe is habit forming...

☐ **SHELDRAKE**: Yes, the whole of nature is habit forming. You could see the whole thing as a gigantic theory of habit. The enormous power of habit in moulding reality. Reality is created by the law of habit...

☐ **FT**: In the book you have a diagram of a row of spheres, the first sphere throwing its influence forward along a time axis to all the others...and the second sphere likewise, until the last sphere of the sequence is being influenced by all the others. You use this as a model of how influences can accumulate from past forms. You also say this resonance cuts across space and time. Such a process of influence or resonance would be simultaneously acting, or universally immanent, not a linear action...

☐ **SHELDRAKE**: The trouble is that when we talk about time we are forced into analogical or metaphorical language, and these words, like 'across', 'through' or 'in', are taken from spatial senses—spatial metaphors applied to time. It may be a completely inadequate way of thinking about the problem. This is one of Bergson's great points—that the way we think about time is extremely misleading. We tend to think of it as a spatial dimension, whereas that's not the true nature of time at all. It is something quite different with properties of its own, manifested in memory for example. If you think of time as a spatial dimension, you could say these influences work *across* or *through* time—but if you abandon that way of thinking about time you could say that the past is everywhere always, and that the past is simply present. If the past is just behind the present all the time, as one undivided totality, the whole thing compressed on the present, as it were, like a telescope. This has a bearing on our conception of time—the natural philosophy of time. I think it is better to think of it as a past which is collapsed onto the present, and always present. In that way the word *accumulation* becomes more natural.

☐ **FT**: This telescoping of time is what I was getting at when I mentioned that time does not seem to pass in the unconscious realm in the same way as it does in the conscious. Because of this our immediate perceptions and reactions are being modified continually by the whole of our accumulated experience, as though each event or perception in our conscious and unconscious memories had just happened. Associated memories are usually thought of as would create a field. If there was a field for alcoholism, the minute someone started drinking too much this field would work on him. He'd enter into resonance with it and be pulled more into it. This would work for good habits as well as for bad, and for bad ways of thinking as well as good ways of thinking. It does mean that most thought would fall into already established grooves, as would most kinds of actions...

'adjacent'—a spatial metaphor again—where, if your theory is applied to mental phenomena, they only need resonate with each other.

☐ **SHELDRAKE**: Yes, I do think that. The problem is how one expresses such an idea.

☐ **FT**: Observations of action across time on an unconscious level influenced Jung into forming his theory of an acausal connecting principle, very like the idea of your morphic resonance, which he called 'synchronicity'.

☐ **SHELDRAKE**: Yes, but Jung's idea is very misleading. You have to ask why he said it was 'acausal', In *Synchronicity* [23] he explains why. He took an extremely narrow and conventional view of energetic causation. He thought causation could only be defined as the kind of energetic causation understood by physics, and he confined the use of the word 'causation' to that kind of causation. But he wanted to talk about something else which was also causative but which wasn't causal in the physical or linear sense...so he called it an "acausal connecting principle". Now, if in fact he'd said: "There is another kind of causation which is non-energetic,"—which he could have said despite his choice of words—it would have been very similar to what I'm saying; that there is a formative causation which is different from energetic causation. It's an interconnecting principle, and an interconnecting principle is a kind of cause. He confuses matters by saying it was a non-causal cause.

When he talks about telepathy and so on, the word 'synchronicity' might mean something different. I think Jung again confused two things when talking about 'meaningful series' of events of the kind Paul Kammerer studied and things like telepathic communication. They are not really analogous, but Jung forced them into the same framework. He said it was a "meaningful coincidence", but telepathic communication could be completely causal. It's only a coincidence when you assume in advance it's not causal. To say that telepathic communication between someone in distress and a friend or relative is coincidence is to utterly stretch the normal meaning of the word. It is much simpler to think in terms of one event causing the other.

☐ **FT**: Fort toyed with a model of how phenomena arose along Aristotelian lines and which worked a bit like your TV set analogy. His ideas developed from his huge collection of notes and involved an abstract regulating force he called 'The Standard'[24]; but he was not so much interested in the repetition of forms as in the mysterious way growth unfolded, regulated in an unknown way by an unknown pattern which must exist but whose location is also unknown. He wrote: "A tree cannot find out how to blossom, until comes blossom-time...no part of a growing plant needs guidance of its own devising, nor special knowledge of its own, as to how to become a leaf or a root. It needs no base of its own, because the relative wholeness of the plant is relative baseness to its parts." In other words he is describing a hierarchy of situations in which any level may act as the organizing model to the level below it—which is a process you have now articulated scientifically.

Fort applied this sort of model to human society, suggesting that simultaneous inventions, or the coincidental filing of patents, was a sign that at the right time the whole will bring forth the appropriate development from its parts. One is led to consider two major interpretations: inventions or developments may arise by chance or design on the individual level and the usefulness of the innovation then spreads by telepathy, morphic resonance, or whatever; or according to some unknowable cosmic plan, when the time is right, the innovation is 'given' from outside, from some eternal realm as it were, and this development may seem to arise spontaneously in every human mind, or whatever, only a small number of which could take the matter further in the physical everyday realm. One could even have both, in a situation where a 'Standard' or high-level morphogenetic field actually inhibits the spontaneous arising of developments on the lower-level fields under its organizing influence, perhaps acting to 'kill off' premature or anachronistic devleopments excepting those at the 'right time'. Fort's particular example is that famous line about steam-engines. For centuries kettles had "blabbed their secrets", he wrote, but "A social growth cannot find out the use of steam-engines, until comes steam-engine-time."

☐ **SHELDRAKE**: Since I'm a theist I think there *is* an outside influence. In cases of simultaneous invention it is very difficult to distinguish between one person who picked up external influences and a second person who picked it up from him telepathically—or that the external factor influenced several people at the same time. Jung didn't want to admit telepathic-type connexions because he didn't think they could be explained causally...so he had to have the idea of something outside acting on two things at the same time to explain telepathy. There is no need to have that.

☐ **FT**: But there are synchronistic events which only involved one person so you couldn't say that telepathy, in the normal sense, was involved—unless we are in contact telepathically across time with our future and past selves.

☐ **SHELDRAKE**: People have favoured synchronicity explanations because they didn't want to have to introduce causal or telepathic type connexions. I don't know what Fort's reasons were, but Jung's were quite invalid. He simply swallowed, hook, line and sinker, the standard chemical and physical theories of causation of his day, without considering that they could be expanded.

□ **FT**: Fort, like you, thought of it as only one of several potent possibilities, which at that time could not be supported any more than any other theory. Jung never went so far as to describe how his synchronicity could actually affect material things or bring about coincidences in the physical realm—but your idea of morphic resonance fills the gap to some extent. If you are willing to accept the likelihood of forces like psychokinesis, could there not be some form of psychokinetic involvement in our own genetic development?

□ **SHELDRAKE**: You mean psychokinetically altering genes...?

□ **FT**: Yes. Perhaps the archetype of a species can influence the development of its individuals, or the formation of new morphogenetic fields, within limits, by something analogous to psychokinesis?

□ **SHELDRAKE**: Yes, that's how I think it works. Two things here... First, the morphogenetic field, in so far as it's a system of repetition, isn't what gives rise to new forms. It simply repeats things which have already happened. But on the question of how super-archetypes make the transition from the purely creative conscious realm outside nature, as it were, to inserting these ideas within nature, *that* could be a form of psychokinesis, yes. But the morphogenetic fields are psychokinetic in the sense that they order quantum probabalistic events and cause things to happen. You could say they are *like* psychokinetic fields, but the word introduces the 'psychic' element, which I don't need.

□ **FT**: ...and the 'kinesis' side of the word implies something energetic...

□ **SHELDRAKE**: Yes. So it's not really a good word for the action of morphogenetic fields.

Actually I think most kinds of psychokinesis can be explained in terms of motor-fields. Because the motor-fields spread out the whole time. Everything in our field of perception comes within these fields which act either on our brains, as they normally do to bring about movements, or if the brain is 'blocked', if you don't act, then it could act directly on an external object...and you'd get a psychokinetic event.

□ **FT**: One of the main problems argued over by parapsychologists is this business of "exteriorization" of force. Nandor Fodor once described poltergeists, in his theory, as "bundles of projected repressions". It seems to me that you are offering a much more wholesome, or embracing, alternative. One has to consider the whole field of which the agent is perhaps like the nucleus of a cell...

□ **SHELDRAKE**: Exactly. Bergson, in *Matter and Memory* says this...that we're the center of our perceptual field which spreads out around us. When I look at a candle, there is a field, embracing me and the candle. The perception of the candle exists there [points at candle] in

Some Implications.

The sure sign of the advent of a new paradigm is the extent of its influence. A new paradigm should harmonize data and observations previously in apparent disagreement or apparently unrelated. It should shed new light on existing thought (eg. Einstein's theories did not render Newton's utterly invalid but simply showed up the limits of their applicability). A paradigm should also bring within the area of serious scientific study subjects or phenomena previously thought anomalous. The hypothesis of formative causation does all these. It applies to both animate and inanimate nature and provides a new context for some long-standing problems in a number of sciences, especially life sciences.

We list below just a few of the subjects in which we can see an immediate application of the idea of morphic resonance between formative fields. Others will undoubtedly be added as the usefulness of the paradigm spreads.

• IN MEDICINE: post amputation 'phantom limb' sensations; acupuncture meridians; limb regeneration; psychosomatic disorders; spontaneous remissions and healing; etc.

• IN PSYCHOLOGY: instincts; intuitive skills; the nature of memory; behavioural conditioning and reflexes; accelerated learning; 'body images'; apparent body memories of old traumas; gestalt theories; 'mass hysteria' and mass panics; the power of ritual and symbol; substantiation of the Collective Unconscious; transmission of archetypes; etc.

• IN SOCIOLOGY: belief systems; the cumulative effects of shared belief; progressive achievement and record-breaking in athletics; simultaneous inventions; etc.

• IN PSI RESEARCH: telepathy, 'psychic healing'; astrological 'types'; telepathic or shared hallucinations; ghosts and apparitions; materialization phenomena; synchronicity and coincidence; reincarnation; 'resonance' during group meditation; etc.

Further evidence of the vitality of Sheldrake's theory is the way it relates to some esoteric philosophical problems at the leading-edge of physics and psychology, as pointed out by the *Brain/Mind Bulletin*: "In his synthesis, Sheldrake refers to physicist David Bohm's 'enfolded order' and physical chemist Ilya Prigogine's proof of an ordering principle in entropy itself. The idea of morphic resonance is compatible with the idea of holographic reality, [but] Sheldrake doesn't require a holographic theory of brain function, because he doesn't think memory is confined to the brain itself."[14]

that field—it's not somehow inside my brain. These perceptual fields are extended things, and space is in a sense built up by these projections.

□ **FT**: This relates to the mind/body problem too. Because we see from a point in physical space we tend to believe objects are external to us, that is separate from us...but the Hindu view would be to think in terms of a totality relating the seer, the seen and the act of seeing...

□ **SHELDRAKE**: ...Exactly...

□ **FT**: ...and you say this forms a field, which in turn structures or orders the events connected to its parts.

□ **SHELDRAKE**: Yes, that's how motor-fields work. I talk about it to a slight extent in my book but I didn't want to develop it there. I thought it would probably be going too far too fast.

□ **FT**: From what we've talked about so far the implications of your work will be far-reaching—far beyond the note on which you end the book. Obviously, as you say, the book was intended to introduce the ideas to biologists and physical scientists. How far do you see these implications extending, whether the theory is proved experimentally or not?

□ **SHELDRAKE**: Some experimental psychologists are also taking up my challenges. One is Prof Steven Rose of the Open University. One is in Canada and another in Chile. They are all rat people. I have not come across any chemists yet to do the crystal experiment.

I think, if it's proved experimentally, there will be a sort of band-wagon effect in science, and lots of people will begin working experimentally on this kind of problem.

□ **FT**: You could say this would be the sort of accumulation your theory predicts. We might call it Sheldrakeism![25]

□ **SHELDRAKE**: If the experiments work it will mean a new research programme in science and science will become quite different. We can't imagine what will happen.

□ **FT**: Well, at one stroke, you will have extended the scope of science to include many subjects until now regarded as paranormal or anomalous...

□ **SHELDRAKE**: But if the experiments don't work and go on not working then it would indicate to me that the kind of casual connexion through or across time which I'm suggesting doesn't happen, and that the whole world is based on transcendent archetypes which are somehow present everywhere and essentially changeless..whereas right now it is only speculation. The failure of the experiments would be as interesting as their success. Such a failure would provide actual evidence for a Platonic view of things. The failure would show that the possible way of looking at things with connexions across time is not the main way things happen, although there may well be some instances of it. Things would then depend on changeless archetypes somewhere outside time...

so we'd have the transcendent, the metaphysical, bearing down on reality much more immediately.

But I think the view, of casual connections through time, is more attractive for a number of reasons. The idea that morphogenetic and motor fields work in and across time fits much better, firstly with the idea of cumulative evolution (because if they are eternal it would be difficult to understand evolution in nature), and secondly, it fits much better with the phenomenon of memory (because memory is something which occurs in or across time.) So I think that reality connected across time is much more likely.

But in spite of that, if the experiments don't work, and then one thinks up new kinds of experiments which ought to work and don't, one would be forced to the view that reality depends on timeless changeless archetypes... Whereas I think we live in the echoes of creative acts from the past—that is, they impinge on reality, and the echoes of that impingement persist through time—but creative acts may also happen now.

□ **FT**: Perhaps the creative act of you conceiving this theory or hypothesis will eventually create the environment for it to be proved, or the phenomena which proves it?

□ **SHELDRAKE**: That would be introducing a highly psycho-kinetic element. One could say that our expectations about nature will govern the way the experiments work and reality happens. I actually think that in particle physics this is what's happening. New theories are thought up about quarks and gluons, and when they do experiments in highly unstable states of matter which are subject to very subtle influences which could well include psycho-kinetic forces...then they discover these new particles, usually a year or two after they've been postulated theoretically. This could well be an example of this kind of thing...

□ **FT**: This recalls Joseph Chilton Pierce's notions that reality itself is hierarchical, with 'everyday reality' being formed by concensus [26]. The trouble is that before we can contribute to that concensus, we have been thoroughly indoctrinated with it from the moment of our birth. According to Pierce children may develop highly individual forms of reality, but by the time of our adolescent revolution we have aquiesced to the adult concensus, or at least are only able to rebel against it in term of its own language, so we become agents of it, perpetuating it.

If I want to levitate [straining sounds] I find I can't. Although my idea has as much validity as any other, it is in fact a feeble thing competing against the accumulated inertia of millions of other minds who in a myriad little ways are constantly reaffirming to themselves 'the way things are', which happens to be a concensus in which levitation has no practical value. If I could invest my idea with whatever it is that makes things real I might have some success...

☐ **SHELDRAKE**: I could agree with that...

☐ **FT**: Pierce suggests that the numbers of people who subscribe to an idea could be as important a factor in reifying the idea as the intensity of belief. While a saint, or someone in an altered state of consciousness, may be able to do things which are 'non-ordinary', to use Pierce's term, he says groups of people who subscribe to the same idea, reinforce each others' beliefs to the extent of creating a new reality, a new concensus. He cites Jesus's words to the effect that his teachings will come alive wherever two or three people gather together in his name...

☐ **SHELDRAKE**: Heavens, yes! This is the essence of the Christian faith...that the Church is the body of Christ, the assembly of the faithful...and the idea of the 'kingdom of God' precisely refers to a state where the concensus reality, or concensus state of consciousness is raised to a new level in which things are seen in a new way...and the idea of Jesus passing through first into this new state, and by that act making it possible for all to pass through... and the idea of the communion of saints, which is the community of all faithful people, refers precisely to the growth of a body of people who've been through this change making it easier for others to follow. And when the whole human race is transformed—well not everyone; some are sloughed off in the apocalyptic view— you'd finally have not only a transformed human race but a new universe, the 'kingdom of God'.

•

NOTES AND REFERENCES

1) **Thomas S.Kuhn**, *The Structure of Scientific Revolutions* (1962, 1970) University of Chicago Press, Chicago.
2) **Rupert Sheldrake**, *A New Science of Life: The Hypothesis of Formative Causation* (1981) Blond & Briggs, London; (1982) JP Tarcher, Los Angeles.
3) **Rupert Sheldrake**, 'A New Science of Life', *New Scientist* 18 June 1981, pp766-8.
4) **Gustaf Stromberg**, *The Soul of the Universe* (1948).
5) **Harold S.Burr**, *Fields of Life* (1972), published in the UK as *Blueprint for Immortality* (1972) Neville Spearman, London.
6) **Curtis Fuller**, 'I See by the Papers', *Fate Magazine* April 1982, pp7-16.
7) **Walter Carington**, *Telepathy* (1945) Methuen, London.
8) **Alister Hardy**, *The Living Stream* (1965) Collins, London.
9) **Henri Bergson**, *Creative Evolution* (1911) Macmillan, London.
10) **Hans Driesch**, *Science and Philosophy of the Organism* (1908, 1929) A&C Black, London.
11) **Henri Bergson**, *Matter and Memory* (1898, 1911) Allen & Unwin, London.
12) **Damon Knight**, *Charles Fort: Prophet of the Unexplained* (1970) Doubleday, NY; Gollanz, London.
13) Anonymous, 'A Book for Burning', *Nature* 24 Sept 1981, pp245-6; and correspondence, 'Incendiary Subject', *Nature* 15 Oct 1981, pp506, 594.
14) 'A New Science of Life', *Brain/Mind Bulletin* 3 Aug 1981, a complimentary copy of which may be had by sending a self addressed envelope and stamp or international postal reply coupon to B/MB: Box 42211, Los Angeles, CA 90042, USA. Also of help in this exposition were: 'M-field Controversy Hotting Up', *B/MB* 26 Oct 1981; 'Nobelist Sees Legitimacy in Sheldrake's Theories', *B/MB* 23 Nov 1981.
15) Unfortunately we don't have copies of these references on file.
16) **R.Semon**, *The Mneme* (1921) Allen & Unwin, London.
17) 'Single-minded', *Fortean Times* 35, p44.
18) **Ian Stevenson**, *Twenty Cases Suggestive of Reincarnation* (1966) American Society for Psychical Research, NY.
19) **Geoffrey Hodson**, *Fairies at Work and Play* (1925) Theosophical Publishing House, London.
20) **John Michell & Robert Rickard**, *Living Wonders: Mysteries & Curiosities of the Animal World* (to be published Oct 1982) Thames & Hudson, London.
21) **Max Freedom Long**, *The Secret Science Behind Miracles* (1948) Huna Research, Vista, California.
22) **Marie-Louise von Franz**, *Number and Time* (1974) Rider, London.
23) **C.G.Jung**, *Synchronicity* (1972) RKP, London - also in Collected Works vol 8.
24) *The Complete Books of Charles Fort* (1941, 1975) Dover, NY, p557.
25) According to *B/MB* [14] 26 Oct 1981, one reader of the *New Scientist* article wrote [15] that he had published a hypothesis very like Sheldrake's 20 years earlier. "We both talked of a 'resonance' influence that could pattern probabilistic events into similar forms, independently of spatio-temporal separation. Is this duplication of the hypothesis evidence for itself?"
26) **Joseph Chilton Pearce**, *The Crack in the Cosmic Egg* (1971) Julian Press, NY, (1973), Pocket Books, NY; *Exploring the Crack in the Cosmic Egg* (1974) Julian Press, NY, (1975) Pocket Books, NY.
27) **Lyall Watson**, *Lifetide* (1979) Hodder & Stoughton, London, pp156-8.

Editor's Note: I would like to thank John Michell for letting us use his flat for the interview; the John Innes Institute, Norwich, for providing the 'Composite' photo and permission to use it; and the *Brain/Mind Bulletin* for permission to excerpt their 'Special Issue' [14] although in the end I did not use as much as I thought I might. *B/MB* is essential reading for me and I recommend it to all who need to keep up with the very latest discoveries and discussions on topics related to reality and consciousness. It comes out every 3 weeks and costs $15/yr (US) or $22 elsewhere airmail, from the address in [14] above. Although not cited here, bibliophiles might wish to know that a slightly rewritten version of the *New Scientist*[3] article appeared in *Science Digest* Oct 1981. pp54-7; and *New Scientist*'s own comment on the infamous *Nature*[13] editorial appeared in *N.Sci* 1 Oct 1981 •RJMR.

AMERICA MYSTICA
25
• by Michael Hoffman •

THE TRUE VINE

In the fecund summer of 1776, in the tavern-Masonry town of Boston, a teenage Quaker girl hallucinated. She spoke of angels and talking heads. In autumn she went into a coma, but after three days "arose" as if from the dead, and proclaimed to her startled relatives and friends that her name was no longer Jemima Wilkinson, but the 'Public Universal Friend'.

She founded her own American religion. Professor Wisbey, who has written her only credible biography, describes her teachings as "an interesting blend of practical, familiar biblical axioms and obscure mysticism"[1]. The latter included bibliomancy, geomancy and telepathy. Wisbey says 'The Friend' (as she came to be called), predicted the 'Dark Day' of May 19, 1780 when a late morning darkness fell over southern New England. Eye witnesses reported seeing copper red or yellow clouds amid the premature night-tide and of experiencing a "smoky smell".

Jemima first attempted to settle her rapidly growing community of followers in Massachusetts but encountered stiff resistance. She moved instead to the Quaker stronghold of Philadelphia where, apparently, the City of Brotherly Love had none to spare for its sister. It seems the Philadelphians were ill-disposed to the fact that The Friend controlled a community of women *and* men. One critic called her "a one-woman power". The resentment was compounded when it was learned that Jemima gave the highest positions of authority and trust in her society to members of her own gender who pledged to abstain from sexual relations with men. To top it all, The Friend and her 'Faithful Sisterhood' wore "masculine costumes". Before she was booted out of the Pennsylvania metropolis, a French aristocrat, the Marquis de Barbe-Marbois, recorded in his journal that this remarkable Matriarch had telepathic powers.

Jemima then moved to the wilderness of the Genessee Country in western New York state. The Red Indians of the region were hostile to whites generally and the state authorities in particular. But The Friend was openly welcomed and dubbed *"Shinnewawna gis tau, ge"* or 'Great Woman'. Her first settlement was in a cave complex near the western shore of Seneca Lake. Her ability to live peacably with the natives and establish a foothold for her community would prove to be her undoing. Masonic land speculators put her and her community through every imaginable harrassment. When The Friend passed away or "left time" as the Faithful Sisterhood said, this male secret society appropriated most of the matriarchal community's land. Curiously, the men and women who were tricked by the

A rare portrait of Jemima Wilkinson, the 'Publick Universal Friend' [from Wisbey's biography.]

Masons into compromising Jemima, exhibited a high incidence of unhappy early deaths in the throes of unknown maladies, while those who kept the faith with The Friend enjoyed remarkable longevity.

After the cave complex, The Friend founded her New Jerusalem in the center of an aboriginal ritual site. Actually, New Jerusalem was bounded on the southeast by a 14 acre pre-Columbian megalithic complex. This site, in turn, is directly aligned with an ancient earthenwork ten miles northwest. This latter area is adjacent to a tall hill where beacon fires would have been plainly visible at the 14 acre complex, at what is today Bluff Point.

The Bluff Point megalithic construction was destroyed in the latter half of the nineteenth century, with some of the stones having been pulled down by farmers and others used in the construction of the Wagner mansion. The ley-hunter and co-creator of a modern megalithic monument near Ithaca, NY, Chuck Pettis, map-dowsed an 1880 survey document of the Bluff Point site and reported that two leys continue to intersect the area.

The original fourteen acre parcel contained several stone circles and squares, dozens of walled compounds enclosing them and a single 8 feet tall, three feet wide, pointed monolith at the northwestern portion. This "sentinel" stone was exactly aligned with the earthenwork ten miles further northwest. The Friend's community lay between them and it is hard not to imagine The Friend, who used to ride in a carriage marked with the old half-moon crescent symbol of the Goddess[2], conducting private meditations and rituals in what must have been a fourteen acre megalithic wonderland. Pettis reports that one ley line goes directly down into the spot where once stood the eight foot stone, and another traverses a series of

recumbent stones near the monolith. So, it would appear this has been a "live" site for some time.

In the Spring of 1794, Jemima built a large and imposing three-story clapboard house one mile west of the beacon hill and earthenwork. When I visited this earthenwork site, the "locals" informed me that science classes from a nearby high school annually visited the complex to do lab tests on its still sparklingly-pure spring water. There are also abundant pockets of natural gas around it. Sometime after 1794, The Friend began a cemetery 300 yards southeast of the earthenwork and directly on the alignment with the Sentinel Stone at Bluff Point. This was a burial place for her most faithful sisters and their stones remain today.

Jemima was a superb equestrian, mid-wife, herbal healer...and warrior—she and her sisters once overpowered two Masons in a brawl and sent them running for their lives. As 1815 approached and The Friend's thoughts turned to the task of leaving time, not to mention the ever-widening pattern of harrassment from the corrupt patriarchy, she took long rides into the countryside on her horse. This portion of western New York, bounded on the east by Seneca Lake and in the west by Canandaigua Lake is something of an enchanted realm, or was in 1815. Pioneers sometimes wrote of seeing alien animals ("lions with erect tails"), of alchemical-like gold at the bottom of misty Guyanoga Valley. It seemed that a month didn't go by without some ploughman turning up an Indian skeleton so old the Iroquois had no knowledge of it, and of course the eerie stone circus at Bluff Point still stood in its multi-acred splendor, radiating power engineered by a race long disappeared.

But there was yet another power site between the lakes and one that this writer thinks

may hold a clue to yet another enigma surrounding the life of The Friend. In her rides through forest and valley, The Friend became aware of the Bare Hill/Serpent Mound site on the pinnacles overlooking Canandaigua Lake in what is today Middlesex. At Serpent Mound a snake-like string of stones winds up Bare Hill where the Seneca Indians say their people sprang, like maize from mounded earth.

Officially, no one knows where The Friend is buried[3], but following a hunch, I asked Chuck Pettis to map-dowse the area and his findings seem to suggest that The Friend is buried within the Middlesex-Serpent Mound area, in a place the old-timers call "Vine Valley".

And despite a nuclear army base twenty miles to the east and the usual wages of a christianised and alcohol-sotted populace, there remains a mystical resonance, in those still-sparsely populated grounds where once trod the Public Universal Friend, and before her a race of megalithic builders. She must still be there, if the sentiments of an 1840 folk-song are at all accurate. It is titled, "A Wonderful Dream" and contains a strange blend of Reincarnation lore and tales of our Friend.

●

Michael A. Hoffman

NOTES

1— **Herbert A. Wisbey,** Pioneer Prophetess (1964: Cornell University Press).

2— Her carriage is currently housed at the Granger Homestead museum in Canandaigua along with one the Marquis de Lafayette stole from a prosperous Babbit.

3— All kinds of explanations are given for the mystery. Some say two men connected with the Masons removed her body from its original resting place at the clapboard house. Others claim the grave is anonymous in keeping with a Quaker custom. Many of The Friend's relics are at the Oliver House museum in Penn Yan and lovingly maintained by Yates County historian Virginia Gibbs.

ON THE TRAIL by Loren Coleman

KANGAROOS ACROSS AMERICA

Not since 1977[1] have I sat down and overviewed the phantom kangaroo situation. A lot of hopping has happened since then in North America, and some interesting developments have occurred. The visitations of the uncatchable kangaroos generally follow an April to August pattern, so before the 1982 flap gets off the ground, let us examine the recent mystery kangaroo sightings.

Wisconsin was hit by one of these wacky waves in 1978; Ontario and New Brunswick were treated to kangaroo visits in 1979; and during 1981, a virtual explosion of incidents occurred in Utah, Oklahoma, and North Carolina.

David Fideler and I finished our April 1978 article with these words: ".... it seems safe to say that somewhere in the American countryside a mystery kangaroo is just waiting to spring into action." As *Fate* was hitting the newstands, the phantom kangaroos had indeed sprung into action in Wisconsin.

The most startling result of the Wisconsin drama was the first photograph of a phantom kangaroo – a mostly unheralded picture, published here for the first time in the Fortean literature. But prior to the photograph being taken, a series of kangaroo close encounters occurred.

The fifth of April, 1978, is the first recorded date of a Waukesha, Wiskonsin, area sighting. On that day, at 6:45 a.m., east of Highway A, on East Moreland Blvd, witnesses Wilcox and Kroske saw

a kangaroo. This was followed by the April 12th, sighting by members of the Haeselich family of nearby Pewaukee Township.

"It was pretty quick. It was hopping. We knew it had to be a kangaroo," Jill Haeselich told a reporter at the time.

Jill, her husband Peter, and his mother, Esther, were sitting in the dining room eating supper about 6:15 p.m. when they spotted the kangaroo in their back yard. It disappeared over a hill as Peter tried to pursue it. "It was so fast," Jill recalled.

The next day, at 4:45 p.m., William J. Busch was returning home from his job as a social worker at a Waukesha County residential school when he saw his kangaroo. Busch was driving on Highway 83, when about 15 feet in front of him, a three foot tall creature with a "slightly odd-shaped" head, little front legs, and long back feet scampered across the road.

Three days later at 3 a.m. on April 16, Greg and Janet Napientek saw a kangaroo as they were driving home along Highway A, east of Wausecha.

"I've seen deer before. I know what a deer looks like. I know it was a kangaroo", Janet Napientek observed.

Up in their hilltop home on Sierra Drive in Brookfield Township, near Waukesha, the Nero family has a good view of the nearby wooded terrain. On the 23rd of April, around 10:45 a.m., Lance Nero was having toast and coffee when he glanced outside to see *two* kangaroos hop out of the woods, across a road, through part of a field, and across another road. Lance and Loretta

Nero, plus members of the Waukesha County Sheriff's Department discovered tracks left behind by the animals. Some deputies tried to quickly debunk the tracks by saying they were made by deer or cow, in spite of their appearance.

Veteran cryptozoologist Mark A. Hall interviewed the Neros and found them to be bright and sincere people. They showed Hall five casts, and he described the tracks to me: "Generally the tracks have a two-pronged fork appearance with two knobs at the rear of the 'fork handle'. The tracks were impressed into mud at a new housing development which accounts somewhat for the depth of them." Measuring two of the casts (see accompanying photographs), Mark Hall found this range in length, 5.75 inches to 6.0 inches (14.5 cm to 15.5 cm); and width, 2.75 inches to 3.125 inches (7.0 cm to 8.0 cm).

As if the tracks of a phantom kangaroo were not enough, on the 24th of April, 1978, a good photograph of one of the elusive beasts was taken. At 5:20 p.m. on that Monday, two 23 year old Menomonee Falls men spotted a kangaroo in the bush near Highway SS and Highway M. They took two SX-70 Polaroid color photographs. One photograph is blurry, but the other clearly shows a kangaroo-like animal (see accompanying photograph). The two men refused to give their identity to a reporter in 1978, fearing public ridicule.

The clear color Polaroid picture shows a tan animal with lighter brown front limbs, hints of a lighter brown hind limb, dark brown or black patches around the eyes, inside the two upright ears, and possibly surrounding the nose and upper mouth area. The animal compares favorably with Bennett's wallaby or brush Kangaroo[2] a native of Tasmania, found from the snowy summits of lower valleys. The Wauseska phantom

A B&W version of the colour polaroid print of a wild kangaroo [from files of Loren Coleman.]

also looks like the black-tailed or swamp wallaby[3] a marsupial inhabiting the wet dense gullies from Queensland to SE South Australia. Or, of course, it could be some undiscovered form of mammal we have as yet not imagined. Anything from Hall's Giant Monkey, to Coleman's North American Ape are monstrous possibilities.

Still, whatever they are, they continued to be seen in Wisconsin in 1978. At 2:30 a.m., on the 24th of April, Tom Frank saw one near Highway C in Merton Township. On the 9th of May, at the Camelot Forest housing development, Waukesha County's last kangaroo of 1978 was sighted.

Later in the month of May, some 185 miles northeast of Waukesha, in Eau Claire County, Wisconsin, another kangaroo was spied. On the 21st, a Sunday night, an Eau Claire woman was returning home, on Highway 12 between Augusta and Fall Creek, when she saw a creature the size of a man hopping across the road.

So ended the 1978 Wisconsin kangaroo accounts.

Canada was the site during the warm months of 1979 for some more mystery kangaroo visitations.

Early on the morning of the 31st of May, a police officer radioed the station to report he had sighted a kangaroo in the Markham Road — Finch Avenue area of Scarboro, a section of Toronto, Ontario. A Metro Toronto Zoo official, asked for his opinion said: "We're definitely not missing any wallabies or any other kind of creature and we haven't sent anyone out to look for anything. It's likely just a rabbit with long ears".

A few days later and several hundred miles to the northeast, another kangaroo popped up.

Roy Hanley, a guard at the Acadia Forest Products, Ltd. mill in Nelson-Miramichi, New Brunswick, saw a kangaroo at 3 a.m. on the 5th of June, 1979. Hanley was on duty at the time when he came upon the creature.

"I was standing no more than 10 feet from him. As far as I'm concerned it was a baby kangaroo", Hanley told reporters. "It was about 3 to 3½ feet in height, had large powerful looking hind legs, small front paws, a long large tail, big droopy ears, and a greyish-brown coat".

A taxi driver and her passenger also had seen a kangaroo near the mill, and other encounters were reported from Millton and Douglasville, New Brunswick, near the Maine border.

The Hanley sighting stimulated interest in the folk collection of the *Songs of the Miramichi.* Folksong No. 47 is entitled, "The Wild Cat Back on the Pipe Line," and tells of the many people who saw a strange animal on the pipeline. One passage goes:

"The next one that saw it, his name was LeClair.

He said 'twas no monkey, nor neither a bear,

For he came from Australia and knows it is true,

For he saw many like it, 'twas a big kangaroo".

This song, written by Jared MacLean, is dated 1948, and gives a good deal of historical backdrop to the recent kangaroo reports out of New Brunswick. The title of the song, "The Wild Cat Back on the Pipe Line", further demonstrates how the kangaroo and phantom panther accounts often merge. Along with the reported encounter between Herman Belyea and an erect panther in 1951 in New Brunswick, strange, upright, kangaroo-like animals appear to have a lengthy history in this part of Canada, separate from the eastern Bigfoot/ Windigo lore.

1980 was an uneventful phantom kangaroo year. I have yet to find one good report for that twelve month period. Ed Barker of KGO radio, San Francisco, recently told me that a crew of his searched Golden Gate Park, probably in 1980, after some San Franciscans reported they spotted a kangaroo there. Even

the 1980 accounts are phantoms.

(In August 1980, a large escaped zoo wallaby showed up on Connie Forster's New Westminster, British Columbia, porch. It was soon returned to the Stanley Park Zoo. Five days later, a New Hampshire newspaper ran a photograph of a dog impersonating a kangaroo chasing a Frisbee, under the headline, "Why is He Hurling a Pie at a Kangaroo?" A final coincidence behind both incidents is that the British Columbian wallaby and the New Hampshire dog happened to have the same name, "Rocky".)

1981 produced a bumper crop of kangaroo stories. Beginning in June, they stretched into October, from the Rockies to Appalachia.

Ray Ault saw the year's first 'roo early in June. Rancher Ault was out with his sheep near Cedar Fort, Utah County, Utah, when he was spooked by an animal jumping six feet straight in the air. "I was checking the sheep up the canyon and off to the side of them I saw something jump straight up. I thought that was a little strange. I got closer to the animal that jumped and it looked me right in the eye. Then jump...jump...jump...off

it went," Ault said.

Ray Ault was certain it was a kangaroo, and commented, "I've seen kangaroos in the movies and on TV and there was no mistaking it. It looked like a big kangaroo rat, kind of yellowish with some dark on the ears. Who knows where the thing came from?"

The Utah rancher was scared at first, but then began to worry about what his friends would think. "Of course they all thought I was crazy and they said I'd been hanging around in the sheep pen too long. But after I described everything they finally believed me," Ault said later.

From Tulsa, Oklahoma, a new twist was added to the usual mystery kangaroo tales. On Monday, the 31st of August 1981, a blond bearded man went into a Tulsa cafe, ordered a coffee, and told the waitress, Marilyn Hollenback, he had just hit a kangaroo. She laughed for 20 minutes, she later said. The unidentified man also told Tulsa Police officers, patrolman Ed Compos and his partner Sgt. Lynn Jones. The officers and the waitress then looked in the back of the man's truck and saw a 3½ foot kangaroo. The skeptical cafe patrons were convinced. But there is more. The man told them

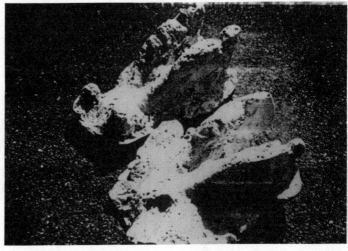

Lance Nero and plaster casts of the Brookfield kangaroo [Photos: Mark Hall.]

there were two kangaroos because he swerved and missed one. The man, his dead kangaroo and his truck drove away, never to be seen again. Officer Ed Compos told reporters, "I wish I had taken a picture of it. I told the whole squad and they are laughing about it. There was a dead kangaroo! Everyone saw it."

An Owasso, Oklahoma family came forth later in the week insisting they frequently had to dodge three foot tall kangaroos while making early morning rounds delivering newspapers.

Finally late in September 1981, something happened which frequently occurs in the midst of a mystery animal flap. Namely an exotic animal which could not realistically be confused for the reported creature is captured, and the media/officialdom uses the alien animal to "explain away" the mystery beast sightings. Just such an event occurred on the 27th of September, 1981, a Sunday, when a 25 pound Patagonian Cavy or Mara was caught. What this particular South American rodent was doing in Tulsa, Oklahoma, no one could guess, but it fits well into the pattern of such Fortean things.

Reflecting historically for a moment, we only have to go back to 1974 to find two good examples of this. During the Chicago kangaroo flap, a kinkajou was seized. This wee South American procyonid was exploited by the skeptics, and immediately utilized as a convenient candidate to debunk the widespread series of kangaroo reports. During the same year, an incredible something attacked and killed dogs, cats and rabbits in Arlington County, Virginia. This mystery beast flap was detoured by the capture of a palm civet. Exotics appearing in the middle of monster sighting waves have become a classic trait I have begun to more and more frequently observe. Not too surprising, then, that a

Patagonian cavy should turn up in Oklahoma when the news began to talk of kangaroo capers.

From Oklahoma, the kangaroos next made an appearance in North Carolina. Near Asheville, home of the famed Brown Mountain Lights, a kangaroo was seen on Friday, the 9th of October 1981, near a Biltmore, North Carolina motel. Police and reporters gave chase.

"I was afraid someone might shoot it!" exclaimed motel desk clerk Jeff Greene.

The kangaroo was neither shot nor caught. It, like the scores before it, disappeared into the morning dew, and this one was not seen again around the motel.

Mystery animals take many forms. Phantom kangaroos are apparently the latest incarnation, and just as surely as I put these words to paper, there is another one out there ready to bound into our consciousness. Perhaps we

should pause a moment and consider the little joke these newest members of the cryptozoological tribe may be playing on us. For, you see, the zoological genus to which the flesh and blood wallabies and kangaroos belong is termed "Macropus", and that literally means "Big Foots"!

●

Loren Coleman

NOTES

1 – *Loren Coleman* and *David Fideler's* "Phantom Kangaroos: A Catalogue and Analysis of Reports", *Anomaly Research Bulletin*, No. 7, September 1977; and our "Kangaroos From Nowhere", *Fate*, April, 1978.
2 – *Macropus rufogriseus bennetti,* and
3 – *Wallabia bicolor*, after *John Gould, Kangaroos,* NY, Doubleday, 1973.
Watch for Loren Coleman's *Weird Excursions Across America* due out late in 1982 from Charles River Books, Boston.

The black Zoobox was seen in Dublin during the first few months of 1981. I encountered it myself, flapping darkly around Henrietta Street; pecking at bruised fruit on Moore Street; sticking up its four fine horns at Trinity College; menacing the ducks on St Stephens Green; enveloping nightjars at Slattery's in Capel Street; pleasing groups of city punks on O'Connell Bridge. Then, very suddenly in May, it was floated and flown across the rolling water, again, to Amsterdam (where it achieved a certain amount of theatrical notoriety).

I hung around Dublin for a little while, then travelled through the sweet counties of Kildare, Offaly, Roscommon, Galway, Clare, Tipperary, Limerick, Cork and Kerry; carrying a special leg-bone from a friendly puck goat by the name of Giles. We...the bone and I... rested for a while near St Gobnat's Well and thought of that blessed lady blowing a

A sky-clad witch wades into Lough Learne [Photo: Doc Shiels/FPL.]

swarm of wild bees from her mouth to chase and sting a gang of vandals. That was at hotel to turf-smoked shebeen.

Now, it should be explained that the Shiels tribe is fairly well known in south-west Ireland. The sight of my tall hat and the more or less musical Ballyvourney, close to the spot where a phantom 'lynx' has been encoutered. My good dog Toby—ex Punch and Judy performer—started a huge hare on the mountain road, no more than a hundred yards from 'lynx corner'. It was the biggest hare I had ever seen...up to then.

A small replica of the original Zoobox...a black box-kite... slipped into Ireland as the big one slipped out.

In May, in the Kingdom of Kerry, in the town of Killarney, where rooks and roy-stons congregate as thick as thieves, there was also a gathering together of our rough band, family and friends, eager for adventure. Most of the summer was spent in that corner of the land, adventuring. We heard tales of Fairies, Cluricaunes, Leprechauns, Phoukas, Formorians, Dullahans, Sheeries, Gruagachs, and Peisthas, alive-alive-oh, from an assortment of story-tellers in all manner of settings, from super-smart

sounds of our various instruments are familiar and welcome to many's the cultured Munster eye and ear. We earn a kind of living as travelling entertainers; a calling which opens many interesting doors, though it must be admitted that a few of the less interesting kind have been slammed in our faces. It's a way of life which brings us into contact with all kinds of people, on the road, at fairs, in pubs and so on. A lot of our friends are travellers too...gypsies, horse-traders, music-makers, tinkers, circus and show folk...our paths cross time and again. When we meet, we usually have a few jars and a bit of an old session, the 'crack' being the main thing. In short, we have, perhaps, a better chance of hearing (and telling) strange tales than anyone in the 'normal' nine-to-five kind of job.

Ireland is throbbing with Fortean phenomena but, Ireland being Ireland, 'events' and 'encounters' of a Fortean kind are usually described or dismissed as blarney-ridden folklore. I'm half Irish (on my father's side) and half Scottish (God bless my sainted mother!), so I'm probably guilty of a certain amount of Gaelic prejudice, but I wouldn't like to think that I

was easily conned by any quaintly romantic Celtic bullshit. Fairies seem to thrive in Ireland, and why wouldn't they? I have spoken to dozens of intelligent, believable men and women who have had first-hand, personal dealings with the *Sidh*...not little green men from Mars or Venus, but home-grown little green men from Muckross or Ventry. These things reported, usually, in a manner which suggests that they are matters of fact rather than fiction.

For example, there was the girl from Cahirciveen who was walking home from work, one dark December evening, when she saw a tiny man with brown skin and a long nose mounted astride a black cat which bounded across the lane in front of her and leaped over a wall. That was supposed to have happened in 1980, and I had the story from a whistle player in Listowel. Also in that town, I heard about two brothers who, after a night on the booze, were driving back to their farm on a lonely country road. The vehicle, a small pickup truck, suddenly stalled and couldn't be re-started. One of the brothers got out to take a peek under the bonnet, then, as soon as he lifted it, a ball of blue flame, big as a football, shot up from the engine with a crackling sound and flew away into the night sky with the speed of a rocket. This happened very close to a fairy rath. The truck started again a few minutes later and the brothers, though shaken, were soon safely home. They both stopped drinking afterwards... for a whole month!

Then there was the tale of a Sligo fiddle player who had learned a set of tunes from a fairy piper he had met by a waterfall on the Owenmore River, near Ballysadare. And the old tinker woman who wore a lucky ring made from fairy gold, a personal gift from the little people, a reward for helping them in some mysterious way. There were more, many more, tales of this kind and I think I half believe at least half of them.

A couple of miles outside Killarney town, at a place called Lissyvigeen, there's a circle of stones, known now as the 'Seven Sisters'. Many times that summer we recharged ourselves and the little Zoobox there, with a pishogue and poteen. Then we headed for the haunts of O Donoghue Mor, to call up the Great Worm of Lough Leane. The lake is very beautiful, magically magnetic and redolent with atmosphere. According to tradition, it is a gateway (one of several) to the enchanted country Tir-na-n-Og; and home of the phantom chieftain, O'Donoghue, who is said to appear once every seven years, at Beltane. It also contains the Great Worm of Peiste More, a three-headed water beast of gigantic proportions, guardian of the O'Donoghue gold. Lough Leane is connected, by the Deenagh River, to Lough Lackagh, about three miles north-east of Killarney, where a horned, snake-necked monster has been seen and reported in recent years.

The month of June saw me back in Cornwall for a while. One day I was drinking with Peter Redrove, the writer, and he told me he had once seen a 'shimmering pisky'. Peter

knows about these things...and he is, by no means, daft. A few weeks later I was in Lancashire, where I encountered a Fylde Coast witch who told me about 'dancing goblins' she had seen in the sand dunes near Lytham. A wise lass, she advised me to get back to Ireland, fast, instead of going to Scotland, to Loch Ness, where I was heading at the time, with a big strong fellow called Allan Pickard. After some thought, I took the witch's advice and booked a ticket on the B+I ferry. Allan continued northwards, arrived at Loch Ness, had a quick look around the monster exhibit at Drumnadrochit, then suddenly collapsed with pneumonia! By that time I was sipping perfect Guiness in Courtney's Bar, Killarney.

At Puck Fair, in August, we met Rich Crowe from Chicago, keen to go hunting the curious Kerry Carbuncle. We met Mrs Dooley, the 'Original Gypsy Lee', keen to put a curse on some of the Killorglin elders. We met old shadow, the happy toothless balladeer, keen to give voice to his latest. We met mad Pan O'Donoghue, artist keen to trade portraits for pints. We met rakes of people, all keen to enjoy the good crack. We met King Puck himself, huge, horny and handsome. But I've told you about Puck before. The 1981 version was as wild as ever. Our little black Zoobox was there; and the evening sky over Killorglin town was filled with pink, saucer-shaped, lenticular clouds.

After Puck, I experimented with what I must call the Irish Rope Trick, related to the Indian version, of course, like so many things which connect Ireland with India. It was, I suspect, first performed in Ireland, centuries ago, by some shamanic gypsy or travelling trickster. One fine day, I mean to master that particular feat.

We returned time and again to Lough Leane, with a trio of witches, to raise the triple-headed monster. Several times, unusual disturbances broke the

smooth surface of the lake, near the island of Innisfallen. At night, sitting around the fire, we heard weird noises, animal sounds, faint music, laughter and whisperings, convincing us all of a fairy presence...expecially around midnight. One misty dawn, Chris and I were suddenly scared awake when a large 'thing' brushed against our tent before splashing into the lake. It was a stag, king of the local herd, keeping an eye on us.

In September, after a wild week in Tralee at 'the Rose' festivities, we staggered back to Killarney hoping for a rest. A telegram was waiting at Courtney's Bar, announcing the arrival of Clive Cooke, journalist, and his assistant, Jan. They had flown over from London to interview and photograph us for a newspaper series on monster hunters. I think Clive and Jan enjoyed their short stay in Kerry. We sent them home with well-earned hangovers, and decided to forget about having a rest.

For a little while longer, the weather was fine and we made a good living. Then, very suddenly, the summer ended and violent storms lashed the Kingdom. One terrible night, the wind ripped a great hole in our old tent and very nearly whipped it away over the mountains. The outdoor life, now, was neither healthy nor comfortable. All the wealthy tourist-punters had disappeared and busking money was hard to come by in Kerry. So the tribe split up. Some took off for sunnier parts of the world. Some, like Kate and Lucy, stayed in Ireland and found 'respectable' employment, frying chips and washing dishes. Others, including Chris, Toby and myself, returned to Cornwall for the winter. Before leaving Ireland, however, I took the goat bone and flung it far into the waters of Lough Leane where it will do its work quietly until we next decide to invoke the Great Worm.　　●

Doc Shiels.

This column is open to any reader who wishes to express an opinion, or to speculate, upon any topic related to the content or interests of FT. However entries must be typed and limited to no more than two pages.

ENERGY FROM SPACE

Space contains energy, which can be tapped directly. Most people think of space as being empty, but this has been scientifically demonstrated to be as inaccurate as the long-cherished belief that the earth is flat and the sun revolves around it. Space contains energy because it is actually composed of energy. The structure of space is energetic. Throughout the universe space consists of diffused energy, which can be tapped directly and cleanly and effectively, thus rendering both nuclear fission and fusion obsolete as energy sources. One of the many things rendered obsolete by this new concept is the power over people the power companies possess at present. If energy can be derived from space itself, once one has the proper equipment there is no longer any need to be plugged in to a central power station, or to pay anyone anything whatsoever for the energy. Those gigantic monopolies that entire populations are obliged to be dependent on are now doomed to extinction like the dinosaurs.

One would think that a discovery of this nature would make front page headline news world-wide. One would like to think that things have changed since the Inquisitors silenced Galileo. Let us consider what happened to the man who discovered this when he tried to make his findings public.

To begin with, his academic credentials: René-Louis Vallée studied under Louis de Broglie at the Ecole Supérieure d'Electricité de Paris, where he obtained his diploma in 1951. He studied Einstein's work from the original texts. He got an additional degree from the same institution in the electronic treatment of information. His speciality is mathematical logic, in particular binary analysis based on the work of Blanchard. He was employed by the Commisariat à l'Energie Atomique as an engineer for nearly twenty years. He is the author of four books, published by Masson. His first published article appeared in 1956 in a review named *L'Onde Electrique*, consisting of comments on Maxwell's equations. He is the author of numerous articles on relativity and the problem of instantaneity. In 1962 he published a paper expressing doubt as to whether "c" is really constant. Many of his articles have been published and distributed by the Commisariat à l'Energie Atomique. He taught at the Institut National des Sciences et Techniques Nucléaires, where he was Professor of Electronics.

Now that we have some idea of the man's background, let us proceed to an examination of the circumstances surrounding his discovery.

What Vallée discovered was that physical space is an energy structure which can be quantitatively defined. Matter has its origin in this energy structure, which contains the potential for manifestation of the physical, chemical and biological principles of everything which exists or which could possible exist in the universe. Vallée announced his discovery as the synergetic theory. The Commisariat à l'Energie Atomique published his original paper on synergetics and continued to support his research until its implications began to be realised.

Mr. Vallée's troubles began when he asked a group of physicists at work on the "Fusion" project at the Fontenay-aux-Roses plant to verify a precise point of his synergetic theory. They were working with a torus of the "Tokamak" type, which was made in Russia. The operation consisted in using the torus to observe the emission of slow neutrons from deuterium plasma after an electron-nucleus interaction. To his astonishment, his request upset the team of physicists, who had already discovered experimentally that these slow neutrons were present, but had decided to say nothing about them for the time being as they were unable to explain their origin. The result of the experiment had been dismissed as erroneous. Mr. Vallée suggested that they try using nitrogen 15 in the torus instead of deuterium of hydrogen, so that after each discharge they could obtain the reconstitution of the radioactive isobars "beta", which would prove both the reality of the energetic structure of space and the possibility now open to us to exploit it directly. The physicists became extremely upset. It was at this point that Mr. Vallée realised that the peaceful and distinguished academic career he had devoted his life to was doomed.

One could write a book about the way he was hounded from his job and excommunicated by the orthodox scientific community, the

Cont on p65

Australia's Lizard Monsters.

Australia was once called 'the attic of the world', the curious fauna and flora discovered there seemingly forgotten by time. If the known wildlife is strange how much more so is the unknown. Over the years the name of **Rex Gilroy** has stood out as someone who has not only studied and written about the mystery animals of Australia, but pursued them in the field as well. Unfortunately his researches have had little exposure outside Australia. We hope to remedy this; the present article being the first of an occasional series in FT. **Rex Gilroy** has been interested in Bunyips, Yowies, lake monsters etc for most of his life, and is curator of the Mount York Natural History Museum in New South Wales.

Over the years, I have collected a growing number of reports from the inhabitants of remote farming areas bordering the vast, inaccessible rainforest and scrub-covered mountain ranges of northern New South Wales and far north Queensland, suggesting that enormous reptiles—giant-sized monitor-like lizards—inhabit this region.

These stories date back far into the last century. In fact, Australian Aboriginal traditions preserve legends of these creatures dating back thousands of years, to a time when there were larger reptilian monsters, or "Bunyips". Similar reptilian monsters have been known to the natives of New Guinea for as long.

There is also a possibility that an even larger form of monitor-type giant reptile was known to the Australian Aborigines in pre-European times. Known as *Mungoon-galli*, the Aborigines insist these monsters grew up to 50ft and inhabited a particular remote area deep in the far northern New South Wales forests in swampier regions. Were these merely an exaggeration of the better known 30ft monitor, or some other creature of Neodinosaur classification?

The mystery 30ft giant monitors are also claimed to exist in at least a couple of areas further south in the eastern Australian mountain ranges, around the Wallangambie Wilderness a still unexplored region covering hundreds of square miles north of the Blue Mountains, and to the north-west around Capertee—where some farmers have been known to carry rifles with them when searching for strayed cattle in the dense scrub thereabouts.

On one occasion a few years ago, an unarmed farmer, searching for strayed cattle on horseback, saw one of these reptiles in the act of eating a cow it had just killed, at a distance of 100 yards from him on the edge of a paddock bordering dense forest. By the time the farmer had returned with his rifle the beast had fled.

Six years ago, in 1975, a group of bushwalkers reported finding large reptile tracks and tail marks in a gully on the edge of the Wallangambie Wilderness, which they followed for some distance through the scrub without seeing the creature who had made them.

In another incident, late one night early in 1980, a truck driver was forced to slow down to a stop on a remote stretch of the Bilpin Road, which borders the southern fringes of the Wallangambie Wilderness, when a 20ft length monitor moved across the road in front of his vehicle into scrub.

On December 27th 1975, a Cessnock farmer sighted a large monitor lizard moving through dense scrub near his barn; it was, he said, at least 30ft in length, of considerable bulk, perhaps over 2,000lbs in weight, and of a mottled greyish colour with a number of dark stripes running barrelwise down the creature's back and along the tail. It stood about 3ft off the ground on four powerfully built legs. The neck was long, at least 2ft thick, the head about 3ft in length.

Near the scene of this incident stands the Wattagan Mountain Range. Sightings of these giant monitor lizards in this region can be traced back to the year 1830, when the first Cedar timber cutters entered the range. Sightings of the monsters and discoveries of their tracks persist hereabouts to the present day. Occasionally the beasts have been known to wander from this range into nearby Quorrobulong, where in 1974 a bushwalker saw a 27ft long beast moving among trees near an orchard.

The giant monitor phenomenon has already attracted the attention of a number of naturalists in many parts of Australia, who have flocked to the regions where the monsters have been reported seen. In early 1979, one herpetologist, Frank Gordon, drove his four-wheel drive Land Rover deep in the Wattagans along one of the rugged tracks accessible only by off-road vehicles early in 1979. Stopping his Land Rover next to a 6ft high embankment on the driver's side, he got out and proceeded to climb down a nearby embankment to search a swamp for water skinks. After two hours of searching he finally gave up and returned to his vehicle.

As he climbed back into his seat he noticed what appeared to be a large "log" lying along the top of the 6ft embankment next to him. Although he could not recall having noticed it before, he thought nothing of it. However, as he started his engine, the "log" suddenly rose up on four powerful legs and dashed along the the embankment to disappear into the nearby forest, leaving the reptile hunter in a state of mild shock. The monster, he said, literally dwarfed his vehicle, which was 17ft in length— the huge reptile that had been lying on the embankment was he estimated between 27 and 30ft in length.

Throughout the many years that I have spent researching strange animals throughout Australia and the Pacific region I have gathered a vast number of such reports. For example, a similar case of 'mistaken identity' happened to two farmers during 1975, also in the Wattagans Mountain Range. They happened to be driving their four-wheel vehicle through the forests one morning, when, ahead of them, they saw what they thought to be a log which must have fallen across the road.

Alighting from their vehicle they proceeded toward the obstruction to lift it off the road— however before they could do so, the "log" slowly rose up and walked off the road and into the surrounding forest. The road was a good 20ft wide, and as the head and tail of the creature had been obscured from view by road-side grass, it must have been much longer.

During an expedition I led to the Atherton Range, inland from Cairns in far north Queensland, a jungle-covered mountainous region 4,000ft above sea level, during June 1978, I gathered a number of accounts of 15-20ft length giant monitors, which, say local farmers, are quite numerous, living in regions still largely inaccessible to man. They have occasionally been known to stray on to farm land and have been known to attack livestock. Further giant monitor lizard stories also emanate from the Gulf of Carpentaria and Arnhem Land from time to time.

But what are these reptilian giants? Certainly the prodigious lengths reached by these beasts contradicts the accepted lengths of typical monitors in Australia, which normally grow up to 6-8ft; specimens of 10ft, or even 12ft are not unknown in some oversize examples. I saw one 12ft example in Hartley Valley, New South Wales in 1965.

The enormous proportions of the 30ft monsters can therefore match only one species—the Giant Australian Monitor, *Megalonia prisca*, thought by scientists to have become extinct several thousand years ago, and the ancestor of the equally fearsome, though smaller, Komodo Dragon of Indonesia, which grow up to 9ft.

Based upon fossil remains of *Megalonia*, scientists estimate the reptiles weighed up to 3,000lbs. *Megalonia's* fossil record can be traced back to the Eocene period, between 40 and 60 million years ago.

There is plenty of fossil evidence to show that *Megalonia prisca* was once widespread throughout Australia as late as the last ice-age, when a land-bridge with mainland Asia would have enabled the species to spread northward through New Guinea into Indonesia where the smaller form now survives. Tales of 30ft monitors however continue to emanate from the vast unknown interior of New Guinea up to the present.

The disappearance of the creatures from all but the eastern Australian mountain ranges was not only due to the growing arid conditions that followed the close of the last ice-age: the Aborigines preserve traditions of their ancestors having hunted the creatrues for food.

What the species actually is, we will only know when we are able to examine either a skeleton, a fresh carcass, or a living specimen— but does anyone know how to catch a 30ft giant lizard?

•

Rex Gilroy

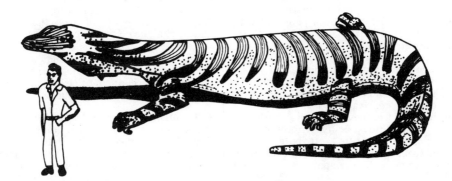

Artist's impression, based upon witness descriptions, of the mystery 30ft giant monitors reported from New Guinea and eastern parts of Australia. [Photo: R.Gilroy.]

Close Encounters: A Mythic Perspective.

If the so-called 'close-encounters' have any real basis in human experience this component must of necessity be universal, arising in people of all times, places and cultures, giving rise to analogues of the 'encounter' experience. **Steve Moore** one of the editors of FT, offers his thoughts on the claims of ancient Greeks that they had actually met their gods, in this case Castor and Pollux.

A typical representation of Castor and Pollux, in warrior garb, mounted and with their distinctive star-topped egg-like helmets. [Engraving: by kind permission of Mary Evans Picture Library.]

INTRODUCTION

Readers of these pages should be familiar with the parallels and connections between the UFO phenomenon and myth/folklore. That Jung was in no doubt on this point is amply illustrated by the title of his work *Flying Saucers: A Modern Myth of Things Seen in the Sky*[1]; and the pages of FT have been peppered with articles amplifying this theme. The awkward and unsymmetrical piece offered here, while concentrating more on the mythic aspect, is intended to continue in the same vein.

That the *subject* matter of myth and the UFO phenomenon, especially in encounter cases, show common features I shall expand on shortly. In *form* also they are similar: both deal largely with numinous beings endowed with supernatural/superscientific attributes; each genre contains astonishingly similiar tales from widely differing and unrelated countries and cultures. The tales are frequently paradoxical; both genres are plagued by wild variations in reportage of the same story, and contradictory details; and both types, it must be said, suffer from the downright bigotry of their interpreters. The *study* of myths and UFOs also seem to show strong parallels. Open-minded UFO theorists might find much of interest in GS Kirk's book *The Nature of Greek Myths*[2], especially Chapter 3, where he discusses five 'monolithic' theories of myth-interpretation—monolithic in that the proponents of each theory believed that by it alone *all* myths could be satisfactorily explained.

Without entering into detailed arguments for or against, we might similarly enumerate four 'monolithic' theories of UFO interpretation, and see how they treat encounter cases.

- **1. Misidentification and Hoaxes**; which neatly sweeps the problem under the carpet. Undoubtedly many UFO sightings *are* misidentifications and *some* are hoaxes, but surely not all. It seems rather unlikely that anyone would misidentify being 'kidnapped by aliens', but for this school of thought, encounters, ancient and modern, present no problem: they simply do not happen.

• **2. The Extraterrestrial Hypothesis**; to wit, that we are visited by objectively real spaceships from alien worlds. Many arguments have been produced against this theory—eg. the sheer quantity and diversity of the visitants and their craft; the flagrant absurdity of their actions; their defiance of physical laws as we know them; and so on. This theory takes encounters at face value as meetings with or kidnappings by real space-men/-monsters. Ancient cases, if considered at all, are treated as the same—the assumption being that percipients have mis-interpreted aliens as gods, fairies, etc (this assumption seems to derive from the common view that anyone denied the material benefits of electric toasters and large automobiles must naturally be more ignorant and gullible than the average 20th Century oaf; even the briefest acquaintance with classical literature would put paid to this mis-equation of technology with intelligence). The 'misinterpretation' notion thus provides a direct link to 'Ancient Astronaut' myth theories.

• **3. The Ultraterrestrial Hypothesis**; that entities from 'elsewhere' (be it 'other dimensions', 'different vibrational planes', 'the future' or other ill-defined and easily adaptable areas) are deliberately plaguing us with UFOs, alien-encounters, hairy monsters, and so on, produced by a super-science beyond our understanding and in a deliberately confusing manner. The beauty of this notion is that because it is almost entirely speculation, without evidence of even analogy as to how these effects are produced, it is virtually impossible to argue against without appearing to have a closed mind. To this author, it appears to be a capitulationist get-out; the logic seeming to run thus: "These things are too confusing for us to comprehend. Therefore, they must be deliberately confusing. Therefore, there is no point in attempting to comprehend them". The fallacy here is too obvious to require further comment. Encounters are thus 'explained' as the vile machinations of wicked ultraterrestrial bozos intent on mayhem, by methods and for purposes known only to themselves.

• **4. The Products of the Psyche/Visionary Theory**; in which psychic contents are projected from the individual unconscious in the form of a visionary hallucination, which is moulded by imagery from the collective unconscious of the day. Particularly applicable to encounter cases, and fitting both ancient and modern examples equally well. Objections can be raised (unless encounters are to be hived off from the rest of the UFO phenomenon, as perhaps they should); for instance, its inability to explain physical traces such as landing marks and radar tracks. Also, while much work has been done on explaining the symbolism of visions, little seems to be known about the actual 'trigger mechanism' which brings them about.

So we have four theories, and again none of them provides an entirely perfect solution to the UFO problem (and it must be obvious that I consider most of them *considerably* less than perfect!), yet all of which might have something to offer. The truly Fortean viewpoint would be to acknowledge all these theories without committing oneself to any of them. Regrettably, taken to its logical conclusion, this leaves one unable to say *anything* certain about *anything*.

Let us have an example. Cicero, in his dialogue on *The Nature of the Gods*[3], has one of his characters state: "...Sacred institutions and the divine worship of the gods have been strengthened from time to time. And this is not to be imputed to chance or folly, but to the frequent appearances of the gods themselves". Put simply: "We believe in the gods because we see the gods". Cicero, a consul of Rome and the most respected lawyer of his day, was at least reproducing the common consensus of his time, even if he did provide arguments both for and against the existence of the gods. But what are *we* to make of this, now that 2,000 years have passed? Who at present would believe that the gods of classical antiquity had an actual existence or manifested themselves to mankind? As Forteans we should perhaps hesitate to deny this outright (you never know, after all!). But if we go ahead and deny it anyway, what did our exemplary' classical god-percipient see? We could attempt to explain with any of our 'monolithic' UFO theories, but the same negative arguments would still apply.

Which brings us full circle to the Extraterrestrial theoriests, who adopt a similar 'face-value' attitude: "we know we're being visited by spaceships because we see spaceships" or "I know I was kidnapped by spacemonsters because they looked like spacemonsters". Are spacemonsters any more 'likely' than gods? I'd say they're not— but you'll have to make up your own mind.

Ultimately then, all we can say with any degree of certainty is that the percepitents have the experience of 'seeing something', whether it be ancients seeing gods or moderns seeing space-aliens. That these experiences, separated by two millenia, are at least similiar in nature if not identical in form, I hope to show in what follows. If my interpretation of the material seems to veer toward the 'prodicts of the psyche' theory I trust the reader will bear in mind all the previous provisos—but it behoves me to do so for the simple reason that otherwise I shall have nothing to write.

•

CLASSICAL ENCOUNTERS OF THE THIRD KIND

The case material given below can naturally make no claim to be comprehensive. It has been assembled from some casual reading, but does, I think, provide a sufficient handful of cases to work with. In collecting the actual cases I have eschewed the poets and mythographers, drawing mainly from Greek and Roman essaysists, historians and biographers, and their annotators.

A general look at the material seems to indicate that the major gods and goddesses of the classical pantheon—Zeus, Hera, Ares, Athene, etc—condescend to make comparatively few visual appearances, outside of dream. Encounters seem to fall into two major groups. The first, which we can only touch on briefly here, are with minor nature gods and spirits: Pan, Faunus, satyrs, etc. The second is encounters with demi-gods and deified heroes, of which the most numerous seem to involve the Dioscuri, Castor and Pollux (the latter more properly known by his Greek name, Polydeuces, but as the Romanised version Pollux is probably more familiar, it will be used throughout), and it is upon these twin deities that we will concentrate here. So firstly then, let's introduce the protagonists.

•

A BRIEF BIOGRAPHY OF CASTOR AND POLLUX

The myths surrounding Castor and Pollux are extremely confused and contradictory, with numerous variants [4,5]. Space doesn't permit a full look at these, but the basic tale runs like this.

They were born at Sparta, prior to the Trojan War. Their mother, Leda, was debauched by Zeus in the form of a swan. On the same night, she also slept with her human husband, Tyndareus. As a result she gave birth to either one or two eggs from which hatched four children. The offspring of Zeus were Pollux and Helen (of Troy); those of Tyndareus were Castor and Clytemnestra (the wife and murderess of Agamemnon). In the two egg variant, the male children were in one egg, the female in the other. One important variant makes Nemesis, the goddess of divine vengeance, the mother of the egg, which was then hatched by Leda. Another has it that the egg fell from the moon.

Despite their differing parentage, both Castor and Pollux were known as the Dioscuri, the 'Sons of Zeus'. Castor was mortal, and noted as a warrior and horseman; Pollux was immortal, and noted as a boxer. They were completely inseperable, and among their exploits were: the rescue of Helen when abducted by Theseus; participation in the Calydonian boar hunt; and membership in the expedition of the Argonauts. The Argo being caught in a storm, two flames descended from heaven and hovered over the heads of Castor and Pollux, signalling the end of the storm. This is the mythical origin of their connection with St Elmo's Fire.

Castor and Pollux abducted and married their cousins, the sisters Pheobe and Hilaeira, ladies with lunar connections whose names mean respectively 'Bright Moon' and 'Shining'. This brought them into conflict with another set of cousins, the twins Idas and Lynceus. Either as a direct result of this, or because of a quarrel over the division of spoils taken in a cattle raid, a fight broke out between the two sets of twins, in which all but Pollux were killed. Pollux was elevated to Olympus, but prayed to Zeus that he might share his immortality with his brother, and this they do on alternate days—on the first Castor is in Hades, Pollux in Olympus, on the second Castor in Olympus, Pollux in Hades, and so on. A later tradition placed them both in the sky as the constellation Gemini.

They are said to be the saviours of storm-tossed sailors, flying through the air accompanied by a train of sparrows, or 'on sparrowy wings'. They also oversee travel, hospitality to travellers, horsemanship and war. They were patron deities of the Spartans, worshipped as two upright beams connected by cross-pieces at top and bottom, which is the origin of the astrological sigil for Gemini, and one or both of these wooden beams were carried by the troops to battle. They were also patrons of the Roman Equestrian Order.

The Dioscuri are usually portrayed riding on white horses, wearing white tunics and scarlet or purple cloaks, carrying spears and wearing on their heads the halves of the egg from which they hatched, surmounted by a star.

•

THE MATERIAL
The following cases are presented in roughly chronological order.

• 1 Pausanias records that when he visited Sparta in the 2nd Century AD, a house was still shown that was alleged to have been the home of the Dioscuri, which has later passed (at an unstated date) into the hands of a certain Phormion. The tale went that Castor and Pollux appeared to Phormion disguised as merchants from the Spartan colony of Cyrene, in north Africa. They asked Phormion to take them in and give them the room that they had most loved when they were among mankind. Phormion welcomed them and told them they could avail themselves of the rest of the house, except that one room, which his young virgin daughter was occupying. Next morning, both 'foreigners' and the girl (with all her attendants) had vanished, and in the room were found statues of Castor and Pollux, and also a herb called sylphium lying on the table. (This herb was precious and medically powerful, was said to have magical properties, and was exported in large quantities from Cyrene. It is variously identified as 'herb-benjamin, a type of asafoetida'[6], as *Ferula*[7], and as masterwort

(*Peucedanum ostruthium*), and was thought to be able to open locks[8,9].

• 2 — A hoax appearance of Castor and Pollux, given by Pausanias. Some time prior to the Second Messenian War (between the inveterate enemies, Sparta and Messenia) in 685-668 BC, two youths called Panormos and Gonippos from Andania in Messenia made raids together in Spartan territory. Finding the Spartans celebrating the feast of the Dioscuri in their camp, the Messenian pair put on white tunics, crimson cloaks and wide-brimmed hats, and then rode into the camp on magnificent horses with spears in their hands. The Spartans taking them for the real Castor and Pollux, bowed down and prayed; whereupon Panormos and Gonippos rode through the camp, stabbing at random with their spears and killing many before making their escape to Andania. As a result, the curse of the Dioscuri was said to have been placed on the Messenians, not being removed until after the battle of Leuctra in 371 BC[10].

• 3 — Castor and Pollux were said to have intervened on the Spartan behalf when they were defeated at the battle of Boar's Grave, near Stenykleros in Messenia, in 684 BC. Pursuing the Spartans, the Messenian general Aristomenes was told by the prophet Theoklos not to run past a certain pear tree because the Dioscuri were sitting in its branches. Aristomenes ignored this and on reaching the tree lost his shield; the delay allowing the Spartans to escape[11].

• 4 — Soon afterwards, Aristomenes made a night march on Sparta, but was turned back by visions of the Dioscuri and their sister Helen[12].

• 5 — Hardly worth mentioning, but Herodotus has a one-line reference to one Euphoroion, an Azanian from Paeus (circa 6th Century BC), who received Castor and Pollux beneath his roof, and afterwards kept open house for all comers[13].

• 6 — When the poet Simonides of Ceos was being entertained at a great banquet by the powerful Scopadae of Crannon, in Thessaly (c.515 BC), two young men appeared at the doorway and called him outside. They were said to be the Dioscuri, and no sooner had he left the hall than the building collapsed, killing hosts and guests alike; all save Simonides[14].

• 7 — At the battle of Lake Regillus (498? 496? BC) between the Romans under Aulus Postumius and the Latins, Castor and Pollux were seen on horseback, fighting among the victorious Roman army. A stone at Lake Regillus, still extant in Cicero's day (1st Century BC) bore a mark in the shape of a horse's hoof, said to have been left by Castor's horse[15]. Livy[16] simply says that Postumius prayed to Castor for aid, and afterwards founded a temple in Rome in his honour, the existence of which is proven.

• 8 — Plutarch[17] records the same story as Cicero as well as a variant (or perhaps a different story?) also given by Suetonius[18] who doesn't give the former story. One Lucius Domitius met a pair of god-like twins, believed to be Castor and Pollux, at Rome on the same day as the battle at Regillus, which at the time had not even seemed imminent. The twins were cooling their sweating horses by the spring in the Forum (an odd touch which seems to imply they had ridden all the way from Regillus, unless this is an embellishment by Plutarch), and told Domitius that the battle was already fought and won. The latter being unconvinced, the twins smiled quietly and touched his beard, which turned from black to the colour of bronze, a trait which was inherited by his descendants and fixed on his family the surname Ahenobarbus ('bronze-beard').

• 9 — When the Locrians were at war with the city of Croton, in southern Italy, they appealed to Sparta for aid, and were told they might have the Dioscuri (presumably in the form of the wooden beams?), which offer they accepted. At the battle of the Sagra (shortly after 480 BC), which resulted in complete victory for the Locrians, two gigantic youths in strange dress were seen fighting on their side[19].

• 10 — Plutarch[20] and Cicero[21] record a tale that when the Spartan admiral Lysander defeated the Athenian fleet at Aegospotami, near the Hellespont, in 405 BC, Castor and Pollux appeared as twin stars on either side of Lysander's ship as he was sailing out of harbour to join battle, and shone out over the rudder-sweeps. Lysander afterwards set up golden stars representing the Dioscuri at the oracle of Apollo at Delphi; these disappeared just before the battle of Leuctra (371 BC), in which the Spartans were defeated by the Thebans.

• 11 — The Romans fought Perseus, the last king of the Macedonians at Pydna, Northern Greece, in 167 BC, defeating him and taking him prisoner. Cicero[22] tells us that as one P. Vatienus was travelling to Rome by night along the Salarian Way, from Reate (50 miles from Rome), two young men on white horses, (Castor and Pollux) appeared to him and told him that Perseus was taken prisoner that day. Vatienus proceeded to inform the Roman senate, and was promptly thrown into prison for speaking inconsiderately on a state affair. However, when letters came from Pydna confirming his story, he was released and compensated with land and immunities from military service and taxes. The decree of the senate concerning Vatienus was still in existence in Cicero's day, some hundred years later. Plutarch[23], however, in his biography of Paulus, the Roman general at Pydna, says that rumours of the victory sprang up four days after the battle (and before news could arrive), but does not mention Castor and Pollux in this connection; but then, curiously, goes on to tell the tale of Lucius Domitius (given above) as an example of how these rumours spring up.

• 12 — Suetonius[24], (a man by no means averse to miraculous tales, it must be said) records a story of Julius Caesar's funeral, to the effect that when Caesar's body had been carried into the forum on an ivory funeral couch, and a dispute was taking place as to where to cremate him, two divine forms appeared, javelin in hand and sword at thigh, and set fire to the couch with torches; the populace thereafter making an impromptu pyre by heaping branches, chairs, benches etc., on the blazing couch. Suetonius conjectures these divinities to be the Twin Brethren, Castor and Pollux. The tale is not recorded by other authors.

•

WHAT DOES IT ALL MEAN?

Your guess is as good as mine; which means my guess is as good as yours, so I'm going to tell you what I think anyway.

At this remove in time, it's virtually impossible to judge the veracity or otherwise of the tales presented above. The first two are usually regarded as tales illustrating the stupidity of the Spartans—perhaps collecting all twelve is illustrative of the stupidity of your author. All we can do is take the stories at face-value and proceed from there.

It will be seen from the above cases that many of the basic motifs of the UFO phenomenon are represented in an archaic form: aerial lights, close encounters, landing marks (the hoofprint), relay of information unknown to the percipient, physiological change in the percipient, an abduction, a hoax. To stretch a couple of points, the medicinal herb sylphium might be taken as a fore-runner of later medical examination cases, and St Elmo's Fire as weird electrical phenomena. As far as I'm concerned, this merely indicates that mythic and UFO encounters are two aspects of the same unexplained phenomenon, and that the basic experiences are similar, even if differences in culture provide variations of detail. If anyone wants to take it as evidence that Castor and Pollux were alien spacemen, that's their fault, not mine.

It should also be obvious that we are dealing with human-like apparitions of Castor and Pollux, and not embroidered accounts of St Elmo's Fire. Pliny[25] has it that the electrical phenomena are 'ascribed to Castor and Pollux' (my emphasis), rather than being the gods themselves. I imagine that the fact that St Elmo's Fire signals the ending of a storm has led to its connection with an already extant motif of the Dioscuri as saviours; especially as the majority of our encounters, and of their mythic deeds, take place on dry land.

Before we move to the symbolism of encountering the Dioscuri, let's look at the basic context. War was an everyday experience to the ancients: Livy[26] tells us that in the early days of Rome, as soon as spring arrived, the campaigning season began, and this occurred virtually every year; internecine strife between the Greek city-states was virtually continuous also. Two cities in particular were centres of worship of the Dioscuri, Sparta and Rome, and it is perhaps no coincidence that these two were among the most militaristic of the classical world, nor that Castor and Pollux, with Heracles, were favourite deities among the solidiery. Heracles, too, we might add, was a son of Zeus with a human twin, Iphicles. The same human/divine twinning applies to Idas and Lynceus (Idas by Poseidon). The majority of our cases have some connection with battle; only one has no reference to death.

As AH Krappe points out [27], the ancients believed there was something numinous about twins. They were considered either well or ill omened, but they were certainly not normal. That Castor and Pollux were identical we know from Lucian, who waggishly suggests in one of his dialogues[28] that the only way to tell them apart was by Pollux's boxing scars, and this identicality makes them doubly numinous. They are, in fact, the archetypal twins, and it's no surprise to find them foisted onto the constellation of the same name, even if it did mean changing one of the original Babylonian twins from female to male.

It would be impossible here to cover *all* the symbolism attaching to the Dioscuri, but we can make a few remarks. They were born from an egg, a well-known symbol of the primal unity (as in the legends of the 'world-egg'), which, like the circle or sphere is a symbol of wholeness, non-differentiation, or completeness. With their hatching, that unity is differentiated.

Taking the four children together, Castor and Pollux would represent a positive element, Helen and Clytemnestra a negative one. Let's quickly dispose of the ladies. As murderess (Clytemnestra) and 'cause' of the Trojan War (Helen) they are undoubtedly negative. According to Pliny[29], in opposition to the Dioscuri's connection with St Elmo's Fire and the salvation of sailors, Helen is an 'evil star' responsible for sinking ships. Between the two there is also differentiation: Helen, daughter of Zeus, was divine and went to the Elysian fields after death; whereas mortal Clytemnestra, after being butchered by her own son, simply went, as the Zen koan has it, 'straight to hell like a flying arrow'.

The Dioscuri show a similar differentiation: Castor was mortal, and died; Pollux was immortal and was deified without dying. That they wear the two halves of the egg-shell would seem to indicate that, though differentiated, there was never any real loss of that primal unity; they continued to carry it with them. Their inseparableness adds further weight to this, and also points to the idea that their aspects were complimentary, rather than antagonistic opposites; and that by union of these opposite aspects they achieve wholeness and overcome death. The stars surmounting the egg-hats, symbolising heaven, indicate that the 'heavenly spark' is within both of them. Their clothing provides more evidence: white was the colour of death and mourning, while purple/scarlet was the colour of heaven (thus the 'Imperial purple').

We find the Dioscuri frequently bringing news of the outcome of battles or providing precognitive warnings, and there are mythic grounds for this as well. The astronomer/astrologer Ptolemy describes the constellation of Gemini as follows[30]: the star Castor shares the same quality as Mercury (messenger of the gods and guide of souls to the underworld) and is also called the star of Apollo (the god of prophecy). The star Pollux shares the same quality as Mars (god of war) and is also called the star of Heracles (another war-like ruffian who transcended death and was deified). Oracular news of battle is definitely within their province. Again, we have interesting double aspects. Mercury the underworld messenger, and Apollo the heavenly, solar prophet. And Mars the god-warrior and Heracles the human-warrior.

To see Castor and Pollux *together* immediately puts us in the realm of paradox; by mythic 'rights' this should be impossible, because one is above and one below ground at any given time. To meet them both shows that we are in an area where the normal writ does not run; a borderland zone of human experience, in this case that of life-and-death. Thus they are connected to those events in which this life/death polarity is most starkly highlighted: battles, collapsing buildings, funerals, sinking ships. The emphasis is always a positive one, however (assuming they appear on your side in the battle, of course); even the abduction of Phormion's daughter can be seen in this light, for though the girl obviously winds up dead, she has been 'taken by the gods' rather than suffering a normal death.

But this positive emphasis should not be understood simply as referring to external life, which would be a rigid exaltation of one aspect at the expense of the other. Death is definitely part of the deal, but the promise is of renewed life beyond this. This suggestion of death and renewal is further emphasized by the Dioscuri's strong lunar connection, for the moon, with her waxing and waning and rebirth after the New Moon, is the symbol of resurrection *par excellence*. Helen was worshipped as a moon goddess at Sparta, and pictorially the Dioscuri are frequently represented travelling alongside the lunar chariot of Selene.

A further illustration of this is a pretty conceit of the poet Callimachus[31]. Writing a lament on the death of Queen Arsinoe of Egypt (d.270 BC), he pictures her as having been snatched away by the Dioscuri, flying with them past the moon on the way to heaven and eventual deification; an interesting parallel to the appearance of the Dioscuri at Caesar's funeral, for he too was deified.

On a personal level the Dioscuri, connected as they are with the borderland between life and death, seem to indicate that by a unification of the opposite halves of our own person (always the goal of the mystic), the mortal, bodily part with the immortal part (mind/soul/Spirit), death, or at least the fear of death, can be transcended.

But it is the social level which brings us back to the UFO phenomenon. The prevailing tensions are similar, now as then (fear of atomic annihilation; fear of annual warfare). The 'mechanical' features of the apparitions are similar. And if UFOs are symbolically pointing out an imbalance in modern culture, highlighting an overemphasis on scientific values by providing a super-scientific symbol, were the Dioscuri highlighting an overemphasis on warfare by providing a divine ultimate warrior symbol?

One closing thought: if mortal peril is the thread that runs through historical and modern encounter cases, could it be that those 'medical examinations' beloved of UFO entities are in fact pseudo-autopsies? The contactee being found to be still alive, he or she is then returned to the world...[32].

Whether there's anything in all this, I leave the reader to decide. I tend to think there is, but then, of course, I am a Gemini...

•

Steve Moore.

NOTES
Quotations from ancient authors are given with reference to the original text first, in three sections: Book number (or title for shorter pieces); paragraph number; sub-section (where applicable). These are then followed by usual references to the English translations.

1 In *Collected Works of CG Jung* Vol 10 (RKP, London).
2 **GS Kirk**; *The Nature of Greek Myths* (Penguin Books, Harmondsworth, 1974).
3 Cicero; 'On the Nature of the Gods', Bk 2,2. *Nature of the Gods (etc)*; trans by **CD Yonge** (G Bell, London, 1902) p46.
4 Many variants, with full classical sources, may be found in **Robert Graves**; *The Greek Myths* (Penguin Books, Harmondsworth, 1960) Vol 1, p206-8, 245-52. I have generally followed the simplified version given in [5].
5 *New Larousse Encyclopedia of Mythology* (Paul Hamlyn, Feltham, 1968) p188-90.
6 **Graves**, *ibid*, Vol 1, p248, 251-2.
7 Footnote to **Quintos Curtius**; *History of Alexander* trans by **JC Rolfe** (Loeb Classical Library. Heinemann/Harvard, 1946) Vol 2, p157.
8 Footnote to **Best & Brightman** (eds): *The Book of Secrets of Albertus Magnus* (Oxford UP, 1973) p12.

Cont on p64

...well, seeds and plants embedded in most unlikely places. But watch out! You may find such curiosities growing on you...

ONE IN THE EYE

One day in 1976, 7yr-old Julian Fabricus fell down while chasing butterflies in a field. When he returned home his left eye was inflamed and smarting. His mother took him to their family doctor, in Worcester, South Africa—but he could not find the source of the irritation and gave the boy some ointment. In a few days the smarting went and soon the incident was forgotten.

About a year later Julian complained to his parents that his left eye itched and sometimes his vision was not as clear as it should be. His father looked and saw a white object lodged in the cornea, near the pupil. Occultist Dr Cornelius Kooy, to whom the puzzled parents took the boy said: "I saw what looked like a grass seed which had sprouted and grown two little leaves." The sprout was about 4mm (or about an eigth of an inch) long, and pure white [see photo]. Dr Kooy referred the case to top eye specialist, Dr Solomon Abel, of Cape Town, who removed the seed in a 30-minute operation on 20 Dec 1977. He called in a botanist who declared the intruder to be of the family Compositae, which includes chrysanthemums, thistles and daisies. Dr Abel wrote the case up, and our sources picked it up from the September 1979 issue of the AMA journal *Archives of Opthalmology*. Dr Abel's theory: "The boy's cornea had been punctured, presumably when he fell in the field, and somehow the seed found its way through the wound and became embedded in the iris. There it lay dormant for a year and then started growing. In order for a plant to grow it needs warmth, moisture and oxygen—all these things were available in Julian's eye...I'm pleased to say that Julian now has perfect vision."

Framingham (Mass) *Middlesex News/UPI* 28 Sept; Omaha (NB) *World Herald/UPI* 29 Sept; *S.Mirror* 18 Nov; *National Enquirer* 20 Nov; *Weekly News* 15 Dec 1979; *Awake* 22 Feb 1980.

ROOTS

This eye-watering story brought back memories of my grandfather threatening that potatoes will be growing in my darkest aural recesses if I didn't clean my ears more frequently. Were he here now I could tell him that that isn't so far-fetched, and quote the case Edmund Parish, in *Hallucinations and Illusions* 1894, cites from earlier authorities, of a man whose right-side auditory hallucinations ceased on removal of a sprouting grain of corn from his ear-wax. Ah, but had I come back to my grandfather with this *then*, I'd have collected a thick ear of a different sort.

Slightly more bizarre is one of the first clippings ever sent to us (when we were called *The News*). It concerned a 5yr-old

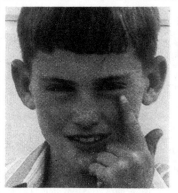

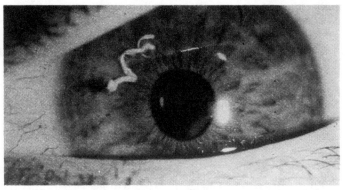

Julian Fabricus, and a close up of the sprout in his cornea. The dark area at its lower end is the wound through which the seed entered. [Photos: David Barritt/Nat.Enquirer 20 Nov 1970.]

Alsatian dog operated on to remove a fist-sized tumour on the rib-cage. During the operation Dr Kenneth O'Toole, of the Veterinary Medical Center, in Milwaukee, discovered to his surprise the tumour had been caused by a sprout about three inches long. Just how it had got inside the dog's flesh was a mystery, but Dr O'Toole thinks a seed entered a wound. The clipping—from the Knoxville (Tenn) *News-Sentinel* 4 Aug 1974—contained two marvellous photos; one of the forlorn dog, Baron von Faust by name, and the other of the offending sprout in the open palm of Dr O'Toole's hand. We tried, for several years, to trace these photos and had no luck. Perhaps someone in or near Milwaukee could locate the

Veterinary Medical Center and ask on our behalf?

In our files of embedded plants we had a few other notes, and we give them here for amusement... During the extensive flooding in water-logged winter of 1976/77 in England came a report in several newspapers that sheep on Cotswold Park Farm, near the Gloucestershire town of Guiting Power, were growing their own lawns. Their damp fleece sported a fine two-inch high crop of grass, sprouting from lodged seeds. No doubt farmers will tell us this is not that unusual but this is the only reference we have to the phenomenon. *Sun, Express & Star* 26 Feb 1977.

Morning Glory seeds, trapped somehow inside a tree,

were reported to be blooming from the trunk of an evergreen at Rocky Ford, Colorado. *New York Times* 7 Feb 1970, cited in *INFO Journal* 6 p28.

We have a couple from Ripley too, from the 6th series of paperback *Believe it or not!*: a goldfish was found at Fortuna, California, with a tiny hawthorn shrub rooted into its head (p113); and a Mrs Joseph Riede, of Denver, Colorado, reported an almond sapling growing from a flavoured candy bar (p128). Hmmm... Colorado again!

All of which proves that, for plants, home is where the roots are.

Credits-*Loren Coleman, David Dunthorn, Chris Hall, Anthony Smith, Joe Swatek* ●**RJMR**

While the evidence for much strange phenomena remains elusive and somewhat etherial, what we call 'true mysteries of the physical body'—like spontaneous combustion (more of this soon) and the incorruption of corpses—occur within the area of conventional sciences, like biology, and in the last quarter of the 20th century all we can really say about them is that they happen. Here are two such enigmas which confound orthodoxy: stigmata and impossibly long fasts

RECENT STIGMATA AND INEDIA

☐ An olive grove on the outskirts of the small hilltop town of El Escorial, in Portugal, is daily attracting flocks of people from the surrounding countryside. The object of their attention is Ampara Cuevas, a 43yr-old mother of 7, who was ordered by the Blessed Virgin Mary (BVM) in a vision to recite the Rosary in public at this spot. Exactly when this initiating vision

occurred is not reported, but one gathers it might have been in November 1980.

According to Francisca Herranz, the wife of a local baker, it was on a day in that month that she noticed Amparo standing entranced in her shop with drops of blood on her forehead. "We made her sit down," says Mrs Herranz, "and we saw that blood was also coming out of her hands and ribs." This stigmatic trance lasted "almost 2 hours", and

since then has been repeated on the major feast-days of the Catholic Church, especially those falling on a Friday, the traditional day of Christ's death. In contrast to the public recitation, the stigmatic attacks are kept as private as possible, attended only by relatives and close friends, who say that most of the usual forms of traditional wounds suffered by Christ are manifested: bleeding from hands, feet, side of breast, knees and forehead. A witness, Mrs Feliza Jimenez, claims she saw the stigmata on Good Friday 1981, when a relative of Amparo let her into the stigmatic's bedroom. She said: "I saw her on the bed, her flesh as white and cold as marble. It's hard to believe if you don't see it with your own eyes."

It seems that at the appropriate times Ampara enters an ecstasy during which the stigmata appear and conversations are held with BVM and Christ. The description of the stigmata is vague—at one point they are described as "scars", and at another as "bleeding like sweat". The reporter met Ampara—a "stocky, youthful" woman who works as a maid—during one of the regular 9am recitations in the olive grove to the south of the town. Replying in "a matter-of-fact way" she said she was in other respects an ordinary person. "As a child I had a strong feeling about the Virgin, perhaps because my mother died and I had a rough time with my stepmother. Still I was not overly religious and almost did not know how to pray." Then she smiled: "But I'm learning now." The morphology of this instance of stigmatic phenomena and its onset is fairly typical, except that it has begun rather late in the stigmatic's life, and appears to compensate for a humdrum life during which intense religious feelings did not find satisfactory expression. An unhappy childhood is a factor that crops up frequently in the lives of visionaries and psychics, but the full significance of this observation has yet to be explored.

UPI/Waukegan (Illinois) *News-Sun* 15-16 Aug 1981.

☐ A Portugese ecstatic of a different kind is described in the *Sunday Mirror* 21 March 1982, in a brief journalistic portrait of 17yr-old Maria Rosalina Viera (see photo). On 28 November 1975, when Maria was about 11yrs-old, she had a vision of Christ in which, she says, he asked her to fast for the sinners of this world. "I was lying on my bed when suddenly this voice called out to me. I knew immediately who it was." Unfortunately the reporter, Wensley Clarkson, did not ask about, or at any rate, does not tell us about, the medical or family history of the girl, so we have no idea of her personality or whether she repeats the usual 'mystery illnesses' and 'spontaneous cures' noted in the histories of so many other ecstatics and stigmatics.

Since that vision, over six years ago, it is claimed, Maria has not taken any food and water, and thousands of pilgrims, who believe her to be a living saint, flock to her mountain village of Tropeco, not far from Oporto in the north of Portugal, to touch her hand. Clarkson was shown into Maria's room by her mother Elena. In the small whitewashed room, bedecked with religious images, the pretty dark-haired girl lay on a snow-white bed. He is told that she is paralysed from the waist down and has never left her bed in that time. She looked well, but tired, and smiles serenely. "When I was younger," she said, "I wanted to get married and have children. But God has made me content to live like this...At first when I stopped eating I felt hungry but that quickly disappeared. Now I don't need food or water. I don't even remember what it tastes like."

At first Maria's parents were suspicious. They sat outside her room for many days and nights in the belief the girl was sneaking food into her room, but Maria never left her bed. "It was at this point that we accepted that this was a miracle," said Elena. Maria's father had been openly hostile to this upsetting of their lives, recalls Elena. "He thought she was wicked and wouldn't talk to her for a long time. We tried forcing food down her throat. But she was sick." This detail is met with in accounts of other mystical hunger-strikers, as Father Herbert Thurston has called them, and indicates a hysteria-like condition called hyperaesthesia in which the sufferer reacts out of all proportion to the stimulus. One of Thurston's examples, in in his *Physical Phenomena of Mysticism* (1951), is Domenica Lazzari, an Italian girl who abstained from food for 12 years until her death in 1848. In her case a doctor put a crystal of sugar on Domenica's tongue and precipitated a fit of vomiting and choking which lasted 20 minutes. Other cases could be cited.

Maria has been studied for 5 years by kidney specialist Dr

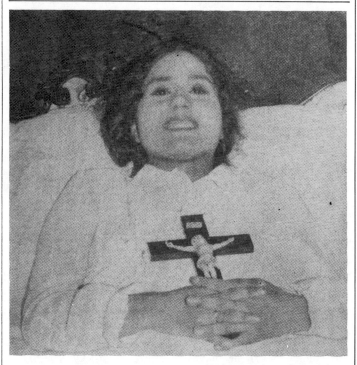

Maria Vieira has not left her bed in six years. [Photo: S.Mirror 21 March 1982.]

Orlando A. Ferreira, of Braga, and his psychologist wife Maria, and both are convinced the girl's phenomena are genuine. They compare the girl's highest weekly output of urine, just 50cc, with the amount produced by the Northern Ireland hunger-strikers in the Maze prison on the last day of their fasts. "Even though they took some liquids, in some cases they produced more than six times Maria's amount," said Dr Ferreira. A London urologist, Mr John Wickham of St Bartholomew's Hospital, approached by Clarkson for comment, said he simply could not accept the facts as stated. "It is impossible for anyone to survive if they are only producing 50cc of urine a week. I can see no explanation for this woman being alive if her claims are true." Explanations aside, we refer the good doctor to Gould and Pyle's *Curiosities and Anomalies of Medicine* for a number of pages of examples of enforced, accidental and voluntary fasts for long periods, usually measured in days or months and very rarely exceeding a single year, in which the bodily excretions are severely diminished, Maria Ferreira discounted the possibility of fraud in the present instance. "I have seen Maria Vieira try to refuse gifts, and, when people insist, all the money goes towards a new church." A Vatican spokesman is credited with the most reasonable conclusion: "There have been many other cases like this which have remained a mystery—perhaps because they are absolutely authentic."

☐ Back in FT33 on page 34 we mentioned the case of Alfonsina Cottini, who at the time (November 1980) was aged 78 and who allegedly had not eaten nor drunk for 11 years, nor excreted anything in that time. On this basis she has become the center of a cult which believes she is a saint, and coachloads of the faithful

trek to the tiny Alpine village of Craveggio, near Lake Maggiore in Italy, hoping for miraculous cures at her bedside. As reported by us earlier there were allegations that not only had some people made huge profits from the affair, but swindles were going on, and Alfonsina herself was a fraud, eating and going to the toilet in secret at night. But as far as we know nothing has been proved either for or against the case.

A note we missed earlier appeared in the *Sunday Times* 9 Nov 1980 and alludes to the widespread belief that Alfonsina has been in some kind of strange sleep for those 11 years too. The report says: "Alfonsina is an extraordinary sight stretched out on her small iron bed...on her back... surrounded by hundreds of photographs and mementoes left by her visitors. Eyes closed, she breathes heavily and wears a blissful smile." In the photo that accompanied the report one wonders if the 'smile' is not necessarily one of bliss but more due to leaving her false teeth out. The reporter, Dalbert Hallenstein, mentions that a 3-man judicial inquiry does not seem to have found evidence of fraud, but, oddly, found that Alfonsina emitted "discharges of remarkable potency." Exactly what these discharges were one hardly likes to imagine or inquire.

☐ Putting the above cases in the mystical shade is the story of Marthe Robin, a French woman who died on 6 Feb 1981 aged 78. She seems to have been a genuinely humble and pious woman, credited with the establishment of over 50 religious retreats on five continents. When she died over 8000 mourners converged on her small village of Chateauneuf-de-Galaure, near Valence in southern France to pay her homage, and two local priests, Fathers Jacques Bondallaz and Raymond Peyret, immediately began the task of compiling a

dossier on Marthe for the inevitable Process of beatification.

When she was about 20yrs-old Marthe was struck down by polio, or a polio-like disease. Up until that year, 1923, it is said, she was a normal peasant girl, but after it she was partly paralysed and slowly going blind—our photo of her dates from this period. About four years later, in 1928, Marthe fell down in her kitchen and became paralyzed from the neck down. Then events took a dramatic turn, because from that day she was totally bedridden, and in the 53 years up to her death ate nothing except a consecrated Communion wafer once a week. That's right, a 53 year fast, which as far as I can recall without checking beats the long fasts of St Lidwina (28yrs), Domenica

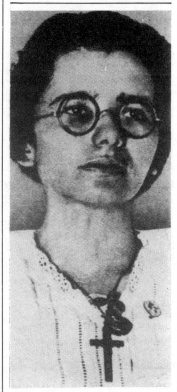

blind and paralysed — Marthe Robin, before she developed stigmata, in about 1928. [Photo: Nat.Enquirer 19 Jan 1982.]

dal Paradiso (20yrs), Nicholas von Flue (19yrs) and others discussed by Thurston. In many of these cases one also finds that the only things to pass the inedic's lips is the wafer and wine used at Holy Communion, or consecrated water. Indeed the stigmatic Theresa Neumann, who was no bedridden invalid, who fasted for at least 8 yrs observed by medical men, would gag on everything else but the consecrated items.

Father Bondallaz, one of the directors of the religious retreat in Chateauneuf founded by the friends of Marthe, who had given her Communion since 1931, said: "This is the only food she has eaten in 50 years. Her body has been

motionless and needed no other food than the Eucharist. I have no concern about whether it is medically possible to live on such little food or not. I can only confirm that it is true and that she ate nothing else. Upon her death her body was literally skin and bone, almost completely dry." Since that fall in 1928 Marthe could only move her head and speak, but managed to deliver sermons to visitors when she was not in ecstasy. In 1930 a priest first noticed her stigmatic wounds, in hands, feet, side and forehead, which have since sppeared and bled every Friday without fail, according to the priest.

In the farmhouse where Marthe lived her whole life, she

was looked after by her devoted sister, Celine, aged 92 at Marthe's death. Celine said: "It is true she never took food. She could talk only very slowly and to help her I would dab a wet sponge to her lips. This was the only water she took. She lived on by the grace of God." We would like to learn a lot more about the case of Marthe Robin, and ask any of our readers, especially those in France, to tell us of any studies or reports. This account compiled from: *National Echo* (M'sia) 11 Feb 1981; *National Enquirer* 19 Jan 1982.

□ **Credits:** *Miss C Brett, Peter Christie, Loren Coleman, Peter Hope Evans, Mark Hall, Michael Hoffman, J Lang, Scott Parker, Ion Will* ● **RJMR.**

OUT OF PLACE

You don't have to go down to the woods, these days, to get a big surprise. Here are a few recent tales of bears, or phantom bears, and their witnesses, for whom the encounter was no picnic.

FURRY FIGMENTS

According to Anthony Dent, whose book *Lost Beasts of Britain* (1974) is a respected authority in such matters, the last native bears of Britain lived around the 8th century; bears mentioned subsequently in histories, and some of the earlier ones, being importations. Nevertheless there are records of bears being seen, or leaving tracks, in remote or wild parts from time to time—but whether these animals are remnants of secret tribes or escapees we cannot say.

1981 was a good year for bears in Britain, not exactly common at the best of times. Apart from the saga of the bear (werebear or alleged bear) on Hackney Marches (below),

we know of at least two escapes. Very early in 1981, a full grown Grizzly, called Hercules, went on the run during the filming of a TV commercial on the Hebridean island of Benbecula. It is a barren waste, and when Hercules was recaptured just over three weeks later he was exhausted, wary and starving. In April 1981, four Brown bears escaped from a safari park near Loch Lomond—three were recaptured and the fourth shot when it evaded the nets. All of which supports our general contention that exotic animals in the landscape cannot always be explained by assuming that a domesticated or pet animal had escaped or been let loose, because these

usually fare very poorly indeed. In these pages we have referred to other bear reports— Yorkshire, Feb 1975 (FT9), and Norfolk, June 1979 (FT30) —but one we seem to have missed occurred in 1976...

On Saturday 12 June 1976 something huge and hairy scared children playing in a sandpit at Vandyke Road, Leighton Buzzard, in Bedfordshire. Mrs Maureen Walsh, of Nelson Road, said: "My children rang back into the house screaming that they had seen a bear in the sandpit." She went back with them and found large pawprints in the sand, and "then, in the distance, we saw a large black object trundle into the woods." Mrs Walsh phoned the police. The police saw the tracks but made no comment upon them. They mounted a search of the area, and because they found nothing, they put the sightings down as a "figment of the imagination." This was reported in *S.Express, S.People* both 13 June; *Beds & Bucks Observer* 15 June 1976.

FT contributor Bob Skinner contacted the *Beds & Bucks Observer* shortly after the Sunday paper reports (13th) only to be told to take the story "with a pinch of salt". He was told the children were "just publicity seekers", because one of them had appeared in the paper in another connection not long before. Bob's own impression was that the whole thing was 'explained-away' in an off-hand but predictable manner. So it goes.

THE HACKNEY HORROR

Similar disbelief followed the claims of four boys more recently. Aged between 9-13 they were out walking dogs on the evening of Sunday 27 December 1981, on the flat scrubland of London's eastern suburbs, called Hackney Marshes, when they encountered "a giant great growling hairy thing". When it reared on hind legs, says 13yr-old Tommy Murray, "I stood there for about 10 seconds and then ran like hell." Earlier the boys had stumbled across three separate sets of similar-looking tracks in the 2-inch deep snow, and Tommy, who is seriously interested in wildlife and wants to be a zoo-keeper, had no trouble in identifying the prints. They were made by a bear. Then they met a middle-aged couple with a dog, and asked them if they knew there was a bear about; "They said 'Yes, it's up there' and told us to go away because it was dangerous," added Tommy. "And they threw snowballs at us to frighten us." But kids being kids it only intrigued them more. Seconds later, "We heard the bear growling. I shone my torch on it and saw it sideways in the dark. My dog Lassie did not want to go near it."

They told their parents, who told police, who began an extensive search the next day. About 50 policemen, a number of marksmen and dogs, and even a helicopter wandered around this 5000-acre snow-covered wasteland which forms the Lea River valley in East London. One animal expert said a bear could live wild here, despite the fact that the Marshes are ringed by industrial and housing estates. But all they could find were a number of sets of unusual tracks; one on either side of the river, and one on an island in the middle.

The tracks were tentatively identified as bear prints by London Zoo and RSPCA officials. Most of the prints had deteriorated because of the slight thaw [see photo of tracks] and others were obliterated by the prints of the cameramen, reporters, children, dogs, etc etc. Nevertheless, the police took seriously the idea of a bear on the loose and continued the hunt.

On the 28th, things looked up a little. An allotment shed was found damaged, as though a bear might have broken in for night shelter—and the manager of a sports complex found another set of prints. And Tommy showed police a tree with large claw marks in its bark. But no further sign of a bear could be found and the search was called off. Then came news that a large group of children had seen the bear—but none of our sources give any details. In view of the fact that the police search resumed immediately only to be called off again after half an hour we can assume the new sighting was dubious.

The search resumed on the 29th with gloomy feelings. On previous performance there was not much hope of tracing a large animal. The lack of an early capture had led people to speculate that the police had been hoaxed, leading to a huge waste of taxpayer's money. As a drizzle completed the erosion of the tracks the hunt was finally abandoned.

On the night of the 29/30th, a man giving his name as 'Ron' called the *Sun* to say that the whole affair had been dreamed up in a pub by himself and friends, with the help of a rented bear suit. He had made two appearances in the suit, he claimed, once in front of the boys, and another occasion when passers-by laughed to see him (or the bear) clamber from the back of a van. Police tried and failed to find any record of hirings of bear suits from theatrical costumiers about that time. One proprietor pointed out that it would be impossible for a man to make convincing bear prints in such a suit because the feer are made to fit over shoes. "A hoaxer would make footprints, not paw prints," he said.

The police never did trace the couple who allegedly also saw the bear; or the bear-foot confessor; nor did the people who might have seen the bear-faced hoaxer come forward—

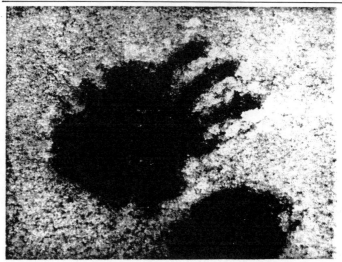

One of the mystery paw prints found on Hackney Marshes. [Photo: Associated Newspapers.]

just a few of the many loose ends to this story.

One of the Chief Inspectors who coordinated the hunt told us: "Although I didn't see the boys myself, I'm reliably informed that they were very frightened by what they saw. They were not hoaxers, although, of course, they may have been hoaxed. The search itself was interesting...it was winter and there was about two inches. I saw three sets of prints that to me were very strange. One line of prints [was] on an island which had a perimeter fence and a locked gate. The other two lots were near marshalling yards. All three were on virgin snow and could not have been made by a [hoaxer] because no other prints were near them or led to or from them. *But* these prints could easily have been misinterpreted by all who saw them [because] the snow had begun to melt and then re-frozen. A man went to London Zoo and secured a footprint of a bear on a piece of cardboard. When this was placed next to a [mystery] print there was little similarity. The real bear print was bigger and a slightly different shape. Police dogs which

usually go bananas at a whiff of a Kray Twin, took no notice whatsoever."

"The searches were inconclusive but that was not necessarily the reason they stopped, nor was the alleged confession by the alleged hoaxer. The trouble with a live bear is that, unlike most things police search for, it is not static and can cover 15 miles in a night. There are so many ways off Hackney Marshes if you're a bear that after one full day of searching a second would be pointless without a further sighting to assist... There were no more credible witnesses. In my opinion the boys were frightened by something that was probably someone dressed up as a bear."

The strangest detail came from young Tommy pondering the comparison of his bear-like apparition with a picture of a Brown bear: "The one I saw had thin legs, and I don't think brown bears have legs like that." Perhaps those who suggest that Mystery Animals teleport here from other worlds are right in this instance, and having winter-vacationed our visitor teleported back to wherever bears have thin legs.

Sources: *Shropshire Star* +29 Dec; *D.Express, D.Mirror, D.Star, D.Telegraph, Sun* 28+ 29+30 Dec; *Guardian* 28 Dec; *D.Mail* 29 Dec; *D.Star* 31 Dec 1981.

HEADLESS IN HACKNEY

The Hackney Hunt was given an added bizarre dimension by the discovery of the bodies of two bears in the same Lea River in Hackney earlier that same month. Weir-keeper [is this a clue?] Alan Farmer saw what he thought were two corpses in the river, on the morning of 5 Dec 1981, and called the police in case they were suicides or victims of East End gangland killings. Police frogmen and other officials on the scene were somewhat surprised to find the bodies were animal and not human, and that they had been decapitated and skinned. They were identified as two fully-grown brown bears, firstly by a vet and then by a bear expert from London Zoo. Someone recalled that a travelling circus had recently been in the area and a search for it was instigated. I don't know if they found them, but as one RSPC man pointed out performing animals represent a considerable investment and no circus would dispose of such a valuable animal by selling them for their furs, as was suggested. It was also doubtful that the bears were victims of underhand taxidermy—though this was the reluctant conclusion of the police—because the animals' paws would also be needed. This mystery too was never solved. *News of the world, S.Express* 6 Dec; *D. Telegraph* 7 Dec 1981.

Seemingly related, is the small item in the Cambridge *Evening News* 4 Dec 1981 that same week two dead whippets were found in a field near the town's Fairview estate—both had been skinned!

Though bears no longer exist, officially, in British wilds, up until fairly recently there used to be a flourishing bear grease industry based in London. At its peak in the mid 1800s many thousands of bears were imported from Russia, until the fashion for natural oils and grease on the hair gave rise to new industries. The year of the bear, 1981, also saw this bear's grease pot-lid fetch a record £2970 at Sotheby's, with its grim design disturbingly evocative of the discovery of two skinned bears in the Lea River later that year. [Photo: courtesy of Sotheby's Belgravia.]

Credits: *Anthony Bell, J&C Bord, Peter Christie, Mike Dash, John Michell, Nigel Pennick, Michael Shadrack, Bob Skinner, Nigel Watson* ●RJMR

It's nearly seven years since we last told you tales of 'homing rings' (*The News 11*). Although a theme firmly rooted in mythology (see 'Honest Codfish' in *Phenomena* by Michell & Rickard) instances continue to be reported as evidenced by the following. Next time, we'll have homing wallets, specs and false teeth!

Brenda Rawson lost her diamond engagement ring on a beach in St Annes, Lancashire, in 1961. She and her fiancé, Christopher Firth, sifted through the sands on six successive weekends without success. They married the next year and continued to check with police lost-and-found files whenever they returned for holidays.

In 1977, Christopher's uncle died, and he discovered through a solicitor that he had a long-lost cousin John, who lived not far away from his own home in Yorkshire. In July 1979, in a conversation about metal detectors, John told Brenda that one of his children had found a diamond ring at St Anne's, 18 years before. It was her ring. (*D.Mirror, D.Star* 19 July; *Pretoria News* 21 July 1979.)

□ □ □

Thekla Aanen of Larkollen in Norway lost her gold ring set with a diamond while swimming in the Oslo fjord in 1976. Three years later her grandson Robert went fishing in the fjord and brought home a 10 pound cod. When Thekla gutted the fish for supper, she found her ring, according to the newspaper *Moss Dagblad*. (*Evening News* [Harrisburg, PA] 19 July; *Sun.Express, News of the World* 12 Aug 1979.)

□ □ □

Mrs G.Gudebrod of Hillingdon, California, lost her wedding ring on a beach picnic. A year later, her husband brought home a crab caught on the same beach. Mrs Gudebrod found her ring fixed to one of the crab's claws. (*Weekend* 14-20 May 1980.)

□ □ □

Mrs Rosemary Clatworthy of East Huntspill, Somerset, lost her wedding ring while hand-feeding a calf on her father's farm. Two years later, the calf, now a fully grown cow, drowned in a ditch. Slaughter-men found the ring in the animal's stomach. The same thing happened to an Icelandic farmer, who got his ring back after a year, when it was re-covered from the stomach of a cow he had sent for slaughter. (*D.Telegraph, D.Star* 14 Feb 1979; *Surrey & Hants News* 25 Nov 1980.)

□ □ □

J.A. of Basingstoke wrote to the *Sunday Mirror* (27 April 1977) that he had a quarrel with his fiancée in a country lane at night. She gave him back the engagement ring, and he hurled it over a hedge into a meadow. They searched for it by torchlight without success.

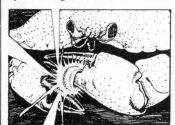

Illo by Baz Hurrell

Six months later he dreamed he saw the ring inside an old shoe in the meadow. He went back and found the ring in the shoe.

□ □ □

The gold signet ring which Linda Robson, 29, lost as a child, turned up after 25 years. When workmen started de-molishing her former home in Errol, Perthshire, her father returned and found the ring among the debris. (*D.Mirror* 10 May 1978).

□ □ □

Dress designer Susan Eagles, 27, of Manchester, lost a gold ring which had been given her on her 21st birthday. Eight months later, her flat mate bought a ring at an auction for £28. Susan recognised it as her own. (*Sun.People* 4 Mar 1979.)

□ □ □

In 1897, the Dock and Harbour Master of Newport, Monmouthshire, married a Miss Hunter of Newport. They spent their honeymoon at Dawlish in Devon, where she lost her gold bracelet in the sea. They re-visited the beach in 1925, and while sitting in deckchairs, spotted a glint of gold in the sand as the tide went out. It was the lost bracelet. The Harbour Master's neice tells the story in the *Sunday Express* (13 July 1975.)

□ □ □

Mrs Felicity Chiddicks lost her £400 engeement ring in the sea off Penzanze. 2 days and 5 tides later, on 31 August 1981, she found it three inches down in the sand, with the help of a metal detector.

Also that summer, Tony Green lost his gold wedding ring while bathing at Barmouth in North Wales. Three weeks later his family returned to the beach, and his daughter Mandy, 13, found the £100 ring in the sand.(*D.Telegraph* 1 Sep + 22 Sep 1981.)

□ □ □

Credits block:
Credits: *Larry Arnold, Peter Hope Evans, Chris Hall, Chris Holtzhausen, Valerie Martin, Paul Screeton, Anthony Smith, Paul Thomas, Steve Wrathall.* ● PRAdeGS.

It always astonishes us how enigmas continue in the face of skepticism. No one has satisfactorily explained how objects and animals can rain from our skies in the way they do, and yet instances occur right up to the present day. The volume of contemporary data can be judged by the fact that this is a topic we have featured more than any other since our inception. Here are some plummeting fish, crabs and peas. Next issue: ice, dust and non-meteoric material.

FALLING FROGS

The following three stories were missed, somehow, from previous collations.

• Paul Thomas wrote to us about the experience of a very old lady, told to him at an Atlantean meeting. In the summer of 1912, the lady and her sister lived in Oswestry, in the north of Shropshire. One day they were caught in a heavy rainstorm, during which so many "baby" frogs fell that they became frightened and ran back to their cottage. When they emerged a couple of hours later the sun was shining and all the frogs had gone. We wonder how many others have an experience like this to tell? Perhaps there is someone living still in Oswestry who remembers the incident? Thanks to Paul we can note this one, even if the details are understandably vague after all this time.

• The London *Evening Standard* 21 May 1921 records a fall of "thousands" of small frogs during a thunderstorm on the North Front of Gibraltar. The frogs, scarce at the best of times on The Rock, could be seen in great numbers in hedges for several days. The item mentions "a similar incident" about 7 years previously (1914)? which was followed by a shower of sand coating whole areas with a pink deposit.

• By some oversight we omitted the well-known shower of frogs in Soviet Central Asia, which happened on an unknown day just prior to the earlier reports from the Tass newsagency on the 5th or 6th of July 1979. It occurred over the village of Dargan-Ata, on the Amu Daria River in Turkemni — though these names were given a variety of spellings (eg: *Soviet Weekly,* which ought to know, called the village Dragan-Ata.) Despite the widespread reporting there are no other details to the story — an omission I find incredible and sadly predictable — except for a vague explanation that this "not uncommon" phenomenon is caused by a whirlwind. *UPI, D. Telegraph, Shropshire Star, D. Mirror, D. Express* 6 July; Lincoln *Star* (Nebraska), *Melbourne Herald* 7 July; *Soviet Weekly* 21 July 1979.

CRABS

• Cliff Davies (see photo) discovered the crabs in the garden of his home in Lime Grove, Killay, Swansea. "We had a tremendous storm with hailstones — I've heard of things coming out of the sky like this but nothing like this has happened to me before." Mr Davies found the dead one then his dog found the live one, which he now intends to free on the nearest beach, five miles away. "I don't think they walked here," he said. They measure one-and-a-half inches across the shell and about three inches from claw to claw. The dead one was pretty mangled. Attempts, by the newspaper, to find an explanation were in vain, but interestingly, the spokesmen they contacted at both the London Weather Centre and the National Museum of Wales (NMW) both acknowledged the subject of fish rains. Mr Piers Langhelt, of the NMW, even said he'd heard of similar incidents, but not "in the last few days." Sadly,

Cliff Davies with the crabs that dropped in. [Photo: Western Mail.]

the otherwise excellent *Western Mail*, who had this story in their 29 Sept 1981 edition, failed to put a date to the incident, but I guess it must have been within 2-3 days prior to the 29th.

PEAING DOWN

• Torrents of veg from the sky are not exactly common, but as readers will know, we've had a few in recent years... mustard cress, dried peas, maize and beans, etc, in Southampton in 1979 [see FT29p38, where in fact the recipient's name is Roland Moody, not as we had it, Mr Rowland] and hazelnuts in Bristol in 1977 [see FT26 p48f] — and the whole subject is reviewed in *Living Wonders* [see Book News, this issue].

This time the target was the tiny hamlet of Dan-y-Bryn, at Tonna, in Glamorgan, stimulating us to wonder at the number of falls recorded for Wales and the West Country (NB. the crab fall in South Wales, above). And once again the *Western Mail* missed out the date in reporting the event — I guess it to be on the 7th or 8th April 1980.

Mr Trevor Williams (see photo), a pump operator for Calor Gas, was in his garden when the shower began. He heard them splash in his pool, and thought the sound unusual for rain. "I couldn't believe my eyes," he said, "I expected hailstones, but there were peas everywhere. They were bouncing off the greenhouse and house roof in their thousands. The storm lasted several minutes and I was able to collect several jam-jars full of peas." There is no indication of the extent of the fall, but from reading between the lines it seems to have been extremely localized.

A Meteorological Office spokesman, Roger Hunt, was contacted and explained, authoritatively, that such events are the products of mini-whirlwinds, which had lifted and carried the peas "less than 10 miles." Just how he arrives at this distance beats me. Besides, who dries peas in heaps in the open air these days? Mr Williams told the paper that he knew of "... nothing in the vicinity, like a market garden or pea stockist, to explain it. I haven't a clue what caused it," he added. We challenge Mr Hunt, and the resources of the Met Office, at Bracknell, to give a single instance of winds of any kind lifting a heap of objects like peas and keeping them together in the air for about 10 miles and then, with uncharacteristic delicacy depositing them, or most of them, in a localized area. If that's too easy, then let him explain how the peas that were lifted, and only peas apparently, stayed dried during their transit in moisture-laden winds and clouds. *Western Mail* 9 April; *Sunday People* 13 April 1980.

Correspondent Paul Thomas, who sent us this story, says he's sure he heard about a shower of peas and beans in East Anglia in 1980, which, if not a distortion of the above and the Southampton multi-veg fall, would put it about the same time as the Tonna pea shower. Does anyone know any more about the doings in East Anglia?

FISHFALLS, LOTS

• Our oldest story, here dates back to 1916, and was told in a letter to *Weekend* 3 April 1980 (or perhaps 1970, the date is uncertain) by 76yr-old Rita Bell. In 1916 Rita was 12, and spending the holiday with a cousin in Sunderland, Co. Durham. On a wet and blustery day, the cousin asked Rita to take some documents to a town center bank. On her way home the storm broke and as Rita struggled to open her umbrella..."the incredible happened. Dozens of frozen fish, each the size of a large sardine...came down with such force that my umbrella was

A bewildered Trevor Williams holds some of the dried peas that rained down on him. [Photo: Western Mail.]

torn to ribbons." To back up her story, Rita said, she carried with her to the present day a tattered newsclipping of the story from the front page of the Sunderland evening paper. Unfortunately of the two identical clippings we have from *Weekend*, from two different clipsters, one has been dated 1970, and the other 1980. But since this is a secondary source it won't matter too much, because we have instigated a search for the original 1916 report. Even so, we might draw a blank. When we asked Paul Screeton if he could help, living as he does not far from Sunderland, he pointed out similarities of this story to that recorded in *Nature* 19 Sept 1918, and given on page 13 of *Phenomena* at the top of column 2—only here the date of the event is reliably given as 3pm on Saturday 24th August 1918. It seems likely that despite having her "tattered newsclipping" Rita Bell may be confused about the date, or simply never noted the date on the clipping. So it goes.

• More convincing is the experience of Fred Swindon, an Industrial Officer for the city of Sheffield, on the morning of 23 Feb 1981. Setting off to work, he was getting into his car, at his home in Stainborough, when he found six small cod-like fish on the driveway. They were "snub-nosed", alive and about 2-3 inches long. "It's a mystery where they came from. We wondered whether some boys had been out fishing and left the fish... as a joke, but there was no water on the drive," Swinden said. Twenty minutes later he was driving along the M1 between Barnsley and Sheffield when another fish appeared on his bonnet, wriggling. He stopped and put it in a windscreen-washer bottle he keeps as a spare. "The fish which appeared on the car must have been lodged in a groove near the windscreen and it was dislodged by the slipstream," he

wondered. "They may have been dropped by a bird." Either a feeble shower of fish fell near Swinden's car, one lodging by his windscreen—or more preposterously he was followed by the phenomenon which had deposited six in his drive and pelted with the seventh on the way to work? If we accept teleportation, they need not have fallen, but like the miraculous goose eggs (above) of Niagara, they could have simply appeared where they were found, perhaps a few seconds prior to their finding. Story from: *D.Mirror* 24 Feb; *Barnsley Independent* ? Feb 1981.

• Next, a correspondent to *The Countryman* (winter 1959) cited a story from the Sydney *Morning Herald* of 18 April 1959, that: "Hundreds of fish, about 4 inches long, fell into the main street of Woodburn, NSW, during heavy rain. Schoolchildren gathered handfuls, while some residents threw many into the nearby Richmond River. A garage proprietor, E.E.Hardaker, said there were about 50 fish in the gutter outside his premises. He put a dozen in the river but the others were dead."

• Finally, a story from South Africa. Mike Blore, of Thornton, was watching TV when he heard repeated "splashing sounds" from the direction of his pool. To his surprise, he found 8 dead sardines and 2 live catfish. He blames pelicans. "They are known to carry fish in their bills," he explained carefully. *The Star* (South Africa) 4 May 1981.

JUST FOR THE HALIBUT?
• To close, we have a story to strain your credulity, but we are assured, by John A. Clark, that it did indeed happen. At 8.15pm on the evening of 8 Feb 1981 Mr Clark was in his garden, in Barnes, south London, when something "swished" by his head and exploded on his 6ft larch-lap

fence. He investigated. "The missile had been partly forced through the larch lap and much of it was left on my side of the fence. I gathered the pieces of the missile and made notes," said Mr Clark in a letter to Francis Hitching, who forwarded the letter to us.

"It had been a complete portion of grilled halibut in oil (rather than white sauce or butter)," continued Mr Clark. The impact was strong enough to break the fence post, but "the skin did not completely disintigrate." Mr Clark collected enough meat, skin and fin to reconstruct the plummeting portion: "It was 6ozs of fragments, very cold but not frozen (ambient temperature was 52°F), very fresh—and even tasty."

"My first thought was that it was the remains of a dinner hurled about by a looney neighbour. The impact was against this, as was the speed." Mr Clark then checked what neighbours' roofs he could, and even sniffed through letterboxes for tell-tale smells of fish —but nothing. The trajectory of the fish, he reckons was north to south, over his house, *across* the flightpath into Heathrow airport and "counter wind", The idea the food came from an overhead plane seems unlikely, as Mr Clark asks: "Do they hurl 1st class grub out of airplanes 5 minutes from Heathrow?" With an excellent grasp of the etiquette of the extraordinary, Mr Clark explains why he wrote to Hitching after reading his *Atlas of Mysteries*: "I saw no point in claiming authenticity with the *Barnes & Mortlake Advertiser* as my means of accreditation." Quite right! Even we, who are schooled in the way of fishfalls have never heard a case involving grilled halibut before!

Credits: *Greg Axford, WR Benedict, Janet & Colin Bord, John A Clark, Peter James, J Lang, John Michell, Michel Parry, Paul Pinn, Anthony Smith, Joe Swatek, Paul Thomas, Andy Townsend, EL Weathers, Dwight Whalen, Colin Wilkinson, Ion Will* ● RJMR

BEHAVIOURAL CURIOSITIES

In FT36, **Paul Sieveking** surveyed recent cases of voluntary withdrawal from society to cellars or the open countryside. In this related installment he turns to the Gothic horrors of family incarcerations. But first some cases of the 'Oblomov syndrome' — retiring to bed for inordinately long periods.

OBLOMOV SYNDROME

Presley Bishop came home from work depressed on 1 October 1978 in Littleton, Colorado, and went to bed. He stayed there for three years, during which time he wore a hole in the bed, lost 9 stone, grew a beard down to his stomach and fingernails six inches long. In August 1981 his widowed sister Bernice, in desperation, called in the cops and he was moved to a nursing home bed in Denver. Asked by police how he felt he replied: "Fine." It was the first word he had uttered since he had taken to his bed. (*D.Star* 27 Aug 1981.)

In 1932 a young Russian woman in England came down with flu and was instructed by her doctor to stay in bed and rest until he saw her again. Unfortunately, he forgot to come back and the woman was still in bed 40 years later.

Her mother looked after her until she died, and then a brother-in-law took over. She was eventually seen by another GP and referred to gerontologist Dr Peter Rowe at Taunton in Somerset. It took seven months to persuade the by-now 74-year-old "flu" victim to get back on her feet. Dr Rowe described the case in a 1978 issue of *The Lancet*.

However, this lady doesn't hold the Oblamov record. In the winter of 1917, an old woman of 94 died in Scarborough, Yorkshire, after days illness. She had taken to her bed 72 years before, when her father had forbidden her to marry her fiancé. Once she got up, to leave Cambridge for Scarborough. She was always in perfect health. Of course, others might have stayed in bed even longer. There's no Oblomov section in McWhirter's *Records*; the nearest we get is almost 66 hours on a bed of nails by Strombo the Maniac in 1977... (*Het Volk*, Sweden, 10 Oct 78; *Weekend Australian* 21 Oct 1978; *Reynolds Illustrated* 14 Jan 1917; *Guinness Bk of Records* 1980.)

Florence Nightingale, after becoming famous for tending the sick, spent the last 50 or so years of her life in bed and in perfect helath. A Victorian cousin of mine, Dr Herbert Sieveking, LRCP, who had founded the Victorian Hospital in Cairo, spent seven years in bed in London until his death in 1923, declaring that he was "fed up with buttoning and un-buttoning".

THE FEARFUL OUTDOORS

Sometimes, acute agoraphobia keeps its victims indoors for years: 20 years, in the case of Sidney Stevens, 35, of Hoxton. In 1978 he attacked his mother who looked after him, and was sent to his sister in Hackney. I expect there are hundreds like him. (*D.Telegraph* 2 Nov 1978.)

Arnold De Loughrey, 77, a weekend night-porter in Widnes, Cheshire, failed to turn up for work in January 1981. Firemen broke into his house and found him dead from a heart attack. The house was full of evil-smelling garbage, and in a "nest" of newspapers and rubbish which reached up to two feet from the kitchen ceiling they found his 77-year-old wife Edith wearing the tattered remains of a 1940's dress, and with long matted hair and 8 inch fingernails. She clawed and growled at her rescuers until given a sedative and taken to hospital.

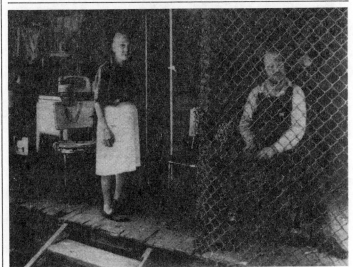

Mrs Georgia Chandler keeps an eye on her son Gerald in his chain-link pen on their shack porch. [Photo: Nat.Enq 7 July 81.]

Fortean Times

Agoraphobia had kept her in the house for over 30 years. Mr De Loughrey's employer remarked: "I couldn't understand how Arnold had always turned up smartly dressed for work until the police opened a garden shed. In it were found his suit and shirts which he used to wear to work." (*D. Express, S.People* 19 Jan 1981; *Globe* 24 Feb 81.)

■ ■ ■
KEEPING IT IN THE FAMILY

Gerald Chandler, 44, a retarded Kentucky mountain man, has been kept in a cage by his aged mother for the last 14 years. "I keep him locked up because he's simple, and to protect him from the outside world," she says. A neighbour down the road in the village of Stinnett remarked: "In these parts we believe in keeping family troubles in the family. 'Taint nobody else's business to look after him." This attitude is found all over the world, and accounts for the majority of domestic incarcerations. In the Chandler case, social workers have agreed to leave things as they are, since removing the son to an institution would probably be fatal for both mother and son. (*Nat.Enquirer* 9 Oct 1979 + 7 Jul 1981.)

Patrick Henry, one of the great civil leaders of the American Revolution, famous for having said "Give me liberty or give me death", confined his wife Sarah in a base-ment room below a trap door during the last years of her life. After 20 years of marriage, she developed a keen hatred of her husband and children, and although she was cared for tenderly, her condition worsened. Eventually she was locked in the basement until her death in 1775. Patrick Henry was greatly affected by her death, gave up all reminders of her and never spoke her name.

Carmine Ferretti was struck dumb and semi-paralysed by meningitis when he was seven. His parents locked him in a seven-foot-square pigsty at their farm near the town of Atri on the Italian Adriatic coast. The parents died in 1948, and Carmine's brother and his two sons continued to keep him in the sty. He was discovered in 1976, after 60 years of confinement, dressed in rags, lying on a heap of straw. Fiorangelo and his sons were sent to jail. (*D. Mirror* 19 Jan 1976; *New Thrill* [M'sia] 11 Mar 1978.)

Pedro da Silva was also confined in a pigsty, naked and manacled at the ankle, for 43 years. As a young man, Pedro had been the best wood-cutter in his home town of Dom Basilio, Brazil. But he began to suffer constant stomach cramps, and became increasingly violent. Then he ate a pig's head stew and started bleeding profusely from the nose. He beat up all the local boys, and tried to kill his best friend and his father. "Pedro threw rocks at us and would run wild in the forest, just like a savage animal," his sister recalled. "He even chewed sticks and twigs." Psychic healers could do nothing for him, and finally his sisters chained him in a pigsty. When he was found in 1981 his five senses were almost extinguished. He was unable to talk, and his skin had turned yellow. (*Nat.Enquirer* 17 Mar; *Singapore Post* 2 June 1981.)

In 1979 police went to a house in West Seneca, a suburb of Buffalo, New York, where

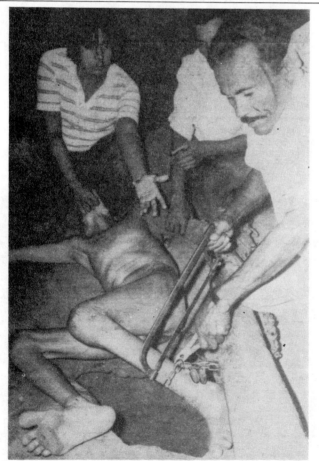
Police freeing Pedro da Silva, chained to a log in a pigsty for 43 years. [Photo: Nat.Enquirer 2 June 1981.]

they found Erwin Moll, 69, naked and emaciated, whom they believed had been locked in the attic for 50 years. His sister Agnes said this was because he was simple-minded. (*Toronto Sun, Niagara Falls Review, D.Telegraph* 31 May 1979.)

Amelia Colautti, 39, was another attic prisoner. Her parents in Trieste, Italy, locked her there for 30 years because, according to the *Daily Mirror* of 22 May 1980, "they were ashamed of her slight" (end of item). I guess we shall never know what they were ashamed of.

Giovanni Portapluglia, a noblewoman from Castell Arquata, 20 miles from Piacenza in northern Italy, was chained in a cupboard in the mediaeval family mansion by her parents in 1940, because she showed signs of insanity. When the parents died, Giovanna's brothers decided to keep her hidden to preserve "family honour and dignity." She was discovered by police in 1980 as the result of questions by an inquisitive villager. They were guided to her by the smell that came from the tiny room where she was held captive. "She was surrounded by excrement—in indescribable conditions" said a policeman. The 65-year-old-woman was a "human larva, with deep-sunken eyes in a small emaciated face, disfigured by starvation." She was incapable of speaking, and was carried into the sumptuously furnished main hall after her wrists had been freed from a heavy chain. Her brothers were arrested and charged with unlawful restraint and maltreatment. The rumours in the village were that she was locked up, not because of madness, but because she had committed incest with her father; or because the family wanted her money. (*Guardian, D.Telegraph, D.Mirror* 10 Nov; Ontario *Standard* 15 Nov 1980.)

Also in 1940, another Giovanna was locked up by her family in the village of Bultei, near Sassari in Sardinia. The brothers and sisters of Giovanna Lucia Tiana thought she was possessed by the devil, and for the next 37 years she was locked up in the cellar without a light, amid rats and filth. She was released in 1977. (*Lanazione* 15 May; *Times* 16 May 1977.)

The aptly named News Horufu was also said to be possessed by an evil spirit, and for 10 years had been chained naked to a tree 70 miles northeast of Salisbury in Zimbabwe. In 1980 the demented man was freed and treated by Mrs Jelly Chari, one of the country's 30,000 traditional healers, or "witch doctors". In March 1981 a smiling News left her clinic to return to his village. He said he was looking forward to rejoining his parents and helping with the ploughing. "There is no need to chain me any more" he said. (*Pretoria News* 21 Jan; *Observer*, 15 Mar 1981.)

Fernando Mendes, 19, of Casal Brancas in Portugal, was found in 1980, also tethered to a tree. His parents were backward peasants living in abject squalor in a three-room, fly-infested shack. His father was retarded, and his mother, who claimed Fernando was violent, first began tethering him 7 years earlier. "If I had not tied

News Horufu, chain ed to the tree for 10 years [Photo: Pretoria News 21 Jan 1981.]

him up, he would have simply run away" she said. The youth was put into a local mental hospital and gave no indications of a violent temperment.

When Juan Ruiz was discovered the following year, he had spent 18 of his 22 years tied to a leash in the family barn in Planes, in the Spanish province of Alicante. Juan, who has been retarded since birth, can't be set free because the only institution in the area is for children and he can't be put there. "He might kill himself if he gets out", said his mother. "Being tied up doesn't hurt him, and we look after him well." (*Nat.Enquirer* 25 Nov 1980; *Globe*, 5 May 1981.)

Vincie Jones was born deaf, and spent the first eight years of his life locked in a cupboard by his mother, who believed he was better off where he

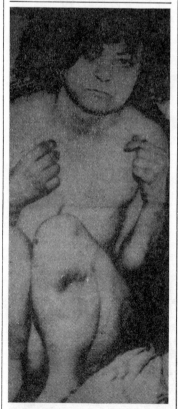

Helen Karioti, as police found her after 29 years captivity in darkness. [Sun 8 Nov 1978.]

couldn't harm himself or others. A Chicago welfare worker found him in 1973, with the mind of a baby and no speech. In 1980 he had fully recovered, and graduated from eighth grade. (*Topeka Capital* 23 June 1980.)

■ ■ ■

A GRIM CHILDHOOD

A quite extraordinary case of family imprisonment—in this case the whole family—is told by Bruno Bettelheim in the *American Journal of Sociology* (March 1959). The story is given to explain the particularly wild and violent nature of Anna, one of the autistic children he treated in the Orthogenic School. Anna's parents were Polish Jews who spent the whole of the Second World War hidden in a dugout under the farmhouse of a gentile peasant friend of the father. The mother, who found the father utterly unattractive, had rejected him for years while he courted her hopelessly. Only after all her family had been exterminated by the Nazis did she join him in his hideout. The father wove sweaters in the hole during the day (which the farmer sold), and the loom was dismantled every night so that they could lie down to sleep.

Several times the Germans shot into the farmhouse, and searched the place, but they didn't find the hidden Jews, who had a daughter, Anna, in the Spring of 1943. The baby was not allowed to cry since any noise would have given them away, and so one of the parents had to hold a hand over her mouth. They left their hole with the Russian occupation in 1945, but by that time Anna was unmanageable. Not surprising really, growing up in a hole with parents who were so ill-matched and in a state of constant dread. After the mother's milk ran out, the baby had nothing to eat except raw vegetables, because cooking was impossible.

■ ■ ■

DOMESTIC ATROCITIES

First of all, three horror stories

from Greece. In 1951 the parents , two elder sisters and brother of Eleni Karioti, 20, locked her in the six by eight foot square cellar of their home in the village of Kostalexi near Lamia, in central Greece. She had already been confined to the house for the previous two years. She was finally found, naked and filthy, in November 1978, after 27 years in the cellar. She was suffering from malnutrition and couldn't speak. Her crime was her wish to marry a war-time resistance hero while there were still no suitors for her sisters Olympiada and Maria (who are still unmarried). In 1980, a Greek court cleared the brother and sisters, since they had only been obeying the instructions of their parents. (*Guardian, Sun* 8 Nov 1978; *Reveille* 6 Jul 1979; *D.Star* 10+11 Jan 1980.)

In December 1981 Chrisostomos Voyatzis, 48, was charged with keeping his 86-year-old mother in the henhouse to stop her quarrelling with his wife; and the previous August, Constantina Maltesou, 80, was found naked in a barn in the village of Kypselli Methanon where she had been locked for six months by her sisters.

Constantina had been a national celebrity in 1970 when she married her 85-year old Romeo, Christos Ladros. Three years later she divorced and returned to her sisters Eleni and Stamatina, who made her sleep in the barn with the family's sheep. This went on for eight years, until she was no longer able to walk, whereupon the sisters locked her in the barn continually. The villagers, who knew all about it, claimed they did nothing because the sisters threw stones at them. A Greek newspaper claimed that Constantina could no longer "speak or feel anything." (*D. Telegraph* 19 Dec; *Guardian* 19 Aug 1981.)

Charlotte Elaine Mottinger was held prisoner by her mother in Long Beach, California, for 20 years, following the death of her father. She was frequently beaten, bound hand and foot and locked in a bathroom for days at a time. Police finally released her in June 1979. She repeatedly asked them: "You're not going to drown me, are you?" Apparently her mother had told her that if she ever talked to police they would beat her and drown her. The mother said Charlotte had been locked up because she was retarded and diabetic, but this was not true. She had been fed mostly on a concoction of rice, corn, bread and water. When released, she appeared to be about 15, although she was 33. (*St Catharine's Standard, Toronto Sun* 29 June 1979.)

Elizabeth Farmer was locked up and tortured by her sister in New York for 20 years. She was padlocked in her bedroom in 1961 when Mary Farmer claimed she had been stealing from her. She had a small quilt to sleep on, a bucket for a lavatory, and was fed on hamburger scraps. She was often beaten with a stick and rope. When rescued in September 1981 she weighed 5 stone, and was incapable of speech. (*D.Star* 3 Oct 1981.)

Maria Jose Roudaut was locked in the garden shed in Nantes for six years by her parents, after they found she had been stealing pop records. "So we shut her up for her own good." The house was up for sale in 1970 when she was finally discovered. Gendarmes broke down the door. The smell was foul, and the young woman was chained to the floor. Her hair fell below her waist and her nails were six inches long. She was taken to hospital, and her parents to jail. (*Titbits* 12 Jan 1980.)

■ ■ ■
ENTOMBED LOVERS
Marcello Montesi lived with his Belgian mistress Chantal de Ryke in Ancona on Italy's Adriatic coast. Then he fell for another woman and for a time all three lived together. Mont-

esi tired of Chantal and bricked her up in the garage where she was found, a living skeleton, ten months later. Every two or three days a tin of corned beef had been pushed through a small hole. That was all he had eaten.

For nearly eight years a Portugese businessman, Antonio Verissimo, 65, kept his secret love affair from his fellow villagers in Alhos Vedros near Lisbon, by locking his mistress and their two daughters in a farm shed. Vivelinda Rodrigues, 48, was discovered and released in the summer of 1981 and was hospitalised for severe nervous disorders while her daughters Ana, 7, and Rosa, 8, were cared for by nuns. The girls could not walk properly and knew only a handful of words. Verissimo was not arrested: police said they had no justification for detaining him. (*Weekend* 19 April 1978; *D. Telegraph* 6 July 1981.)

■ ■ ■
THIS DANGEROUS WORLD
Parents sometimes lock up their children to "protect" them. Miroslav Kolak, a Yugoslav religious fanatic, kept his eight children imprisoned from birth because the outside world was evil. When police raided Kolak's home in Melbourne in November 1980 they had to scale a 13 foot high wire fence and penetrate an elaborate security system including searchlights, sirens and electronic eyes. The eldest child, 21-year-old Alexander, had somehow managed to escape in the summer with two brothers and a sister, and had reported the situation to welfare authorities. Neighbours said they were unaware of the existence of the children. (*New Standard* 7 Nov 1980.)

Umberto Cannuci also wanted to protect his family from "the world's corruption." For three years the righteous Sicilian locked up his wife and two teenage daughters, with only the Bible to read. In November 1981 police freed them from their steel-barred cell

Vince Jones, 15, deaf and mentally retarded, spent his first eight years in a closet. [Photo: Topeka Capital (AP) 23 June 1980.]

after Umberto, 43, had threatened a nun with a knife. He had let his family out of their room for an hour a day and they took exercise in a sealed courtyard at knifepoint. All this he did because "Voices" had commanded him to do so. (*D.Express* 24 Nov 1981.)

Mothers do it too. In 1977 police released two sisters, aged 12 and 19, in Bayreuth, West Germany, who had been confined to the house all their lives by their mother, to stop them catching diseases. And the NSPCC told of a case in 1981 where a young mother had kept her three children locked up at home for two years because she was convinced that they would be killed or injured in a road accident. (*Guardian, D.Mail* 13 May 1977, *D.Telegraph* 2 Jun 1981.)

☐ **Credits:** *Hubert Adamson, Ronny Blomme, Christ Holtzhausen, Peter Hope Evans, Alexis Lykiard, Valerie Martin, Lorenzo Massai, Andy Townsend, Dwight Whalen, Ion Will* ●**PRAdeGS**

INTRUSIONS

By Hilary Evans.
Routledge & Kegan Paul (Henley-on-Thames, Oxon; 1982); £5.95 pb, pp206, index, bib, photos, illus.

Those of us acquainted with Hilary Evans are well aware of the range of his interests and reading, and know he is capable of making considerable contributions to the study of most areas of the anomalous, and this book certainly justifies our confidence in him.

Intrusions is a book about society's attitude towards the paranormal as represented by two mainstreams, an 'official' line and the concensus of popular beliefs, the two often being diametrically opposed. Most of the material revolves around the history of spiritualism and its precursors in witchcraft and religious or mystical phenomena. As the discussion nears the present it includes psychic research and ufology. Not only is this a useful overview of the psychological and social dramas created by the intrusion of the paranormal into the lives of men, it is studded with insights. Significantly, such intrusions are seen by the orthodox view as threatening to undermine their monopoly of authority in the realm of knowledge of this world, whereas to the mass of ordinary people they are mainly taken as confirmation of ancient, traditional beliefs in the multiplicity of worlds and beings. Essential reading for all wishing to make some sense out of this bewildering world and the veritable Babel of explanations.

RJMR.

UFO STUDY

By Jenny Randles.
Robert Hale (London; 1981) £7.95 hb, pp271, index, refs, illus, plates.

ALIEN CONTACT:

Window on Another World

By Jenny Randles & Paul Whetnall.
Neville Spearman (Sudbury, Suffolk; 1982) £5.25 hb, pp207, index, bib.

Few people can have contributed more to British ufology in recent years than Jenny Randles, who, in a short time, has become a leading worker for FSR, BUFORA, UFOIN, ASSAP, and ufology in general, and is probably the nearest there is to that form of pundit to whom the media turns for a quote on a given subject. Apart from her public relations work she is a tireless investigator and her reports seem to pop up everywhere these days.

UFO Study is a straightforward book, subtitled 'A Handbook for the Enthusiast'. There must be many motives for becoming a ufologist, and those who have had the bug a long time will say it's a kind of madness — but that wouldn't attract many willing minds among young readers, so I guess this approach, implying ufology is a kind of hobby, is about right. The book is pitched toward British youngsters and Jenny's writing is neither patronizing nor dull, though long-winded in parts.

The beginner will find everything he needs here, and much excellent advice on how to investigate UFOs, from learning where to find reports, field work, interviewing, writing reports, and where to send them. Case histories are given, of classic British cases (many here are publicly for the first time). Photographic and historical work are also covered, and there is an extensive history of ufology, and the 'new ufology' with its psychological and parapsychological leanings, to place the study in some perspective. Jenny, finally, reviews significant theories fairly, making a reasonable plea for the young investigator to be careful, impartial, and responsible.

American readers will find here an excellent review of British ufology, both its philosophical development and as represented by 'Ten Significant Cases'. The book is very sensible and if not bought personally or as a present should be stocked by every school library...and inquiring children sould be pointed in its direction without delay.

Alien Contact is quite a different book, being a case study of the experiences of the Sunderland family of North Wales. The first part is a blow-by-blow account of the family's close encounters, in the sweltering summer of 1976, with several UFOs and their occupants, following which various members of the family experience paranormal phenomena, ranging from out-of-the-body trips, distortions of time and reality, poltergeist-like phenomena and apparent visits to somewhere quite unlike planet earth. It is in the second half of the book that the reader gets the full benefit of the experience of Jenny and her colleagues as UFO investigators and theoriests, when they analyse the Sunderlands' extraordinary story, which is so at odds with what we accept as everyday reality that even the rich genre of the UFO is too narrow a context for it and the authors are obliged to reach into other areas of the anomalous for comparison.

The difference between the two parts of the book are great: the latter is a careful exposition of fact and opinion, while the former suffers from being 'written-up' in the techniques of fiction. British books on British ufology are rare things and often botched for one reason or another. For all its faults (which are mainly stylistic and should be no obstacle for the serious researcher) this has got to be one of the best research cases for years, and a good book for the reader of *UFO Study* to move onto as an extreme example of the CE4 strangeness. It is a book with many loose ends and unanswered questions, and while the affair has left the Sunderland family with an inspired optimism that the future will contain the answers, the rest of us will have to settle for having our thoughts provoked — and that is something this book does very well.

RJMR.

THE UNFATHOMED MIND:
A Handbook of Unusual
Mental Phenomena
Compiled by William R. Corliss.
Sourcebook Project (Glen Arm, MD 21057, USA; 1982) $19.95 hb, pp754, illus, index.

I have been looking forward to this volume in Corliss' amazing series of fat reference works for a long time, and the waiting has been worth it. Once again we see an admirable selection of reports, observations, data and research from the frontiers of a science (psychology, this time) as the product of Corliss' grand sweep through scientific literature as a whole, supplemented with sources less well known. As science marches on, its priorities shift according to new areas of interest and the changing needs of society, as a consequence of which much data, knowledge and experience gets left behind, dumped or forgotten because no one could judge its relevance at the time. Corliss' programme is designed to collect this valuable material, which would otherwise be lost or unavailable to most of us.

Once again it would be impossible to discuss the full range of phenomena dealt with, but the list of subjects includes: automatic writing and drawing; speaking in tongues; multiple personalities, and the use of hypnosis to probe them; spirit and demonic possession; possession by animals; the Windigo psychosis; vampirism; amoks and berserkers; jumping and other manias; mass hysteria and delusions; self-induced delusions; folie a deux; hypnotic behaviour, including telepathy under hypnosis; dreams, including induced dreaming and somnambulism; meditation and altered states of consciousness; deja vu divination; clairvoyance; eyeless sight, precognitions; memories of past lives; telepathy; word blindness; calculating and musical prodigies; hypnotic regression; lucid dreaming; eidetic imagery; memory; genius; Hallucinations, apparitions and illusions; induced hallucinations, including scrying; out-of-the-body experiences; near-death experiences; hysterical blindness and other effects of the mind upon senses; mental control of pain; psychosomatic phenomena; healing and the power of the mind; stigmata and other body effects with mental or psychic origins; lunar and other influences on mental illness; the seat of intelligence; psychokinesis and mental control of psychical processes. Phew!

It almost goes without saying that this is an indispensible reference work, of immediate interest to those studying these phenomena, and a worthwhile addition to public and school library shelves. Corliss ought to receive some kind of award for his services to Fortean publishing, but all I can drum up right now is my deepest appreciation for this and the other volumes in the excellent Handbook series, available from him at the above address.

RJMR

THE NATURAL HISTORY OF THE MIND
By Gordon Rattray Taylor
Granada (London; 1981); 2.50 pb; pp370, index, bib, notes, illus.

The achievement of this book is something that has been needed for a long time — nothing less than possibly the most complete overview of the latest thoughts and discoveries about the mind and brain. Taylor has a long-standing interest in the frontiers of science — remember his successes of the 60s, *The Biological Timebomb*, and *The Doomsday Book*? - as well as a well-deserved reputation as a scientific journalist, and was described by one reviewer as "an unpretentious polymath". His considerable erudition in the sciences and philosophy presents here a series of state-of-the-art summaries on such topics as pain, perception, ego and self-awareness, split-brain research, the nature of personality, multiple-personalities, thinking and memory, hypnosis, parapsychology, meditation, hallucinations, so-called photographic memories, the power of imagination, the structure of the brain and its chemical and electrical processes, mental illnesses, and the nature of phenomena of the unconscious to name just a few.

Taylor has great style. His paragraphs are concise statements of fact, reference and well-thought-out opinions — it engrossed me, and actually excited me with new insights. What I value most of all, and which comes across clearly, is that this book was a labour of love by someone deeply interested in the curiosities and

history of his subject, and not just its demonstrable facts and achievements. It is one of the most balanced and far-reaching books I've read for some time.
RJMR

SEARCH FOR THE TASMANIAN TIGER
By Quentin Beresford & Gerry Bailey.
Blubber Head Press (Box 475, Sandy Bay, Tasmania, Australia 7005; 1981); Aus$8.95 pb, pp54, Bib, index, plates, illus.

THE TASMANIAN TIGER
By Steven Smith.
Wildlife Division, National Parks & Wildlife Service of Tasmania (Box 210, Sandy Bay, Tasmania, Australia 7005; 1981); Aus$6.00 pb, pp134, photos, maps, graphs.

SAVAGE SHADOW
By David O'Reilly.
Creative Research (Box 137, North Perth, WA 6006, Australia; 1981); Aus$4.95, pp262, photos.

Australia's mysteries do not often make the headlines in the northern hemisphere, and relevant publications are rarely seen, so it is particularly pleasing to be able to review three 1981 publications on two of the continent's perennial mysteries – the Tasmanian tiger and the cougar. The Tasmanian tiger (or thylacine, or marsupial wolf – *Thylacinus cynocephalus*) was/is a carnivorous marsupial, that is, it looks like a dog or wolf, has a striped back and a long tail, and carries its young in a pouch like a kangaroo. Sadly, it was hounded towards extinction in its chief territory, Tasmania, because the settlers believed it was a threat to the sheep. The last recorded killing of a thylacine in the wild was in 1930, but there still persist reports of sightings fifty years later, and the animal (if it really does still survive) is now under government protection. *Search for the Tasmanian Tiger* records the story of the thylacine in the past and the present. The book is well illustrated with many rare

photographs and engravings, is very readable and at the same time thorough, and is highly recommended.

The Tasmanian Tiger - 1980 is more technical, being 'A report on an investigation of the current status of thylacine *Thylacinus cynocephalus*, funded by The World Wildlife Fund Australia'. It is large in size, 11½x8" as compared with *Search's* almost 8"-square format. There are many graphs and statistics, and a few photographs, including a section on other animals recorded during the physical search for the thylacine, which will be of interest to those who have ever wondered what Tasmanian devils, possums and bandicoots look like. Full of useful facts and figures, and recommended to the reader who prefers a report prepared by zoologists rather than journalists.

Savage Shadow deals with a greater enigma. At least the thylacine is a native Australian animal. The cougar is not – but hundreds of sightings have been made, and farmers in the south-west have for decades had to put up with attacks on their stock. David O'Reilly has taken the journalist's approach to the mystery and partly turned his material into a novel. The first sentence reads: 'Dennis Earnshaw sat bolt upright in bed, every nerve in his body tingling.' But despite this unpromising start, the book does contain plenty of hard facts. The mystery animal's method of killing shows that a big cat is at work rather than a dog, and footprints, and claw marks, hairs and excreta all tell the same story. Eye-witnesses describe a large cat-like animal – sometimes tawny, sometimes black – with a long curly tail, and there seems little doubt that some kind of big cat is indeed living successfully in the Australian bush. If O'Reilly's book had been more like Beresford & Bailey's in presentation, it would have been far better. But nevertheless the facts are there if you can dig

them out from among the superfluous story-telling. The book is sparsely illustrated with photographs of dead animals. Again it would have been better for having the wealth and variety of illustrations that enhance *Search for the Tasmanian Tiger*.
Janet Bord

MYTHICAL MONSTERS
By Charles Gould.
Wizards Bookshelf (Box 6600, San Diego, CA 92106, USA; 1981); $18.50 (+ overseas postage of $1.40) hb, pp412, index, engravings.

What a splendid idea; to publish a facsimile edition of Gould's classic work, first published in 1886. The new edition has a utilitarian binding instead of the impressively blocked original with its brocade-like endpapers, but then the Wizards Bookshelf have added a thorough index and scattered notes. The Wizards, who are new to us, seem to be devotees of H.P. Blavatsky's *The Secret Doctrine*, and embarked on a project to reprint a variety of documents and books which are referred to by Blavatsky, and incidentally doing us all a favour by making available some marvellous classics, of which this is one.

Gould was the son of the famous ornithologist, John Gould, and travelled the world as a young naturalist. Among his many contributions to cryptozoology are his reports from Australasia on the mysterious *bunyip* in Tasmania, and the elusive Queensland marsupial tiger-cat, and the moas of New Zealand, but only the latter is mentioned, and then only briefly, in this book. If you don't know *Mythical Monsters*, it contains seminal chapters on the antiquity of man; on whether the Biblical deluge is a myth; on the unicorn, the Chinese phoenix and a fine study of the dragon in Europe, China and Japan. There is also a long survey of the case for the sea-serpent, important to the subject because Gould open-mindedly discusses the opinions of his scientific colleagues, and because he was the first to collect SS accounts from the Far East.

An admirable venture and worthwhile book.

RJMR.

THE SUBTERRANEAN KINGDOM
By Nigel Pennick.
Turnstone (Wellingborough, N'hants; 1981 pb, pp160, index, bib. glos, illus.

THE LOST WORLD OF AGHARTI
By Alec Maclellan.
Souvenir Press (London; £7.95 hb, pp231, bib, plates.

HOLLOW EARTH MYSTERIES
By Floria Benton.
Future Press (Elkton, MD, USA; 1981 - available from Arcturus Book Service, 263 N. Ballston Ave, Scotia, NY 12302, USA - $4.95 + 85¢ P&P (overseas orders add $1.00 P&P) pb, pp107, illus.

HITLER'S SECRET SCIENCES
By Nigel Pennick.
Neville Spearman (Sudbury, Suffolk; 1982) £6.50 hb, pp182, bib, plates.

Nigel Pennick has long been fascinated by subterranea, and *Subterranean Kingdom* is a marvellous compendium of the lore and history he has collected about man-made underground structures, whether real, like crypts, caves, catacombs, mines, tombs, chapels, earth-houses and hypogea, or legendary like the stories of secret tunnels attached to ancient and sacred sites all over the world. Most of the book is devoted to the subterranea of Britain, which is absorbing enough to read about, but made more exciting by frequent digressions into tantalizing titbits: the secret city of Ivan the Terrible, found while tunnelling was in progress for the Moscow underground; the vast tunnel system beneath the Andes; the maze of tunnels beneath Paris and Rome; the 'official' mysteries of tunnel/ shelters under London; the Hellfire Club complex; and those perennial favourites, the underground city of Agharti, (said by various authors to be under Tibet, Outer Mongolia, the Hindu Kush, or Afganistan) and the Hollow Earth idea.

While Pennick warns us to treat these last two as mythical — possibly folk-memories of underground dwelling complexes, etc, in our megalithic past — Floria Benton is an unashamed apologist for the real existence of a civilization (or two) inside the Hollow Earth, which she ambiguously equates with the legendary city of Agharti, which in turn is often confused with its 'twin', Shamballa, in a rambling discussion of Atlantis, Theosophy, UFOs, Venusians, degenerate but technologically advanced subterranean races, and Nazi occultism. For example: the builders of the vast global network of tunnels and caves linking these mysterious cities to other sites (Maclellan has a map of this on his endpapers) are variously the ancient gods, spacemen, Atlanteans, giants, and a super-race, and so on. To Benton though, the ancient gods were an Atlantean super-race of giant spacemen.

Benton begins her little typed book with a statement of her belief: that the earth is a hollow shell, virtually "in orbit around a central sun"; the inner surface is colonized and linked to our surface world by tunnels and by huge openings at the poles. If this makes a nonsense of conventional ideas of geology, gravity etc, then gravity, etc, must be rethought, she argues imperiously. The rest of the book summarizes evidence for and against the Hollow Earth, and is entirely biased towards her beliefs. This of course is an author's privilege, but it is hardly convincing stuff. While she is critical of data mitigating against the HE hypothesis, she does not apply criticism to the supporting data she has selected. Typically her defense of Von Daniken against the scorn of his critics, is to employ scorn, again, against their statements.

Maclellan's is altogether a more rational approach, examing basically the same source material, though he is more knowledgeable about the fictional and pseudo-mystical literature on Agharti than on UFOs (where Benton is vice versa). What disturbs me is the over-reliance by Benton and Maclellan on authors who are extremely unreliable sensation-mongers at best: Von Daniken, Ray Palmer, Dr Raymond Bernard, Richard Shaver, Robert Charroux, Peter Kolosimo, Eric Norman and the dubious self-proclaimed 'Messenger of Buddha' Robert Dickhoff — these are hardly the authorities for hard facts that she thinks. Another disturbing trend is that a number of classical works of fiction — among them, Bulwer Lytton's *The Coming Race*, Jules Verne's *Journey to the Center of the Earth*, W.G. Emerson's *The Smoky God*, and the haunting *Etidorpha*, an 'inspired' book by John Uri Lloyd — which are searched by these authors for confirmation, and then cited as almost-proof. In this Floria Benton abandons herself to utter credulity at times.

Maclellan's interest in the subject began with an eerie experience while caving in Yorkshire — deep in the earth he was first intrigued, then terrified, by a mysterious green light and a humming which grew to shake the earth. He then gives us the benefit of his search for understanding these events in terms of underground civilizations. Part of the book is a research into the curious 'Vril Power' which so obsessed some Nazi occultists, and which first came to light in Bulwer Lytton's novel in 1875, and was enlarged upon by Blavatsky in her *Secret Doctrine* (1888), as a universal latent force or energy which could be controlled by adepts for beneficial or destructive purposes. It was a belief in the existence of Vril and Agharti, and the hidden power of a temporal ruler known as 'The King of the World' whose seat was Agharti, that inspired the formation of the Vril Society, a pre-Nazi organization which found favour with Hitler, as did the Thule Society in its own search for the Northern Atlantis.

It is left to Pennick's deceptively casual study of Hitler's quest for the hidden knowledge of the ancients, *Hitler's Secret Sciences*, to suggest a reason why we should take seriously the preposterous but exciting ideas of underground worlds, lost races, strange energies and mystical visions of the future. It is precisely because Blavatsky, Hitler and many others treated them seriously, believing them to be symbolically if not literally true, and they in turn influenced multitudes of believers, affecting the course of history and the fate of millions.

Although Pennick's coverage of Agharti is not as extensive as Maclellan's, he does place it in the context of the Nazi interest in the 'golden' age of secret ancient civilizations generally. With great erudition and insight Pennick unfolds facet after facet of the occult and mystical traditions adopted by the Nazi movement. There were expeditions to find these lost worlds, scientific programmes to recover the ancient magic, propaganda to reeducate the masses with the new religion, and strange embassies which, even now, remain unexplained but which hint at Hitler's search for occult power (eg: the discovery of hundreds of bodies of Tibetans in the ruins of Berlin after Hitler's suicide.) The intricacies of this vast and complex subject, which reaches into almost every aspect of folklore, magic and mysticism, cannot be adequately summarized here, and I urge you to read the book. The publishers claim *Hitler's Secret Sciences* will be a best-seller in the tradition of its precursor *The*

Spear of Destiny by Trevor Ravenscroft — time will tell, but it is certainly on a par with it. Pennick is to be commended too for his level-headed approach to the subject, many aspects of which must still fill thousands of people with revulsion. This is not one of those gosh-wow books of misplaced adulation, but an able perspective, full of insights, of one of the most bizarre movements of all time. It is without doubt also a disturbing book, as, at every turn of the page, one finds it almost impossible to conceive what our world would now be like if the Nazi's had succeeded with their mad dreams. Even more disturbing, as Pennick makes clear, the vestiges of these strange beliefs and secret societies are still with us, and "the final chapter in the weird history of Nazi occultism has yet to be written."

RJMR.

MEGALITHOMANIA
By John Michell.
Thames & Hudson (London; 1982) £8.50 hb, pp168, index, plates, illus.

Following on from John's *Little History of Astroarchaeology* here is the other side of the official history. It is not so much a book about 'old stones', as a book about people who were obsessed with them; people whose careers were made or smashed by their love of the stones; people who excavated them, worshipped them, suppressed them, or thoughtlessly destroyed them; people who have surveyed, photographed, painted or drawn them; and people who have theorized and explained them, some successfully and others hopelessly wrong.

In John's inimitable style, erudite and entertaining, this book is something of a celebration, a visual feast of engravings, drawings, paintings (eight in colour) and photographs. It is clear that while the effect of ancient stone sites all over the world exert a strange influence upon scientists,

anthropologists, archaeologists, etc. is to set them quibbling or scoffing, their effect upon artists and poets is quite the reverse, inspiring them with vision and imbuing their work. with that ancient energy they assert still crackles around these magical megaliths.

If nothing else, this book is a wonderful collection of portraits of tombs, mounds, circles, standing stones and other structures, many of the illustrations with people in period costume, reflecting the great changes in social attitudes towards the stones; whether, for example, they were indeed tombs, celestial calculators, temples, military or trade markers, healing sites, the homes of spirits or elementals, or simply relics of a long dead tribe.

There is much humour here too — eg: Magnusson's disasterous interpretation of cracks in the Runamo rock (see FT35 p14) as runes, and an amazing comparison of no less than 9 interpretations of the Dighton Writing Rock, in Massachusetts. But the humour here is gentle and full of compassion for the human condition, which, thank God, is large enough to encompass cranks of all persuasions. A beautiful book for collectors and scholars.

RJMR.

EARTH RITES
By Janet & Colin Bord.
Granada (St Albans, Herts; 1982) £8.95, pp273, index, bib, notes.

For years now the Bords have colonized that area between folklore, ufology, earth mysteries and Forteana, and seem to have made it their own. *Earth Rites* leans heavily towards the folklore quadrant and shows the Bords to be as widely read in that area as they are in the others.

The earth rites in view are to do with fertility — perhaps one of the greatest obsessions of our ancestors, whether of themselves, their land or their livestock. This was not wholly a self-centered preoccupation, but seen as a symbiosis. Fecundity and vitality, as exemplified by the cycle of growth and decay, and sexuality, were the product of man and deified nature working together so that fertility was exchanged for worship and respect of natural forces. Mainly British customs are dealt with, although digressions into the beliefs of other cultures are included, and the impression is that the forms of such ideas were remarkably universal. It is also fascinating to see apparently innocent traditions — like cheese-rolling, confetti, 'wild' football and circular dancing, to mention just a few — revealed as degenerated forms of fertility rites.

The book has long chapters on the cult of the Earth Mother; archaeological evidence for fertility cults; the folklore of fertility; standing stones shaped like sexual parts: the carvings inside churches on the themes of sexual exhibitionism, the 'green man' and dragons; holy wells and sacred trees; the agricultural cycle: ritual sacrifice and the divine victim; folk customs which are often vestiges of older fertility practices; ending with the Bords' own view of how the fertility culture operated in the context of earth energies.

Earth Rites is copiously illustrated, many of the photos taken by the Bords themselves. It makes an excellent addition to the folklore section of your library.

RJMR.

VELIKOVSKY'S SOURCES
by Bob Forrest.

This project is not likely to please the supporters of Velikovsky, because Bob's aim is nothing less than examining every classical and Biblical citation and reference used by Velikovsky in support of his radical, dramatic and hotly contested (by some outraged scientists) theories about the origin of Venus and the nature of some of the global catas-

trophes remembered in the various race mythologies. Bob is a stickler for detail and down on this level, it seems, Velikovsky's quotations do not stand up all that well when compared directly with the original material. Bob shows them side-by-side and thus provides an indispensible reference work for any study in this field. The project so far consists of 3 continuously numbered volumes — part 1 (81pp), part 2 (pp81-164), part 3 (pp165-248).

The work is privately printed on stencils on A4 paper, and available at £4.50 ($18.00) the set of 3 vols, including p+p. UK orders to Bob at: 53 Bannerman Ave, Prestwich, Manchester M25 5DR; US orders to Bob Schadewald: Route 1, Box 129, Rogers, MN 55374, USA. Dollar cheques should be made payable to R. Schadewald.

At the time of writing other volumes have been planned, including one containing any postal discussion of the main work.

TRANCE AND SUBJEC-TIVITY + JAZZ by Dave Reissig (16pp, litho): two brief papers, being the Jungian thoughts of Dave on these topics. It was quite coincidental that we received Hunt Emerson's strip for this issue, virtually covering the same topics, shortly after this booklet arrived.

AN INVESTIGATIVE RE-PORT INTO THE ALLEGED ALIEN BODY PHOTOS by The Ohio UFO Investigators League Inc. (52pp, litho, photos): the controversy rages. We have heard from those who have asserted the photos show an authentic burnt alien UFO pilot, now a member of the triumvirate of UFO groups who teamed up to investigate and release the photos, gives their conviction that the entire story was fabricated by the original source of the story, one Willard McIntyre, from fragments of other crashed-

Saucer stories and several declassified photos showing the unhappy conclusions of a rocket, fired at White Sands with a monkey passenger. These conclusions are argued awkwardly but sensibly, and highly likely. Price $6.00 (+ $2.00 overseas postage), from OUFOIL: Box 436, Fairfield, OH 45014, USA. *RJMR.*

Cont from p 3

form of folklore still in the making. More follows below, and next issue Paul Begg will review an important new book on the subject. For a note on Curious Facts see 'Help' column, this issue—Ed.]

I've been following the odd 'whale tumour' stories you've related with interest, and have seen the one about the people on holiday in France with the dying grandmother several times in print.

However, I actually had this story related to me—in all seriousness—as a P.S. in a letter from a friend. Most interesting is that although it had, of course, happened to some "friends of friends", the unlucky victims were from Melbourne in Australia, which is where I received the letter from. So where did the story start?

Richard Cotton
Knighton, Leicester.

I have just turned up a couple more 'Tumour in the Whale' type stories which I think might interest readers:

Firstly there's the 'Impossible Barricade' story. The latest example is in the Pope's visit to the Philippines, where the dictator, Marcos, is alleged to have put up miles of white-washed walls alongside the road to Manila from the airport to block out the Pope's view of the shanty-towns. This is a re-run of the tale told when King George V went to Liverpool to open the Mersey Tunnel, and the 'false flat fronts' said to be erected alongside the railway into Rome by Mussolini to fool Hitler in the 30s. All were supposed to mask slums, but in reality it would have been cheaper to clear the slums than spend such an effort on masking them.

The second story is about railways. I have heard it applied to three separate events. When the Lynton and Barnstable Railway, a bankrupt narrow-gauge line in North

Devon, was slated for closure in 1935, it is said that a delegation of local worthies went to see the general manager of the Southern Railway at Waterloo in London to protest. He is said to have asked them how they got there. When they answered 'by car', he showed them the door and closed the line forthwith. The same story is told of a visit to Dublin of petitioners from the west of Ireland, who, asked by Dr C.S.Andrews, the railway boss contemplating closures, answered likewise. Also the story applies to the notorious Dr Beeching in England.

Obviously these tales are further examples of that category.

Nigel Pennick
IGR, Cambridge.

PREDICTABLE PLOTS

The attempted murder of Pope John Paul made me re-read your article on popes (FT27).

A few days afterwards I found the following paragraph in the Swedish newspaper *SDS* (17 May 1981)—you have probably seen it in English newspapers:

"On the same day as the attempted murder of pope John Paul II—but in the morning—a weekly magazine in Columbia published an article that predicted an attempt to slay the pope. The magazine, named *Cromos*, introduced 'an expert on occultism' Marcellus Toe-Gucor, and quoted him: 'an act of violence will be committed against the Pope'. The magazine warned the Pope and his bodyguards for large crowds, and stated that a religious or political fanatic would try to take his life."

Marcellus is quoted as saying, "I saw it in the Pope's palm."

My own guess is that such "predictions" have been published several times each year during the last 20 years. (I cannot prove that.)

In *My Life and Prophecies* Mrs. Jeane Dixon states:

"During this century one pope will suffer bodily harm. Another will be assassinated. The assassination will be the final blow to the office of the Holy See. This pope will be the same one who will be chosen in the not too distant future, but whose election will not be approved by the Roman clergy. His influence, however, will be such that he will win out over the objections of his opponents. While this pope will be the last one ever to reign as singular head of the Church, the beginnings of this change will occur with one of his predecessors who will give far-reaching power to the cardinals. These same cardinals will use their powers to replace him with one more to their liking." (page 167, Bantam 1970).

Almost all of Mrs. Dixon's "prophecies" in that book however, are *shamelessly STOLEN* from H.C.Roberts' notorious mis-interpretations of Nostradamus! (E.g. cf III:65, IV:11, V:15, 46, 92, VIII:19, etc.)

There is one coincidence however: the head of the Catholic Church in Poland being severely ill at the same time as John Paul II was shot.

Sven Rosen
Eslov, Sweden.
[We had Sven's letter on file since May 1981, but the recent attempt on the Pope's life (on 12 May 1982) during his visit to the site of the BVM apparitions at Fatima, Portugal, made the letter topical again. The recent attempt, by a priest armed with a bayonet, protesting about reforms of traditional Catholic rites, occurred on the anniversary of the shooting of the Pope at the Vatican in May 1981 by a Turkish assassin —Ed.]

THE GHOST IN THE BATHROOM

At the age of 11 I was fascinated by the subject of the supernatural. A voracious reader, I read everything I could get my hands on on the subject. I was particularly intrigued by accounts of children my age in whose presence objects flew across the room. I read that this was not an unknown phenomenon in youngsters on the brink of puberty and that in the Middle Ages children to whom this happened were considered to be witches and were buried alive, just for being the innocent victims of a poltergeist.

While I was truly interested in this phenomenon, I was also truly frightened of it. I certainly never wanted it to happen to me.

One evening while taking a bath, I was luxuriating in the steaming hot water, the bubbles and the total relaxation after a hard day at school and hours of gruelling homework. My mind was a day dreamer's blank. I reclined in the bathtub facing a large metal clothes hamper. Fifteen minutes into my bath the hamper slowly rose straight up at least two and a half feet off the ground, momentarily paused suspended in mid-air, began to sway for several seconds, crashed down to the floor and began to violently rock from side to side.

My first impulse was to scream for my parents and run from the bathroom but being exceptionally modest, I would rather have faced the workings of an unseen poltergeist than to dash into the living room naked.

My mother, attracted by all the noise, called up the stairs to inquire of its source. There was no way I could tell her that the clothes hamper just rose in the air. I would have been punished for lying. I just said, "Oh, nothing" and stayed in the tub, by now too scared to leave it.

Then it happened again. This time the clothes hamper rose slightly, settled down with a shudder and began more subdued rocking than before.

Enough was enough. I quickly rose, put on my pyjamas as fast as I could and joined my family in the living room. I kept my heavy secret

to myself.

To overcome my fear of our only bathroom, I tried to rationalize this happening as inadvertant telekinetic occurrance brought on by my latent mental energy. My totally relaxed, tuned out state did not allow for the release of this energy so it was directed to the only object in my direct view. Over and over I made an effort to talk myself into this line of reasoning. After all, I had read a lot on the subject and this was a theory some scientists were offering. In the far reaches of my mind I suspected a poltergeist was behind it but if I was to get through childhood and adolescence using that bathroom I had to be logical.

In time my trepidation of the bathroom gave way to normalcy but I never again let my mind wander aimlessly while taking a bath. I told no one of the experience, neither friend nor family. It

When I grew up and recalled the incident, now more informed on the subject of psychic phenomena and having added a few more parapsychological episodes to my life, I concluded that the rising of the clothes hamper was not the result of mental energy seeking an outlet but was in fact the work of an unscrupulous spirit who harnessed that energy and used it to frighten a child through a telekinetic manifestation.

No one understands why children, particularly girls, who are on the verge of puberty are the targets of these restless spirits. Even in children who are constantly being subjected to this phenomenon one finds that it tapers off or stops altogether with the onset of adolescence.

I just know that as a result of my own experience many years ago I do not own a clothes hamper and if I ever do get one it won't face the bathtub.

Connie van Hundertmark
Kew Gardens Hills, NY

SHATTERING EXPERIENCE

When I was about ten years of age I was at my friend's house, in Meanwood Road, Leeds, and we were playing a game when I accidentally knocked his mother's vase off the mantlepiece, whereupon it smashed to pieces on the hearth. I bent down to pick up what I thought was half of it and found it back together again. The room then went very cold and dark and when I looked out into the garden the trees were blowing violently—but only in the garden. Then to our amazement a green hand moved across the window from outside. We both ran from the house as the doors slammed behind us.

To this day (I am now 26) I can't explain it and can only put it down to a psychic experience.

Graham Pouncy
London.

Cont from p39

9 **Pausanias;** 3.16.2-3. Pausanias; *Guide to Greece;* trans by **Peter Levi** (Penguin Books, Harmondsworth, 1971) Vol 2, p54-5.
10 **Pausanias;** 4.27.1-3. *ibid* Vol 2 p163-4.
11 **Pausanias;** 4.16.5. *ibid* Vol 2 p140.
12 **Pausanias;** 4.16.9. *ibid* Vol 2 p141.
13 **Herodotus;** 6.127. Herodotus; *The Histories;* trans by **Aubrey de Selincourt** (Penguin Books, Harmondsworth, 1972) p433.
14 Footnote to the 'Aetia' of **Callimachus.** Callimachus; *Fragments;* trans by **CA Trypanis** (LCL. Heinemann/Harvard, 1975) p47.
15 **Cicero;** 'Nature of the Gods'. 2.2. and 3.5. *ibid* p46, 109.
16 **Livy;** 2.19-20. Livy; *The Early History of Rome;* trans by **Aubrey de Selincourt** (Penguin Books, Harmondsworth, 1971) p125-7.
17 **Plutarch;** 'Aemilius Paulus'. 25.2-5. *Plutarch's Lives;* trans by **B Perrin** (LCL. Heinemann/Harvard, 1914-26) Vol, p421.
18 **Suetonius;** 'Nero'.1. Sutonius; *The Twelve Caesars;* trans by **Robert Graves** (Penguin Books, Harmondsworth, 1957) p209.
19 **Justin;** 20.3.8. quoted in *The Oxford Classical Dictionary* (2nd Ed. OUP, 1970) p354. This work has been used throughout for checking various details.
20 **Plutarch;** 'Lysander'. 12.1. and 18.1. *ibid* Vol 4 p261, 281.
21 **Cicero;** 'On Divination'.1.34. *ibid* p176.
22 **Cicero;** 'Nature of the Gods'.2.2. and 3.5. *ibid*

23 **Plutarch;** 'Aemilius Paulus'.24.4-6. and 25.1-6. Vol 6, p419-23.
24 **Suetonius;** 'Julius Caesar'.82. *ibid* p47.
25 **Pliny;** 'Natural History'.2.37. *Pliny's Natural History;* trans by **Bostock & Riley** (Bohn, London, 1855) Vol 1, p64-5.
26 **Livy;** *ibid;* passim.
27 Quoted in *Larousse* (see note 5).
28 **Lucian;** Dialogues of the Gods'.25 (26). *Lucian* Vol 6; trans by **MD Macleod** (LCL. Heinemann/Harvard, 1961) p351-3.
29 **Pliny;** 'Natural History'.2.37. *ibid* Vol 1, p64-5.
30 **Ptolemy;** 'Tetrabiblos'.1.9. Ptolemy; *Tetrabiblos;* trans by **FE Robbins** (LCL. Heinemann/Harvard, 1940) p49.
31 **Callimachus;** 'The Deification of Arsinoe'. Callimachus; *ibid* p162-5.
32 And while we're having afterthoughts, we might briefly return to the encounters with fauns and nature deities. One notable feature of this class of tales is that fauns (etc) were frequently encountered or captured by armies on the march. And an army is perhaps the most rigidly disciplined mode of 'civilised' behaviour known. So do the faun-encounters represent another basic area of opposing tensions; between civilisation and nature? And have they been replaced in modern times by the Bigfoot and other hairy monsters?

And lastly, a tip of the battered hat to Karl Kerenyi and Lucian of Samosata.

Help!

Any reader or researcher requiring help in research, questions answered, or contacts on Fortean topics, may do so free in this column. Just send the details, on a separate sheet, keeping it brief.

■ I am looking for books, research papers etc, on **physical immortality,** **Breatharianism,** fasting, psychokinesis and consciousness expansion. Would like to correspond with serious researchers in these area. C.R.Kaelin: 89-44 217St, Queens Village, NY 11427, USA.

■ Doc Shiels is contemplating a book on the **mysteries and wonders of golf** (see his column in this and next issue) and is collecting information, references and anecdotes connected with the folklore of golf, haunted golf links, freaks of performance (holes-in-one etc), bizarre golfing characters, and any odd or synchronous connections involving golfing people, objects, sites, and events. Doc Shiels: 3 Vale View, Ponsanooth, Truro, Cornwall.

■ I am planning to draw together all the cases of toads and other **animals found alive in rocks, coal,** solid tree-trunks etc, details of experiments designed to test the longevity of toads, etc, and the various explanations which naturalists and others have applied to the phenomenon. To this end I would be very glad to receive any references on this anomalous and strange topic, particularly details of little known cases or instances outside the UK. I will also need help in translating Latin and French sources. Bob Skinner: Squirrels, The Horseshoe, Banstead, Surrey SM7 2BG.

■ Does anyone know what happened to the rest of the **Index of Possibilities** series of books? First published in 1974 by Clanose Publishers Ltd., Energy and Power were the first of a planned series of five titles. Scott Parker: 5775 Kristin, Beaumont, TX 77706, USA.

[By one of those curiostities of happenstance Clanose occupies the same building as Open Head Press and our art director Richard Adams, so we got the following statement from Michael Marten of Clanose: "I'm afraid this projected 5-volume series of everything you ever wanted to know about everything only ran to a single volumn—

the first, subtitled 'Energy and Power'. Further volumes never achieved publication due to financial, physical and intellectual exhaustion of the authors. They have since gone on to produce a number of books on other subjects, including Worlds Within Worlds *(Secker & Warburg/Holt, Rinehard & Winston, 1978), a fascinating collection of scientific photography, and* Curious Facts, *the book, from the samepublishers (1981), 'an avalanche of the irrelevant' which is totally indispensible." - Ed.]*

Truss Fund.

…in which we gratefully acknowledge the heartening support of the following whose donations will be applied where they will do most good.

Richard T.Crowe, Mike Dash, Kathleen Francis, Ron Gauntlett, Dr Mia Gerhardt, B.F. Greene Jr, M.D. Hine, Francis Hitching, Nick Maloret, Mike Rowe, Udo Schlegel, Mike & Linda Ward, D.K. Watson, and Steve Wrathall — Thanks one and all.

Cont from p 2

search; another instalment of extracts from the *Gentleman's Magazine* by Peter Christie; a new data section we call 'Reflections' recording incidents which follow the themes of recent issues (a sort-of 'reflexive universe' department); and some good columns, letters and usual stuff.

Next issue will be just as good. Wait and see.

BOUND BACKISSUES
The response to our idea of a special facsimile bound edition of FTs 21-30 has been sufficiently good to warrant us seriously investigating the

practicalities and financing of such a project. Based on the success of that volume, we would do the same for FTs 1-20 in one volume, and may even offer bound collections of FTs beyond FT31, when sufficient have accumulated. We'll keep you posted.

TYPESETTING SERVICE
Our valued setter, Cecilia Boggis recently bought a deluxe composer which can do virtually anything required by a small-magazine editor, or anyone else for that matter, who requires neat, dense, good-looking setting. I urge anyone interested to inquire after a costing, to Cecilia at 11

Ashburnham Road, Bedford (telephone 0234 211606), or BM Bozo, London WC1N 3XX. This is not a solicited ad, but a recommendation out of appreciation for her help to us, the results of which can be seen on the pages of this and recent FTs.

EXCHANGE LISTING
The usual listing of exchange journals had to be omitted from this issue, partly for lack of space, and partly for lack of time to compile it. It will appear in a revised form next issue, so please bear with us.

•

Bob Rickard

Cont from p31

attempts made to buy him out or silence him. The long agony he endured makes one wonder whether things have really changed all that much since Galileo and Giordano Bruno. Mr. Vallée had committed the unforgiveable sin of contradicting orthodox dogma as defined by the Commisariat à l'Energie Atomique, and was anathemised. Although he was not physically

poisoned, the story bears resemblance to the ordeal of Karen Silkwood. Similar tactics were employed.

Those interested in finding out more about his work can obtain his writings and further details from the Societé pour l'Etude et la Promotion de l'Energie Diffuse (SEPED), 16 bis rue Jouffroy, 75017 Paris, France.

George Andrews.

BACKISSUES

ALL AT SINGLE ISSUE PRICE
(SEE LEFT)

- **FT31** – The Chinese Wildman; Gateways to Mystery; The Touch of Death; UFO muggers; mystery big cats; ball lightning; synchronous names; little people; fake doctors; Forteana from China; comix.
- **FT32** – The Mississauga Blob; Old Ives' Tales; Gateways (pt 2); occult murder; mystery big cats; fairy tales come true; Forteana from India and China; child sacrifice; mystery panthers in USA and Australia; comix.
- **FT33** – The Enfield Poltergeist; mythology of UFO abductions; Gateways (pt 3); mass hysteria at Nottingham; simulacra; coffin stories; Jeoff Watson's Nessie pix; UFOs; Forteana from China; giant snakes; comix.
- **FT34** – Congo dinosaur hunt; lake monster names; phantom hitch-hikers; interview with Dr Jean Bolen on synchronicity; the Welsh 'puma'; mystery big cats; beached whales; animal saboteurs; nature follows art; ice falls; inept crimes; Trashkashic records; odd Irish doings; giant squids; comix.
- **FT35** – The Myth of Darwinism; an SHC from 1744; The Runamo Runes; Forteana from Malaysia and China; spontaneous combustions; antiquities; strange trees; magic fuels; frog and stone falls; mystery big cats; bizarre bacteria; TV science; occult murder; Fortean travel in USA.
- **FT36** – Anomalistics; Photos of Jesus; Runamo Runes; Gent's Mag extracts; hermits and wildmen; strange tales; toads in holes; bleeding statues and visions; the Buddha's UFO; DIY surgery; coin, ice and sand falls; ASSAP and CSAR; jellyfish in the sky; Forteana from China; USA monitor lizards; Nessie; comix.
- **FT37** – Australia's Lizard Monsters; energy from space; encounters with Greek gods; interview with Dr Rupert Sheldrake on a New Science of Life; a female prophet; Irish oddities; mystery USA kangaroos; UFO hallucinations; falls of crabs, frogs, peas, fish; visions, stigmatics and fasting; plants in odd places; mystery UK bear scares; talking polts; reflections; homing rings; locked-up by friends and relatives,

• • •

Founded in 1973 and first called *The News*, FT's humble beginnings have become legendary — well, out of print anyway! We now have high quality xerox facsimilies of the **first** twenty issues of *Fortean Times*.

Fortean Times

Issue No. 38 | The Journal of Strange Phenomena. | PRICE: £1·25 $3·00

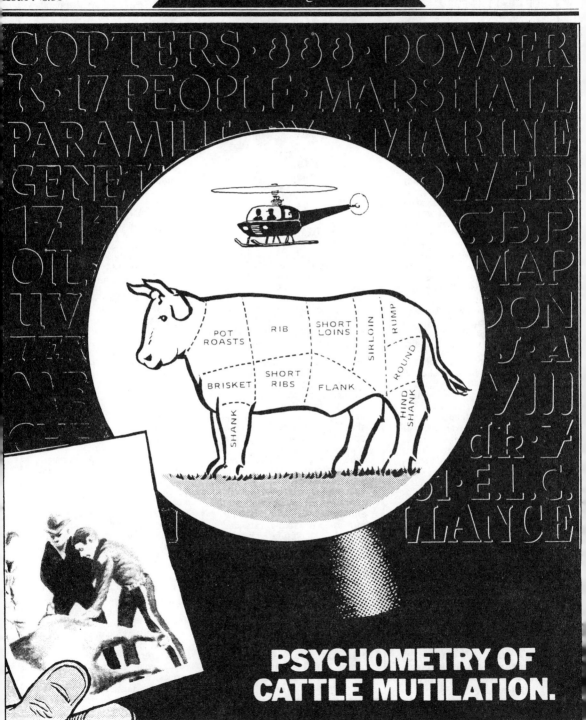

PSYCHOMETRY OF CATTLE MUTILATION.

Books from FT.

Fortean Times

BM-Fortean Times
London WC1N 3XX.

The Journal of Strange Phenomena.

Autumn 1982
ISSN 0308.5899

GANG OF FORT

Editor Robert J.M. Rickard
David Fideler
Steve Moore
Paul R.A. deG Sieveking
Art Dir. Richard Adams
ComixEd. Hunt Emerson

SPECIAL CORRESPONDENTS

Australia Greg Axford (Vic)
Paul Cropper (NSW)
Rex Gilroy (NSW)
Tony Healy (ACT)
Richard King (Vic)
Belgium Henri Premont
Canada Dwight Whalen (Ont)
Mister X (Ont)
England Richard Cotton
Peter Christie
Peter Hope Evans
Alan Gardiner
Chris Hall
Valerie Martin
John Michell
Nigel Pennick
Paul Screeton
Anthony Smith
David Sutton
Andy Townsend
Paul R. Thomas
Finland Tuuri Heporauta
France Dr Bernard Heuvelmans
Greece Anastasios D. Panos
Ireland Doc Shiels
Robert Anton Wilson
Japan Jun-Ichi Takanashi
Malaysia Ahmad Jamaludin
Dr C.H. Yeang
Roving Ion A Will
Scotland Roland Watson
Jake Williams
S. Africa Chris J. Holtzhausen
Sweden Ake Franzen
Anders Liljegren
Sven Rosen
USA Larry E. Arnold (PA)
Tom Adams (TX)
Loren Coleman (MA)
Richard T Crowe (IL)
Ron Dobbins (AZ)
Mark A Hall (MN)
Steve Hicks (KS)
Michael Hoffman (NY)
Phil Ledger (CN)
Kurt Lothmann (TX)
Gary S Mangiacopra (CN)
Joseph Swatek (NB)
Paul Willis (MD)
Joseph W Zarzynski (NY)
USSR Vladimir V. Rubtsov
Wales Janet & Colin Bord
Yugoslavia Milos Krmelj

Reprosetting Mostly by Cecelia Boggis:
11 Ashburnham Rd, Bedford.
Photosetting Wordsmiths: 19 West End.
Street. Somerset.
Printed by Golden Valley Publications
Piccadilly Mill, Lower St.
Stroud. Glos.
Overseas Overseas Postal Services Ltd.
Mailing 2-8 Hornsey St.
London N7 8HF
Sub & Label Anagram
Computing 316A Richmond Rd.
Twickenham TW1 2PD

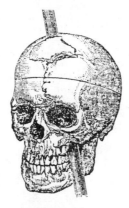

Cover art copyright
Jay Kinney

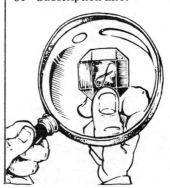

TICK, TICKA TICKA TACK TOCK TACKA

Janet & Colin Bord, Paul Burd, Nigel Cassell, Tom Costick, Mike Dash, Alan Gardiner, W Gaworzewski, Mia Gerhardt, Ethel Gold JW Goodes, Robyn Gurney, Chris King, JT Kirkwood, J Lang C Maitland, Valerie Martin, Graham McEwan, Frank J Palmer, Mike Rowe, Kevin Ryan, RE Sinclair, HN Stiles, Alan Thomas, WK Vannan, Roger Waddington, and David Whalley.

Thanks to to all those who've bought books and backissues — what profit we make goes towards the running costs.

10 YEARS OF FT

As we enter our tenth year of reporting contemporary Fortean events, I'm in no doubt as to how we made it. I've moaned a lot in that decade about our precarious financial situation, but there has never been a shortage of offers of help and monetary support, from astounding amounts (eg £200, and recently $500) to more humble figures which have been appreciated just the same. Our thanks to you all. A more loyal and supportive readership an editor could not wish for.

Following my appeal for help last issue, so that we could obtain chunks of the mailing list of *The Unexplained*, we have received further support and donations. In fact what we have decided to do is to place 5000 FT blurbs in the mailing of the next binder for *The Unexplained*, and this should happen in December sometime. The idea is to reach committed readers with minimum hassle, and if it works we'll try it again.

So, by FT39 we should be in a position to say how near we are to our 'survival' figure of 2000 readers. If we exceed that we're in clover, and our decade year will see important developments. We have already asked Hunt Emerson to design a special celebratory envelope for our 1983 mailings — so watch out!. Our actual anniversary issue will be a special issue, looking forward and backward. We are planning a few other surprises too.

SUBSCRIPTIONS

Due to the difficulty of guaranteeing 4 issues a year, I implied in various places, last issue, that you could renew for as many issues as you like at our new price of £1.25 *pro rata*. Most of the renewals have sensibly plumped for the round sum of £5 for 4, and most of the rest have chosen £3.75 for 3. But to renew for less causes us problems: eg we have to pay for each alteration to our sub/ mailing database maintained for us by Anagram, and no sooner are these entered than they lapse — or so it seems to us drudges who have to deal with the paperwork. So, if you can, please renew for 4, or not less than 3 issues. Thanks.

TRUSS FUND

Thanks to the following for their valuable support, every penny of it put to good use:

SHELDRAKE SEQUELS

Our interview with Dr Rupert Sheldrake (last issue) went down well, to judge from the majority reaction. Sheldrake himself told us that it was more satisfying, and turned out better, than any other interview he'd done on his recent USA lecture tour. Very gratifying that. However our plans to reprint it as an offprint in the 'Occasional Papers' series, have had to be modified. We simply don't have the money to re-publish it as a booklet, so we'll be doing it in xeroxed form — available from Jan 1983.

In the meantime, you might like to know that Sheldrake's book, *A New Science of Life*, will also be available in the New Year, as a Paladin paperback (£1.95).

Sheldrake-mania seems to have taken root....with at least two prizes offered for ways of testing the hypothesis of formative causation. *New Scientist* are offering £250 (see *N.Sci* 28 Oct 1982 p249 for details) — and the Tarrytown Group, of New York, are offering a dazzling $10,000 (for details, write: Robert L. Schwartz, *Continued on p.60*

FORTEAN TIMES is an occasional journal, intended to be quarterly, of news, notes, reviews and references on all manner of strange phenomena and related subjects and philosophies, continuing the work of Charles Fort (1874-1932). The views of contributors are not necessarily those of FT and vice versa. Published from BM–FORTEAN TIMES, LONDON WC1N 3XX, ENGLAND. **SUBSCRIPTION INFO:** see index for page. **RIGHTS:** all articles and art are the copyright of the authors and artists – everything else in this issue is copyrighted throughout the universe by FT. Uncredited material is by the editors. **SUBMISSION** is invited of articles, art, cartoons and news clippings. FT assumes no responsibility for submissions, but all reasonable care will be taken while in FT's possession. **ADVERTISING** and **SALES:** enquiries to the above address, or ring the editor on 01 552 5466.

RUSSIAN BALL LIGHTNING

I have been studying the problem of visiting our Earth by extraterrestrials in ancient and modern times during the last 15 years. From time to time my articles on the subject matter have been published in various journals and annuals here and abroad. Two years ago I have defended by dissertation "Philosophico-methodological aspects of the problem of extraterrestrial civilizations" and now am trying to enlarge it to a book. I try to keep abreast with Western ufological and Fortean literature.

Our Moscow Lenin Library has all the books by Charles Fort. Recently the Library has obtained three issues of your splendid journal *Fortean Times* (Nos. 24, 25 & 27) and I ought to tell you I had the pleasure of getting acquainted with them. To my mind, this is the best Fortean periodical I know. Please accept my heartfelt congratulations on this occasion.

To my great regret I have no possibility to read the FT regularly, but even some odd issues of it have been very interesting for reading and useful for my work.

I think you will be interested to know that I have been contributing during several years to our *Tekhnika-Molodyozhi* journal answering the readers' letters dealing with various unusual phenomena. The journal has a special section "Anthology of Mysterious Cases"; that's why many readers write to the Editor of it describing inexplicable events having been occured to them. These include many real Fortean phenomena. Some of the readers' letters have been published in the TM – 1976, No. 10; 1978, No. 11; 1982, No. 1, etc. I hope the translation of the letter by S. Yevdokimov published in TM, 1978, No. 11, p.52 under the title "Pulsating ball from a ruined plug socket" will be of some interest to you:

This event occurred in Leningrad, later in 1960. The room I lived in had the only window that overlooked the Grecheskaya square. On the right of it, on the wall there was an old large plug socket made of white-glazed clay. The fabric insulation of the wires loosened with time, and when the plug was taken out, the socket often gave sparks. Yet I neglectfully postponed the repair.

A certain evening of that winter I needed to take the plug out of the socket. I failed to do so for some time because it stuck there very tightly. At last I however managed to draw it out, put it on the table and turning back, stopped dead.

Out of the socket hole, quite slowly, appeared something looking like a soap bubble. Growing some 40mm in diameter, it separated from the socket, went up about 10 centimeters and stopped in the air. Its colour was like that of a soap bubble. The only difference was that besides bluish colours, it was also milk-white. White stains were small, but constantly moved about on its surface. There seemed to be something as-living in the bubble; it looked as if there was some vibration inside. The white spots were surrounded by concentric rounds of irregular shape. Their colour ranged from very light-blue near the white spots to very dark blue away from the centre.

The bubble made neither sound, nor smell. It was opaque, and its shape was like an irregular sphere, continually changing though very little. Besides, the ball emitted gentle scattered light which magnetically attracted my eye.

While seeing this queer sight, I lost the sense of time, and I cannot say how long it lasted – seconds or minutes. At last, it vibrated several times about the vertical axis, stopped for an instant and moved, quite smoothly, straight to the second finger of my right hand. I did not fear, I cannot tell why, and did not move to avoid the contact. The bubble softly touched my second finger, penetrated under the nail and, quickly shrinking, disappeared noiselessly.

I felt warmth in my finger, that spread through the hand and the arm to the whole of my body (except the head) and also disappeared. I recovered from the stupor, looked at my finger, then stared at the socket and the plug, and sat down on the sofa. My hands and feet were slightly trembling.

After that event I set a new plug socket, fixed it well and made good wire insulation. Many years have passed since, but I remember all what happened as clearly as if it had been yesterday. I had no wit-

Continued on p58

Psychometry & Cattle Mutilation: Four Psychics & Their Readings.

Bizarre mutilations of cattle have occurred in a number of US states for nearly two decades. Despite reports and investigations into this continuing horror story — with its weird catalogue of organ removals, bloodless corpses and precise surgery — we are no nearer learning the identity of the mystery mutilators. The saga is an unresolved morass of baffling data, grim evidence, and complex as well as conflicting theories involving rumours of UFOs, pagan or military cults, scientific or governmental conspiracies, secret experiments, and so on. In a bold effort to 'see' beyond this impasse, New Jersey researcher **Peter A. Jordan** conducted an experiment: asking psychics to study photos of a case he investigated himself and to give a psycho-metric reading. These impressions, whose relevance you will have to decide for yourselves, is here published for the first time. Peter Jordan is a free-lance writer and lecturer on ufology and psychic research, and founder/director of the Association for the Study of Unexplained Phenomena (ASUP), Flushing, NY.

PREFACE

Five years of research into the unexplained has taught me several valuable lessons. Above all else, however, I have learned that the most spontaneous and instinctual methods of re-search often lead to the brightest discoveries. Whether investigating a putative haunting, or analyzing the spectacular claims of a UFO con-tactee, I could not escape the conviction that an investigation guided purely by intellect was empty. I quickly learned to appreciate moments of intuition which came across my path, and to grab hold of them as vigorously as I did the familiar logic of the philosopher's trade. With each new case I explored, the less I discarded as meaningless and irrelevant, and the more I came to view as symbolic and vital. In a sense, I was *reborn.* As was the case with the venerable Sufis, I yearned for greater progress in the co-evolution of Science and Spirit, and searched for signs of an impending "paradigm shift." I had been disappointed before. There would be no such drama. Only more struggle. On account of this struggle, I have developed new eyes. For that, I am grateful. It is with these new eyes that I am able to dream.

INTRODUCTION

In June of 1979, I became actively involved in the investigation of unexplained cattle mutila-tions. My primary source of information at that time was New Mexico State Police Officer Gabe Valdez, who kindly furnished me with a set of photographs taken on the ranch of Manuel Gomez, a rancher living in the northwest town of Dulce. Gomez, according to Valdez, had been the hardest hit in New Mexico by the mutilators, having lost 6 of his cows since 1976. The photographs I received from Valdez, in addition to depicting the alleged "surgical in-cisions" of the classic mutilation, also showed a series of odd, circular tracks discovered in the vicinity of the carcasses. Firmly etched into the hard dirt road, the imprints, which measured four inches in diameter, were shaped like "suction cups," and had been found arranged in what police described as a "tripod" pattern.

After extensive investigation, Valdez said that the origin of the strange prints "could not be determined."

Like many other ranchers affected by the mutilation phenomenon, Gomez was hopeful that a good, "logical" explanation would be found for the anomalous events in Dulce. Un-fortunately, the mystery stubbornly refused to respond to reason, thus prompting a wave of vast speculation. Gomez was told by some that his cows had sucumbed to "natural predation," and that the so-called "surgical incisions" were, in fact, produced by the sharp teeth of either foxes, badgers, coyotes, or magpies. Others pointed their fingers at local "cultists," linking the mutilations to "clandestine , pagan rituals," a claim widely made in other mutilation areas throughout the United States. Still others argued that the government was conducting secret tests on our livestock, using the repro-ductive organs as "bio-indicators" for monitor-ing the effects of fallout and other possible environmental hazards. Predictably, a small per-centage conveniently used the bioindicator theory to nourish their own *extraterrestrial* hypothesis, simply replacing the word "govern-ment" with the words "alien superpower." UFO enthusiasts found this particular theory appeal-ing, since, they reasoned, it helped to explain the absence of any *leaks* in the curtain of secrecy surrounding the mutilation phe-nomenon.

Gomez was not impressed, however, with much of this speculation. He denounced the predator theory as "nonsense," claiming that predators are physically "incapable" of per-forming incisions as precisely as in the mutilations, and also thought it "unlikely" that any government agency would go through such "expense and trouble" to conduct research that could more easily be accomplished by *purchas-ing* the cattle directly from him. At this juncture, Gomez is willing to give a small measure of credence to the popular cult and alien theories, though, he admits, "the motive, in either case, is still very unclear." "No matter how I look at it," says Gomez, "I can't find a

The Gomez land. Along the ridge of mountains Officer Valdez has himself witnessed UFO activity – typically a "bright, glowing orange light moving silently and slowly". Valdez also claims that the appearance of the light systematically precedes mutilation activity in the area [Photo: PAJ.]

single reason why they would pick me. All the places they might have gone to, all the other ranches they could have hit, and they come to *me*. Why? No one's given me a good answer yet."

THE EXPERIMENT

Upon learning of the Gomez mutilations, I was inspired to do something that I suspected had not – until that time – been seriously considered. My plan was to study the mutilation problem *from the perspective of the psychic.* Aware of the intellectual discomfort experienced by parapsychologists in coping with the capricious nature of psychic perception, I enlisted the aid of, not one, but *four* sensitives as a means of insuring proper control in my experiment. Each psychic was selected on the basis of a willingness to be put, as it were, "to the test," and, more importantly, on a well-established reputation for accuracy. The psychics were consulted on an individual basis, usually in the privacy of a home or apartment, and at no time was the psychic made aware or brought into contact with others involved in the experiment. Information supplied to the psychics beforehand was sparse, with historical information reduced to a minimum. The psychics were made aware of the fact that "several animals have been found dead in New Mexico," and were told that "circumstances surrounding these deaths pose something of a mystery." Beyond this, no detailed information was furnished *until* the completion of the experiment.

Material submitted to the psychics for the purpose of psychometry [object reading through a paranormal (extrasensory) means] consisted of approximately 22 photographs (slides) obtained through New Mexico State Police, and pertained almost *exclusively* to the incidents reported by Gomez in Dulce. The majority of these photographs were of actual carcasses, though several depicted the circular tracks mentioned earlier. One miscellaneous photograph, taken on July 24th, 1975, was incorporated into the target population, and showed an unidentifed helicopter which was sighted in Elbert County, Colorado. This Colorado county had experienced an intense wave of mutilation phenomena during that year and produced one of the *only* authentic photographs of the so-called "mystery helicopters." Speculation that helicopters were in some way connected to the mutilation events prompted me to include this extraneous slide in the psychic readings. It should be noted, that this was the *only* photograph which did not pertain to the Dulce group. Psychics were discouraged from *visually* inspecting the slides, but were free to touch them in any way they saw fit. Of the four, only one psychic, Nancy Fuchs, indicated a preference for viewing the slides in a conventional way (on a projection screen), and this was the only instance in which such an exception was made. All impressions received by the psychics were recorded on cassette tape, with the average reading lasting 60-75 minutes.

The purpose of this experiment was to try to establish the origin and purpose of the mutilations by drawing upon the resources of four, highly gifted psychics. I did not know what to expect. My research into the Gomez mutilations strongly suggested, however, that conventional explanations such as normal predation or Satanic ritual were not persuasive. Likewise, claims that aliens from another world were responsible seemed irrational (why so *many* killed?) and sensationalist. However objectively I looked at the situation, *nothing seemed to fit. A mystery without a meaning.* The following are verbatim transcripts of an experiment in psychic perception which frustrated every expectation I put before it. I present them here to the reader in their entirety. Hopefully, they will shed new and important light upon one of the most baffling mysteries of our time, a mystery which, if the psychics can be believed, *may* contain a meaning of profound importance.

•

RONALD MANGRAVITE
Mr. Mangravite is a professional chemist. He manages a consulting laboratory, and is also the current president of the Jersey Society of Parapsychology. Mr. Mangravite is a psychic who specializes in "psychic healing," and has participated in many experiments focusing on this subject. He lectures extensively on the paranormal, and conducts workshops on meditation and self-development. An active member of Mensa, Ron's readings strongly reflect his technical expertise, and are often replete with references to physical science.

Date: June 9, 1979
This animal has been dead a few days. The decomposition is going irregularly, some parts are decaying faster than others. Some parts are quite slow. I seem to be getting a read-out of the body itself — the abnormalities. There is an overload of some of the electrolytes in the system which may be due to the injection of a citrate. Definitely getting an overload of some of the alkaline earths. There's something wrong with the blood. I seem to be picking up a higher portion of plasma which may be lymphatic fluid. It may be that some of these things do have a very abnormal lymph system. I'm getting imagery of the thing being lifted. I get very sharp, surgical knives. Two men working on the animal. They're only cutting out one or two parts instead of a major chunk. They're in black. Jumpsuit-effect. Shiny black nylon. Wind. Chopper wind. Their hair is flying. Platform. May be 10' by 10'. It has a low wall. One wall is either missing or is hinged to go either

up or down. The winchline is coming down from the chopper. They just winch it up and then flip it onto the platform. The cow is just dragged up alongside and then they can haul it. The men doing this are skilled, trained, ex-military and they're not scientists this particular crop. They're simply highly-skilled in how to handle the bodies and how to take stuff out of them. I get the impression that some of the analysis has got to be done directly in the copter. Some thing is going to be done with the tissue. Some of the sample is going to be processed in the copter and some is going to be brought someplace else. The stuff in the copter can be done with some kind of spectrophotometric system. I'm getting an impression of a device in the copter which will analyze by light. This could be UV or flourescence. Wait a minute. Flourometry connection here. The word which pops into my head about these people is decommission. I get the impression that they are people that are paramilitary, who *could* be military, but let's say they are ex-military or people who are working in a governmental level, but are not governmental employees. They would be hired by someone working through a governmental agency. The site of the animals is important. The copters are either brown or grey. Also getting an underground implication. Something spreading through the soil and through the earth. This is

Rancher Manuel Gomez [Photo: PAJ.]

New Mexico State Police Officer Gabe Valdez. At left is Dave de Witt, New Mexico free-lance journalist, author of the 'factional' work The Mute Strategy *[Photo: PAJ.]*

part of what they're trying to monitor. Impression of dual-engine. Feather-blades to change the sound. Helicopter was in Asia. The helicopter was one supposedly shot down in a Vietnamese war. It was either not lost or not damaged as badly as it was supposed to be and was segregated so that it could now be made available. Marine. Ex-Marine. Copter. Once had silver paint. I don't know whether the whole copter was silver or whether it was an insignia. Silver has been covered. It had a gun-placement, or opening. A gun-pod. There is something there now. There's some kind of thing there that's quite odd. It's designed to send signals. It has weapon-like properties. A national group is behind all of this. Some kind of radiation impression. I wonder if certain of the elements are being removed selectively because they're elements which may carry or indicate radio-activity. They are experimenting with different analytical techniques.

ELISABETH LERNER
Mrs. Lerner is a professional psychic who, for 20 years, has successfully collaborated with law enforcement officials in all facets of criminal investigation. She is routinely consulted on police cases involving homicide, burglary, rape, and missing persons and has been widely praised for her uncanny accuracy. She is a self-proclaimed follower of the pagan religion known as "Wicca," and has established a national reputation as a highly-gifted and articulate sensitive. She is well-educated, with a university degree in engineering, and is also regarded as an authority on the subject of Early American antiques. She currently resides with her husband in New Jersey.

Date: April 22, 1979
I believe we will discover that these mutilations involve a network of non-American people, as well as perhaps some *paramilitary* forces here

who *do* appear to be American. This represents a serious invasion of American privacy. I do see non-American Indians very clearly, and they are part of this secret project. I get the name Stevenson, and the name Victor. There appears to be person with a boyish face, very bright, with the hands of a small child. He, I believe, was responsible for the actual cutting of the animals, operating some sort of mechanical device. The word Annide. The word Carmine or Karmine. The symbol dk. I perceive someone on a horse, as part of a trio. This is for sure. These mutilators appear to work in groups of three, with functions divided between them. Each seems to head in a different direction, in order to accomplish a specific task. A new wave of mutilations will, I believe, strike near a place in the southwest or New Mexico, wherever mink or weasals are raised. There is also an uncompleted dam near this next site, and I get the name Pelitta (or tto) in connection with it. This place is close to the border of New Mexico, towards the Gulf Stream. Any towns in southwest New Mexico with the name Annover or Andueo? I get this name strongly. The initials E.L.C. in connection with these future mutilations. The Hobart Company involved in this. Three huge, donut-shaped objects with whirring lights will be seen in connection with these new mutilations. 888. A woman with red hair, in her 40's, runs the aircraft. Pressurized vents somehow keep this lighter-than-air craft in the air for a considerable time hovering over the site area, so that men may be alighted from it for the actual procedure. If I had to establish a time for these new mutilations, I would be inclined to say that they will occur at the time of the new fold, whenever this might be. It's definitely spring, I can definitely state this for certain. I see the rooster crowing, which I believe is a police officer investigating the case. This signifies a breakthrough in research; something

Officer Valdez near Mutilated carcass, at Corinth, NM [photo: PAJ.]

will be discovered at this new mutilation area which ties some loose ends together to form a more coherent picture. The mystery will, I believe, be solved in the near future.

I get a picture of what appears to be an abandoned convent, or perhaps it is a mission at this time. I do know the courtyard has a bell over the entrance gate. I get very large white hats on the sisters that used to be there, and may *still* be there. I also get a place where there is much fun and pleasure, as if a bar is not too far away. I would advise looking in an abandoned area, where once there had been a ghost town, now taken over by officials of the United States. If this is not our government, perhaps it is Mexican, because of the khaki-colored uniforms, with ginger-colored leather across the chests. A cap that looks like a navy officers cap, but it's dark and there are epaulets on the shoulders. So it could well be a Mexican government. Did any of these mutilations occur around our Xmas time? Near the end of November? The reason I say this is because I see packages that were gaily-wrapped during the time these mutilations were going on. Some festivity surrounds these mutilations. I am getting a spotlight, as if I were at the border where there would be an entrance gate with four officers as guards. A gate is down, that you cannot go through, unless authorized to do so. I know that time is of the essence in these mutilations, because I keep seeing an engineer with a stopwatch, almost pushing a plunger saying, "This is it, this is zero hour." Lighter-than-air kind of apparatus are used. I thought, at one time, these were balloons, but now feel that it is any lighter-than-air object which does not contain heavy machinery or motors one could hear. They, by using this object, can drop any kind of chairlift, whereby two or three parachutists could be lowered, and be lifted back aboard by rope or taut string. Colored lights could defray a person's knowledge of what is occuring during this procedure, causing the person to become engrossed with the lights, which is what people *think* is, or are, UFOs. I keep getting a piercing, comet-like flashing in the sky, as if fireworks were going off, but on a larger scale. I definitely feel these are man-made. I see strings or ropes descending from a balloon or lighter-than-air device, explaining how these people got there without any apparent detection. I am also seeing what appears to be a shower of a slight film, which might have spilled by accident out of one of these chairlifts used in the procedure. This would create a sort of dusting of the area, the ground, and the animals. The swelling of these animals I know positively to be caused by something which they ingested orally. A chemical is swallowed by mouth. The area in which these animals are found is controlled, that is to say, something has been done to *affect* the soil composition itself, precipitating some of these biological reactions. Somehow, before being marketed for sale to the general public, some of these cattle are marked for experimental purposes and for testing at a later date. The experimenters wish to observe changes within these marked animals under normal stress conditions, something not possible within the confines of a laboratory. Removal of the vital organs tells me they are interested in the sensitive parts of the body, and are testing out various nerve drugs. The experimenter, I feel, wishes to remove the blood as quickly as possible, in as natural state as possible, and had to keep it *hot* for some reason. I see a saddle being slipped under the cattle for it to be hoisted, by men who are dropped from a stationary object. The animal is hog-tied, just long enough for the mutilation to occur, and, most importantly, in order that a tranquilizer be injected. Something injected in the animal acts as a form of muscle-relaxant. The veins of the animal must be kept in a certain order; a heart attack must be prevented. The reason seems to be that the blood can only be fully drained when the veins and arteries are *completely* relaxed. Whatever the animal is injected with conflicts with the elements found in its daily diet, and causes a violent reaction. The tongue appears to have swelled horribly as though by poisoning. A chairlift is definitely used here, and is dropped from a blimp-like object.

Someone with the name "Empeda." I'm getting a laboratory. I see three technicians working there. I'm getting a man who is almost bald, short black hair, just over the ears, and little black hair going over the nape of the neck. Something "veydante". Large tower in the air. Very high. Could be radar or laser beam. This is positively *Mexican*. I am getting the faces or masks of a festival that takes place there just before our Xmas. Piñata seen around this at time of the mutilations. Wherever there would be dancing in the square near the borderline, I feel this important radar-controlled or laser-controlled tower exists. Look there. Also, I feel they are cross-breeding the animals, forming a sort of blood-bank for animals, in order to produce a more perfect breed of cattle, that would be less nervous, and would be a heavier cow in the years to come. This is all government funded. Any town near this mutilation where they, at one time, might have had a flogging block? Criminal justice would have been brought to the center of town. I am getting people in stocks, as in the public square of yesteryears. A large letter K comes around this, or the town itself has the letter K in its name. Someone with the names "Kielman" and "Kelman". Someone Joseph, who writes his name with a great flourish. The Joe first, then the rest of the name very small. I'm getting an institution where there are many Lincoln Continentals and Cadillacs. This is definitely a laboratory. Also, some sort of strange bird, maybe a

rooster, as a symbol. This is right nearby. This laboratory institution has a cyclone fencing around it and most things are conducted *underground*, rather than on top of ground, bringing me to a Colorado place. Something about a whistle that is controlled, blowing over this compound. Seems like it is a steam whistle, but it is very loud. This whistle has three sections before blowing. It is the size of a bucket. Someone with the last name "Audler". Someone with the first name "Mase". The Department of Agriculture must know something about this experiment taking place. I'm getting a shaking of the animal just before it dies. Anyone with a herd coming up should take note of whether their cattle are experiencing a shaking or palsy-like syndrome, as though having a fever or chill. A day or two after the animal develops this shaking condition, it is disembowled in the way described before. I see the number 1714. I get monkeys, and various kinds of primates. I see a girl with long blond hair, twisted at the nape of her neck. I am getting someone with the last name "Audli."

I want to go to a place that says "Pesk' Pecc", near a place where there is a well in the courtyard. I'm getting a building that one might think of as the capital of the city with a tiny spiral at the top. Something like half an eggshell extending above the ground, some sort of structure. I see three such structures, very large, something like one hundred feet wide. Circular in shape. Domes above the ground. Some kind of pipes near them that have walkways on them, as if they were connected to oil wells, or oil deposits. Something here having to do with oil companies. These are laboratory related in some way. The Roman numerals IVIII. Someone called Stephano, the name Whitmore and Lilly pharmaceuticals. Are there any atomic or jet-rocket labs nearby? I'm getting something jet-propelled. I'm also getting something that folds up in the way of a walking platform, that extends from one triangular area to another. This assures the experimenter of no footprints.

MP 1936 on a vehicle, that seems to come around a military installation. Small jeeps. Last name "Plento." Blood is used, I believe, for transfusion purposes, in order to understand how chemicals are affecting human organisms, in the event of germ warfare. I feel the government wishes to protect some mineral content which exists in this particular region, and to prevent people from purchasing, buying, or developing this land. This may be a thought-scare, for people to stay away from this area. This area is definitely controlled. This may involve more than one governmental agency, and includes study of germ warfare, as well as nuclear fallout. Blood must be kept warm, this is absolutely essential, so time is very important. A precise schedule must be adhered to. Men are dropped from a stationary object, into a chairlift, towards the earth. The planes do not come from a great distance, nor do the lighter-than-air ships with the lights. They are within twenty miles of these mutilations. There must be a central installation in the area which governs this entire military project. Two governmental agencies involved, perhaps, because of the difference in coloring of the uniforms. One seems Mexican, one is not. The experiments concern breeding, and the effects of toxic chemicals in both the air and in food on animals and humans, as well. Also, testing for fall-out, to determine any possible adverse biological reactions, and if animals can be bred to resist these reactions. The areas in which these mutilations occur are being tested for chemical imbalances in the air and soil. A new outbreak can be expected as we come into a new fold, in the spring.

Date: February 9, 1980
Scotsman, or Scotch-speaking people around this. Is this near an Indian reservation? Impression of Indian, could be Mexican. Face of an Indian child. The name of Hartman comes around this. Or Hartmann. Somebody studying water facilities in the area, because I see the dowsers. Dowsing rods in two different men's hands. Is there an iron ore plant around here? Refining gravel plant, maybe. See the big funnel they would fill with gravel for sorting out ore and minerals. Either sand or gravel connected to this. This area at one time must have had gold or some precious minerals around it, cause I see balance scales and ore dust and nuggets. Are they planning to dam up the water in order to produce more electricity? I feel like they are building a dam. They are controlling water pressure. Military men with brown caps. The top is definitely drab-olive, yet darker than our own, so it is really not our government represented here. Something I don't understand. Seems to me like head Army officials. Impression of young Indian-appearing children. Is there a school nearby? Children 5 to 7 years old. C.B.P.—name of a man seen as heading this operation in particular. Wears brown military shoes. I keep getting Army. Does this area have limestone deposits, or funny-colored stones nearby? The water seems to be turning strange colors. Discoloration towards the beach or shore and it seems yellowy-green. The number 1161 comes around this. Somebody sitting on a swing-like device. Balloons used. Do they grow grapes around this area? Something about vineyards. Some big oil company around this, Exxon perhaps, about 5 or 6 miles away off a main route. Many micrometers around this. Everything measured in detail. Engineering project. Definitely around an oil field because I see big domes where you can walk up on side rails. Little ladders on this dome. Chemical engineering connected very strongly. Two buttons on military cap. Airfield near mutilation site. The number 7. Could be 7 o'clock.

Time when plans are made for attack. Place where oil crosses in a type of "X" pattern. Chemical engineering again seen as connected to a mutilation. Large letter J and large letter A. Not seen as a violent action, but as something for the "greater good." Termination of a trial or test. This is weird. I don't know what mustard would mean to this. Makes the cattle dizzy and makes the eyes and nose feel like it's all clogged up.

Date: February 28, 1979
(The following reading pertains to the Colorado chopper slide.)
Periscope on bottom of craft. Comes out of the belly. Telescopic. Extends downward. Army. White star on end. WWII. Pilot's headpiece. High altitude. This chopper is called the "shark". Painted like a shark. Jaws design. Something about a vacuum. Vacuum effect. Man with blond hair. English features. High forehhead. Wears a square ring. Gold ring. Insignia. Insignia reads C.B.P. Has something to do with ammunititon. A boat. Turrets on war boats seen. This is definitely an Army person, but why would I say he has a five-leaf cluster? That's a Colonel. Oak-leaf cluster. V.I.P. Something about ZIP. Not zip code, something else. Large letter Z. Something about a mountain lion and experimentation.

•

NANCY FUCHS
A registered nurse by profession, Nancy Fuchs is a psychic who specializes in the diagnosis of animals. She has assisted police in locating animals reported as lost, and conducts classes and workshops in psychic development around the country.

Date: March 10, 1980
Dusk scene. Man talking about some animal's throat. Something missing. I feel he's very bewildered at first. Some parts of animal missing. Disarrangement. Color of cow is off, somehow. Very frustrated. Went to authorities. No satisfactory answers given. Authorities said something about a wild pack being responsible. He liked these cows very much. Heartsick. Lost as a result of this. Very hurt. Aimless. No explanation given. Being tossed off to predators. Something about burying the carcasses. What happened to the carcasses afterwards? He's talking about having to destroy them. Smell of burnt flesh present. Some parts saved for analysis. Carcasses destroyed later. His life never the same since. Nothing but worry now. Lost about ¼ of his herd. Some which were among his favorites. Possibly could have 5 or 6 mutilated in near future. (Moves on to slide of circular prints.) Something shaggy and furry-like. Cylindrical-like object. Something human-like about this. Surrounding it are long white things, almost fur-like. Personality controlling this. Pieces of metal over metal. Cylinder with

strips of metal over it. In the cow is inserted a long, thin object going into the jugular vein. Metallic, rod-like instrument used to immobilize the animal, causing it to fall. Arm projection used again. Very powerful energy flow emanating from this. Metallic extension with elbow used during operation to throw animal down. No struggle. Discharge emanating from this extension. Electrical discharge of some sort. Tingling sensation. Voltage discharge. Must have been several prints in area. Separation between them. One and a half feet, perhaps. Something that walks, for sure, along the ground. Feeling of tremendous anger and hostility. Directed at Gomez. Show of power and vengeance. Projection revolves at base. Revolutions made. Small, pinpoint projections come out of the bottom. Spurs? (Proceeds to carcass slides.) Jolt of electricity went right through this animal. From the neck or head down. Super high-voltage. Mineral distribution rearranged somehow in animal's system. Something wrong with the eyeball. One of them. Eye is sucked out. When the energy goes through the eye is dislodged. A vacuum effect. All mineral content is dislodged. Research implication. Minerals needed for research. Gomez land ever in trouble? Mineral deposits there? I hear people saying "We will come back." Gomez knows someone is determined to gain control over his property. Any premonitory dreams experienced by him shortly before the mutes? Government action. Intimidation of Gomez. Machine used. Arrowhead surgical, drill-like bit used to make cuts. Any of these prize cows? Breeding and genetics involved. Expansion of ownership by government-related individuals. Embryos. Thousands of samples needed for this breeding facet. Cross-breeding. Animal dies in seconds. Rapid, high-speed drill or blade used. Army backbround. Marshall something or other. Something associated with the "horn". Military background. Plastic over the shoes. Liquid-filled, leaves no prints. Stopwatch used. Man in late fifties. Marshall. Army. Cap with black rim and gold braiding. Pompous. White-haired. Very influential. Walks into the Pentagon whenever he pleases. Commission given 15-18 years ago for mutilation project. Was overseas then. Friend of General McArthur. Grand Marshall. Lives in the Dakotas. Money invested. High-priority issue. Tall. Heavyset. Only 17 people know of this. Project with 2½ million allocated early on in game for breeding experimentation. Late 1960's. Thru the Pentagon. Person who backed this bill is spearheading the new research. More and more money invested each year. All major oil companies backing this heavily. (Moves on to slide Colorado chopper.) White liquid used as a fuel. Home base is California. Plain, bucket seats. Man with dark shades. Near a border. Dome-like structure where choppers are housed. (Proceeds to additional carcass slides.) Work is completed in

about 6 minutes. Impression of animal being dropped. Plastic bags used to preserve tissues removed. Tissue samples. Puncture marks made for tissue sample. Hear mutilators discussing plans to intimidate ranchers into leaving property. Land wanted. Want to destroy ranchers prime source of income: the cows. Map pinpointing mutilations in future seen. Red pins used. Indicates a northerly trend. Oil companies wish to seize control of more land. This is part of solution. Cartels wanted on mineral deposits as well as oil deposits. Animals prepared in some way 3 or 4 months in advance. Project initiated in either 1966 or 1967. Techniques perfected over the years. UFO beliefs fed by mutilators. John Mitchell connected to this. Also, Howard Hughes. Barett or Barnett associated. Sources of money derived from a variety of companies and individuals. Drifting on some kind of lighter-than-air device. Done very quietly. Eartips taken for study under microscope for vessel activity. Small vessels of ears of some importance to these people. Saudi Arabia. Uranium connection. Metal detectors used for mineral exploration. Something that sparkles in soil. Picture is extremely complex. Faction-ridden. Partly interested in speeding up the level of growth in cattle, and in developing livestock that require less food, and, hence, less money. Pancreas important in all this.

•

ALBERT THOMPSON
Mr. Thompson (A pseudonym. Real name withheld by request.) is a New York psychic who specializes in trance mediumship. He is considered to be very gifted in the area of psychometry, and has been tested extensively at the American Society for Psychical Research.

Date: July 12, 1980
The name Helen or Helenville connected. Something about fences. The fences have not been disturbed or broken? The name Meyer. German name. Possibly Meyers. Any distinctive German population out in this area? German-connection. Has anybody been out there who is a dowser, a person with a stick? A feeling of where is it, where is it, where is it? (Makes motions over the table with imaginary dowsing rod.) Somebody's looking for something. Exploration for something beneath the surface of the earth. Animals know where to go instinctively, and know where what they require is. Water is of importance here. There may be a correlation between oil, water, and gas. They all require *hollow* spaces beneath the earth. Uranium connection. Something about radioactivity. Any reports of missing persons out in this area? This is a *strictly terrestrial phenomenon.* Impression of khaki-green uniform worn by military man. Army. (From slide of Hine's copter photo) Runs on Diesel and some other kind of fuel, and it runs partially on *com-*

Mutilated carcass at Dulce, NM [Photo: PAJ.]

pressed air. Two different kind of motors attached to this thing. Forced-air entry. Man piloting this thing has dark glasses and a crew cut. Cap looks like this: ⌐⌐ . He is talking by radio. Canvassing. Surveillance. Radio communication to someone on the ground. Someone out there has an installation underground.

All underground. (Moves onto some slides of carcasses) Something worn on shoes which masks footprints. Something big and spongy. Distributes weight over a wide area. Little balloon-shoes. This has all been conceived by the military-industrial complex. Something here about nerve-gases. Not just looking for things above the ground, but experimenting with certain kind of chemical as well. Some portion of the government or a large governmental installation is planning to *move* into this area. Almost like re-locating Washington, D.C. to this area. *Major* re-location. Geologically, they are conducting surveys regarding earthquakes, and other earth-related phenomena, because of nuclear facilities needed in the area. The government has a great deal of interest in this land. They would like this land very much. Any offers or bids for land? Who is Howard Baker? Check him out. Connected for sure. (Looks at slide of suction print) Does this occur in any round pattern? Or in a triangular pattern? I believe this is a *tripod base.* They use this to set down. (Holds slide of Gomez

cemetary plot). Any recent burials there? May be something buried there which causes the glow. (Glow phenomenon explained to Mr. Thompson beforehand. P.J.) You may find a stash of some sort. May be a box or something buried there. Any signs of digging around this? I keep picking up Texas for some reason. Panhandle section of Texas. Northern Texas. Anything happening in Mexico? Monterey, Mexico. Strong connection there. Renosa, Mexico, too. Next immediate area to be hit will be Texas. The Panhandle area.

•

CONCLUSION
The readings compiled for this report — considering the *notorious* unreliability of psychic perception — demonstrate what I have found to be a most remarkable uniformity of opinion regarding the anomolous Gomez mutilations. Though of *vastly* dissimilar character, attitudes, and philosophical world-view, all four psychics were nonetheless unified in their belief that the mutilations stemmed from a massive, covert operation led by what is described as the "military-industrial complex."

That not so much as even the slightest support was given to the popular predator, cult, and alien theories, comes as an extraordinary surprise, and, barring instrusion by possible *unconscious* preferences of the experimenter, is difficult to explain. (The so-called "experimenter effect", wherein attitudes of the researcher influence or predetermine the outcome of the psychic's reading, is thought to occur frequently in parapsychological research.) All the more surprising is the fact that two of the psychics were inclined to accept the possibility of "close encounters" with occult and alien forces, but failed to establish any such connections during their readings. Each psychic was firmly committed to the view that the mutilations were terrestrial in origin, though practically all sensed that phenomena *suggestive* of extraterrestrial involvement had been introduced as a means of creating confusion and uncertainty.

Obviously, these readings, in and of themselves, prove little, since confirmation of the material is largely an impossibility at this time. The readings may, however, someday prove to have important value in supplementing UFO and veterinary research by suggesting *new* methods of approach to the mutilation problem. We may discover that, while relying upon a suspiciously "noisy" and imperfect mode of perception, psychics such as those used in this project *are* capable of leading us into uncharted territory where solutions to the mutilations mystery may be found. If we are *extremely* fortunate, we may discover that the descriptions and names given by the psychics in these readings are actual "blueprints" of the mutilation story as it continues to unfold before us. Only time will tell.

Working with these four psychics has been a rewarding experience, and has profoundly enriched my own perspective on the mutilation subject. I thank them all for their invaluable contribution, and appreciate the time they devoted so kindly and unselfishly to this experiment. Together with their assistance, *and* the assistance of State Police Officer Gabe Valdez, I was able to accomplish something for which I felt there existed an important need.

POSTSCRIPT

The reader may be interested in considering some rather surprising "correspondences" that seem to exist between parts of the psychic material and facts both central and peripheral to the mutilation subject.

• 1 - Mangravite mentions a "citrate" injection. The presence of citric acid (an anti-coagulant) *was* discovered in a mutilated carcass in New Mexico which was examined in 1978 by Los Alamos Laboratory.

• 2 - Mangravite speaks of a device carried in a chopper "which will analyze by light." This, he says, could be "UV or flourescence". An experiment conducted on some of Gomez's cattle in 1978 *with* ultraviolet light revealed that some of the cattle had bright flourescent "splashes" on their backs and top sides. Speculation is that the animals are marked in advance for "pickup" at a later date.

• 3 - Lerner mentions the Hobart Company. Among other products, Hobart manufactures a wide assortment of industrial *meat slicers and choppers.*

• 4 - Lerner associates balloons, blimps, and other "lighter-than-air" devices with the mutilations. In the spring of 1979, Valdez investigated a sighting of a low-flying plane that was seen hovering over a herd of cattle near Dulce. With assistance from the Air Traffic Control Center in Longmont, Colorado (where the plane allegedly took off from) Valdez was able to determine that the plane belonged to a world-famous *balloonist* (he succeeded in making the first Trans-Atlantic flight in a balloon) who is also the owner of a New Mexico based *mining* outfit which specializes in the exploration of uranium.

• 5 - Fuchs mentions the name of John Mitchell. (in later work with Fuchs pertaining to *Iowa* mutilation cases, the name once again appears — Fuchs says she very definitely associates the name with the former Attorney General) In July 1980, the *Washington Post* reported that Mitchell is now connected with a company called Global Research International, Inc, which has been chartered, according to the article, "to assist and advise those seeking to do business with foreign governments or foreign commercial enterprises." The article also states that James M. Tully, a *former Marine Corps* officer (see Mangravite transcript) works out of the office with Mitchell. Mitchell, for some reason, refuses to provide details on the operation.

• 6 - Thompson mentions a dowsing connection. (so does Lerner, in fact). In 1980, rancher Robert Blake discovered a branch that had been fashioned into the shape of a dowsing rod lying next to the mutilated carcass of a 16-year old registered quarter horse. Again, a possible implication that the mutilators are involved in some sort of *geological prospecting.* In the Fall 1980 issue of *Pursuit,* New Mexico writer and researcher, Dave De Witt, gives serious consideration to this hypothesis, and says support for it (though circumstantial) can be found in reference books dealing with the subject of biogeochemistry.

Obviously, a much *larger* sample of psychic subjects is required as a basis for speculation on the mutilation subject. While the recurrence of certain patterns *is* evident in this initial study, such patterns may not persist in future trials, and therefore ought *not* to be accepted as proof that a terrestrial-based conspiracy is the answer. Research with additional psychics is continuing, and may suggest alternative solutions to the problem. Complete findings will be made available to the public in the near future. All comments, suggestions, and information are welcome, and, of course, will be held in strict confidence.

•

Peter A. Jordan

"Cattle! Do you know where your calves are?"

Avoid unwanted and tragic Cattle Mutilations in your family!

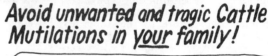

From Cover-up Lowdown #1, *by Jay Kinney & Paul Mavrides. All rights reserved. Published by Rip Off Press Inc, Box 14158, San Francisco, CA 94114, USA. Reproduced by kind permission.*

THE ISOTOPE MYTH.

The Periodic Table has always seemed one of the essential and immutable dogmas of that prince of sciences, Physics. While researching artifact dating methods, **Dr Don Robins,** an inorganic chemist, "stumbled upon" the discovery that Mendeleyev's Table was largely mythical, and has been almost wholly, and quietly, superseded by concepts more suitable for today's physics. Yet it is still an article of faith for many physicists . . .

It is often said, and with reason, that the construction of the Periodic Table was one of the greatest triumphs of 19th Century chemistry. The seemingly absurd suggestion that a list of the chemical elements in order of atomic weight — the mass relative to the hydrogen atom — should show up remarkable periodicities and even allow new elements to be predicted from 'gaps' in the Table gradually won acceptance, and the originator of the Table, Mendeleyev, was lionised, whilst the earlier protagonist of the idea, Newlands, remained in ignominy.

One of the major objections to the Periodic Table was that for periodicity to be observed, the places of certain pairs of elements had to be reversed — for example, Argon (39.95) before Potassium (39.10) — without any convincing reason other that to maintain this periodicity. Another interesting feature of the Table was that most elements had atomic weights that were very close to whole numbers, or were whole numbers. It had already been observed, during the early days of atomic weight determinations, that these near-integral values might mean that all the elements were simply agglomerations of hydrogen atoms. This statement formed the substance of Prout's hypothesis, put forward in 1815. It was subsequently ridiculed by the scientific establishment, since many elements had atomic weights that were decidely not integral numbers (eg) Chlorine 35.45).

The answer to these riddles came about in the early decades of the 20th Century with the parallel developments in radiation chemistry, atomic physics and mass spectrometry. The understanding of the structure of the atom — a tiny dense nucleus surrounded by a tenuous cloud of electrons — led to the realisation that a subtle difference existed between the nuclei of the atoms of some substances, and this difference was explained by the existence of isotopes.

An isotope of an element has the same number of positive protons in its nucleus and the same number of extra-nuclear electrons as that element. It differs in that it contains a different number of neutrons in its nucleus. Thus, it is chemically indistinguishable from its fellow atoms, and only exhibits slight physical differences, since it has a different mass. When the term 'isotope'. was originally coined, it was used to bring some order to the overwhelming number of radioelements identified during the heady days that followed the discovery of radioactivity. Many of these elements were indistinguishable from each other, but were supposed to be different because they came, by transmutation, from different radioactive parents. The end result of this confusion was that samples of Lead were obtained from different radioactive sources each with different atomic weights — which made nonsense of the periodic table.

So, the chaos of radioelement chemistry was resolved by suggesting that isotopes were formed, but it was soon discovered that this phenomenon was not restricted to the 'heavy end' of the periodic table, where the naturally radioactive elements, such as Radium and Thorium were concentrated, since most elements throughout the periodic table consisted of a stable mixture of non-radioactive isotopes. For example, the element Tin contained no less than 10 isotopes, Chlorine contained two, whereas Sodium and Fluorine contained one single isotope.

So it was now inadmissable to talk of elements, but of mixture of isotopes in most cases, and the deviations from whole numbers could be explained by fortuitous mixtures of isotopes, as could the earlier shift of anomalous element pairs by Mendeleyev in his formulation of the Table. Further study showed that, with the exception of the radioelements — which decayed spontaneously and thus changed their isotopic mix — the other stable elements showed fixed patterns of abundances, chemical reactions, etc., which were supposed to take place without shifting this pattern of isotopic species.

Within a short while, the old dogma of precise atomic weights was thrown overboard and a new one of immutable isotopic mixes substituted for it, *without questioning.* While the exception of the radioelements was tucked away out of sight, it rapidly became standard knowledge that the isotopic mix of an element could never change. Very seldom was this law questioned or even explained, and the increasing number of exceptions that were uncovered, and are still being uncovered, have hardly dented the edifice of the new dogma.

It became common, therefore, to talk of 'age abundances' of the individual isotopes that made up the elements in the Periodic Table, and while convincing arguments could be put forward to explain why certain isotopes should be very stable in terms of the microstructure of the individual nuclide – as the particular isotope that went towards the make-up of the atom was now termed – the observation, that for the non-radioactive elements the isotopic abundances appeared to be always a fixed ratio, hardly ever excited speculation or theoretical justification.

Variations in abundances were discovered, however, when certain light radioactive isotopes were identified in nature. The discovery of these 'atomic clocks' – whose timing mechanism depended upon the decay of the radioactive species giving a measure of the age of the sample by a knowledge of the decay rate of the radio-isotope. Carbon-14 and Potassium-40, among others, have proved invaluable in dating archeological and geological sequences, and these have generated their own specific dogmas about the occurrence, transference and concentration of natural radionuclides. These discoveries, momentous as they were in chronometric science, did not infringe the basic tenet of isotopic immutability, since they invoked radioactive decay; but further work with light isotopes such as Deuterium and Tritium – the 'heavy hydrogens' – showed that various physical techniques such as boiling and fractionation could lead to isotopic enrichment, enabling two forms of water – 'heavy' and 'light' – to be separated. The two forms were of demonstrably different chemistries: heavy water had a much higher boiling point and density, for example, than ordinary water. These differences,and the separation of the species, were rationalised by the suggestion that since hydrogen was the lightest element – one proton, one electron – the addition of a neutron to make deuterium made such a large relative difference in mass that the differentiation of properties was possible.

These observations, together with refinements in Mass Spectrometry – the most precise method for measuring isotopic abundances – also revealed other elements that showed a variable isotopic composition where this variation could not be ascribed to radioactive decay of an unstable species. Oxygen, atomic weight, 16, was the first of these heavier elements detected to show abundance anomalies. Normally oxygen consists mainly of O^{16}, with very small traces of O^{17} and O^{18}, and it was observed that geological deposits derived from marine fauna had tiny but real differences in their O^{16} and O^{18} abundances which could be related to ancient ocean temperatures. Broadly speaking, the higher the temperature, the smaller the fraction of O^{16} to O^{18}, since the lighter isotope was more volatile in its compound.

More recently, sulphur-containing substances in geological deposits have been shown to exhibit similar abundance anomalies, and careful analysis of the minute differences in the abundances of the various sulphur isotopes has been used to give a vivid picture of remote geological events. An interesting sidelight here is that a recent paper on this topic has demonstrated a vast climatic catastrophe at the end of the Permian age. [1]

It may well be argued that these tiny discrepancies in oxygen and sulphur abundances are also 'light element effects'; but heavier elements also show these anomalies, as demonstrated in recent work in cosmology. The theory, put forward by Fred Hoyle and others [2], suggest that organic matter may form in stellar dust clouds, and survive the extremes of conditions by accreting siliceous coatings. The meteorites known as Carbonaceous Chondrites contain this type of structure, and they are also noteworthy for containing noble gases, principally Argon and Neon, which exhibit large abundance anomalies – which in turn argue for an solar system origin – by comparison with the composition of the sun and outer planets by spectroscopy. More recent work has shown that other meteorites exhibit abundance anomalies which argue that the planetary system was formed by the explosion of a nova near the sun in the remote geological past. This hypothesis is argued from anomalies in abundances of metals such as Magnesium and Aluminium. [3]

Various strands of evidence have gradually been accumulating which begin to show that the 'fixed' isotopic composition of elements usually observed is due only to the limitations of analytical devices. More careful searching amongst natural isotopes may reveal anomalies that will show a relation to origin or age, since separation may occur due to diffusion over archeological periods of time even with heavy metals. It may well be that in several years the assumptions of most textbooks, that isotopic composition does not change for other reasons than those of radioactive decay will be demolished, just as the notion of 'precise atomic weights' were before them; and a bewildering pattern of isotopic movement demonstrated in a way that will turn the whole of observable nature into an interlocking system of very sophisticated clocks.

•

Don Robins

NOTES
1) William Holser, 'Catastrophic chemical events in the history of oceans', *Nature* 1977, v267 p403-408.
2) F Hoyle & C Wickramasinghe, *Lifecloud* (JM Dent, 1978).
3) MG Edwards, 'An induced birth for the solar system?', *Nature* 1977,v267 p393-4.

A phenomenon noticed by ourselves, and some of you, from time to time is the occurrence of certain curious events or phenomena immediately following the publication of an issue of FT dealing with that topic. It's a reflexive universe, they say, so we've created this new heading to focus our reflections.

DO IT YOURSELF – FT36

In mid-September 1982, Robert Yarrington and a friend were charged with fraud and grand theft. Yarrington had been paid a total of $210,000, as compensation for losing his left foot in an accident two years ago. But recently a third friend, a woman, ratted on the two for reasons unknown. It transpired that Yarrington chopped off his own foot and asked his friends to stage an auto-accident. *Western Mail* 17 Sept; *Globe* 2 Nov 1982.

9th March - Roger Cox, a 35yr-old father of eight children, cut off his penis, and as his wife joined him in prayer, cast it into a fire at his home at Saron, near Denbigh, Wales. He says he did it so that he can devote himself 100% to preaching, which he does from a double-decker bus. His wife said they had discussed the act for 12 years, and that her husband's jusification was in *Matthew* 19:12, which goes: "...and there are eunuchs who have made themselves eunuchs for the sake of the Kingdom of Heaven." He divulged his sacrifice hoping to scotch rumours and gossip. The man's fateful name will not be lost on connoisseurs of the name game, here. *D.Telegraph, Sun, Western Mail, Shropshire Star* all 18 March 1982.

During a murder trial at the Old Bailey, Robert Draper told how a man paid him £50 to cut off the man's right hand. Leslie Tainton, 32, wanted to punish himself for being unfaithful to his homosexual lover, Peter Faiers. The two met Draper in a pub, where he agreed to do the job, and after drinking to get up courage, they went to Faiers' home in Leeds. Tainton drank wine and sniffed glue as the others tied his arm to a bannister rail, and Draper severed the wrist with two blows of an axe. Draper fled to London where, it was alleged, he killed another homosexual with the same axe in a row over a TV programme (I think television, not transvestite, is meant here). Not quite do-it-

yourself, I know, but almost... *D.Telegraph, Western Mail* 7 May 1982.

Credits: *Larry Arnold, J&C Bord, Peter Christie, Mike Dash, Nigel Pennick, Jeff Saward, P.R. Thomas.*

PHOTOS OF THE GODS-FT36

Our survey of alleged photographs of Christ brought immediate responses from two of our readers.

Rich Crowe, of Chicago, sent us a photocopy of the *Globe* 12 Jan 1982 which featured an image of 'Christ in the clouds' variant 2, differing slightly from my figures K and L (p39) in that it was cropped differently and blocked in differently. The story which accompanied it was given by George Mason, an Annapolis, Maryland, artist, who claimed it was taken by a 16yr-old girl, Robin Aberzinski, from a plane window over Washington DC. No date is given—only that the girl believed it was an angel with a shining face and skeletal hands.

John Peffley sent us a copy of an ad for a book of Apocalyptical prophecy which uses an image much like our figure J (p37) of the 'Christ in the clouds' variant 1. All we know is that the ad appeared in *UFO Review*—no date or details.

RINGS LOST & FOUND – FT 37

A flood of recent cases constitute an interested grouping of this odd penomenon, one of the most persistent themes in both folklore and 'real life'. We give them in brief:

• AP/*Houston Chronicle* (TX) 5 March 1982 – Joseph Cross, of Newport News, lost his ring in 1980 while crossing Hampton Roads, Va. It was knocked off his hand and sank into the channel waters during a storm. Two weeks ago it was noticed inside a fish, caught for a restaurant in Charlottesville, and its owner traced through an inscription.

Sieveking's Selection

Every clipping-sort by the FT editorial team yields up macabre/hilarious items which send us chortling through to the next cup of tea. I intend in this column to present you with some of these, which might otherwise get buried and never be gathered up for publication in one of our thematic news sections. First, then, let me share with you some of my vintage favourites.

• *S.Express, News of the World* 28 March 1982 — Two years after farmer Ferdi Parker lost an antique wedding ring, at Rectory Farm, Lower Swell, Glos, it was found in a cow's stomach, by a vet, during an autopsy on the animal.

• *S.Express* 2 May 1982 — Mrs Jane Hicks was helping her husband with a harvest on their farm at Sennen, a mile from Lands End, when she lost her wedding ring. It was discovered 40yrs later as her son Michael, now 52, was ploughing the field.

• *D.Telegraph* 15 May 1982 — Mrs Marlene Carvell was celebrating the finding of her wedding ring, yesterday, lost 20 years previously in the garden of her Irthlingborough, Northants, home.

• *D.Star, D.Mirror, D.Telegraph, D.Express* 13 Sept 1982 — 11yrs ago Joy Manley lost her ring when she worked in a bedding factory, in Somerset, as a pillowstuffer. It was at last returned to her after Marshall Hazzan, of Wilmslow, Cheshire, investigated an annoying lump in his pillow, found the ring and passed it onto the bedding firm.

• *Sun* 4 June 1982 — Barbara Staton, of Nottingham, returned to a hotel in Torquay, Devon, and found her wedding ring, lost on a visit 4yrs previously.

• *S.Mirror* 18 July 1982 — Pensioner Albert Thornton, weeding a flower-bed at his home in Tolworth, Surrey, found his wife's wedding ring, lost 15yrs before. It was their silver wedding anniversary!

• *D.Express* 22 Sept 1982 — Tony Green was angry when his wife lost her wedding ring during a holiday at Barmouth, North Wales. Three weeks later they returned to Barmouth, from their home in Stourport, to collect sea-shells....and found the ring.

Credits: *Peter Hope Evans, Steve Parker, Nigel Pennick, Paul Screeton, Heathcote Williams, Steve Wrathall.*

•

Bob Rickard

Mourners at the burial of Anna Bochinsky of Moinesti in Rumania were astonished to see the "dead" woman jump out of her coffin while it was being carried with the lid open, as is the custom, from the cemetary chapel to the grave. She ran into the road and was run over and killed by a car.[1]

•

Harold Brown, 22, rushed past a security guard in the 48-storey Transamerica pyramid in San Francisco calling out "I want to see the man at the top. I've been sent by God!" He sprinted to the 29th floor closely followed by the guard, muttered a profanity, spat at witnesses and jumped 300 feet down the airshaft. Shouting "whoopee!" all the way down, he landed on the concrete floor at an estimated 100mph. His t-shirt and jeans were torn off either by the force of the fall or from hitting the sides of the shaft.

For two minutes he lay unconscious, then woke up and laughed a little while. He had broken his thighbones, kneecaps and a heelbone, but, astonishingly, suffered no internal injuries. He hummed "Campdown Races" in the ambulance.[2]

It's amazing the falls which people survive. Terry Bennet, 20, fell 8,500 feet when her parachute failed to open. Hitting a muddy ploughed field, she escaped with a dislocated elbow, two broken wristbones and a chipped ankle.[3]

•

During a ceremony at the Kemper Arena, Kansas City, at which the building's designer, Helmut Jahn, was to receive a citation from the president of the American Institute of Architects watched by 1000 of the Institute's members, the roof of the twelve million dollar building fell in. 26 architects were hospitalized.[4]

•

Arturo, a polygot Panamanian parrot in Chicago which Ida Sabala told police she had stolen, killed, cooked and fed to her 96-year-old grandmother, was found unharmed— although a bit shaken and muttering to his owner in Spanish. Arturo also spoke Italian, English a few German phrases, and was partial to scrambled eggs, rice and potatoes. The alleged birdnapper, police said, had a long-standing feud with Arturo's owner, Robert P. Fox, ever since, she maintained, he stole her dog. I also notice that Mark Tripp of Pasadena was jailed for shooting dead his mother's parrot — because (he said) it grinned at him.[5]

•

Jake Crawford, 28, of Shreveport, Louisiana, thought his teddy bear was possessed by demons, and that its eyes were camera lenses spying on him. So he poured alcohol on it and set it alight. His house caught fire and was badly damaged, and he was charged with aggravated arson.[6]

•

Ape fan George Clark swung into action when police tried to evict him and 13 chimpanzees sharing his home in Birmingham, Alabama. In a four-hour battle he fired at the police while the chimps threw eggs and jam jars.[7]

•

When pensioner Doris Bass of Bournemouth tried to phone her daughter-in law she got space control, a Chinese takeaway, a lighthouse keeper, the Post Office, the police, the hospital accident department a and a phone answering service.

"I didn't dial a number", said Mrs Bass. "All I got when I picked up the phone was these strange voices. The man at space control said he was in the Outer Hebrides. He was very nice and suggested it might be a spacecraft interfering with the line." The Chinese takeaway wanted to take her order, but the lighthouse keeper at Portland, Dorset, was not amused. A Post Office spokesman said "There's no logical answer."[8]

•

Passersby were astonished at the sight of a man, one arm handcuffed to a tree and blood on his face, shouting, kicking and apparently trying to climb up a branch of the tree at North Beach in Durban, South Africa. A beach inspector said the blood on his face was from a fairly deep cut, self-inflicted by throwing a stone in the air and letting it fall on his forehead. The man was taken to a doctor.[9]

•

After years of dismissing stories about alligators living in New York city's sewers, municipal officials found a small alligator in the Kensico reservoir in August 1982. It was taken to the Bronx zoo. [10]

•

According to the *Teddington and Hampton Times*, a man appeared in court accused of using a knife and fork to try and break into an East Sheen restaurant. He told police: "I wanted something to eat."[11]

•

REFS & CREDITS

1) *D.Express*, late 1960's (Lance Sieveking)
2) *D.Telegraph*, 1 April 1978 (Valerie Martin)
3) *Standard*, 4 Feb 1982 (Peter Hope Evans)
4) *Architects Journal*, 13 Aug 1979 (Ion Will)
5) *Hartford Courant*, 3 Sep 1979 (Phil Ledger), *Standard*, 15 Oct 1982.
6) *D.Telegraph*, 12 Feb 1982 (Peter Christie)
7) *Weekend*, 25 Feb-3 Mar 1981 (Andy Townsend)
8) *D.Telegraph*, 16 Feb 1980
9) *Pretoria News*, 23 Oct 1979 (Chris Holtzhausen)
10) *Guardian*, 13 Aug 1982 (Peter Hope Evans)
11) *D.Telegraph*, 7 Oct 1982

Paul Sieveking

Two recent visions of the Blessed Virgin Mary (BVM), one in Yugoslavia and the other in France, show that the genre of religious apparitions is as active and as socially useful as it ever was — one has become the focus of political feelings and the other yet another expression of grass-roots feeling against the reformed rituals of the Second Vatican Council. In each case, too, we feel the lack of psychological or background material on the principal witness — in this the study of such phenomena lags far behind the small advances of ufology.

BVM AT CITLUK

Apparitions of the BVM to six young Yugoslavian children, which have been compared to the famous events at Fatima, Lourdes and Garabandal, began in June 1981 and developed into a major political furor in this Croatian region of southern Herzogovina on the Adriatic coast, centered on the tiny mountain village of Medjugorje near the town of Citluk. We were hoping to bring you a report by our Yugoslavian correspondent, Milos Krmelj, but this has not arrived yet—so we rely on our clippings for this summary.

The series of apparitions began on 24 June when two boys and four girls, aged between 10-17yrs, went on a ramble up a nearby hill called Podbrdo. They reached the hilltop meadow at about 6.30 pm. We draw our account of what happened next from the report in the Catholic newspaper *The Wanderer* 21 Jan 1982, by Father Milan Mikulich, pastor of a church in Portland, Oregon, who visited the scene on 23 November 1981, and saved for us by Michael Hoffman.

Regrettably, Father Mikulich does not describe how the apparitions first came to the authorities' attention

–just that, at about 6.30pm, "Our Lady appeared to them, holding the Child Jesus in her arms." One boy later described the apparition as "dressed in gray clothes reaching to the ankles. Her shoulders were covered with a white mantle, and her head surrounded by a brilliant crown of stars." The October AP reports said the girls described a golden-haired Madonna "floating over the meadow". According to Fr Mikulich the children waited, "somewhat frightened and embarrassed, "For the vision to disappear. Instead the lady spoke "in a calm and persuading voice "words of peace and universal brotherhood. After delivering her message she asked the children if they had any particular requests. The youngest boy, Jakov Colo, asked that his friend Danial, paralyzed from birth, be cured, and the lady promised satisfaction "soon". Mikulich continues: "Before disappearing in the skies, encircled by a bright cloud, the Madonna instructed them: 'Children, come to find me during the following days on this mountain because I have other things to reveal to you."

Between that first day in June and Mikulich's visit in November, the apparition appeared daily at 6.30pm to the children except for four days–though it is not clear whether all the children saw the vision on each occasion. At each appearance the lady delivered the same message: prayer, pennance, fasting on Fridays, reception of the sacraments and confidence in God. Mikulich adds: "She also revealed five secrets which the children were to convey personally to the Pope. The local bishop, Pavao Zanic, visited the Holy Father in early December; the results of that visit are yet to be seen and heard." At first the visions took place in the same mountaintop meadow, but when people "were no longer allowed to go there", they continued in the childrens'

homes, and in church at the appointed time. Mikulich's phrase here is the only allusion he makes to the political developments that followed.

It seems that little Daniel did indeed gain some kind of remission or cure, and as news of this and the apparitions spread the pilgrimages began. About 6000 attend the church services every Saturday and Sunday, and at times there would be up to 30,000 in the meadow hoping for a sight of the BVM themselves, or a cure, or at least to touch or see the visionaries. Then the local authorities thought matters were getting out of hand, threatening the peace of the area, and worse. Inevitably, when they acted to prevent or break up the daily gatherings and fenced off the site, things got out of hand for real. At first the apparitions had escaped the notice of the regional papers but as the crowds grew, so did the official ridicule in the government-controlled press. The visions were called "scientifically impossible", and the Catholic Church accused of using the event for "political purposes". In October, 11 people were expelled from the Communist Party and 48 others were "officially warned" because they visited the site of the apparitions on the mountain. The visions were denounced as a "publicity trick" by the government's Commission on Church Relations, and "a typical manifestation of superstition and the result of childish fantasies" by the local Communist Party. Then a friar, Brother Jozo Zovko, was imprisoned for "slandering the socialist state" in a sermon. Inevitably the national government were "quick to identify the visions as part of a nationalist plot." They allege that Brother Jozo–who was already accused of taking a group of young people to the Catholic Youth Olympics in Rome and allowing them to wear the symbols of the

Ustashi Croatian separatist movement–and several bishops called on Croatians, during Masses at Citluk, to "shed 40 years of darkness"–an allusion to the period of Communist rule in Yugoslavia. During this controversy Ustashi slogans have appeared on walls around Citluk, and bands of youths, said to be from a "Croatian neo-Nazi group" have wandered the streets singing rebel songs.

Meanwhile the numbers of the faithful have grown, and a numberof cures reported. Vida Ivankovic, the oldest of the girls, told Father Mitulich that in their visions they pass on the petitions of sufferers, and the lady tells them in return who will be cured and who not. Bishop Zanic is mindful of his position, saying: "The children do not seem to be lying. The problem remains: is this just a subjective experience of the children or is it a supernatural thing? If it is from men, it will fail; but if it is from God, it will not be stopped." His lack of outright endorsement does not result from ecclesiastical fence-sitting but the Church's deliberately cautious approach to reports of miracles. This was emphasised by the Bishop of Zagreb, who added: "When some apparently supernatural facts occur, it is necessary to walk with feet of lead..." Father Mikulich discovered that the apparition asked the boys to become priests and the girls nuns, and at the time of his visit two girls had already enlisted, one boy was doing priest-studies, and a boy and a girl intended to take orders shortly.

Continuing the parallels with earlier BVM vision cases is the promise, made at Medjugorje, by the shining form, that she will give "a visible sign" of her visitations "when least expected". Students of vision phenomena will note the detail (as far as we can tell) that the apparition never proclaimed herself to be the BVM. Appearing as she does in the iconographic attributes of the Virgin the Catholic community make the assumption naturally, as does Father Mikulich, who refers throughout to the figure as "Blessed Mother", "Our Lady" etc. As the apparition at Lourdes did to Bernadette, the vision at Medjugorje gave an enigmatic reply to the question, often asked, of who she was. She said: "I am the Queen of Peace."

Additional sources: AP/ Rochester (Minnesota) *Post-Bulletin* 22 Aug; AP/*Guardian* 18 Oct; AP/Houston (Texas) *Chronicle* & AP/Lewiston (Main) *Daily Sun* 26 Oct; *Sunday Standard* 15 Nov 1981.

THE VIRGIN AND THE CABBAGE PATCH

This second case came to light at Easter 1982 when thousands made a pilgrimage to the French village of La Talaudiere, in Loire, south-west of Lyons. They were trekking to this "grim little village dwarfed by giant slag-heaps" (As one reporter described it) to the site in the back-garden of a tumbledown cottage — which is home to a blind, retired coalminer, Jean Piegay, his equally aged wife and their five children — where one of the girls, Blandine, aged 14, claims she first saw the BVM on 31 October 1981. Since that date, Blandine says, she has had 31 visions of the BVM. Once, according to her mother, Aimée, an apparition began while they were seated around their plastic-covered kitchen table. "There was a shining white light and my daughter asked us to leave the room."

The cabbage patch where Blandine first saw the apparition is wedged between the cottage and a chicken shack, and bordered on one side by an orchard and on the other by a polluted stream — an altogether bizarre site for celestial revelations. Blandine describes her vision as "a tall, gentle lady, young and very good, dressed in a large blue and white veil." It is not clear

whether the entity in the vision identified herself as the BVM, or whether this is Blandine's interpretation, or that imposed by her pious family when Blandine told them of her experiences — Catholic theologians will place a great weight on such distinctions — but the Lady certainly delivers grandiose demands: eg, that a basilica be built on the spot, and that Blandine refrains from sweets and cakes. Already there is talk of miracles — water is said to have gushed "mysteriously" from a hole dug in one corner of the patch, but it was "bone dry" when observed somewhat cynically by the *Sunday Times* reporter shortly afterwards.

Father Perard, the parish priest, has reacted with some hostility to the events. According to the girl's mother he told her not to believe what her daughter said, adding that she was a dreamer and "should not be encouraged to look at too many pictures of the saints." The neighbours, who are as happy as neighbours anywhere would be with the uninvited nuisance of crowds jostling around their homes, have reacted with disbelief. One dismissed Blandine as "a little girl who suffers from epileptic fits." Nor has the spectacle found favour with the Bishop of St Etienne, Monsignor Paul Pousset, in whose diocese the town is. He attributes the visions to "girlish fantasy". "Anyone going to La Talaudiere because of the supposed visions defies my express wishes," he fulminated. The Church's cold reception of this alleged appearance by the mother of their God is hardly unexpected. It is due in part to a well-founded caution, but we suspect another reason is the seeming endorsement by the Queen of Heaven of a strong anti-Papal movement, according to the messages passed on by Blandine, who says that the Lady told her she prefers Masses to be said in Latin, and priests to wear cassocks. These are two of the main aims of the

increasingly popular Traditionalist movement, led by the ex-communicated Archbishop Lefebvre, who has publicly abominated the 'modernization' of Church ritual by several recent Popes. The Piegays, however, are defiant of 'official' criticism. "God is with us. We have more faith than certain priests," said Madame Piegay.

The first reports of the apparitions were in the Paris paper, *Liberation*, for 13 and 14 April 1982, which we have not seen — perhaps one of our French readers could locate these for us? The same paper for the 16th reported a curious development. According to opthalmologists in the area there had been a steady stream of pilgrims, returning from the Easter vigil a few days before, requiring attention for varying degrees of blindness. One eye-specialist spoke of "serious and frequently irreversible damage to the retina." It seems that many of the visitors to La Talaudiere stared at the sun for long periods, in expectation, I would guess, of seeing a 'solar miracle' similar to that reported at Fatima, when the sun was said to "spin" and "descend" and which some ufologists have claimed was a UFO event.

The last note we have is a sad sequel. Crowds again gathered on 18 April 1982, hoping to witness the supposed regular weekend apparition. Instead, old Jean Piegay materialized at his back door and announced to the hoardes trampling his garden that because the people were not sufficiently reverent the BVM would henceforth appear only in the privacy of Blandine's bedroom.

D.Mirror 14 & 19 April; *Liberation* (Paris) 16 April; *Sunday Times* 18 April 1982.
Credit: *Jean-Louis Brodu, Peter Christie, Loren Coleman, Mark Hall, Michael Hoffman, Nick Maloret.*

•

Bob Rickard

Headlines. An occasional feature.

Giant toad menaces California

VENTURA, California — An adult female almost ... (UPI) — The poisonous ...

THE JOY OF BEING HIT IN THE EYE BY A GOLF BALL

GIANT RODENTS STILL ON RUN

Keepers at Kilverston Wildlife Park, Suffolk, are using bananas, apples and carrots to try to tempt home five escaped capybaras—a breed of rodents—wh...

Mad Thai King Buried in Cave

BANGKOK, Thailand (UPI) — Thailand's legendary King Takson was either placed in a velvet bag and beaten to death with sandalwood clubs (official records,) or spirited away by loyal retainers and quietly buried in a limestone cave (legend.)

The regent of the late 18th century was considered officially mad because he thought he could fly.

HARTFORD COURANT (CT) 29 OCT 78

YOGURT ATTACK SOURS WEDDING

By Our Athens Correspondent

An elderly Greek couple were sentenced to three months' jail yesterday for smothering a bridegroom with yogurt as he walked up the aisle with his bride. They said they wanted to restore their daughter's dignity after she had been ditched by 28-year-old Mr Costas Trontzos. 31 JAN 81

Man moved 300 tons of tabernacle in vain

From Our Correspondent Swindon

Mr Stanley Frost has lost his appeal to ...

GAGGED WOMAN USES NOSE TO PHONE POLICE

6   THE STANDARD. Thursday, December 11, 1980

Sofa hits man

HONGKONG, Tues. — STRAITS TIMES 21 JAN 81

ARABS BUY SAND

Witch boils boyfriend

CHICAGO (AP) — A 45-year-old woman who said she had turned from witchcraft to Bible ...

testimony on Kleinfelder's self-proclaimed rel...

Skipper to the rescue as it rains pigeons

Vatican is to reexamine Galileo's heresy

Masked woman who scares the poor

MANAGUA, (Nicaragua), Sun. — A woman who puts on a grotesque gorilla mask and frightens people in the dead of night has been branded an opponent of Nicaragua's leftist revolution because she only attacks poor people. PENANG STAR 2 FEB 81

MADONNA WATER · PRODUCT OF ITALY

Will Pope's intestine go in church vault?

HAUNTED MONOPOLY BOARD   WIN £3

FLYING FISH 'TO BEAT IMPOTENCY'

23 SAILORS PREGNANT ON U.S.S. STORK

Vet coughs up bullet after 65 years

A STUNNED war veteran has coughed up a bullet that had been lodged inside him for more than half a century. Ilija Sesum, 90, of Yugoslavia, was wounded in a World War I battle near the Italian-Austrian border in 1916. During a recent illness Sesum coughed for two hours and — incredibly — dislodged the bullet. Sesum, who lives near Belgrade, said he felt just fine afterward.   TORONTO STAR 23 JUNE 81

DAILY MIRROR, Saturday, November 7, 1981   PAGE 9

Yard hunt werewolf

A MYSTERIOUS "werewolf" is terrifying children and old folk living in a block of flats.

The ghostly figure, wearing a wolf mask and brandishing a long knife, has been seen running along the roof and leaping from window ledge to window ledge.

He also crouches on top of the lift to the flats, opens the escape hatch and howls down at the occupants.

KHRUSHCHEV'S FALL 'MADE HIM CRY FOR WEEKS'

20   Lowestoft Journal, Friday, May 22, 1981

FT wins the long battle

We had planned to have a long section on cases of families forced to flee their homes by polt infestations, but as usual we ran out of room and something had to be postponed to next issue. Just room enough, though, for a couple of good yarns about speaking spooks

A SLIMY TALE
According to the Cape *Argus* (South Africa) 9 Sept 1981, a Grabouw woman believes she is being terrorized by an evil *tokoloshe* spirit, which speaks to her in a high-pitched voice, and appears disguised in various forms. The woman, Maggie Hendricks, 38 [see photo], said the problem started the previous year when she heard eerie sounds of an animal running about on the roof of her house, on a farm near Grabouw, followed by the clanking of chains. This conventional debut was followed by more bizarre phenomena. One day a voice shouted: "I love you and want you." Then she began to find "frog slime" and earthworms in her food and was pestered by an "itchy irritation" in her throat. In July she began a series of strange vomitings—needles, balls of human hair, earthworms and pieces of broken bottle—culminating on the 3rd Sept 1981 with a frog "as big as a man's hand" and three tadpoles. A police sergeant said he saw Mrs Hendricks vomit knife blades without any sign of bleeding. "I have felt a lot of pain in my throat," says Mrs Hendricks, not surprisingly.

More recently the persecution has involved her clothes and shoes being torn, and she has given up work in case she is attacked at her workplace. Wooden crosses decorate all her belongings and one dangles from her neck. Aubrey Bosman, a furniture salesman and part-time evangelist, says they know the man responsible for sending the *tokoloshe,* but can't prove it. "He is a man in the neighbourhood who wanted Mrs Hendricks," he said.

THE TALKING TOILET
A woman leans over a dental spitoon. "Shut your mouth," said the spitoon. A few days later a man is lying prone in the same dentist's chair, when a voice, not the dentist's, commands from the surgery basin: "Open you mouth wider, stupid." A woman patient using the dentist's toilet was shocked when a voice from beneath her boomed: "Move your behind, I can't see a thing."

And so on, for 11 months, up to 90 times a day, a mystery voice, in a gruff Bavarian accent, tormented the surgery of Dr Karl Bachseitz, in the small West German town of Neutraubling. For a while punning journalists had a fieldday with such headlines as: 'Poltergeist hits a nerve', 'Dentist's teeth on edge', and my favourite 'A voice of unknown extraction'. When it first manifested, the untraceable voice hinted at horrible deaths for the dentist's wife. But while the voice abuses and insults the dentist and his patients, it is sweetness itself to his 17yr-old secretary Claudia Judenmann. "Claudia, I love you," croons the electric socket near her desk. The voice, which calls itself 'Chopper', manifests mainly on the telephone, usually breaking into Dr Backseitz's calls with obscenities. But when Claudia checks in on Monday mornings, the phone rings and there is Chopper inquiring if she has enjoyed her weekend. The voice even contradicts her, appearing to know exactly where she went and what she said.

The strange case came to light in February 1982 when the desperate dentist, at his wits end, filed a suit against unknown persons for injury and harassment, and called in the Bavarian Office of Criminal Investigation, in Regensburg. On 23 Feb, West German TV showed a film taken during the investigation on which the 'spook in the spitoon', as the phenomenon was called, could be heard burbling to Claudia from a plughole and over a phone. The doctor called in Post Office engineers but they could find no technical or electronic origin for the voice. They even disconnected the phone, then, in best horror story tradition, it rang. Yes, Doctor, it's for you. Someone called Chopper... One engineer is said to have said of the voice, "Either he is a technical genius, or the whole thing is a case of parapsychology..."

Inevitably Germany's distinguished poltergeist hunter was called in, Prof Hans Bender of Freiburg University, who should know what a case of parapsychology looks like if anyone does. It was Bender who identified another secretary, Annemarie, as the unconscious agent of the Rosenheim poltergeist in 1968, which also included weird phone phenomena. The *Express* (4 March) described the scene when Bender, an eminent 74yr-old, arrived at the door of the surgery.

"Bender is here. I'm scared. He wants to kill me," wailed the washbasin. "Don't worry, the professor won't hurt you. He just wants to talk to you," soothed Claudia stroking the rim. And when Bender concluded his 'interview' and was leaving, the voice called out: "Come back Bender. Help me. Release me." Benders canny comment: "That sounds like the voice of a being in distress."

The Public Prosecutor of Regensburg, Elmar Fischer, announced that the riddle had been solved—it had been a silly, prolonged practical joke involving "voice projection". Then, in a move every bit as baffling as the rest of this case, he named names but made no arrests. He accused Dr Bachseitz himself, and Claudia, of "feigning a crime", whatever that is, for which they could face up to three years prison.

Could it have been a hoax? Could love, or something else, have driven a 60yr-old respectable dentist so mad that he indulges in exceedingly clever but silly tricks which would have the certain result of ruining his business, and then be stupid enough to alert the police? Though the case has many similarities with the Rosenheim case, and could have been modelled on it, somehow I don't think it was. Three teams—police, engineers and parapsychologists—went over the place without finding evidence of trickery...and Dr Backseitz's actions are invested with a victim's desperation. I'd like to know more about the young secretary's role in this, too. But, my Fortean funnybone tingles at the name Backseitz. How perfect for the victim of a talking toilet!

Le Soir (Belgium) 17 Feb; *Guardian* 18+25 Feb, 5+9 March; *S.Telegraph* 21 Feb; *Western Mail, Shropshire Star* 25 Feb; *D.Express* 4+5 March; *Sun* 9 March 1982.

Credits: *J+C Bord, Mike Dash, Henri Premont, Mrs Jesse Prisman. PM Smith, Paul Thomas* • RJMR

Poltergeist-tormented Mrs Maggie Hendricks, with Aubrey Bosman, holds a cross over a pair of shoes mysteriously ripped apart. [Photo: Cape Argus 9 Sept 1981.]

Help!

Any reader or researcher requiring help in research, questions answered, or contacts on Fortean topics, may do so free in this column. Just send the details, on a separate sheet, keeping it brief.

☐ Researcher seeks data/correspondence from others concerning **underground sounds** of unknown origin, directly, indirectly, or not related to UFOs. Such sounds, ostensibly, are not quake related. Greg Long: 310 Armistead, Richland, WA 99352, USA.

☐ Anyone interested in *Earthworship* and relevant activities and discussions please contact Brian Riley: 'Pagan Wessex', 10 Laura Place, Bath, Avon.

☐ I am looking for any information on the following topics: the **'Philadelphia experiment'**, the **'men in black'** syndrome, and the **Ummo letters.** I would also be interested in hearing anyone's opinions on these subjects. Stephen Hurley: 25 Stourbridge Rd, Halesowen, West Midlands B63 3TV.

☐ **Penetralia** – collecting materials, written and drawn, concerning the inner/hollow/under Earth. Tero contactees, dero victims, ray mech operators, megalith wizards, geomantic romantics, macrobe witnesses, spelunkers, lesser and demigods, weather witches, Titans, Atlans, mutants, space-farers, time-travellers and all parties connected to Gaean mysteries in the Shaver tradition are invited to contact *Ki-ina's Arena*: the NEW Inner Earth Polemic – c/o Telluric Ric: 248 E. 2nd St, New York, NY 10009, USA.

New species continue to be discovered at a stirring rate, though obviously more frequently among the lower orders. Here is a selection of notes which have come our way — we have others but your editor has temporarily misfiled them (blush!) — of discoveries which have been lost and re-sighted years later.

ANIMALS

● Tree-climbing giant skunks, as big as Alsation dogs, were discovered in the jungles of northern central Java. They could be prehistoric survivors, said B.O. Nainggolan of the Central Java Animal Lovers' Association, who obtained a killed specimen from shepherds in the Ungaran highlands. 'BO' discovers skunks?

Star (M'sia) 15 May, Times Wire Service/*Los Angeles Times* 14 May, *St Petersburg Times* (Fla)14 May 1977.

● A rare sub-species of gold monkey, called the snow monkey, last seen 100yrs ago, was rediscovered by Chinese zoologists in northern Yunnan province, near Tibet, in November 1979.

Ta Kung Pao 17 Jan 1980.

● Small numbers of a rare deer, the black muntjac, have been sighted again in eastern China. The species was described on the basis of one specimen sent to London in 1885. By 1920 only two other specimens had been found, and until 1965 it was thought extinct. But then sightings of *Muntiacus crinifrons* were

made during forest clearances and the destruction of their secret refuge again raised fears of their extinction. The new sightings — 56 mixed specimens have been seen since 1972 — are in reforested areas and are now under strict conservation protection.

Journ. Nat. Hist Nov-Dec 1980 p803; *Times* 12 Nov 1980.

● A colony of miniature muntjacks, the size of terriers, has turned up in Sherwood Forest, Notts. They are thought to be descended from a group which escaped from Woburn Abbey wildlife park during the 1939–45 war. Where (on earth?) they have been in the meantime, and why their migration has gone unobserved until now is not ventured upon. Perhaps they teleported?

D.Telegraph 21 Nov 1981.

● Long-horned 'kouprey', thought to be the oldest form of cattle, similar to those featured in prehistoric cave paintings, have been sighted again in Thailand, near the Cambodian border. They were last seen in the early days of

the Vietnam war. The World Conservation Center, in Switzerland, urges the capture of this small group of males and females in order to breed them back from near extinction. Come back Frank Buck!

D.Telegraph, Guardian 14 Aug 1982.

BIRDS

● The stork-like glos ibis, believed to have been extinct for the last 60yrs has "inexplicably" reappeared in "open spaces" south of Colombo, Sri Lanka. Police have warned against capturing or killing the birds, around 30 in number.

S.Express 26 June 1977.

● The white-winged guan (*Penelope albipennis*), slightly larger than a pheasant, has been found in "considerable" numbers in northwest Peru, in the Andean foothills, says the World Wildlife Fund, after a presumed extinction since 1877. They were previously known only from three stuffed ones in museums.

UPI/*Dallas Morning News* (Tx) 23 Oct; *D.Telegraph* 22 Dec 1977.

● The same on-going ornithological survey, in Peru, which turned up the guan (above) followed up with the discovery of a tiny owl, hitherto unknown to science, and named the long-whiskered owlet, after its distinctive facial feature.

D.Telegraph 30 Jan 1978.

● A colony of "a thousand or more" of the yellow-fronted gardener bowerbird, believed extinct for nearly a century, has been discovered in a New Guinea rain forest, by Prof Javed Diamond, of the University of California Medical School, during an ornithological survey of the largely unexplored Gutier mountains for the Indonesian government.

UPI/*D.Telegraph* 11 Nov 1981.

● A University of Kansas team visiting a coastal region of Argentina, in 1979, found a new species of steamer duck, then spent two years verifying their discovery of this unusual white-headed, flightless bird.

AP/Lincoln (Nb) *Journal* 26 Nov 1981.

INSECTS Etc

• A unique species of fly which turns the (dinner) tables on spiders -- it marches into the web and attacks the spider — has been discovered at Hengistbury Head, Dorset, and nicknamed Superfly (*Acrocera globosus*).

D.Express 3 Dec 1976.

• A snail that flourished in Pleistocene times has been rediscovered in a cave in northeast Iowa. *Discus macclintocki* was only known before now in fossil form, and these specimens, about 100, form the only known extant colony.

Des Moines Register (Iowa) 15 July; UPI/Omaha (Nb) *World Herald* 16 July 1978.

• *Eresus niger*, "one of the world's most beautiful spiders", last seen in 1906, has turned up in Dorset. Two males were trapped, at a secret location, by Rowland Snazell, of the Institute of Terrestrial Ecology, at Furzebrook Research Station, Wareham. Dorset sounds like its infested with undiscovered creepycrawlies!

Observer 10 Feb 1980.

• After two years of research, Dr Alan Brennen, University of Wales, announced the discovery of a new midge, found on a stretch of the River Wye. Although not yet named, it is "thought" to belong to the Denicryptochironomoid family.

Western Mail 2 June 1982.

• A type of hairy snail -- ugh! — thought to have died out 10,000yrs ago, has been found alive and well near Brentford, Middlesex, of all places.

D.Mirror 3 Sept 1982.

Credits: *Gary L. Abbott, Tom R. Adams, Peter Christie, Loren Coleman, David Fideler, Bill Grimstad, Chris Hall, Dr E.C.Krupp, Valerie Martin, John Michell, Tony Roberts, Doc Shiels, Joe Swatek, Paul Thomas, Ion Will.*

Bob Rickard

MEDICAL CURIOSITIES

A singularly dispensible item, it is said, is a hole in the head. Here a few tales of people who have survived having a little sunlight into their innermost cranial recesses. Next in this section: 'Frozen in death'—and don't say we didn't warn you.

Before we get to....uh....the point here are a few quickies.

☐ Three-year-old Anthony Kosaczek, cut free by firemen after impaling his head on iron railings outside his home in Askern, Doncaster, was said to be "satisfactory" in hospital.

S.Express 18 April 1982.

☐ At a school sports day at Keyningham, near Hull, a javelin was blown off course by wind and struck Michael Beadle, 13, in the head. He was taken to hospital with the 3" point still lodged in his skull.

D.Mirror, D.Star, D.Telegraph 2 July 1982.

☐ Albert Jones, 30, of Thame, Oxon, was accidentally shot in the head with a crossbow bolt. It was removed at the Radcliffe Infirmary, Oxford..

D.Telegraph 4 June 1982.

☐ James Wallace, 23, was driving in Memphis, Tennessee, when something flashed through his open window to hit him on the head. Without realizing the full extent of the injury he drove himself to the nearest hospital, where doctors found a 5" long knife blade was buried up to the hilt in his right temple, with minimal damage to brain and optic nerves.

S.Express 27 June 1976.

☐ Robert Deckard, 10, was playing with an old umberella when the point of a loose rib struck his brother, Tippu, under his left eye. Seeing only a speck of blood there, his mother simply comforted the 8yr-old boy and put a bandaid beneath the eye. The next day Tippu complained of dizzyness and nausea. He was taken to a local hospital, in Los Angeles, but when a small object showed up in a brain x-ray a doctor laughed it off as something that must have been on the x-ray table beneath the boy. Six days later Tippus was feeling worse; nor could he chew properly because his jaw felt numb, he said. He was rushed to Los Angeles Children's Hospital where neurosurgeon Frank Anderson removed a half-inch long piece of metal from Tippu's cerebellum in a 4hr operation there days later. It was the tip of the emberella rib which had penetrated through the eye societ 5" into the boy's brain, missing the optic nerve, arteries and vital areas, and was left behind, lodged dangerously near the brain stem, when the rib was withdrawn.

S.Express 27 March 1977.

A NAIL ON THE HEAD

☐ Kenneth Blount, 17, was working with other carpenters on the frame of a house in Baton Rouge, Louisiana, on 18 July 1979, when a colleague above him yelled, losing his footing and dropping a pneumatic hammer. It landed on Blount's head; the impact triggered the hammer which punched a nail deep into his head, midway between the crown and right ear. Blount said later: "I heard the hiss of air, but....I just thought I'd been hit by the hammer. I reached up expecting to feel a bump on my head, but instead....I felt the head of the nail. 'Oh, God, no," I thought, 'That thing is right inside my skull!' Strangely enough there wasn't much pain. I tried to pull the nail out, but it wouldn't come. It was in there pretty tight."

Blount's workmates panicked when they realized what had happened. "I had to keep them calm for my own sake," he said. The nail was eventually removed at Our Lady of the Lake Medical Center, in the city, by neuro-surgeon James Poche, who was astounded by Blount's "dumb luck". There was little tissue damage and Blound recovered well after the 2hr operation. He vowed to wear a safety helmet in future.

S.Express 18 Nov; *Nat. Enquirer* 20 Nov; *Weekly News* 1 Dec 1979.

☐ A powered nail-gun also nearly did for Linda Archipolo, of Massapequa, NY. The 18yr-old waitress was working in the local Burger King when a spot on the wall behind some diners exploded with a shower of concrete chips. Linda's boss stormed next door where he discovered some cretin putting up a poster with the gun. After complaining, he returned and asked Linda to clear up the mess. As she bent over the table a second nail ripped through the wall and was driven into her skull.

Linda was rushed to the Nassau County Medical Center with the nail protruding from her head. There was a "hell of a lot of damage" said neuro-surgeon Robert Degler. She was in a deep coma and not expected to recover – but now, against "staggering odds" she is making an "amazing" recovery, moving her eyes, attempting to speak, snapping her fingers to attract attention, etc. There is some hope that she will walk and talk again, eventually.

Globe 14 Sept 1982.

BRAIN ON A STICK

☐ When rescuers investigated a car which slammed into a tree on Hyde Park Avenue, Boston, Mass., on 1 May 1981, they gasped with horror. Inside was 39yr-old John Thompson, his head pierced through by a 7ft steel crowbar, used to shift granite blocks. It had been on the back seat and flew forward on impact and was now protruding about 3ft from just above his left eye. Paramedics supported the bar with sandbags and cut it fore and aft with a grinder saw, keeping the metal cool with water to avoid cooking the man's brain.

Thompson was still unconscious when he arrived at Boston City Hospital trauma center, where he had the good fortune to be attended by neuro-surgeon I. Joseph Ordia, who cut the left scalp along the parting, picked out the fragments of shattered skull and "lifted out" the segment of bar. "I have never seen such penetration in anyone's head before'" Ordia said. "I have only read about something similar in medical journals once before." The 40lb bar had smashed its way through the mid-brain just above the brain stem (see photo) and the damage has left its effects – nevertheless, Thompson is recovering beyond any of the expectations made when doctors first saw him. "He wakes fully. He understands everything we say to him. He obeys simply commands. He

Dr I. Joseph Ordia, of Boston City Hospital, uses a 7ft broom handle to demonstrate how the steel crowbar was driven through the head of John Thompson. [Photo: by Joe Dennehy from Boston Globe *5 May 1981.]*

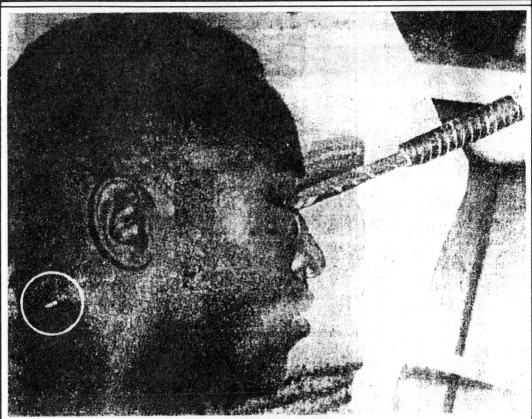

Yes....you're seeing it correctly. Just be thankful we can't print in colour! This Lupane tribesman of Rhodesia, came home to find his wife with a lover. He chased the man into a dark hut and ran right onto the lover's spear. Just not my lucky day, he thought as he trudged 8km to the clinic at St Paul's Mission, including wading through the waist-deep Shangani River. After a doctor cut off the main shaft (after he took the photo, it seems) the unfortunate man was sent to Mpilo Hospital, in Bulawayo. Bolt cutters were used to remove most of the protruding iron spearhead, and the rest, including the barbed head, was drawn through the wound. Bet he didn't need anaesthetic either! He was released after 35 days, suffering from "slight headaches". (Undated, unnamed South African paper – our guess: Rand Daily Mail *mid 1970s.)*

can move his left arm and leg strongly and pick up his right leg, but he can't move his right arm. With the help of therapy teams, father of three, Thompson was able to recover sufficiently to be allowed home to convalesce, and he struggled out on crutches, just three months after the accident. Despite some paralysis and difficulty talking doctors say there is hope for improvement.

Boston Globe, UPI/Lincoln (Nb) *Star,* AP/*Kansas City Star* 5 May ; AP/St Catherines (Ont) *Standard* 5 May & 28 July; *Globe* 26 May; *Star* (?) 9 June 1981.

□ Carpenter Michael Melnick, 29, of Reseda, Calif., fell 10ft through the floor of a house under construction in Malibu, in Feb 1981. After hitting the ground he tried to lift up his head but couldn't – there was 6" of rough-surfaced steel rod protruding from between his eyes, the other end buried in the concrete floor. The five-eigths of an inch thick rod, used for reinforcing concrete, had gone through his head from the base of his neck. He remembers lying there trying to figure it out. "When I finally realized what had happened to me, my heart just dropped. I was sure I was going to die."

His colleagues, including his father, tried to keep him calm by rushing about in complete panic shouting encouraging phrases, like "Oh, my God!"

Melnick went into shock when lifeguards from nearby Zuma Beach sawed through the rod at ground level. Melnick says he will never forget the sound echoing and vibrating inside his head. At Westlake Community Hospital, neuro-surgeon Paul Ironside removed the iron from inside Melnick's skill, rebult his shattered nose and repaired tear ducts, nerves, muscles and what tissue damage he could. Doctors, certain there would be permanent if not fatal damage were baffled to find this not the case. After 7 months Melnick's most serious aftereffects are psychological: nightmares, insomnia, fear of falling. There have been some "physical complications" but these were not specified. Melnick is said to be seeing a psychiatrist – this is a new hallucination on us!

AP/Lincoln (Nb) *Star* 25 Sept; *D.Telegraph* 26 Sept 1981.

'IS YOUR BRAIN REALLY NECESSARY?'

I'm willing to venture that the historic case alluded to by Dr Ordia (above) is the classic case of Phineas P. Gage, who at 25, was a railway foreman, somewhere in the USA. On13 Sept 1847, while placing a charge in a hole, a premature explosion drove the tamping-iron through his skull (see engraving). The 13lb, 1¼dia, 3'7" long rod entered point first and passed completely through. He lost parts of his skull and some brain matter, but a few hours later was still rational enough to ask after his work. For several days he discharged bone and brain bits through his mouth, then passed into delirium and lost vision in one eye. Gage recovered rapidly, and even tried for his old job. His employers rejected him not because he wasn't fit, but because "the most efficient and capable foreman" had changed into a truculent, brutish, untrustworthy simpleton. His friends said he was "no longer Gage". For those interested, the main write-ups of this case are: *Am.Jour. Medical Science* (Philadelphia) July 1859; *Brit.Med.Jour.* 21 April 1888; *Boston Medical & Surgical Jour.* 18.

Other examples of similar accidents resulting in substantial damage to, or even loss of, brain substance are given in chapter 10 of Gould & Pyle's *Curiosities & Anomalies of Medicine* (1896). In most cases where the injury is survived there is some recovery,

mentally and physically, though very rarely does that recovery approximate to the pre-accident normality. The question raised is just how much of our brain matter is essential to normal functioning at any time? The answer must be that we simply don't know much about the living brain fuction in its 'global' mode (to use computer jargon).

The skull of Phineas Gage, showing the passage of the iron bar and the area of frontal bone dislodged by its passage [BMJ 21 April 1888].

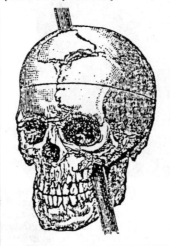

Part of the answer may be the discovery of the ability to relocate specific brain functions in other parts of the brain, but whether this means that the available matter is shared out in a new proportion, or that there are unused or 'spare' areas of matter which can be cultivated in the event of accident to other parts is not yet fully understood. This versatility was shown dramatically in a documentary – originating in Sweden, I believe – called 'Is your brain really necessary?' (*ITV*, 11 May 1982, 10.45pm), in which several patients were described who had "no detectable brain" or minimal brain tissue; facts confirmed by the latest brain-scanning techniques. These tecniques also helped to show that some functions had reloc-

ated in the remaining brain tissue. We saw:
• Sharon – during a routine check on a brain fluid valve a huge cavity where brain tissues should have been was discovered. A Prof Lorber said her brain had disappeared or become paper-thin in the frontal cortex region. She was otherwise functioning normally.
• Roger – who had only 5% of his brain left, but who still got a 1st degree in maths. The whole area where speech and feelings are usually located were missing.
• Stephen – his absence of brain was demonstrated by holding a light behind his head, like a dull pink goldfishbowl. He, nevertheless, obtained 5 O levels. Later his brain was found to have "returned" or "regrown" or "reflated".

The results, suggests Prof Lorber, suggest that it is quality, not quantity, which counts in the old grey stuff. Weird!

HEAD CASE

As an absurd postscript to the above, I must mention the amazing luck of the Irish, visited upon one John Delaney, 56yr-old father of four, passing a building site in Coventry St, Birmingham, on 16 Aug 1979. A huge coping stone, weighing at least a hundredweight, fell two floors to land square on his head. Horrified police, ambulancemen and doctors expected the man to die from massive brain damage from the force of the blow from the huge concrete block – but not so. The very next day, Delaney sat up in bed, in the Birmingham Accident Hospital and said: "I've got a bit of a headache, that's all." It merely fractured his skull, for which he received 17 stitches. Now there is one lucky Irishman.

D.Express 18 Aug 1979.

Credits: *Larry Arnold, Peter Christie, Peter Hope Evans, Steve Hicks, Chris Holtzhausen, Valerie Martin, Laurence May Jr, Joe Swatek, Dwight Whalen.*

●

Bob Rickard

As you well know, one of our many areas of interest is the way in which ideas or images from the world of human art and invention are reflected by life and nature. It would be simplistic to suggest that nature actually imitates art — anyone who studies these whimsical events soon realizes that each is a nexus of complicated connections and causal chains whose meaning or value cannot be explained as the product of mere chance. There are many forms of simulacra within this genre, and we were struck, recently, by this example of resonating image.

The picture (above) is a familiar one. It is one of a number of drawings, done by Maurice Sand for his mother's — the French novelist, George Sand — book, *Legendes Rustiques* (1858), popularized in Montague Summers' classic study, *The Werewolf* (1933). It illustrates one of those marvellous pieces of medieval gossip which pass for history in Olaus Magnus' *Historia de Gentibus Septentrionalibus* (1555) — a book which includes many categories of Forteana — which alludes to "a certain wall" in the region of Latvia, where "some thousands of werewolves come together, that each of them may try his nimbleness in leaping."

In the course of our usual scavenging for clippings I noticed the following strikingly similar photograph (below) in the *National Enquirer* for 19 April 1977 (Cr: Gary L. Abbott). It shows a number of meerkats — a small dark brown South African resident, related to the mongoose. They have little hair on their bellies and love to stand, exposing themselves to the sun on chilly days.

If you have collected or noted any other weird conjunctions or replications of images, we'd like to hear from you with a view to showing them in FT.

•

Bob Rickard.

A miscellany of notes this time, ranging from the 18th century to the present day, from blazing mops to blazing bodies, with a couple of strange poltergeist-like cases thrown in.

PYRENEAN PYROTICS

It began at 5.30pm on 6 August 1979. Madam Gaby Bourdat was herding six cows along a lane near the remote French village of Seron (Haute Pyrenees) when she smelled smoke. Looking around, she saw it billowing out of a downstairs window in an abandoned farmhouse belonging to her neighbours, the Lahores. She alerted them and the fire was quickly put out. Within two hours, two more fires broke out, but this time in the Lahore's modern farmhouse opposite. In the month that followed about 90 mystery fires began in the Lahore's house, and noone has been able to discover why.

The Lahores were quickly nervous-wrecks. For a while 20 gendarmes camped near the farm, but despite round-the-clock vigilance no physical arsonists was discovered. At the same time the case came to the attention of a steady stream of psychologists, exorcists, mediums and psychics, none of whom had any more success in solving the mystery. According to several witnesses the fires begin in a similar way: "First comes the smell of smoke. An object is discovered with a circular charred spot, which is smoking. It bursts into flames and is rushed out of the house, where the family, friends, investigators or gendarmes stamp it out or douse it with water from a line of buckets." Each bucket has a rosary in it — no one's taking chances!

One day 32 separate fires sprung up within the house — towels, sheets, clothes, furniture — the number could be higher (our earlier report mentions 80 fires in a week). As the search for external agency failed, some speculated the fires were being set by someone in the family. Besides father Edouard Lahore, 59, and his wife Marie-Louise, are their sons Roger, 29, and Jean-Marc, 24, and a foster daughter Michelle, 19, who came to live with the family six years previously. "Ahah!" I hear you mutter. Rivalry among the brothers for the girl's attention was indeed rumoured the cause, by villagers, but none of the investigators, as far as we know, commented on this. Sexual tension or frustration, repressed into the subconscous, figures in quite a few poltergeist cases, as do spontaneous outbreaks of fire — but without the facts it would be useless to assert much more.

The official investigations failed to find any culprit — even the usual tack of officialdom out on a limb, the blaming of the most available likely candidate, did not happen in this case. The prefect of police, an investigating judge, and Gregoire Kaplan, head of the Laboratory for Physical Analysis in the town of Pau, could not even discover how objects were set alight! Even Michelle's clothes burst into flame while she was wearing them.

Edouard Lahore took it all stoically. "They say it could be paranormal. They say it could be rays....or the Devil. I don't know." But by the time of our last report he was happily showing reporters over his house. "See the bedstead? See the two big charred sections? That was Tuesday morning; the other was Wednesday evening."

D.Mirror 16 August; *D.Mail* 11 Sept 1979.

PSYCHIC ARSON?

A strange case, reminiscent of the dark days of the witch persecutions, has been playing out in Italy. On 2nd August 1982, Carole Compton, aged 20, from Aberdeen, was arrested and held in jail in Livorno accused of trying to murder Agnese Cecchine, the 3yr-old Italian girl, for whom she was engaged as a nanny, by setting fire to her cot. Her case was taken up initially by a Scottish lawyer, Lawrence Nisbet, who was on holiday nearby when he heard of the arrest. Nisbet was told by Carole that she was not even in the room when the fire happened. "She was having breakfast with other members of the family. The child was not burned because she was sleeping on the other side of the cot. There was a similar fire the night before in the grandfather's bedroom when Carole was having dinner with the family." At their home on the Isle of Elba, the family's grandmother accused Carole of being possessed by the Devil, and began a series of nightmare allegations that Carole had set the fires using the 'Evil Eye' or witchcraft. Nisbet said that the authorities did not take these charges seriously, but asked for a psychiatric examination of the girl on 17 Sept.

When next Nisbet saw Carole, she said the behaviour of the inmates of Livorno added to her misery. They were constantly trying to get her to take drugs or to take part in lesbian activities. Nisbet is reported to have said later that "There is evidence that something strange is going on. She has now admitted there were unexplained happenings on the day of the fire. A bowl jumped off a table and a glass fell for no reason." We also learned that Carole had gone to Italy to be with her fiancé, Marco Vituloni, but he broke off the engagement "recently".

Then came a report (4 Oct), via Carole's mother, who had been in touch with Italy by phone, that the psychiatric examination was positive — whatever that may mean. The report puts it quaintly: "[She] has been cleared by a psychiatrist of allegations that she can start fires by mental powers." What a jumble of assumptions and misunderstandings in that sentence! Mrs Pamela Compton continued: "This talk of her starting a fire by her mental powers is a load of rubbish. [It] is good news, but I haven't yet heard the results of the forensic tests." Forensic? Probably on the charred bedding. Mrs Compton said Carole's hearing was set for the 4th Oct. But the last we've heard (25 Oct) Carole was still in jail awaiting trial.

The Sun, D. Telegraph 9 Sept; (Scottish) *D.Record* 9-11 Sept; *S.Times* 3 Oct; *Shropshire Star* 4 Oct; *The Sun* 25 Oct; Aberdeen *Press & Journal* 7, 13, 16, 29 Sept 1982.

SMC?

As caretaker Victor Webber opened up the Leasowes Sports Center, in Kent Road, Halesowen, on 22 March 1981, he smelled smoke and called the fire brigade. They discovered a blazing mop in a broom cupboard. There was nothing near it to show how it caught fire. "It had not been used for some time. Heaven knows how it started. It looks like one of those cases of spontaneous combustion," he said. Fire brigade spokesman said: "We took the mop outside and put out the flames. It's a mystery. There were no electrics or anything around it which could have set it off." Peculiar how

many of these odd fires seem to begin just prior to being discovered!

We sigh, and reach for a new file, and scribble 'Spontaneous combustion of mops'.

(Wolverhampton) *Express & Star* 23 March 1981.

READING SHC

Early on Sunday morning, 12 Nov 1978, Maria Gmiterek, aged 8, hammered frantically on her neighbour's door. Mrs Elizabeth Randall, of Baker Street, Reading, said: "The little girl came running in, saying something was wrong with her mummy. I ran back with her and smelt smoke in the house, and then Maria said there had been a fire. She said her mother was in the basement, and when we got down there she was lying on the floor. Marie ran to me sobbing. She just said: "Is my mummy dead? My mummy has turned to ashes."

Mrs Randall returned to her home to comfort the child, now in great distress. Meanwhile, Maria's brother Peter, aged 11, went across the road to call an ambulance, and returned to wait with Mrs Randall. "He was trying to be very grown up, trying to help, but the little girl was heartbroken. It was terrible in that basement. I don't want to see anything like that again. It's bad enough for an adult to see, but imagine what it must be like for a child to find her mother like that." The children's father died six years previously. The dead woman had lived in Baker Street for nearly 16 years. Mrs Randall who said Mrs Lucy Gmiterek's hands were "so shak y", said she thought the woman had been in the basement "trying to do a bit of washing" when she "must have knocked a fire over." Working on the same supposition the forensic boys were examining an oil fire "found in the house". At the inquest, her doctor, Rojand Shukla, said Mrs Gmiterek, 49, had suffered from acute fits of depression and hysteria.

Sometimes she shook so much she could not stand up. She had a pain in her back "for which no physical cause has been found." Since 1971 she had the occasional blackout. The post-mortem at the Royal Berkshire Hospital, on 13 Nov, showed the cause of death to be shock due to extensive burning.

Several times in the reports, the woman's body is described as "charred" — and, of special interest to us is the statement that "Police and fire experts are known to be puzzled why Mrs Gmiterek should have burned to death while the rest of the room was only barely damaged...." In the first report, the girl, Maria, was said to have stumbled upon the grim scene; the "charred remains" of her mother were "lying on the stone floor of the basement....but police say there was only slight fire damage to the building." As you know by now, it can take an intense and sustained fire of 2-3000°F quite a while to incinerate a human body. This case deserves further investigation.

Reading Chronicle 14 & 17 Nov 1978. The inquest note is undated but from the same peper and before 5 Dec 1978.

ANOTHER IPSWICH INCIDENT

Peter Christie told us that a shortened version of his 'Grace Pett' article [FT35p6-9] appeared in the *East Anglian magazine* for Jan 1982, which drew the following letter in response in the February issue:

"In 1796 John Constable sketched the ruins of an old cottage in Capel, Suffolk, and across the top of the picture he wrote: 'Curious circumstances happened in this cottage a few years since, a poor woman being burnt entirely to ashes.' The remaining words are not very clear, but it looks as if mention is made of the terrific heat that must have been necessary but nothing else was burned or even singed in the cottage. Can anybody give any date or any definite proof of what really occurred? The original picture is in the Victoria & Albert Museum, South Kensington."

Peter adds: "So far no-one has responded to this letter — but this second case so near Ispwich [where Grace Pett was fatally charred in 1744] is interesting. One wonders if SHC cases are concentrated in certain areas?"

Readers may remember that Larry Arnold pursued this notion in a 3-part article on his ideas of 'leynes' or alignment of SHC sites [FT22p6-12; FT23p6-9, 16].

Speaking of Larry Arnold.... Last year he investigated one of the most astounding cases of SHC survival we have heard of, Jack Angel, a travelling salesman visiting Savannah, Georgia, in Nov 1974, went to sleep in his truck and didn't wake for four days. When he finally woke up he was seriously burned in parts — his right hand was charred and had to be amputated, there was a hole burned deep into his chest and more burns on his back, groin and legs. Could have been worse! Larry wrote the case up for *Fate* Sept 1982, but nevertheless we are glad to have is his special report next issue.

DID SHE, OR DIDN'T SHE?
The headlines shouted 'Woman in flames', and 'Woman walk-

ing Chicago street bursts into flames, dies.' It's the sort of headline that gets a Fortean reaching for his scissors on reflex. But the story that unfolded is elusive, enigmatic and confused.

The incident happened in broad daylight on a busy street in Chicago's South Side on 5th August 1982. According to a public statement made by police sergeant George Owen, a witness, Winfield Gattlin, 45, of Merrillville, Ind., was sitting in his car with his girlfriend, and noticed the woman cross the road in front of him. When he next looked she was about a block away and she was aflame, standing on the sidewalk near 4052 South Wells Street. Gattlin said he got out of the car to help her but the burning woman collapsed. By the time police arrived the woman's body was "scorched and disintegrating". Detective Dan Fitzgerald, of the Brighton Park Violent Crimes Unit, said: "She was completely burned; I mean scorched. It was obviously not just a case of her clothing catching fire. We really don't know what happened here. She could have been carrying something flammable or doused with something flammable." But despite efforts police and fire department investigators could find no trace of "accelerants" in the vicinity of the remains.

They acknowledged, however, that the fireman's efforts to douse the blaze could have dispersed any evidence. The fire-fighters themselves first thought it was a "rubbish fire" and were "stunned" to discover "the body of a woman, burned beyond recognition." Owen said: "The body was small enough to be a child's, but there was a lot of gold dental work in her mouth" The only other evidence were scraps of a blouse, and her purse, said to be untouched by the blaze. The body was found with hands in front "in a boxer position", said Owen.

This sensational news of a seemingly authentic SHC case was flashed around the world, and items appeared in most papers the next day. One consequence is that the Chicago authorities were deluged with inquiries from people interested in SHC. One caller to the police, from Cornell University, gave them chapter and verse on a number of incidents including the famous case of Mrs Reeser of St Petersburg, Florida in 1951. Could this informant be someone we know? Or are there a lot more SHC researchers out there unknown to us?

Enter the Cook County medical examiner, Dr Robert Stein, assigned to do the autopsy. Before he begins his

---

This account of the inquest on an SHC case appeared in the Australian paper, Adelaide Observer *15 Sept 1883. On the same page is the report of a dead sea-monster cited by Fort (*Books p609*), so Fort must have seen it and noted it, yet he never used it. We reproduce it here for your interest.*

ADJOURNED INQUEST.—On Monday morning the adjourned enquiry into the circumstances attending the death by burning of Mrs. Murphy, a widow, at Norwood, was conducted and closed. It appeared that the deceased, who was an unusually corpulent and somewhat eccentric woman, lived by herself, and had a comfortable annuity, besides some little property. She seems to have been rather careless [with candles and matches, those articles being found in drawers amongst clothes, and in various parts of the house. Owing to her non-appearance about the house, and not responding to the calls of neighbours and the tradespeople, some anxiety for her safety was created, and on the back door being broken open her dead body, covered with burns, was found extended on the floor of one of the rooms. The singular feature in the affair was that, although the body was severely burnt and half-consumed, and wearing apparel was found in various parts of the house, the body was clothed in a nightdress which was uninjured, and one hand showed no marks of fire except a scorched thumb. There was no evidence, however, to confirm any suspicion of violence or robbery. Money was found in deceased's desk, in a reticule, and in a common bag, which, hanging by one handle to the knob of a door, had its interior quite exposed. The Jury found that the deceased came to her death by burning, but that there was not sufficient evidence to show how it happened.

investigation he publicly states his disbelief in SHC. "There's never been an authenticated case reported," he announced *ex cathedra*. "Such theories make nice fairy tales." Regarding the witness, Stein said he doubted the man's credibility. In this fashion, since time immemorial, have the 'experts' dismissed the testimony of witnesses. So confident are they of the superiority of their opinions they do not even bother with *all* the facts, their vaunted impartiality, or the history of similar incidents. It was this same arrogance that led the Academician, Lavoisier to dismiss sightings of meteorites as the collective aberration of peasants.

However, Stein, after the autopsy, comes up with some astonishing facts. The woman, was black, 5ft 2 inches, and about 45 years old, with dentures and five gold caps. She had been dead "at least 12 hours" before burning. Somebody must have doused her body with an accelerant and set her ablaze. His reason for believing she was dead was that there was no soot in her lungs or windpipe, nor carbon monoxide — so she was not breathing during the fire. The body was uniformly burned on the skin and the internal organs were undamaged, said Stein. The body was partly decomposed, and he was unable to determine any other cause of death, eg stabbing or strangling. Forensic tests found traces of an accelerant "possibly gasoline".

In the original reports, Sgt Owen said that the witness, Gattlin, "wasn't paying too much attention." It is possible that in the time he looked away from the woman crossing the road he lost track of her, and on looking up to see the fire asssumed the victim was the woman he'd just seen. But if the woman had just burst into flames, how did Gattlin miss seeing whoever doused her and torched her. And what about his statement that he saw her standing in flames then falling down? Was Gattlin

hallucinating? On the other hand, from what we know of previous incidents, authenticated as far as possible, SHC, whatever it is, is like no ordinary combustion or death by fire. A rapid disintegration is frequently reported, as is actual shrinkage of the body and bones in process (this happened to Mrs Reeser's skull). And if the process of SHC occurs on a molecular level, or lower, the disintegration and chemistry might well give rise to strange new hydrocarbon compounds, some of which may indeed be similar to "traces" of gasoline. This is altogether an exciting mystery,

and we can only urge the likes of Larry Arnold to get their gasmasks on, magnifying glasses out, and try to elucidate the full and true facts.

UPI/*D.Telegraph*, Chicago *Sun-Times* 6 Aug; *Chicago Tribune* 6 & 7 Aug, Chicago UPI/Albuquerque (NM) *Journal* 6 & 7 Aug 1982.

Credits- *Larry Arnold, Janet & Colin Bord, Peter Christie, Lucius Farish (UFONS), Alan Gardiner, Brian Hain, Mark Hall, F Hudson, J Lang, Jonathan Mullard, Paul Screeton, Mike Tuppen, Jake Williams, Howard Wolinsky.*

●

Bob Rickard

- by Michael Hoffman -

In 1930 an obscure tribal chieftain, Ras Tafari (Amharic for "Head Creator"), was crowned Emperor of Ethiopia as part of a line of succession dating back to Solomon. In the twenties, Jamaica, W.I. Black activist Marcus Garvey had prophesied, "Look to Africa where a Black king shall be crowned." The 1930 coronation of Haile Selassie I prompted King George V of England to give the golden "Scepter of Judah" as a gift, via his son, the Duke of Gloucester. While in Ethiopia, the Duke allegedly got drunk and ate "tall grass", revealing himself to be "the reincarnate King of Babylon, Nebuchadnezzar"[1].

The magically empowered Scepter had been stolen from the black race by Marc Anthony and Julius Caesar who used it to make Rome

omnipotent. Somehow it got into British hands. After receiving the English gift Selassie "sent a mysterious emblem back to England"[2]. King George's subsequent paralysis and death is said to have been related to his laying eyes on the African emblem.

Selassie was the leader of a secret society, Niyabinghi ("Death to Black and White Oppressors"), that was partly a drumming fraternity and partly a mystical paramilitary organization[3]. The society originally took hold in east-central Africa in the 19th century and was named after an assassinated Hamitic queen from Tanganyika. Niyabinghi warriors attacked European colonial outposts from 1919 to 1928.

Meanwhile, back in Jamaica, a millenarian sect of violent black hippies with snake nests for hair, led by Kingston preacher L.P. Howell, were worshipping Selassie as the "Living God" (*Rev; 5:2.5; Joshua* 3:10) demanding repatriation to Africa styling themselves Niyamen and Rastas. The police reacted by promptly "committing Howell and every Rasta they could arrest to terms in mental asylums on charges of lunacy" [4]. Thus was born the cult of Rastafari.

When Howell was released in 1940 he acquired a mountainside mansion and there with 1500 faithful planted marijuana cash crops, thumbed his nose at the authorities and became an outlaw. In 1954, after years of skirmishes, Howell's empire was razed and its leadership and cadres scattered over the island. By this time the Rastafari had developed a reputation as menacing, Gorgonian devils whose chief activities were disembowelling tourists and smoking drugs. In 1963 this reputation increased dramatically when a gang of Rastas went beserk near Montego Bay, hacked up a gas station attendant, torched the gas station, sacked a motel and killed one of its guests. Hence it was with some trepidation that official Jamaica prepared, in the spring of 1966, for the state visit of the Rasta God the Conquering Lion of Judah His Imperial Majesty, Haile Selassie I.

On April 21 a solitary white dove flew over the assembled multitude, including thousands of Nuyamen, followed by a gentle rain of benediction and then Selassie's jet winging in from the East. The Rastas ripped up the red welcoming carpet (it had been defiled by Queen Elizabeth II), stormed the plane and generally went bonkers. Selassie appeared at the door of the aircraft with tears in his eyes (though from joy or terror it is not known). Several present reported visions, miracles and conversions. Among the latter is the account of a woman who told herself, as Selassie drove past in a motorcade, that she wouldn't believe he was God unless she saw the imprint of the crucifixion nails. At exactly the moment she thought that, Selassie turned his waving hand toward her, revealing the black imprint of a nail wound in his palm.[5]. But some very dread Rastas, too stoned to attend the occasion were less enthusiastic. Said one. "If he was God he wouldn't need a plane to fly to Jamaica"[6]. The Emperor himself apparently had reservations too. In response to the Rasta hope for repatriation to Ethiopia, he is reported to have stated that the last thing his country needed was thousands of lazy drug addicts who didn't pay taxes.

In 1974, amid charges that he permitted mass starvation and had stashed millions in Swiss banks, Ethiopian army officers deposed Selassie. They would have liked to have executed him but "were superstitious and fearful of his powers"[7]. He died of natural causes on August 27, 1975. Rastas say he is not dead. In an interview with CBS News a university-trained journalist turned Rastaman informed Dan Rather than he believed "literally" that Selassie still lives. When reminded of the reports of Selassie's death, the man replied, "Well, you and I know what the press can do".

The Rasta creed is based on the belief that Christ was a Black man and Selassie was his 72nd incarnation. They say the inhabitants of Israel are "imposters" and "false Jews" of whom the Scripture says "Woe unto them that call themselves Israel and are not". Blacks are the true Hebrews. The Bible has been falsely interpreted and is benevolent only when understood in light of the mystic revelation of Rastafari. They don't cut their hair, shave, use alcohol or deal with corpses because they are Nazirites (*Numbers* 6:1-27). Samson, Samuel, John the Baptist, Jesus and the early Christians wore matted hair and beards. Their communion sacrament was marijuana. Their chalices were pipes and chillums out of the smoke of which manifested Jah Rastafar. The tangled lock s are "high tension wires which transmit divine energy and inspiration" [8]. They are also symbols of racial pride and affirmations of the principle that, "As a man destroys his hair, he destroys himself, his divine energy. He will na produce nothing"[9]. Marijuana is referred to as ganja and the highest sacramental form of it is called "Kali-weed". These terms are products of the intercourse, in the 19th century, between Jamaicans and indentured servants from India. The synchronicity of Medusa-haired Bible-believers using "Kali-weed" in their anti-"Babylon" rituals is interesting in that the symbolic East Asian image of the goddess Kali is that of a change agent and destroyer.

For a millenarian cult, Rastafari has temendous cachet in religion, politics and especially music worldwide. Their reggae ("regular") music tops the pop charts in London, NY, LA, Paris and parts of the Third World. The best known Rasta musician was the late Bob Marley, who is believed to have been the reincarnation of the Biblical Joseph, received the Order of Merit and a state funeral from Jamaica (rumor has it he was killed by radioactive lasers beamed from between stage footlights). Reggae's popularity is intriguing given the cult's notion that Babylon shall fall by the power of words. They cite the *Genesis* account of the creation of the world with words: "Let there be light" and say that when enough people chant God's name ("Jah" as in Halleluj*ah*) — Jah Rastafari — destruction will swiftly ensue.

In the opening segment of a CBS News piece on Rastas, a chant against the Pope was featured. The sect regards him as "Imperial Wizard of the KKK, Godfather of the Mafia and General All Around Anti-Christ"[10] who keeps alive the wor d-power of the Roman Empire. Latin. Ironically, the man who took another stab at killing the Pope, *Sede Vacante* Father Juan Krohn, did so because he thought there wasn't enough Latin. [This was on 12 May 1982 at Fatima, Portugal: 65th anniversary of the BVM apparition on the site in 1917, and exactly one year after the gun attempt on John-Paul II in Rome—Ed.]

When Pius XI blessed the invading Italian armies converging on Ethiopia in 1935 he was "thereby tipping his hand as to the extent of his complicity in the supernatural struggle for power"[11]. Rastafari emphasize the cultivation of mental power. One has to wonder how much this played in the fact that two days after Rasta/reggae superstar Bob Marley/Joseph died, Pope John Paul II was gunned down.

Not only the power of sound, but elemental forces as well — Rasta Peter Tosh (who says he is always surrounded by 7 protective ghosts) — "My Father flash lightning, roll thunder, cause the bloodclot (evildoers) to quake....five years from now will be a different age"[12].

There is a report that a tribe of American Indians auspiciously located at the Havasupai Indian Reservation at the bottom of the Grand Canyon, eighty miles north of Flagstaff, Arizona, have converted, *en masse*, to the mystic brotherhood of Rastafari. "Rebel Music", a Marley reggae composition, has been adopted as their tribal anthem along with the chanting of "Jah Rastafari" [13]. Recalling D.H. Lawrence's dark fantasies about the "dire implications of this powerful southwestern landscape for the old European view"[14], any day now I almost expect to see Selassie-in-the-flesh, along with his snake-

locks troops, sacking the Vatican, Wall St, & the Kremlin to the boom of burra drums and reggae guitars, creating a tidal wave of word, sound and elemental power stretching from Ethiopia to the Grand Canyon.

●

Michael Hoffman

NOTES

1) Stephen Davis and Peter Simon, *Reggae Bloodlines*
2) Ibid.
3) *Jamaican Times,* 7 Dec 1935.
4) Davis and Simon, Op.Cit.
5) *Rolling Stone,* 27 May 1982.
6) Davis and Simon, Op.Cit.
7) Ibid.
8) Tracy Nicholas, *Rastafari, A Way of Life.*
9) Ibid.
10) *Subway News* (Boston), Autumn, 1979.
11) Ibid.
12) *Oui* magazine interview, ca. 1980.
13) *Rolling Stone,* Op.Cit.
14) Jim Brandon, *Weird America.*

U·F·O commentary by **Nigel Watson**

Given the slenderest clues to the nature of surrounding objects we identify them and act not so much according to what is directly sensed, **but to what is believed.** [1]

Mountains often seem to be the home of strange monstrous beings who easily elude the attempts that are made to capture them. Sometimes there are explanations for such sightings. For instance, mountaineer W.H.Murray relates an experience he had in the Cairngorms which was originally puzzling but had a mundane explanation: 'When we started on

the last rise to Cairn Toul there came a wider clearance than usual. Suddenly Mortimer gripped my arm and pointed uphill through the misty column. "Look!" he exclaimed, "Two men crossing to Glen Einich." Upon looking up at the slope I was duly surprised to see two climbers a long way ahead of us...I watched them traverse a full fifty feet from east to west across the snow-slope, one about ten yards in front of the other...We advanced and saw them halt, apparently to wait for us. At a hundred yards' range they turned out to be two black

boulders. So great was our astonishment that we failed even to laugh at ourselves.' [2]

The rocks appeared to move due to what is called the autokinetic effect. This happens when there are a lack of visual clues for a person to detect the movement, or lack of movement, of an object. In normal circumstances we can tell if something is moving or stationary by referring it to the total visual field. Some think that the autokinetic effect is caused by a slight imbalance between the neck and eye muscles, which conveys the feeling of eye movement; since there is no real change in its position, the brain interprets this as a movement of the object or objects in the ambiguous visual field. So here, according to Dr Helen Ross [3], we have an explanation for certain observations of ghostly figures, abominable snowmen, and monsters who haunt mist strewn mountains.

The autokinetic effect does have a bearing on certain kinds

of UFO reports, particularly lights in the sky (LITS) reports. Stars often seem to move about in the sky in a way which is not expected of them due to the autokinetic effect, and this phenomenon was first noted by Von Humboldt, the astronomer, in the 1850s. You can experience this phenomenon for yourself, especially if you can focus upon a star that does not have any prominent objects in the same field of vision that might distract your observation. A more controlled method of experiencing this effect is to stare at a dim light in a darkened room. After a moment or two the light may appear to move.

An example of how the autokinetic effect relates to UFO sightings can be seen in the reported observations of erratic moving German airships over Britain in 1913. The anticipation of seeing a German airship, combined with the misperception of a common celestial object, worked wonders as can be seen in this extract from the *Doncaster Chronicle*, 28th February, 1913; 'The airship scare has spread to Doncaster. On Tuesday night a crowd of several hundred people gathered at the central tram terminus, at the junction of St. Sepulchre Gate and Station Road, and scores of them persisted that they saw an airship in the sky, moving, and lighted. Unprejudiced observers, however, were just as positive that the object of their attention was the brilliant star (sic), Venus, which must have been somewhat distressed at the attention she was receiving.'

On the same night (the 25th February, 1913) according to the *Sheffield Independent* of the 26th February, in Hull: 'Crowds of people gathered in the centre of the city and outside the Paragon station, and watched with the keenest interest the strange craft for upwards of an hour, when it disappeared in a westerly direction...the airship's lights were easily distinguishable, and at times were quite bright. Occasionally a patch of red was visible. The ship altered her course frequently, and at times appeared to be stationary.'

But it seems 'that the light which the crowd saw was a bright star.'

In Sheffield, on the same evening, three men walking along Abbeydale Road, saw Venus in the west. 'Then', reported the Sheffield *Daily Telegraph* of the 27th February, 1913, 'the trio played an old but always successful jest. They stood looking until others joined them, talking the while in non-committal fashion on airships in general. When a crowd of respectable dimensions had gathered, the original trio slipped away, leaving the new-comers gazing at the glowing planet and reading into its rays all sorts of horrid fancies and tragical possibilities.'

In these 1913 instances the autokinetic effect could well have been to blame for the alleged movement of the 'German airship'. Mental expectations, aided by jokers like those in Sheffield, along with the autokinetic effect (or other kinds of phenomena which cause perceptual distortion) can have a powerful influence upon human affairs which are not always easy to predict.

In this context it is worthwhile to note that in experiments it has been found that people who see little autokinetic movement are more likely to live their life 'in a close, vivid, direct, interactional involvement with the people and things around (them).' They give an "attentional priority to external stimuli'. On the other hand those who see a lot of autokinetic movement 'the more likely it is that a person experiences himself and his world with more detachment and with more subjectivity.' They give 'attentional priority to internal stimuli', Another interesting result of this research was that: 'The more autokinetic movement seen, the more elaborate, vivid, and compelling was the phantasy evoked in the autokinetic situation.' [4]

In another study[5] an attempt was made to correlate 'particular exponents of attentiveness-inattentiveness with specific facets of externalization-internalization' in order to understand attentional processes based upon the psychological disposition of the subject, using the autokinetic effect as a stimulus.

From this research it appears that the auto-kinetic effect is not just the result of as yet little understood neurophysiological determinants, but is also conditioned by the psychological state of the subject.

In the real world outside the laboratory the autokinetic effect can have some very serious consequences for aircraft pilots who might mistake stars or ground based lights for those of moving aircraft[6]. Another aspect of this effect is to induce pilots into believing that UFOs are in their vicinity, and this could be the explanation for some of the aerial encounters enshrined in the UFO literature.

To conclude, we can see that even when we are dealing with what might at first seem a simple UFO sighting involving a light in the sky many varying factors can come into operation. The social setting, the psychological and physiological state of the witness, the situation, etc., can have as much significance as in more elaborate UFO reports. This is confirmed by reference to the 1913 'airship' sightings as outlined above, or by more contemporary reports which indicate that celestial bodies, such as Venus, can give rise to reports of Adamski-type scout-ships scaring housewives [7]. Lastly, the autokinetic effect could be responsible for certain types of entity reports such as those reported by mountaineers or people in similar situations where perceptual clues are lacking[8].

•

Nigel Watson

REFERENCES

1) Gregory, R.L. *The Intelligent Eye*, Weidenfeld & Nicholson (1971) p11.

2) Murray, W.H., *Mountaineering In Scotland,* Dent (1947) pp 140 & 214.

3) Ross, Dr Helen, *Behaviour and Perception in Strange Environments,* G.Allen & Unwin (1974).

4) Mayman, M. & Voth, H.M., 'Reality Closeness, Phantasy, and Autokinesis: A Dimension of Cognitive Style', *Journal of Abnormal Psychology* (1969) Vol. 74, pp635-641.

5) Bush, M., Hatcher, R. & Mayman, M., 'Reality Attentiveness-Inattentiveness and Externalization—Internalization in Defensive Style', *Journal of Consulting and Clinical Psychology* (1969) Vol. 33, pp343-350.

6) Pitts, D.G., *'Visual Illusions and Aircraft Accidents',* SAM-TR-67-28, USAF School of Aerospace Medicine, Brooks Air Force Base, Texas (1967).

7) Randles, J., 'Vendetta with Venus', *MUFOB*, Nos. 14 (Spring 1979) pp15-18.

8) Not everyone is convinced of the importance of the auto-kinetic effect in relation to UFO sightings, **Anthony Durham and Keith Watkins** in 'Visual Perception of UFOs: Part 2', *(Flying Saucer Review,* Vol. 13, No. 4, 1967) state that; 'Under normal conditions we think it unlikely that this illusion would give many UFO reports, except that excitement or old age may exaggerate the illusion.' (p25) Unfortunately, when UFO sightings are made 'normal conditions' do not usually prevail!

Doc Shiels Words from the Wizard

When a Twister a-twisting will twist him a twist,
For the twisting of his twist, he three times doth untwist,
But if one of the twines of the twist do untwist,
The twine that untwisteth, untwisteth the twist.

★ ★ ★

To a busking thimble-rigger, such as myself, the archaeological term 'Cup and Ring marks' invokes a picture of a group of 'marks', meaning 'gulls' 'punters', members of a 'hedge' or audience, ready to be hood-winked by a presentation of the 'Cups', meaning the old 'shell game' or 'Cups and Balls', and the 'Rings', meaning the Chinese 'Linking Rings'....two of the oldest conjuring tricks in the world, and the two which I happen to use more than any others when busking. The term also describes a type of megalithic decoration, those carved concentric circles, spirals and rings which, along with straight, serpentine, or zig-zag lines, are so familiar to ley-hunters, geomancers and students of ancient Celtic history. I suspect a lexilink....a kind of private coded message, nudging me into a semantic examination of those symbols, both lexically and visually.

★ ★ ★

Let's begin with the spiral, that spinning, twisting, coiling shape. Etymologically, it is Greek, signifying the breath of life, or spirit. We can read it as the coiled serpent or worm; and the coil means power, as in an electrical induction coil, a transformer, producing high voltage from low votlage. A worm is spiral, like the copper pipe used as a condenser in a poteen still....illicit spiral spirit, the holy water of life. Another worm is the helical groove in a shaft, as used in gear arrangements, where it meshes with a zig-zag toothed wheel. Energy and power. Think of the coiled steel spring, storing potential energy when compressed, releasing it when....sprung! Suddenly, upwards, unexpected, escaping, leaping, jumping, Spring Heeled Jack!

★ ★ ★

Jack be nimble, Jack be quick, Jack jump over the candlestick.

★ ★ ★

Now, there's a thing. Old Jack the springer. Jack-in-the-Box. Jack the Jackass, male and jackphallic. Jacko Jackanapes, the hairy ape. Jackdaw, the thieving black crow-bird. Black Jack, the knave of cudgels. Jackpudding, the fool. Jack Frost's twisting ferns on the winter windows. Jack O'Lantern, the pumpkin-head or ignis fatuus. Jackstones, knucklebones. Jack Tar with his pitch black curly pigtail. Jumping Jack Flash, the gas-gas-gasser. Jumping Jacky jiggy-doll. Crackerjack, the zig-zag, fork lightning firework Jack-ladder, a rope ladder to the sky. Jack Ketch, the rope twisting hangman. Jack-knife, zig-zag sharply. Jack the Ripper, rip-rap, R.I.P., jacking off in the jacks, the rippler.... rip-tide....Rip Hepple? Help!

★ ★ ★

Jack: A hydraulic device for exerting a large force to raise things.

★ ★ ★

Jack and Jill went up the hill to fetch a pail of water.

★ ★ ★

Hydraulic? Water? Interesting!

★ ★ ★

Spring Heeled Jack had claws

on his fingers to rip off women's clothes. He had red eyes, pointed ears, and he spat blue flames in women's faces. He wore a black helmet and a black cloak. He had a large 'W' embroidered on the front of his jump-suit, and some say he was the Marquis of Waterford, playing pranks in fancy dress. 'W' is the 23rd letter of the alphabet....twenty three skidoo, Weishaupt and Wilson! Wilson (viz: Robert Anton, Kenneth, and Colin) is a name with weird worm and wizardry associations, so we will keep it in mind; but back to Jack. The 'W' or double-U could, in fact, be a double-V....or even a zig-zagging triple-V. *VVV* was the title of a famous surrealist magazine, published in the nineteen forties. Issue No.2-3 (significant?), with a cover designed by the arch-dada Duchamp, contained an article by William 'Voodoo' Seabrook, a 'Prognostication by Paracelsus' annotated by Kurt Seligman, and a piece on H.P. Lovecraft by Robert Allerton Parker. Keep that in mind as well; and think of 'V' for Vampire, 'V' for Viper, 'V' for Vaulting.

* * *

Zig-zag, jig-jag, jagged rip-saw blade. Joking Jack, jiggling up and down, jig-a-jig, the dancing gigolo, on a boozing jag, or a jazzy gig, spinning like a gig-top. Reeling drunk, jiggery pokery Sheela-na-gig. Irish jigs and Irish reels as played in County Waterford, in monster-haunted Munster.

* * *

A reel can be a spook, too, a spiral winding of film or re-cording tape, for example. A disc recording has a spiral groove, and dada Duchamp made magical roto-reliefs by painting eccentric and con-centric circles on gramophone records. When they revolved, a three-dimensional pattern was eerily created.

* * *

There's an old Dublin busker, a harmonica-blower, by the name of Jacko, who sleeps in a cardboard box. And

there's a famous Irish 'box' (button accordion) player called Jacky, in a group called De Dannan. A Jack-in-the-Box is sometimes called a 'Jacky Jump Up., and a well known song from County Cork is 'Johnny Jump Up' which celebrates the effects of a powerful kind of cider (Cork screw....applejack?). The song has been recorded (spirally) by the Cork singer (and box player) Jimmy Crowley....and Crowley is an interesting name.

* * *

Crow.... Ley.... straight as the crow flies.

* * *

Twist about, turn about, and do just so, Every time I wheel about I jump Jim Crow.

* * *

Crowley's band is called Stoker's Lodge. Ireland's most famous Stoker was Bram, who wrote about someone who slept in a box. Think of the silent film *Nosferatu*, with Max Shreck as the vampire.... pointed ears, sharp claws, Max-in-the-Box. The 'Lodge' could be the Golden Dawn, with which Stoker is said to have had connections, as did Aleister Crowley.

* * *

The 'A' in Aleister Crowley's signature is a phallus. Reversed, this sign becomes the 'Spectacle' shape on the 'hood' of a cobra. It is also a common megalithic symbol. Another is the line rising from the centre of a circle or spiral, which could be seen either as a repre-sentation of a snake in a snake-charmer's basket, or the Indian/Irish Rope Trick. It can also be read as a long-necked serpent rising up through the concentric ripple rings in a Celtic lake. St. Patrick ban-ished all the serpents, including zig-zag patterned vipers, from the shamrock shores....but he was a Paddy-come-lately, and we are dealing with pre-Christian powers. Remember, we Celts come from the Indus Valley. The Rope Trick is reported in some very old Irish folk tales which tell of a

(Jack) hare being made to run up the rope 'air ladder', chased by a hound, a milkmaid and a boy. Snakes and Ladders! Other so-called Cup and Ring markings look very much like Houdini-Style handcuffs or leg-irons....and Jack-in-Irons is a giant, manacled, bogie man. Testicles, spectacles, miracles, manacles....what else?

* * *

A wiggling sperm....or a wilting spoon? 'Do as thou wilt shall be the whole of the law'. Wiltshire-space-shuttle-wood-henge-hinge-swing-pendulously. A silver spoon in the Great Beast's gob, with brewer's droop. Pissed as a newt and neutered by the uric gelder. What a bender!

* * *

You see how it keeps working? The romping, punning, lexi-linking, visulinking, synchron-istic symbolism. One of the things that Crowley did with the brewery gelt was to purchase Boleskine house, over-looking Loch Ness, and call himself MacGregor (like his chum, Mathers....another funny fellow). Did I say 'brewery'? Yes....Aleister's puritanical dad was a brewer of ale. Ale....as in Ale-ister....or even in Dinsd-ale. Two Loch Ness names containing booze. Now, let's push it further. I often contain the stuff myself and my favourite tipple is Guinness.... Ireland's crow-black marvelous brew. G....U....IN....NESS. There's a pretty phrase. The 'In Ness' part is obvious enough, but what do we make of 'G' and 'U'? Uri Geller and Uri, perhaps? Godzilla of Urquhart....the Gargoyle Underwater.... Gro-tesquely Upstanding.... Goblin Universe? Take your pick, it's a wide open game with very few fixed rules. G.U. could be Guy Underwood (or Geodetic Uffington), the gyrating, un-dulating dowser. Spinning us back to the Cup and Ring marks. 'G' for Grail.... 'U' for Uther, the Pendragon and father of Arthur. Arthur the father of Guinness. Cup and Ring.... Holy Grail and

Round Table. A. Guinness, brewer to the magi. Real Guinness is brewed in Dublin (Duibhlinn, meaning Black Pool), and the town was built below a fenced ford (whence its current Irish Gaelic name, Baile Atha Cliath) where an ancient trackway crossed the Liffey. The brewery at St. James's Gate (gateway to the West) was purchased (by Arthur Guinness, in 1759) from the brewer, Rainford, a name which lexilinks to Waterford and other significant watery fords.

* * *

A. Guinness....that's a mixture of 'genius' and A.N.S. (my initials, folks!). How about 'A' for Awe, 'N' for Ness and 'S' for Shiel; three Highland lochs, famous for their monsters? The 'genius' is the 'genius loci' or guardian spirit of a place, and the word is derived from the Arabic 'Djinnee'....a demon sometimes found in a bottle.

* * *

Maybe some megalithic marks are bent spoons? Uri is lexi-linked and visu-linked with beer and surrealism. For example, we can obtain the anagramtic advertising phrase 'Mr Uri's Ales' from the word 'Surrealism'....and the name 'Uri' is contained in the middle of 'Maurice'.... 'Burton' being the beery surname. The word 'Uruisg' is Gelleric Gaelic for goblin, demon or monster. Uri's harshest critic is the Amazing Randi, whose real name, Randell Zwinge, can be turned into 'And Geller winz'. Salvador Dali anticipated the 'Geller Effect' in several paintings, the most obvious being 'The Persistance of Memory' (1931) with its wilting watches .... 'the camemberts of time and space', said Dali, giving a new meaning to the idea of a 'running' watch. 'Time and space' invokes (apart from Yuri Gagarin) Albert ('watch-chain') Einstein.... of Z-URI-CH (birthplace of Dada and Joyce's 'Ulysses'). 'Einstein' means, literally, a 'stone' or a beer mug. The American writer Gertrude Stein introduced Sir

Peter Scott's mother, the sculptress Kathleen Bruce, to some of the early surrealists.... but enough of that.

* * *

'Monster Hoax by Sir Peter.S.' is a cruel but splendid anagram created from Scott's zoological Latin *Nessiteras Rhombopteryx* ....which can also be turned into (as I discovered when my No.1. Nessie picture appeared on the front page of the *Daily Mirror*) 'Tony's ESP Beats Hex.... "Mirror"'. Scott is a name long associated with magic (Michael, Reginald, and Sir Walter, for instance).... but enough of that, too.

* * *

During the writing of this piece (April 1982), a beautifully Fortean twist suddenly occurred, as these things will. One day, I popped down to Maguire's pub for a lunchtime jar of the dark stuff, and fell into conversation with a man from Cork. I asked him if he had heard of the Ballyvourney Lynx (see FT 34). My friend, misunderstanding, replied that he wasn't aware of any links at Ballyvourney but was familiar with the nine hole course at Macroom. For a moment I looked at him in dumb puzzlement until it dawned on me that he was talking about golf links. 'Oh....I meant the animal, the tufty-eared lynx.

Get some g-r-r-r in your game with Lynx. Bred in the U.S. and set free in the UK by Trendan Sports. Bell Lane, Uckfield, East Sussex TN22 1QL Tel: Uckfield (0825) 61266

Nothing to do with golf,' said I. 'Don't be so sure of that,' said he, enigmatically. Links.... lynx....links? That night, having a bit of a nose for things pretentous, I picked up a book which I had first read about seven or eight years ago, *Golf in the Kingdom* by Michael Murphy. It described the author's mystical adventures on the links at 'Burningbush' in the Scottish kingdom of Fife. The hero of the tale is a strange shamanic figure, a golfing pro named Shivas Irons (and there's a name for lexilinkers to conjur with), who changed Murphy's vision of the world. The book, though teasingly truncated, is packed with signs and clues relating to things I had been writing about. All night I thought about golf....a game I hadn't played for nearly thirty years....becoming more and more convinced that it contained some profound and important secret. Next day, in a newsagent's shop, I opened a golfing magazine, and there, staring me in the face, was a surrealist photograph of a yellow-eyed lynx! It was an ad for Lynx golf clubs (see illustration), and it gave me quite a turn....it *had* to mean something. Since that moment (two weeks ago. I'm writing this at Beltane), I have been obsessed with the mysterious, royal and ancient game.

★ ★ ★

Hickory.... Dickory.... Doc!

★ ★ ★

Today, armed with a bag of antique, hickory-shafted clubs and a half a dozen battered pills, I'm off to the green fields of Pelean for two hours of ritual May Day hooking, slicing, topping and divot cutting. It's perfect golfing weather. The grass on the hill puts springs on your heels, and the gorse blossom is burning bright. By the time this reaches the printed page, I'm hoping that my grooved swing will be smooth and rhythmic, my drive long and straight as a ley-line, and the ball rolling merrily into the cup, for a bogey at least, on each and every hole of each and every Kerry course I mean, most earnestly, to play.

●

Doc Shiels.

This column is open to any reader who wishes to express an opinion, or to speculate, upon any topic related to the content or interests of FT. However entries must be typed and limited to no more than two pages.

THE WHIRLWIND THEORY OF FISH FALLS

Over the past few years there has been considerable discussion in the pages of FT about falls of fish, frogs and other unusual matter. There has been some reluctance to accept the conventional whirlwind explanation of such falls. Certainly there have been some cases which, if correctly reported, are difficult to ascribe to a whirlwind, but I believe that Forteans should accept the standard explanations if they clearly fit the facts (then we are on stronger ground when we produce genuinely anomalous data) and that the whirlwind theory does fit the facts in the case of fish and frog showers at least. In the past some scientists have gone so far as to deny the existence of these remarkable showers — see Frank Lane's *The Elements Rage* — but, as Lane observes, this view is so obscurantist as to imply an inability to evaluate evidence properly. Some frog showers, however, in which the frogs were not actually seen to fall, were probably nothing more than swarms of young frogs that had emerged as a result of a rainstorm.

Forteans have raised objections to the whirlwind theory that seem to me unnecessary. In issue 1 of FT, p.9, for instance, is the comment that the whirlwind theory "does not explain the extraordinary selection that goes on. Often the fish, toads, worms, whatever are of the same size; or in the same state living or dead; or uniformly of the same species (often completely foreign to within thousands of miles — and if they did stay up there, 'tens of thousands' of them, by some means, how could they stay alive for that time?"

There seems to me nothing remarkable about the creatures all being the same size. Sticklebacks in a pond *will* be much the same size, and so will young frogs and toads that have just metamorphosed from the tadpole state; and I cannot see how the fact that they are all alive or all dead is a problem. As to uniformity of species, a pond or stream may well contain thousands of minnows and no other fish, or thousands of young frogs and no toads. In any case, how many times have the specimens been looked at carefully enough to make sure that they *were* all the same species? In the South Wales fish fall of 1859 [FT30p38-42], where the fish were examined properly, more than one species was found. And if you saw hundreds of fish wriggling on the ground would you notice a few water beetles and pond snails mixed in with them? (apart from the fact that the insects might have flown away, or been segregated by the whirlwind).

The problem of 'foreign' species is more difficult, but I would like to see more evidence that the creatures really were alien to the district. Whirlwinds, at least in Britain, do not usually last long enough to transport anything more than a few miles. There can be no question of a whirlwind carrying specifically North African fish to Britain, for instance. But because whirlwinds are usually short-lived there does not seem any difficulty in explaining how the animals (even fish) stay alive in the air. Where dried fish have fallen I assume they were removed from a dried up lake.

In FT13, on p.8 is the statement "We admit that some frogs have fallen by whirlwinds — others have been seen falling with no whirlwind about." Presumably the frogs are released when the whirlwind dissipates; also it must be remembered that the tornado type of whirlwind does not always have a visible funnel cloud. However, it is true that not many of the fish and frog showers were seen to be accompanied by a whirlwind, so it may be as well to put on record some that were.

I came across the first example several years ago in *The Excitement*, a little book published at Edinburgh in 1830. In probably about 1760, we were told: "They were surrounded with water spouts, one of which was very near, and they fired to disperse it. The roaring was tremendous, and presently a torrent of water poured on the ship, which brought down with it many fish and sea weeds." About a year ago I found a second case in *Whitaker's Almanac* for 1937, which was probably quoting *The Times* for 23 January 1936. *The Times* stated: "Violent whirlwinds accompanied a storm which broke over Florence on Monday, and among various objects which were seen spinning in the air were some big fish which had evidently been drawn out of the River Arno."

Last Autumn, on 27 September 1981, there was a possible fall of two crabs at Killay, near Swansea [see FT37p48—Ed] Reporting this in the *Journal of Meteorology* for December 1981 Dr. Terence Meaden mentioned three other relevant cases: a fall of four crabs near Canterbury on 19 July 1829, associated with a local 'hurricane'; a tornado and fish fall in September 1838 near Jedburgh in southern Scotland; and a waterspout off Hong Kong on 29 September 1839 which deposited seaweed and a few fish on the land.

Recently I was sent a letter by a Mr or Mrs E. Singleton who had witnessed a whirlwind near Newton-le-Willows, Merseyside, around 1947. This letter was in response to an appeal of mine in the *Manchester Evening News* asking for reports of whirlwinds. "I saw flocks of birds suddenly appear from behind me. Looking back the reason was obvious, for approaching rapidly was a whirlwind which was carrying all sorts of debris. I threw my two children to the floor and lay on top of them while the wind passed by about 30 yards away. It travelled directly over a huge pond which was locally known as Thompson's Pit. Half the water together with the fish, frogs and weed was carried away and was found deposited on house tops half a mile away.... We have laughed about it since but at the time it was a most frightening experience."

•

Mike Rowe
Tornado & Storm Research Organisation.
Flat 2, 2 Wilton Avenue,
Southampton.

ON THE TRAIL
by Loren Coleman

THE URBAN JUNGLE

(During the first week in October 1982 reports out of Hoboken, New Jersey, told of an apelike creature quickly labelled "Monkeyman". Unlike the locale for the Bigfoot accounts from the Pacific northwest, Hoboken is not a heavily forested wilderness area. Instead it is a one square mile community of 43,000 people situated on the Hudson River, not far from New York City.

"Seems that a fellow who hadn't been shaving much lately was spotted hanging around a Hoboken playground", noted the *New York Post*. The stories about the thing developed to the point, the paper went on, so: "within days, mysterious hunchbacked Monkeyman — half ape, half human, all rumor — was terrorizing school hallways, throwing students out of windows, and killing a teacher."

The explosive nature of the tales surprised school officials, and police authorities. Soon the "wipe" was in full force to bury the entire story. Public Safety Director, James Giordano, flatly told the press: "There is no Monkeyman, no students missing, no children missing. We went looking for him — he wasn't even in the streets. But how do you stop a rumor that's spreading like wildfire?"

Detective Commander Patrick Donatacci continued this line of thinking in his comments. "It's just a vicious rumor that got out of hand. It's a strange thing — once they hear something, they don't believe the truth when they hear it. They'd rather believe fiction."

On Friday, October 15, the local authorities were still so upset by the Monkeyman accounts they formed a task force to enlighten all teachers and principals as to the facts or nonfacts behind the case. As the New York Post cleverly put it: "In an effort to kill a monster that never existed, cops in Hoboken, N.J. are spreading the word around grade school that Monkeyman is a lot of monkey business." Safety Director Giordano's three man Juvenile Aid Bureau were given a task they probably never could have imagined they would be assigned, namely to wipe out an entity entitled Monkeyman.

This current monster has echoes of other shadowy beasts of the urban jungle. In a recent issue of FATE magazine I noted the wave of "phantom clown" accounts* which swept across many widely separated Midwestern and Eastern United States cities in May of 1981. Some bizarre creatures, however, have also been encountered in the last couple of decades in the concrete morass of America. Some of these incidents have been more amusing than frightening.

ST. LOUIS' THING
In 1963, from about the 9th of May until the 23rd of that month, St. Louis, Missouri and Centreville, Illinois were engulfed in flap after flap of strange monster stories.

Several youngsters reported a "halfman, half woman with a half bald head and a half head of hair." The thing was said to be a sometime resident of the Ninth Street housing project, and would disappear into an old subway on 12th Street. Sounding more like a "dero" on an excursion from the underground than a cryptozoological specimen, this St. Louis "thing" was taken seriously by the police.

"Those kids were sincere. They saw something," said Patrolman Bill Conreux of the St. Louis Police Department. "Supposedly it scuffed with a man near the Patrick Henry School."

Soon thereafter, on the 18th of May 1963, Centreville, Illinois, just across the Mississippi River from St. Louis, was visited by a bizarre denizen of the unknown. Police received fifty calls about a monster reported in the area. One man, James McKinney, said the monster, which he described as half man and half horse, was in front of his house. Reports died down with only three calls to the police coming in on the 23rd of that crazy month in 1963.

EMBASSY ROW'S ELUSIVE LION
If a "Monkeyman" in Hoboken and Centaurs in the St. Louis area were not enough, then a lion loose in the District of Columbia may convince you some strange phantom inhabitants of the urban jungle are making themselves known.

On the tenth day of August, 1982, uniformed Secret Service officer Leonard G. Gooch spied a mysterious feline "about half the size of a full grown lion" scurrying between the stately mansions along Massachusetts Avenue N.W., and disappearing behind the Iranian Embassy. Over fifty law enforcement officers, National Zoo vets, and other official searchers did some intensive searching with no luck. Yes, one "gray fox-sized" animal was flushed out of the woods, and humorous news accounts tried to quip that the beast might turn out to be a field mouse. However, with a police helicopter hovering over head as this latest creature disappeared into the annals of urban phantom critters, we must guess the answers hardly lie in the realm of mice.

A HIGHRISE ELEPHANT
Years of stories of phantom pachyderms have issued from the ancient Indian grounds around Baraboo, Wisconsin. Such tales sit nicely in the minds of cryptozoologist and folklorist as the possible remembrance of massive mastodons and thus seem plausible. Or within the conceptual framework of the parapsychologist maybe these ghostly tuskers could be explainable as haunts from the Ice Age voids of America. But how in the world are we to include rumors, sightings, and bureaucratic search parties of a small invasion of his home territory by such a large uncatchable? But here we have it, the New York Times and other Big Apple papers of May 3, 1979, informing an unsuspecting public of the reports of a little elephant seen near a warehouse in the Bay Ridge area of Brooklyn, New York. The classic search party — individuals from the Bureau of Animal Affairs, City Health Department and the American Society for the Prevention of Cruelty to Animals — looked and questioned and looked and queried, all to no avail. Even local television station, Channel 5, sent up a helicopter, another classic part of the safari syndrome which came out in Washington, D.C.'s lion hunt as well, without results.

Dr. Howard Levin of The New York City Bureau of Animal Affairs probably thought he was pretty close to finding his quarry at one point, for he asked one Bay Ridge resident: "Have you ever seen an elephant about the neighborhood?"

After solemn consideration the man answered, "What kind?" •

Loren Coleman
[*See 'A Circle of Clowns' p16]

BOOK ALERT!

by JANET BORD

Recently the publishing scene has been quiet so far as Fortean Books are concerned, perhaps recovering from the euphoria engendered at the time of publication of *Arthur C. Clarke's Mysterious World* when it seemed that the media could not get enough of Forteana. However, the double event of the birth of this column and the publication of Bob Rickard's and John Michell's eagerly awaited follow-up to *Phenomena, Living Wonders*, perhaps heralds a new era in Fortean books. At any rate, there are a number of good things lined up for you to read, some of them iminent as I write, others still only in embryo form.

I will start with books which are due for publication during the autumn and winter of 1982, and of course *Living Wonders* must head the list as it is essential reading for all Forteans. The first publication is the U.K. hardback, from Thames and Hudson in October 1982, price £8.95. Next will be the U.S. paperback (no hardback), due in March 1983 from Thames and Hudson, Inc., followed in October 1983 by the U.K. paperback edition, again from T&H. There will also be a German hardback edition, from Econ Verlag.

Another well-known Fortean, Loren Coleman, also has a new book out this winter,

Weird Excursions Across America, to be published by Charles River Books, Boston. Loren is also a contributor to another American book due during the autumn — *Sasquatches and Unknown Hominoids*, edited by Vladimir Markotic (publisher unknown). The book will include chapters by 17 specialists on different aspects of Bigfoot and his kin.

Four new UFO titles are also due this autumn, two originating in Britain being Paul Devereux's *Earth Lights* (Turnstone, £9.95, October) and a 64-page study by Steuart Campbell of a strange Scottish case: *Close Encounters at Livingston* (BUFORA Case History No. 1, £5.25, October). From North America comes *The Andreasson Affair: Phase Two, The Continuing Investigation of a Woman's Abduction by Alien Beings* by Raymond E. Fowler (Prentice-Hall); and *In Advance of the Landing: Folk Concepts of Outer Space*, by Doug Curran (McClelland & Stewart, Toronto). Curran is a photographer who has travelled widely since 1977, studying and photographing people and objects relating to outer space, including people who build rockets in their barns, or quietly make preparations for the landing of extraterrestrial beings.

The Camera Never Lies, subtitled, 'A Book of Bizarre

and Unusual Photographs' and coming from Webb & Bower in November 1982 (price £4.95) is an unknown quantity which sounds as though it might contain some material of interest to Forteans. Those who have read Andy Collins' amazing tale *The Sword and the Stone* and wish to learn more should look out for *The Green Stone* by Martin Keatman and Graham Phillips, due from Neville Spearman late in 1982. Three new paperbacks from U.K. publishers are *Recollections of Death* by Dr. Michael B. Sabom (Corgi, October), *Poltergeist* by Colin Wilson (New English Library, December, £2.25), *Mysteries from Forgotten Worlds* by Charles Berlitz (Granada, January 1983, £1.50).

Moving further into 1983, the prolific Jenny Randles has two new books for publication, preceded by a paperback edition of her *Alien Contact*, duefrom Coronet in February. In the summer Robert Hale will publish her *UFO Reality* in hardback (the final and possibly the best book in her UFO trilogy. Jenny comments: 'I regard the book as about as far as I can go with the UFO subject', but I doubt her pen will be still for long, and we look forward to reading more of Jenny's thought-provoking work). Also mid-year Granada will publish (in paperback only) Jenny's *The Pennine UFO Mystery* an account of UFO activity in an area of northern England since 1972, culminating in the strange case of a policeman abducted from his patrol car and bringing in general information on abductions, hypnotic regression, and the piezo-electric effect.

Probably most of the following books will also be published during 1983. Those readers who, like me, were brought into the 'earth mysteries' and 'strange phenomena' fields through reading John Michell's classic work *The View Over Atlantis* will be delighted to learn that *Continued on p48*

A Circle of Clowns.

Man has always been intrigued and mystified by the way the events in his life occasionally form meaningful clusters, in which seemingly unconnected incidents and data from the most unexpected quarters appear to relate to each other significantly. **Bob Tarte** and **Bill Holm** send us this example on the themes of clowns and the number 22. They invite readers with odd stories of clowns or 22 to write to them at: 15 Prospect SE, Grand Rapids, MI 49503, USA.

"I think we are cattle."
Charles Fort

"I think we are Bobo's cattle."
R. Charles Tarte

In February, 1981, while Robert Tarte and William Holm were driving through a vaguely rural region of north-east Grand Rapids. Tarte swore out loud that he saw a mailbox near the road bearing the name A.CLOWN. A few days later the two men scoured the area for the mailbox without success.

On the night of March 25 they were within blocks of Tarte's apparition after an evening of video games at the Crystal Cue, when a battered white Chevy pulled up alongside Tarte's Subaru. The Chevy carried a plump, grizzled driver and bore the title BOBO THE ROLLER CLOWN in large letters above the fender. Two clown faces and the motto TAKE A CLOWN TO LUNCH adorned the front door. At the sight of Bobo in his car, Tarte pulled into the lot of a supermarket where the two men struggled to catch their breaths.

For one full year Tarte and Holm had been haunted by clowns—but never in such intimate, terrifying circumstances. The barrage had mainly consisted of clown photos on newspaper feature pages; magazine covers; clowns known selling products on television; and through Hollywood personalities like Mickey Rooney and Anthony Newley using clown characters to revitalize their careers. According to Tarte, the blitz had been initiated by a scene in his super-8mm film "Monsters", where Holm sat fully dressed in a bathtub contemplating the globe through a clown mask and giant comic sunglasses.

As the phenomena developed, the clowns threatened to merge with other coincidences and symbols, notably the ghostly number 22. Holm claimed Bobo was the latest taunting expression of the Lord of 22. Tarte, then untouched by the number which gnawed at Holm, disagreed. However, the flesh and blood appearance of the Roller Clown convinced both men beyond a doubt that whatever the force was, it was authentic, personal, and had a name.

One week after the shock of Bobo's car, a Peter Sellers' film, "The Bobo" was scheduled on a cable-tv-satellite channel from Atlanta. Prophesying a revelation, Holm insisted they watch. But when the tv was switched on at 2:20 the film wasn't on. In its place was the inexplicable rebroadcast of a tennis match that had just ended on another station. Elsewhere on the cable dial there was an absurd amount of news and features about race car driver Mario Andretti.

That night they sought consolation at the Northtown Theatre in the newest film by Jerry Lewis, one of their least favorite matinee stars. "Hardly Working" turned out to be the tale of an out of work clown named Bo, effectionately **known as Bobo. When Bobo met his girlfriend at** a tennis match—a mockery of Tarte and Holm 's interrupted afternoon— Tarte sighed, "If Mario Andretti comes on, I'm leaving." Moments later, as Bo sped through a residential neighbourhood in his mail truck, his movie buddy exclaimed, "Who do you think you are, Mario Andretti?"

The mailman connection was underscored when "Hardly Working" appeared later at the Northtown with "The Postman Always Rings Twice." Earlier that year, Holm's friend Steve Williams wrote him an annoying letter from Cloquet, Minn., with an address he had found containing an inordinate concentration of 22s: 1222 N 22nd Street, Arlington, Va., 22202. About the time of the Bobo sighting a complicated web of circumstances landed Williams a job he had not sought as a legislative aid for Congressman Harold Sawyer in Washington, D.C. He now lives on 3rd Road in Arlington within blocks of the address he jokingly sent Holm. Nearly every morning he leaves his apartment for work to find a Yellow Cab outside bearing the phone number 527-2222. The number for the police department in Arlington is 558-2222.

Williams should have known better than to tweak the nose of the Lord of 22. He was, after all, the man who first discovered the 22 phenomenon while a law school student at Wayne State University. On his way to class one day he got stuck in a traffic jam behind Detroit bus number 2222 while his car radio was playing the theme from "Room 222" ("And how many times do you ever hear *that* on the radio?" demanded Williams).

Another of Holm's friends, Dave Bartek—then of Flint, Michigan—had experienced his own brush with the forces of Bobo before Holm had mentioned the Roller Clown incident. One day after Holm had been troubled by a number of clown related occurrences, Bartek called Holm at work over the toll-free WATS line at IBM he had grown to abuse.

Holm related some of the recent clown stories to his friend. They had been weighing heavily upon Holm and he needed to talk it out. Bartek listened patiently. Then, with a strange calm in his voice, he said, "Well, that explains why I saw what I saw." A short time earlier he had been staring out his window at work and saw a clown hitchhiking. A few days later from the same window he saw a clown on a bicycle; in the parking lot the license plate of the car closest to Bartek read number 222.

Bartek now lives on N.22nd Street in Phoenix, Ariz. He left Flint for a new job on June 22, owing $22,000 on his Michigan condominium. Bartek, who complains of frequently leaving his body at inconvenient moments, has experienced the most eccentric clown activity of any of Tarte and Holm's friends. Recently, after seeing clowns in a Phoenix shopping mall, he returned to his car, a light blue Ford Fairmont with a white interior, to find it encircled by two dozen balloons colored white and blue.

Dennis Keller, a Grand Rapids cartoonist and book collector, was also assaulted by clowns after hearing the tale of Bobo. Once, after spotting a clown in front of the Masonic Temple a scant block from Tarte and Holm's apartment, two clowns smoking cigarettes passed in another car. Keller, the first to notice the unsettling *ordinariness* of most of the clown encounters, would later play a key role in the punchline of Bobo's 18-month long joke.

Meanwhile on June 13 Tarte and Holm planned to attend the Pan Pagan Festival in Southern Michigan with David Fideler. Fideler cancelled due to rain. Eager to leave town for the day the two men drove to the resort town of Saugatuck on Lake Michigan. Tarte was interested in finding Toys Ahoy and combed the streets with Holm for the shop. Along the way they passed a clown. When they finally got to the store it was closed, but the owner, there on an errand, let them in for a moment. Soon it became clear why fate took them inside. The last entry in the guest register near the door was MR. BUM THE CLOWN signed in a bold hand some two weeks earlier on Memorial Day.

Since the clowns wouldn't leave them alone whatever they did, the men decided to try and get the jump on Bobo. Thumbing through the phone book, Holm came upon a K.Bobo listed two blocks down Prospect, the street he and Tarte lived on. Plucking up their courage, the pair drove through a light drizzle past K.Bobo's

home. Directly in front was parked a Mr.Jolly ice cream truck decorated with clownish figures. It sat there every night throughout the summer. Sometimes there were two.

Thereafter Tarte and Holm were unable to leave their apartment day or night without Mr. Jolly trucks crossing their paths. One June morning the van was illegally parked for hours outside Holm's window at work. Bartek chose that day to phone from Flint and tell Holm he was quitting IBM—and giving his resignation to his supervisor, a Mr. Jolly.

Then on June 16 the ceiling fell in. Holm stumbled across an article on the "Names and Faces" page of the Detroit Free Press about a man so obsessed with the number 22 that he had changed his name to LOVE 22. According to the story, 22 was arrested in New Orleans for selling phony $22 bills adorned with his picture for 22 cents to finance his 1984 Presidential campaign— since 1+9+8+4=22. This was the first confirmation of the 22 curse beyond Holm's tiny circle of friends, and Holm was stunned.

The news troubled Tarte, but worse was to come. When Tarte called Fideler with Holm's 22-calibre bombshell Fideler countered with a missile of his own. *FT* columnist Loren Coleman had that day sent him an announcement of a coast-to-coast Fortean Alert; the subject: phantom clowns. Their personal torment had gone national.

Tarte immediately phoned Coleman, introduced himself, and began meticulously detailing the events that had led up to that moment. An intrigued Coleman answered with his reasons for interest in the clowns—a wave of clowns in vans trying to kidnap children in St. Louis, Kansas City, Pittsburgh, Boston and Denver. Coleman was writing these up for *Fate* magazine.

After that night it was as if something had burst, bringing an incessant rain of clowns and 22s. The atmosphere at Holm's office at Grand Rapids Magazine grew especially turbulent. Co-worker Bonnie Hanger got a porcelain clown music box from her mother on her 22nd birthday. Holm's boss John Brosky was downtown in Kalamazoo when a golf cart carrying two clowns drove slowly by. They wore name tags. HI, I'M BOBO, said the driver's; HI, I'M JOHNO, the passenger's. Then, the following poem from New York was inexplicably submitted for publication: "A raving beauty / Got into a stew, / She finished a contest / Raving 'Oh, 22!'"

For a week in September Grand Rapids was briefly in the national news as hoardes of politicians and tv personalities arrived for the opening of the Gerald R. Ford Presidential Museum. Tarte speculated it was a good week for an appearance by Bobo. Holm said he feared an assassination attempt on Ford or Reagan. A few days later on Sept. 21 the Grand Rapids Press reported the murder of a local man named (Henry) Ford witnessed by Danny Bobo.

Though the clown activity was constant, it seemed to have lost its intensity—more background hum than thunderclap. Both men speculated that Bobo had done all he could, that a new cycle of symbols was on its way instead. They tried to stand back and grapple with what had happened. "Bobo," insisted Holm, "is an agent of the Lord of 22, who is probably the First Cause, the Earth Spirit. Only by playing with the absurdities of clowns in popular culture could he get my attention so I could realize his or her power and be saved." Tarte took Bobo's appearances personally, bearing them a grudge. "The unrelenting presence of a Cosmic Clown is a slap at my Catholic-bred agnosticism," he sulked. "Only a figure as stupid as Bobo would make me long for an intelligent deity."

Just when it seemed Bobo had finished with their lives, Keller phoned Tarte and invited him to his house to meet a friend, Arlene Samrick. Urged by Keller to unburden himself of the clown saga, Tarte reluctantly started to unfold the strange events to 'Sam'. No sooner had he begun, however, when 'Sam' said blandly, "Oh, Bobo the Roller Clown. He lives on Four Mile by the Stop 'n' Go."

At first light the two frightened men piled bravely into Tarte's Subaru and headed for the neighbourhood where Tarte thought he'd seen the A.CLOWN mailbox seven months previous; near where they'd encountered the Roller Clown car. Parking near the Stop 'n' Go convenience store, they set out on foot armed with Tarte's high speed auto-focus SX-70, walking towards a group of mailboxes. There they found it. The last one read BOBO in two-inch high letters, and on the front the name Leo Torpey. The box looked freshly painted, as though another name—such as A.CLOWN—might have been covered up.

The events had come full circle. They had exploded out of one clown in a car, spread to their friends, then across the country, only to collapse again into a flesh and blood Bobo, the punchline of a year-and-a-half long joke. Tarte and Holm saw the house. They saw the mailbox that said Bobo. But they have not gone back since then.

The circle was complete. It was time to move on.

Bob Tarte - Bill Holm

Continued from p45

Thames and Hudson are to publish a new and revised edition with new photographs. John is also revising *City of Revelation* for T&H; and there is to be a German edition of *Ancient Metrology*. T&H will also be publishing archeologist Myra Shackley's *Wildmen*, a study of the possibility of Neanderthal survival in Asia, and probably also containing data on wild men worldwide. Still in the 'alien animals' field, verteran lake monster hunter Lionel Leslie has written *The Water Horse*, to be published by Colin Smythe Ltd. It will concentrate on Irish lake monsters, but comparisons will be made with monsters elsewhere. Obviously aimed at the mystery-hater, *The Loch Ness Mystery Solved* by Ronald Binns is to be published by Open Books Publishing in 1983, price £7.50. It is said to contain a unique collection of photographs, and we shall be particularly interested to see this one, which we doubt lives up to its title.

Penguin Books have two paperbacks with Fortean overtones scheduled for 1983: John Gribbin's *Future Weather* and Leslie Fielder's *Freaks*. 1983 may also see the publication of some high-quality UFO books in the States, namely: Michael Persinger's *Predicting UFO Events and Experiences* (Praeger), William L. Moore's *The Roswell Evidence: Traces of a UFO Crash-Landing and Cover-Up*, and William L. Moore and Stanton Friedman's *Visitors From the Cosmos: Evidence and the Extraterrestrial Hypothesis* (Harper Row).

My final category is 'books in embryo' – those which are still being researched or written, or for which the authors are seeking publishers. Mystery animals are popular: Di Francis, who has actively researched big cats in the Dartmoor Area, is (according to a press report) working on *Close Encounters of the Cat Kind*, while Graham J. McEwan and Chris Hall are together writing *The British

Puma. Graham McEwan (20 Berkeley Drive, Wallasey, Merseyside, L45 1HN) would be glad to hear from anyone with relevant information. Australian Fortean Tony Healy has written two books describing his search for mystery animals worldwide, and I hope next time to be able to report that he has been successful in finding a publisher. In the States, George Eberhard is preparing a bibliography on mystery animal phenomena, including UFO-related material; and finally, we will end as we began, with our industrious editor Bob Rickard, who is actively gathering material for a second volume of *Photographs of the Unknown*.

Writers with books in progress or scheduled for publication, and who would like to give the rest of us something to look forward to, are invited to send details to me c/o FT.

Janet Bord

PROFESSOR CLASPROOT'S

FACTS YOU MIGHT FORGET

I THINK THERE'S A **KNACK** TO THESE HERE **TIBETAN SINGING BOWLS**. SOMEHOW THIS ONE LEAVES SOMETHING TO BE DESIRED.

WELL NOW, WHILE WE WAIT FOR A TOUCH OF MYSTERY, HERE'S A LITTLE **SYNCHRONICITY**

JACK THE RIPPER WAS AT LARGE. THE YEAR WAS **1888**.

BRAHMA HE'S MAKING EYES AT ME ♪

ON AUGUST 8th **EIGHT** MEMBERS OF SEVENOAKS SOCIETY FOR PSYCHICAL RESEARCH MET...

@POKKETTZ '81

AT **88** OCTOBER AVENUE...

AT **8 O'CLOCK** A SEANCE BEGAN...

A SPECTACULAR SESSION! NO LESS THAN **EIGHT** OBJECTS MATERIALISED...

APPARENTLY, **GIFTS** FROM THE **INFINITE!** EACH OCTAGONAL SLIVER WAS INSCRIBED THUS...

UNFORTUNATELY, **EIGHT** DAYS LATER

A PASSING DOG NAMED OCTAVIUS **ATE** THEM...

PAH!

♪ IF YOU'RE ♪ HAPPY AND YOU KNOW IT CLAP ONE HAND... ♪

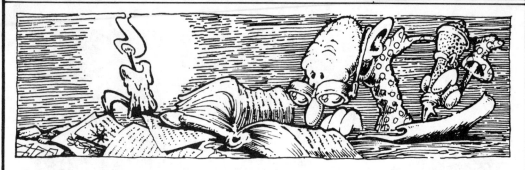

MIND OVER MATTER

By Walter and Mary Jo Uphoff
New Frontiers Center. Oregon, WI 53575, USA, & Colin Smythe Ltd, Gerrards Cross, Bucks, UK, 1980; $6.95 (UK price unknown) pb, pp256, photos.

Since Uri Geller first took the international media by storm, back in 1973, psychokinetic spoon-bending has become as popular a 'psychic' parlour game as reading tea-leaves or playing with Ouija boards. Hundreds of people, throughout the world, suddenly discovered that they had Gellerish powers after seeing Uri on the box. Thousands of perfectly good knives, forks and spoons were wilfully vandalised in the name of PK. And I added metal bending to my 'Supernaturalist' cabaret act.

In the nineteen-sixties, a hard-drinking, ex-hotel worker called Ted Serios made 'Thoughtography' famous by 'thinking' recognizable images onto Polaroid film. Ted's PK power seemed to cause peculiar chemical reactions in the photographic emulsion. Within a very short time, many other 'sensitives' found that they could make thoughtographs too. Today, metal bending and thoughtography are favourite study areas for parapsychologists investigating PK.

In this, their latest book, Walter and Mary Jo Uphoff present the results of several experiments involving the young Japanese psychics, Masuaki Kiyota and Hiroto Yamashita. Masuaki is the 'star' of *Mind Over Matter* (his younger friend, Hiroto, seeming almost to be playing 'Shipi' to Masuaki's 'Uri'), though other well-known paranormalists, such as Matthew Manning, Jean-Pierre Gerard, Nina Kulagina, Silvio etc, crop up throughout the book. Walter Uphoff first met Masuaki Kiyota in 1976, when acting as a kind of travelling talent scout for Alan Neuman, the TV producer, who included a section on Kiyota in his documentary programme *Exploring the Unknown,* shown on NBC-TV that year as a 'Hallowe'en Special'. The Japanese boy was 14 years old when Uphoff first encountered him in his Tokyo home, and the veteran investigator was astounded by the youngster's ability to twist spoons and project images onto Polaroid film. On returning to the States, Uphoff corresponded regularly with the boy. Then, in March 1979, he went back to Japan, with Mrs Uphoff, for six days during which he put Masuaki and Hiroto through their paces. Nippon Television tested and filmed the boys, during Uphoff's visit, with interesting results. During the Summer of 1979, Masuaki and Hiroto arrived in the USA and demonstrated their psychokinetic abilities to various interested parties, at the New Frontiers Centre, Oregon, Wisconsin; the Mayo Clinic, Rochester, Minnesota; and the Washington Research Centre, San Francisco. The scientists who observed, studied and/or tested the lads included Prof. John Hasted, Dr Jule Eisenbud, Russell Targ and Harold Puthoff ... familiar names in the weird world of PK. From the evidence quoted in this book, the American tests and demonstrations do not seem to have been spectacularly successful.

Like many psychical researchers, Walter Uphoff is very sensitive towards those who are openly skeptical or critical in their opinions of PK. The Committee for the Scientific Investigation of Claims of the Paranormal comes in for quite a bit of stick, and James Randi (arch-enemy of Geller and Serios) is seen as irritatingly hostile. In his foreword, Dr Berthold Schwartz suggests that 'the reader, if not amused, might become incensed at reports of · chicanery and grossness perpetrated by the so-called 'exposers'. But he can read for himself and decide'. This reader was amused by the section in which Walter Uphoff recalls an occasion when Uri Geller 'fixed' a broken watch held by Mary Jo: 'How can Geller be accused of trickery when he was about fifty feet away and did not see or touch the watch? This watch ran for about thirteen hours and stopped the following noon, about two minutes after it was shown to David Hoy, a rival of Geller.'

This seems to imply that my old pal, David, should be regarded as being in the enemy camp; but regular Forteans will remember that Hoy was a member of the 1977 'Monstermind' team, which succeeded in raising Nessie by what some people regard as psychokinetic means. David often uses PK, and was well established as a famous professional psychic long before Geller arrived on the scene (see *Super Psychic: The Incredible Dr. Hoy* by

John Godwin). Maybe I should, at this point, also mention the fact that Randi approved of my monster hunting activities ... so I'm not quite so biased against him as the Gellerites seem to be. I have followed his career for over twenty-five years, we have many mutual friends, and I'm sure that Randi is totally sincere in his attitudes towards Geller and Serios. At the same time, 'exposers' of pseudo-psychics have, in the past, been known to plant damning evidence of 'fraud' ... and Randi himself has said, 'I've never claimed to be honest'.

In my opinion, the 'safeguards against fakery' set up in many of the Kiyota/Yamashita experiments described by the Uphoffs, were virtually nonexistent or, at least, extremely loose. To be fair, Walter Uphoff says that he prefers to begin testing a subject under informal conditions, gradually tightening the security as things progress. Experience has shown that this is often the best procedure, as many PK subjects feel uncomfortably inhibited by some of the tough restrictions which have been imposed on them. If investigators are seen or felt, by a psychic, to be 'hostile', then the psychic will probably think 'why bother?'. After all, the genuine psychic *knows* what he can do, and hours of tiresome testing can seem boring and pointless. I tend to believe that most, if not all, lab tests for ESP and PK are self-defeating, they don't prove a damn thing one way or another, but it really doesn't matter. As Lyall Watson has said: 'The search for validity through proof is fundamentally foreign to magic' ... but science demands proof, time and time again. The photographs of the two Japanese boys, taken during test and demonstration sessions, are studies of profound boredom. Masuaki and Hiroto are fed up to the back teeth with those earnest scientists, including the friendly ones, and it shows. No wonder that even polite Japanese kids would

occasionally become angry or want to take time off for a game of Space Invaders; and it isn't really surprising that, sometimes, a psychic ... especially an impatient, hyperactive youngster ... feels tempted to cheat, to come up with quick results in order to escape the claustrophobic parapsychology lab. I'm not suggesting that Masuaki or Hiroto ever resorted to trickery, but I wouldn't blame them in the slightest if they did.

It is quite possible and practical to imitate the so-called 'Geller Effect' through the application of fairly standard conjuring techniques. Trick methods of metal bending, thoughtography, design duplication, watch manipulation etc have been described by James Randi, Milbourne Christopher and others, in books readily available to the general public. More sophisticated and secret methods for imitating telepathic and telekinetic effects have been published in the specialist conjuring journals for many years. A method for bending glass rods, by seemingly psychokinetic means, was published in *The Jinx* as long ago as December, 1934 (spoon and coin bending goes back much further); and an interesting item appeared in the March, 1907, issue of the *Wizard,* announcing the fact that Dr Herschell intended to demonstrate his 'new apparatus for photographing thoughts' at a Magic Circle get-together ... that's three years before the 'discovery' of thoughtography by Japan's Prof. Tomokichi Fukurai. A significant point emerges: the tricksters appear to have imaginatively anticipated the main specialities of our present-day PK superstars!

The thing that impresses me most about Masuaki's style of spoonbending is the tight twist he puts in the metal. This effect would be very difficult to achieve by means of trickery, under laboratory test conditions. Very little effort is required to simply *bend* a spoon, physically, but it would

be an immensely powerful man who could, with his bare hands, put a double twist in the handle of a heavy tablespoon, and he would have to be a master of misdirection to do it, unnoticed, in the presence of an investigation committee. Guy Lyon Playfair, discussing the Enfield poltergeist in *FT33,* mentions a curtain being paranoramally twisted into a tight spiral. He writes: 'This spiral, or vortex effect, kept turning up, and may be an important clue to the mystery of poltergeist power.' I agree, and it is that very effect which, more than anything else described in the book, suggests that Masuaki Kiyota's PK power is authentic. The spiral ... an ancient 'power' symbol ... crops up with amazing regularity in the history of magic and the paranormal. It's a sign to watch out for.

A spiral 'swirl' sometimes appeared in the thoughtographs of one of Prof. Fukurai's psychic subjects, tested between 1910 and 1913. A similar pattern has been seen in some of the Serios pictures, but I don't know if it has ever happened in Masuaki's photographic work. Frankly, I'm not too impressed by the boy's efforts in this area, and the pictorial evidence presented by the Uphoffs is disappointing, but I admit that I know very little about thoughtography and I have never tried it myself (contrary to a minority opinion, my monster pictures are *not* thoughtographs). One of Prof. Fukurai's early subjects had a doppelganger known as 'The Goblin', Geller received messages from Spectra, and Masuaki is visited by 'a life' without a body (who, nevertheless, appears wearing a round hat and a gown 'as a clergyman wears'), called Zenafu. If these ethereal entities can be seen or 'imagined', a good thoughtographer should be able to come up with a portrait of his familiar spirit. In fact, the imagery of most thoughtographs is depressingly banal when one would expect it to be rather exciting. Some years ago, when asked to produce a picture of the Arc de Triomphe, Ted Serios created a picture of a Triumph motorcar 'in which he was more interested'. We are told that Masuaki is interested in heavy rock music and McDonald's hamburgers, so why doesn't he come up with thoughtographs of his favourite rockers and images of succulent steaming burgers instead of those draggy, out-of-focus, postcard views of the Statue of Liberty or Tokyo Tower? I'm surprised that thoughtographs display such a lack of imagination, that they are not more obviously 'Surrealistic' or even pornographic. If I happened to suddenly find that I was a thoughtographer, I certainly wouldn't be content to produce murky views of public monuments, I'd try to deliver something far more exciting and entertaining.

Certain individuals can push the power of PK well beyond the level of bent keys or everted tennis balls. In 1979, a psychic friend of mine, Marc Poelsky, created something of a sensation around Central New Jersey when he caused a minor earthquake. At 11.20am he concentrated, for ten minutes, on 'disturbing the ground'; at 11.31am, the earth moved . . ; and Marc had to make a public apology for the damage he had caused! Now *that* was a spectacular piece of PK, the kind of PK depicted in movies like *Carrie* and *The Medusa Touch,* the kind that cannot be faked by sleight of hand. This is the type of heavy stuff which sometimes happens, spontaneously, in cases of 'possession' and poltergeist activity, and it's a type of PK which should have been, but wasn't mentioned in *Mind Over Matter.*

The destructive potential of PK is discussed (a psychic, could, in theory, trigger a nuclear bomb or knock a missile off course), along with some familiar-sounding stories about secret government research programmes and military interest in people like Masuaki, but the darker side of psi-power is not investigated very deeply. PK *is,* very often, destructive . . . and it annoys me that this is thoughtlessly encouraged by so many PK enthusiasts. A bent spoon is not some kind of magical talisman, it's just a distorted object, whether it has been warped by mind or muscle. There is something amusingly self-contradictory about those who express delight, in 'the same breath, at having their broken watches repaired and their door keys broken by the wonderful powers of PK. Yes... I've warped many a key myself, but I feel that there is a 'wrongness' about it, and the last time I included metal bending in my public performances was Dec 31st, 1974. There is a strong element of conscious or unconscious vandalism in PK/ poltergeist activity ... things are broken far more often and more easily than they are mended ... the power is quite unpredictable and extremely difficult to control with any real accuracy. I say this from a basis of personal experience, and it is one of the reasons why I am dubious about the usefulness of PK in healing. The Uphoffs are keen to promote the healing potential of PK, but I cannot share their enthusiasm. Genuine psychic healing is, of course, a good and praiseworthy thing, but the 'power' it employs is not the same as that which bends metal. I certainly wouldn't relish the thought of having my physical ailments 'treated' by a spoon-warper ... speaking as an ex-member of the spoon-warping class.

Doc Shiels.

LIVING WONDERS:
MYSTERIES & CURIOSITIES OF THE ANIMAL WORLD
By John Michell & Robert J.M. Rickard
Thames and Hudson (London, 1982) £8.95 hb, 176pp, name index, 170 photos and illus.
In this attractive and finely written tome John Michell and Bob Rickard have produced a follow-up to their earlier success from the same publishers, *Phenomena* (1977). The new book deals with animals, or in view of some of the odd things they describe, perhaps seemingly animate entities might be more correct. *Living Wonders* is a marvellous bestiary of the bizarre creatures at large, if not in the wide, wide, world, then at least in the fertile acres of the human imagination. If some of these things are not the result of over-stimulated hippocampi then the world is a great deal odder than they think in South Kensington.

They have packed what seems to be a slim volume so full of material, that it is even difficult to give a potential reader an idea of what they cover. The book is divided into four parts, two dealing with mysteries, and two with curiosities of animal life. The first part deals with Cryptozoology, beginning with a "little history" of this not-so-new science. This is excellent, a model of its kind. All the old familiar heroes — Gesner, Gosse, Sanderson, Fort, Heuvlmans, Keel — are covered, as well as some more minor writers.

Then they survey, briefly but concisely, a whole range of mysterious creatures, the Kraken, Ape-Men, Neo-Dinosaurs, and others. Some of the material may seem familiar, but it is the great virtue of this book that new information of great interest and importance appears everywhere. Likewise the illustrations. These have been selected with great care and attention (and designed into a very handsome format). For instance, they have used Bernard Heuvelmans' photo and the drawing based on it, of that errant Neanderthaler, the Ice-Man of Minnesota, rather than the inaccurate version by Ivan Sanderson which has done duty elsewhere. And the photograph of the skull and scalp of that long notorious creature the Bunyip of the

Murrumbidgee found by James Stuart leaves no doubt that this was indeed a deformed colt's head and not "the real thing".

In the second part, 'Hints of Teleportation', the book moves away from what South Kensington might regard as just about reasonable to deal with the quite unreasonable, and often random-seeming, way in which Old Dame Nature sprinkles animals from foreign countries or ancient days about with a fine disregard for zoogeography. To this are added accounts of rains of fish and frogs, toads alive in rocks, and so on.

Part three deals with such wonderful creatures as talking cats, counting horses, and other freaks. And so, lastly, to various controversies and curiosities of animal behaviour. Here some old legends receive new critical scrutiny and come out very well. These include the notorious Man-Eating Tree, modern Jonahs, animal courts, wakes, funerals, and battles, and mass-suicides. As a tail-piece there is added accounts of monkey bridges (they twine their tails together to hang over the gorge), and rat kings (where several rats become entwined by their tails).

Altogether, a weird and wonderful panorama, which will give any Fortean food for thought, and leads for new research. Some of the events reported are infrequently observed patterns of behaviour — the rat king for instance — which are so seldom seen that they hardly feature at all in the literature. In the 19th century there were more places in which such events could be reported. *The Field*, for example, then "the country gentleman's paper", carried a natural history column where odd events found a home for well over half a century. Now they receive treatment by the wire services and end up as fillers bereft of detail in the popular press. A sad decline.

The other class of reports —

the talking animals and loyal pets — are always popular. They are curiosities — but it is the mysteries which must be the real meat for readers of this journal.

The authors distinguish two lines on research in this area: a rationalistic one including Gosse, Oudemans, Willy Ley, Heuvelmans (and the present reviewer, as the authors themselves observe). The other line, includes Sanderson, Fort, Keel, the Bords, and tends towards a more occult explanation for some of these animals. And here is the crux. Since at least the 1950's it has become clear that the old explanations will not always do. Nor will the idea that what cannot be rationally explained must be a fraud or a hoax.

The search for a new kind of explanation is on. And here the authors make great play with Rupert Sheldrake's theories. The hope is that there may be some all engrossing theory to encompass all these phenomena. Charles Fort would surely have snorted at this. For as soon as a global theory is accepted the facts to overthrow it will make their appearance.

And now we must insist that John and the esteemed editor of *Fortean Times*, will start on a new tome, *Strange People*.

Peter Costello

EARTHLIGHTS
By Paul Devereux
*Turnstone Press
Wellingborough, N'hants,
1982; £9.95 hb, pp256,
photos, diags, index, refs.*

This book has been brewing inside Paul Devereux, editor of *The Ley Hunter*, for more than a decade. His personal search for understanding the nature of UFOs began in the hippy heyday of 1967, with a UFO that turned into a startling vision of a figure in the sky, likened to Leonardo's 'universal man'. This is also the starting point of the book, as supporting testimony is given by other witnesses. Paul has

never doubted that what he and his friends saw was objectively real, despite the differences in interpretations of detail and meaning. The second chapter parades a number of summaries of different types of UFO experience (based on Hynek's classification), which are severely scrutinized for signs of a common denominator. Chapter 3 takes the criticism further, and positively rages with Paul's frustration and disappointment at both the weakness of the main theories of UFO origins, and the unthinking servitude of their proponents. Paul creates a further category of UFO phenomena to bring together the high-strangeness accounts of shape-shifting UFOs and their associated and equally shifty entities, stimulated by his original vision, in which the "glowing figure formed out of the UFO material itself." Other examples of these 'proto-entities', as he calls them, are given; much of the case-histories being refreshingly new.

Paul then argues that abduction and close-encounters of the complex kind should be separated from the reports of unidentified aerial objects and lights. Once they are shorn of their psychological, cultural and conceptual overlays — these are imposed by the witnesses and researchers — the 'pure' phenomena can be seen to be similar to such bizarre electro-magnetic phenomena as ball lightning. Paul doesn't say they *are* BLs, but by the time you follow his argument into the following chapters you might accept that UFOs and BLs could have the same ultimate origin in the complex and invisible world of the geomagnetosphere of this Earth. Building upon the work of Persinger & Lafreniere's *Space Time Transients*, in which they argue that UFOs and other kinds of Fortean phenomena occur in regions of seismic activity, Paul develops a detailed study of a number of 'window' regions in England

and Wales, correlating a huge amount of UFO data (supplied by BUFORA) with the investigations of his ley-hunting colleague, geologist Paul McCartney. They find a high correlation between UFO activity and areas of 'mineral enrichment' with its associated faults (not necessarily visible on the surface) and geotectonic stress. Geological stress, it transpires, causes electrical changes in certain rocks, and these fields extend into the atmosphere. Lights, auroras, glows and 'fireballs' have all been seen during quakes, not to mention more baffling co-incidences (eg. meteors with quakes). It is a pity that Fort's insight into this correlation is not recognized here.

The centrepiece of this reasoning are experiments fracturing lumps of granite which generate tiny balls of light in the process. The effects of these alterations in the electro-magnetic environment upon man and animals is considered, and authorities cited to show that living organisms are indeed influenced by such invisible forces both terrestrial and extraterrestrial (eg. solar flares). In summary, Paul believes that "UFOs are Earth phenomena" and that seismic forces not only generate or precipitate the luminous UFO forms and their associated electro-magnetic effects, but that these forces also subtly influence our perception, imagery and thinking about them.

Practical UFO investigation, then, must take into account geology, as well as meteorology and astronomy. But more than that, there is the ancient landscape. Paul has discovered that those same regions of high seismic and UFO activity also have the greatest concentration of stone circles and other megalithic structures. Drawing on evidence that the invisible Earth forces can be detected by certain psychics (eg dowsers), and even under some circumstances enhance psi abilities or precipitate hallucinations or visions, Paul amplifies

an idea put forward originally by John Michell — that the shamans of the megalithic era ("ancient geopsychic wizards") used a combination of observation, intuition, ESP and inspiration to locate the most effective sites for their monuments. And these artifacts were not merely ornamental or religious, but practical places, where men might commune with the forces of nature in the form of "atmospherically sustained pictorial representations of the fundamental powers of the mind and of physical nature...." The whole society and its non-material technology would be sustained by direct symbiosis with the forces of the natural world to help them in their daily life. But nature changes, irrevocably, and the decline began. By the time of the Druids 'The Knowledge', as Paul calls it, was fragmented and dispersed by the rise of "patriarchal, left-brain" type cultures.

This vision of ancient society may seem to have little to do with UFOs on the surface, but many researchers have found links between them beneath the bedrock of phenomenology. *Earth Lights* is the best expression to date of current thinking. By bringing together material from many areas tangential to hard-core ufology Paul lays claim to formulating the most comprehensive paradigm for genuine unidentified aerial phenomena, and we thank him for that. Paul's writing is as intense as his belief, and he makes no secret, nor apology, for his personal investment in his thesis. The dangers of this position, for Paul, are justified because he has deliberately chosen to be provocative. The book will undoubtedly provoke strong reactions, for and against his ideas, and it will be talked about for a long time. One criticism will be about the lack of discussion of the psychological, psychic, sociological and cultural dimensions of UFO experiences. I'm sure Paul would

agree about their importance, and say they were beyond his present brief, which was to prove his conviction that "These phenomena exist, and there has to be a function in nature that produces them." I can't agree with the publicity blurb that this paradigm 'encompasses *all* aspects of the problem" — there are many questions left begging — but this is certainly the most solid and literally down to earth contribution to understanding the UFO enigma for a long time. Essential reading, I'd say. RJMR

THE BIGFOOT CASE-BOOK
By Janet & Colin Bord. *Granada, London, 1982; £8.95 hb, pp254, index, bib, photos, illus. US edition is by Stackpole Books, Harrisburg, Penn; S14.95 hb, S10.95 pb.*

North America's version of the Yeti, called Bigfoot or saquatch, only achieved notoriety worldwide in the last decade, but patient researchers have dug out reports of sightings dating at least from the early 19th century, and which exceed in number, as the Bords point out, recorded sightings of Yeti. The second half of their book is a massive chronology of 1000 Bigfoot reports (1818-1980), each with a summary and details of location and bibliography.

The first half of the book is a history of the 'wild man' of North America, examined in 20-yr chunks by putting the spotlight on the most interesting cases. These invariably involve sightings, close contact or even conflict with huge hairy ape-like creatures. The high-strangeness cases often include disturbing paranormal phenomena which if not caused by the creatures indicate a series of synchronistic events worthy of further investigation. The authors have on file many more cases than are included here, and decided to omit most incidents in which a giant humanoid footprint was the sole (no pun intended) feature, for these are common enough, except when a creature has been seen to make the imprint. The Bords spend little time on theories here, referring the reader to their recent *Alien Animals*, the main aim of the present book being to compliment that work with detailed case data.

Bigfoot Casebook is the result of a commendable and prodigious reading programme, and although it may not be every Fortean's cup of tea, it belongs in the library of every cryptozoologist, and zoologist for that matter. *RJMR*.

ELOHIM'S NURSERY
By David Medina.
Regency Press, London, 1981; £6.00 hb, pp158, index, bib, photos.

As a sequel to Medina's previous book on the Ark of the Covenant, he has scoured the Bible and some other ancient texts in further support of the 'ancient astronaut' thesis. It forms a very interesting collection of citations alluding to strange goingson; though I for one reserve judgement on it being evidence of visiting extra-terrestrials. It is additionally thrilling to see Paul Devereux's vision of 1967 (see review of *Earth Lights*, above) interpreted as a message or craft from the ETs! *RJMR*

OTHER WORLDS: SPACE, SUPER SPACE AND THE QUANTUM UNIVERSE
By Paul Davies.
Simon & Shuster, (NY; 1982) $5.15 pb.

If quantum physics continues along its present course, Charles Fort will begin to seem as conservative as Charles Darwin. Relativity, after all, only asked us to credit that a second in the coordination system of Observer A is equivalent to a million years in the system of Observer B; but quantum mechanics asks us to believe truly strange propositions. The quantum realm is

the field of mathematical physics in which a hypothetical particle is blandly named the *quark* (after *Finnegans Wake*) and the researchers engaged in trying to find it refer to their work jovially as "the hunting of the quark" (after Lewis Carroll.) Surrealism, by comparison, is stodgy and old hat; 'Pataphysics' is left at the post; even Discordianism is tame stuff next to the quantum universe.

What is strangest of all is that quantum theory is based on the greatest number of successful experiments and the tightest mathematical analysis of any science that exists. If there is such a beast as hard demonstrable truth anywhere, it is in this mad world of paradoxes, of waves that act like particles, particles that are only "virtual", universes that may be only mathematical fictions or may be as real as this one, and logic that goes beyond *true* and *false* to include *maybe*.

Prof. Paul Davies has written one of the best popular introductions to this pixillated and perplexing subject. Unlike Gary Zukov (*The Dancing Wu Li Masters*) and Michael Talbot (*Mysticism and the New Physics*), he is not trying to prove that quantum mechanics confirms the truth of ancient mystic teachings; unlike Prof. Paigel (*The Cosmic Code*), he is not trying to prove that it does not confirm the mystics after all. Prof. Davies merely shows that the results of quantum experiments and quantum math are extremely queer, no matter how you interpret them, and definitely cannot be reconciled in any way with what we used to call common sense.

Among the many interesting topics Davies discusses are: the Schrödinger's cat paradox, which shows that under some circumstances a cat can be both dead and alive (or neither dead nor alive); the "catastrophe of the infinite regress" of John von Neumann which shows that any attempt to

escape from the notorious quantum uncertainty leads to more uncertainty; Wigner's problem of the experimenter's friend, which leads inexorably to the conclusion that physicists cannot only not escape recognizing mind as part of their subject but must even accept mind as perhaps their only real field of study; the Einstein-Rosen-Podolsky demonstration which leads to a kind of monism strangely familiar to Forteans and may explain what Jungians call synchronicity; Wheeler's super-space which makes faster-than-light travel at least theoretically possible; and many similar topics which are all guaranteed to drive both the fundamentalist theologian and the fundamentalist materialist to run into the night screaming and howling incoherently.

Basically, it seems, the results of both experiment and math in the sub-atomic realm have led to results so startling that the physicists themselves cannot agree on what the data *means*. Among a plethora of competing theories four schools seem to cover most of the ground: (1) The Copenhagen Interpretation of Bohr, which in effect reduces physics to a branch of human psychology: we are not talking about the universe, this school says, but about how our brains necessarily build models of the universe. (2) The multiple universe theory, promulgated chiefly by Everett and DeWitt, which claims that everything that *can* happen *does* happen: there are many parallel worlds, as in science-fiction. (3) The monists, led by Bell and Capra, who are in effect agreeing with Fort and Buddha: All is One. "There is no difference between anything," says Dr. Nick Herbert, a proponent of this school, only half joking. (4) The Hidden Variable group, led by Dr. David Bohm, whose position is so subtle that any simply description will seem like a caricature; but basically, like Plato, they accept the universe as a crazy shadow of something that does make sense in its own realm, outside space, time and sensory perception.

This book is not only a very readable and entertaining introduction to the most advanced and complex of all sciences, but is also a good weapon to turn on anybody who says any of your own interests are too weird to be taken seriously. Just open to page 130, read aloud the cat paradox and ask your querent if he or she can come up with a better answer to that which the physicists have found in the 47 years since Schrödinger first published it.

Robert Anton Wilson

OTHER BOOKS RECEIVED;
★ **BAALBEK** by Friedrich Ragette. History, plans and excavations of this massive temple-complex in Lebanon. *(Chatto & Windus, London, 1980; £9.50 hb, pp128, index, bib, illus).*
★ **THE GRIMOIRE OF ARMADEL** by S.L. MacGregor Mathers. A classic of ceremonial magic, with introduction by Francis King. *(RKP, London, 1980; £6.95, pp79, illus).*
★ **DRAWING ON THE RIGHT SIDE OF THE BRAIN** by Betty Edwards. 'Drawing' in both senses of the word. Fascinating discussion of the artistic talents of the right half of our brains. Very well presented. *(Souvenir Press, London, 1981 (original by JP Tarcher, Los Angeles, 1979; £6.95 hb, pp207, index, illus, bib, gloss.)*

★ **ANCIENT METROLOGY** by John Michell. John's definitive exploration of the sacred numerology of Stonehenge "and of the whole world therein symbolized." *(Published by the author and Pentacle Books: 11 Powis Gdns, London W11, 1981; Hb: £7/$14, pb: £3/$6, postage extra; pp48, bib, diags.)* There might just be some of the limited edition of 504 copies left. Enquire.
★ **NAVEN** by Gregory Bateson. Transvestites and ritual homosexuality among the Iatmul people of New Guinea. 2nd edition. *(Wildwood House, London, 1981; £4.50 pb, pp343, bib, photos, gloss.*
★ **MAYAN DREAM WALK** by Richard Luxton & Pablo Balam. A 'new' view of Mayan hieroglyphics and their meaning for Mayan shamans. Fascinating. *(Rider, London, 1981; £4.95 pb, pp247, rec reading, gloss, plates, illus.)*
★ **DOOMSDAY 1999AD** by Charles Berlitz. Mostly nonsense. A sorry waste of publishing resources. *(Souvenir Press, London, 1981; £6.95 hb, pp226, illus.)*
★ **COMPLETE BOOK OF PRACTICAL ASTROLOGY** by E.O.Hammack Jr. With the aid of this book, it is claimed, you "can know for certain what lies ahead....until the year 2000." *(Parker Pub Co, West Nyack, NY, 1981; £8.40 (US price unknown) hb; pp220, tables).*

★ **INTO THE BLUE** by Alexander McKee. Good aviation mysteries, much of it new to us....and not a 'Flight 19' in sight. *(Souvenir Press, London, 1981; £8.95 hb, pp296, refs, plates.)*
★ **LOCH NESS MONSTER** by Tim Dinsdale. New (4th) edition, with new material and good colour cover of Doc Shiels' Nessie photo. *(RKP, London, 1982; £4.75 pb, pp218, plates, illus.)*
★ **THE CONCORDANCE OF HIGH MONARCHISTS OF IRELAND** by John Michell Radical traditionalist, mystical, geomantic, sane solution to the troubles of this long-suffering land and people. The proposal: a federation of the four ancient provinces, presided over by a High King in a central city-state. *(Price: 50p/$1.50. Published by the author from 11 Powis Gardens, London W11; or from Martin Brennan, 274 68St, Brooklyn, NY 11220, NY).*
★ **LID OFF THE CAULDRON** by Patricia Crowther. A handbook for modern *witches. (Frederick Muller, London, 1981; £6.95 hb, pp156, index, plates, illus.)*
★ **MARIE: VOODOO QUEEN** by Margot Arnold. Fiction but seemingly well researched. *(Granada, London, 1981; £1.95 pb, pp461.)*
★ **CAUSE OF DEATH** by Frank Smyth. A fascinating forensic history of 'murder under the microscope'. *(Pan, London, 1982; £1.75, pp252, index, plates.)*

Classified Exchanges.

FT welcomes an exchange of publications with those of mutual interest and for mutual advertisement. This listing represents exchange publications received since last issue. A full list will be published every fourth issue — indermediate issues will simply record new titles and data changes as they are received.

FORTEAN

● **Anomaly Register** [#4,5] - free with the mailorder booklist issued by Wm Corliss' Sourcebook Project, and now dedicated as a supplement to his projected series of phenomena catalogues (see Janet Bord's 'Book Alert' next issue). W.R. Corliss. The Source-

book Project: Box 107 Glen Arm, MD 21057, USA.
● **ASSAP News** [#4] - news letter of the Association for the Scientific Study of Anomalous Phenomena. Details of memb. from Janice Bagnall: 6 Colwyn House, Cosser St, London SE1 7BY.
● **Common Ground** [#4,5,6] - studies at the fringe

of human experience. 4/yr; UK:£4; E:£6; foreign: $15
(bills only). [Pay: Kevin McClure.] CG: 14 Northfold
Rd, Knighton, Leics.
- **Creature Chronicles** [#5] - bigfoot etc. 4/yr.
US:$6; foreign:$8 (US drafts). [Pay: Ron Shaffner.]
Hominid Research Group: Box 12049A, Cincinnati,
OH 45212, USA.
- **End Times Bulletin** [#1,2] - monitoring end of the
world beliefs. UK:£2; foreign:$6 (bills only). [Pay:
Kevin McClure.] ETB: 14 Northfold Rd, Knighton,
Leics.
- **INFO Journal** [#40] - one of the two oldest
Fortean journals, looking healthier than for a long
time. 4/yr. UK:£5.00; US:$10.00. INFO: Box 367,
Arlington, VA 22210, USA.
- **ISC Newsletter** [#1:1. 1:2] - organ of the new
International Society of Cryptozoology. 4/yr. Memb
enqs to ISC: Box 43070, Tuscon, AZ 85733, USA.
- **Jour. Meteorology** [#7:67. 68. 69. 70]. 12/yr.
UK:£14.50; foreign:£17; institutions add £3. Artetech
Pub.Co: Cockhill House, Trowbridge, Wilts BA14
9BG.
- **Lantern** [#38] - 4/yr. UK:£1.50; foreign:dollar
equiv (bills only). [Pay: Borderland Science Research
Group.] Lantern: 3 Dunwich Way, Oulton Broad,
Lowestoft, Suffolk NR32 4RZ.
- **Ness Information Service** [#52,53] - 12/yr.
UK:£2.50; foreign:$9.00; [Pay: Rip Hepple.] NIS:
Huntshieldford, St Johns Chapel, Bishop Aukland, Co
Durham DL13 1RQ.
- **New Atlantean Journal** [#10:2] - 4/yr. US:$5;
foreign:$12, inc 3 backissues. NAJ: 5963 32nd Ave
St Petersburg, FL 33710, USA.
- **Science Frontiers** [#21,22,23] - fortean abstracts
from current sci. lit. Free to customers of Sourcebook
Project. See *Anomaly Register* above.
- **Shaverton** [#4:2] - hollow earth mysteries Shaver-
style. 4/yr. US:S9; foreign:$10 (S), $13 (A). [Pay:
Richard Toronto.] S: 325 Coghlan St, Vallejo, CA
94590, USA.
- **Tri-County UFO Study Group Newsletter** - also
Bigfoot & some Forteana. Details from TCUFOSG:
Box 2, Sebring, OH 44672, USA.

EARTH MYSTERIES
- **Northern Earth Mysteries** [#18,19] - 5/yr. UK:£2.
[Pay: Philip Heselton.] NEM: 170 Victoria Ave, Hull
HU5 3DY.
- **Quicksilver Messenger** [#6,7] - 4/yr. UK:£4. E:£5;
US:$16 (bills only). [Pay: Chris Ashton.] QSM:
Garden flat. 46 Vere Rd, Brighton, Sussex.
- **Stonehenge Viewpoint** [#47,48] - 6/yr. UK:£5
(2yr sub), SV: c/o 3rd flr, 35 Gt Russell St, London
WC1. US:$8. SV: 2821 De La Vina St, Santa Barbara,
CA 93105, USA. Canada: US$10.
- **Terrestrial Zodiac News** [#1] -revived after 2yrs.
4/yr. UK:£2.50. [Pay: Anthea Turner.] TZN: 8
Eynsford Court, Hitchin, Herts SG4 9JS.
- **The Ley Hunter** [#93] - Britains oldest EM journal.
3/yr. UK:£3.75; E:£5; foreign:$13 (S), S18 (A). TLH:
Box 13, Welshpool, Powys, Wales.
- **The Templar** [#2] - goemancy of circular sacred
buildings. 4/yr. UK:£3;25; IGR: 142 Pheasant Rise,
Bar Hill, Cambridge CB8 8SD.

PSI
- **Int. Jour.Paraphysics** [#16:3&4] - rates unknown.
Benson Herbert: Paralab, Downton, Wilts.

UFO
- **AFU Newsletter** [#23,24] - new format, English
trans. from Swedish, bibliographic organ of Archives
for UFO Research (AFU). 3/yr; Swedish Kr35 or
equiv. AFU: Box 11027, S-600 11 Norrkoping 11,
Sweden.
- **APRO Bulletin** [#30:7,8] - Memb/yr: U$:S15;
foreign:$18. APRO: 3910 E. Kleindale Rd, Tuscon,
AZ 85712, USA.
- **BUFORA Bulletin** [#5] - rates unknown. Contact
Memb. Sec, Miss P Kennedy, 30 Vermont Rd,
London SE19 3SR.
- **Centre Update** [#1] - OSEAP's resources centre
bibliography, reviews, abstracts & book news. see
OSEAP Journal below.
- **Earthlink** [#11] - 4/yr. UK:£3; foreign:£4/S9
(bills, IMOs only). E: 16 Raydons Rd, Dagenham,
Essex RM9 5JR.
- **Inforespace** [#61] - 4/yr. in French. Enquire:
SOBEPS: Ave Paul Janson 74, 1070 Bruxelles,
Belgium.
- **Journ. Transient Aerial Phenomena** [#2:3] - pub
by BUFORA, free to members. Apply to BUFORA
above.
- **Magonia** [#9,10] - 4/yr. UK:£2; US:$5; other
countries £2.50 equiv. [Pay: John Rimmer.] M: 64
Alric Ave, New Malden, Surrey KT3 4JW.
- **Northern UFO News** [#94,95.96.97] - currently
being enlarged to include *Case Histories*, as NUFON
changes into UFO Research North. UK:£4.20 for 6.
[Pay: Jenny Randles.] NUFON: 8 Whitethroat Walk,
Birchwood, Cheshire WA3 6PQ.
- **OSEAP Journal** [#1:1] - of the Organization for
the Scientific Evaluation of Aerial Phenomena. Rates
include *Centre Update* above. 2/yr of each. UK:£5;
foreign:£6 (IMOs). OSEAP: 170 Henry St, Crewe,
Cheshire CW1 4BQ.
- **UFO Aspect** - Danish report in English. No info.
Free UFO STudy: Bragesgade 26 D 3, DK-2200
Copenhagen N, Denmark.
- **UFO Newsclipping Service** - monthly facsimilies of
reports, some Forteana. UFONS: Route 1, Box 220,
Plumerville, AK 72127, USA.
- **UFO Research Australia Newsletter** [#3:2,3] -
6/yr. Aust:A$10; foreign:A$12 (S), A$24 (Oz
currency draft only). UFORA: Box 229, Prospect, SA
5082, Australia.

OTHERS
- **Church of the SubGenius** - '82 convention pros-
pectus, has to be seen to be disbelieved. SubGenius
Foundation, Box 140306, Dallas, TX 75214, USA.
- **Prytania** [magic, philosophy, esotericism. 4/yr.
UK:£3, Biophysical Research, 126 Bevan St,
Lowestoft, Suffolk NR32 2AQ.
- **Walrus** [#19,20] - official organ of the non-
material world. 3/yr. UK:£2.25. W: 142 Pheasant
Rise, Bar Hill, Cambridge CB3 8SD.

**Please mention Fortean Times when you
respond to these listings.**

Continued from p3

ness, and nobody believed me – so odd it all seemed. One of my listeners said that if it had been a ball lightning, it would have exploded and killed me.

Yet I am quite convinced of reality of what had happened, for I have never suffered from hallucinations. Can my spoilt plug socket have indeed worked by chance as a generator of ball lightnings?

The second letter (by L. Pechyonkin) published in the same issue of the TM deals with an enigmatic case of "the meteorite doctor" (the treatment of eczema with the aid of a meteorite). If you take interest in the case I could translate it for you too.

Allow me once more to express my admiration about your splendid journal and to wish you personally and your colleagues every success in all your endeavours.

Vladimir V. Rubtsov
Kharkov, USSR.

CAT ENCOUNTER
In 1964 I lived with my parents in rural Surrey. I was 17 years old. Rumours of the 'Surrey Puma' were rife at that time but I paid little attention to them.

One day I was returning home from a party at 1am in the morning – a short cut home led through woods and fields. It had been a long walk and I had had little to drink. As I neared home I walked across a field to reach the field behind my house. Between the fields two woods met forming a narrow copse. As I passed through this wood I heard the noise of an animal running towards me within one wood. I stopped, to see what it was, thinking it might be a fox (of which I had seen plenty).

The noise got louder and closer and suddenly a large beast rushed headlong out of the woods towards me. I froze to the spot and my hair seemed to stand on end. The animal was obviously a large cat and appeared to be oblivious of me,

having to swerve at the final moment to avoid me. It was panting hard and I could smell the warmth of its breath in the night air. In a flash it was past and the sounds receeded into the distance.

Needless to say I sprinted all the way home. I related the story to my family in the morning and they assumed I was drunk. Nobody really believed me, although my sincerity led them to believe I had seen something – but not a puma. But I know I saw something – puma or panther, I couldn't say, but something similar.

For the next week I walked the long way home by the road. The following week my fears subsided and I decided to take the short cut. As I walked through the field I was nervously looking all around me. Something at the top of the field caught my attention. It was moving stealthily in the long grass, keeping pace with me. A large cat-like animal was stalking me! Again I sprinted home. I never crossed the fields again at night until much later, and have never made public my experiences. It is the only strange thing that has ever happened to me.

Timothy Blewitt
Hove, Sussex

OLDEST READER?
I will be 75 next birthday and have a hunch I am your oldest subscriber.

I got a kick out of 'Oblomov Syndrome' [FT37p51]. One of my cousins spent 20 years in bed. Nothing wrong – just tired! She got up when she was almost 50 and lived until her 70s.

John H. White
Denham Springs, Louisiana
[Do we have any readers older than John? If so, we'd like to hear from you. During our near-decade of publishing FT we have discovered, and been discovered by a number of people who were members of the old Fortean Society, 1931–1959 – Ed.]

MOUSE REWARD
As the readers of the Fortean Times well know, mice have long been used as subjects in laboratory experiments.

One result of the knowledge gained from these experiments is that it is often possible to determine the mechanism of damage in a member of the same species injured by an otherwise unknown cause. (For example, the effects of microwave radiation are especially easy to identify.)

Because of this fact, I hereby offer a reward of $50.00 for copies of each published description of mice killed or injured as the alleged result of their proximity to a UFO.

Any reference to cases where mice were affected by a UFO will also be most welcome.

Jan Eric Herr
6250 Stanely Avenue,
San Diego, CA 92115
USA.

MURDER MYSTERIES
Regarding Michael Hoffman's article on occult murders in 35 I have substantial material which dovetails perfectly with his. (No pun intended!) My material includes animal mutilations, murders committed by Richard Chase of Sacremento, with characteristics almost identical to Mr. Hoffman's and much material concerning cattle mutilations. I also have an unsanitized version of the "Flickenberger Report" and other items of interest.

My own research uncovered a disproportionate number of victims of mass murderers who are close to law enforcement. Daughter of prosecutor. Daughter of a police chief. BLM land surveyor supervisor. Wife of a deputy Sherrif. Large numbers of military personell in several locations. Etc. etc.

In addition to Son of SamBianchi, et al, one might include Ted Bundy, a social worker and official close to the Governor of Washington, whose killings followed an astrological sequence. Incidentally, only the early killings follow the occult pattern. Once into killings, the killers almost universally depart from the pattern for later killings.

The double-initial pattern also appears in Bundy, in part of the killings, following victims: Brenda Baker. Brenda Ball. Laura Lehi. Carin Campbell. Kathy Kliner, injured and Lisa Levy, in one incident. Six out of thirty isn't a pattern, but is disporportionate to the distribution of double initials in the population. There is, for example, not one single double initial in the Chase series. Bundy is known to have been involved in the occult, as were some of his victims.

The Flickenberger Report goes into great detail about killings of animals and humans by a "Satanic Cult" using the name Church of Satan. So does the book, *Michelle Remembers*. Neither are related to Anton LaVey's outfit.

Edwin Austin
Mutilation Data Center
Orange, Calif.

RAIN OF GOLFBALLS
In April 1976 when tracing a disused footpath I was crossing rough and unfrequented ground about one mile west of Saundersfoot, South Wales, at an altitude of about 150 feet, map reference SN230052, when I noticed a golf ball in the grass and looking around I picked up about a dozen within a small area. I thought at first that the balls might have been lost by a careless and affluent golfer practicing but later decided that no golfer in his senses would practice on such rough ground when there was a smooth field a few yards away so returning to the place a few days later and searching more carefully I discovered more balls making about 30 in all. Many of the balls had been trampled into the ground by cows which use the place and were barely visible so probably more could have been found by digging.

The balls varied from apparently new, clean ones to badly battered; I gave them away to local golfers. The place where I found them is on the side of a valley which slopes at about 30°. It is rectangular, about 50 by 30 yards and is in the corner of a large field but separated by a hedge with gaps in it. The surrounding hedges are wide belts of brambles with shrubs and trees. I found no balls outside this area.

I considered the possibility that these balls could have been transported from Tenby golf links, a distance of about 3¼ miles, by magpies which flock in this area during the spring. Though I have never seen seagulls there I thought they might have done it. The seagulls around here dig cockles out of the sand; carry them up to a height of about 30 feet and then drop them. Apparently this causes them to open. I wrote to the Royal Society for the Protection of Birds about this but their reply was that it was unlikely that birds were responsble.

I continued to visit the place during 1975 but found no more balls. Much rain prevented me struggling through mud to reach the site during January and February but when I got there in early April there was a new supply of balls just as in the previous April and again I collected about 30. I then looked forward to a regular supply of balls each April but since 1976 I have not found any.

Lacking any tenable explanation for the foregoing experiences, I pushed them to the back of my mind, until, recently I read in *Phenomena*, about the fall of golf balls in Florida in 1969 (p18). I realise that this is a weak case. No one saw the balls arriving and no one saw me collect them and I could have planted them there myself, so I doubt that you can make use of it even though the fact that it occurred twice makes it extra mysterious.

A.T. Ryland
Saundersfoot, Dyfed

STRANGE FEELING
Two friends of ours had a strange experience in September 1982 near their home in Rearsby, Leicestershire, which one of them described as follows: 'It was very nearly dark — overcast sky and a slash of orange sunset over Charnwood. We were just outside the village walking along a farmtrack (with Hopkins, of course [their dog]) between two potato fields. Very cold wind. Then, for a split second, we both felt a warm breeze on our faces. We both agreed afterwards that had we been alone we would not have trusted our own senses. Any idea what it was? No buildings nearby, no trees, no birds.'

If any reader can throw light on this experience, we would be glad to hear.

Janet & Colin Bord
Montgomery, Powys

TULPOID CATS
Interesting that the early sightings of the Scottish 'Lioness' (or Puma... or black panther... or whatever) should have been near Bettyhill... a name with some UFO connexions. The beast is obviously some kind of *Cait Sidh*. Compare the description given by Donald Mackenzie (FT26p43): 'About the size of an alsatian, dark coloured and had a white chest', with the one from J G Campbell, quoted in Katherine Briggs' *Dictionary of Fairies:* 'Large as a dog, black with a white spot on its breast'. Katherine Briggs also gives some information on the Highland demon-cat 'Big Ears', describing how its claws made clearly visible marks upon a stone on which the creature appeared. Perhaps *taghairm* has been revived? Taghairm is described by Miss Briggs as 'Perhaps the most horrible of all recorded magical spells'; an invocation of the huge demon-cat which involves the roasting alive of a good many 'normal' cats. The word itself seems, according to my shaky Gaelic, to mean 'I come'. **Doc Shiels,**
Ponsanooth, Cornwall.

EDITORIAL
Continued from p 3

Tarrytown conference Center, East Sunnyside Land, Tarrytown, NY 10591, USA). The *New Scientist* competition closes 28 Feb 1983, and will have two runners-up prizes of £100 each. The condition is to describe the experiment only, not to perform them, so that the effects of the very first experiment can be monitored elsewhere in the world.

REQUESTS FOR BOOKS
Some readers, under the impression that we sell the books we review, have sent orders for these books. All review copies received are put in the Fortean Times Library, which will one day be available to genuine researchers. The only books we sell are those we advertize with FT's address, and so far these have been confined to our regular ad page. These are books in which we have a direct interest, written by some among us, or basic reading (like Fort's *Books*). We'd like to develop an FT mail-order book business for new and second hand Fortean books, but we'd need some capital (though you *can* start small in this trade), but more importantly, some mug who will take it on on our behalf. Any mugs out there who want some home-work? Write in and we'll talk it over.

In the meantime, here are the few mail-order addresses known to us who might be able to help you (speciality in brackets):

Arcturus Book Service: 263 N. Ballston Ave, Scotia, NY 12302, USA. (Ufo, Fortean).

Lionel Beer: 15 Freshwater Court, Crawford St, London W1H 1HS. (UFO).

Compendium Books: 234 Camden High St, London NW1 (General).

Oracle Books Ltd: 62D Stamford Hill, London N16 5BR. (Occult).

The Sourcebook Project: Box 107, Glen Arm, MD 21057, USA. (Fortean).

Ms S.R.Stebbing: 41 Terminus Drive, Beltings, Herne Bay, Kent CT6 6PR. (UFO).

If readers know of any other mail-order shops, please let us know.

ERRATA
FT37
• In the 'Classical Encounters' article, p39, col 1, para 3, the line should read: 'But this positive emphasis should not be understood simply as referring to eternal life,'; not 'external life'.
• There were a number of spelling errors in the Sheldrake interview, and a line of text missing from col 1, p17 — these will be restored for the xerox (see 'Sheldrake Sequels' above). Ooops.
• Doc Shiels wishes to dissociate himself from the spelling errors in his column last issue, including odd transpositions, in the first 4 paras. Mea Culpa — that's what happens when we rush. This issue has been rushed off its feet even more, with little time for proofreading. We try....but ....well, you know....
FT36
• Under the heading 'Christ in the Clouds 1' the reference to fig K should be 'fig A' which will be found on p32.

REFERENCES
Some readers have suggested a modification to our method of referencing which will better help those benighted souls who have to look them up for research. We delight in recording some obscure publications, and that's the problem. How can someone in South Bend look up the *South China Morning Post*, or someone in Neasden check out the *Rising Nepal*? Many of these stories have commonality through the newswires, so in future we will prefix our references with the initials of the appropriate news agency: Associated Press (AP), Reuters (R), United Press International (UPI), Press Association (PA), etc, where this info is known.

NEXT ISSUE
For FT39 we have something out of the ordinary: a lead article by Robert Anton Wilson on synchronicity in Joyce's Finnegan's Wake — also a long delayed review of some north of England toad-in-the-hole cases by Paul Screeton. There will also be a collection of short reports, sent by different people, of some peculiar creatures sighted; and a summary of recent developments at monster-haunted Lake Champlain. Among subject for our notes are: spectacle-snatchers, shoe-painters and other compulsives; weird plants; more UK cat sightings; evictions by poltergeists; mass-hysteria outbreaks (if we can get that together); and a miscellany of Fortean oddities which arrived too late for inclusion in *Living Wonders*. Oh....and much more, as always.

YOU CAN LOOK HIGH AND LOW FOR FT

– but the only way you'll be certain of getting it these days is by subscribing (or renewing your sub).

All overseas readers get an airmail service (on subs only) at surface rates; that means within 2 weeks of publishing instead of the usual 6-8 weeks.
• **SUB RATES** - 1 year or four issues: (UK) £5.00; (Overseas) $12.00.
• **SINGLE COPIES** - (UK) £1.25; (Airmail) $4.00 – we can send a recent issue plus our literature to a friend or potential subscriber at these rates.
• **PAYMENT** - payable to Fortean Times. Dollar cheques acceptable, but a sterling cheque drawn on a London bank is better (ask your bank for one). Rates include postage and bank charges. If you think your order has gone astray, let us know.

BM-Fortean Times
London WC1N 3XX, UK

BACKISSUES

ALL AT SINGLE ISSUE PRICE (SEE LEFT)

• **FT31** – The Chinese Wildman; Gateways to Mystery; The Touch of Death; UFO muggers; mystery big cats; ball lightning; synchronous names; little people; fake doctors; Forteana from China; comix.
• **FT32** – The Mississauga Blob; Old Ives' Tales; Gateways (pt 2); occult murder; mystery big cats; fairy tales come true; Forteana from India and China; child sacrifice; mystery panthers in USA and Australia; comix.
• **FT33** – The Enfield Poltergeist; mythology of UFO abductions; Gateways (pt 3); mass hysteria at Nottingham; simulacra; coffin stories; Jeoff Watson's Nessie pix; UFOs; Forteana from China; giant snakes; comix.
• **FT34** – Congo dinosaur hunt; lake monster names; phantom hitch-hikers; interview with Dr Jean Bolen on synchronicity; the Welsh 'puma'; mystery big cats; beached whales; animal saboteurs; nature follows art; ice falls; inept crimes; Trashkashic records; odd Irish doings; giant squids; comix.
• **FT35** – The Myth of Darwinism; an SHC from 1744; The

Runamo Runes; Forteana from Malaysia and China; spontaneous combustions; antiquities; strange trees; magic fuels; frog and stone falls; mystery big cats; bizarre bacteria; TV science; occult murder; Fortean travel in USA.
• **FT36** – Anomalistics; Photos of Jesus; Runamo Runes; Gent's Mag extracts; hermits and wildmen; strange tales; toads in holes; bleeding statues and visions; the Buddha's UFO; DIY surgery; coin, ice and sand falls; ASSAP and CSAR; jellyfish in the sky; Forteana from China; USA monitor lizards; Nessie; comix.
• **FT37** – Australia's Lizard Monsters; energy from space; encounters with Greek gods; interview with Dr Rupert Sheldrake on a New Science of Life; a female prophet; Irish oddities; mystery USA kangaroos; UFO hallucinations; falls of crabs, frogs, peas, fish; visions, stigmatics and fasting; plants in odd places; mystery UK bear scares; talking polts; reflections; homing rings; locked-up by friends and relatives,

• • •

Founded in 1973 and first called *The News*, FT's humble beginnings have become legendary – well, out of print anyway! We now have high quality xerox facsimilies of the **first** twenty issues of *Fortean Times*.

LIVING WONDERS

Mysteries & Curiosities of the Animal World · John Michell & Robert J. M. Rickard

· THE LOST AUSTRALIANS ·

· AVIAN ABDUCTIONS ·

· MAN-EATING TREES ·

Following the worldwide success of their previous book, *Phenomena* (1977), John Michell and Robert Rickard have again joined forces to produce a detailed study of strange and unexplained aspects of animal life. Old ideas, long thought to be discredited, are re-examined in the light of modern evidence, and the authors have drawn on a wide range of sources, from mythology to the records of early naturalists and the latest press reports. With 170 illustrations £8.95

· THAMES & HUDSON ·

· CALCULATING HORSES ·

· CANINE LOYALTY ·

Fortean Times

ISSUE No.39 The Journal of Strange Phenomena. PRICE: £1·25 $3·00

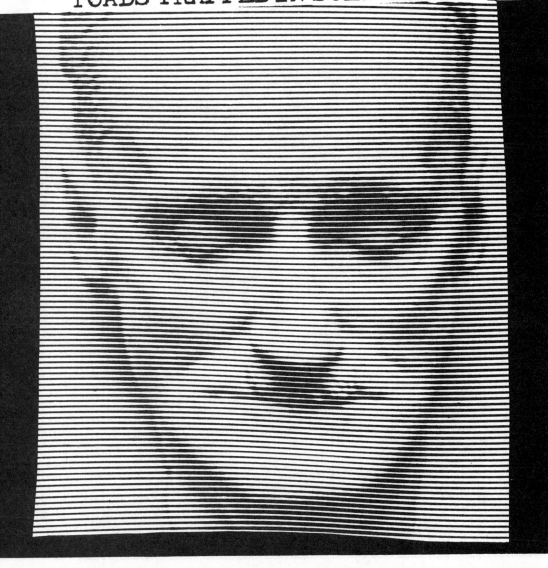

ROBERT ANTON WILSON ON JAMES JOYCE

JACK ANGEL: HE SURVIVED HELL'S FIRE

TOADS TRAPPED IN SOLID ROCK

Books from FT.

- **THE COMPLETE BOOKS OF CHARLES FORT** – Comprising *Book of the Damned* (1919), *New Lands* (1927), *Lo!* (1931), and *Wild Talents* (1932). Still the greatest single compendium of baffling and strange phenomena ever written, covering almost every subject on our list and many others besides. Fort's style has been called bewildering, intoxicating, impenetrable, stream-of-consciousness and one of the most brilliant of his day. This is a tour de force of iconoclasm, challenging the complacency of dogmatic science and religion with embarassing data and exciting ideas, but written with disarming wit and wisdom. This is a 1974 reprint of the 1941 edition compiled for the old Fortean Society, with a new introduction by Damon Knight, and the old index. Hardcover, 1125 pages. Because of its bulk we are offering this only to UK and European readers. US readers are advised to obtain it from Dover Books, NY. £15.00.

- **PHENOMENA: A Book of Wonders** by John Michell & RJM Rickard. Recommended introduction to the philosophy of Charles Fort, and the historical and thematic continuity of 57 varieties of strange phenomena, from stigmata levitation and fairies to showers of frogs, wild children and ball lightning. 216 illustrations, many collected together for the first time anywhere. Large format paperback. Price includes post & packing. UK: £3.90; Overseas surface: $8.00.

- **SIMULACRA** – An erudite survey of the varieties of spontaneous images in nature. One of the most remarkable Fortean books around – inspires art, psychology and mysticism. Illustrated with 196 photos collected by the author, John Michell, over many years. Soft cover only, 128 pages. Virtually unobtainable in USA. UK £3.80; overseas surface $8.00.

- **LIVING WONDERS** – The authors of *Phenomena*, John Michell & Robert Rickard, explore some mysteries and curiosities of the animal world, from folklore, and mythology to the records of early naturalists and explorers and contemporary reports of strange animals and stranger behaviour. Topics include: a little history of cryptobiology sea-serpents and other marine enigmas, lake-monsters, the return of extinct animals, prehistoric survivals, animals out of place in Britain, mysterious animals of Australasia, theories of animal distribution and the evidence for animal teleportation, explanations for rains of frogs & fishes, showers of insects and other animals, falls of seeds and veg, swarms and dearths of insects, creatures imprisoned in rock and wood, animals found far out at sea, talking cats and dogs, calculating horses, winged cats, life-saving pets, animal benefactors, canine loyalty, martyred animals, homing animals, abductions by eagles, man-eating trees, modern Jonahs, animals courts and funerals, animal battles, mass-panics and animal suicide, bird hibernation, imprinted eggs, how rats steal eggs, rat kings & monkey chains. Paperback pp176, 170 illus, name index. UK £6.00; overseas surface $10.00.

- **PHOTOGRAPHS OF THE UNKNOWN** – An unparalleled collection of over 300 photographs on sea and lake monsters, Bigfoot, ghost lights, natural UFOs, haloes and parhelia, falling objects, UFOs, computer analysis of UFO photos, possession, stigmata, bleeding images, spiritualist phenomena, thoughtography, Kirlian photography, apparitions, portraits of Christ, pain immunity, firewalking spoon-benders, levitation of objects, human levitation, apports, poltergeists. Many in full colour; many never before published, many never collected before. Plus essay on paranormal photography. An excellent visual reference for paranormal and Fortean photos. By Bob Rickard and Richard Kelly. Large format paperback, 144 pages. UK: £6.50; overseas surface $13.00.

- **MAN BITES MAN: The Scrapbook of an Edwardian Eccentric.** Edited by Paul Sieveking from the press clipping albums of George Ives. The weird, the dubious, the heroic, the horrific, and the hilarious. Much of Fortean interest. Large format hardback. 160 pages. Profusely illustrated with 584 facsimile clippings from 1890 - 1950. UK £5.00; overseas surface $10.50.

- **WILDMAN** – A compendium on the Chinese equivalent of Yeti and Bigfoot. Three articles newly translated from original Chinese, with new photographs, & 12 illustrations from old Chinese books. 'A Challenge to Science' the original article by Yuan Zhenxin and Huang Wanpo, with new material. 'I Witnessed a Wildman Mother and Child in the Chestnut Forest' by Fan Jingquan. 'Does the Flying Saucer Exist?' by Zhou Xinyan. Also 'A Brief Bestiary of Chinese Hill-monsters' compiled from Chinese literature by the booklet's editor Steve Moore. FT occasional paper No. 1. 24 pages, FT format. UK: £1.00; Overseas surface: $2.50.

Fortean Times

BM-Fortean Times
London WC1N 3XX.

The Journal of Strange Phenomena.

Spring 1983
ISSN 0308.5899

GANG OF FORT

Editor Robert J.M. Rickard
David Fideler
Steve Moore
Paul R.A. deG Sieveking
Art Dir. Richard Adams
ComixEd. Hunt Emerson

SPECIAL CORRESPONDENTS

Australia Greg Axford (Vic)
Paul Cropper (NSW)
Rex Gilroy (NSW)
Tony Healy (ACT)
Richard King (Vic)
Belgium Henri Premont
Canada Dwight Whalen (Ont)
Mister X (Ont)
England Richard Cotton
Peter Christie
Peter Hope Evans
Alan Gardiner
Chris Hall
Valerie Martin
John Michell
Nigel Pennick
Paul Screeton
Anthony Smith
David Sutton
Andy Townsend
Paul R. Thomas
Finland Tuuri Heporauta
France Dr Bernard Heuvelmans
Greece Anastasios D. Panos
Ireland Doc Shiels
Robert Anton Wilson
Japan Jun-Ichi Takanashi
Malaysia Ahmad Jamaludin
Dr C.H. Yeang
Roving Ion A Will
Scotland Roland Watson
Jake Williams
S. Africa Chris J. Holtzhausen
Sweden Ake Franzen
Anders Liljegren
Sven Rosen
USA Larry E. Arnold (PA)
Tom Adams (TX)
Loren Coleman (MA)
Richard T Crowe (IL)
Ron Dobbins (AZ)
Mark A Hall (MN)
Steve Hicks (KS)
Michael Hoffman (NY)
Phil Ledger (CN)
Kurt Lothmann (TX)
Gary S Mangiacopra (CN)
Joseph Swatek (NB)
Paul Willis (MD)
Joseph W Zarzynski (NY)
USSR Vladimir V. Rubtsov
Wales Janet & Colin Bord
Yugoslavia Milos Krmelj

Reprosetting Mostly by Cecelia Boggis:
11 Ashburnham Rd. Bedford.
Photosetting Wordsmiths: 19 West End.
Street. Somerset.
Printed by Golden Valley Publications
Piccadilly Mill, Lower St.
Stroud. Glos.
Overseas Overseas Postal Services Ltd.
Mailing 2-8 Hornsey St.
London N7 8HF
Sub & Label Anagram
Computing 316A Richmond Rd.
Twickenham TW1 2PD

Cover art by
ad Press

Editorial

TICK TICKA TICKA TACK TOCK TACKA

THIS ISSUE

Firstly our ritual apologies for the lateness of this issue. I know the wait will have been worth it for most of you, and you'll be glad to see FT has swelled to 64 pages. Even so we've had a hard job to pack in all we intended.

We have two new columns. I've decided to split off the strictly editorial business (which is mainly to keep you informed about FT itself) and give myself space in which to extemporize more generally on our subject matter. We also extend a welcome to Mike Crowley, all-round trivia expert who will go boldly to the front-line of science where no trivia expert has gone boldly before.

And next issue we'll be joined by Kevin McClure, editor of *Common Ground*, who will be monitoring beliefs in the end of the world. The industrious Kevin started *End Times Bulletin* but after several fascinating issues has had to fold it because of time and financial problems. We liked ETB so much that we promptly offered Kevin the chance to continue his doom-watch as a column in FT.

PLANS

Well, some of what we have planned for this anniversary year will be visible already. You will have met Hunt Emerson's envelope on the way in, and then, hopefully, have noticed the improvement in paper quality (the new paper is also cheaper than the thin stuff we used to use to cut down air-mailing costs!)

Our actual anniversary issue – FT41 – will take a different format from our usual method of presentation. The entire issue should be taken up with pieces of varying length by a galaxy of Fortean writers. For example, we are honoured to have something from Dr Bernard Heuvelmans on the cryptozoological dimensions of mythical monsters; Robert Anton Wilson on Fort's prose style and philosophy; and John Keel on Ray Palmer one of the forgotten founders of the mythology of UFOs. Many other items have been promised, and should make FT41 a sought-after and useful issue for a long long time.

Finally, we've had several requests to publish our system of clippings categories. The system we operate right now is,

in my view, not very satisfactory, and I'm in the process of a complete rethink as part of our work towards our computer database.

FT GIRO ACCOUNT

Several of our European readers have got into horrible muddles trying to pay their subs, what with Euro funny-money, weird currency controls, varying bank commissions etc. To ease matters we have opened a GIRO account through which money can be sent through postoffices with ease. This mainly applies to our subscribers in Europe and the EEC. The GIRO account number is **507824008**.

LIVING WONDERS

A word of explanation. Thanks to all those who ordered *Living Wonders* from our ad last issue. Unfortunately, supplies of the hardcover dried up quickly due to T&H underestimating the demand, and it is doubtful if hardcovers will be available in the near future. To cope with the unsatisfied demand, T&H have brought the release of the paperback forward from September to this April, and we should have supplies even as you read this. We hope those who ordered hardcovers will accept the paperback and a refund of the difference, and still get the same enjoyment from it.

ASSAP LIBRARY

One of the main aims of ASSAP (the Association for the Scientific Study of Anomalous Phenomena – see back to FT36p28), and the one your editor has been most active in supporting, is the founding of a national library of reference material covering the whole range of paranormal phenomena. I'm pleased to *Cont on p.22.*

FORTEAN TIMES is an occasional journal, intended to be quarterly, of news, notes, reviews and references on all manner of strange phenomena and related subjects and philosophies, continuing the work of Charles Fort (1874-1932). The views of contributors are not necessarily those of FT and vice versa. Published from BM–FORTEAN TIMES, LONDON WC1N 3XX, ENGLAND. **SUBSCRIPTION INFO:** see index for page. **RIGHTS:** all articles and art are the copyright of the authors and artists – everything else in this issue is copyrighted throughout the universe by FT. Uncredited material is by the editors. **SUBMISSION** is invited of articles, art, cartoons and news clippings. FT assumes no responsibility for submissions, but all reasonable care will be taken while in FT's possession. **ADVERTISING** and **SALES:** enquiries to the above address, or ring the editor on 01 552 5466.

OLDEST READER?

I am sorry to disappoint John White [FT38p58] but I was 75 *last* year. I have been chasing the mysteries since I was about 12 and have spent most of my spare time on them, apart from learning nine languages and following one or two material hobbies.

My only definite conclusion is my astonishment at the enormous amount which man still has to learn.

How pleased I am to see FT arrive through the letterbox. Keep up the good work!

William Brereton
Barton-on-Sea, Hants.

Yes, you have at least one reader older than 75 year-old John White. As of February 9, 1983, I will be 78. I am a retired chemist, a freelance writer, home-maker, grandmother, and an enthusiastic Fortean! My husband and I are a couple of odd-balls—but you would like us!

Iola B. Parker
Oakland, Maryland.

I will be 78 next birthday and there are probably older readers. I suggest you tell Mr White to keep going a bit longer. He might go to bed for a few years like his cousin!

I wonder why you repeated my letter about the rain of golfballs [originally in FT34p44] last issue[FT38p59]? It is a pity you did not add a note saying that if anyone encounters the same phenomenon they should *keep at least some of the balls* as it might be possible to trace their origin, when and where they were sold etc. from their makers. Not

realising their possible Fortean connection I gave mine away and the principle recipient has since died.

A.T.Ryland
Saundersfoot, Dyfed.

[We are gratified to learn of so many senior citizens among our readers, and that they find FT enjoyable.

As for repeating Mr Ryland's letter...put it down to brain damage (all those brickwalls I come up against, you know). I have written out 100 times: 'I must pay attention,' and in reparation for my bludner I've added a special note to our 'Falls' section, this issue – Ed.]

PHOTOS OF CHRIST

I was pleased to see that you reprinted my *Saucer News* material about 'Christ in the Snow' and the various versions in your FT36. I was the editor and publisher of this zine during its final days on earth. My connecting the picture with UFOs, I later noted, was in the fine tradition of the multigenesis claims.

I obtained the original [sic] 'Christ in the Snow' photo from a restaurant menu, on which it was printed verso to the bill of fare.

Gray Barker
Jane Lew, W.Virginia

BOBO (GOLF) LINKS

Fortean Times #38 arrived on the 23rd of December, but I did not have a chance to look it over until after the yuletide drama was over. Therefore, while "previewing" it last night, as I usually do before sit-

ting down one night to digest it, I was struck by the odd series of literary and related events FT seemed to trigger.

First, I was immediately drawn to Doc Shiels' last passages (on page 41) about lynx, links, and golf. Next, my fingers naturally turned to "A Circle of Clowns" as I did quite a bit of research on that subject in 1981. Obviously I had heard about the pre-phone call (from Bob Tarte to me) material, and skipped to the lower middle part of page 47. Well, I could not believe it, but there was a note about a sighting of two clowns in a golf cart, one with the magic name Tarte had zeroed in on, "Bobo". Leaping through the rest of #38, I discovered two letters by the Bords and Shiels which seemed must reading, but first I was drawn to the missive next to theirs – a communication on a rain of golfballs!! Were you playing some kind of Fortean game on us by placing Doc's letter on tulpoid cats next to Ryland's one on golfballs?? By the way, as I was reading about the golfball rain, Arnold Palmer was appearing in a TV ad on my set.

Well, I thought it was over, but as I placed my FT#38 safely away for future reading, I magnetically was attracted to a book of fairy tales of my wife's. I thought, now this looks nice and light, something to put me to sleep. Ha. The stories were all unknown to me, so I "randomly" picked "The Lost Half Hour" by Henry Beston. I almost dropped the book when I dis-
Cont on p62.

Synchronicity and Linguistics in Finnegans Wake.

1982, was the centenary of the birth of James Joyce, and we were very glad, at the tail-end of last year to receive this look at the way in which Joyce exploited the multi-dimensional properties of words and meanings, by **Robert Anton Wilson**, who claims Joyce as a significant influence on his writing. Synchronicity is a term coined by C.G.Jung for manifestations of meaningful coincidence. Back in FT17 Anthony Bell introduced us to the very Fortean game of 'lexi-links', the punning and plays on words, phonemes and symbols that occurs in almost every report of paranormal phenomena and the people and places involved. From time to time writers in FT have returned to the subject of word-play, among them Doc Shiels, whose offering this issue also — coincidentally (naturally) — celebrates Joyce.

Perhaps no novelist in history has been more concerned with synchronicity than James Joyce. As Samuel Beckett, a great fellow novelist who knew Joyce intimately, told Professor Richard Ellmann, "To Joyce reality was a paradigm, an illustration of a perhaps unstatable rule...It is not a perception of order or of love; more humble than either of these, it is a perception of coincidence." Over a hundred synchronicities appear in Joyce's *Ulysses*. When Joyce worried that he might die without finishing *Finnegans Wake*, he selected James Stephens to complete it, not on any literary grounds *per se* but because Stephens had been born on the same hour (6am) of the same day (February 2) of the same year (1882) and in the same city as Joyce (Dublin), had the same first name and had a last name which differed only by one letter from the first name of Stephen Dedalus, Joyce's alter ego in *Portrait of the Artist as a Young Man* and *Ulysses*.

Finnegan's Wake is in many ways an extension and enlargement of the forbidden and "unthinkable" areas of human experience first explored in *Ulysses*. It is more "difficult" than the earlier book, much more obscene, more experimental in styles, much funnier, and contains many, many more synchronicities. I intend to demonstrate in a forthcoming book that the *Wake* contains literally thousands of synchronicities; this paper is an introduction to that subject. We will focus especially on linguistics because, as Mark Patrick Hederman has noted, "In...*Finnegans Wake*, language is the main character, before whom all the other characters, the author and the reader are required to give way."

Finnegans Wake is a dream, and a dream requires a dreamer. As early as 1923, Joyce selected the name Earwicker for his dreaming protagonist; he had seen the name on a tombstone in Sidlesham, England, while on holiday. In *Stephen Hero* Joyce's autobiographical Stephen Dedalus had said that even a clock on a storefront could contain an "epiphany" or revelation; in *Ulysses* Stephen went further and defined God as "a shout in the street." It was consistent for Joyce to seek deep meanings in a casual tombstone.

What follows is neither correct nor consistent etymology; Joyce believed that the unconscious has not either/or logic and uses every possible meaning.

Earwicker might derive from *Eire-weiker*, dweller in Ireland. The Middle English *weiker* is cognate with Latin, *vicus*, a way or road. Synchronicity has already appeared, because Joyce had planned from the beginning to base *Finnegans Wake* on the linguistic theories of Giambattista Vico, whose name also derives from *vicus*. To commemorate this first "happy coincidence" the word vicus appears in the first sentence of *Finnegans Wake*.

Earwicker sounds much like "Earwigger"

and Joyce's dreamer seems to fear that his neighbors maliciously pronounce it that way behind his back. The earwig is reputed in folklore to *cause dreams* by crawling into the ears of sleeping people. Thus, the association Earwicker-earwig is appropriate for a book of dreams.

Earwicker owns an inn in Chapelizod, a Dublin suburb. The only other wellknown novel about Chapelizod is Sheridan Lefanu's *House by the Churchyard*, in which a character named Hyacinth O'Flaherty gets involved in a duel in Pheonix Park because of a misunderstood conversation *about earwigs*. By incorporating this into the *Wake*, Joyce makes Lefanu's novel a partial key, by synchronicity, to his own novel.

Before leaving Hyacinth O'Flaherty and House by the Churchyard, it is worth noting that "Hyacinth" was Oscar Wilde's code name for Lord Alfred Douglas in a love poem; Earwicker's dream partically concerns repressed homosexuality. Churchyard in Danish is *kierkegaard;* the philosopher Kierkegaard suffered from compulsive masturbation and morbid fears that this habit would cause insanity. Earwicker shares these fears and when Joyce describes him as being "on the edge of selfabyss" he is punning on both self-abuse and Kierkegaard's favorite metaphor of the Abyss.

Ear*wicker* thinks of himself as a Dubliner (indeed, Chapelizod is in County Dublin). The original Gaelic name for Dublin was *Baily atha Claith,* "town of the ford (bridges) of hurdles." The hurdles were bridges made of tree bark twined in a *wicker* pattern.

In the course of the dream Earwicker is repeatedly attacked by neighbors bent on lynching him or burning him alive for his real or imagined sexual "sins." These nightmarish sequences always refer back, through puns, to the ancient Celtic rituals in which human sacrifices were burned in *wicker* baskets.

Earwig in French is *perse-orielle*; Joyce sometimes calls Earwicker "Pearse O'Reilly," punning on this, but *Pearse* and *Reilly* are also two of the Irishmen shot by the English for staging the Easter uprising in Dublin post office, 1916.

The title of *Finnegans Wake* comes from an old Irish ballad in which Tim Finnegan falls from a wall, appears dead and suddenly rises again, alive, when splashed accidentally with whiskey. This is an Irish folk-equivalent of the myths of Jesus, Osiris, Dionysus etc.: the primordial archetype of Death and Resurrection. Thus Pearse and Reilly not only refer to Earwicker by a French pun but link synchronistically to the Resurrection theme, since they were part of the Easter Uprising.

Earwicker's name also contains an *ear*; as Joyce's eyesight failed and eleven operations were necessary to stave off total blindness, it became a critical commonplace to stress the aural aspect of his writing and to compare him to those two other blind bards, Homer and Milton. When asked to make a sketch of Joyce, Brancusi produced an abstraction based on the spirals of the *inner ear*. (Joyce's father, seeing this in a Dublin newspaper, said "Jim has changed a great deal since going to Paris.") Since "it darkles (tinct! tinct!) all this our funnanimal world" in the *Wake*, we have only our ears to tell us what is happening, by listening to the "soundsense" of the languages.

There seem to be only two *incidents* in *Finnegans Wake*, although they go through so many permutations and combinations that they eventually link on to all the major themes of myth, art and philosophy,

The first incident, which probably took place the morning before the night of the dream, happened when Earwicker, crossing Pheonix Park, felt the need to retire to the bushes to answer a call of nature. After taking his pants down, the misfortunate man suddenly noticed two young women who had retired to the bushes for a similar purpose. Whirling around, he noticed three British soliders who saw, or might have seen, whatever happened: Joyce describes Dublin as a "gossipocracy;" the dream continually has the neighbors, told of the incident by the soldiers, accusing Earwicker of any and all possible (and impossible) offenses, beginning with voyeurism, exhibitionism, masturbation, making homosexual overtures to the soldiers and going on to such elaborations as: murdering the soldiers, cannibalistically eating them, plotting to assassinate the Pope, etc.

In the second incident, which happened perhaps a half hour later, Earwicker, still in Pheonix Park, encountered a tramp who asked the time, in one version, or else produced a gun and attempted to rob him, in another version. In both versions, the clock in a nearby church struck noon just then. Earwicker is blonde and the tramp was brunette; this will become important in dream logic as we proceed. In both versions, Earwicker responds to the tramp with an impassioned but illogical denial that he has incestuous desires for his daughter, Isobel.

The girls in the bushes were urinating; by Freudian displacement this becomes Noah's flood. The three soldiers then become Noah's sons, *Ham*, Shem and Japhet, who saw Noah naked after he got drunk. Of these three Noah cursed only one, *Ham*, because the other two averted their eyes. Earwicker curses all three soldiers for seeing him partly naked.

Ham (the meat) derives from the pig; the pig is on the Irish shilling, a coin which passes through Earwicker's hands all day long as he serves drinks to the customers in his bar.

Ham also suggests Hamlet. Earwicker's full name is Humphrey Chimpden Earwicker and Humphrey, believe it or not, derives from Hamlet (see Brandan's O'Hehir's *Gaelic Lexicon to Finnegans Wake*.) According to one version of the Hamlet legend, Hamlet did not die when he killed his uncle, but survived and went on to become king of Danish Dublin.

Some eccentrics believe that Bacon wrote the plays attributed to Shakespeare. The dreamlogic synchronicity linkage is now Ham-pig-Bacon-Shakespeare-Hamlet-Humphrey Chimpden Earwicker.

Shakespeare's parents were John and Mary; so were Joyce's. This is punned on and elaborated at least a dozen times in the *Wake*.

Shakespeare is considered homosexual or bisexual by many writers; Earwicker worries that the soldiers think he was making overtures to them by lowering his trousers.

Earwicker's disgrace occurred, remember, in Phoenix Park. Joyce identifies the spot exactly: "By the magazine wall. Where the maggies seen all." The magazine was the subject of a satiric poem by Jonathan Swift.

> Behold this proof of Irish sense
> Where Irish wit is seen
> Where there's nothing left that's worth defense
> They build a magazine.

Swift had ambiguous romantic involvements with two ladies named Esther (Johnson and van Homerigh were their respective last names.) Joyce then creates the following correspondence: Swift = the guilty man in the Freudian bushes; the two Esthers = the two young ladies; Peter, Jack and Martin (in Swift's *Tale of a Tub*) = the three soldiers.

Joyce commented to Harriet Weaver that Swift and Sterne should have exchanged names, because Swift's writings were stern while Sterne's were swift. This joke appears dozens of times in the *Wake*: "he sternly struck his tete in a tub...and swiftly took it out again," "the siamixed twoatalk used twixt stern swift and jolly roger," etc.

Swift suffered from glaucoma. The German name for this disease is *die Sterne*, the star.

Joyce also suffered from glaucoma, the star, and had played with the German-English pun as early as the poem 'Bahnhofstrasse,' written after he had his first painful eye attack on that street in 1918:

> *Ah, star of evil! star of pain!*
> *High hearted youth comes not again*

Glaucoma derives from Greek *glaucis*, shining, and is an epithet for Athene, who was an owl goddess and is always shown with an owl in Greek statuary. Athene is also the patron of juries. When the jury sits to judge Earwicker they utter "a plethora of uluation." Uluation means to moan like an owl; in Jungian terms the jurors are invoking the owl-totem of wisdom to guide them in their deliberations.

Lawrence Sterne, the other half of the Swift-Sterne system, has many synchronistic links to the *Wake*, all exploited by Joyce. Sterne wrote *Tristram Shandy*: Howth Castle in Dublin,

which plays a huge role in the *Wake*, was built by Sir *Tristram* Armory de *Lawrence*. The patron saint of Dublin is St. *Lawrence* O'Toole. There is another Dublin in *Lawrence* County, Georgia; its motto "Doublin' our number all the time" appears on the first page of the *Wake*.

Tristram is the Gaelic form of Tristran. In the legend of Tristan and Isolde, Isolde hails from Chapelizod, where Earwicker lives; Chapelizod is corrupt Gaelic for Chapel of Isolde.

There are two Isoldes in the legend – Isolde the Fair, from Chapelizod, and Isolde of the White Hands, from Armorica in France. When Joyce writes of "Sir Tristram...rearrived from North Armorica," he includes both a reference to this legend and part of the name of the builder of Howth Castle, Sir Tristram Armory de Lawrence. Immediately following is "laurens county's gorgios," which completes Sir Tristram's name and locates the other Dublin in Lawrence County, Georgia. If there are two Isoldes, two Esthers and two Dublins, this is only partly Freudian distortion of the two girls in the bushes; it also refers to the fact that Earwicker has twin sons, Shem and Shaun.

Swift, incidentally, had a private name for Esther Johnson; he called her Stella. That also means star, in Italian, and links to the Sterne-star-glaucoma system.

Shakespeare, Swift and Sterne, already in synchronistic mesh with the *Wake*, all have S as the first letter of their names. Joyce named his autobiographical hero Stephen Dedalus, which begins and ends with an *s*. *Ulysses*, which starts, "Stately, plump Buck Mulligan..." and concludes "yes I will yes," begins and ends with an *s*.

Both incidents in Earwicker's nightmare – the first, with the 2 girls and 3 soldiers, and the second, with the tramp – happened in Phoenix Park. The brunette tramp addressed Earwicker as *"ouzel fin,"* which is phonetic Gaelic for "my blond gentleman."

Pheonix Park is an anglicization of Gaelic *finnishce pairc*, "field of bright waters." The waters bring back the urination theme. The phoenix was a bird who allegedly rose from its own ashes, after burning itself, thus bringing back the resurrection theme. Together water and fire introduce the alchemical *koan*, "water and fire are one."

The *finn* in *finnische* and the *fin* in the tramp's salutation evoke Finn Mac Cool, hero of Ireland's principal epic cycle. Finnegan, in the ballad, is Finn-again, as Joyce tells us explicitly: "Hohohoho, Mister Finn, you're going to be Finn again."

Finn Mac Cool's wife, Graunia, eloped with a handsome young warrior named Dermot. The aged Finn pursued them and they hid in a cave on Howth Hill. Thus we come back again to "Howth Castle and Environs," the phrase which concludes the first sentence (and includes the initials of Humphrey Chimpden Earwicker.)

The romantic triangle of Finn, the aged king, Gaunia, the faithless wife and Dermot, the young rival is repeated in the triangle of King Mark, Isolde the Fair and Tristan. Joyce does many variations on this synchronicity, and complicates it further by introducing also King Arthur, Guinevere and Launcelot. This theme is based on ancient rituals of flight-and-capture in marriage ceremonies, according to folklorist Gershon Legman, who also says it survives in the risqué jokes about the honeymoon couple and the man in the lower berth who interrupts their love-making. In Chapter II, Joyce combines all of these, and adds the pattern of the young stranger who is invited to have intercourse with a priestess and is then hanged (as an embodiment of the god) to make the crops grow. When Joyce writes, "They'll be tieing the knot any minute now," his language is deceptively simple for once, but both the Sacred Marriage (hierogamy) and Human Sacrifice are being invoked, on the Jungian legel, while Earwicker's sexual guilt and his fear of punishment are also there, on the Freudian level.

Finn Mac Cool's last name sounds like *cul*, which is French and Latin for ass-hole, the part of Earwicker most visible to the three soldiers in the bush incident. When Joyce writes "how coolious an epiphany," he puns on *cul* and *Cool*, caricatures his own doctrine that anything can be a revelation to the artistic mind, and includes again the intitials, HCE, of the dreamer.

Cul is also part of *felix culpa* ("joyous sin"), a phrase from the Mass for Holy Saturday. This refers to the sin of Adam and Eve which is happy because it called forth the Redemption through Jesus. Thus, fall and resurrection appear again: Holy Saturday precedes the rising of Easter Sunday.

When Joyce addressed Earwicker as "foenix culprit," we have the sin in Phoenix Park, the sin of Adam and Eve and the cul-Cool semantic system. When Earwicker confesses to the jury, he says "Guilty, but fellows culprits," implying we have all sinned with him (as in the hymn, "In Adam's fall/We sinned all"); he is also punning on *felix culpa*, and admitting he enjoyed it ("*happy*" sin"); and the cul-Cool association is still there. In the children's games of Chapter 9, primitive fertility rituals are reenacted, climaxing in "May he colp her, may he colp her, may he mixandmass colp her," which would make a good chant for a sex ritual except that it includes Irish Catholic guilt, since it sounds like "*Mea culpa, mea culpa, mea maxima culpa*" (my sin, my sin, my most grevious sin), a Catholic prayer; cul-cool are still there.

When the hero becomes "Old Fing Cole," he combines Finn Mac Cool with Old King Cole, who called for his fiddlers three, as Earwicker's sin summoned the punishment of the three

soldiers as eyewitnesses.

Returning to Pheonix Park: that was the scene of the infamous Phoenix Park murders of 1882 (the year of Joyce's birth), in which a revolutionary group, the Invincibles, killed two innocent men while trying to kill the English Lieutenant Governor, Joyce's childhood hero, Charles Stewart Parnell, was accused of conspiracy in connection with those murders; he stood trial, and was acquitted, when the letter implicating him was proven to be a forgery. All through the dream, Earwicker keeps waiting for a letter from Boston, Mass. (birthplace of the American Revolution) which he hopes will clear him of all charges relative to his own Phoenix Park Atrocity.

Parnell eventually fell from power when the Catholic Church repudiated him after he was found guilty of adultery. Part of the evidence concerned Parnell's having lived in an English hotel with Kitty O'Shea under the name "Mr. *Fox*." The *fox-hunt*, another paleolithic blood sacrifice, appears again and again in the Wake, usually to the tune of "John Peel." (Peel also contains a reference to nudity.) The main fox-hunt theme, however, occurs through systematic distortions of Oscar Wilde's description of that sport as "the uneatable pursued by the unspeakable." Joyce has about a hundred versions of this, of which the funniest is "The Turk, ungreekable in pursuit of armenable," which combines Wilde, homosexuality and the cultural peculiarity that most Europeans believe Greeks are especially prone to that habit, whilst the Greeks claim it is the Turks who are the *cul*prits. The Greek-Turkish-Armenian war of the 1920s is also included.

Parnell and Wilde were both Irishmen; both were persecuted and disgraced for sexual scandals when Joyce was very young and impressionable; both are verbally linked to the fox-hunt. Both lived on Stephen's Green in Dublin, and we know how important the name Stephen was to Joyce.

In Joyce's early short story, 'Ivy Day in the Committee Room,' one of the characters compares Parnell to a phoenix rising from its own ashes. What rose from Parnell's ashes was Easter 1916.

Earwicker was seen by three British soldiers, who are popularly called "tommy atkinses." One of the witnesses against Wilde was a Fred Atkins, a male prostitute.

The dark threatening figure of the brunette tramp often merges into the ancient Celtic bear-god. "What a quhare soort of a mahan," Earwicker says at one point, *mahan* is Gaelic for bear. Sometimes this figure becomes Bjorn Bjornssen, Norwegian folk-hero, because his name means bear bearson. Puns on the Latin *ursa*, bear, also abound. Glasheen concludes that the bear-god is one of the major figures in the *Wake*.

The bear blends with Giordano Bruno, Neopolitan philosopher burned for heresy in 1600, because of the pun bruin-Bruno. As burned heretic Bruno is another phoenix; Copernican astronomy, which he avowed, rose from his ashes.

Bruno taught an evolutionary dualism which held that everything eventually becomes its own opposite; as the name Phoenix Park contains both fire and water. "In filth, sublimity; in sublimity, filth," Bruno once said: this could almost be the motto of *Finnegans Wake.*

Bruno usually signed his works "Bruno of Nola." Dublin in Joyce's day had a Brown and Nolan bookstore. The opposites who struggle throughout the *Wake* go by many names — Earwicker and the tramp, Mutt and Jute, Ondt and Gracehoper, Butt and Taff, Shem and Shaun, Mercius and Justius, tree and stone — but most often they are Brown and Nolan. When united, these opposites become Bruno of Nola again. Bruno has been taken apart and put together again, to illustrate his own philosophy.

Bruno's first name was Giordano. In English, Jordan is a river, tying onto the urination theme by Freudian symbolism; and in Cockney slang, jordan is a chamber-pot, making the link explicit.

Bruno also suggests Latin *bronn*, thunder — which brings us back to Vico.

Vico, whose writings were influenced by Bruno's, held that both languages and religion were inspired by thunder, language being an attempt to imitate the Thing roaring in the sky and religion an attempt to propitiate it.

Thunder strikes ten times during Earwicker's dream. The link is thunder-Vico-vicus-weiker-Earwicker.

Like Joyce himself, Vico had a morbid fear of thunder, induced by childhood trauma.

Like Finnegan in the ballad, Vico once fell off a wall, was pronounced dead, and rose when they were getting ready to bury him.

Like Joyce, Vico believed that poetry arose out of creative etymology ("incorrect" etymology, in acadamese.) Like Joyce (and Benjamin Lee Whorf), Vico believed that a radical change in language could alter our perceived realities.

The 50ish Earwicker is afraid of the young tramp. Finn Mac Cool struggles to get his wife back from the younger warrior, Dermot. Old Mark of Cornwall loses Isolde to young Tristan. Vico, who had a long court battle with his own son, said that revolutions are rebellions of the sons against the fathers.

Nineteen years before beginning the *Wake*, Joyce taught school on Vico Road, in Dalkey, County Dublin. Seventeen years before the *Wake*, Joyce taught on Via Giambattista Vico in Trieste.

Vico, who wrote of sons displacing fathers, said every verbal coincidence was a poem showing a new reality. Joyce, who derived his name from Latin and French roots for joy, al-ways reminded people that, in German, Freud also derives from joy, *freude*. Freud agreed with Vico about rivals being Oedipal sons.

Let us consider this entire synchronicity-network in relation to one of the minor characters in the Wake, General Pierre Cambronne (1770-1842.) All that most people remember about General Cambronne, and all that concerns dreaming Earwicker, is that Cambronne said *"merde"* when asked to surrender. That is enough to make him a powerful symbol.

The first time the thunder strikes in the dream it includes the letters "-konnbronn-," which contain Latin *bronn*, thunder, and sound like Cambronne. The thunder-crash is then dream-distorted into "the great fall of the offwall" — Finnegan's fall in the ballad, Earwicker's offal falling, or Humpty Dumpty smashing. This rapidly becomes the Battle of Contarf (April 23, 1014) in which the Irish king Brian Boru defeated the Viking invaders. The two girls and three soldiers are there, hidden, in the date.

A tour guide takes us around Clontarf, blending Brian Boru's death (he was killed by a fleeing Viking after his army had won) with 'Humpty' Chimpden Earwicker: "He was poached on that eggtentical spot...Load All-marchy...Onheard of an umscene...erde from erde." General Cambronne is in the elided *merde* and the Freudian concept of war as anal aggression is strongly implied.

Cambronne continues to appear in various guises throughout: "Brum! Brum! Cumbrum!" cry the cannons at Waterloo, page 9. "Cumbrum, cumbrum," they repeat on page 134. On page 421 we find: "Sept out of Hall of that, Ereweaker with the Bloody Big Bristol. Bung. Stop. Bung. Stop. Cumm Bumm. Stop. Come Baked to Auld Aireen."

General Cambronne mingles with Earwicker's defecation in the park, the possible etymology of wicker from *weiker* and *vicus*, and the strains of "Come Back to Erin," a meaningful song to the exiled Irish author of all this.

Cambronne's anal imagery gradually merges with the case of an anonymous Russian General about whom Joyce heard from his father. It seems that John Joyce knew a man named Buckley who served with the Royal Fusiliers at the Battle of Savastapol during the Crimean War. At one point, Buckley got a bead on a Russian General and was about to shoot him, when the general took down his pants to relieve his bowels. "It made him look so human that I couldn't shoot," Buckley said. But when the general finished and pulled his trousers up again, he became an enemy officer once more, and Buckley shot him dead.

In Joyce's version, Buckley claims he shot the Russian General for his crime of "homo-sodalism." The gun fires twice: "Cabrone! Combrune!" The Russian general, making *merde*, is becoming Cambronne, saying it, and both blend with the Russian Bear (*brune*.) Since Buckley is Gaelic for youth and Joyce emphasizes the general's old age, this has Oedipal overtones and recalls Vico on politics as the war of sons against fathers.

The murder of the Russian bear/Russian general exfoliates to include Brian Boru at Clontarf, by way of the pun Brian-bruin; Cain and Abel; Napoleon and Wellington at Waterloo (Earwicker's sin in Phoenix Park was near the Wellington monument and *water* symbolizes urination, while *loo* is slang for a toilet); climaxing finally in "the abnihilisation of the etym," suggesting the atomic bomb that didn't go off in real time until six years after *Finnegans Wake* was published. (Joyce's assaults on language, to find "the nest of evil in the bosom of a good word" are also included in the ab-nihil-ization of the *etym*.)

The general's death is part of a cycle of "eggburst, eggblend, eggburial and hatch-as-hatch-can," which includes Vico's cycle of history, Humpty Dumpty again and the permutated initials of Humphrey Chimpden Earwicker.

If Earwicker is simultaneously man, mountain (Howth Hill), insect (earwig) and egg (Humpty Dumpty), he is a walking text of evolution. His story includes, we are told "weatherings and marryings and buryings and natural selections." When Isobel, his daughter, tries to justify her pubescent urges she evokes "the law of the jungerl" and calls on the great evolutionist in the tones of a popular song, "Charlie, you're my darwing." Earwicker attempts to restore Irish Puritan values by urging her to turn her mind to improving literature, such as *The Old Curiosity Shape* and *Doveyed Covetfilles*, which, alas, only reveals his own guilts. When Earwicker becomes a bee and asks a wasp to "commence insects" with him, more repressed truth comes out, but it is all very natural, is it not? As Hyacinth, Earwicker is most guilty and most natural; never mind that that was Wilde's name for Douglas — is it not normal for a hyacinth to be seen "pollen himself" in the Spring?

One of the more mysterious characters in the *Wake* is a shadowy Eugenius who keeps popping up at odd moments. Adaline Glasheen has finally identified him as Eugenius Schaumann, who happens to have shot another Russian general, Ivan Bobrikoff, governor of Finland on June 16, 1904.

June 16, 1904, was the day which Joyce immortalized in *Ulysses*; it was also the day on which he met Nora Barnacle, who was his mistress for 27 years and his wife for 10. They met in front of Oscar *Wilde*'s house on Stephen's Green, diagonally across from the house where *Wellington* once lived, near where a bust of James Joyce now stands. Nora was working at the time in *Finn's* Hotel.

Oscar Wilde was the first proponent of the theory that Shakespeare was homosexual.

Suit Claims Leprechaun Kidnapped

DUBLIN (Reuters)—What may be the first lawsuit in history involving the kidnapping of a leprechaun is being threatened by a Dublin couple.

Kathleen and Mick Maguire claim they found the fairy in question under a mushroom in Dublin's Phoenix Park last August.

They admit he was dead but they and their neighbors promptly pronounced him "a real little leprechaun with perfect features and one leg crossed over the other."

What it was the Maguires found they promptly put it in a bottle and took a booth at the Crumlin Fun Fair to display the sprite for the public.

Folks paid threepence a look and in seven weeks the Maguires collected £35 ($98)

But one day, Kathleen says, four country lads came to look and snatched the bottle away, and to this day no sign has been seen of them.

The Maguires hired a lawyer who sent a letter to Gordon Hunt, manager of the fair, claiming the fair was liable for the loss of the leprechaun and demanding £100 compensation.

Hunt insists he was not responsible.

Another Phoenix Park coincidence. We were amused — but not surprised — when this clipping arrived in the same week as Robert Wilson's Joyce/synchronicity MS. [It is a Reuters report in Niagara Falls Review *(Ontario) 20 Oct 1953. Credit: Dwight Whalen.]*

Shakespeare, like Brian Boru, died on April 23.

Brian Boru was blonde and the Vikings were called *dugalls* which means "dark foreigners," making them brunette, like the tramp who threatens Earwicker .

A mysterious voice cries *"More pork!"* several times in the dream. This may be a voice heard earlier in the evening, from a customer in Earwicker's inn, but it links with the ham-bacon-Ham-Bacon-Shakespeare chain and also with Swift. Swift met Esther Johnson at *More Park*.

Nora's voice appears on the first page of the Wake, combined with the voice that spoke to Moses: "nor avoice from afire..." The place where she worked as a chamber-maid is invoked on the last page: "There's where. First...Finn, again!"

The week *Finnegans Wake* was published, the Russo-Finish War of 1939 broke out. Joyce wrote to his friend, painter Frank Budgen, "The prophet is vindicated. The Finn again wakes and Buckleys are coming from all directions to shoot that Russian general."

These synchronicity-systems all link to each other, making the *Wake* a model of the inter-connectedness of all things claimed by mystics (and by Bell's Theorem in modern physics.) Thus, the man who forged the letter implicating Parnell in the Phoenix Park murders was Richard *Piggott*, thus linking Parnell to the ham-bacon-pork system. Two girls and three castles (military symbols) appear on the Dublin coat-of-arms, suggesting Earwicker's guilt about 2 girls and 3 soldiers. Ireland is a living synchronicity, being converted to Christianity in 432 (by St. Patrick) and containing 4 provinces divided in 32 countries. If Earwicker is both Hamlet and Humpty Dumpty, he easily becomes "omlette," combining guilty prince and smashed egg. Hamlet-Gertrude-Claudius is the same triangle, with more Freudian over-tones, as Dermot-Graunia-Finn, Lancelot-Guinevere-Arthur, Tristan-Isolde-Mark, soldiers-girls-Earwicker. When Joyce wants to link cuckolded King Mark with Mark Twain (by linguistic dream-association) another synchronicity appears to help him: Twain wrote of Huck *Finn*... And *Twain* suggests *twin* and Earwicker has twin sons...

And so on, *ad infinitum*? It seems so; and that is Joyce's singular triumph. The physical universe currently appears to be finite, but it is infinite *in its aspects*, as Korzybski argued, because we can always see new connections and relations between its elements. This "infinite regress" in our relation to the universe, our interminable analytical ability to find ourselves in new relations with everything, has no model anywhere in art, except in *Finnegans Wake*. Even Escher only suggests infinite regress for a short while; then we see how the trick was done. *Finnegans Wake* creates the illusion of infinity at a higher and higher level, the more we study it. The synchronicities exfoliate outward, beyond the book to Joyce's other works, to the whole universe.

Thus: in *Exiles*, Richard Rowan, the character based on Joyce, cynically suggests that in a hundred years the "Americans" will build a statue of him in Dublin. 100 years after Joyce's birth, in 1982, an executive of American Express donated the money for a statue of Joyce in Stephen's Green. In *Ulysses*, Stephen, deserted by Lynch, mutters a phrase from the vulgate Bible about Judas going to hang himself; Vincent Cosgrave, the model for Lynch, committed suicide a few years after that was written. Earwicker has a television set in his bar, in the *Wake*, published in 1939; real television sets only began to appear in real bars around 1949, ten years later. The Russian General is "blown to Adams" in a sequence Joyce wrote about ten years before Hiroshima. *Levin*, Latin for thunderbolt, appears many times in the Wake in connection with the Vico-thunder theme; the first book-length study of Joyce was written by Prof. Harry Levin of Harvard...

And in Dalkey, where Joyce once taught school on Vico Road, a young man was arrested while this article was being written less than a mile away in Sandycove. The young man was charged with two murders and a burglary. One of the murders occurred in *Phoenix Park*. Because the accused young man was arrested in the apartment of the Attorney General, the Attorney General, although accused of no crime, has had to resign. Rumors much akin to the dream-blurred sexual scandals of *Finnegans Wake* are rife. One hundred years earlier, the Phoenix Park murders of 1882 similarly brought about the near-downfall of another Irish politician, Parnell, who was proven innocent, but later fell anyway for sexual irregularity. Since Joyce was born in 1882, this second Phoenix Park murder mystery marks his centennial with deep shadows of the nightmare themes of the *Wake*.

•

Robert Anton Wilson

PHENOMENOMIX

HUNT EMERSON

NOGWOOD PUSTULE HAD PRESENTED HIS DELIGHTED FIANCÉE BEENA FLEEP WITH AN ENGAGEMENT RING!

OH NOGGY! ITS BWOOTIFUL!

SNURK

THEY CELEBRATED THE EVENT WITH A TRIP TO THE SEASIDE!

SIGH

SNURK

SUDDENLY....

NATURALLY, BEENA WAS HEARTBROKEN...

WAAAAAH

..AND NOGWOOD WAS NONE TOO PLEASED EITHER!

FOUR NICKER THAT RING PUT ME BACK!

SNURK

SO YOU CAN IMAGINE HIS SURPRISE SOME MONTHS LATER WHEN HE OPENED A PACKET OF FISH FINGERS AND FOUND....

EEEEE! WELL I NEVER!

"WELL" YOU MAY THINK - "WHAT A HAPPY ENDING!" BUT IT WAS NOT THE END, FOR THE FISH FINGER THAT BORE THE RING, WAS BACKED UP BY A WHOLE HAND OF FISH FINGERS BRANDISHING WRITS FOR BREACH OF PROMISE!

writ

FISH FINGERS

POOR OLD NOGWOOD FOUND HIMSELF OBLIGED TO TAKE IN MARRIAGE NOT THE HAND OF HIS BELOVED BEENA, BUT FIVE FROZEN FISH FINGERS.

Moral: WIMMIN IS TRUBBLE

Jack Angel, SHC Survivor.

As rare as cases of SHC are, instances in which the victim survives the strange fire are even more scarce. Here, **Larry Arnold,** possibly the leading researcher into SHC looks at some SHC survivors, and reports on the startling story of Jack Angel.

Jack Angel — SHC survivor [© 1983 by Larry E. Arnold/ParaScience International. All rights reserved.]

The evidence for self-igniting people threads a meandering, often convoluted trail through the last 500 years of human history, and may extend right to the very edge of time where the mists of memory become lost to pre-history. Its exploration has engaged some of the world's best medical minds in bitter controversy, requires at times a near (even temporary) cessation of credulity, and promises to be among the more provocative and profound adventures yet undertaken by sciences.

Spontaneous Human Combustion is, as most forteans but few physicians know, the process whereby a person suddenly ignites without contacting an external source of fire and then may be reduced to ashes while nearby combustibles paradoxically escape largely unsinged. Classically, the person who becomes a human fireball leaves behind an extremity or two — feet, ankles, maybe the lower legs, hands, perhaps a shrunken skull — and a mound of sweet-smelling powdery-ashed bone and tissue burned more completely than a crematorium normally achieves.

Fire marshals and medical professionals generally despise (and dismiss) SHC. It raises too many disquieting questions and baffling mysteries they are untrained to address, let alone answer. They would probably detest Jack Angel...not for who he is but for what he *did* one day in November 1974.

Angel was no criminal or murderer, but a travelling clothing salesman earning a comfortable £35,000 annually. He was successful, healthy, jovial, and happily married. The future looked heavenly for Mr. Angel.

Then something unimaginable occurred. Some would say impossible. In one presumably brief moment Jack Angel managed single-handedly (we mean that literally) to alter his life and medical history. Jack Angel did battle with the hellish fire of SHC...and lived to tell the incredible incendiary tale.

On Tuesday, 12 November 1974, Angel parked his motorhome that he'd converted into a garment showroom at the Ramada Inn in Savannah, Georgia. Pushing aside racks of clothes samples, he sheeted the sofa cushions, donned pajamas, and retired for the night — and a nightmare from which he'd never escape.

Around noon on November 16th — four days later — he awoke.

His right hand was burned black on both sides, from the wrist to his fingers. "It was just burned, blistered," he stated. "And I had this big explosion in my chest. It left a hell of a hole. I was burned down here on my legs and between my groin, down on my ankle, and up and down my back. In spots!"

Feeling no pain, Angel got up, showered, and dressed in the clothes he had laid beside his bed four days before. Unlike his body, Angel's pants and shirt were not touched by the mysterious fire; nor was the sheet on which he slept.

Staggering "like I was drunk," Angel recalled being told, he left the motorhome and entered the motel's cocktail lounge, A waitress immediately remarked about her customer's right hand. "Yeah, looks like I got burned," Angel muttered, still only half-conscious of his injuries and insensitive to pain. Minutes later, Angel lost all consciousness and collapsed on the floor.

"The next thing I knew," Angel told us, "I woke up in the hospital. And there's some doctor, maybe an intern, he's there with a pair of tweezers pulling skin off my arm."

Angel was in shock, unable to speak coherently. The physicians appeared shocked too. One doctor, Angel vividly remembered, "explained to me I wasn't burned externally, I was burned internally. And he called it a burn."

Around midnight the bafflingly burned patient abruptly regained full consciousness, and with what Angel called "excruciating pain." He began asking, then demanding, answers to his predicament. None were forthcoming.

He called his wife, telling her to examine the motorhome for signs of electrical faults (like blackness around outlet sockets or scorthing on any of the dozens of hanging garments). "There wasn't anywhere that you could find [burn] spots on the clothing, " he said of his wife's search. "There was no evidence of any fire in that bus." Once Angel had staggered away from it, that is.

Perplexed by his injuries and displeased with his treatment, Angel insisted he be transferred to a hospital renowned for its burn center. The diagnosis remained the same, however.

"Mr Angel presented himself to the hospital with a severe burn injury of the hand and minor injury of the chest wall," said Dr. David Fern, one of the burn center's physicians. "This was a third-degree burn which damaged the skin severely and most of the underlying muscle of the hand, causing a total anaesthetic hand." Fern declared the ulnar nerve "completely destroyed," with the median nerve showing "questionable viability." The burning that caused necrosis in the victim's hand continued up the *inside* of his right forearm, as well.

"They treated me for an *internal* burn," Angel said of his doctors.

The hand failed to respond to antibiotics, and became septic. Faced with many months of painful skin grafting and reconstructive surgery, Angel elected to have the burned hand and lower forearm amputated. During the next fortnight amazingly rapid healing occurred, and by mid-January 1975 Angel was discharged from the hospital.

Restoring normalcy to a life disrupted by what several physicians independently diagnosed as internal burning wasn't easy. Questions remained. What caused the horrific fire that blackened his hand and burned up the inside of his right arm, and created explosion-like wounds in his chest without damaging all the surrounding clothing? Why was there initially no pain? SHC *was* impossible, wasn't it? Angel wanted answers.

Enter the partners of a Georgia law firm known for its expertise and success in liability litigation, Thomas L. Clark and William C. Bowman (pseudonyms). They thought they had the answer: as Angel had been asleep and alone in his motorhome, certainly a design error or equipment malfunction caused the incendiary injuries they told him. If Angel agreed, they were willing to take the case on a contingency fee and would file suit against the manufacturer. Angel would get his answers at the lawyer's expense, and get two-thirds of the settlement as a throw-in. He agreed. "We engaged in litigation right away," Bowman said. They sought $3,000,000 in damages.

Now all their high-powered law firm had to do was find the cause.

First, the motorhome was examined again for faulty wiring. "But that proved not to be the case," Bowman admitted. Nor were there reports of lightning during the fateful period, nor overhead powerlines in the vicinity that could have somehow conducted electricity to Angel through the vehicle's chasis.

The lawyers then hired one of Georgia's prestige engineering and technology laboratories to inspect the motorhome from top to bottom. They did, literally; eventually dismantling the vehicle right down to the wheelbase.

Nothing rational — even irrational — could be discovered that suggested a plausible link between the motorhome and the cause of its owner's baffling burns. The laboratory's detailed report concluded by speculating Angel went outside the motorhome and became scalded by a jet of pressurized hot water that gushed through a safety valve he had opened when allegedly adjusting the water heater.

"They told me that somehow I had been burned by steam!" exlained Angel, throwing up his shortened arm in exasperation. "Well, steam again is an outside burn. And I wasn't burned outside. I was burned internally. The thing didn't make sense!"

The lawyers, confronted with their rapidly nearing day-in-court, were becoming exasperated too. "It was driving us crazy trying to find out what happened," Clark declared. The fact the engineers' report, on which their case had to be built, admitted its 'scalding water scenario' couldn't be verified left the lawyers as empty-handed as their client's right arm.

What began 2½ years earlier as a hot case for the legal team fizzled before their eyes and their single-handed client. Angel's attorneys withdrew the case from the court docket just one week before the scheduled trial. To quote Clark: "We just could not place the approximate cause... We never could come up with enough to keep us in court."

★ ★ ★ ★

In *The Sign of the Four*, Sherlock Holmes advises that "When you have eliminated the impossible, whatever remains, however improbable, must be the truth." What remained in the Angel case was, however improbably, SHC and its survival.

On the basis of both medical and (by default) legal testimony, Jack Angel had self-ignited and burned from the inside out. Furthermore he initially suffered no pain, suggesting confirmation of our belief founded upon other SHC events that this pyrophenomenon circumvents or disengages the body's neurosensory system. Also absent was the noxious odor characteristic of burning human flesh — another trademark of SHC.

Unlike the overwhelming number of historical SHC cases, such as the classic SHC of Grace Pett laudibly researched by Peter Christie in FT36, Angel survived the fearsome fire within. "The only explanation is that I was a victim of spontaneous human combustion," he has said recently after years of confronting the mysterious incident that significantly alterered his life yet stopped short of fatally transforming him into a fireball.

Is Jack Angel, now in his 70s, the only person to escape these frightful enflamings with his life? To the further consternation of Conventionalist scientists, the answer appears to be no.

★ ★ ★ ★

Heretofore the most widely known case of SHC survival occurred to Professor James Hamilton, a mathematician at the University of Nashville, Tennesse.

Walking home in the brisk winter air of January 1835, Hamilton was suddenly afflicted by a stinging sensation in his left leg. "Directing his eyes at this moment to the suffering part," chronicled Dr. Overton in the *Transactions of the Medical Society of Tennessee* (1835), "he distinctly saw a light flame of the extent at its base of a ten cent piece or coin, with a surface approaching to convexity, somewhat flattened at the top, and having a complexion which nearest resembles that of pure quicksilver."

Overton continued by telling how his patient, thinking to smother the flame by restricting its oxygen, "applied over it both his hands open, united at their edges, and closely impacted upon and around the burning surface." Whether by fortuitous chance or a triumph of rationalism, "the flame immediately went out."

As with Angel's physicians, Dr. Overton viewed the burn as being internal when treating his patient. Supporting this belief was the fact Professor Hamilton's silk and woollen drawers next to his legs had a small hole burned through the fabric at the point where the leg enflamed but his outer woollen pantaloons escaped with merely a "slighly tinged...dark yellow hue" on the inner layer of broadcloth.

About five score and seven years later, Paul V. Weekly rented a hotel room in Sioux City, Iowa. Sometime during the following night his foot began to itch, and Weekly threw back the covers to see what was the matter. A lurid blue glare from flames leaping out of his toes illumined the room, according to the fortean journal *Doubt* (June 1943). Without citing a source for the incredible event, *Doubt* said Weekly wrapped the bedsheet around his foot and extinguished the flames, after which he went back to sleep. Later an itchy foot (or feet) re-awakened him...and Weekly once more had to contend with a hot foot (or feet), which he did in the same fashion as before, afterwhich he again slept without further incident.

Weekly must certainly be considered in the running for the Guiness championship of Remaining Cool Under Fire. But beyond that, nothing can be said about this astonishing tale of apparent SHC survival.

What *can* be said is the pyrophenomena persists in plaguing people, and some continue to survive...occasionally more than once!

One evening around October, 1980, Mr. Jones of central California sat on the edge of his bed, his wife standing beside him. "I looked down and smoke was billowing from his arms as though something was on fire," she told us. "We both started frantically trying to put it out. Suddenly it was gone." There was no odor, no heat or tissue damage, but much smoke. He confessed it happened once before, when he was driving his car.

Almost the same thing happened — twice — to a Chicago, Illinois, woman in May 1981. In a two-week period dense odorless smoke gushed from beneath her blouse sleeve. Her garments were not singed, though they did get soaked as she frantically doused her arm with water from the kitchen sink.

A 31-year old Toronto woman, living alone in a 20th floor apartment, went to bed about 2:30AM on 19 June 1980. She awoke at her normal time four hours later, but there normalcy ended. During those 240 minutes portions of her thighs and abdomen began developing 2nd and 3rd-degree burns. Six months of agonizing skin grafting was needed to repair

the scar tissue caused by an unidentified blaze to which night clothes and linen were immune. This lady was terrified her body would re-ignite on the first anniversary of her self-searing, she told us. It did not.

Once was also enough for U.S. Navy airman Jeanna Winchester, who on 9 October 1980 suddenly burst into yellow flames while riding in a friend's car in Jacksonville, Florida. Before the fire died out it burned over 20% of her body: her right shoulder and arm, neck, side and back, and across her stomach and breast. "There was no other fire damage," reported patrolman T.G. Hendrix.

In central New Jersey, a young wife cradled her infant child in the back seat of a car driven by her husband. The tranquil afternoon drive in 1981 was suddenly shattered by an explosion — "It was like a boom!" — within the lady that left one side of her neck severely burned. Whatever the cause, it left her shoulder-length blonde hair unsinged and the baby untouched as well. Her physician blamed the seatbelt.

★ ★ ★ ★

We've interviewed more than a dozen individuals in the past two years who claim to have experienced SHC in a variety of sometimes similar, oftentimes outrageous and even nonsensical, and always astonishing ways. Some cases severly test credibility, yet the years of investigating pyrophenomena have prepared us to expect the marvellous and to respect the bio-energetic magic within *homo sapiens*.

"I don't understand the whole damned thing," Jack Angel said near the end of our interview with him, as he waved the stump of his right arm before our eyes. "I don't know anything about human combustion theories. But something has to cause it, doesn't it?"

The search for survivors of hell's fire continues...and for remains of those who didn't beat the Blaze within. Someday that search, with cooperation from fire and medical officials, and particularly from forteans themselves, will find the answers that Jack Angel and others ask about their enigmatic enflamings.

●

Larry Arnold

★ ★ ★

DEVILS SAFE
- Australia's new Labour prime minister, Bob Hawke has honoured his pre-election promise and halted the construction of the Gordon River dam in southwest Tasmania. This was the project that TV botanist David Bellamy went to jail for when he joined protesters in the paths of the bulldozers. The area to be flooded had some 29 plant species special to it, and a recent study of it found more than 1000 invertebrate ground dwellers new to science. It is also one of the last habitats of the Tasmanian devil, now officially extinct on the mainland. (*Times* 20 Jan 1983). Dr Bellamy won our admiration by claiming the area to be one of the few regions in which the Thylacine (Tasmanian wolf or tiger) might exist if any specimens are exant. Since the massive slaughter of their numbers at the turn of the century fewer and fewer Thylacines have been seen, and no good sightings have been recorded for many years now. Recent government and World Wildlife Fund studies have expressed the fear the remarkable creature may already be extinct. But just in case it isn't ready to roll over yet, a bit more jungle has been saved for it to hunt in.

THE DEVIL'S WALK IN DEVON
- The classic Fortean story of the mysterious trails of hoofprints through parts of Devon on 8th Feb 1855 is not yet dead, for just recently a letter appeared in the *Daily Mirror* (2 Feb 1983) on the subject. Its writer, signing himself 'Graham' of Slough, Berks, explained that it was all a trick, performed with great acrobatic skill by the Romanies of the area to drive away their rivals, the Didikais and Pikies. The whole theory set out by Graham is so exactly that set out in an excellent article on the subject by Ray Manners, in the Oct 1982 *INFO Journal*, even down to the use of stilts like extending step-ladders, that I thought Graham must be an unsuspected reader of that venerable Fortean journal.

Ray's piece was based on a story sent to them years ago by a member, from *In the Life of a Romany Gypsy* by Manfri Frederick Wood (RKP, 1973), and both article and book are well worth reading. Then a second letter, from Danny Smith, "a travelling gentleman of Herefordshire," in response to Graham's, was printed by the *Mirror* (18 Feb 1983), confirming the story as the widely-believed reason that Didikais and Pikies call 8 Feb 'The Night of the Mulo's Walk': Mulo being a term for the Devil himself. Danny Smith also mentions that the operation took 15 mths to prepare (Wood says 18mths) and that 400 sets of stilts were used. This figure agrees with Wood's account, but the main difference is that Wood (who admits a faulty memory) places the event in Somerset, not Devon.

There seems to be a modern tradition among the Romanies now that they were responsible for the tracks, but they could after all have cleverly exploited a genuine mystery that was well publicized. I'm not entirely convinced either way, but these are the best approximations to a solution to this ever-popular and cracking good yarn.

CLIPSTER'S DREAM
- By all accounts Mr W.E. Ashley Brown was a clipster from the Fortean mould. He was a former deputy editor of the *Sunday Express*, and had accumulated more than a million clippings during his 55yrs in Fleet Street. On his retirement he had a building

FALKLANDS FORECAST
- It was interesting to see how 'Old Moore' *nearly* prophesied the Falklands conflict. Though not a prediction of the actual fighting, all the elements appear in the drawing to go with 'June 1982', showing the Islands, Argentina and a sinking ship. Not bad when you consider that *Old Moore's Almanac* is published the previous year (by William Walker & Sons, Otley Yorks.) The actual confrontations began in April 1982, following the notorious landing of the 'scrap merchants' on South Georgia on 18 or 19 March. **(Credit:** *Jitendra* **)**

erected in the garden of his Bournmouth home, and employed a staff of six to tend the treasure trove. Each item was trimmed of margins, folded and ironed flat and tucked into its own white envelope, and the rows of mahogany filing cabinets with their 47,000 index cards was called the Ashley Library.

Among his thousands of categories are such choice subjects as 'Crimes detected through opera glasses', 'The etiquette of undersea weddings', 'Sports abandoned because of earthquakes', and 'Deaths associated with the performance of Tchaikovsky's Pathetique symphony.' It is obvious he took the same sort of delight in human crankiness as George Ives, and the potential here for many *Man Bites Man* type collections is obvious.

Brown died in 1972 and this fabulous collection, in which many a TV game show question was researched, languished until recently, when his widow Mrs Ivy Brown, 82, decided to sell it off through the National Union of Journalists newspaper.

Had ASSAP Library [see p2] known of this collection and its sale, and had the bucks, it would have been a marvellous foundation for its own clippings library. But it didn't. It was very nearly in Fortean hands though. TV personality Jeremy Beadle, a good friend to FT, tells me he was the only bidder to begin with, and had he acquired it, would have allowed FT free access. But sadly, through a misunderstanding with an intermediary, Mrs Brown thought he was no longer interested.

It was quickly bought at a snip price of £5000 by Graham Nown, a freelance journalist, who plans to base a few books on it. He promised Mrs Brown that he would add to it and function as a library again. The collection weighed about five tons and needed an articulated lorry to shift it. These details are from *Guardian* 23 Feb 1983.

When I spoke to him, Mr Nown was beginning to realise the complexities of allowing access to the cabinets, now housed in his home in Southport Merseyside, without disrupting his working or family life. It would be a crying shame if the Ashley Library became inaccessible by default. We hope to establish a relationship with Mr Nown and encourage him otherwise, and to discover the Fortean nuggets in this clippings motherlode.

•

Bob Rickard.

It's happened to everyone at some time or another, or at least to a friend of a friend — that which was thought irretrievably lost is found in a way which beats the odds. Coincidence? Or do inanimate objects have homing powers too?

TEETH AND GLASSES

Roy Peters, 55, of Bristol was swimming in 15 feet of water at Beer in Devon when he opened his mouth and his top false teeth fell out and sank. When he went back to the resort (we are not told how much later this was) he found that a set of dentures had been washed up in a gale and handed in to the beach café. He tried them on a found they were his. (*Reveille*, 4 Feb 1977)

☐

Tim Dinsdale has told us that many years ago his uncle lost his false teeth while bathing at Borth on the Welsh coast. About three months later, another member of the family trod on them while bathing — and they were put back into service.

☐

In 1976 skin divers found a pair of spectacles in Torquay harbour, and they were recognised by onlooker Colin Hill as the pair he had lost 8 years before. (*Sunday Mirror*, 19 Sep 1976)

☐

Bill Lees wrote to the *Sunday Express* (13 Nov 1971?) about his glasses which he had lost in the sea off Benidorm in Spain when he dived off a pedallo about 150 yards out from the beach. He only realised later that he must have been wearing them when he dived in. During the night he had a feeling he knew exactly where they were, his daughter bought some diving goggles and they rowed out and found them in about 15 feet of water.

☐

Dr Peter Callaghan accidentally cast his spectacles into the water while fly-fishing on the River Ystwyth. Will Jones was a neighbour of the doctor in Llanilar, near Aberystwyth, but he was unaware that he had lost his glasses. Several days later Will was out fishing and reeled in the missing specs. (*Western Mail*, 16 July 1982)

SWALLOWED WATCHES

Brian Potter's uncle Dennis owned a small farm, and one day a cow nuzzled against his stomach, took his fobchain in his mouth and swallowed it, watch and all. Later than year (which year is unspecified) the farmer died.

More than two summers later, Brian Potter found the watch, next to a small fresh cow pat. It was still going, though it was four hours slow. A vet suggested that the cow's breathing and stomach movements had somehow kept the watch wound up. (*D.Mirror*, 6 Nov 1979)

☐

A Ukranian woman was helping her husband set up his angling gear by the River Dneiper in the summer of 1979, when she unwittingly dropped her gold wristwatch in the water. Her husband's first catch of the day was a 7 pound pike, and the watch was found still ticking in its belly. (*D. Telegraph*, 16 Aug; *S.People*, 26 Aug 1979) This item reappeared in the *Daily Express* on 9th September 1982, when the fisherman was named as Alexander Taran. This time however the watch was lost "days earlier. It was still going and showing the correct time." Which proves, once again, what scant regard journalists have for the truth.

☐

Paul Watson, a Texas cattle farmer, dropped his gold wristwatch in a river while out fishing. Three days later his son Jack, 13, went fishing near the same spot with some friends. Jack caught the only fish of the day, and the lads prepared to cook it over an open fire. They gutted the fish...and, you guessed it, there was the watch. We are not told whether it was still going. (*Weekend*, 18-24 Mar 1981).

HOMING BOOKS
Mrs S. C. M. Hill of London wrote to the *Sunday People* (27 July 1980): "My mother bought some children's books at a jumble sale, intending to read them to my young neice when she came to stay. Later when she examined one of the books more closely, she saw my name and address on the fly-leaf, written by me when I was five 25 years ago. There was also a half-finished letter that I had been writing to an aunt still between the pages."

☐

And Mrs E. Owens of Bristol wrote to the *Sun* (?) (22 June 1980): "My brother wrote from Canada asking if a book of his was still around at home. It wasn't — we thought it had been sent to a jumble sale years earlier. A week later in a second-hand book shop I spotted a copy of the book my brother wanted. Opening it to see the price I found his name on the fly-leaf."

OF CASH AND WALLETS
"For years I carried in my purse a lucky sixpence with my initials on it" wrote Mrs M Coyle of Glasgow (*Sun*, 19 Aug 1971). "The day before I went to Ireland on holiday, I accidentally spent it. Two days later, in a small Irish village, I had the sixpence back in change."

☐

Mrs Kathleen Jackson received a pound note in change while shopping in her home town of Huntingdon, Yorks. On it was written in ballpoint: "9 for bank 1 for Andrew." Next day Mrs Jackson and her family drove to a caravan site near Kirkcudbright in Scotland for a holiday. She parted with the note while shopping for food, overcoming an odd compulsion to keep it. Five days later, back in Huntingdon 200 miles away, she got the note back at her local greengrocers. There was no doubt it was the same note. The handwriting and position of the message were identical. The note, serial number AX27 743180 was one of 657 million in circulation. (*S.Express*, 22 Aug 1982). [Bob Tarte — see 'Clowns' in 'Reflections' this issue — also tells of a banknote with a meaningful message — Ed.]

☐

P. West and his wife were on holiday in Oban in 1976 when the wife realised her handbag was missing. They retraced their movements without success and reported the loss to the police. Later that same day the police brought them the bag with its contents intact, including £5. It had been found in a bar, although the Wests never went into bars. "Did someone find it, take it there, and then, like my wife, lose it?" mused Mr West in a letter to the *Sunday Express* (8 Aug 76).

☐

Gunner Tom Waterloo Dando, fresh back from the First World War, lost his prized war medal in a mill pond at his home village of Ackworth in Yorkshire. He became a miner, married, and raised four children. He never forgot the medal and often went looking for it up to his death in 1942. In 1979, an elderly man knocked on the door of Tom's son, also called Tom, by then aged 60. "Did your father ever lose a medal?" he asked. It transpired that the man's daughter had found it in her vegetable patch. The mill pond had been drained after 1945, and the land bulldozed, levelled, seeded and built on. Yet still the medal turned up, after 60 years. (*S.Express*, 7 Oct 1979)

☐

Ken Kay had his wallet stolen from him in 1943. 38 years later it was found under the floor-boards at Ken's old billet in Swanage, Dorset. The contents were intact, apart from the week's pay. Builder's wife Diana Jordan traced him through the post office, and sent it to him in Hawarden, Chester.

Karl Regul had his wallet stolen by a group of drunken soldiers in 1946. 30 years later, it was found hidden in a ceiling support seven feet from the floor when an old base hospital was being torn down at Fort Meade, Maryland. Again, everything was there except the money. The base carpentry foreman tried in vain to get in touch with Regul using hs old address. Then a policewoman read about it in an AP story printed in the Lancaster, PA, *New Era* and got in touch with Regul, a tool and die maker in Warminster,

PA. (*D.Star*, 1 May 1981; *Times Herald* (Newport News), 27 Nov 1976).

☐

Young David Hatter from Little Shelford near Cambridge lost his wallet containing 12 dollars when on holiday with his parents in Miami in 1979. He was certain it was somewhere in the Ford Mustang they had hired, but it couldn't be found anywhere. Enter Mr Ralph Renton, of Oldham, Greater Manchester, who runs Renton's Garage and imports Ford Mustangs. He was using one of the Mustangs and had a puncture. Hunting for the wheel brace he put his hand down by a wheel arch in the boot and found the wallet, along with David's address. He posted it on. "I think it is absolutely the most honest thing I have ever heard of", said David's mother.

But Kenneth Herring was more honest, the temptation being greater. He was fishing in the Platte River in Michigan when he reeled in Harold De-Witt's wallet containing 2,750 dollars. Herring, unemployed, returned the wallet and got 50 dollars reward. (*D.Telegraph*, 9 Oct 1979; *Burlington Free Press*, 31 Oct 1980).

☐

Angler Gordon Jenkins of Blackpool dropped his wallet into the sea off the North Pier. Six months later a Danish trawler retrieved it – with a soggy £10 note inside – in the Irish Sea, off Wales, and sent it back to him.

John Crow had to wait only four months for a boat to fish up his wallet – containing cash and a bankers card – lost at Cullercoats, Tyne & Wear.

Jean Turnbull had her wallet containing £80 stolen at Chester's Gateway Theatre. 11 days later and 200 miles away it was trawled up in the Irish sea. The cash was gone, but her passport, driving licence, birth certificate and photos were intact. It was handed to the police in Whitehaven, Cumbria, who traced the owner through a council wages slip. (*Sunday*

People, 9 Dec 1979; *Weekly News*, 19 Jan 1980; ? *D. Mirror*, undated.)

☐

In 1979 while on a lecture tour in America, Tim Dinsdale lost his wallet in Boston. He searched all his pockets about ten times without success. Back in Britain, about six weeks after his return, he put on his suit and found the wallet in the breast pocket – "which, so help me God, had been searched umpteen times

in Boston: when there was *nothing* in it." (Letter to FT). (Compare with the temporarily disappearing trout in *Sieveking's Selection*.)

Credits: *Gary Abbott, Peter Christie, Richard Cotton, Mike Dash, Tim Dinsdale, Chris Hall, Peter Hope Evans, Paul Pinn, Sam, Paul Screeton, Bob Skinner, Anthony Smith, Paul Thomas, Andy Townsend, Nigel Watson, Ion Will, Steve Wrathall, Joe Zarzynski.*
•

Paul Sieveking

It is some time since we had a festival of fetishism, so here are a few modern outbreaks of the loony lusts and cranky compulsions that amused Fort so much. May we present our carnival of curious cravings...

CLOTHING COLLECTORS
TROUSERS

☐ A phantom debagger struck at a fire station in Anadarko, Oklahoma, for the second time, stealing the crew's trousers as they slept. *D.Mail* 16 March 1979.

☐ A 17yr-old student, sleeping in Victoria Station, London, had his trousers stolen while he slept. He was wearing them at the time. *D.Telegraph* 13 Aug 1979.

UNMENTIONABLES

☐ We have so many instances of men stealing womens knickers off washing lines, or breaking into apartments for the purpose, that we conclude the panty-snatcher is not so unusual. But before we go on to less common cravings I must mention the "bearded man" who, four times in one week, was discovered trying to cut underwear off sleeping students with a razor blade at the University of Illinois, Chicago. *D.Star* 10 Aug, *S. People* 31 Dec 1978. ...and

Devon again, where police were baffled by the night prowler in Torquay who used to pin £1 notes to panties on lines. *D.Mirror* 8 Dec 1979.

SHOES

☐ In Hilleroed, Denmark, a 70yr-old man was jailed for stealing 5,000 shoes over 7 years. He declined to give a motive. *Sun* 31 Aug 1978.

☐ A 10yr-old girl was robbed of just one shoe by a "young man", in Mexborough, Yorks. *D.Star* 10 March 1979.

☐ Our next fetishist operated on the University of Virginia campus, at Charlottesville, and had a thing for clogs. Since 30 Dec 1979 he had swiped the clogs off at least six girls after tackling them at the knees. AP/*Sun* (Vancouver, BC) 28 Feb; AP/*Fort Meyers News* (Fla) 29 Feb 1980.

COLOURFUL CHARACTERS
TOE PAINTER

☐ A young man, identified by Los Angeles police only as 'Leonardo Da Toenail' was caught after a number of complaints from young women, in the library of the University of Southern California, that someone had painted their toe-nails different colours. Da Toe-nail was not a student but posed as one. He would follow his chosen ones into the library and sit opposite them, apparently deep into work on a project. He would drop something and under the table surreptitiously daub the object of his desire. Something else clatters to the floor, and the other big toe would be coloured. When arrested, Da Toenail had 16 pots of nail varnish about his person. Police believe he was responsible for a similar outbreak of 'phantom pedimania' at the California State University, at Dominquez Hills. Later charges were dropped when no one wished to testify. LATS/*Omaha World Herald* (Neb), AP/*Niagara Falls Review* (Ont) 19 March; *D. Telegraph, D.Mail* 20 March; *D.Star* 29 April; *Lincoln Star* (Neb) 18 June 1981.

STRANGE ASSAULTS

☐ Luigi Longhi, a shampoo fetishist, was jailed in Denmark when his kink drove him to murder. He had picked up a girl hitchhiker who agreed to let him wash her hair. But by the time he began shampooing it for the fifth time she got worried and her resistance led to her death. Longhi kept the body for nine months until it was discovered by workmen. *Sun* 12 Mar 1983. We have a lot of notes on people who have kept bodies for long periods and we'll give these in the near future.

☐ We have a number of clippings about George Mitchell, an American Negro with a compulsion to step on the feet of white women, each mentioning a different crime and arrest. They all agree that he has been in and out of jail — more than 40 arrests in 13 years — for putting his foot down. No sooner is he released than he dons his Cuban heels and steps out. Once he even

slipped away from two officers, while on a visit outside prison and stamped on the first ladies' feet he saw. George can't explain his urge: "I'm just walking along when this feeling starts — step on this foot! step on that foot!" Right now he's getting treatment, but I've a feeling we haven't heard the last of him. AP/*New York Post* 19 March, UPI/*New York Post* 5 May 1980; *Sun*, UPI/*Hongkong Stnadard* 25 Jan; *Weekend* 7 Oct 1981.

BREAST STABBERS

☐ Paris — Police were hunting a "sex maniac" who preyed on well-endowed women, plunging a hypodermic needle into breasts. *D.Mirror* 1 Feb 1978.
☐ Malaya — A bra salesman was arrested after admitting to stabbing the breasts of more than 20 women with a needle. *D.Express* 11 Sept 1978.
☐ Malaya, again — A Chinese youth — "a timid boy from a good family" — was charged with stabbing two women in the breasts with a 2" pin, and cutting a third on the breast with a razor blade. *Straits Times* (Singapore) 11 June 1981.

TOUCH AND GO

☐ Colchester — Police were hunting a nuisance who rugby tackles girls and runs off. *S.People* 23 July 1978.
☐ Cyclist Terence Cocks assaulted at least 17 girls in 4 weeks, in Cheltenham, Gloucestershire. Riding or pushing his bike up to them, he would quickly squeeze their breasts and pedal off fast. *D.Mail* 19 Oct 1979. Perhaps some names *drive* their owners into weird obsessions. Here we have a Cocks; and one of our knicker-stealers was an Edward Horn, and in one of Paul Sieveking's 'Name Game' compilations a few issues back we had a naughty headmaster called Jack Mount.
☐ Shy David Brook, son of a policeman, of Weymouth, Dorset, was funny about women's legs. His technique, though stylish, has a hint of desperation about it: he'd writhe on the ground, pretend-

ing to be ill, and grab the legs of girls who came to help, smothering their knees in kisses. *News of the World* 1 Feb 1981.

UNHELPFUL HANDS
TEETH

☐ Venkat Ali settled down to sleep during a long wait for a departure at Heathrow, and put his teeth on his suitcase. They were gone when he woke up. "I'm broken hearted," he wailed. Aye, and toothless to boot! *D.Telegraph* 9 Sept 1981.
☐ Later that same month... high drama on the streets of Luton, Beds. Bus driver Giovanni Vitale was concentrating on negotiating traffic lights when a young man reached into his cab, stuck his fingers into Giovanni's mouth and deftly hooked out his dentures. The top set broke in the ensuing struggle, but the teef-theif got away with the bottoms. Later, Giovanni thought he saw the young man in a crowd and drove his bus to a phonebox and begged the police to come. They never did. *S.People* 27 Sept 1981.

☐ Imagine the shock of the boy's mother! Her son, Robert Pizzitola, 10, of Colorado Springs, had gone to a Disney matinee and come back minus four good teeth. Robert, who was with his younger brother, said later that a man sat down with them and identified himself as "Dr.Bob" (shades of the Muppet Show, and the Sub-Genius guru). As the boys continued to watch the movie, Dr. Bob molested Robert's molars. Seemingly without instruments — Robert could not remember any — the dentomaniac whipped out his teeth with no pain and no bleeding. There is a hint of some secret oriental art about this. When the fang fiend was arrested, Robert J Brantley (for it was he) turned out to be a mere car mechanic. He admitted two similar offences. UPI/*Grand Rapids Press* (Mich) 20 Sept 1978.

SPECTACLES

☐ Back in our last roundup of rude boys [FT28p11] Paul Sieveking summarized the saga of the Thornton Heath spectacles snatcher which occurred in three distinct flaps: 1975 (11 incidents), 1976 (30 incidents) and 1977. Two years later, in Feb 1979, John Hansford, of Thornton Heath, admitted, in Croydon Crown court (just days after FT28 came out, in fact) to stealing the glasses of 38 women since 1977. He said he began operating in 1977. This makes me speculate (sorry) that he might have been copying the 1975-77 frame-fetishist whose felonious MO was regularly in the local papers throughout that period. Hansford added a quirk of his own: after hooking off the spex he would hurl them to the ground and stamp on them before the very (blurred) eyes of his victims. Sometimes he would wear a black mask and brandish a knife. Once he even strolled into a house and broke the glasses of an astonished housewife. *D.Telegraph, D.Mirror, Sun* 3 Feb 1979.

HAIR SNIPPERS

Our tailpiece to this selection concerns mainly hair snipping. The reader might like to contrast the following cases with Steve Moore's accounts of the hair snipping panics in China — see 'Tales from the Yellow Emporium' this issue.

☐ A 'Mad Scalper' caused panic in Dijon, France, in early July 1969. At first women were too embarassed to come forward, but after one victim went to the police, others followed. Full of Gallic charm this loony would sit beside pretty girls in secluded places and compliment them on their hair, then ask for a lock for his collection. When the girl reacts to this suggestion with anything other than compliance, the man quickly jumps upon her, and having bound and gagged her, whips out his shears and cuts off most of her hair. *D.Mirror* 16 July 1969.

☐ Joseph Smietana, of Hobart, Indiana, was charged with the unlawful practise of medicine. Posing as a hospital doctor he rang up at least 15 women in Lake County saying their husbands had just been admitted with a potentially deadly hair disease borne by parasites and that their houses were now under quarantine. He was convincing enough to get these women to cut off their hair and wash their scalps with lye solution. One woman waited by the phone for hours with her hair in five separate bags, and another had shaved a large circular area on each side of her head as instructed. Police said: "There could be more women who didn't report it because they were too embarassed." UPI/*Centralia Sentinel* (IL) 27 Jan 1977.

☐ Police arrested a 23yr-old man in Rapid City, South Dakota, and charged him with cutting women's hair without their permission. He sat behind them in cinemas and kept his trophies in boxes at home. *D.Telegraph* 13 Jan 1979 Later, in October, the same man, David Mordhorst, was charged, in Wyoming, with burglary and cutting the tresses off at least three women as they slept. *D.Mail* 1 Nov 1979. A year later, Mordhorst was again arrested, this time in Hopewell, New Jersey, charged with cutting a waist-length braid of blond hair off a Princeton girl as she jogged. AP/*Omaha World Herald* 11 Dec 1980.

☐ Writing in *Nursing Mirror* (no date), Dr Arthur Miller reported the case of a woman who for 24 years was compelled to tug and pull out other people's hair, even that of the doctors, nurses and fellow patients of the various institutions she was sent to. Giving her long-haired dolls, the enforced wearing of boxing gloves, and punishment did not moderate her impulses. Now, doctors at Norah Fry Hospital, Shepton Mallet, Somerset, claim they have cured her by putting a crash helmet on her whenever she feels the urge

to pull hair. But they confess they don't know the origin of the compulsion, nor why the cure works. "It seems to have a calming, not a punitive effect," says Dr Miller. "It is not strapped on and she makes no attempt to pull it off." *D.Star* 11 June 1979.

☐ Surat, India — A young "superstitious" man was charged with snipping of the braids of 22 girls with scissors. He said he had vowed to offer 120 braids to the goddess Khodiar in return for an extension of his mother's life and prosperity for himself. *Statesman* (Calcutta) 18 June 1979.

☐ Police in Robertsbridge, East Sussex, are hunting a mystery assailant who told a girl of 19 he had a gun. He forced her to her knees in a doorway and began hacking off her waist-length hair. *D.Express* 12 July 1979.

☐ A mugger attacked Robert Stewart, in Bournemouth, and failing to find his wallet, made off with his toupee. *D.Star, D.Telegraph* 14 April 1981.

☐ We end with a very mysterious story. Leonard Bowie was jailed by Glasgow High Court for attacking and scalping a 40yr-old woman, leaving a bloodstained knife and hairclippers by her unconscious body. A bizarre dimension to this incident is added by the information that three years previously, the victim, Mrs Anne Reilly, was found guilty of killing her husband because of his craving for "unnatural sex". Whether these two incidents were linked in other ways is not ventured into. *Sun* 25 Feb 1983.

Credits: *Peter Christie, DW Clarke, Claudia Egypt, Peter Hope Evans, David Fideler, Chris Hall, Jasper, Martin Kottmeyer, David MacAdams, Valerie Martin, Al Rosenweig & Phyllis Benjamin, Anthony Smith, Linda Suto, Joseph Swatek, Andy Townsend, Joseph Trainor, Roland Watson, Dwight Whalen, Ion Will.*

•

Bob Rickard

Our last collection of ice from the sky was in FT34 — here are those for the last two years. Next time, in this section, we'll have showers of dust and stones.

EDITORIAL
Cont from p2.

report that the ASSAP Library has been given shelf-space in its first home in Purley public library, south London. Its holdings will eventually be available by inter-library loan through the reference sections of any public library in the United Kingdom, which immediately sidesteps the formidable access problems faced by members of organiz-ations with libraries fixed in one place. It will be some time before the Library will reach functional proportions, but the main growth will come through donations or legacies of private collections. John Rimmer, our colleague at the helm of *Magonia*, who works at Purley Library, tells me that books, runs of journals and other publications are already arriving, which include some desirable items.

If you would like to donate books or magazines, whatever, almost anything will be wel-come at this stage. You can deliver it in person (but please pre-arrange this with the library) or you can post your offering to **The ASSAP Library, c/o Purley Library, Banstead Rd, Purley, Surrey CR2 3YH.**

TRUSS FUND
Thanks to the following for their valued donations: Mahmoud Alliho, Sid Birchby, David Dunthorn, Judith Gee, Jerry Lucci, Ray Manners, Steve Mooser, Sue Rose, David Sutton, Mike & Linda Ward.

NEXT ISSUE
The main feature will be a miscellany of data on some of the themes in *Living Wonders*, which has surfaced since publication: rat kings, winged cats, hibernating birds and others; we will also have a collection of reports on sight-ings of really bizarre animals; more of Paul Pinn's follow-ups to stories in previous FTs.

•

Bob Rickard

1981

• **6 Jan - Truro, Cornwall** - Ice lump "the size of a person's head" fell on the vegetable garden of Mrs Elizabeth Cross, in Bodmin Road. The ice con-tained air bubbles described as "unusual air hole patterns." *West Briton* 12 Feb 1981.

• **April - Southern China** - Storm damaged huge area de-molishing 10,500 houses, with hailstones up to 30lbs. Five people killed, 225 injured. *D.Telegraph* 15 April 1981, citing the *Canton Evening News.*

• **16 May - Stockport, Cheshire** - Block of ice 1ft square, est. weight 101lbs, landed on canvas awning over china stall owned by Cyril Knapper. *Stockport Advertiser* 21 May 1981.

• **31 May - Mussoorie, India** - Two children killed and 12 injured as giant hail pelted this hill station area in early hours. *Calcutta Statesman* 1 June 1981.

• **June - Wirral, Cheshire** - About mid-morning, Mary Nickson, 95, was sweeping her front bedroom carpet, when a frightening crash shook the house and she staggered back as plaster rained down. Through the choking dust she saw a gaping hole in the ceiling near where she had been stand-ing moments before, and on the floor was a "football-sized" chunk of ice surrounded by more fragments. Police took the ice away for analysis, and later said it contained coffee, sugar and detergent. *S.Express* 21 June 1981.

• **24 June - Anerley, Kent** - A block of ice (different accounts compare it to a rugby ball and a football) smashed a 2ft hole in the roof of a house in Stem-bridge Road, South London, as Philip and Kay Wells watched TV downstairs, at 7.50pm. Had the ceiling not stopped the missile it would have landed on the bed of their son Joe, 5, who, with his younger sister, slept through the "ear-splitting crash". Kay Wells rescued what she could - an irregular-shaped lump weighing 11lb 9oz, which she kept in her fridge. She says it is "slightly discoloured", and, believing the ice to be waste from a plane, that it "might have been coffee." Another piece was later found 40ft away in the garden. *S.Express* 10 July; *D.Telegraph D.Star* 25 June 1981.

• **10 July - Enontekiö, Lap-land** - A violent hailstorm, called the worst in living memory, devastated an area near the mountain of Ounast-unturi while other parts of Lapland enjoyed hot weather. The stones, averaging 2" diameter, came down with such force they badly bruised hardy reindeer keepers, blinded their flocks, stripped trees of their leaves, and punched 2" deep holes into the clayey soil. (Rovaniemi) *Lapin Kansa* 12 July 1981.

• **28 Sept - Yateley, Hamp-shire** - A large ice block hurtled out of the sky into a shattering collision with the front garden of the Pearce family home in Greenleas Close, during the afternoon. No estimation of size is made, but it made a 3" dent in the lawn. Another piece was found under a car 20ft away. Mrs Joan Brazier, who lives opposite, said: "It was uncanny. I heard a noise and saw this object coming down at a terrific speed. It plunged through the trees and smashed into the ground." *Fleet News* 2 Oct; *Farnborough News* 23 Oct 1981.

Correspondent Chris Hall notes that just 11 days later, on 9 Oct, the Fleet area just to the south of Yateley, had a hailstorm "of unusual severity", with stones up to ¼" dia. in 1" drifts.

1982
• **12 March - Tecumseh, Oklahoma** - Lloyd Basden crossed the road to his neighbours opposite, the Hinsons, and told them that earlier that morning he heard "a roaring noise" and saw something fall from the sky behind their house. Mr A.C. Hinson went with Masden for a looksee and found a small crater recently knocked into sloping ground about 200yds north of the house. It contained a block of ice roughly 30lbs, which had split into several pieces. (Carlisle, PA) *Evening Sentinel*, (Little Rock, AR) *Gazette* 16 March; (Tuscon AZ) *Daily Reporter,* (Boston MA) *Herald American* 17 March, all UPI; (Tecumseh, OK) *County-Wide News* 18 March 1982.
• **23 July - Stuart, Florida** - As Mrs Edith Turner sipped her morning coffee in her kitchen, an 'ice bomb' estimated to weight 100lbs, smashed through her roof. 100lbs is BIG compared to others we've recorded, and yet this case attracted little media attention, so we have no further details. Note: not coffee-ice this time, but a nice try! UPI/*Houston* (TX) *Chronicle* 25 July 1982.
• **25 July - Northampton** - Just two days after the Florida fall a "huge" chunk of ice fell from the sky into the garden of Mrs Dorothy Medhurst. *D.Star* 26 July 1982.

MYSTERY GOLF BALLS
The curiosity of the employees at a waterworks at Sutton, in Surrey, soon turned to alarm as the golf balls which had been mysteriously accumulating in their grounds over several weeks continued to appear. Two men, on separate occasions, were narrowly missed by speeding, ricochetting balls. The men believe they are under seige, but know not from whence the balls come. There is not a course within miles, and attempts to identify the trajectory (supposing the balls were being hit out of a nearby garden) have failed utterly. Could this be one of those legendary golf ball falls? *S.Express* 26 July 1981.

Credits: Larry Arnold/PSI, Janet & Colin Bord, Anthony Barber, Peter Christie, Loren Coleman, Jenny Dawson, Peter Hope Evans, Chris Hall, Tuuri Heporauta, Jitendra, Nick Maloret, Valerie Martin, KJ Neilson, Scott Parter, David Rees, Paul Screeton, Doc Shiels, Bob Skinner, Anthony Smith, Joseph Trainor, UFO Newsclipping Service, Steve Wrathall.

•

Bob Rickard

*Pamela Pearce & Steven, 18mths, look at bits of the ice-bomb preserved in a plastic bag [*Fleet News *2 Oct 1981; reproduced by kind permission of the Aldershot News Ltd.]*

They read more like 'Whale Tumour stories, but accounts of people found dead in life-like poses are true enough, and give more fuel to the argument that fact may give rise to fiction and folklore. Here are a few still lifes (or should that be still deaths?) found lurking in a remote corner of our filing system.

☐ Our first item is two incidents which came out of New York in the bitter winter of 1980/81 (remember?). Firstly, 47yr-old Jessie Smalls was found in her kitchen, in the Bronx, literally frozen stiff. A waterpipe had burst encasing her in a shroud of ice, and NYPD officers had to chip her out to cart her off. Secondly, Sally Brazell, a 59yr-old hospital worker, was found dead in her Brooklyn apartment, which had been without heat since November. She was found in a sitting position on the floor near her bed. *D.Telegraph* (UPI) 22 Jan 1981.

☐ On 11 Feb 1981, a cleaner, at work in St Mary's church, Thorpe, Surrey, was surprised to find a smartly-dressed woman kneeling in a pew. Some time later, the cleaner realized the woman had not moved, and on investigation thought she looked dead. She told the vicar who called an ambulance, and sure enough they found the woman to be dead. The woman had no identification with her, nor was she known locally, so at the time of the report her identity and cause of death remained unknown. *D.Express* 12 Feb 1981.

☐ In April 1982 the body of a man, wearing only underpants, was found on a beach at Woolacombe, North Devon. He was kneeling, with his head buried in the sand. Police established his identity as Michael Townsend, an appar-ently fit 60yr-old from Bath. A police officer told the coroner's inquest that at 3.15pm on the day (no date given) of the death, he was on the cliff at Marine Drive and watched through binoculars as a man slowly walked out to sea. The officer, John Iddes, thought it was odd that the man appeared to make no effort to swim, but losing sight of him, assumed he had returned to shore. at 3.40pm the body was discovered in the strange position on the beach. With some understatement the coroner concluded: "This was a most unusual death." *North Devon Journal-Herald* 22 April 1982.

☐ On 22 May 1981, Colin and Kathleen Lovelock died in a fire in a coach on the forecourt of a coaching firm at Baginton, near Coventry. The couple both worked for the firm, and according to colleagues, Kathleen, 28, had gone into the coach as her husband prepared it for a trip to Holland. According to police, Colin, 40, had splashed petrol inside the coach and set it alight, and then held his wife down on the rear seat. The couple, who reputedly had a stormy marriage, were found in positions suggesting they were struggling with one another while suffocating. Workers tried to rescue them but had found the doors locked. A bizarre suicide or death pact is suspected. *D.Mail* 23 May 1981.

☐ Police investigations into the death of an RAF officer and his young family believed they too suffocated. The bodies of Adrian Ray, 32, his wife Brenda, 30, and their two sons aged 3 and 5, were found in the positions in which they had died at least four days earlier, in their snow-covered caravan, on a site at Waidring, in Austria's East Tyrol. A Dutch tourist saw a dim light

The soldier who had his block knocked off, in the battle of Beaumont, 1870. An illustration featured in William Corliss' Strange Life sourcebook (BOB.002) and Incredible Life (p167).

in the caravan and noticed there was no sign of movement within over a long period. Officers dug their way to the caravan where they found Brenda at the sink in the midst of the washing up. Adrian was seated on the bed with one child on his lap; the other child was in his cot. It is thought that snow blocked their ventilators causing a build-up of carbon monoxide. The family lived in Cheadle Hulme, Cheshire. *The Sun, Wolverhampton Express & Star* 31 Jan 1981.

☐ Our last review of this genre of strange deaths was back in FT21 (p12). Incidentally Paul Pinn has followed up several of those old cases and his results can be read in his article next issue.

Apart from the tragedy of the Ray family (above) the more spectacular instances of body attitudes after death are in the past. William Corliss in his volume *Strange Life* and *Incredible Life* cites fully a paper from *Knowledge* 1884 (p115–7) by a Dr C.E. Brown-Sequard on the subject. One of the most dramatic instances on record was observed by Dr Rossbach just 24hrs after the battle of Beaumont, near Sedan, in 1870, involved a soldier who had most of his head taken off by a cannon-ball while in the act of drinking from a tin cup (see illu). The American Civil War also generated examples (given in this paper): eg. a man killed while climbing over a low fence; and another in the act of mounting his horse.

☐ One of the earliest items clipped by one of the editors, (no date or source, unfortunately) concerned a British sergeant found at Spion Kop, during the Boer War. He was standing in the attitude of taking aim with his rifle, his finger ready on the trigger, when he had been shot through the head. A Boer, thinking to take the rifle for himself, struggled with the dead man's rigid hands, trying to prise them open. As he did so the

rifle went off, shooting the Boer through the heart. A dead shot, you might say!

☐ To close this selection, I add a note of my own, gleaned from Flammarion's *Thunder and Lightning* (1905). It seems a clergyman named Butler saw lightning hit a tree, at Everdon, Warwickshire, under which 10 harvesters sought refuge in a storm. Four were killed. "One of them was found dead, still holding between finger and thumb a pinch of snuff he had

been in the act of taking. A second had one hand on the head of a small dog, also killed, and still sitting on his knees, and in the other hand a piece of bread; a third was sitting, his eyes open, facing the direction from which the storm came."

Credits: *Peter Christie, Peter Hope Evans, Valerie Martin, Paul Pinn, Anthony Smith.*

●

Bob Rickard

MUSIC HATH CHARMS...
☐ This first item needs no editing or comment. It comes from the *Houston Chronicle* (19 Dec 1982). "A man scaled a 10-foot concrete wall at the Honolulu Zoo, stripped to his underwear and played a harmonica for an elephant, police said. The police officer who arrested the man said Empress, a 51-year old female Indian elephant, apparently didn't like the music and cornered the man. He was charged with cruelty to animals. The policeman said he couldn't name the tune."

ANOTHER VOCIFEROUS TREE
☐ Back in *Fortean Times* 35 I described the crying Pecan tree of Alabama which sounded like a puppy. Now, thanks to the admirable research work of Mike Dash on an early nineteenth century weekly called *The Mirror of Literature, Amusement and Instruction*, I can tell you about the groaning

elm tree of Baddesley in Hampshire, that sounded like a "person in extreme agony". (*The Mirror,* Vol XIX, No.554, 30 June 1832).

"It was a young, vigorous tree, and, to all appearance, perfectly sound. In a few weeks the fame of the tree was spread far and wide; and people from all parts flocked to hear it." These included the Prince and Princess of Wales, so all this must have happened prior to 1820, when gouty George became king. Naturalists vied with one another in offering explanations. "Some thought it was owing to the twisting and friction of the roots; others thought that it proceeded from water, which had collected in the body of the tree; or, perhaps, from pent air: but the cause that was alleged appeared unequal to the effect...it was thought to groan least when the weather was wet, and most when it was clear and frosty; but the sound at all times seemed to come from the roots."

The tree groaned for eighteen or twenty months, and a pamphlet was written about it. A man named Forbes then bored a hole in the trunk in an effort to discover the cause, after which it never groaned again. Its roots were dug up and examined, but nobody was any the wiser.

If any readers have further tales of audible trees, I would like to hear from them.

MISSING FISH

☐ Stephen LeBaigue had three fish, two gold and one silver. He had kept them in a tank in his room for about two years. When he woke up one morning, the silver one had vanished. The door was locked, the window closed. Could the goldfish have eaten their tank mate, after having co-existed for two years (and longer, elsewhere)? And leave no trace, not so much as a left-over bone?

When Steve told me about it, I mulled over the old problem of teleportation. Perhaps fish get shunted around on the etheric or something, fulfilling some arcane balance sheet? Back in *The News* No.2 (January 1974) Bob Rickard glimpsed behind teleportation "an idiot, albeit a cosmic one." This was prompted by two stories, both sent in by Anthony Smith. One was undated, but came possibly from the *Daily Mirror*, sometime in 1969: thousands of roach, perch, bream and gudgeon disappeared from a pool belonging to a works angling club in Smethwick, Staffs. After finding only a few "tiddlers", the club members called in the police. Chief Inspector Kenneth Cocayne said: "Samples of pool water have been sent to the public analyst." End of story.

The other item came from the *Daily Mirror* of 30 August 1968. A large wartime watertank in a town centre was found by firemen sent to empty it to contain 250 plump roach and perch. How they got

there was a mystery.

An apparent *temporary* fish teleportation was noted in *The News* No.9. 8,000 trout, averaging eleven pounds each, vanished from a brick-pit near Barton-on-Humber in Lincolnshire. Police were baffled, but blamed "several people" with large nets, according to the *Scunthorpe Evening Telegraph* (2 May 1974). The next day the fish were back, and the headline in the same paper was *Detectives Trace Trout*.

In October 1980, ninety goldfish vanished from an enclosed courtyard behind Catley's garden shop in Devizes, Wiltshire. The shop owner George Day ruled out the shop cats who lapped the water but had never been known to touch the fish. Herons had been known to take fish from ponds in the area, but with plant in the tank would have been unlikely to have snatched all ninety. (*Chippenham Times, & News,* 3 Oct 1980)

In November 1982, Mrs Pam Shepherd of Sedbury near Chepstow in Wales, decided to transfer fifty baby goldfish from her garden pond to a tank indoors, to prevent the adult fish eating them. For ten days they grew nicely; then, one lunchtime when she returned from work, they had all gone. At nine o'clock that morning she had looked at the fish, locked the house and shut the windows. There were no cats or dogs and her children were at school. (*South Wales Argus,* 24 Nov 1982). For those who like measurements, Mrs Shepherd gives some in a letter to the *Mirror* (8 Nov 1982). There were "about forty fish, each about a half inch long". They were in "a twelve inch deep tank in about four inches of water." Well, forty or fifty, they all went somewhere...

More discussion of vanishing fish will be found in the 'Evidence of Animal Teleportation' chapter of *Living Wonders* by John Michell and Bob Rickard.

Whilst on the subject of goldfish, I must mention a small sect in Bognor Regis called the Spiritual Organisation for the Teachings of the Master. This was set up by an Irish army clerk in his thirties, Herbert John Yarr, known to his diciples as Ishvara, who claims to be "the greatest incarnation of God in the history of man — a true perfect master". His hundred or so devotees, many of whom have reached sainthood, believe that he once restored his pet goldfish to life. Or so said the *Telegraph* of 17 March 1980.

UP AND AWAY

☐ Last time I recounted how a parachutist survived an 8,000 foot drop sans parachute. Now comes a tale of a parachutist who shot *up* 6,000 feet while practising for the Commonwealth Games opening ceremony in Brisbane.

Rick Collins, 29, was sucked upwards by a thunder cloud's fierce turbulence just after his main 'chute opened, and was bombarded by huge hailstones, as lightning zipped past him. "I knew these cloud formations could extend up to 25,000 feet and at that height I would pass out through lack of oxygen," he said.

"There was also the danger that I would suffer serious injuries from the hailstones that were smashing into me so I decided to release my main chute at 12,000 feet and freefall down to a safe altitude. I had my arm around my face to protect me from the hail which was then coming up at me as I dropped. I was watching my altimeter wind itself down to 1,500 feet. I grabbed my ripcord and pulled it." He landed in a field some five miles east of his stadium target. (*D. Telegraph*, Sep or Oct 1982.)

MHUNGU VENOM CURE

☐ Kenneth Hampson was driving through the bush north of Bulawayo in Zimbabve when a Mhungu (cobra) got under his car bonnet and spat a jet of venom into his eyes. The

Mhungu has a spitting range of six feet, and the venom is deadly for some creatures and can cause blindness in human beings. A bystander "grabbed me and pushed me over to his wife who was breast-feeding a baby and told her to squirt milk into my eyes," he said. This neutralised the neurotoxins in the venom and saved his sight. (*Int. Herald Trib & Guardian,* 1 Dec 1982). And

that rounds off the meal of ostrobogulous oddities for the time being. (Ostrobogulous means bizarre, so I discovered from Vol. III of the OED Supplement, published last Summer).

Credits: *Mike Dash, Peter Hope Evans, Ian Murray, Scott Parker, Paul Thomas, Ion Will.*
•
Paul Sieveking

Phenomenal ripples from previous issues...

CIRCLE OF CLOWNS – FT38

☐ Just as we published FT38, Bob Tarte, author of the above-named article (p46-48), wrote with the news that the real Bobo T. Clown, alias Leo Torpey, had died recently in Grand Rapids, followed a few days later by a rare visitation of a bolide-type meteor in the pre-dawn hours.

Bob adds: "One of Bobo's surviving relatives has the last name of Tartal – too close to my own for comfort. This is bothersome considering that in the past two months I've been overwhelmed by Turtle co-incidences. Cataloging the convolutions of the Lord of 22 since the article would be almost impossible, but one rather creative enmeshment is

worth recording. During the stellar period of Bobo/Lord of 22 activity described in the musty article I submitted, I received a $1 dollar bill with the legend 'Kim 22' written on it. Natch, there had been a spate of wrong numbers on the telephone here and at work asking for Kim...but this was nothing compared to my shock upon seeing, in the *National Enquirer* several months ago, a story on a woman named Kim who met her husband by writing her name and address on a $1 dollar bill! Postscript to that: last week, while at a friend's house, the babysitter for his children arrived, a teen-ager named Kim Tuttle. It is a perpetually swirling soup of correspondences."

FRENCH BVM – FT38

☐ Yet another sequel to the sad story of the Virgin of La Talaudiere, which had appeared to Blandine Piegay, aged 14, who erected a statue on the site of her vision in her backyard vegetable patch – see FT38p22. It seems that shortly after the reported episodes the 2ft high, 6lb plaster statue was stolen. The *S.Express* (28 Nov 1982) reports the discovery of the statue at the St Etienne football stadium in Paris, after their match with Nancy. St Etienne were doing badly in the league table, so it is probable that a worried fan brought the statue to the match hoping to change his team's luck. St Etienne lost. Such is the fate of the sacreligious.

Through a circuitous series of contacts, which involves a French correspondent of Hilary Evans', we learn that Blandine's visions were preceded by some interesting poltergeist-like phenomena. Among them were visitations of an angel called Nicole who predicted that the visions would start shortly after Blandine began menstruating. We hope to find out more about this intersting case.

THE TALKING TOILET – FT38

☐ We told the tale of the poltergeist, plaguing a German dentist and his pretty assistant, calling itself 'Chopper' on p24 last issue. We have since learned that Claudia, the assistant admitted culpability on a German TV talkshow, 'Frank Elstner's Roundup of People in The News in 1982', she said that she and her boss had played along with an unknown third party who used to phone the dental clinic for weeks in a strange voice. One day, she says, she answered, imitating the funny voice and the 'conversation' began. She added that she now has a new job and is very sorry for the trouble she has caused. There is something suspicious about this seeming confession. For a start, Dr Backseitz, whom God preserve,

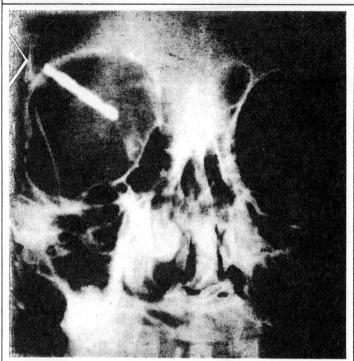

X-ray of Villicana's skull showing the position of the bit. [Globe 14 Dec 1982.]

was elderly and with an undoubted reputation for respectability – would he just play along, throwing his life's work away for a doubtful laugh? Personally, I think not. Claudia's apparent confession has all the hall marks of those other marvellous confessions wrung out of the frightened, bewildered, ordinary people who find themselves the focus of paranormal phenomena Both Claudia and the dentist are still under threat of prosecution from the state who, apart from their annoyance at being caught up in such strange business, incurred the expences of the police, scientific and other investigations. It is in the state's interest to have Claudia conveniently confess and the whole matter may be dropped quietly now she appears to have done so. I don't suppose anyone is seriously trying to trace the mysterious third party! *Rheinische Post* (Dusseldorf) 10 Jan 1983.

HOLES IN THE HEAD – FT38

□ Over the last few months we have accumulated quite a bit in our impalings file, but we'll concentrate here on 3 incidents which were reported just after our look at the subject of head-penetrations last issue [FT38p27-30].

□ Miguel Villicana, 52 slipped while carrying a drill, in his auto-repair shop in El Centro, California. His head hit the drill, and unknown to him the bit penetrated his head and snapped off. "I didn't feel any pain, other than you would have from banging your head," he said. Villicana spent the next 15 minutes on the floor looking for the broken bit. Afterhalf an hour the cut on the side of his head was still bleeding, so he went home to put ice on it, and when that didn't work, his son drove him to the hospital. "I nearly died of fright when I saw the x-ray," he said. The bit had pierced his speech center, narrowly missing arteries and stopping short of the brain

stem. Dr Travis Calvin removed the bit in a five-hour operation and Villicana walked out two weeks later. "I'm feeling fine," he said. "Believe me I know I have an awful lot to be thankful for." *Globe* 14 Dec 1982.

□ Building contractor David Wright, 54, fell off a ladder onto the drill he was using, working on a flat in Toronto. When he came to, he soon realised the drill bit was deeply embedded in his right forehead and that he had lost a lot of blood. Even though he was sure he was dying. Wright struggled to his feet, careful to hold the body of the drill steady, and had the presence of mind to stand in front of a nearby mirror. Because the bit was firmly jammed his only hope was to squeeze the trigger gently and remove the bit. "I kept saying to myself, 'Oh, my God, whatever I do I have to do it right because any mistake would be fatal." Keeping his nerve and a steady hand, Wright managed to pull the whirling bit from his skull, and bleeding profusely, put out the lights and shut the door of the flat and went upstairs to his own, from which his wife called an ambulance. Doctors found the drill had gone in 8cm (2 inches), and removed a tiny fragment of bone from the brain tissue. *Shropshire Star* 24 Feb; *Rheinische Post* (Dusseldorf) 25 Feb 1983.

□ Fear and loathing in Trento, north-eastern Italy. A 71yr-old priest was in a coma after a group of "religious fanatics" hammered a four-inch nail into his head. Father Armando Bison was also battered with the hammer while in his church. The bizarre sect called itself 'Ludwig' after the mad king of Bavaria, and claims responsibility for the deaths of two other priests, a prostitute and a homosexual, a tramp and two drug addicts whom they burned alive. *D.Mirror* 2 March 1983.

FIRE-PRONE NANNY – FT38
□ The sad story of Carole Compton, the Scottish nanny

at the center of rumours of having startled fires by witchcraft was told on FT38p32f. Since then the case has developed interesting dimensions. Firstly, on 20th January 1983, Carole was formerly charged, in Bolzano, of three attempts of murder and arson, setting fire to the bedding of Agnese Cecchini, aged 3, on the island of Elba. Because the press focussed attention on the sensational accusation of witchcraft, and pointed to fires in the house of a previous employer, Carole was further charged, on two counts, of similar attempts on the life of Emanuele Ricci, aged 2, in Rome. Carole's Italian lawyer, Sergio Minervini, firmly blames the press for the mess she is in. He stresses the charges are strictly of attempted murder and arson, not of witchcraft, magic or poltergeists. But the discussion continues.

An article by Robin Lustig, 'Witch-hunt in Italy' (*Observer Magazine* 16 Jan 1983) adds much more background to the case, including testimony that few if any of the fires broke out in the presence of the girl; in fact the first occurred while she was with her charge in the garden. It also confirms the references to poltergeist-like phenomena in the Ricci house during Carole's stay. After 3 fires, the services of the bewildered girl were quickly disposed of, and she went to the Cecchini house where she was arrested after two more un-explained fires. According to Lustig, Agnese's father, Luigi, hates foreigners, and her mother lives in fear of him — hardly an encouraging climate for a confused girl trying to recover from a disasterous love affair, who hardly spoke Italian, and who was alone in a close-knit community of relatives who were not backward in expressing their dislike of foreigners (especially those who brought trouble) and disapproved of the Cecchini's having a nanny in the first place.

It is ironic that in order to

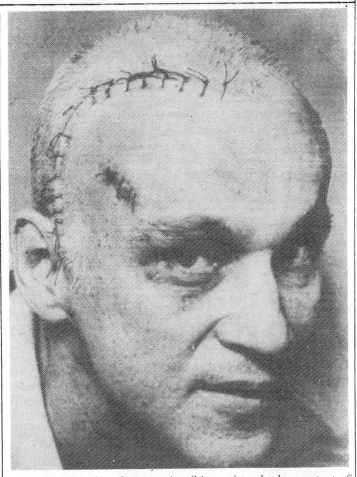

David Wright, after the operation (big scar) to check on extent of damage (small scar). [Globe 22 March 1983.]

prove the girl innocent — ie: the girl did not deliberately start the blazes with known means — the defence may well provide a good case for the likelyhood of spontaneous fires. It is doubly ironic that the psychic phenomena researchers, who are interested in the girl as an unconscious source of the fires started by some paranormal means and who can point to a stack of well investigated cases, including poltergeist-type cases involving spontaneous fires, are thus making Senore Minervini's job more than usually difficult. For example: the *News of the World* 13 Feb 1983, quotes the polt expert, Prof George Owen, of

Toronto: "I am much inclined to believe that the girl is guiltless (of arson) and is in fact one of the very many persons of both sexes who have been, to their own misfortune, centres of Recurrent Spontaneous Psychokinesis (RSPK). They are unaware of their own power."

Another interesting wrinkle, caught by FT's clipster network, is the story of Teresa Hunter, another Scots girl who nannied for the Cecchini's, in The Scottish *Daily Record* 29 Oct 1982. Teresa left their employ three days before Carole took over. She says that she learned that at least *three previous nannies* left the Cecchini's *because of unexplained fires.* But Teresa thought the explanation was likely to be fairly down to earth: "The grandmother was really weird. She hated nannies. In fact she may have started the fires. She used to smoke a lot and sometimes left lighted cigarettes down, forgetting where she'd put them."

Perhaps so. In which case, I hope, for Carole's sake, Sr Minervini has this information. But what about the un-explained fires at Carole's previous job at the Ricci's? Interesting, isn't it? Meanwhile, Carole, who has been in prison since 5 August 1982, waits for her trial-date to be set.

Credits: *Janet & Colin Bord, Hilary Evans, John Fullerton, Brian Hain, J Lang, Kevin McClure, Nigel Pennick, Paul Screeton, Doc Shiels, Anthony Smith, Bob Tarte, Roland Watson, Steve Wrathall, Ion Will.*

•

Bob Rickard

Paradigm Lost
Philosophies of Science by MIKE CROWLEY

PARTICLE PAIRS

As far as we can tell it will never be possible to create a perfect vacuum. Not because of any deficiency in the available technology but because, at the subatomic (or quantum) level of reality, there is a wonderful weirdness in the way matter works. For even if it were technically feasible to empty a container of all its atoms, there would be no way of preventing particles such as electrons and protons from appearing out of the void, existing briefly, interacting with each other then disappearing again, flickering in and out of existence like a cloud of fire-flies. This phenomenon (and many others) is described by a theory called quantum mechanics which, incidentally, has been more extensively verified than any other single scientific theory.

One way in which matter might arise spontaneously is in the "two-particle system" or "particle-pair" in which two particles are created simultaneously and possess a degree of complementarity as if one is yin to the other's yang. For instance, an electron/positron pair (a positron being the anti-matter equivalent of an electron) appear, fly apart, have a momentary existence as independent entities, then each exerts a fatal attraction on the other and they are both annihilated in the resulting collision. An alternative description offered by Richard Feynman is equally valid, very elegant and gives a good example of quantum weirdness: a particle travels forward through time (thus appearing to be an electron), reverses time-direction (apparent annihilation of particle-pair), travels backward through time (thus appearing to be a positron) and reverses direction once more to become an electron again (apparent creation of particle-pair).

Particle-pairs do not always originate in this spontaneous and haphazard manner but this phenomenon affords a good example of why Einstein refused to accept the quantum theory. It was not, as is so often suggested, that the conclusions drawn from the theory were simply too bizarre, it was the very nature of those conclusions which he found unacceptable. The theory predicts that at the subatomic level of reality the commonsense laws of cause-and-effect break down or, to put it another way, events occur for no reason at all.

This is what got Einstein's goat, "God does not play dice" was his famous observation on this subject. At first he probably assumed that contradictions would soon be discovered in the quantum theory but instead it went from strength to strength. So it was that in 1935, along with co-workers Podolsky and Rosen, Einstein wrote a counter-blast [1] to quantum mechanics which attempted a reductio ad absurdum in the form of a thought-experiment. In it they described the creation of a particle-pair and showed that by the application of quantum-mechanical rules the fate of each particle is inextricably bound up with the other in such a way that if the state of one is altered then the other immediately responds. Perhaps the import of that last sentence has not yet reached you. The crucial word is "immediately", meaning "with no intervening time interval". Now "immediately" is a good deal faster than the speed of light which Einstein had determined as the speed limit of the cosmos 30 years before in his special theory of relativity.

This Einstein-Podolsky-Rosen (EPR) effect was thus held to be impossible and as it was rigorously derived from quantum mechanics it was claimed that the quantum mechanics had been invalidated. Of course, the quantum scientists reserved judgement on these claims. After all, the quantum theory had more experimental verification than the theory of relativity, and it was just as likely that relativity was wrong.

Until last month. In February 1983 a French team *Cont on p.43.*

The ET Law.

Almost unnoticed the US Congress passed a law, in 1969, which creates a new class of criminals, those who have unlawful contact with extraterrestrials. At least, this is the interpretation offered by **George Andrews**, who comments on the loophole through which it could be made applicable to UFO contactees.

A SURPRISE PACKAGE FROM UNCLE SAM
Dr. Brian T. Clifford, who is employed by the Pentagon, has just announced that contact between U.S. citizens and extra-terrestrials or their vehicles is strictly illegal, and that according to a law *already on the books* anyone guilty of such contact automatically becomes a wanted criminal to be fined $5,000 and jailed for one year. According to Dr. Clifford, whose commanding officers have been assuring the public for the last 35 years that UFOs are nothing more than hoaxes and delusions to be dismissed with a condescending smile: "This is really no joke, it's a very serious matter."

There are two points I wish to make:
* **1211.101 Applicability.** *"The provisions of this part apply to all NASA manned and unmanned space missions..."*

I could dismiss this whole controversy as a tempest in a teacup if the above passage contained the word "only", so as to read: "The provisions of this part apply only to all NASA manned and unmanned space missions...". However, it does not contain that one little word which would have made such a big difference. If the government was suddenly faced with the accomplished fact of an undeniable overt ET visitation, in the absence of any other legislation pertaining to this particular subject, this regulation could therefore be construed as being applicable to all space missions, NASA or non-NASA, whether of terrestrial or extra-terrestrial origin. As it stands, this law is applicable to UFO contact. The meaning would have to be stretched, but the loophole does exist.
* **1211.102 Definitions. (b) (2):** *"Touched directly or been in close proximity to (or been exposed indirectly to)..."*

Even without including "indirect exposure", anyone involved in a UFO close encounter would become eligible for indefinite quarantine under armed guard according to the above. By including indirect exposure, the NASA administrator is empowered to make the definition mean just about anything he wants it to. An example of indirect exposure is given, but an example is not a definition. Unless indirect exposure is defined precisely, it can mean almost anything. The possibility is not specifically ruled out that other types of indirect exposure than the example given might be considered

valid grounds to "quarantine" a citizen or group of citizens.

This legislation was put through Congress without having been mentioned to the tax-paying citizens Congress is supposed to represent. Thus from one day to the next we learn that, without having informed the public, in its infinte wisdom the Congress of the United States has created a whole new criminal class: UFO contactees. The lame excuse offered by NASA as a sugar coating for this bitter pill is that extra-terrestrials might have a virus that could wipe out the human race. This is certainly one of the many possibilities inherent in such contact, but just as certainly not the only one, and in itself not a valid reason to make all contact illegal or to declare contactees criminals to be fined and jailed immediately. The primary effect of such a law would not be to prevent contact (which is often involuntary), it would be to silence witnesses. If enforced, the law would prevent publication of contactee reports except under cover of anonymity, and unleash a modern Inquisition in the Land of the Free. However, it is unenforceable, so obviously absurd and unfair that the public will refuse to accept it.

The law is an ass. The citizens of the United States will greet it with a resounding Bronx cheer, laugh it out of court, and oblige Congress to repeal it. Those in the unenviable position of trying to enforce it will find themselves like people with sieves trying to stop the ocean tide. If there had never before in human history been contact with extra-terrestrials, extreme precautions might be advisable, but contact cases in recent years number in the thousands and tens of thousands. Are all these normally law-abiding citizens to be declared criminals from one minute to the next, fined, and automatically jailed for one year? What other laws has Congress passed surreptitiously without informing the public?

What other surprises have our trusted representatives prepared for us? No matter what they may be, one thing is for sure: contact between humans and extra-terrestrials has been occurring at periodic intervals ever since the Sumerians built the ziggurats, and will continue to occur whether the Pentagon likes it or not. •

George Andrews

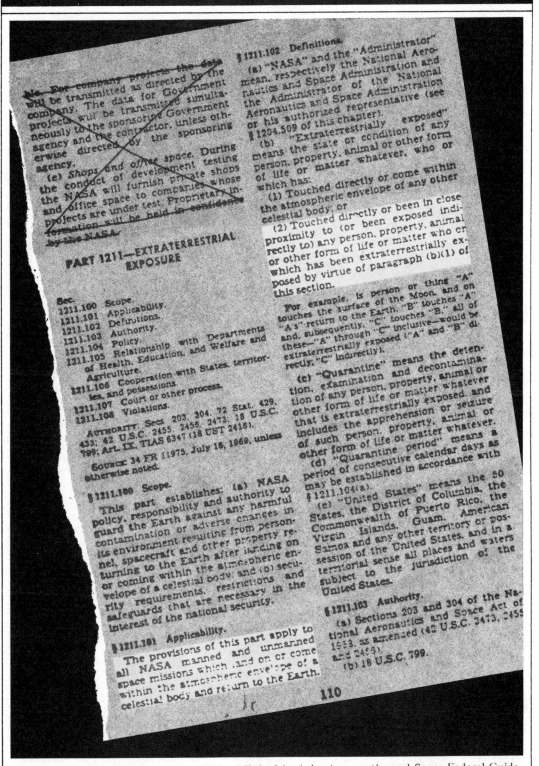

will be transmitted as directed by the company. The data for Government project will be transmitted simultaneously to the sponsoring Government agency and the contractor, unless otherwise directed by the sponsoring agency.

(e) *Shops and office space.* During the conduct of development testing the NASA will furnish private shops and office space to companies whose projects are under test. Proprietary information will be held in confidence by the NASA.

PART 1211 — EXTRATERRESTRIAL EXPOSURE

Sec.
1211.100 Scope.
1211.101 Applicability.
1211.102 Definitions.
1211.103 Authority.
1211.104 Policy.
1211.105 Relationship with Departments of Health, Education, and Welfare and Agriculture.
1211.106 Cooperation with States, territories, and possessions.
1211.107 Court or other process.
1211.108 Violations.

AUTHORITY: Secs. 203, 304, 72 Stat. 429, 433; 42 U.S.C. 2455, 2456, 2473; 18 U.S.C. 799; Art. IX, TIAS 6347 (18 UST 2416).

SOURCE: 34 FR 11975, July 16, 1969, unless otherwise noted.

§1211.100 Scope.

This part establishes: (a) NASA policy, responsibility and authority to guard the Earth against any harmful contamination or adverse changes in its environment resulting from personnel, spacecraft and other property returning to the Earth after landing on or coming within the atmospheric envelope of a celestial body; and (b) security requirements, restrictions and safeguards that are necessary in the interest of the national security.

§1211.101 Applicability.

The provisions of this part apply to all NASA manned and unmanned space missions which land on or come within the atmospheric envelope of a celestial body and return to the Earth.

§1211.102 Definitions.

(a) "NASA" and the "Administrator" mean, respectively the National Aeronautics and Space Administration and the Administrator of the National Aeronautics and Space Administration or his authorized representative (see §1204.509 of this chapter).

(b) "Extraterrestrially exposed" means the state or condition of any person, property, animal or other form of life or matter whatever, who or which has:

(1) Touched directly or come within the atmospheric envelope of any other celestial body; or

(2) Touched directly or been in close proximity to (or been exposed indirectly to) any person, property, animal or other form of life or matter who or which has been extraterrestrially exposed by virtue of paragraph (b)(1) of this section.

For example, is person or thing "A" touches the surface of the Moon, and on "A's" return to the Earth, "B" touches "A" and, subsequently, "C" touches "B," all of these—"A" through "C" inclusive—would be extraterrestrially exposed ("A" and "B" directly, "C" indirectly).

(c) "Quarantine" means the detention, examination and decontamination of any person, property, animal or other form of life or matter whatever that is extraterrestrially exposed, and includes the apprehension or seizure of such person, property, animal or other form of life or matter whatever.

(d) "Quarantine period" means a period of consecutive calendar days as may be established in accordance with §1211.104(a).

(e) "United States" means the 50 States, the District of Columbia, the Commonwealth of Puerto Rico, the Virgin Islands, Guam, American Samoa and any other territory or possession of the United States, and in a territorial sense all places and waters subject to the jurisdiction of the United States.

§1211.103 Authority.

(a) Sections 203 and 304 of the National Aeronautics and Space Act of 1958, as amended (42 U.S.C. 2473, 2455 and 2456).

(b) 18 U.S.C. 799.

110

The ET Law — a facsimile of Part 1211 of Title 14 of the Aeronautics and Space Federal Guidelines, *passed by an act of Congress on 16 July 1969, just before the first moon landing.*

The recent publication of *Cat Country* (see 'Reviews' this issue) introduced us to the work of **Di Francis,** whose quest for the 'British Big Cat' began with her attempts to track down the phantom felines of her native Devon. Well, that should be not-so-phantom felines, because Di has some controversial ideas about the nature and identity of these creatures...so we invited her to stand on the...

NOT SO MYSTERIOUS CATS

For the past three years I have been carefully studying the case of the mystery cats of Britain, and have interviewed hundreds of witnesses as well as spending a great deal of my time tracking the animals in the wilder areas of the country. I should like to take this opportunity to lay to rest at long last the ghost of these animals. They are not spirit, or out of this world, creatures. They do not vanish, leave no trace or fly off to another planet. They are in fact, very large and rather beautiful animals that have been living and breeding throughout our countryside undetected by the scientific world. And the only reason they have been undetected is because the scientific world would not get out of their comfortable chairs and take the situation seriously. If a housewife walking along a country lane spotted one, then she was mistaken; because she didn't have a university degree, how could she be expected to know a fox from a large cat! If a farmer spotted one running across his land, well he would recognise a fox without a degree, but of course, he was no doubt on his way back from the local pub. And if the police reported a sighting, Ah then, that was a different matter; the officer had seen a real large cat, but no doubt some idiot had let it escape and kept quiet about the situation. The fact that the sightings seldom

matched existing known big cats was put down to bad eyesight or witness mistakes. No one appeared to notice that witnesses all over the country were apparently suffering from identical eye defects.

So what is the animal and what does it look like? There are still a number of pieces missing from the jig saw – and will remain missing until we actually capture one – but enough is known to draw a reasonably accurate picture. The cat is leopard-size, about five to six feet long when adult, with a heavy long low slung body but with a neat puma like head, pricked ears and a flat catlike face. The legs are short and powerful, the paws large with graded pads rather like a hand with a thumb and three fingers and the tail long, thick and blunt ended. The colour-ation is very varied, ranging from ginger or fawn through all shades of brown to chocolate, jet black, silver and charcoal grey, and a combination of colours in striped animals such as silver grey with black markings, fawn with brown or even gold and grey. Variations of colour appear in all the breeding groups. For example a group I have studied in Wales consists of a large silver grey animal with dark thin stripes and rings on its coat, a jet black large one, two silver grey with dark stripes and rings on small cub sized animals, a large reddish brown animal and a large silver grey with a white chest but no markings. In Scotland, in one small forested area, fawn and reddish brown cubs and adults, a jet black adult, a chocolate brown adult, gold striped and ringed cubs and a gold striped adult have been seen. At the time of the so-called Surrey puma sightings there were seen on the estate at Bushylease Farm a puma coloured animal, a jet black panther and a fawn cat with dark brown stripes and spots. All these groups of animals are breeding within their own territories and the picture is the same throughout the country. Certainly there could be feral black panthers and fawn pumas, but not grey or striped known big cats. Unless one is willing to believe that we also have a number of tigers living happily alongside escaped pumas and black leopards. And even that wouldn't explain the silver grey animals.

However, despite the problems with colour, the animals are certainly flesh and blood, not spirits and despite comments to the contrary, they do leave tracks. And the tracks don't only reveal the graded pads, they also appear to show non-retractile claws and the only known cat with this trait is the cheetah. So we are left with believing that we have tigers, cheetahs, *Cont on p42.*

Cont on p42.

BOOK ALERT! by JANET BORD

No sooner had I written last issue's column than the information given began to be out of date. So I will begin by updating my previous column, giving revised publication dates where known. According to the Thames and Hudson spring catalogue, the U.K. paperback edition of *LIVING WONDERS* is due on 25th April, price £4.95. Also in the T&H catalogue and scheduled for the same period are *WILDMEN: Yeti, Sasquatch and the Neanderthal Engima* by Myra Shackley (£7.50), and *THE NEW VIEW OVER ATLANTIS* by John Michell (£8.95). Neither Loren Coleman's *WEIRD EXCURSIONS ACROSS AMERICA* nor Vladimir Markotic's *SASQUATCHES AND UNKNOWN HOMINOIDS* appears to have been published yet, and more information on these will be given in a later column. Douglas Curran's *IN ADVANCE OF THE LANDING* has also been delayed, until the autumn of 1983.

Recently two new major publishing projects have been announced. The first volume is already available in William R. Corliss's Catalog of Anomalies, and he plans to publish at least 24 more, at a rate of two per year, 'until we cover all of science'. Bill certainly sets his sights high, and, incredibly in these days of big ideas and

small achievements, he does what he sets out to do. He has already published 16 invaluable volumes of anomaly source material, and reports that he has on file 25,000 articles and other items from the scientific literature, with 1,500 added each year. So we can look forward to a regular stream of books from the Anomaly Data Research Center (P.O. Box 107, Glen Arm, MD 21057), the first of which, *LIGHTNING, AURORAS, NOCTURNAL LIGHTS AND RELATED LUMINOUS PHENOMENA* ($11.95) sets very high standards. Customers will also receive 'The Anomaly Newsletter', a regular progress report.

The other new project is a series of large-format paperback books under the series heading 'The Evidence for...'. The project is sponsored by ASSAP and the books will be published by The Aquarian Press, commencing probably during the spring of 1984. The first four titles are likely to be: John Rimmer on 'alien abductions', Janet & Colin Bord on 'Bigfoot and his kin', Kevin McClure on 'visions of the Virgin' and Hilary Evans on 'UFOs'.

In the last column I mentioned that Di Francis was thought to be working on a book about British big cats. This has now surfaced as *CAT

COUNTRY: The Quest for the British Big Cat* (David & Charles, £4.95), and will be published when you read this. The advertising for the book claims that photographs show that the cat is an unknown species, and a £500 reward is offered 'for the first big cat to be captured alive!' (Have they forgotten the Scottish puma trapped by Ted Noble in 1980?)

Two new books to be published by Souvenir Press this spring are *ADVENTURES IN IMMORTALITY: A Look Beyond the Threshold of Death* by George Gallup, Jr., with William Proctor (April, £7.95), and *THE GUADALUPE MADONNA: Myth or Miracle?* by Jody Brant Smith (May, £7.95). The first book uses the scientific resources of the Gallup Poll Organisation in yet another 'startling new look' at life after death, and includes hundreds of personal testimonies. Jody Brant Smith's book also invokes science, in an attempt to determine whether the image of the Virgin Mary on a 16th-century Mexican cloak is a 'genuine miracle'.

Although it is now 12 years since he died, archaeologist, psychic researcher, dowser and explorer T.C. Lethbridge has not been forgotten, and in March Routledge & Kegan Paul will reissue two of his books in paperback: *THE POWER OF THE PENDULUM* and *THE LEGEND OF THE SONS OF GOD* (both £2.95).

Finally, more books written and seeking a publisher, or scheduled for publication at some future time, or in the process of being written. Two of them are UFO books. Jenny Randles has teamed up with David Seargent in Australia to write *UFOS WORLDWIDE* ('a social comparison between the development of the UFO movement in Australia and Britain, with reference sections on other nations, e.g. France, U.S.A., Russia'), but this book is still seeking a publisher
Cont on p.43.

The Enigma of Entombed Toads.

It is easy to scoff at the notion of living toads found in cavities in rocks, but, as the authors of **Phenomena** and **Living Wonders** show, such stories are universal and form a class of phenomena which poses very real physical, geological and biological questions. While the mystery awaits its solution, Forteans continue to collect the evidence. Here **Paul Screeton** presents some cases he unearthed during research into some enigmas of north-eastern England.

Can a toad be entombed in stone for centuries and be none the worse for its enforced hibernation upon release? Persistent tales suggest this is so and seemingly defy categorization as myths or rumours. A Hartlepool case is central to the thesis that such is possible and real, and that such stories need not be relegated to the level of apocrypha.

Under the headline 'An Extraordinary Toad' in the *Hartlepool Free Press* of April 15, 1865, the following was printed:

"During some excavations which are being carried out in connection with the Hartlepool Water Works, the workmen on Friday morning found a toad embedded in a block of magnesium limestone, at a depth of 25 feet from the surface of the earth and eight feet from any spring water vein.

"The block of stone had been cut by a wedge being reduced by workmen when a pick split open the cavity in which the toad had been incarcerated. The cavity was no longer than its body.

"The toad's eyes shone with unusual brilliancy and it was full of vivacity upon its liberation. It appeared when first discovered desirous to perform the process of respiration but evidently experienced some difficulty and the only sign of success consisted of a 'barking' noise which it continues to make at present on being touched.

"The toad is in the possession of Mr Horner, the president of the Natural History Society, and continues in as lively state as when found. On a minute examination its mouth is found to be completely closed, and the barking noise it makes proceeds from its nostrils. The claws of its forefeet are turned inwards, and its hind ones of extraordinary length, and unlike the present English toad.

"The Rev. Taylor, incumbent of St. Hilda's Church, who is an eminent local geologist, gives it as his opinion that it must be at least 6,000 years old. This wonderful toad is to be placed in its primary habitation and will be added to the collection in the Hartlepool Museum.

"The toad when first released was of a pale colour and not easily distinguished from the stone, but shortly its colour grew darker to a fine olive brown."

A number of aspects here are worthy of comment. Firstly, though it resembled its surroundings, its change of colour discounts the possibility that it had been misidentified as not being released from the rock. Secondly, as we shall see, this was no isolated discovery and it fits the general rule in such cases that the amphibian fits exactly into the cavity of its discovery. Thirdly, it is established that amphibia hibernate in deep mud at the bottom of ponds or sink themselves into the ground to spend the winter, but megnesium limestone is quite a different mater. Such strata were laid down aeons ago, the heat and pressure involved in forming such stone must have been immense; plus, of course, if we are to accept the Darwinian evolutionary hypothesis amphibia were not at the time of laying down of such rockbeds even so much as a twinkle in the Creator's eye.

The unusual brilliance of its eye I am not qualified to speculate upon, or the curious barking sound, equally the closed mouth and the odd nature of its legs and feet, but the description makes it clear that this individual was not a native to these shores and, perhaps, not known anywhere on Earth.

Where the age of 6,000 years comes from is unclear. The Rev. Robert Taylor subsequently wrote: "I should infer that it had been there six times that number." Yet, if one accepts a uniformitarian viewpoint, the stratum of limestone is vastly older, having been laid down by sea creatures not pond life.

The same edition of the newspaper obviously had a member of the staff quick off the mark to consult the cuttings file for, under

A quarryman points to the hole in a rock from which a toad escaped, as his astonished fellows, who were breaking the rock, look on. [From Philip Gosse's Romance of Natural History *(1861) which contains possibily the first collection and examination of stoned toad stories.]*

the heading 'The Toad Again', Hartlepudlians were reminded:

"The world now had another story of a toad in a hole... Illustrations of the toad's perilous passion for holes abound in our literature and, if we turn over the leaves of our local chronicles numerous examples present themselves.

"We read of the discovery within the last hundred years, of live toads in all sorts of possible and impossible situations; in the solid slate of a quarry in Barnard Castle, in a block of free-

stone at Blyth, in a limestone block at Saeham and at Ryhope, and in a seam of coal down a deep pit at Sunderland.

"Embedded in sport at Bamborough, in the heart of a stone wall, a toad was released in 1809 after a lapse of 16 years; torpid and drowsy, dazzled in the sun, some minutes were required for the recovery of his juvenile animation, and then he crawled away with an air of unconcern.

"Another of his race, profiting by repairs, emerged from the battlements of Flambard's

Bridge in 1828, and gave rise to unavailing speculation as to his antiquity. A beech tree at Shawdon and an American oak at Blyth fell into the hands of sawyers, when a 'living toad' started out of each of them, and exchanged a life of solitude for the publicity of a paragraph in Sykes or Latimer.

"It is remarkable, certainly, that after the world has grown so old and research so long on foot, there should still be controversy as to whether a breathing animal can live for centuries in the heart of solid rock, excluded from the air."

The discovery was on April 7, 1865, and the account in a Leeds newspaper added that James Yeal, of Dyke House Quarry, was superintending excavations.

Additionally the report was communicated in an 1865 issue of *Zoologist,* in which Mr E Birchall stated that it was not a "myth" and also mentioned that a report in the *Sunderland Herald* had quoted the Rev. Taylor as saying the toad was still alive.

In fact, Mr Taylor addressed himself to the editor of the *Stockton and Hartlepool Mercury* on April 19, 1865, feeling he had been misquoted over the time factor of the entombment. He also chose to follow a catastrophist geological argument to account for the toad's incarceration, believing the "living toad was caught in the finely comminuted sediment, and sealed up alive and kept there for numberless years. How it is that all this time it lived, I leave to the naturalists to determine — they often contend among themselves about things of much less importance."

He then vouches for the veracity of the report in the newspaper and adds "for the satisfaction of the toad's kind friends who inquire after him", that it is healthy, "and as if he would have no objection to live a thousand years longer in his new situation."

This being in a small aquarium in Hartlepool Museum, where numerous visitors had inspected it.

Mr Taylor added: "For the satisfaction of those who have not heard of him, I may state that he cannot be accused of gluttony, for he has no mouth. For a few days after his deliverance he seemed to pine, but they plunged him into water, whence be began to puff out and swell like the mother frog who would rival the ox in size.

"His only support seems to be water absorbed through his carbunkled skin. When first delivered from his confinement he seemed like a new born babe to struggle in his attempt to breath. He utters a barking noise, like a little dog, from his snorting nostrils. He has most beautiful eyes and, should he die, we hope to find Shakespeare's 'precious jewel' in his head.

"Save some clumsy difference in his hind feet, he has a brighter skin than his other bretheren. He is now in a glass case with a moist grassy turf and in apparently high enjoyment of life."

Mr Taylor adds another salient point about the discovery. The men who found the toad "assert that he exactly fitted the mould, and it is not the only instance of such occurrences about five years ago the like happened in another part of the rock."

In fact, accounts of entombed amphibia date back to classical authors and discovery of frogs and toads in closed cavities in trees are far from unknown. A 1976 issue of *Zoologist* reproduced a cutting from a South African newspaper recording that when the bark of a broad tree was being sawn a hole going inwards was found, the size of a wine glass, from which the sawyers scraped out 68 small toads each about the size of the upper joint of one's little finger. They hopped away healthily, yet all around them had been solid yellow wood with nothing to indicate how they got there or received sustenance.

Now we come to the crux of the matter.

Presuming we accept the evidence and the veracity of those involved in the discovery of incarcerated amphibia we must consider the possibilities of how this puzzling phenemenon manifests. Is it naturally, unnaturally or phenomenally?

• 1—The hibernation mechanism is such that virtual immortality is guaranteed.

• 2—Geological dating is wildly innacurate or amphibia have been around during periods palaeontologists do not acknowledge. Earliest toads date from Tertiary rocks so, where entombment occurred in older rocks, were the toads contemporaray with their fossil companions — who had not survived? Or would a catastrophist geology in preference to the orthodox uniformitarian model explain the presence better — though not the longevity?

One explanation is that a toad could find its way into a crevice in limestone and while hibernating the dripping of water holding carbonate of lime in solution would seal it in. When it was released finders would not make a distinction between the original stone formed under the ocean aeons before and the encrusting stalagmite whose formation was still continuing. To them all would seem contemporaneous solid limestone.[1] But then this does not apply to examples of other stone, coal, and certainly not a tree.

• 3—Nature can violate "the 'logical' laws we try to impose with some low frequency, after the fashion of the 'forbidden transitions' in quantum physics," as William R. Corliss has postulated.[2]

• 4—But a certain A. Wilson, writing in *Knowledge*, represents the blinkerdom of the cult of science by claiming that what is really to us a repeating and observable phenomenon is simply a matter of rumour. In his opinion: "The usual story is that of some quarrymen who, blasting stones, see a live frog or toad hopping about, after the blast, among the debris. Because the toad is found thus it is assumed that it came from the interior of the rock. Not a particle or evidence exists to show in such a case that the animal had anything to do with the rock."[3]

All of which leaves us no nearer a solution, but it is another challenge to our comfy concepts of reality. It gives a neglected branch of life some degree of dignity for being the focus of a special bizarre behavioural mechanism in the larger than life continuum of phenomenal reality.

Frogs and toads emerging from rock may be a surprise and if you wish to disbelieve and choose to imagine a lurking terrestrial toad near a quarryman's pick had been there ready to hop out obligingly at the exact moment of the blow, then my final "case" should disturb such a conception.

It is recorded that during railway tunnelling in France a large boulder was broken to release an extraordinary creature from a cavity. The creature, the size of a goose with hideous head and harp teeth; shook its wings, gave a hoarse cry and expired. It had four legs joined by a membrane terminating in talons.[4]

Yes, this living – albeit briefly – fossil was identified by a naturalist/palaeontologist as being a pterodactyl!

The stratum was Jurassic limestone, which fits the period of that flying reptile's age according to evolutionists. But it is also of some nagging interest that the constituency of the rock was limestone, that favourite habitat of other creatures.

If there can be frogs and toads, even pterodactyls, in limestone, then who knows but one day the blasting of a limestone quarry will set free an example of Tyrannosaurus Rex?

But as any scientist present would reassure you, the dinosaur must have been there unnoticed beforehand, for you do not find toads, frogs or reptilian carnivores in rocks...

•

Paul Screeton

References:
1) Worhen, A.H., *American Naturalist*, No.5, 1871.
2) Corliss, W.R., *The Unexplained: A Sourcebook of Strange Phenomena* (Bantam, U.S.A., 1976.)
3) Wilson, A., 'Toad in a Hole', *Knowledge*, 1881.
4) Michell, J., and Rickard, R.J.M, *Phenomena* (Thames & Hudson, 1978.)

Fortean Extracts From
The Gentleman's Magazine:

St JOHN'S GATE.

Lond Gazette
Londō Jour.
Fog's Journ.
Applebee's ::
Read's :: : :
Craftsman ::
B. Spectator
Grubstreet ¶
W.ly Register
Free = Briton
Hyp = Doctor
Daily Court.
Daily = Post
Dai._ournal
Da. Post-boy
D. Advertiser
EveningPost
S: James's Eb.
Whitehall Eb.
Lōdon Ebēīg
_lving = Post
Weekly Mis=
cellany.

Yozk 2 News
Dublin 6 :::
Edinburgh 2
Bristol :: : ::
Norwich 2 ::
Exeter 2 : : :
Worcester : :
Northamton
Gloucester : :
Stamford : :
Nottingham
Bury Journ.
Chester ditto
Derby ditto
Ipswich dit.
Reading dit.
Leeds Merc.
Newcastle C.
Canterbury
Manchester :
Boston ::: ¶
Jamaica, &c
Barbados :

Or, MONTHLY INTELLIGENCER.

...being the second installment from the pages of *The Gentleman's Magazine,* founded in 1731, and compiled chronologically for us by Peter Christie.

1737

• The year 1737 started with some odd but not Fortean events—how else would you describe a jealous husband sewing up his wife's genitals to keep her chaste while he was away? Of more immediate interest to readers of this magazine was the report concerning a rather remarkable centenarian.

July 31. Was living in St. Margaret's Parish Workhouse, Westminster, Mary Patten, aged 136 Years, whose only Food wa: Milk. The Trustees have had her Picture taken, to succeed her, when she dies. (page 449)

• A little later in the year the Irish had a challenger to this old lady—who, though not so old, certainly seemed more virile!

October. Marriage—Andrew Newton, aged 117, lately in Ireland—to a young Woman of 19, who is big with Child by him; he has a Son living above 80, and is as hail and hearty as any Man of 50 in the Kingdom. (p.637)

• The following month of November 1737 saw an extraordinary entry;

November. Exeter. Some Fishermen near this City drawing their Net ashore, a Creature of human shape, having two Legs, leap'd out, and run away very swiftly; not being able to overtake it, they knock'd it down by throwing sticks after it. At their coming up to it, it was dying, and groan'd like a human Creature: Its Feet were webb'd like a Duck's, it had Eyes, Nose and Mouth, resembling those of a Man, only the Nose somewhat depress'd; a Tail not unlike a Salmon's, turning up towards its Back, and is 4 Feet high. It was publickly shewn here. (page 703)

The next year saw another capture of a similar animal on the South Devon coast (see below: 1738, July 12).

1738

● In April, a precis of a report from a Government committee was printed. The committee had been set up to "examine the Causes of the present notorious Immorality and Profaneness". Things don't change much apparently! Amongst the witnesses questioned was one Peter Lens who,

...professes himself to be a Votary of the Devil, that he hath offered Prayers to him, and publickly drank to the Devil's Health; that he had at several times uttered the most daring and execrable Blasphemies against the Sacred Name and Majesty of God; and often made use of such obscene, blasphemous, and before unheard of Expressions, as the Lords Committees think they cannot even mention to your Lordships, and therefore chuse to pass over in Silence. (page 219)

Satanism in the eighteenth-century was rarely made so public—the penalties were harsh and one always ran the possibility of being lynched by incensed Christians. Peter's oaths must have been shocking indeed if they could not even be reported to the hardly lilywhite members of the House of Lords.

● A few months later another enigmatic creature was caught in south Devon;

July 12. Exeter. A strange Fish was taken just without Exmouth Bar, by Robert Heath, (the Person who caught 2 Fishes by People in general called Mermaids in September and May last) supposed by many to be the Triton, or Merman, of the Antients, being four Feet and a half in Length, having a Body much resembling that of a Man, with a Genital Member of considerable Size; together with jointed Legs and Feet, extending from his Belly 12 or 13 Inches, with Fins at his Thighs, and larger ones, like Wings, in the Form of which those of Angels are often painted, at his Shoulders; with a broad Head in uncommon Form, a Mouth 6 inches Wide, Smellers, or kind of Whiskers, at his Nostrils, and two Spout Holes behind his Eyes, through which he ejected Water, when taken, 30 and 40 Feet high. (page 378)

Several points in this report are of interest, especially the previous capture in May which does not appear in the *Gentleman's Magazine*. The mention of whiskers and spout-holes suggests a type of seal but what about the "jointed Legs and Feet" and the "Wings"? Unfortunately, as with many of these eighteenth century

wonders, I know of no engraving or drawing of this true nondescript.

● Passing on, there is a full account of a tremendous storm that passed over England on July 25 1738. Amongst the details listed are hailstones "as big as Walnuts" that fell at Dunstable and Uxbridge and injured several people. Of interest are the concluding sentences;

Between three and four a'Clock in the Afternoon, they had a like Storm of Hail, about Bungay, in Suffolk, preceded by an uncommon Clap of Thunder. The Windows of the Churches were shatter'd, the Corn laid flat, Turkeys and other Poultry kill'd in great Numbers. (page 379)

Bungay of course, experienced a similar clap of thunder in the sixteenth century only at that time a giant black dog appeared in the local church and killed several people. [See illustration of the contemporary report on FT29p14— Ed.] Bungay would appear to attract particularly fearsome storms.

● The year 1738 closed in Fortean terms with a report on,

A Strange Creature taken in a Wood in Guinea, is brought to Town; 'tis a Female, about four Foot high, shaped in every Part like a Woman, except its Head which nearly resembles that of an Ape! She walks upright naturally, sits down to her Food, which is chiefly Greens, and feeds herself with her Hands as a Human Creature. She is very fond of a Boy, and observed to be always sorrowful at his Absence, is clothed with a thin silk Vestment, and shews a great Discontent at the opening her Gown to discover her Sex. (page 492)

This is probably an orang-utang though one wonders if, just by the faintest chance some enterprising sea captain had managed to obtain a real 'Wildman' (or woman)? As with so many of these reports, however, there is no later follow-up and we are left with supposition and unanswered questions.

1739

● As the *Gentleman's Magazine* entered the ninth year of publication so its record of Fortean events continued unabated. In the January edition for 1739 came news of an event that happened on the 30th of December in the previous year. In the West Riding of Yorkshire there was a,

...sudden and violent Earthquake, the moveable utensils rattling and rolling out of their Places, and People fearing to be tumbled out of their Beds. It seem'd as if the Earth had mov'd out of its Place in a Line parallel to the Horizon, and again return'd to its former Situation with reciprocal Vibrations, which ended in a Minute or two with a hizzing hollow Report, and a Quivering of all Things on its Surface. (page 75)

The final detail about the noise that accompanied this event is of some interest. Corliss in his valuable series of *Sourcebooks* reprints many similar items that make mention of noises associated with earth movements—both before and after the event.

• Once more centenarians featured in the magazine pages. In April 1739 died,

> *A Tenant of the Lord Lovat's in the Scotch Highlands...aged 126; he retained his Senses to the last so as to give distinct Orders relating to his Funeral.* (page 216)

1740

• The year 1740 was curiously empty of Forteana though William Duell, a convict, had reason to be grateful either to Providence or to the clumsiness of the hangman. After being hung at Tyburn his body was brought to a surgeon for dissection,

> *but after it was stripp'd and laid on the Board, and one of the Servants was washing him in order to be cut, he perceived Life in him, and found his Breath to come quicker; on which a Surgeon took some Ounces of Blood from him; in two Hours he was able to sit up in his Chair, and in the Evening was again committed to Newgate.* (page 570)

A later note revealed that he was transported for life—a true return from the dead, or at least half-dead?

1741

• If 1740 was quiet 1741 was marked by a series of unusual "natural" atmospheric phenomena. The first of these occurred in August and was related by a correspondent as follows,

> *On the 28th Ult. happened a violent Storm of Thunder and Hail in the South East parts of the West Riding of Yorkshire, part of Nottinghamshire and Lincolnshire. The Hail-Stones were generally as large as Musket-Balls, many as big as Pigeons Eggs, and some two or three Inches long, and an Inch Diameter, of various Shapes, like broken Isicles, which tore and cut up the standing Corn, and beat, as with a Flail, the Corn that was reaped; broke off large Branches of Trees, and tore up some by the Roots; knocked down and broke the Heads of several People, and killed Birds and Hares. Thus it raged 10 miles in Length, and 1 in Breadth, and did much Damage 40 miles in Length and 2 in Breadth. The Hail lay in Heaps half a Yard deep 2 Days after like Ice. The loss of the poor Farmers is computed at 4000£ and a Collection is proposed for their Relief.* (page 441)

In the following month a similarly destructive storm passed over Huntingdonshire and Norfolk as well as another over Kent. On December 11 a report came from 'Bushy' in Herts. about a fireball,

> *At 45 Minutes after 12 (the Sun shining) appeared at Bushy, a Ball of Fire 45 deg. high in the Clouds, which run about the seeming Distance of 4 yards and then disappeared. It grew larger as it ran, and ended in appearance, as big as a man's Hand. The same Phenomenon was seen at Reading, and several other Places. Its course was nearly from West to East.* (page 664)

Just to finish off the year Mother Nature achieved her most spectacular series of phenomena in Kent only a week after the Bushy event on December 18th.

> *About Noon a large Ball of Fire was seen to pass over Canterbury, which was follow'd by a Storm that broke almost all the Windows in the Town, and the next Morning three Suns appear'd in the Sky attended with a Rainbow inverted, which lasted from nine to twelve, to the great Astonishment of the Inhabitants.* (page 664)

To be continued

•

Peter Christie

SOAPBOX
Cont from p34.

pumas and leopards living and breeding happily all over the country, or ghosts that produce cubs, allow photographs to be taken, make kills and leave tracks and droppings. Or, more simply, I believe we have an addition to our native wildlife that we just hadn't taken notice of because it normally makes a point of keeping out of our way.

I'm sorry to throw cold water on the many fanciful theories regarding the British Big Cats, but perhaps knowing so much more about them, we can now appreciate a new and beautiful animal that inhabits our woods and forests and together we can help protect them as a species, thus ensuring they remain to delight us for another thousand years.

•

Di Francis

This column is open to any reader who wishes to express an opinion, or to speculate upon any topic related to the contents or interests of FT. However submissions must be typed and limited to no more than two pages

Fortean Times

PARADIGM LOST
cont from p.30

led by Alain Aspect at Institut d'Optique Theorique et Appliquée near Paris established once and for all that the EPR effect is a reality and that signals can pass instantaneously between the particles of a "two-particle system".

But if all the matter in the universe was simultaneously created in the "Big Bang" then the whole universe is just an infinitely complex version of a "two-particle system".

As David Bohm, the theoretical physicist who devised the modern form of the experiment (using photons with complementary spin-states) said, "It may mean that everything in the universe is in a kind of total rapport, so that whatever happens is related to everything else; or it may mean that there is some kind of information that can travel faster than the speed of light; or it may mean that our concepts of space and time have to be modified in some way that we don't now understand. Yet whichever interpretation you choose, the experiment establishes once and for all that physics as we know it is unfinished"[2].

•

Mike Crowley

Credits and References:

(1) Einstein, A., Podolsky, B., Rosen, N., "Can Quantum-Mechanical Description of Physical Reality be considered complete?", *Physical Review,* 47, 1935.

(2) *Sunday Times,* 20.2.1983.

BOOK ALERT
Cont from p.35.

CLEAR INTENT by Larry Fawcett & Barry Greenwood has found a publisher (Prentice-Hall), but is still being written. The subject is the U.S. government's role in UFO research, and the authors are using material obtained through requests under the Freedom of Information Act. Two 'works in progress' with strong UFO links are Anders Liljegren's on the Swedish 'ghost fliers' of 1946, and Jean Sider and Jean

Giraud's on the U.S. airships of 1896-7.

I close with three lake monster books, two of them imminent, the other, in the author's words, 'in the lap of the gods'. Due during 1983 are Lionel Leslie's *THE WATER HORSE* (Colin Smythe Ltd), mentioned last time, and an English translation of *MONSTERS IN QUEBEC LAKES: Myths and Troublesome Realities* by Claude Gagnon & Michel Meurger (already available in French,

published by Montreal publisher Editions Internationals/Alain Stanke). Due in 1984, or '85, or '86...is Tim Dinsdale's next book, *LOCH NESS AND THE WATER UNICORN,* and we all hope that the events Tim is awaiting, to enable him to complete the book will occur during this auspicious year of 1983, which marks the 50th anniversary of the monster's naming, and Tim's 50th monster-hunting foray.

•

Janet Bord

WORDS FROM THE WIZARD
cont from p.49

smack in the centre of a perfect fairy ring. Should have shouted 'fore', I thought, oddly nervous. Leaving the ball as a kind of gift, to God knows who, I went back into town, straight into a pub and was soon drinking the black wine of the country. Then a woman's voice said loudly, 'that's your man', but it sounded like 'that shaman', and I looked up to see the barmaid pointing me out to a stranger. He turned out to be a travelling balladeer, and he knew a lot about the 'little people'. Now, it all means something or nothing at all. 'Nothing is not,' said old Crowley, none too brightly... but... 'Nothing is better than nothing,' said Sam Beckett, darkly, and who am I to

disagree? • *Doc Shiels*

NOTES AND REFERENCES
1. John Updike. *The New Yorker,* 1972.
2. Sigerson Clifford. 'The Legend of Puck Fair' from *Legends of Kerry,* Geraldine Press, Tralee, 1972.
3. Peter Dobereiner, on Dooks, from 'Golf in Ireland' in *The Golfer's Bedside Book,* Batsford, London, 1971.
4. Richard Cavendish, *The Black Arts,* RKP, London, 1967.
5. Richard Davies. Ed. *I've Seen a Ghost.* Hutchinson, London, 1979. Full chapter on 'Spooks'.
6. Philip José Farmer. *The Image of the Beast* and *Blown,* Essex House, Hollywood, Calif. 1968, and Quartet Books, London, 1975.
7. Robert Shea and Robert Anton Wilson. *Illuminatus.* 3 volumes. Sphere, London, 1977.
8. Robert Anton Wilson. *Masks of the Illuminati.* Sphere Books, London, 1981.
9. Tristan Tzara. 'Zurich Chronicle 1915 to 19', *Dada Almanac,*

Berlin, 1920. Around this time (1915–20), the Polish medium, 'Franek Kluski', was materializing his, sometimes 'headless', pythecanthropus. 'Kluski' was known to Conan Doyle and to the early surrealists.
10. Stan Gebler Davies. *James Joyce: A Portrait of the Artist.* Davis-Poynter, London, 1975.
11. AJ Bell. 'Lexi-Links: Nature's Play on Words', from *Fortean Times.* No 17. 1976.
12. Old Irish music hall song. Now heard mostly in Dublin pubs.
13. Kurt Schwitters, *Anna Blume,* Hanover, 1919.
14. James Joyce. *Finnegans Wake.* Various editions since 1939, including Faber, London. Interesting comments on the Wake are to be found in *A Reader's Guide to Finnegans Wake* by William York Tindall, Thames & Hudson, London, 1969.
15. Old music hall song... *Finnegan's Wake* (note the apostrophe, missing from the title of Joyce's book). Now heard mostly in Dublin pubs.

ON THE TRAIL by Loren Coleman

THE STRANGE CASE OF THE TWO CHARLIE WETZELS

1958 in the United States was a relatively uneventful year. Most noteworthy, perhaps, was the launching of the Explorer I from Cape Canaveral, and the creation of the Bank Ameri-card. Things moved slowly in Eisenhower's America. Meanwhile, in Forteana America, a few births of another kind were occurring. The modern era of Bigfoot accounts began in 1958. On the 27th of August of that year, Jerry Crew and his men, literally his crew, reported some strange incidents as they were building a new lumber access road near Bluff Creek, California. Soon photographs of giant seventeen inch long plaster casts of human-like tracks were being carried nationwide by the media, and the modern out-burst of Bigfoot accounts was launched.

Three months later, and six hundred miles away, an eerie encounter was to occur in southern California which soon took on an aberrant but classic place in the Bigfoot literature. This was the Charles Wetzel sighting. The details of the story are familiar through the writings of Barker, the Bords, Green, Sanderson, and others, but during 1982, I was able to personally interview Wetzel and his family, coming up with some interesting new information.

Charles Wetzel, born 8 July 1934, was driving his two door green 1952 Buick Super near Riverside, California, when he saw "it". Saturday, the 8th of November 1958, is a night

Charlie told me he would not soon forget. He even remembers which radio station — Los Angeles' KFI — he had tuned in on the car's wireless receiver. Slowly, Charles Wetzel neared that part of North Main Street where the Santa Ana River infrequently overflows its banks. The road dips at this spot, and sure enough, water was rushing across the road. So Charles slowed down.

Quickly, however, he was struck by two sensory events which caught him offguard. First, his radio started to trans-mit lots of static. He changed the stations, he told me, but to no avail. Next he saw what he thought was a temporary danger sign near the flooded site. Before he could think twice about all of this, Charles Wetzel saw a six foot tall creature bound across his field of vision and stop in front of his Buick. It had a "round, scarecrowish head like something out of Halloween", Charles told reporters at the time. He described it then and now as having no ears; no nose; a beaky, protuberant mouth; and fluorescent, shining eyes. The skin was "scaly, like leaves, but definitely not feathers," Wetzel reaffirmed in our 1982 talk. (Gene Duplantier's 1958 drawing of the creature Wetzel saw, gives a feel for how bizarre the thing must have looked.)

The entity was waving "sort of funny" with its incredibly long arms, and seemed to be walking from the hips, almost as if it did not have any knees. Wetzel remembers another detail not chronicled

at the time — that the legs stuck out from the sides of the torso, not the bottom. It made a gurgling sound mixed with a high-pitched scream. When it saw Wetzel, it reached all the way over the hood and began clawing at the windshield. Terrified, Charles Wetzel grasped his .22 High Standard pistol he kept in the car because he was on the road a lot at nights. Clutching the gun, but not wanting to break the one barrier he saw between himself and the beast, the frightened Californian stomped on the gas. "Screeching like a fucker," as Wetzel graphically put it, the creature fell back from the hood, and was run over by the Buick. Wetzel could hear it scraping the pan under the car, and later police laboratory tests demonstrated something had indeed rubbed the grease off from the under-side.

Police used bloodhounds to search the area, but were only left with sweeping claw marks on Wetzel's windshield to ponder. However, the next night a black something jumped out of the underbrush near the same site, and fright-ened another motorist. In recent years, strange three-toed "Bigfeet" have been reported from surrounding areas of Southern California, one of the most current being the Buena Park smelly eight footer seen emerging from a drainage ditch in May, 1982. But it is the Wetzel sighting from River-side that has remained the atypical but classic southern California case, having been widely discussed and debated by Bigfooters since 1958.

Not until 1982, however, when researcher Ray Boeche passed along a yellowed news clipping to me did I learn that *another* Charles Wetzel had seen something strange. For years I had encouraged Boeche, as I have many others, to search their local newspaper libraries beyond the realm of lake monsters and bigfoot accounts, into the whole weird world of creatures filling the zoo surrounding us all. I was thus happily amazed to discover this Charles Wetzel was involved with one of my favourites, the mystery kangaroos. And the long forgotten Nebraskan incident had taken place in *1958!*

So I got on the telephone, and interviewed this new Charles Wetzel. The elements of the story are as straightforward as this man of the Plains. Charles Wetzel, born 29 March 1888, was at his Platte River cabin, near Grand Rapids, Nebraska, that Monday, the 28th of July 1958. Wetzel reported the thing he first took to be a deer was chasing some dogs which in and of itself he thought was kind of strange. Then he got within ten yards of it, and what he started to take to be a kangaroo bound away with ten foot leaps. Charles Wetzel described the animal or whatever as about six feet tall, brown, with large hind legs and small forelegs which barely touched the ground as it jumped. Wetzel told me the kangaroo stayed around the cabin for several minutes, but finally departed when Wetzel tried to get closer, first on foot, then in his car. The kangaroo disappeared into an alfalfa field.

Wetzel's report was not an isolated event in 1958's Nebraska. Sightings of kangaroos came in from towns, sometimes 100 miles distance from each other, including Endicott, Stanton and Fairbury. Charles Wetzel, a successful Grand Rapids businessman, operated a brewery soon after his sighting, and even entitled one of his products 'Wetzel Kangaroo Beer'.

In talking to both the Nebraska Charles Wetzel and the California Charles Wetzel, I discovered that both have sons named Charles, but neither family knew of the other. So what are we to make of this bit of synchronization of Wetzels, both named Charles, in 1958, both encountering creatures vastly beyond the norm?

After much head-scratching, I thought it would be best to attempt to understand some kind of underlying pattern via the name "Wetzel". Now, monsters do not seem to be seen by people with the most common names, but why would a couple of Charlie Wetzels be picked? 'Wetzel' is a German name, a corrupted form of 'little Varin' from 'Warin' — meaning 'protector'. Therefore, are we to assume some elemental insight from the fact 'Wetzel' literally and simply means 'little protector or guardian'?

Next, I went to search how often and where 'Wetzel' is used geographically. In the United States of America, there is but one use of 'Wetzel' — namely as the proper name

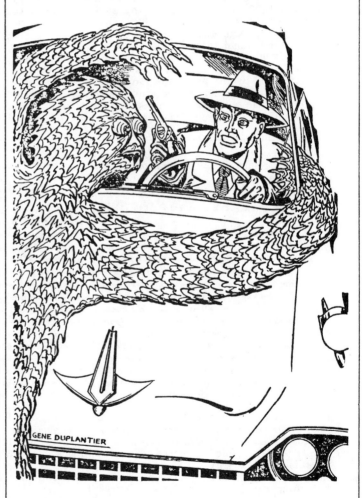

Drawing by Gene Duplantier of the California Wetzel incident, for Flying Saucers *Feb 1959. Reproduced by GD's kind permission.*

of a county in northern West Virginia. I was not too surprised to find that the folklore of Wetzel County is filled with a long history of ghost stories, or to note a few curious Fortean items in the surrounding area. By now, I was not shocked by what might be in show via a Wetzel. Interestingly, while perhaps not a hotbed for Forteana, the Wetzel County locale has a lot to offer. Nearby Sisterville, West Virginia, is well known as one of the few eastern American cities visited by the phantom airships of the 1890's. Moundsville, just north of Wetzel, is the site of a significant earthen mound built by persons unknown, Mounds are still being discovered in the area, as evidenced by the one recently found there when a glass factory was cut out of the hills. The bordering counties in Pennsylvania (Greene and Fayette) are the seat of many strange big hairy hominoid and UFO accounts, especially in the last few years. All in all, Wetzel County probably feels very at home in the state of the Flatwoods Monster, and Mothman.

And speaking of Mothman, John Keel was one of the first among us to start looking at this whole issue of name selectivity. Some form of choosing is occurring beyond the limits of our understanding — be it the Reeves noted by Keel, the Lafayettes discussed by Bill Grimstad, or the Wetzels mentioned here. The name game sometimes centers on people — be they Ambroses, Suttons or Wetzels — and other times on places — be those Decaturs, Dovers, Leeds, Logans, or Fayettevilles. These names pop up again and again.

Variations on the magnetic names above and dozens of others appear in some as yet undiscovered way to attract frequent bouts with poltergeists, creatures, ufos and related phenomena. The laws of probability do seem to malfunction in the midst of Forteana, for the Smiths, Jones and Johnsons, at least in the USA, are not the most frequent witnesses of the more bizarre encounters. Two Charles Wetzels saw two quite wonderfully weird creatures in the same year, 1958. Why are we not surprised any longer?

I would expect that somewhere across America there is a 'little guardian' who soon will have another meeting with a monster, and perhaps because of that encounter, the elementals will have been held back yet another day. Something is collecting Charles Wetzels!

Postscript

Shortly after completing my column on the Wetzel name, the Chamber of Commerce of Wetzel County, W. VA. sent me a short, old, undated item. The extract shown gives yet another insight into the mysterious history of the locale.

An incident occured in 1845 that must have aroused dreams of wealth. A man presented himself to the community and remained a while without any apparent means of support. Having no occupation, he was arrested under the vagrancy law and to obtain his liberty was compelled to state his business to the town officers. Thereupon he showed papers from the French Government. By this it was ascertained that he was the accredited agent of that government sent to this community to search for $87,000.00 supposed to have been buried below the creek during the French and Indian war. It is thought that he did not find the money. Shortly after this, another incident occured in the same line. A Mr. Watkins of Monongalia county sold his farm there for 1,000 silver dollars, and came to this settlement, the silver, which weighed over 60 pounds, was too heavy to carry about his person, so he set aside $40.00 for his immediate use and buried the remainder at the foot of a pawpaw bush, 60 steps from the river bank, midway between the mouth of the creek and a point opposite Texas run; when he returned for his money, it could not be found.

What I found of interest in the two buried treasure incidents is their connectedness to patterns running through other Fortean events. Strangers appearing in towns, giving out "disinformation," and leaving a wake of questions in their path occurs frequently. It happened in the 1890's airship, the 1960's Mothman, and the recent era's Men-In-Black encounters. Wetzel's 1845 "Frenchman" falls right into this category.

And what of a Mr. Watkins hiding and losing 960 silver dollars weighing over 60 pounds, placed 60 steps from the river under a pawpaw tree? The name Alfred Watkins comes to mind when thoughts of hidden power points are mentioned, and Watkins Glen, New York, is the site of re-occurring disappearences.. Indeed, Bill Grimstad must be credited with noting "Watts" and its derivations as names having entanglements with certain phenomena. A Watkins in Wetzel dealing with 960/60/60 fits all too comfortably into the cryptologic we have begun to rediscover.

•

Loren Coleman

FORE...TITANIA!

In the merry month of May, in the year of 'eighty two, my golfing career was abruptly banjaxed when I was clubbed and clouted by a group of patriotic SUN readers, near Falmouth's waterfront. It had something to do with the Malvinas...sorry...the *Falklands* business, and my Hibernian connections, resulting in a fractured skull, badly bruised ribs, and a crushed right hand. After six weeks of painfully interesting treatment, my physiotherapist recommended accordion-playing as being 'probably good' for the injured hand, but warned that golf-playing could be 'probably bad'. I made the mistake of experimenting with one-handed golf...and dislocated my sinister pinkie!

Falkland is the name of a Scottish town in the golfing kingdom of Fife. The world's most southerly golf course is at Stanley, in the Falkland Islands, and Stanley is the name of a Scottish town in the golfing Tayside region, next-door to the kingdom of Fife.

□ □ □

'Golf is of games the most mystical, the least earth bound, the one wherin the walls between us and the supernatural are rubbed thinnest.'
John Updike[1]

□ □ □

I was attacked again in July (whilst busking in Falmouth. Theraputic thespianism?) by a trio of unionjackbooted morons, wearing 'Bash the Argies' T-shirts. After smacking two of their closely cropped heads with my accordion (theatre of cruelty, or the absurd?), I managed to escape. Prince Philip had just arrived in town, aboard HMS '*Londonderry*' (!), to start the 'Tall Ships Race'. Falmouth was bedizened with red, white and blue John Bullshit, and heaving with bellicose True-Brit boozers, ready and willing to deliver a bit of 'backlash' (psychic or otherwise) to any thick Paddy whose presence reminded them of recent 'outrages' against the Crown. Remembering that the 'father' of the Argentine Navy, Admiral William Brown, was a native of Foxford, Co Mayo...as was my paternal grandfather...I decided that my most prudent course would be to get the hell out of Cornwall and head back to Erin. Then, as Christ and I were about to cross the water, Jon Beckjord...sasquatch-scatologist and seer...arrived in Ponsanooth. He tried to cajole us into a Nessie raising expedition, all expenses paid, but we declined. Jon set off for Scotland and we set off for Ireland.

At the beginning of August, the Kerry newspapers carried front page headlines concerning an assassination threat to Killorglin's pagan goat king. A letter, posted in Swansea on July 26th, read:

Dear Sir,
I want to warn you that I am coming to Eire to assassinate your foolish King Puck. Your tribe shot my great friend Lord Louis Mountbatten. I will not be known in your town but at 12 o'clock on Aug 10th I will kill your King... 12 o'clock at

night. I am the Black Hand of the World.

(signed Black Hand.)

As things turned out, King Puck's throne, high above Killorglin town, was better guarded than Queen Elizabeth's bedroom in Buckingham Palace (and *that* little caper, with its drinking and smoking, had Irish/Cornish connections, through Fagan and Trestrail).

While Puck Fair was in full swing, the Garda DS found a large patch of 'home grown' cannabis on a mountainside, just a few miles outside Killorglin. Locally, the stuff is known as 'Kerrygold'.

□ □ □

'The mountains around Killorglin were favourite feeding-grounds for the goats as some special herb that grew there was greatly to their liking, for it put extra silk in their coats and added another inch to their horns.'[2]

□ □ □

I wondered if, in the Indian Rope Trick, the shaman gets himself high on a rope twisted from Indian hemp? Packing my dudeen with twist, taking a rope, a jug, and a fiddler, I made my way to the seaside golf links known as Dooks, about eight miles from Killorglin, and, there, conducted a few experiments in PSI ('Paddy's Surrealist Intoxications'). The fiddler, Ashley C. Drees, played some lively reels and I coaxed the rope into a perpendicular pose. It seemed, somehow, fitting to attempt the Irish Rope Trick at Dooks, a place which atmospherically encourages a very special kind of golf.

□ □ □

'It was a dreamlike experience, playing over the rolling hills and guessing, often wrongly, which hollow would harbour a green. I did not see another human all day.'[3]

□ □ □

We were close to Lough Caragh and Lough Acoose, where monsters dwell. Meanwhile, back in the UK, Nick Witchell presented news from the South Atlantic to his TV audience, and, perhaps, between bowdler-ised bulletins, gave occasional thought to the fate of the Pategonian plesiosaur. Witch-ell is a name which adds 45 inches (an ell) to 'witch'. 4+5=9. The BFPO number for Falklands troops included an ominous 666, which reduces numer-olically to 9 (6+6+6=18. 1+8=9). Old Crowley killed the cat nine times, once for each of its lives. My name, Anthony Nicol Shiels (anagram of 'Only a hit in Loch Ness') has 18 letters, 1+8=9. A golf ball has 333 dimples, another numer-ological 9. Each dimple is 0.0135 in, or 0.34425mm, in depth, reducing again to 9. The ball is 1.62 in or 41.31mm in diameter...a further 9. The golf ball is a formal symbol of the moon, with its dimple craters; and golf, remember, is or was the first human game to be played on the moon (by Alan Shepard).

□ □ □

'Netsah and Hod are balanced and combined in Yesod, 9, the sphere of the moon.'[4]

□ □ □

After the three lunatic days and nights of Puck Fair, our tribe returned to base-camp Killarney. In Foley's Restaurant, I discussed golf, the rope trick, and related topics with a few pals. Some interesting facts emerged: Arthur Conan Doyle was obsessed with golf. He believed he introduced the game to America (in 1894.... though, actually, golf had arrived in the USA a few years earlier). Conan Doyle's golf bag was pale purple (a mixture of red, white and blue?). His mother's name was Mary Foley ('Mary F'!). He had a long series of arguments on the subject of spooks with Harry Price (my wife's maiden name was Price). Harry Price was fascinated by the Indian Rope Trick, which was demon-strated to him by a magician called 'Karachi', whose 'real' name was Arthur Claud Darby (same initials as Arthur Conan Doyle...and Ashley Christopher Drees). Darby is an Irish/Scottish name, and Conan

Doyle was a Hibernian Scot (so am I). Handcuffs are known as 'Darbies'. Harry Houdini, the 'Handcuff King', was very friendly with Conan Doyle. Conan Doyle once saw a sea-serpent off the Greek coast (and Houdini once 'escaped' from the belly of a beached sea monster). Conan Doyle's uncle, Richard Doyle, painted pictures of fairies and designed the cover of *Punch*. Houdini, early in his career, presented a Punch and Judy show (so did I). Conan Doyle believed in fairies (and the Cottingley photographs). He was educated by the Jesuits (so was James Joyce, who will eventually play a significant role in our cosmic musings), at Stonyhurst School (so was a cousin of mine, Dr Alexander McEwan, who may eventually play a significant role in something or other). Bram Stoker was friendly with Conan Doyle...and I once wrote a play, *Spooks*, about Count Dracula and Sherlock Holmes. The full story of that little adventure has been published elsewhere.[5]

When I left Foley's, I strolled down the High Street and played a few tunes outside Moriarty's emporium. Two kindly fellows who, within minutes put silver into my hat were Tommy Doyle, a well known Kerry footballer, and Johnny Sherlock, a travelling man. Moriarty, Doyle and Sherlock are not particularly uncommon surnames in Ireland, and it was only when thinking about it later that I was struck by their remarkably Fortean juxtaposition (and perhaps I should proffer the in-formation that excellent tweed deerstalker hats and curly briar pipes are for sale at Moriarty's). Names and numbers, para-normal parallels and portent-ous puns...the game's afoot!

Arthur Conan Doyle...ACD ...or AC-DC, the eclectic body electric? Holmes and Watson, ohms and watts, the buddies electric who elected to detect. Holmes was a CD or Consulting Detective, that is to say a private dick, and John Watson

a doc, as was AC Doyle. The names Conan Doyle, Sherlock Holmes and John Watson can be anagrammatized into such telegrammatic lines as: 'O NO! WHAT? JOHN KEEL LANDS COY LOCH NESS ORM!' or 'JOKE ON LOCH NESS AND LOCAL MONSTER. OH, WHY?'. From a Fortean lexi-linker's point of view, that sort of thing is pregnant with portent. The fact that the word 'lexilink' was coined by AJ Bell, and the character of Sherlock Holmes was based on Dr J Bell (Conan Doyle's old teacher), may also be signifi-cant. Bernard Heuvelmans, writing of Doyle's encounter with a 'young plesiosaurus' off the Greek coast, says: 'The one seen by Sir Arthur and Lady Conan Doyle is very like what Mackintosh Bell saw through equally clear water'. 'Bell' happens to be high on my personal list of curiously re-curring fore and surnames. 'Wilson' is another.

My nick name (and my middle name is Nicol or 'Nick'), at junior school, was 'Earwig' (because, in a match-box, I kept earwigs as pets). 'Nick' (along with variations such as Nicholas, Nicholson, Nicklaus, Nicol etc) is another favourite in the Fortean nom-enclatura, but 'Earwig' is HC (Hoy...Charles?) Earwicker, Here Comes Everybody, or Haroun Childeric Eggeberth, from Joyce's *Finnegans Wake*. James Joyce, with what Frank O'Connor called his 'assoc-iation mania', is the supreme lexilinker, and *Finnegans Wake* is the lexilinker's bible. Haroun Childeric Eggeberth evokes the Fortean characters Herald Childe (from Phil Farmer's 'Exorcism Rituals'[6] and Hagbard Celine (from Shea and Wilson's *Illuminatus* triology [7]), who are both far more interesting to the crypto-zoological literati than Doyle's pithecanthropoid Prof. Challanger. Herald (the harbinger) Childe (child of supernature...plus E for Earwicker?), superdick, is 'much closer to Holmes than

Greystoke'[6].Hagbard (witch-poet?) Celine (from Cellini, the 'smoke and shadow' demon-raiser; but with an E for Ear-wicker) was 'related distantly, to the Greystokes.' [8]. Greystokes...Tarzan (of the pithecanthropoids?) was, according to Farmer, the 'natural' son of Jack the Ripper (never far from our thoughts, and involved with Holmes in several post-Doyle pastiches). In *Masks of the Illuminati*, Wilson introduces another member of the Grey-stoke clan, Sir John Babcock (Bab, as in Babel, Arabic 'gate' plus 'cock'), who gets involved with James Joyce, Aleister Crowley and Albert Einstein (a different 'AE' from the Celtic twilighter), in the dada city of Zurich.

□ □ □

'The pipes dance the renov-ation of the headless pythecan-tropes' Tristan Tzara[9]

□ □ □

After Syliva (the silvery sylvan spirit) Beach ('Strand' in Ire-land, like the magazine which published Conan Doyle) pub-lished Joyce's *Ulysses*, Crowley tried, without success, to get her to publish his memoirs.[10] In the *Wake*, Joyce calls Einstein 'Winestain' (almost an echo of Crowley's *White Stains*) and, to quote William York Tindall, 'Relativity rules Joyce's time-space continuum, as it rules Einstein's'. Joyce was terribly afraid of catching a heavy dose of thunderclap, so he carefully avoided golf courses...most dangerous places during electric storms. In 1916 Tristan (a Cornish Arthurian connection?) Tzara linked Zurich's dada Cabaret Voltaire with the 'Thermal Golf Mystery'[9], thereby linking golf with thermions and Tony Bell's 'rodballs'[11]. Joyce also had an exaggerated fear of dogs, and carried an ashplant or blackthorn stick with which to defend himself against troublesome curs.

□ □ □

'I cut a stout blackthorn to banish ghosts and goblins,

Rattlin' oer the bogs, I frightened all the dogs, On the rocky road to Dublin.'[12]

□ □ □

'Trickle trickle triss,' says Joyce, in the *Wake* invoking both Molly Bloom and Anna Blume. 'Anna Blume, you trickle beast,' says merz-dada, Kurt Schwitters, and makes me wonder.[13]

Joyce is the name of one of the fourteen tribes which formed the oligarchy of medieval Galway, and 'Joyce's Country' is the name by which a large area of that beautiful county is known. There are more lake monsters in Galway than in any other of the thirty two counties of Ireland. Robert Anton Wilson makes James Joyce involve himself with the 'Loch Ness sea serpent' (described by the Laird of Boleskine...Crowley... as 'practically a household pet'), and 'Mother Goose', the 'horror of Horrors'. Clever fellow, Wilson (it's that name). Crowley (self-elected 'King of Ireland' and manager of the 'Ragged Ragtime Girls') puts a rodballing 'Io' (input/output) in bed with the goat god Pan... 'Io Pan Io Pan'... and conjures up, for me, a golfing Nora Barnacle (Mrs Joyce) teeing up at Ballyconneely for nine cabalistic holes with King Puck, ending with an albatross at Goose Green. Nora (not-either-a) Barnacle (after either the barnacle goose, eaten and enjoyed on Fridays by Galway clerics; or from the goose barnacle, a crustacean with feathery appendages, said by some ancient cryptozoologists to be a kind of barnacle gosling). Nora was regularly goosed by her affectionate gander..not just on Fridays.

□ □ □

'There I met an old man Who would not say his prayers. I took him by the left leg And threw him down the stairs.'

□ □ □

'"An Irishman is not drunk", Joyce proclaimed dogmatically, *"until he can fall down three*

flights of stairs and the coal shute without hurting him-self."' Robert Anton Wilson[8]

Goosey goosey Greystoker, gravestaker, Brimstoker. Stately, plump Bram Stoker was a close neighbour of Oliver Gogarty, the Buck Mulligan of *Ulysses*, and he pops up in *Finnegans Wake...* 'Dracula nightout.'[14]

□ □ □

'Bad luck to your sowls. D'ye think I'm dead?'[15]

□ □ □

The Wilson and Shiels photo-graphs of Nessie are, at the time of writing (Jan'83), just about the best. Kenneth Wilson, a surgical spirit, snapped the famous classic. Kenneth Campbell(in *Masks of the Illuminati*, a murderous Scouse with an Ilford accent, the Liverpool Mangler), you may remember, did theatrical things with Wilson and Shiels. Campbell (a most campano-logical name) is in the lexilink catalogue, and Ilford has photographic connections. In my play *Gallavant*, Ken Campbell was 'King Gamble, the roman candle man', who dangled a pet 'worm' on the end of a dog leash (which was draped, authentically, round King Gamble's neck).

So...still in Killarney, I squeezed my busking box, out-side Crowley's shop on New Street, and thought of Foxford. Earwicker, the wicca/wicker man was, like Parnell, a foxy gent. Forteans are foxy, too, and these quasi fortuitous connections carry some im-port. Joyce knew that a pater-noster could conjure a panther monster; that Holmes (Sherlock) could meet Holmes (Oliver Wendell) at the break-fast table; that Mother Guinevere Goose loves Father Arthur Guinness; that a quark in the park (Pheonix) is worth nine fnords at the ford (Fox); and that Professor Richard Owlman is never far away.

The summer slipped by and, one day in late September, I was playing a solitary round of *Cont on p.43.*

AMERICA MYSTICA

by Michael Hoffman

ELECTRONIC BABYLON

The Public Broadcasting System aired a Valentine's Day (check the intials of the latter) examination of *God's Banker*, Roberto Calvi, the Propaganda-2 masonic cabal and the Vatican on national television.

One learns to watch American TV news shows for what they don't say. We learn something from the manner in which the waters are muddied. In this case Calvi, P-2 and the Vatican fit into a tightly PBS-constructed 'fascist' pigeon-hole, forgetting, on the other side of the conspiracy spectrum, the fascism that renegade intellectual Susan Sontag describes as having a "human face" (communism).

So Calvi & Co. are neatly portrayed as buddies of the fascists we all love to hate, forgetting to remark along the way, upon the high irony that not so long ago talk of masons secretly manipulating the world was the sole province of 'fascists'.

The PBS TV documentary does not mention that not only is P-2 linked to Latin American Banana-Republic juntas but to the drug and gun-running activities of the worker's paradise known as Bulgaria. Even more revealing of the partisan tilt of the broadcast is hostess Jessica Savitch's failure to tell us who or what 'Propaganda-1' was. Perhaps because that outfit from the 19th century was peopled by architects of state socialism, the usual background information

was ommitted.

When one of Calvi's banks — this one in Switzerland — is closely scrutinized in Ms. Savitch's breathless fashion, her attitude of thoroughness becomes transparent. For this is a notorious money 'laundering' financial institution with intimate ties to Meyer Lansky's Murder, Inc. empire in the Bahamas. Incredibly enough for a nationwide broadcast, absolutely no mention is made of the late Lansky's connection to this P-2 bank.

Still, for its subject matter alone, *God's Banker* is a landmark broadcast, a kind of *schlock* murder-mystery thriller and eminently entertaining if viewed as 'faction' rather than hard-boiled news.

Continuing in the fantasy realm, Canadian movie director David *Cronen*berg (*Scanners*) is dropping not-so-veiled hints about 'our' electro-teat future. His *Videodrome* is concerned with a unique TV signal that produces "physical transformations" on the body of the viewer. Recently in real-life, some adolescents in Florida and the mid-west experienced epileptic fits after marathon sessions before a video game machine. Medical authorities claimed the youths were "predisposed" to epilepsy anyway and yet, one wonders about the level of intimacy produced by the video game machine/human player interface. Is the emerging rapport capable of/or calculated to/prepare people for more intensive human/

machine relationships? If the relatively crude electronic games now available have the capacity to stimulate even pre-disposed epileptics into seizures, will the state-of-the-art gear of the future directly beam into memory centers or erogenous zones? The potential for hypno-tech is staggering: "After seeing enough hypnotizing movies...a fantasy life develops" (John Hinckley). If Hinckley sprayed President Reagan with bullets on the basis of mere movies...shudder. The best American research in this area that I know of has been done by Ron Steele, author of *The Mark is Ready– Are You?* Ron's work is inspired by his Biblical fundamentalism but his data is darn good. For his latest publication list send him a dollar or an International Postal Money Order for same (P.O. Box 187, College Place, Washington 99324, USA).

In our 'Twilight Language' department for this issue we have another tidbit from videoland. The CBS TV show *"Magnum p.i."* has been sending cryptic smoke signals to the group mind (or is it all just an inside joke?) ever since January 6. That's when the sidekick of the hero, 'TC' started turning up with a magical headpiece. Specifically, 'TC' has been sporting a baseball cap that's emblazoned on the front with the *Sigil of Baphomet*, the Hi-sign of latter-day Templar Aleister Crowley and the signature symbol used by "Sovereign Grand Commanders" of Scottish Rite masonry when composing lodge documents. It looks like this:

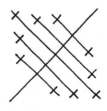

Now why would the down-to-earth, strictly rational *Colombia* Broadcasting System adopt a 'mojo' for its TV series? Isn't its all-seeing *Ayin* (Eye) logo enough of a whammy? Just how hot is the network's ratings war getting? Pistol-hot methinks: *Magnum p.i.* hit the top of the Neilsen-survey (of U.S. TV show popularity) just after 'TC' donned his magic-hat.

If some of you have noticed that utopia-as-perennial-heresy is a persistent theme of mine, permit me to gloat over yet another example of Paradise Lost:

Peter Gebhardt is a film and video collector; but not just of any old celluloid. A sample from Peter's movie catalogue: *Blood Spattered Bride, Eaten Alive, Nightmare in Blood, Raw Meat, Torture Dungeon, Wizard of Gore; Gore, Gore Girls; Texas Chainsaw Massacre* etc. etc. Almost night-and-day Peter screens his video gems in a house whose walls are decked with gruesome movie lobby posters and stills from the world's most sanguineous horror films. Scenes of blood and savage cruelty vibrate

throughout his home constantly (although in person Peter is bright, courteous and pleasant).

Peter lives in Oneida, New York at a place called the 'Mansion House' which, in less complicated days was the home to one of the most highly touted 'perfection' cults in America, John Humphrey Noyes' Oneida Community. Peter Gebhardt is the 19th century Noyes' great-great grandson.

•

Michael Anthony Hoffman II

TALES FROM THE YELLOW EMPORIUM
=ORIENTAL FORTEANA BY STEVE MOORE=

In the sixth chapter of *Wild Talents* Fort, at the end of a discussion of western hair-clippers, spends a couple of pages describing a pig-tail cutting panic in China in 1876 [1], which can be summarised as follows: The panic seems to have started at Nanjing (Nanking) in May 1876: that invisible agencies were cutting off people's pig-tails, generally instantaneously and without the owner's knowledge. The panic spread to Shanghai and Hangzhous (Hangchow) during the summer, and men in Shanghai, fearing attack from behind, held their pig-tails in front of them. Quack doctors offered charms, soldiers were stationed on the streets. The use of acid to remove the

queue was mooted, as it was thought impossible to cut it with shears without the victim feeling anything. Suspects included the charm-sellers (hoping to stimulate business), mischievous children, missionaries, etc. But while it's a typical case, Fort only tells one tale. There are more.

The earliest case I have found so far dates from 477 AD, when the *History of the Wei Dynasty* records laconically that 'fox-elves cut off the people's hair' [2]. In 517 AD, the same work records another outbreak in the capital, Luoyang, beginning in the spring and terrorising the population. In the sixth month (approx July), the empress-dowager Ling

issued a decree that all persons found cutting hair should be whipped outside the gate of the Thousand Autumns by the chief of the guards[3]. But we have a more detailed account from the *Record of the Temples of Luoyang* by Yang Xuanzhi of the 6th century [4]. How much literary invention there might be in this brief tale is impossible to tell, but it records that a professional mourner, Sun Yan, who lived in the coffin-makers and undertakers quarter of Luoyang, married a woman who went to bed fully-dressed. This went on for three years until Sun undressed her while she was asleep, and found she had a three foot long tail like a fox. Afraid, Sun divorced her but as she left she cut off his hair and ran. Pursued by the neighbours, she turned into a fox. After this, more than 130 citizens lost their hir; the fox would change into an attractive looking woman, and when passers-by stopped to talk, she would cut off their hair. This source gives the start of the disturbance as the 4th month (approx May), and says that it stopped in the autumn, though no reason is given for its cessation.

In old China, foxes were thought to be supernatural

creatures, capable of changing themselves into human form, usually to plague mankind is some way.In literature they are portrayed as beautfiul fairy seductresses and sexual vampires, while in everyday life their activities seem to centre round poltergeist-type hauntings and acting as possessing spirits. Hair-cutting is typical of the sort of viciously mischievous pranks attributed to them.

In 1221, when the Taoist alchemist Chang Chun was travelling west to visit Chingiz Khan, his party met a retainer of the mongol prince Chinkai, Li Jianu, who told them that at some previous time a spirit had cut off his back hair in the Altai mountains, to his great alarm, though whether this was a fox or some other mountain spirit is not made clear[5].

Supernatural foxes are also known in Japan, where the hair-cutting tradition is similarly attached to them. The *Kiyu Shoran* (date and author unstated), a book of strange happenings, records that a fox named Benkuro once lived in Yamato province. This fox was in the habit of cutting women's hair and breaking earthenware pans[6].

Nozaki also has some rather vague references to a hair-cutting panic in Edo (Tokyo) 'during the life of the artist Utamaro' (1753-1806). This outbreak was also attributed to fox-spirits, who were thought to cut women's hair as a pledge when assuming the forms of beautiful ladies[7].

However, foxes were not the sole cause of hair-cutting in Japan. We have a picture (see illustration), of unstated date, of the snipper-clawed, snapping-beaked Kami-kiri, the hair-cutting monster. While it's obviously not a fox, we have no further details, unfortunately, except that its attentions were thought to be a punishment for vanity [8].

Returning to China and more recent cases, though, we find that the 'fox-explanation' seems to have gone out of fashion, and that the victims (especially in later times) are usually men. It should be remembered that during the Qing dynasty (1644-1911 AD), China's Manchu conquerers decreed that all men should wear their hair in a pig-tail, and that to cut this off was taken as a sign of rebellion. To lose one's hair therefore put a man in a very awkward position; on the one hand, this might provide an explanation for the beginning of the scares (a wild

story made up as an excuse by someone with short hair); on the other, it also explains why the panics were taken so seriously when they were in full flow.

There was a panic in 1768, which started in the eastern Jiangsu and Zhejiang provinces, spreading in the south as far as Yunnan, Guizhou, Sichuan, Guangxi and Guangdong provinces, and in the north as far as Jilin; and between 9th October and 29th November was considered so important as to be the subject of a number of Imperial edicts. These edicts also make reference to a former case in Zun-hua, Hebei province (no date) where a number of heretic sects were found, and punished as being responsible for the hair-cutting. Indeed the government seems to have regarded both the zun-hua and 1768 panics as being entirely the work of rebellious sects, eager to stir up fear and trouble and promote a revolution. But there is also mention that the authorities in Jiangsu had arrested two Buddhist priests who had been distributing charms and written papers said to counteract the evil. These were charged with misleading the people, and another explanation was offered: that the entire panic had been started by charm-sellers, hoping to make a killing by selling protection against their own rumours [9].

Things appear to have been quiet until 1812, when an Imperial Censor, Yong Chun, reported that the evil had broken out again in capital. His statement was found to be untrue, however, and he was degraded [10].

There was another panic in August and September of 1821 that, amongst a number of other rumours, tail-cutting was rife in

The Kami-kiri, the Japanese hair-cutting monster. After a print (date and artist unstated) in Keij's Japanese Grotesqueries.

Shandong province. 'Heretical villains' were blamed again, and apart from cutting hair, they were said to cut the sex organs from young boys and girls. Charm and medicine-sellers were dong a thriving trade in protectionary measures [11].

Another edict, dated 12th September 1844, informs us that there was an outbreak of tail-cutting in the city of Taiyuan, in Shanxi province, and that the culprits were said to 'vanish like spectres'. De Groot points out that in most of these panics, it's likely that the 'heretical sects' were probably not thought of as physically cutting hair themselves, but using spectres to do so for them. For this, sorcery could be added to their crimes, as well as sedition[12].

De Groot also describes the 1876 outbreak, mainly with reference to Xiamen (Amoy) in Fujian province. There are tales of respectable gentlemen having lost their queues in broad daylight, usually in noisy streets, or at the theatre, in bazaars and shops, and even in their own homes with the door securely barred. Opinion was divided as to whether the miscreants were men or spectres. Tumults arose and a numberof persons, usually alleged to be heretics, outlaws and outsiders, were arrested. (As a cynic, the thought occurs to me that perhaps the government started such rumours as an excuse for a purge of undesirables, but I have nothing to support this). Some persons were said to have seen the phantom clippers, and realised that they were tiny and made of paper, and the use of paper-men by sorcerers was the basis of several other panics, which perhaps we'll go into another time [13].

De Groot quotes a book by a certain Mr Holcome[14], which asserts that such hair-cutting panics occurred almost *every year* in various parts of the empire, and quotes numerous 'absurd' stories. That someone was walking down the street when his queue dropped off and vanished without anyone being near him. That another man put his hand up to his queue and found that he didn't have it anymore. That one man got into conversation with a stranger, who vanished suddenly, taking the man's queue with him. That another glanced at a child, and when the child returned a steady gaze, the man's queue faded from sight, leaving only a odour of burnt hair. Cures included: a yellow and red cord braided with

the hair; medicine to be taken internally; medicine, half of which was to be taken internally, the other half to be thrown on the fire.

Since the 1911 revolution, most Chinese have worn their hair short, which is no doubt one reason why we don't hear too many tail-cutting stories these days. But what can we make of these reports? The only underlying theme that I can see is one of emasculation; from the fox-enchantress who emasculates her partner with prolonged debauchery, to the symbolic emasculation of cutting off a braid of hair, to the rumours of organ-cutters. This doesn't work with the Japanese cases, of course, which feature women victims...but there only women wore their hair

Cont on p.63.

U·F·O Commentary by Nigel Watson

FOOLS AND HORSES?

One of the great reasons for rushing to subscribe to *Flying Saucer Review* in the late 1960s and early 1970s was due to the appearance within its pages of the many controversial, yet stimulating, articles written by John A. Keel. The main substance of his ideas on the subject of UFOs were embodied in his book, *Operation Trojan Horse* which was published in Britain by Souvenir Press in 1971. It is hard to calculate what impact it had on ufology as a whole, but along with *The Flying Saucer Vision* by John Michell (1967) and Jacques Vallée's *Passport to Magonia* (1970), it led ufo-

logists in Britain to take more interest in high strangeness UFO incidents and to devote time to studying folklore, parapsychology, demonology, etc. The effect of these books can be seen in the pages of the *Merseyside UFO Bulletin* which emerged as a local UFO magazine and finally ended up as a vehicle for the publication of detailed studies of the paranormal in general; its new name, *Magonia*, reflects this change in direction. Less dramatically, other ufologists, UFO publications, and groups, have been influenced by the attack on the extraterrestrial hypothesis (ETH) so that today, in Britain, there are very few outright proponents of the ETH.

I must admit that when I first read *Operation Trojan Horse* in the early 1970s I was most impressed by Keel's arguments, and as a consequence of his ideas and others of a similar nature I became interested in the British phantom airship sightings made in 1909 and 1913, and in high strangeness UFO encounters.

Recently when working on a writing project I took the opportunity to read *Operation Trojan Horse* again. Again, Keel's brash, impulsive, incredible lynching of the ETH sent my brain cells reeling as I eagerly turned over the pages. Fortunately I survived the journey and I am able to report my findings to whoever has the courage to read on...

Primarily Keel's book is a launching point for exploring many aspects of the UFO enigma, which were ignored and neglected by most ufologists up to that time. Indeed, even today it can be used as a source of inspiration for the UFO investigator or researcher who wishes to examine and take into account many facets of the UFO problem which might lead to some fruitful conclusions. However, Keel's research and conclusions about the UFO phenomena are very contentious and must be taken with a big pinch of salt. In particular, I find the alleged statistics he presents throughout the book to be virtually meaningless.

As a dabbler into the fine art of searching for UFO reports in dusty old newspaper files or in blurred microfilm reels, I find that Keel's speculation, which seems to have been widely accepted, that some form of super intelligence manipulates the UFO phenomena to have very little foundation. In his analysis of the USA 1896-97 mystery airship wave, he states that: *Some kind of explanation for the mystery airship had to be tendered. This could best be done by staging deliberate landings in relatively remote places and contacting a few random individuals, telling them the "secret invasion" story, and letting them spread the word.*

This, according to Keel, was done in order that these sightings would act as a smokescreen for, perhaps, some form of survey of the USA without attracting attention to their goal. Since Keel then goes on to quote Charles H. Gibbs-Smith, the late well-known aeronautical historian, to the effect that the only passenger carrying aerial vehicles in existence in the USA in 1897 were nothing more than "free spherical balloons" it seems ludicrous to my mind that the ultraterrestrials should employ airships to avoid attention. If, as he says, "the objects and their occupants appear to be able to adopt a multitude of forms" why didn't they disguise themselves as spherical balloons which would not have attracted the massive newspaper publicity the airships attracted?

In Keel's defense he does state that the ultraterrestrials and their craft reside in hidden parts of the electromagnetic spectrum and deliberately transmogrify into physically solid objects, or manipulate our minds, in an attempt to slowly educate us (a theme explored by the film *2001: A Space Odyssey* and by John Michell in *The Flying Saucer Vision*). Whether this is for our benefit or not, Keel does not know.

If the intelligence behind the UFO manifestations are capable of discovering everything there is to know about individuals and their society, and are able to manipulate what we see and what we think, then how can we be sure that what Keel has to say is any more valid than the ETH or any other kind of hypothesis? This I think is the main problem with the views that Keel expresses in this book, and in his other writings. They inevitably lead to mental bankruptcy and impotence since we cannot believe what we see or think, which is exactly the philosophical corner Descartes painted himself into! The academic question of the validity of our perceptions is tricky enough, but in everyday life we can determine a concensus opinion of the nature of reality without too much trouble. However, even a rudimentary concept of the nature of reality for the sake of everyday existence is put into question when Keel-type views are believed. This no doubt leads to, or causes, the mental imbalance of contactees which Keel mentions, and to the disillusionment of those involved in UFO research generally.

On the other hand, the idea that alien intelligences or forces are directly involved in our lives can be very supportive and exciting to many people. It can be an adventure to see UFOs, be followed by Men in Black, or have your telephone tapped, etc. And of course there is always the possibility that you might solve the UFO riddle, if you fancy your chances against the forces of the unknown. This could possibly explain why many teenagers are attracted to this book, which is the very sector of the population Keel, paradoxically, warns are in most danger if they become interested in the occult (a warning which is liable to encourage people to do just the opposite!).

As I said before this is a book which can help in finding new lines of research and is deliberately controversial. How seriously we take it is revealed by this quote from the Apollo II astronaut, Neil Armstrong, which Keel used at the end of his book: *Mystery creates wonder, and wonder is the basis for man's desire to understand. Who knows what mysteries will be solved in our lifetime, and what new riddles will become the challenge of the new generations?*

•

Nigel Watson

Classified Exchanges.

FT welcomes an exchange of publications with those of mutual interest. This listing represents exchange publications received since last issue. Symbols: # = issue number; Pay = to whom cheques should be made if different from title, O = overseas rate; E = European rate; all rates inland or surface unless indicated; NFC = no Foreign cheques, many offer airmail rates, so inquire. Please mention FT when writing to listings.

FORTEAN

- **Anomaly Newsletter** #3 – news of Sourcebook Project publications. Free to customers. Anomaly Data Research Center, Box 107, Glen Arm, MD 21057, USA.
- **Ancient Skills & Wisdom Review** #17 – Possibly the only review journal covering all fields. 4/yr. UK: £2, US $6.00. Pay: Paul Screeton, 5 Egton Drive, Seaton Carew, Hartlepool, Cleveland TS25 2AT. Shortly to be retitled "The Shaman".
- **Bulletin of the Tychonian Society** #34 – Advocates of a geocentric universe. Free on request, but donations welcomed. Ed: Walter van der Kamp. 14813 Harris Rd, RR 1, Pitt Meadows, BC V0M 1P0, Canada.
- **INFO Journal** #41 – 4/yr. US:$10.00, UK:£5 in US funds. INFO: Box 367, Arlington, VA 22210, USA.
- **ISC Newsletter** #1:3 – from International Society of Cryptozoology. 4/yr. Memb. US$25.00pa. ISC: Box 43070, Tuscon, AZ 85733, USA.
- **Journal of Meteorology** #71 – 75 - 12/yr. UK £14.50, O:£17. Artetech Pub. Co: Cockhill House, Trowbridge, Wilts BA14 9BG.
- **Lantern** #39 – 4/yr. UK:£1.50, O:$4.00. NFC. Pay Borderline Science investigation Group. Lantern: 3 Dunwich Way, Oulton Broad, Lowestoft, Suffolk NR32 4RZ.
- **Nessletter** #54, 55 – Essential for news and theories of lake monsters. 12/yr. UK:£2.50. O:$9.00. Pay. Rip Hepple. Ness Information Service, Huntshieldford, St Johns Chapel, Bishop Auckland, Co Durham DL13 1RQ.
- **Pogonip** #00,0 – Forteana from France, mostly in French. Write for details. Jean-Louis Brodu, BP 195, 75665 Paris Cedex 14, France.
- **Pursuit** #57-59 – Essential for serious Forteans. Journal of the Soceity for the Investigation of the Unexplained. 4/yr. memb. US $12, O:on application. SITU: Box 265, Little Silver, NJ 07739, USA.
- **SIS Review** #5:2 – Journal of the Soceity for Interdisciplinary Studies, essentially for the discussion of Velikovsky type material. 4/yr. Memb enqs to Bernard Prescott, 12 Dorset Rd, Merton Park, London SW19.
- **SIS Workshop** #4:4 – an informal journal of discussion of Velikovskyan topics to supplement *SIS Review*. Free to membs – as *SIS Review* above.
- **Stigmata** #18,19 – continuing investigation into animal mutilations. 4/yr. US:$5. O:$10, US funds only. Project Stigma: Box 1094, Paris, TX 75460, USA.
- **Zetetic Scholar** #9,10 – Formidable, authoritative, academic discussion of the whole range of Fortean and paranormal subjects with emphasis on dialectic debate and bibliographies. Essential for Forteans. 2/yr. US:$12, O:$18, US funds only. Journal of the Center for Scientific Anomalies Research: Dept of Sociology, Eastern Michigan University, Ypsilanti, MI 48197 USA.

UFO

- **APRO Bulletin** #30:9,10; 31:1,2 – 12/yr. Memb: US:$15, O:$18. APRO: 3610 E. Kleindale Rd, Tuscon, AZ 85712, USA.
- **BUFORA Bulletin** #6 – 4/yr. UK:12.50. But for this membs also get *J-TAP* and *Probe*. BUFORA Sec, Miss P Kennedy, 30 Vermont Rd, London SE19 3SR.
- **Centre Update** #2 – Bibliographic & resource news supplement to *OSEAP Journal*. Rates on application. OSEAP: 170 Henry St, Crewe, Cheshire CW1 4BQ.
- **Earthlink** #12 – 4/yr. UK:£3, US:$9, NFC. Earthlink: 16 Raydons Rd, Dagenham, Essex RM9 5JR.
- **Inforespace** #62 – 4/yr, in French. Inquire to SOBEPS: Ave Paul Janson 74, 1070 Bruxelles, Belgium.
- **Magonia** #11 – Essential reading. 4/yr. UK:£2, US:$5. Pay: JOhn Rimmer: 64 Alric Ave, New Malden, Surrey KT3 4JW.
- **Malaysian UFO Bulletin** # 4– Our apologies to editor Ahmad Jamaludin for overlooking (in previous issues) his excellent coverage of UFOs from S.E. Asia. 2/yr. For exchange with other scholars and journals only. A. Jamaludin; Makmal Diagnosa, Veterinary Dept., Kuantam, Pahang, Malasia.
- **Northern UFO News** #100 – New format, new address. Essential for up-to-the-minute UFO news. 6/yr. But Jenny forgot to put her rates in this one. Apply to Jenny Randles: 9 Crosfield Rd, Somerville, Wallasey, Wirral L44 9EH.
- **Odiseja** #29-31 – Apply to Milos Krmelj, Milcinskega 6, 61000 Ljubljana, Slovenija, Yugoslavia.
- **Probe Report** #8.9 – One of Britain's brightest new UFO journals. 4/yr. UK:2.50, O:£3.50. Probe: 16 Marigold Walk, Ashton, Bristol BS3 2PD.
- **Newsletter** #1:12 – Report of the Tri-County UFO Study Group. 12/yr. US:$10. TCUSG: Box 2, Sebring OH44672, USA. This same group also offer a UFO Comminicators Collectors Catalog, listing hard to get UFO & Fortean books, mags and tapes.
- **UFO Research Australia Newsletter** #3:4 – The top UFO mag from Oz. 6/yr. Aust:A$10, O:A$12, Aust. funds only. UFORA: Box 229, Prospect, SA 5082, Australia.

EARTH MYSTERIES

- **Archaeoastronomy** #5:1,2 – Bulletin of the Center for Archaeoastronomy, with special emphasis on the Americas. 4/yr. US:$12, O:$15. Center for Archaeoastronomy: Space Sciences Building, University of Maryland, College Park, MD20742, USA.
- **Caerdroia** #9-11 – Everything to do with mazes and labyrinths; a commendable effort. Shortly to have a new address. Meanwhile, inquiries to Jeff Saward: 53 Thundersley Grove, Thundersley, Benfleet, Essex SS7 3EB.

Cont on p64.

LIGHTNING, AURORAS, NOCTURNAL LIGHTS AND RELATED PHENOMENA
Compiled by William R. Corliss. *The Sourcebook Project, Box 107, Glen Arm, MD 21057, USA; 1982, $11.95 hb, pp242, indexes, drawings.*

BALL LIGHTNING AND BEAD LIGHTNING
By James Dale Barry. *Plenum Pub. Co., New York & London; 1980; £18.59 hb, pp298, index, bib, photos, diags, tables.*

Barry's is the most thorough study of these two anomalistic lightnings to date. Interest in the subject among scientists and scholars dates back at least 300 years and there is such a wealth of literature on them — the bibliography here runs to an incredible 86 pages — that the fact that we know so little about the phenomena is as mystifying as these tantalizing lights themselves. The book is undoubtedly a valuable reference. The main part of the book is composed of critiques of the known photographs of alleged ball or bead lightning (most of which seem doubtful). The latter half of the book discusses the resistance of the scientific establishment to these phenomena, and the considerable laboratory experimentation of attempts to reproduce the effects. Barry concludes that there are indeed phenomena of this nature to study, and that the descriptive term 'lightning' may have misdirected much of the attention from what might be called an anomaly of plasma physics.

One noticeable lack is any consideration of ball or bead lightnings in folklore. Perhaps this criticism is unjust — as a physicist, the author is addressing the problem from the fields of atmospheric physics, geology, meteorology and plasma physics — and we should now be calling for a book length treatment of curiosities of lightning from the folklorist's point of view.

Corliss, as you know , is one of us — by which I mean he has a fine appreciation of anomalies, and his collections (see past reviews of the Sourcebooks and Handbooks) are justly world famous. See 'Book Alert' (in this issue) for some additional information on Corliss' new enterprise, of which this is the first volume, known as The Catalog of Anomalies. Barry may have thought he was out on the frontier of knowledge about ball lightnings, but there are items in Corliss's work which are weirder still, and not listed in Barry's massive bibliography: for example, BLs with long tails, BLs with diverging rays, BLs which fragment, double and triple BLs, rod-shaped BLs, giant and tiny BLs, transparent BLs and those which appear to be made of "fibres of light wriggling like a mass of eels ", and opaque or even black BLs. To these Corliss adds cases of BLs playing poltergeist - like tricks, the physiological effects of impact with the human body, and an alleged correlation of incidence with solar activity.

The fact that these phenomena are absent from Barry's study only shows the importance of Corliss' work, and is not intended to disparage Barry's excellent study. Corliss'

Catalog, of course, is, on the other hand, not intended to be a study, but rather a collection of sources and references on unusual phenomena, and differs from his earlier compilations in their layout and higher proportion of modern material. The three-letter classifications of subjects is still in use, so correspondences to the earlier works can be made — but in time The Catalog, which will run to 25 or so volumes, will supersede them. Another new feature is the set of guidelines which prefix each subject, intended to help the reader assess the value of the data, and its relevance and degree of anomaly relative to mainstream science. Again the sheer quantity and quality of data precludes a full discussion here, and the scope of this deceptively small volume is best given by an outline of the other contents...

The major subject categories are Aurora-like phenomena, BLs, Diffuse electrical discharges, Lightning anomalies, Low-level meteor-like phenomena, Nocturnal lights, and Marine phosphorescent displays. Some of the subcategories, chosen at random, are: black auroras, pillars of light, auroral smell; intermountain discharges, luminous aerial bubbles, quake lights, whirlwinds of fire and smoke, flashes detected by satellite, lights on clouds; horizontal lightning, lightning figures, superbolts, tubular lightning; low-level meteor-like objects; low-level nocturnal lights (of the will-o'-the-wisp type); phosphorescent bands and wheels in the ocean, milky seas; coloured rays emanating from ships. To make the book even easier to use, there are indexes to time of event, place of event, subject, source and first author of the citation. No serious Fortean or anomaly researcher can afford to be without this intended series, and if you baulk at the cost, for Fort's sake lean on your local library to get it. They may be surprised at how popular and useful it turns out to be.

□ RJMR.

CAT COUNTRY
The Quest for the British Big Cat
By Di Francis.
David & Charles, Newton

By Di Francis.
David & Charles, Newton Abbot, Devon; 1983, £4.95 hb, pp152, bib, index, photos, maps.

The search for the British big cat has taken a stride forward as a result of the field-work diligently undertaken by Di Francis in Devon and South Wales. Her findings have confirmed that the people all over Britain who have been reporting big cat sightings for decades were telling the truth; and she has seen and photographed the cats for herself. In *Cat Country* she records eye-witness accounts from Scotland, England and Wales, describes her own experiences while searching for the animals, states her belief that the black dogs of folklore were in fact black cats, and ponders on the seemingly inevitable conclusion that there is a cat of unknown species living wild in Britain. That it is an unknown species rather than a known species like a puma seems clear from the descriptions and the recent photographs, one of which shows long claws used almost like fingers, a detail which may explain the footprints with claw marks which have puzzled investigators for so long. Di Francis is to be congratulated on her achievements, and we

hope she will now be able to obtain incontrovertible proof of the existence of an unknown species of cat. Though we also hope that as a result of its public recognition it will not immediately be hounded out of existence by trigger-happy hunters claiming to be protecting the community.

□ Janet Bord

ENCYCLOPEDIA OF OCCULTISM & PARAPSYCHOLOGY: SUPPLEMENT
Edited by Leslie A. Shepard.
Gale Research Co, Detroit, Michigan 48226, USA; 1982, $70.00, pp231, indexes.

The main *Encyclopedia* was published in two volumes in 1978, and since then there have been four issues of *Occultism Update*, the publication devoted to updating correcting and expanding those tomes. This *Supplement* combines the contents of the four *Updates* into a single alphabetical sequence, and a cumulative index to both the *Encyclopedia* and the *Supplement*. In addition to the corrections and updates (eg. new addresses of organizations and journals), there is a considerable volume of new material.

Over the years I have found the *Encyclopedia* an invaluable ready reference, and I readily commend it to all researchers. However the price will put it beyond the reach of most individuals, in which case they have a duty to encourage their local library to get it.

□RJMR

THE ALLENDE DOSSIER
By Robert A. Goerman.
Goerman Pub.Co., 107 Mile Lock Lane, Brackenridge, PA 15014, USA; 1982, $2.95 pb, pp36.

The indefatigable Fortean investigator is regularly thwarted not only with debunking of frog falls *et al.* by Conventionalists who refuse to examine the evidence, but with frauds all too readily accepted

by most mainstream writers who succeed (if sometimes inadvertently) in establishing the 'factuality' of these myths which then hamper— even misdirect — future research and the credibility of Forteana.

For more than a quarter century the name Carlos Allende has been linked to ufology (and Forteana generally) through the annotated Varo edition of M. K. Jessup's *The Case for the UFO*. Allende, along with two mysterious persons named Mr.A and Mr.B provided fuel for a number of *causes celebres*, including UFO propulsion and the ultra-secret teleportation of a U.S. Navy destroyer escort (or two) witnessed by Allende and later the subject of Moore and Berlitz's *The Philadelphia Experiment: Project Invisibility* (1979).

Who is Carlos Allende, alias C. Christopher Allen, alias Senor Professor & Colonel Miguel Christofero Allende? Was he "an extraterrestrial power who took root on Earth centuries ago," as one book proposed? Is that how he was able to know about and explain so many Fortean proposed? Is that how he was able to know about and explain so many Fortean enigmas (like SHC!)?

Goerman provides the answer, a result of discovering that his neighbors were the parents of Carl Meredith Allen (born 31 May 1925 in Springdale, PA). Allen is no centenarian Alien but is, Goerman demonstrates, an eccentric drifter of high IQ and an appetite for occult/Fortean literature that "gets all twisted somehow." Goerman even discovered a letter written by Allen to his father stating all Varo annotations were penned *"alone by myself with no Mr.A or Mr.B..."*

Thus is doused much controversy and speculation groundlessly engendered over a hoax, one Allen (in his various guises) still tries to maintain even if it requires him to tell Goerman he'll be "too delightfully happy...to blow your empty stupid *head* off."

Unfortunately the discrediting of the Allende Affair has not earned Goerman much praise. "The sad irony that angers me," he wrote us, "is that many 'big name' researchers knew or suspected the truth some time ago and continued to perpetuate this myth regardless of facts. A few seek answers regardless of consequences or horror. Believe me, the world *per se* is not appreciative of these efforts."

Dossier warrents perusal, not persecution. One worries about how many other "Allende Affairs" still exist undiscovered to waylay the gullible and hinder respect for Forteana.

☐ *Larry E. Arnold*

GEORGE ADAMSKI: THE UNTOLD STORY
By Lou Zinsstag & Timothy Good.
Ceti Publications, 247 High St, Beckenham, Kent BR3 1AB; 1983, £6.95 pb (overseas $12.00, airmail outside Europe $3.00 extra), pp208, index, photos.

George Adamski became the most famous contactee in UFO history after claiming that he met the pilots of a Venusian scoutship in a California desert on 20 November 1952. His claim and subsequent antics – including further meetings, alleged hard evidence and films, and the founding of possibly the first UFO cult – almost single handedly forged the link between UFOs and crankery in the minds of both bigoted scientists and the ignorant public. The notoriety didn't seem to bother Adamski, whose fame was boosted when the Theosophist Desmond Leslie told his story in *Flying Saucers Have Landed* (1953). He was even feted by Queen Juliana of the Netherlands and Pope John XXII. As a child Adamski showed a mixture of religious feelings with philosophical interests and a strong

imagination. He wrote science-fiction, elements of which turn up in his UFO accounts, and, in the 1930s, founded a strange 'Christian' Royal Order of Tibet. In a later edition of a book first published in 1936, Adamski instructed that 'The Space Brothers' should be substituted for reference to 'The Royal Order of Tibet', ensuring the continuity, at least in his own mind, of his religious and ufological beliefs. But to the cynical this could be seen as an attempt to fabricate a climate of belief in the aliens he met in retrospect; indeed, this and other so-called evidence (photos of a Venusian's footprint, transcribed conversations, and dubious photos) convince none but the converted.

And yet...Adamski's experiences, and the group that sprung up around him set in motion influences and themes which still reverberate in ufology today, and preposterous though his story is (including his space rides to Mars and Venus), it should not be rejected uncritically. Again, in retrospect, he claimed contact with extraterrestrials during his childhood, and UFO sightings which predate those of Arnold in 1947. Clearly, as a prototype UFO contacee, the character and writings of Adamski are worthy of rigorous analysis and psychological study. Alas, *The Untold Story* is not such a study, though it does offer interesting and valuable materials towards it, and towards our assessment of Adamski in the history of ufology, Lou Zinsstag turns out to be the cousin of C.G.Jung, who introduced the great psychologist to ufology, and Adamski's claims in particular, and precipitated Jung's study, *Flying Saucers* (1958).

Tim Good's portion of this well illustrated book attempts to assess the evidence, but his objectivity falls far short of what so important a saga deserves. For example, he

fails to comment upon the suspicious similarities between the symbols on a negative Adamski said was given to him by an alien in 1952, and some petroglyphs discovered by Dr Marcel Homet in Brazil. Adamski later (in his *Flying Saucers Farewell*, 1961) claimed the similarity was evidence that the Space Brothers had been passing information to earthlings since the dawn of mankind. Because Homet's book was published in German in 1958 (translated as *Sons of the Sun*, 1963), and Adamski's image appeared in the book with Leslie in 1953, the evidence for Adamski's claim looked impressive. However, according to Diane Wirth, in *Pursuit* (Summer 1980), who corresponded with Homet on this question, it transpires that Homet's Brazil expedition was during 1949-50, and that Homet and Adamski were personally acquainted. It is certain that Adamski knew of the petroglyphs before 1952, through Homet's letters or through a European newspaper photograph of them. Yet Adamski continued to feign ignorance of the true origin of the symbols he copied. In *The Untold Story* Miss Zinsstag says Adamski saw the German edition of Homet's book on her shelves when he visited her in 1959, and was "amazed" at the similarity. Did Adamski deliberately hoax this vital evidence for his claims, consciously or unconsciously hoodwinking his millions of believers? If so, what else did he fabricate?

You won't find any answers or clues in Good's part, but in Miss Zinsstag's half, which is a fascinating *memoire* of the people and events in the Adamski story, we have a picture of Adamski as a soft-spoken, thoughtful man who gave every appearance of believing what he said was true, and was remarkably consistent in his statements throughout the remainder of his life, Despite claiming "half a lifetime's work with Adamski",

Miss Zinsstag cannot give any objective or unequivocal proof of the reality of Adamski's claims. She believes in extra-terrestrial life on principle, and her sympathy for Adamski is with his philosophical preaching of cosmic brotherhood.

The authors make the valid point that contactees today are telling "wilder and far more fantastic" stories than Adamski's, and are being investigated seriously. Adamski does deserve a 're-trial', not the least because of the reminiscences of the man in this book, or in terms of personal mystical revelation rather than alien contact. One has to agree with the comment made by Lady Falkender — yes, former PM, Sir Harold Wilson's minder believes in UFOs too — in her enthusiastic foreward to this book, that "Something clearly of tremendous significance happened to this man..." Exactly what that something was, you'll have to make up your own mind.

☐*RJMR*

THE VANISHING HITCHHIKER
By Jan Harold Brunvand.
W.W.Norton, London, 1982; £10.50 hb, pp208, index.
Not about the phenomenon
Not about the phenomenon of vanishing hitchhikers, but an analysis of modern American urban legends. We know them as 'whale tumour' stories (after Rodney Dale's book) or bar-room tales (after Ken Campbell's collection.) Here are such classics as 'The pet (or baby) in the oven', 'The spider in the hairdo', 'The nude surprise party', 'The Kentucky fried rat' and so on. Brunvand is a professor of English, specializing in folklore, and his interest in these stereotyped and unlikely tales — which as Dale points out have all happened to friends of friends (foafs) — is that they represent the folklore-making process in its living contemporary form and not as a collection of remote tribal beliefs. Curiously

he rates the 'Vanishing Hitch-hiker' and the 'Alligators in the sewers' as just that — modern folklore — in much the same way as Dale ignored the reality of frog showers. This is essentially a study of American lore: nevertheless, some stories — like the dead grandmother on the roofrack of a stolen car, phantom cars and trucks, the unzipped fly, etc seem universal and have been around for a long time.

Altogether a fascinating book — very entertaining, too — in the light of our own observation that much of the bizarre behaviour and phenomena we record in FT seems classic material on which to found modern folklore. *RJMR*

A UFO GUIDE TO FATE MAGAZINE
By Gray Barker.
Saucerian Press Inc., Box 2228, Clarksburg, WV 26301, USA; 1981, $9.95 (overseas $19.95), pp100.
After acquiring a micro-computer veteran ufologist Gray Barker had the bright idea of compiling an index to the UFO materials in *Fate* magazine (up to 1980), as an experiment which would familiarize himself with his new toy and at the same time do some useful research. The inputting of data took some time, but, as Gray points out, the supreme benefit comes later when you want to find specific information or compile citations or chronologies. With a good database programme this can be done virtually at the press of a button.

Fate began publishing less than a year after Kenneth Arnold's historic sighting in 1947, and for a long while *Fate* was the leading source of UFO writing. Accordingly the whole series has immense value because it reflected the development of ufology in all its mainstream and eccentric forms. Gray emphasises this value by providing a ready means of analysis and access to this historic collection of UFO

materials. Apart from being of obvious interest to sociologists and historians studying 'pseudo-science' beliefs in general or the UFO phenomenon in particular, there is much here for the ordinary UFO buff and researcher; eg, each section is prefaced by a fascinating little introduction. One can discover the rise in the use of the term 'UFO'; the fashions in beliefs and theories; the popularities of certain authors; the growth in other UFO publications; and the cut and thrust of critics and the criticized. Basically the main database lists titles of articles, books reviews and advertisments by author, subject, issue number, page and date, and the various sections of the *Guide* are print-outs of these sorted into alphabetical or chronological sequence. Added to these are lists of 'typical illustrations' and 'typical advertisements'. For those interested in how it was all done and on what equipment there are some necessarily brief and superficial details.

This project is undoubtedly the forerunner of other similar bibliographical research which will be more common as more researchers get their own micros. Gray Barker's efforts, and this excellent and inspiring result, are to be heartily commended to all interested in UFOs.

☐*RJMR.*

THE COSMIC SERPENT
By Victor Clube & Bill Napier
Faber & Faber, London, 1982; £12.50 hb, pp299, index, refs, bib, illus.
The cosmic serpent of the title is the giant comet which terrorized mankind over 3000 year ago, and which left its image in art, myths, megaliths and religion as an archetype of destruction. The authors, prominent astronomers at the Royal Observatory, Edinburgh, pioneered the idea that asteroid precipitated dinosaur extinction, and here extend their researches into a com-

prehensive history of bombardment from sapce and its effects upon the civilizations of this Earth.

They argue that fear was a prime motive for the migration of megalithic peoples and their construction of stone-circles, etc; that a cosmic interpretation should be put on many myths; that the Old Testament records a real catastrophe; and so on. They admit their ideas are not new — Laplace wrote about the effects of global catastrophes about 200yrs ago — but they are brought together here with the very latest discoveries by modern astronomers, about the solar system, comets, meteors and asteroids.

The result is an authooritative discussion of the major cosmic impacts on Earth, astronomically, geologically, zoologically and historically. The authors are not afraid to face the implications of new data, and for this reason the book is a refreshing, if heavy-going, read. The post-Lyall geological principle of 'uniformity' is drubbed in favour of a more catastrophic view of planetary evolution, for example; and the orthodox chronology of Egypt (the 'clock' by which much Mediterranean history is set) is shown to be several hundred years out of alignment with the majority. The revised chronology of Egypt very similar to that of Velikovsky, but for sounder reasons, say the authors confirms the last great cometary impact in 1369 BC. There are fascinating chapters on prehistoric impacts, 'Comets and Gods', and a detailed look at 'Zeus and Typhon'. The authors end with the acknowledgement that they are only just beginning to investigate the relevance of astrology, mythology, etc to modern astronomical research, and realize that future studies, or at least co-operations between a variety of unlikely disciplines. This is good news, coming as it does from two pillars of the establishment. It's something we've advocated all along. *The Cosmic Serpent* is well worth your study. *RJMR*

THE STONES OF KIRIBATI

By Erich von Daniken.
Souvenir Press, London, 1982. £7.95 hb, pp268, index, bib, colour plates.

The further adventures of Erich.... In this episode he latches onto alleged graves of giants around which nothing will grown on the South Pacific Islands of Kiribati (there are many in British folklore); the work of the Dragon Project logging odd radio-emissions from the Rollright stones (for the latest work see *The Ley Hunter*, and Devereux's book *Earth Lights*) an extraterrestrial skeleton which turned out to be a complete fabrication; the belief that Jesus died in Kashmir; the geometric perfection of stone circles; black holes; extraterrestrial craft (damaged) in earth orbit; micro-organisms from space; ancient Indian flying craft and ruins; the straight tracks of South America; the colossal stones at Tiahuanaco; deformed skulls in the museum of Ica.

It's a better book than his recent offering, containing some interesting material, but padded out with wads of travelogue. It also includes the same old whines — EvD still confuses criticism of his presentation with hostility to the 'ancient astronaut' idea, which he continues to believe is his personal invention. *RJMR*

DICTIONARY OF OCCULT, HERMETIC AND ALCHEMICAL SIGILS

By Fred Gittings.
Routledge & Kegan Paul, London; 1981, £15.95 hb, pp410, bib, diags.

I can't imagine this book being used very often, but when it is needed it will prove very useful indeed. There is a long introduction on hermetic notation, and the main body of the book deals with topics in the manner of a dictionary. There are appendices on medieval and classical notation of sigils; and an index of all the sigils in the book classified, like a Chinese calligraphic dictionary, according to the number of strokes and points.

☐ *RJMR.*

SOUL SEARCH

By Glenn Williston & Judith Johnstone.
Turnstone Press, Wellingborough, Northants; 1983, £4.95 pb, pp256, index.

ENCOUNTERS WITH THE PAST

By Peter Moss with Joe Keeton.
Penguin Books, Harmondsworth, Middx; 1981, £1.50, pp233, index, plates.

Both books claim that a wide range of essentially neurotic problems, including allergies, phobias and obsessions, can be cured or relieved by hypnotic regression to a past life, in which the trauma which initiated the neurosis may be found. Both Williston and Keeton have an unshakeable conviction of the reality of reincarnation based on the results of their work regressing people by hypnosis — Keeton claims over 8,000 of such regressions — during their practices as hypnotherapists, Keeton in Merseyside and Williston in America. Both books offer the reader little or no objective way of assessing the claims (client confidentiality, you see). The Moss/Keeton book does have photos of some of the regressees, but instead of any proof the reader of both books is asked to believe their truth.

There is a great fashion for this kind of 'research' lately, and though it is very interesting there is great danger too from the eagerness with which the apparent access to information not known to the conscious mind is explained by the hypothesis of reincarnation. The glaring obstacle — so pathological applications the conscious mind becomes mislead by misinformation or self-created myths. In the famous case of Bridey Murphy, who claimed to be the Irish former incarnation of Wisconsin-born Ruth Simmons, and who emerged under hypnosis of Ruth, its vaunted usefulness as evidence of reincarnation fell apart when it was shown that the basis of the Bridey personality was a jumble of ill-remembered facts from Ruth's youth. In all cases the bizarre stories of past lives, UFO abductions, astral projection, visits to heaven or hell, etc recovered by hypnosis cannot be shorn of the suspicion that they have been created from the subject's unconsious mind by leading questions from the hypnotist. The very 'guidance' of the hypnotist, and the pre-knowledge that they are about to have a 'past life' session, creates the preconditions for the experience.

But whether you believe these stories of past lives are genuine recollections of a previous existence (very often obvious to more impartial critics — is the technique of "guided hypnotic regression" itself. Alvin Lawson has shown, for example that subjects taken at random and hypnotized can construct a complicated UFO abduction scenario in every way similar to those recovered the same way from people convinced they had really been abducted. And recently the US police and courts were warned about the fact that most crime data recovered from witnesses by hypnosis proved useless and erroneous because there is some evidence that the intrusion of the hypnotic state actually alters the memory. Both are examples of the amazing power of the unconscious mind to fabricate flights of fancy almost immediately and with very little information (what it doesn't know, it will make up). In its benign mode this manifests creatively as inspiration and invention, but in inappropriate or psycho-

some details do check out), or they are recollections of some-one else's gleaned (telephathic-ally?) from the Akashic Record (a cosmic record of everything that's happened) or from the collective unconscious, or they are created by the unconscious mind to 'rationalize' personal neurotic problems, is up to you — both books discuss all these theories to varying degrees, and Soul Search even summarizes both Western and Eastern traditional belief in reincarnation. The caveats aside, I found both books horribly fascinating (eg. narrators accounts of their deaths) — and clearly there is some abreactive value in the process of regression if it has half the success rate that these convinced practitioners claim.
□ RJMR.

BURIED ALIVE
By Dr. Peron-Autret.
Corgi/Transworld, London; 1983, £1.25 pb, pp118.

In contrast to the above two books, this one is about people who really came back from the dead, though as unfortunate victims of catalepsy, poisoning, shock or bizarre drug side-effects. This slim, overpriced volume is a poorly designed translation of a French study of 1973 but I'm glad to have it anyway. It is genuinely horrify-ing: Dr Peron-Autret says, for example, that about 200 coronary victims in the USA are buried alive every day of the year. The main thrust of the book discusses the medical problems of determining death, or detecting faint life in seem-ingly lifeless bodies, and new techniques are called for. What brings the book within our sphere of interest is that the good doctor has a taste for the bizarre and anomalous case. *Buried Alive* is a treasure trove of stories (not properly referenced, alas) of people who cheated the grave, drawn from ancient records right up to the present. Dr Peron-Autret's work on the subject continues, and he ends with a question-naire for those of you who

have survived a wrong diagnosis of death, or who know of someone who has.
□RJMR

SHAMAN
By Joan Halifax.
Thames & Hudson, London; 1982, £3.95 pb, Sources, photos, plates.
THE SHAMAN AND THE MEDICINE WHEEL
By Evelyn Eaton.
Theosophical Pub.House, Wheaton, Illinois; 1982, $6.50 pb, pp212, illus.
THE SHAMAN AND THE MAGICIAN
By Neville Drury.
Routledge & Kegan Paul, London, 1982, £3.95 pb, pp129, index, bib, notes, illus.

Any books on shamanism are mighty welcome, and here we have three. The shaman is a perennial figure, probably as old as human consciousness itself, and because the essence of shamanism is a personal journey through the cosmic landscape of spirits, gods and symbols of natural forces the shaman is alive today where-ever there is spontaneous and natural mysticism. These are three different pictures of the shamanic life. Joan Halifax's profusely illustrated book is a worldwide survey of shamanism, with the striking result that these magical figures are remarkably consistent in their practices, experiences, symbols and cosmology. Against the universal shaman Neville Drury concentrates on the contemporary shamans or their heirs, and his book is a study of how the central parts of Western ritual magic may have evolved from a sort of institutionalized shamanism (ie not a shamanism which has be-come a religious system, but one which nevertheless finds a balance between holding its place in the tribal or social structure and providing the framework for the personal confrontation and mastery of unseen worlds. Evelyn Eaton's book is a first-person account of a modern American Indian *Cont on p.64.*

LETTERS

Cont from p3.

covered the lead character is a simpleton named Bobo. It is a good story, and maybe sometime I will share some of the symbols it is filled with, but for now, Bobo does become a hero after he kills the dragon and rescues the fairy-princess, Tilda. For his troubles, besides getting the usual kingdom and the princess, for some reason, he was awarded the Order of the Black Cat. So, at the night's end, I found myself full circle back to lynx, links, golf, Bobo, and cats.

I am not sure what it all means or where it is leading, but I had some second thoughts on the magic of FT when I turned on the radio this morning. The song playing was "Send in the Clowns"; the next line in the tune after "Send in the clowns" is "Don't bother, they're here"!!

Loren Coleman
Cambridge, Massachusetts.

NEW ANIMALS

Some comments and additions to the notes on "Animals" [FT38p26-27].

It is certainly true, as you say at the beginning of the section, that "new species continue to be discovered at a stirring rate". A few of the most recent zoological novelties of a higher order than the insect/mollusc level are: (a) a new kind of bat in Kenya, (b) a poisonous snake in Australia, (c) a thrush in India, and (d) a jerboa [jumping rodent] in Mongolia. Although these are all fairly small creatures, such discoveries still raise the hearts of those crypto-zoologists who hope that one day we might see the links of Bigfoot and bunyip added to the scientific lists, and raised out of the realm of myth/ hallucination/thoughtform.

Two other species can be added to your account of "extinct" species being recently refound, but one of those you listed should be deleted (see below). The two latest 'Lazari' are (1) the shou — a relative of the British red deer — in Bhutan, and (2) a bird with the unlikely name of "Bishop's O'o" in the Hawaiian Islands...which had last been seen in 1904.

Unfortunately, the account of the glos (sic) ibis's redis-covery in Sri Lanka was rather misleading. The bird referred to is the *glossy* ibis which, though it may not have been seen for 60 years in Sri Lanka, has never been considered an extinct species. It is, in fact, found over a wide range — from North America and Southern Europe to Australia — and as it is known to wander far from its breeding grounds, there is nothing too remarkable about its turning up again in Sri Lanka. So scratch one "mysterious reappearance", I fear.

The most curious report, however, was the first one quoted on page 26...the giant skunks of Java. Until now, skunks have only been found in the Americas, and I wonder if a spelling mistake wasn't made in the original report... with the word SKUNK being put, instead of SKINK. Skinks are a kind of lizard; and if the mystery animal is actually a *reptile*, then the suggestion of "prehistoric survivors" makes better sense. However, I freely admit that a skink the size of an alsatian dog is just as un-likely as a Javanese skunk. So what's the truth of the matter? Is the report a hoax? If not, then this could be the biggest zoological find since the coelacanth was rediscovered: and yet it seems to have gone largely ignored, and I have heard nothing more about these giant "skunks" since the 1977 newspaper reports. Perhaps one of FT's Malaysian correspondents would be in a position to find out more?

Mike Grayson
London

ISOTOPE MISS

The scientific dating processes bother me, too, as does the ease with which scientists in general will assume something constant without really being aware that they are doing it. Nonetheless, I think that Dr. Don Robins is off a bit in his "Isotope Myth" [FT38p16-17].

What he says is probably news to those who have had only beginning courses in chemistry, but he · must have slept through a few classes if he got a doctorate in inorganic chemistry and exited with the picture of the isotope situation which he attributes to chemists and physicists in general. Variations of the isotope mix in natural samples is a frequent topic in *Nature* articles, and the sulphur example that Robins dates as "more recently" was textbook material (i.e. probably more than a decade old) when I took freshman chemistry over 25 years ago. And one of my first jobs nearly 20 years ago was to modernize the design of a plant which separated Boron isotopes using a mechanism which depended upon the iso-topes behaving differently during a chemical reaction. Rather a strange assignment if we all throught that isotopes were chemically indistinguish-able!

Physical isotope separations, like the distillation and dif-fusion mechanisms that Robins mentions, have been in use even longer than chemical separations.

David Dunthorn
Oak Ridge, Tennessee.

ANOMALISTICS

Anomalistics — the inter-disciplinary study of anomalies [FT36p4-10] sounds an inter-esting idea, but its establish-ment as a subject will not be helped by such howlers as appear in Roger Wescott's article.

The goals of science, he says, can be categorised as, in order, description, classific-ation, explanation, prediction and control. Indeed they can. He then goes on to say this means dividing anomalies into anomalies of description, anomalies of classification, anomalies of explanation, anomalies of prediction and anomalies of control, and gives examples of each. Ahem. Does he imagine that a meteorologist, say, divides up weather into weather of description, weather of classification, weather of explanation etc? No, a meteorologist divides his activity into description of weather (rainy, snowy, etc), classification of weather (grouped into patterns), explanations of weather (reasons why), prediction of weather (at least, they try), and control of weather (eg cloud seeding).

This schema works just as well for anomalies. First, description of anomalies – lots in FT. Second, classification of anomalies – for which there are several possible approaches, according to whether you want to classify them by type, or nature of occurrence, or whatever. Third, explanation of anomalies – very variable, this; some anomalies have reasonable explanations, anomalous behaviour of water as a liquid, for instance. Others, the more Fortean anomalies, are quite unexplained at present. Fourth, prediction of anomalies – anyone for Fortean forecasts? We're not very good at this yet. Last and best of all if you can do it, is control of anomalies. Fire-walking is probably a good example – summoning of Great Orms is another (if they come).

But prediction and control are normally things that come after a proper understanding of the whys and wherefores. Even then they can be long-term goals. Man may understand volcanoes perfectly, but predicting eruptions accurately is not possible yet, and no-one knows how to control them at all. With anomalistics we're still at stages one and two, and only groping towards stage three.

Roger Musson
Edinburgh

M-FIELDS

May I draw attention to the similarity of Rupert Sheldrake's theory of morphogenetic fields to the metaphysical teachings of Seth, allegedly an evolved entity communicating through American novelist and medium Jane Roberts. On p.113 of *The Seth Material* (Prentice-Hall), we read 'Consciousness comes first and evolves its own forms.' Again, on p.246 'There is constant creation. There is within you a force that knew how to grow you from a foetus to a grown adult.'

Of course the value we place on these and other statements depends on who or what we believe Seth to be. The several Seth books are collectively a *tour de force*. It is difficult to imagine them being the product of the medium's mind and nothing else.

Perhaps then, Dr. Sheldrake's ideas and Seth's teachings complement and give credence, one to the other.

R.E. Sinclair
Accrington, Lancs

THE NAME'S THE GAME

A couple of issues ago you had a feature on 'synchronous names' [FT31, p37]. Has anyone looked into the opposite, ie inappropriate names – eg: the Welsh football team's manager is Mike England? Maybe the idea is worth persuing.

R.A. Parkes *Hong Kong*

Help!

Any reader or researcher requiring help in research, questions answered, or contacts on Fortean topics, may do so free in this column. Just send the details, on a separate sheet, keeping it brief.

● I want to hear from anyone who has had a **peak experience** ie extreme joy, ecstasy, immense well-being, etc. I get it too and we must talk! Contact me: Adrian Colston, at 'Lynwood', 14 Down Lane, Bathampton, Bath, Avon, BA2 6UE.

THE YELLOW EMPORIUM
cont from p.53

loose; men tying it tightly into a small top-knot which I imagine would defy even the most adept kami-kiri. It would be idle to speculate that, as the majority of panic occurred in the 19th century when colonial interference by the western powers was weakening China, the 'emasculation' of the country was being reflected in the prevailing Fortean phenomena, but who knows? Celestial hints, perhaps?

There are simply a few notes put together one afternoon, and can hardly claim to exhaust the subject.

●

Steve Moore

REFERENCES

1) Charles Fort, *The Complete Books* (Dover, NY, 1974) p875-877.
2) JJM De Groot, *The Religious System of China* (reprint, Literature House, Taiwan, 1964) Vol 5, p598.
3) De groot, *ibid*, Vol 5, p598.
4) Yang Hsien-yi & Gladys Yang (trans), *The Man Who Sold a Ghost* (Commercial Press, HK, 1974) p131. Also, De Groot, *ibid*, Vol 5, p598-599.
5) (Arthur Waley, trans) Li Chih-Ch'ang, *The Travels of an Alchemist* (reprint, Greenwood Press, Conn, 1976) p75.
6) Kiyoshi Nozaki, *Kitsune* (Hokuseido Press, Tokyo, 1961) p178-179.
7) Nozaki, *ibid*, p7, 132, 179.
8) Nikolas Kiej'e *Japanese Grotesqueries* (Tuttle, Tokyo, 1973) p144-145.
9) De Groot, *ibid*, Vol 5, p484-487.
10) De Groot, *ibid*, Vol 5, p487.
11) De Groot, *ibid*, Vol 5, p487-488.
12) De Groot, *ibid*, Vol 5, p489.
13) De Groot, *ibid*, Vol 5, p482-483.
14) De Groot, *ibid*, Vol 5, p483-484, quoting Holcombe, *The Real Chinaman* (1895).

REVIEWS

cont from p.61

shaman. Miss Eaton, of white and Indian ancestry, took the name Mahad'yumi (Way Shower) and is a Medicine Woman of two tribes, having undergone authentic Arapahoe and Paiute initiations. Her book is the story of her life and experiences and her practice as a healer.

Altogether these books paint a picture of the Natural Man, who lives within each of us. The shaman has given us a variety of techniques for coping with non-ordinary reality, and his influence and power is far-reaching and misunderstood. Joan Halifax thinks he is an endangered species, but both Drury and Eaton show, in their various roles as magician/philosopher and healer, that he is very much with us today.
□*RJMR*

OTHER BOOKS RECEIVED

★ **PEACE RIVER** by Michael Walton. A privately printed inspirational tract. *(£10.95 hb; from the author at Melrose, 14 Clinton Rise, Beer, East Devon EX12 3DZ).*

★ **THE ISLAND** by Arthur Guirdham. Convinced of the reality of reincarnation, Guirdham here tells of his life on a Greek Island about 1250 BC, revealed to him clearly as a "far memory". *(Neville Spearman, Jersey; 1980, £4.95 hb, pp176).*

★ **THE WILFION SCRIPTS** by William Sharp/Fiona Macleod. Sharp (1855-1905) had a secondary personality, Fiona Macleod, and both wrote with own distinctive style. After death the two unite and continue their poetry through the mediumship of Margo Williams. Strange. *(Wilfion Books, Paisley, Scotland; 1980, £3.00 pb (+50p p&p), pp127, drawings).*

★ **THE ADULT DEVELOPMENT OF C.G.JUNG** by John-Raphael Staude. *(RKP, Henley, Oxon; 1981, £7.50 hb, pp134, indexes, bib, notes.)*

★ **JUNG: MAN & MYTH** by Vincent Brome. Full of fascinating recollections by people who knew Jung, and a wealth of biographical background details. *(Granada/Paladin, St Albans, Herts; 1980, £1.95 pb, pp327, index, bib, notes.)*

★ **BEHIND WORLD REVOLUTION** by Richard Gilman. The strange career of Nesta Webster, political theorist and writer on the lore and activities of secret societies and subversive movements, and who believed she was a reincarnated French countess. *Insight Books, Box 1784, Ann Arbor, MI 48106, USA; 1982, $7.95 pb, pb111, illus.)*

★ **THE COMPLETE BOOK OF DOWSING & DIVINING** BY Peter Underwood. A very competant survey of dowsing in general and British dowsing in particular. *(Hutchinson/Rider, London; 1980, £5.95 hb, pp229, index, bib, plates.)*

★ **TERRESTRIAL ASTROLOGY: DIVINATION BY GEOMANCY** by Stephen Skinner. Essentially a detailed study of primary forms of geomancy ("using dots to foretell the future") which evolved from the Islamic *raml*. The later half of the book is a manual of various practices. *(RKP, London, 1980. £15.00 hb, pp293, index, bib, plates, illus, tables, diags.)*

★ **EIGHT SABBATS FOR WITCHES** by Janet & Stewart Farrar. *(Robert Hale, London; 1981, £6.95, pp192, index, bib, photos.)*

★ **POWER SECRETS FROM A SORCERER'S PRIVATE MAGNUM ARCANUM** by Gavin & Yvonne Frost. A hodgepodge of European occult traditions by the principals of an American correspondence school on witchcraft and sorcery. Even more bizarre are the stories of psychic power herein. *(Parker Pub. Co, West Nyack, NY; 1980, £7.10 hb, pp217, diags.)*

CLASSIFIED EXCHANGE

cont from p.55.

• **Earth Giant** #1-3 — Erudite journal of Wessex mysteries & antiquities. Mostly EM but many Fortean items in each issue. Formerly called *Picwinnard*. 4/yr. UK:£2.

• **Earthquest News** #5 — Formerly *The Supernaturalist*. Some Fortean items (eg The Fobbing Puma). 4/yr. UK:£3, E:£4, O:£7. Andrew Collins: 19 St Davids Way, Wickford, Essex.

• **NEARA Journal** #16:3 — New England Antiquities Research Association. 4/yr. Memb: US:$8, O:$10, NEARA: Box 313, Barrington, NH 03825, USA.

• **Northern Earth Mysteries** #20 — 5/yr. UK:£2. Pay: Philip Heselton: 170 Victoria Ave, Hull HU5 3DY.

• **Quick Silver Messenger** #8 — RA Wilson interview. 4/yr. UK:£4, E:£5, O:$16. QSM: Garden Flat, 46 Vere Rd, Brighton, Sussex.

• **The Templar** #3 — Geomancy of circular sacred buildings. 4/yr. UK:3.25. IGR: 142 Pheasant Rise, Bar Hill, Cambridge CB3 8SD.

• **Terrestrial Zodiac News** #2:2 — 4/yr. UK:£2.50. Pay: Anthea Turner. 8 Eynsford Court, Hitchin, Herts SG4 9JS.

• **Touchstone** #1— Surrey earth mysteries. 4/yr. UK:£1. Pay: Jimmy Goddard: 25 Albert Rd, Addlestone, Weybridge, Surrey.

OTHERS

• **Prytania** #3 — Esotericism. 4/yr. UK:£3. Biophysical Research: 126 Bevan St, Lowestoft, Suffolk NR32 2AQ.

• **Walrus** #21 — Official organ of the non-material world. Recently liberated from any form of self-control and subscription system. Apply within. Walrus: 142 Pheasant Rise, Bar Hill, Cambridge CB3 8SD.

•

Please mention *Fortean Times* when you respond to these listings.

YOU CAN LOOK HIGH AND LOW FOR FT

— but the only way you'll be certain of getting it these days is by subscribing (or renewing your sub).

All overseas readers get an airmail service (on subs only) at surface rates: that means within 2 weeks of publishing instead of the usual 6-8 weeks.

• **SUB RATES** - 1 year or four issues: (UK) £5.00; (Overseas) $12.00.

• **SINGLE COPIES** - (UK) £1.25; (Airmail) $4.00 — we can send a recent issue plus our literature to a friend or potential subscriber at these rates.

• **PAYMENT** - payable to Fortean Times. Dollar cheques acceptable, but a sterling cheque drawn on a London bank is better (ask your bank for one). Rates include postage and bank charges. If you think your order has gone astray, let us know.

BM-Fortean Times
London WC1N 3XX, UK

BACKISSUES

ALL AT SINGLE ISSUE PRICE (SEE LEFT)

• **FT31** – The Chinese Wildman; Gateways to Mystery; The Touch of Death; UFO muggers; mystery big cats; ball lightning; synchronous names; little people; fake doctors; Forteana from China; comix.

• **FT32** – The Mississauga Blob; Old Ives' Tales; Gateways (pt 2); occult murder; mystery big cats; fairy tales come true; Forteana from India and China; child sacrifice; mystery panthers in USA and Australia; comix.

• **FT33** – The Enfield Poltergeist; mythology of UFO abductions; Gateways (pt 3); mass hysteria at Nottingham; simulacra; coffin stories; Jeoff Watson's Nessie pix; UFOs; Forteana from China; giant snakes; comix.

• **FT34** – Congo dinosaur hunt; lake monster names; phantom hitch-hikers; interview with Dr Jean Bolen on synchronicity; the Welsh 'puma'; mystery big cats; beached whales; animal saboteurs; nature follows art; ice falls; inept crimes; Trashkashic records; odd Irish doings; giant squids; comix.

• **FT35** – The Myth of Darwinism; an SHC from 1744; The Runamo Runes; Forteana from Malaysia and China; spontaneous combustions; antiquities; strange trees; magic fuels; frog and stone falls; mystery big cats; bizarre bacteria; TV science; occult murder; Fortean travel in USA.

• **FT36** – Anomalistics; Photos of Jesus; Runamo Runes; Gent's Mag extracts; hermits and wildmen; strange tales; toads in holes; bleeding statues and visions; the Buddha's UFO; DIY surgery; coin, ice and sand falls; ASSAP and CSAR; jellyfish in the sky; Forteana from China; USA monitor lizards; Nessie; comix.

• **FT37** – Australia's Lizard Monsters; energy from space; encounters with Greek gods; interview with Dr Rupert Sheldrake on a New Science of Life; a female prophet; Irish oddities; mystery USA kangaroos; UFO hallucinations; falls of crabs, frogs, peas, fish; visions, stigmatics and fasting; plants in odd places; mystery UK bear scares; talking polts; reflections; homing rings; locked-up by friends and relatives,

• • •

Founded in 1973 and first called *The News*, FT's humble beginnings have become legendary — well, out of print anyway! We now have high quality xerox facsimilies of the **first** twenty issues of *Fortean Times*.

Fortean Times

ISSUE No.40   The Foremost Journal of Strange Phenomena   PRICE £1·25 $3·00

MORE LIVING WONDERS
THE EXMOOR BEAST

SNAKES ALIVE! WILTSHIRE WHIRLWINDS & MUCH MORE

Books from FT.

- **THE COMPLETE BOOKS OF CHARLES FORT** – Comprising *Book of the Damned* (1919), *New Lands* (1927), *Lo!* (1931), and *Wild Talents* (1932). Still the greatest single compendium of baffling and strange phenomena ever written, covering almost every subject on our list and many others besides. Fort's style has been called bewildering, intoxicating, impenetrable, stream-of-consciousness and one of the most brilliant of his day. This is a tour de force of iconoclasm, challenging the complacency of dogmatic science and religion with embarassing data and exciting ideas, but written with disarming wit and wisdom. This is a 1974 reprint of the 1941 edition compiled for the old Fortean Society, with a new introduction by Damon Knight, and the old index. Hardcover, 1125 pages. Because of its bulk we are offering this only to UK and European readers. US readers are advised to obtain it from Dover Books, NY. £15.00.

- **PHENOMENA: A Book of Wonders** by John Michell & RJM Rickard. Recommended introduction to the philosophy of Charles Fort, and the historical and thematic continuity of 57 varieties of strange phenomena, from stigmata levitation and fairies to showers of frogs, wild children and ball lightning. 216 illustrations, many collected together for the first time anywhere. Large format paperback. Price includes post & packing. UK: £3.90; Overseas surface: $8.00.

- **SIMULACRA** – An erudite survey of the varieties of spontaneous images in nature. One of the most remarkable Fortean books around – inspires art, psychology and mysticism. Illustrated with 196 photos collected by the author, John Michell, over many years. Soft cover only, 128 pages. Virtually unobtainable in USA. UK £3.80; overseas surface $8.00.

- **LIVING WONDERS** – The authors of *Phenomena,* John Michell & Robert Rickard, explore some mysteries and curiosities of the animal world, from folklore, and mythology to the records of early naturalists and explorers and contemporary reports of strange animals and stranger behaviour. Topics include: a little history of cryptobiology sea-serpents and other marine enigmas, lake-monsters, the return of extinct animals, prehistoric survivals, animals out of place in Britain, mysterious animals of Australasia, theories of animal distribution and the evidence for animal teleportation, explanations for rains of frogs & fishes, showers of insects and other animals, falls of seeds and veg, swarms and dearths of insects, creatures imprisoned in rock and wood, animals found far out at sea, talking cats and dogs, calculating horses, winged cats, life-saving pets, animal benefactors, canine loyalty, martyred animals, homing animals, abductions by eagles, man-eating trees, modern Jonahs, animals courts and funerals, animal battles, mass-panics and animal suicide, bird hibernation, imprinted eggs, how rats steal eggs, rat kings & monkey chains. Paperback pp176, 170 illus, name index. UK £7.00;; overseas surface $12.00

- **PHOTOGRAPHS OF THE UNKNOWN** – An unparalleled collection of over 300 photographs on sea and lake monsters, Bigfoot, ghost lights, natural UFOs, haloes and parhelia, falling objects, UFOs, computer analysis of UFO photos, possession, stigmata, bleeding images, spiritualist phenomena, thoughtography, Kirlian photography, apparitions, portraits of Christ, pain immunity, firewalking spoonbenders, levitation of objects, human levitation, apports, poltergeists. Many in full colour; many never before published, many never collected before. Plus essay on paranormal photography. An excellent visual reference for paranormal and Fortean photos. By Bob Rickard and Richard Kelly. Large format paperback, 144 pages. UK: £6.50; overseas surface $13.00.

- **MAN BITES MAN: The Scrapbook of an Edwardian Eccentric.** Edited by Paul Sieveking from the press clipping albums of George Ives. The weird, the dubious, the heroic, the horrific, and the hilarious. Much of Fortean interest. Large format hardback. 160 pages. Profusely illustrated with 584 facsimile clippings from 1890 - 1950. UK £5.00; overseas surface $10.50.

- **WILDMAN** – A compendium on the Chinese equivalent of Yeti and Bigfoot. Three articles newly translated from original Chinese, with new photographs, & 12 illustrations from old Chinese books. 'A Challenge to Science' the original article by Yuan Zhenxin and Huang Wanpo, with new material. 'I Witnessed a Wildman Mother and Child in the Chestnut Forest' by Fan Jingquan. 'Does the Flying Saucer Exist?' by Zhou Xinyan. Also 'A Brief Bestiary of Chinese Hill-monsters' compiled from Chinese literature by the booklet's editor Steve Moore. FT occasional paper No. 1. 24 pages, FT format. UK: £1.00; Overseas surface: $2.50.

Make cheques, money orders etc, payable to **Fortean Times**. Prices include post and packing. Allow up to 10 weeks for surface mail. Send orders to BM-Fortean Times, London WC1N 3XX, UK.

Fortean Times

BM-Fortean Times
London WC1N 3XX.

The Journal of Strange Phenomena.

Summer 1983
ISSN 0308.5899

Contents.

Cover art by ADCO
See 'Rats/eggs' on p5

GANG OF FORT

Editor   Robert J.M. Rickard
  Mike Dash
  Steve Moore
  Paul R.A. deG Sieveking
Art Dir.   Richard Adams
ComixEd.   Hunt Emerson

SPECIAL CORRESPONDENTS

Australia   Greg Axford (Vic)
  Paul Cropper (NSW)
  Rex Gilroy (NSW)
  Tony Healy (ACT)
  Richard King (Vic)
Belgium   Henri Premont
Canada   Dwight Whalen (Ont)
  Mister X (Ont)
England   Richard Cotton
  Peter Christie
  Peter Hope Evans
  Alan Gardiner
  Chris Hall
  Valerie Martin
  John Michell
  Nigel Pennick
  Paul Screeton
  Anthony Smith
  David Sutton
  Paul R. Thomas
Finland   Tuuri Heporauta
France   Dr Bernard Heuvelmans
  Phil Ledger
Greece   Anastasios D. Panos
Ireland   Doc Shiels
  Robert Anton Wilson
Japan   Jun-Ichi Takanashi
Malaysia   Ahmad Jamaludin
Roving   Ion A Will
Scotland   Roland Watson
  Jake Williams
S. Africa   Chris J. Holtzhausen
Sweden   Ake Franzen
  Anders Liljegren
  Sven Rosen
USA   George Andrews (MO)
  Larry E. Arnold (PA)
  Tom Adams (TX)
  Loren Coleman (MA)
  Richard T Crowe (IL)
  Ron Dobbins (AZ)
  David R. Fideler (MI)
  Mark A Hall (MN)
  Steve Hicks (KS)
  Michael Hoffman (NY)
  Kurt Lothmann (TX)
  Gary S Mangiacopra (CN)
  Joseph Swatek (NB)
  Paul Willis (MD)
  Joseph W Zarzynski (NY)
USSR   Vladimir V. Rubtsov
Wales   Janet & Colin Bord
Yugoslavia   Milos Krmelj

Reprosetting   Cecilia Boggis;
  11 Ashburnham Rd. Bedford.
Photosetting   Wordsmiths; 19 West End.
  Street. Somerset.
Printed by   Golden Valley Publications
  The Old Convent. Beeches
  Green.
  Stroud. Glos GL5 4AD
Overseas   Overseas Postal Services Ltd.
Mailing   2-8 Hornsey St.
  London N7 8HI

TICK TICKA TICKA TACK TOCK TACKA

LATE AGAIN!

Despite our good intentions FT does it again, for which our apologies are offered. To compensate, we've made this a bumper 72 page edition.

Producing FT is a very time-consuming business, and unfortunately it competes for my time with a very demanding family problem, and the needs of my two eczematic children tend to come first. I can only ask you to continue being as patient as you have been – it is much appreciated.

Better late than never!

Speaking of which... Some of you have written solicitous notes during the long silences, hoping that FT has not 'gone under', as have so many small magazines recently. I speak for all of us at FT when I say we have no intention of folding our tent. To the contrary, our pointy little heads are still cloggged with ideas... Now read on...

EXPANSION PLANS

After years of thinking about it, and several false starts which, mercifully, never got very far, we embark on a three phase plan, which will culminate in FT as a professional journal with all the trimmings. First comes a developmental period in which we will be overhauling FT's format, editorial practices and seeking answers to distribution, advertising, production and marketing questions.

Next issue, FT41, our anniversary issue, will be the last in the present format. Even so it will be a departure, more in the nature of a celebratory issue consisting mainly of essays specially commissioned from Leslie Shepard, John Keel, Hilary Evans, Ron Westrum, Peter Costello, Bernard Heuvelmans, the Bords, Mr X, Loren Coleman and Doc Shiels, to name a few. This should reach you in December. Alas, that makes for only three isues of FT in 1983. I can only apologise and say that we are doing our best at all times. Hopefully we'll do better with...

THE NEW FT

The first issue of 1984 – FT42 in Jan – will be the first in a new format. It'll be larger (A4) and 48 pages, which in effect will give us the space equivalent of an extra ten thousand words. The change to a larger size has not been an easy decision to take – the present size has valuable charm, handleability and bookish quality – but we want to explore more creative layouts, on top of which the A4 size is a prerequisite for our eventual distribution.

There will be other changes too... We want to explore new ways of presenting you with more current and more varied news reports. We are negotiating regular reviews of the earth mysteries, UFO, psychic research fields by Paul Devereux, Jenny Randles, Kevin McClure and Loren Coleman respectively. Up to now we have been content to leave these subjects to their very excellent specialist journals, but we feel we should include some overview of them because a growing number of you are interested in the Fortean overlap with these relatively distinct subject areas. It is not our intention to supplant the vital work of the other, more specialized mags but to spread our nets widely and channel back the interest to the specialist areas.

Other regular features we are lining up will include Bill Corliss' 'Science Frontiers', gleanings of Forteana from the current science periodicals, to give us those 'hard' anomalies we are often aware we've lacked; and a return of the 'Diary of a Mad Planet' feature we pioneered back in FT27. The new 'Diary' will be compiled for us by Albert Thomas from the prior three months' quakes, astronomical data and worldwide weather disasters and superlatives.

Phase one of our expansion means using our own money, or that invested in us by the encouragingly faithful, in an advertising drive to triple, at least, our subscriber base. If you'd like to help us by donations you are more than

Cont on p 51

TRUTH IN TRASH?

I am delighted to have discovered Fortean Times, and become a subscriber.

I would like to comment on the BVMs reported in FT38. The French BVM seems to have occured in a cabbage patch wedged between a cottage and a chicken shack, and bordered by an orchard and a polluted stream. This is described as a "bizarre" site for celestial revelations. Certainly it seems incongruous, but it's not unprecedented.

In fact there seems to be some odd connection between "miraculous" events of various kinds – not only religious – and rubbish dumps. There is the example of Lourdes – Bernadette saw the "Lady" near a hillside dump. Then one thinks of horticultural inexplicabilities on a rubbish dump at Findhorn, Scotland. John Keel, in his "The Mothman Prophecies" said that fairies, demons, and witches would choose gravel pits, garbage dumps, cemetries, and crossroads for their appearances.

Peter Kells
Springbrook, Queensland

THE MUTILATED HORSE

This is a response to Nigel Watson's piece "Fools and Horses" in FT39p53-54.

Bob Durant, an airline pilot and Fortean, once said that *Operation Trojan Horse* was the "most discussed and least read book in ufology". I'm afraid he is right. Worldwide sales of the book were negligible. Barely 2,000 copies were sold here in the USA and, so far as I know, only a few hundred were sold in the British Commonwealth.

Mr Watson should realize that the book was necessarily cautious because of the nonsensical attitudes of the American ufologists at the time. Associates of Dr Hynek fired off enraged letters to FSR when my article appeared there. Hynek and Vallee made a strenuous effort to force Charles Bowen into shutting me out of the pages of FSR. It has been most amusing to see them reluctantly change their positions over the years. Gradually both Hynek and Vallee have adopted what they once called 'Keelisms' and now they assume the stance I took back in the late 1960's. Too embarrassed and ashamed to use my etymology (I was once a professional lexicographer), Hynek now uses words like meta-terrestrial (impossible usage) because he thinks ultraterrestrial was my invention. Actually, ultra-terrestrial is a respectable word found in most good dictionaries. Metaterrestrial is not... and cannot be used as a substitute.

In any case, while writing OTH I was aware I was dealing with an audience with great limitations. An audience totally unschooled in philosophy and psychology (my two strong points), and largely unaware of basic High School physics (such as the electromagnetic spectrum). So I had to reach down to them, using all kinds of literary devices. Even so, the editors were appalled by the book and it was almost cancelled. It was not "a believer's book",

as they put it. I had to cut the manuscript into two books (*Strange Creatures from Time and Space* is actually one-half of OTH), and I had to rewrite the closing chapter. The editors felt I was much too blunt. My original conclusions were forthright and very candid. I simply explained that the whole subject was a mis-interpretation, that 99.9% of all the UFO literature was pure hogwash. In OTH I had tried to demonstrate how any theory could be constructed when the reader was unaware of the history of man's belief systems. Later I expanded this greatly in *The Eighth Tower* (published in England under the title *The Cosmic Question*). In its original form, about 2,000 pages long, OTH probably would have sold even fewer copies. The editors made me pull all my statistics, developed at the cost of many months of hard work, and I could never find a publisher for that body of material. Nobody wants to read statistical analyses, particularly ufologists.

Basically, what I attempted to do was set up a frame of reference that the reader could, hopefully, understand. Obviously I failed in this. Even now people like Nigel are still assuming that ultraterrestrials are actual entities. What I have said in five books, carefully spelled out and defined, is that *we are the intelligence which controls the phenomena* because the phenomena do not exist in the same way that, say, a Volkswagen exists. Some few astute readers realized that
Cont on p 70

A Reprise for 'Living Wonders.'

After *Living Wonders* (Thames & Hudson, 1982) was delivered to the publishers, the authors, John Michell & Robert J M Rickard, began to accumulate miscellaneous related material which arrived too late for inclusion, and which we give here. We'd like to record a special thanks to Bob Skinner, whose diligence in the pursuit of his own current interest, tales of entombed toads and frogs, turned up many of the notes which follow. In fact he had so many curiosities relating to cats and eggs that he has written these as separate articles which will appear in future issues .Any errors arising out of the annotated notes below should be laid at the feet of **Bob Rickard.**

UNUSUAL HIBERNATIONS

★ There is some discussion of whether swallows can hibernate in *the Edinburgh Journal of Natural History* Vol 1 no 1 p2 (1835), where in such a belief is described as a "popular error"; this skepticism, despite references to the beliefs in the subject by Buffon, Gilbert White and Goldsmith.

★ "On opening the vault belonging to the family of J. Norris esq. in the church of St Peter Mancroft, Norwich on Monday se'nnight, a live bat was found there, of greyish colour, where it had probably lain in a torpid state, companion for the dead, more than 32 years, the distance of time since the vault was before opened." *La Belle Assemblee* Vol 1 p56 (Feb 1806).

★ Apropos torpid birds found underground, the following interesting note appeared in the *D.Mirror* 11 Jan 1983. A robin was found by miners 600ft underground and five miles from the shaft bottom in Britain's largest undersea pit, at Ellington Colliery, Northumberland. The state of the bird is not described, but it was later released unharmed.

★ On LWp164f we gave the account, by Mr Archard, to Peter Collinson, of swallows found torpid in sandy cliffs of the Rhine. While this incident contributed to Collinson's later opinion that some "of the swallow-tribe" hibernate while the rest migrate, he was not always of that view. To the contrary, in *Philosophical Transactions* Vol LI p425 (1760) he attempts to demolish a closely argued thesis, by a J.Th.Klein of "Dantzic", that swallows are *not* birds of passage and in fact at the season of their disappearance retire under water where they spend the winter. In the first place, argues Mr.C., there are no special organs discoverable

in the swallow which would allow it to breathe underwater; secondly, he rightly points out that Klein's analogy of insects which survive underwater is pointless. Thirdly, there is a place on the Thames where swallows congregate in great numbers, and yet no waterman has ever found torpid swallows there in winter (to our knowledge) during the annual winter pruning of the willows. Fourthly, a trusted clergyman friend, who lived near sandy cliffs at Byfleet, Surrey, conducted an experiment on Mr C's behalf. The cliffs were the annual home of great numbers of sand martins, and during winter, the clergyman excavated a 12ft section, containing about 40 holes which lead back into the cliff about several feet to the little chambers used as nests. He found no sign of any bird using the nests as winter quarters.

And yet...

★ American Philosophical Society (Philadelphia) *Transactions* Vol 6 pt 1 No12 p59f: article on hibernation of swallows, by Frederick Antes. *American Academy of Arts & Science* (Boston) Vol 2 pt 1 p96-8: report by S.J. Bruyn on large number of swallows found hibernating in a tree.

★ LWp165: the corncrake found in the Orkneys in the rubble of a demolished wall... fuller reference can be found in John Fleming's *Philosophy of Zoology* Vol 2 p73 (1822), who sites Neill's *Tour through Orkney & Shetland* p204. Other discoveries in Orkney are mentioned by 'W.R. of Wick' in *Land & Water* Vol 9 p188 (12 March 1870), who cites *Historia Naturalis Orcendensis (1848)* by W B Blackie and R Heddel, that "on several occasions when digging up old turf dykes, landrails (corncrakes) have been found in them in a torpid condition." 'WR' gives another landrail case, of January 1861: Robin Scarth, of Bin Scarth, found it in a stone wall being dismantled, and revived it by a fire, but it died later.

★ A bird, thought to be a cuckoo, found apparently hibernating in a ball of feathers in a hollow tree; the bird being largely denuded of feathers. *Land & Water* Vol 21 p291 (15 April 1876).

★ In LW we mentioned the subject of birds supposedly discovered hibernating under water, for which we have several unchecked references. *Medical Repository* (NY) Vol 2 No2 p215f (1800): article by W. Johnson & H. Pollock on the submersion of swallows. *The Naturalist* Vol 2 p361 (1838): swallows seen emerging from Grasmere Lake, Cumbria, in spring, rising in bell-shaped bubbles, each of which burst to reveal a swallow.

★ Another, perhaps more reliable reference to submerged swallows can be found in the notes appended by the translators (Drs Hodgkin & Fisher) of W.F. Edwards' *On the Influence of Physical Agents on Life* (1834), originally in French. Dr Edwards contrived some experiments on hibernating toads, which prompted one of the translators to reflect on the possibility of bird hibernation in general and swallow hibernation in particular. By experimentally chilling a swallow — he placed it in an open jar embedded in ice and salt, and measured a drop in the bird's temperature from 106F to about 86F in an hour — he successfully demonstrated the bird's torpidity. This in turn prompts the translator to cite the experience of a reliable doctor friend of about 50yrs previously (approx in 1780). At the age of nine the doctor lived with his parents on the coast of Hampshire, and one winter morning was playing ball in the yard prior to going to school. The ball fell into a rain butt and the boy reached in to retrieve it: "I felt something which induced me to move it, and found it, on examination, to be a bird in a torpid state, perfectly wet and to appearance inanimate..I remember well leaving the ball and taking my prize to the kitchen fire, which after drying and warming, I had succeeded in restoring to perfect animation my bird..." It was time for school and the boy reluctantly left the bird on a windowsill — it had flown by the time he returned home (p467f).

★ A correspondent to *Notes & Queries* Vol 12 p513 (29 Dec 1855) refers the reader, interested in the question of hirundinian subaqueous hybernation, to the observations of "the celebrated Huet", in Gordonius' *Instinct and Reason definitively seperated* (mid-1850s) p37. We have not checked this out.

★ The same volume of *Notes & Queries* has, for 24 Nov 1855 p413, a letter giving the experience of a friend of the writer: "that on a fine day in autumn, about two years since, she saw a number of swallows successively dive, and

not emerge again, in a well-known river in the north of England."

★ A response to the previous item a few issues later *N&Q* 29 Dec 1855 p512f — brought the expected rebuff. However, the writer, F. Phillott, gives the following account of some swallows who seemed prepared to remain and die rather than migrate. "A North American gentleman, attracted one day, late in the autumn season, by the gathering of a large body of swallows over a particular spot, and having been told that swallows had been seen to *dive into a mill-pond and disappear* [original emphasis], watched their operations; which, after a few significant circumvolutions, were closed by a simultaneous descent into a hollow sycamore tree. The said tree was felled the following year, and revealed the debris of bones, feathers, and other remains of such birds as had not survived, through age or weakness, to renew their spring migration."

★ Can it be that the so-called hibernation of the swallow-tribe and others is some sort of deathwish, and that having chosen to stay behind, in what must be the avian equivalent of a considerable depression, they would seek out some sort of refuge which would allow them a gradual temperature drop into torpidity and eventual death. The dive into water may be a form of suicide. This is supposition, but as evidence of the extraordinary presence of mind of these birds when death approaches, I draw on a fact from a record, by the same Phillott, in *N&Q* 27 Oct 1855 p331, of the severe mortality among swallows during a sudden very cold spell at the end of May that year (1855), during which these birds were found dead "ten or twelve deep on windowsills". At one place they were observed to "fly round a heap of dead or dying companions, and then suddenly dart down, and bury [themselves] amongst them."

RATS STEALING EGGS

★ Our cover illustration is by the great Gustave Doré, originally engraved to accompany La Fontaine's fable 'The Two Rats, the Fox, and the Egg' (Book X, Fable 1)

★ Another note we overlooked occurs in one of the sources we used frequently for other subjects, the marvellously erratic *Zoologist*. In Vol 23 p9431 (1865) we find this unequivocal statement from one Henry Moses of Reading, Berks: "The rector of a parish in Westmorland assured me he had witnessed this feat. Having lost many eggs belonging to a laying hen he was induced to watch to discover the thief. One morning, soon after the cackling bird had given warning that she had deposited an egg, he observed two rats come out of a hole in the hen house and proceed direct to the nest. One of the rats then laid down on its side, whilst the other rat rolled the fresh egg so near it that it could embrace it with its feet. Having

now obtained a secure hold of the egg, its companion dragged it into the hole by its tail, and disappeared. We may now ask how the rats got at the contents of the egg?''
★ From an account of a voyage to the East Indies under Admiral Du Quesne, about 1670, we learn that some eggs disappeared and so a watch was kept on the remaining eggs in a casket. Rats were seen to enter the casket, and while one lay on its back, the other rats placed an egg on its belly. The prone rat was taken by the tail by another rat, whose tail was taken in turn by yet another rat and so on, until a chain had been formed up the inside and down the outside of the casket which was then pulled by four or five other rats until the egg was hauled safely out of the casket. *La Belle Assemblee* Vol 4 p18 (Jan 1808). If true, the degree of organization displayed is astonishing. We also have here a demonstration of a rat chain.

ANIMAL CHAINS
★ An extraordinary example of a chain of rats is given under 'Rats stealing eggs'. A chain of young shrews following their mother, usually by grasping the rump of the one in front, or by biting the base or tip of the tail in front, is a characteristic of some kinds of shrews; a photo of such can be found in E. Walker, *Mammals of the World* (1968). Another, more obvious example is that of elephants trained to walk in procession holding the tail of the one in front, though this has also been observed in the wild.

OUT OF PLACE ANIMALS
Some historical gleanings...
★ In September 1810, a leopard escaped in London. It was caught eventually. *La Belle Assemblee* New series Vol 2 p161 (Sept 1810).
★ In 1812 a "fine racoon" was caught by a stud groom and his dogs after they spotted it in an "aged oak" on the estate of Lord Grosvenor, at Eaton in Berkshire. As usual, the supposition is that it escaped from the menagerie of an unidentified travelling showman. *La Belle Assemblee* New series Vol 9 p110 (Feb 1812).
★ We referred, in the chapters on insect dearths and abundances, on the rare discoveries of insects unusual tó Britain, like locusts. We have no space here to tip out the contents of our errant entomology sack, but I must mention the locusts found at Hurstpierpoint, Sussex, in the midst of the recent winter. No date given, but I guess it happened just after Christmas 1982, when Mrs Heather Thompson, proprietor of the Prime Antiques, found what she at first thought was a large yellow grasshopper on the window-sill of the shop. It was caught and identified as a locust by a biologist friend. Then, 30 more were found in shrubbery near the shop. "They all looked pretty sluggish when they were found and they died after a day or two," said Mrs Thompson.

Their origin, and how they came to be in Surrey in mid-winter is a complete mystery. Eggs hatched in sand in packing crates, or blown off-course from the Middle-East, are two rather ineffectual theories offered. *S.Express* 2 Jan 1983.
★ *Natural History Journal* Vol 3 no 7 p128 (15 Oct 1879): two strange captures in the Thames: "A small turtle was taken by a Kingstonian a few weeks ago, and lower down the river at Isleworth a young crocodile was captured – H.K. Harris.'' This is the first we've heard of a croc in the Thames. Pity it's capture date is so vague.
★ Re. the famous 'Dragon' of St Leonards Forest, Sussex, Leslie Shepard referred to this, in FT29p15, in the context of the ballard and broadside tradition of street-literature, implying that it could not be seriously credited as anything other than invented marvel. But suppose it was based on an attempt to describe, as best as the witnesses could, a misidentification of one of our out-of-place animals? That this might not be far fetched is to the credit of Mike Dash, who found the following fuller account of the case in a pamphlet in the Earl of Oxford's collection (*Harlean Miscellany* Vol 3 p227-231, 1810 edition.)
In August 1614, the approximate time of the case, Horsham was a small market town on the edge of St Leonards forest, which our source calls "a vast and unfrequented place, heathie, vaultie, full of unwholesome shades, and overgrown hollowes...'' The mystery beast roamed an area about four miles around, roughly centered at a place called Faygate. It had even come within half a mile of Horsham. The "serpent, or dragon" is about nine feet long and shaped like "an axel-tree of a cart", that is thickest about the middle and of a lesser diameter front and rear. It is scaley in appearance, blackish on top, a redish underbelly and seemingly a white ring of scales around its neck." Though called a serpent, we then learn it has "large feet" and can run as fast as a man; and on hearing cattle or men will lift its head and neck "and seem to listen and looke about, with great arrogancy." This fearless creature killed a few cattle, a man and a woman and two dogs on different occasions, though apparently, and to great surprise, it did not devour its victims. Locals could only suppose that the 'serpent' was satisfied eating rabbits etc.
My first impression on reading this general description is that it could apply to a large crocodile, and fit in with the British tradition of crocs and alligators we discussed in LW – but there are other details which do not fit this conclusion and which need accounting for, even if they are dismissed as colourful embellishments to a good scare story. Firstly: "There is always in his tracke or path left a glutinous and slimie matter (as by small

Tab VI

Sequitur argilla, post glarea filicea. Distantia O ad litus P est 109½ cubitorum.

Tom I.

EMBEDDED FROGS – *As you can tell from the way this subject was expanded beyond our treatment of it in* Phenomena, *it is far from exhausted yet. Space forbids giving all the new cases we've found, but they will not be lost. We have copied them for Bob Skinner, who, for over a year now, has been seeking out and compiling every findable datum, theory and discussion of the subject with a view to eventual publication. It is a project which had out full endorsement, and we want to encourage any of you who might have some information on frogs and toads etc found embedded in solid stone or wood to send a note of it to* **Bob Skinner**: *Squirrels, The Horseshoe, Banstead, Surrey SM7 2BG.*

★ *However, we cannot resist mention of the latest case, in the light a general feeling that this was a Victorian abberation and doesn't happen any more. In Nov 1982 a gang carving an extension to a railway to the south of Te Kuiti, on New Zealand's North Island, were trimming a rock face of sedimentary mudstone, some four metres down, when one man noticed a cavity in a newly fragmented rock was occupied. Closer inspection revealed in imprisoned frog, which was found to be alive after it was shaken loose onto a shovel. A bridge inspector, Mr L. Andrews, supervising the gang, said he began to believe the claim when the men stuck to the story. "The frog was moist, but not exactly bouncing about," he said. The frog was placed on the bank as they went back to work. Later that day, a drilling machine uncovered another frog in similar circumstances, and this was placed near the other one. Andrews said neither frog could have fallen with loose rock into the places they were discovered.* New Zealand Herald *(Aukland) 9 Dec 1982.*

★ *Our illustration (above) describes a living tomb, found in a quarry in the parish of Vamlingbo, near the port of Burgs Vic, Gotland, in Sweden, on 8th May 1733. The toad was found alive when a quarryman split a stone block quarried from eight cubits down. Our source is* Analecta Transaplina *Vol 1 p177-182 (1741).* [C: Bob Skinner/FPL.]

similitude we may perceive in snailes) which is very corrupt and offensive to the scent..." If the creature had just left water it could leave a wet track, but not for very far. This might be simply an association, like the similar erroneous belief that snakes are slimy. Secondly: "He will cast his venome about four rodde from him..." Crocs do not spit venom like some snakes do.

And thirdly, perhaps oddest of all: "There are... on either side of him discovered two great bunches so big as a large foote-ball, and, as some thinke, will in time grow to wings." The placing of these would be important: if they occur in the pelvic region they might be sex organs; or if at the base of the neck they might be gills (but that would require the animal to be a giant newt or salamander type creature). We are given no information of any use in solving this. The record is signed by two local men and "a widow woman" who have seen the animal, and they say there are many more witnesses.

★ The following suggestion of a 'werewolf' in rural Sussex appeared in *The Country Man* Winter 1957 p635 but it might refer to wolves. "Early in the morning [a friend and I] were riding to one of the first foxhunting meets of the season [ie. Sept or Oct.] and had taken a short cut along a rough track, which is known to have been part of a Roman road, when the horses shied as a gigantic grey wolf-like creature came loping across the field on our off-side. Never checking even to glance at us or to swerve, it crossed the road a few yards in front and vanished over the hill. Mike said: What the devil was that? Looked like a wolf, didn't it? A werewolf.' Fascinated we looked for spoor, but not a trace did we find. We asked all over the district if anyone owned such an animal, or if it could have escaped from a circus or a zoo, but the answer was in the negative." The writer then speculates whether it was in fact the ghost of a giant animal killed long ago on that spot.

★ The above account brought a response, a few issues later, from a Doris W. Metcalf, of that county, who had also seen large grey wolf-like animals in the area before WW2, but accepted them as a surviving remnant of some ancient wolf-fox cross breeding that once stalked the downs and ancient forest of Anderida where Pevensey now sits. She writes: "I always understood they were the last of an ancient line of hill foxes, though I have found them on the marshes too. I first saw one of these huge grey foxes on a summer afternoon near Jevington. My companion and I thought it was a large Alsatian dog as it crossed the track, taking not the slightest notice of us. It loped out of sight into a little hollow in the downs, where we expected to see its owner; but we found no-one and concluded it had gone to ground, as there was an earth there. Another time, when hounds were in the wooded grounds of Glenleigh Manor, one of these huge creatures suddenly appeared walking along the drive a yard or two in front of us. We stood watching it, and the animal stopped too. It did not see us but seemed to listen to the sounds of the hunt before turning and loping off across the marshes towards Pevensey." *The Country Man* Summer 1958 p357.

DINOSAUR SURVIVAL

★ The following tantalizing letter appeared in *Empire Magazine* (Denver, Colorado) 22 Aug 1982, from a Myrtle Snow, of Pagosa Springs, Colorado, who was convinced she had seen "five baby dinosaurs" there in May 1935, when she was three years old. Some months later, she says, a farmer, John Martinez, shot one which

he claimed had taken some of his sheep. "My grandfather took us to see it the next morning. It was about 7 feet tall, was grey, had a head like a snake, short front legs with claws that resembled chicken feet, large stout back legs and a long tail." Now I don't expect orthodox zoologists to drop everything and run after the recollections of a three-year old some 47 years later, but I do hope that some cryptozoologist will look into the case, especially as she claims, further, that: "I saw another one in a cave in 1937, but it was dark green," and "On Oct 23, 1978, as I was returning from Chama, NM, about 7.30pm, in a driving rain, I saw another one going through the field towards the place where I had seen the one in 1937."

BIRD BATTLES

★ W.Hone's *Table Book* Vol 1 p661 (1827): I've not checked to see if this is a garbled version of an earlier similar story, like the great battle over Cork (in LW), but the ref. is to a huge battle of starlings in Yorkshire in 1825, after which 1087 were found dead.

TADPOLE RAINS

In several placed in LW we commented on the comparative rarity of showers of tadpoles among the torrents of frogs and toads from the sky.

★ We are pleased to note another occurrence, being the recollection of 80yr-old Leonard Burrough, as told in the *Maidenhead Advertiser* 4 Dec 1981. He said he vividly remembered the day, in about 1910, when, aged nine, his family uprooted to Maidenhead from Somerset. On the day they moved into a dairy on Market St, a violent storm broke during the afternoon, which was the worst in his memory. The sky became "darker than the darkest night" and the torrential rainfall, thunder and lightning were terrifying. When the storm cleared he wandered round to explore the High St, and was astonished to find it alive with thousands of tiny frogs and tadpoles. I'll try to track down records of this event one day, but our first impression is that the presence of tadpoles gives a good rebuff to those who argue that this kind of phenomenon is due to the rain drawing frogs from hiding places under leaves or in cracks or undergrowth. We hope old Mr Burrough's memory proves reliable.

GIANT GOOSEBERRY

★ Before the advent of the Loch Ness Monster as a focus for 'silly season' news reports, the Victorian equivalent was the hunt for the giant gooseberry, reputedly growing in these isles, and to which we refer on LWp75. Imagine my amusement when, shortly before the publication date of LW, I saw a giant gooseberry sighting in the *Sun* (6 Aug 1982). It was a monster of 2ozs which won top prize at a show in Egton Bridge, North Yorks; yet somehow

GIAN SNAKES – *Although we only mentioned giant snakes in passing (LWp13) we continue to take an interest in them. An extensive correspondence covering most of the known material on this subject, and many new references, appeared in the letter columns of* Science Digest *for about a year – I don't have the beginning date, but it ended with the May 1982 issue. The longest snake mentioned was a truly monstrous 131 foot, 5 ton anaconda from Brazil, but because the condition is for a living specimen of 30ft or more, the $50,000 prize, offered by the New York Zoological Society, still stands. Our illustration is of an incident in the Indian Sunderbands, when a sleeping lascar was resucued from the coils of a boa measuring 62 feet "and some inches" (about the length of the anaconda shot by Fawcett, that we illustrate in LW), from the* Museum of Animated Nature *1856-8 p111.*

not of the terrible proportions of its legendary ancestor.

WINGED CATS

We thought our chapter on winged cats was about as definitive as we could get, but two more references came to light, showing that it doesn't do to be overconfident.

★ Our first case was not what we expected, but of interest nevertheless. It is a reference in Curtis Fuller's regular 'I see by the papers' column in *Fate* (June 1967, p25) to a "flying cat" shot in the summer of 1966 at Alfred, near Ottawa, Ontario. That same night a curious cat was photographed at London, Ontario; but this one had two large fluffy tails which could be mistaken for wings. We'd like to trace that photo.

★ Bob Skinner has found two other references to winged cats, and one to a 'flying cat', and these will be given in an upcoming article on cat curiosities.

FALLS OF WHEAT

★ From J.J Daniell, *History of Warminster* (1879 p 232, 2nd edn) we read: "In the year 1696, or thereabouts, it was a report in Bristol, and thereabouts, that it rained wheat upon this town (Warminster), and six miles around – and many believed it. One Mr. Code, being curious to find out the truth of the odd phenomenon, procured several parcels of it; and upon diligent examination, of them with magnifying glasses, judged from the taste, figure, size and smell that they were seeds of Ivy berries, driven by a strong wind from the holes and chinks of houses, churches and other buildings, where starlings and other birds had laid or dropped them..." Ivy seeds they may well have been, but even this classic piece of explanationism was too much for the original reporter, who added: "...but if so, 'tis strange they should fall in so great quantities and in so many places." Strange indeed! I wonder how the date

Cont on p11

Fig. Rattan Grimalmiche worden bey Mayl. Johann Heinrich Jagern, in dem großbaltßischen Mühlestein under dem Steinrad, und demselben Taleßi zwischen zwey Steinen hervorgestelt.

d. 13ten July 1748.

RAT KINGS – *Since writing our summary of this subject we have discovered what must be the most excellent account so far, Martin Hart's book* Rats *(Alison & Busby, London, 1982; £8.95) in which a whole chapter is devoted to this knotty problem.* Rats – *a translation from German – is a splendid read, informative and amusing. The gaps in our knowledge of the rat are suprising but Hart, who frequently champions them against the cruelties and bad PR inflicted by men through the ages, finds some balance, with the laboratory rats of the Skinnerian behaviourists on the one hand, and the historical gleanings of the rat rampant on the other. The chapter on Rat Kings is the most definitive yet, and lists an amazing 57 incidents between 1564 and 1963.*

On the opposite page is a photograph and X-ray (from the book) of the most recent Rat King, found in 1963, in Rucphen, North Brabant, Holland. It consists of a modest seven black rats; the largest number on record is 28. Despite this recent evidence, how the tails become knotted remains a mystery. It is a real knot – not 'glued' as some suggest – but the needed histological examination was never carried out for fear of damaging so valuable a specimen.

In collecting information on Rat Kings, we were pleased when Bob Skinner passed on to us a Dutch veterinarian journal, belonging to his vet father, containing a fine old print of a King, which we print on this page, courtesy of the editors of Historia Medicinae Veterinariae – *the print was on HMV Vol 5 no 2 p46-7 (1980). The caption reads: "These rats were found at Johann Heinrich Jager's flour-grinding mill, at Gross Ballheiser...hidden under the cogwheels, when they fell out from between two stones on 13th July 1748." Later, Bob drew our attention to Hart's book, and a reference to the Gross-Ballhausen rat (I don't know which of the two place-name spellings is correct). Hart says (p70): "Although it would seem that a copper engraving of this king was made... the print is no longer extant." Naturally we are happy to prove this wrong, and tell Mr.Hart that the lost engraving now resides at the Danmarks Veterinaerbibliothek, in Copenhagen.*

(not given) of the fall squares with the season of ivy berries?

★ The excellent new magazine for earth mysteries of the Welsh Border, *Earthlines*, details two 'grain' falls in the Shrewsbury area: one from 1681(?) of barley-like grain which fell in great quantities; and the other, on 13 April 1597, at 4pm, 'wheat' fell in small quantities at Shrewsbury, Pontesbury and Ludlow.

Cont on p12

ANIMAL TELEPORTATION

Since our accounts of animal teleportation are in the main anecdotes of strange discoveries, or rather discoveries of appearances of animals in strange and opportune circumstances, we suspect quite an overlap with those stories of strange coincidences involving unexpected animals.

★ Just such a synchronicity happened at a banquet given in honour of Houdini by the Los Angeles Society of Magicians (12th April, but what year?) at which many celebrities did turns. A local magician named Robinson was going through the motions of turning a rolled cigarette paper into a living moth, but when the moth was finally produced it was quite lifeless. Suddenly "a living moth appeared from somewhere and circled about his head! It vanished as it came, and a believer might well have decided that it was the astral body of the dead insect..." These are Houdini's own words, from *Houdini on Magic*, edited by W.B. Gibson & M.N. Young (1952 p147-8). Houdini added: "Of course it was a coincidence, but a miraculous one. I was myself startled, and so was everyone else, the performer possibly most of all. I have never seen anything like it in my experience with the art of conjuring."

ANIMAL MARINERS

★ *Sun* 1 Aug 1983: A Labrador dog found feebly paddling towards France, about a mile out of Plymouth. The dog was rescued by a trawlerman who abandoned his place in the Sutton Harbour trawler race to grab it with a boat hook. Failure to trace owner.

THE SEA SERPENT

★ The following interesting item was gleaned from *Diving to Adventure* by Hans Haas (1952 p176f). Haas and crew was moored at Lac, near Bonaire, Curacao, off the Venezuela coast, sometime between the years 1939-45, when a Dr Diemont informed them of a recently beached head "of extraordinary size and mysterious origin" thought to be the remains of a sea serpent. The team set off and located it by its "pestilential stink". "Dr Diemont had not exaggerated; the head was actually very big and very strange. If we had not been absolutely certain this could only be the head of the sea serpent, we might perhaps have taken it for that of an unusually large sea cow." They set to work to strip flesh from the skull but when they succeeded in penetrating the tough hide, "such an abominable corruption poured out that we took to our heels. No matter if it remained undiscovered, we wanted nothing further to do with the head. We hurried back board and recuperated over a second, once more perfectly harmonious breakfast." But I find it incredible that a scientist like Haas, who was on a specimen hunting exhibition for the Vienna Natural History Museum at the time, was either unmotivated, unprepared or unable to take or preserve samples of such epoch-making evidence, or at least to film them, especially since he made a living from documentaries. And why the lack of details, like the date or a more exact description? It seems the stink affected his scientific sensibilities far more than it did his stomach! Does anyone know any more about this case?

ANIMAL LOYALTY & RESCUES

★ A school of porpoises protected Jeff Barry from hunting sharks for nearly 12 hours as he swam to shore using two floating cushions, after his boat capsized in Nassau Sound, off the tip of Florida. *Shropshire Star* 26 May; *Sun* 27 May 1983.

★ *New Standard* (London) 3 Nov 1980: A sheepdog guarded its dead master for 11 days in Spanish mountains. Rescuers found it wounded itself, presumably from defending the corpse, and when the body was taken away, the dog silently vanished into the wilderness

★ *S.Express* 24 April 1983: 3yr-old Oscar Simonet vanished during a picnic near Villacarlos, on Minorca. After 30hrs searchers led by the mayor gave up. But when he got home, the mayor's dog, an Irish setter, would not stop whining and scratching the door, and eventually it was let out and led the mayor to the picnic site. The dog quickly indicated a crevice, hidden under bushes, into which the boy had crawled and fallen three feet, hitting his head. The big puzzle is: how did the dog know someone was missing, and where to look, when he was locked up two miles away at the time of the accident?

★ *D.Star* 12 May 1983: Farmer Alan Elliott was cutting wood near his farm when a huge pine tree fell on him, breaking his back and pinning him down in a small but icy stream. Doctors believe he would have died of hypothermia if his sheepdog, Bracken, had not snuggled up to him for three hours, and then led the search party to him.

★ *News of the World* 31 July 1983: Caroline Osborne was attacked and hacked to death on a tow-path by the Grand Union Canal, in Leicester. Her Labrador dog ran off whimpering back home, but began scratching at a neighbour's door. The neighbour's dog ran off and stood guard over the woman's body, hidden in scrub, for 11 hours, until police discovered the body.

★ *News of the World* 8 May 1983: Nick the Labrador fell in love, or the canine equivalent of it, with a collie he met in a street. The collie's back leg was badly injured by a car, and the pair set up home in a hedge in Mill Hill, London. For two days Nick stood over the collie, and when the lady outside whose house the hedge was put some food out for them, he would take pieces to the collie before he ate any. Then the police arrived to take Nick to his worried owners, but he pined and escaped to join his friend. Taken back once more, he again escaped; but this time he howled and whined when he found the collie gone. It had been taken to a dog's home and put down. All involved were impressed by Nick's devotion to the injured dog.

★ *Sun, D.Telegraph* 14 May 1983: Percy the Chihuahua was given up for dead after he was knocked down by a car. His owner, Christine Harrison, and her father, wrapped him in a sack and buried him in the garden of their Barnsley, Yorks, home. They were quite shocked seven hours later when Mick, a Jack Russell belonging to Christine's mother, dug up the sack and dragged it to their house. They were even more surprised when they realized there was still life in Percy's body, and that Mick's actions had undoubtedly saved him. Oddly, the two dogs were not the best of friends.

★ After those current stories, here's another oldie, gleaned by Dwight Whalen from the *Suspension Bridge Journal* 7 Nov 1885. A lion tamer named Stewart died "of apoplexy" in a room near Paris, and beside him was found the body of a lion, which, it is supposed, died of hunger and grief, unable to leave the side of its master.

LONG RETURNS

★ *Western Morning News* 16 Feb 1983: 8yr-old Tabby the cat was given to an animal home by Ivan Lee, of Barnstaple, when Ivan could no longer afford to keep him. Twelve months later Tabby turned up...but why he took so long to travel just 12 miles, and where he went, remains a mystery.

★ *D.Mirror* 21 July 1983: a French family took their cat, Gringo, with them to their holiday cottage at St Tropez last year, but when they returned home the cat sulked and then vanished. Six months later he turned up at the St Tropez cottage, having travelled 350 miles.

★ *National Enquirer* 5 July 1983: Another French story... When the Ehmig family moved from a Paris suburb to Goudargues, a village about 400 miles away, their white cat, Blanchette, vanished after just three months of country life. Five months later a bedraggled Blanchette scratched at the door of the family's old apartment in Paris. Luckily a neighbour remembered the distinctive all-white cat and notified the family. The cat now stays with Mrs Ehmig's parents in Paris, where she was raised as a kitten.

★ Now here's a new wrinkle... A pregnant heifer was sold by Sidney Krafsow, of Seminole County, central Florida, to Read Hayes, who ranched cattle in the neighbouring Orange County. Over night the cow vanished and returned to Krafsow the following evening, having negotiated 35 miles across fences, rivers, and highways, *Houston Chronicle* ? March 1983.

CLEVER DOGS – *Re. Rolf, the smart dog of Mannheim (LWp109-111), Sven Rosen sent us this portrait of the canny canine from the Swedish magazine* Djurens Rätt *(1916, no 3/4), which said that Rolf was fond of girls with long hair, and hairy zoologists with long beards, or so he is alleged to have told Prof. Ziegler. [C: Sven Rosen/FPL.]*

AVIAN ABDUCTIONS

More stories, which bird experts would rather believe to be mere folklore...

★ *Suspension Bridge Journal*, Ontario 26 Sept 1885: The ten-year-old son of George Johnstone, of Euphemia, was pounced upon by a huge eagle, carried across a road and dropped by a fence. It was said to have been the biggest bald eagle ever seen in the area. If the same eagle was responsible for the next incident, just five weeks later, then young Johnstone had a lucky escape.

★ *Suspension Bridge Journal*, Ontario 31 Oct 1885: On the Thursday prior, the two-year-old child of Jean Rommilly, who farmed near Montreal, was borne off by a large bald eagle, and carried for about a mile, landing on top of a barn. Men with guns followed but before they could reach the child, the eagle had driven its beak into the boy's skull and partly devoured him...and then escaped.

★ *Niagara Falls Gazette*, Ontario 18 Aug 1924: An eagle with a wingspan of eight feet hoisted Fred Cunningham, aged 14 and weighing 97lbs, and carried him five feet before the boy's clothing gave way. Fearless Fred fought the feathered fiend for a while, on a golf course near Chatham, Ontario, and managed to force it against a wire fence, where a man killed it. Dwight Whalen tells us that Chatham is about 25 miles from Bothwell county, scene of the previous incident.

★ The story we quote from Martin's *Description of the Western Isles of Scotland* (1716) on LW p140, of the kidnapped baby called Neil, had, in fact, an ending most appropriate to our tack in that chapter; ie that survivors of avian abduction become singled out after the manner of shamans and folk heroes. Were we able to give the full quote, you would have learned that, "He is still living in that parish, and by reason of this accident is distinguished among his neighbours by the surname of Eagle." An additional, but secondary source for this story is *The Museum of Animated Nature* 1856-8 p255.

ANIMAL FUNERALS AND WAKES

★ *Sunday Express* 29 Aug 1982 – letter from Sally Anne Hardie, 1 Brewers Cottages, Mill End, Sandon, Herts: "On my way to work I noticed, sadly, that a hedgehog had been knocked down and its body lay at the edge of the land alongside the verge. At lunchtime, on my return home, I could see before reaching the spot that the hedgehog's body was still there. However, as I got nearer I noticed some activity beside it. I slowed down and was intrigued to see another hedgehog, of the same size, nudging the body up the verge which runs into a hedgerow. I moved on and left him/her labouring away. On my return, about three-quarters of an hour later, both body and labourer had gone with no more trace than a small tunnel into the hedge – leaving me to wonder: do hedgehogs bury their dead?"

★ *Sunday Express* 12 June 1983 – letter from Mrs KM Battle, Calle Riera, Alta No5, Bianes, Gerona, Spain: "One day last week, as I was driving home, I spotted two green and yellow lizards in the middle of our unmade country road. They are quite common around here, harmless and about a foot long. Usually they scuttle off when they see a car approaching. So I was quite surprised when they made no attempt to move. I slowed down and got out to find that one was dead and the other had refused to leave its side. It moved slowly away when I bent down to pull the dead one to the side of the road. I felt very sad as I drove on. When I returned about an hour later, I found not one but two lizards standing guard over their unfortuante friend. I wonder if these creatures are like swans and magpies, who remain faithful to their mates?"

★ *Suspension Bridge Journal* 17 Oct 1885: "John H. Osborn, of Belleville, NJ, tried breeding quail in an immense wire cage. The third day after the female had begun sitting she died on the nest. The cock was greatly distressed. He dragged the dead bird to a corner and buried it, leaving only the long feathers on one wing exposed. This done he returned to the nest and sat on the eggs and eventually succeeded in bringing out a brook of ten young quail." Cited from the *New York Sun*.

TALKING ELEPHANT

★ Just in case any of you thought the news-clipping on LW p108, of the Soviet talking elephant was a tall story, the case got an explosion of publicity lately. Batir, now 13yrs-old, was discovered talking at night by his keeper six years ago. On 13 July, Tass released a story that Soviet zoologists had confirmed this with taperecordings of about 20 phrases, like "Batir is good. Have you watered the elephant." Et cetera. Another curiosity of this story is that the skeptical reaction of Western curiosity of this story is that the skeptical reaction of Western zoo spokespersons (at its most benevolent) is in accord with the reductionist view of the Young Communist League paper, *Komsomolskaya Pravda*, which said the elephant had merely learned to repeat the admiring words of zoo visitors in order to cadge more food. Only one person referred to in our sources dissented, saying that he believed that the elephant, which had never mixed with others of its race, was not merely parroting but using speech purposively – and he was not Russian, but American! Widely reported AP bulletins of 13 & 14 July: *Globe* 2 Aug 1983.

CLEVER HORSE

★ Doc Shiels chided us for forgetting to mention "the most famous learned horse of them all, Marocco, owned by the magician, Banks in Elizabethan times – see *The Great Illusionists* by Edwin Dawes (David and Charles). These beasties are, of course, 'familiars' in an almost classical sense."

DOG MARTYRS

★ Doc wrote to us further: "The material on St Guinefort (grand lexilinking name for the Guiness-drinking Fortean!) is fascinating, and I'm sure it related to the Celtic 'worship' of great hounds, such as Bran etc, in the Ossianic tales. The Byzantine icon of a dog-headed saint is interesting too... Anubis and the Trickster. Nice Fortean touch, for me, in that the icon bears the Irish word 'POC' (you see...it's not all Greek to me!), which means a male goat, and is a very short step from 'Puck', 'Puca' etc...shapeshifters. I take it as a clue to something."

THE TROLL FROM THE SKY

★ On LWp78 we mention the reference by Bishop Rhyzelius to the strange creature that fell during a storm into the streets of Norkoping, in 1708. Our Swedish colleague, Sven Rosen, said he'd tried to research the case some years back, and sent us what little he found out. "The fall is described by Rhyzelius on pp98-9 of his *Brontologia*, and his source is Gustaf Otto Bilberg's *Almanackia* (1709), where it is given as follows, under the heading 'Prognostica Varia':"

"*Last year, 1708, on the night between August 8 and 9, a great thunderstorm with continuous lightning raged over the country and set many villages on fire, causing much damage. Then, according to testimonies by trustworthy men, it so happened that in Norrkoping, just as the lightning flashed and the thunder and rain seemed heaviest, a strange animal fell from the sky into a street not far away from the chemist's shop. It somewhat resembled a beaver, but its body was a little smaller than that of a full grown beaver, although its head was a bit larger, and its lower jaw a little longer than its upper jaw. It had rather small eyes, short hind legs and tail, and a rough brownish fur.'*"

"This is the original account. Bilberg, who was an astronomer and mathematician, also says that although he was present in the town when it happened, he did not himself see the animal fall. He also hints at a 'ridiculous' rumour that the 'thing' was a troll...a rumour which evidently spread among people who had not seen the animal themselves. Bilberg suggests the animal may have been brought to the place by a whirlwind; although he doesn't know what the animal was or where it came from.

"Rhyzelius also offers a natural explanation: 'A learned scholar who was staying in Norrkoping on this occasion, Herr Dr. Johan R., told me in a letter that a shammy maker the previous evening had poured out into the street a barrel of bad seal's lard, which he (Johan R.) supposed also may have contained a young seal; and when the seal was washed in the torrent, people believed it had come down with the rain.' This theory is also given by Magnus Gabriel Block, a devoted rationalist, in *Om Widunder* (1709), though he is uncertain whether it was a 'flayed or bald young seal'."

It seems to me that the discussion of seals rests entirely upon a supposition, by Johan R., that there *might* have been a flayed seal in the barrel. Both Johan R. and Block seem to have written their accounts at a much later date than Bilberg, who was there and interested enough to make inquiries. Certainly his description, when compared to that of Johan R's (who was also there) seems less dogmatic and more informative. I particularly find interesting the detail that the animal had a rough brown fur, hindlegs *and* a tail, and a protruding lower jaw — nothing like a seal, in other words. Can anyone throw any light on this mystery?

LIVING BLUNDERS

Finally, here are a few corrections to LW — there are others, but we are still checking them out or tracing original sources. The numbers, in order, refer to page, column and paragraph.

★ 15/caption — for 'Mawgawr' read 'Morgawr'.
★ 40/2/2, and 42/1/1 — for 'Bossburgh' read 'Bosburg'.
★ 42/1/1 — for 'John Beckjord' read 'Jon Beckjord', although he now tells us that his name is Erik Beckjord.
★ 45/caption — for 'meaced' read menaced'.
★ 57/caption — for '1836: read '1866'.
★ 57/1/2 — for 'Ingenstre' read 'Ingestre'.
★ 84/1/1 — for 'Lambhurst' read 'Lamberhurst'. This error is in our source, Fort's Books p915.
★ 108/2/3 — for 'And nor he could' read 'And nor could he.'
★ 115/2/2 — for 'peole' read 'people'.
★ 138/1/3 — for 'rarified' read 'rarefied'.
★ 145/1/2 — for 'yet it. ..' read 'Yet it..'
★ 147/caption — for 'Phoenician' read Assyrian'.
★ In the index, 'Westrum' should be 'p53' not 'p52'.

●

Credits: *Janet & Colin Bord, Peter Christie, Mike Dash, Lucius Farish, Alan Gardiner, Chris Hall, John Harney, Ursula Mitchell, Steve Moore, Ray Nelke, Scott Parker, Sven Rosen, Bob Skinner, Anthony Smith, UFO Newsclipping Service, Dwight Whalen, Ion Will.*

●

Bob Rickard

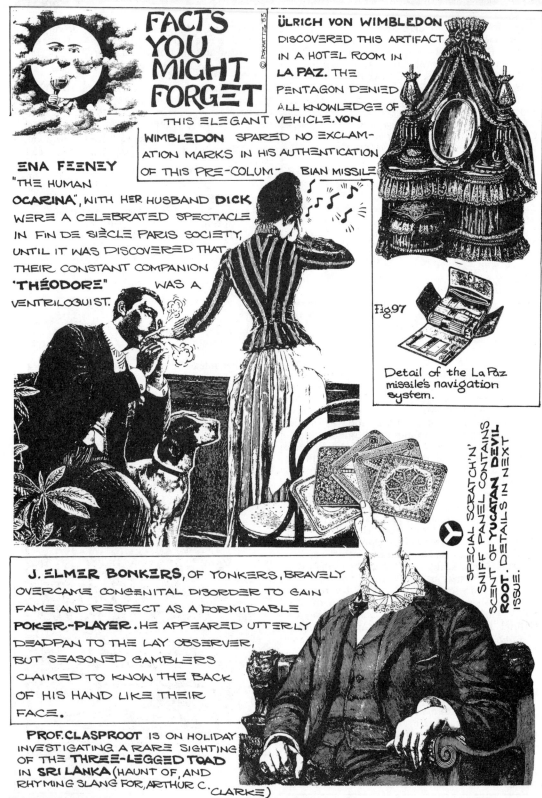

FACTS YOU MIGHT FORGET

© PICKETT'S '85

ÜLRICH VON WIMBLEDON DISCOVERED THIS ARTIFACT IN A HOTEL ROOM IN LA PAZ. THE PENTAGON DENIED ALL KNOWLEDGE OF THIS ELEGANT VEHICLE. VON WIMBLEDON SPARED NO EXCLAMATION MARKS IN HIS AUTHENTICATION OF THIS PRE-COLUMBIAN MISSILE.

ENA FEENEY "THE HUMAN OCARINA", WITH HER HUSBAND DICK WERE A CELEBRATED SPECTACLE IN FIN DE SIÈCLE PARIS SOCIETY, UNTIL IT WAS DISCOVERED THAT THEIR CONSTANT COMPANION "THÉODORE" WAS A VENTRILOQUIST.

Fig 97

Detail of the La Paz missile's navigation system.

SPECIAL SCRATCH'N' SNIFF PANEL CONTAINS SCENT OF YUCATAN DEVIL ROOT. DETAILS IN NEXT ISSUE.

J. ELMER BONKERS, OF YONKERS, BRAVELY OVERCAME CONGENITAL DISORDER TO GAIN FAME AND RESPECT AS A FORMIDABLE POKER-PLAYER. HE APPEARED UTTERLY DEADPAN TO THE LAY OBSERVER, BUT SEASONED GAMBLERS CLAIMED TO KNOW THE BACK OF HIS HAND LIKE THEIR FACE.

PROF. CLASPROOT IS ON HOLIDAY INVESTIGATING A RARE SIGHTING OF THE THREE-LEGGED TOAD IN SRI LANKA (HAUNT OF, AND RHYMING SLANG FOR, ARTHUR C. CLARKE)

Embeddings

We've written some disgusting columns in our time, but this one will really bring a lump to your throat. If you're wondering about the relevance of the heading illo: we like to read it as 'things found inside other things'.

HARD TO SWALLOW...

We've all felt that 'butterflies in my tummy' sensation, and felt the odd 'frog in the throat' but God preserve us from the following revolting fate...

Yeter Yildirim, a 15yr-old Turkish girl, had suffered mysterious stomach pains for five years. In that time she changed from being a happy-go-lucky farmgirl into a moody, withdrawn outcast. Her pains and vivid headaches alienated her friends and caused the family to be shunned by suspicious villagers after she failed to respond to local folk-healers and their magic charms. So Yeter's family moved 80 miles to Ankara where they eventually took her to a hospital. I can picture the scene: the doctors come to her parents clutching the x-rays and say matter-of-factly: "Don't worry, we can easily remove the snakes." "Snakes? What snakes?" shout her parents, staring alternately at the doctor and the girl in horror. Yes, there were three of them − water snakes, it is claimed − "slightly thicker than string and nearly a foot long." The doctors can only surmise that the girl must have swallowed them as eggs while drinking from a stream when she was ten years old, since when they grew inside her.

D.Star 28 June 1979.

Well, that was that, we thought. Over and done with. But last year came a similar story, but harder to swallow somehow. The unfortunate this time was a Syrian woman, Khadija el Reefi, aged 25, of Aleppo. After complaining of severe stomach pains the girl was taken to a hospital where they discovered, to everyone's astonishment, that a six-foot snake was lodged in her intestines. Our source, citing the Syrian daily *Al Baath*, said that the snake "cheeped" like a chicken when it was hungry, and the noise was loud enough for Khadija and people standing near her to hear. Surgery in the Syrian hospital failed the remove the reptile and so the girl was sent to Spain where a second operation similarly failed, despite, it says, using anaesthetic on the snake. We've not been able to discover how the story turned out, and we hardly dare think about it. UPI/*D.Telegraph* 12 March 1982.

THE INDIGESTIBLE FACTS

Out of idle curiosity I wondered what my favourite medical reference, Gould and Pyle's *Anomalies & Curiosities of Medicine* (1896), had to say about animals surviving in the human gut, and was dismayed to find a wealth of disgusting information. They refer to authorities who record the successful passage through the gut of snails, snakes, lizards and even (ugh!) a live spider. More common were the stories of small, usually water dwelling animals vomited up some time after they were ingested in polluted water. In at least two cases, one fatal, snakes had slithered into the throat of a heavy sleeper. There are numerous cases of caterpillars being brought up after swallowing, and more improbably, one each of a mouse and a "young chicken".

Our indefatigable colleague Bob Skinner also provided more references on this subject, again too many to mention fully. In a catalogue of tales of living animals in the human stomach, few of which duplicate those of Gould and Pyle, R.Kirby, compiler of the notorious *Wonderful and Eccentric Museum* (1802-1820) mentions three instances involving snakes, which I'll quote:

"John Christian Frommann, doctor of medicine, and professor of philosophy at the college of Coburg, in Franconia, mentions a poor widow woman, aged 26 years, who lived out of the town in an unhealthy house, frequented by a great quantity of reptiles. This woman being accustomed to sleeping with her mouth open, a snake half a yard long, and of proportion-ate thickness, crept into her stomach. She was attacked with different complaints, which the author describes at length; and by means of various medicines which he administered, succeeded in making her bring it up, and ridding her of such a disagreeable inmate."

"Taberna Montanus mentions the medicine he employed to make a man cast up a salamander, and to bring from a women three frogs she had swallowed. Tragus likewise details those which he used to cause a child to throw up a snake that had introduced itself into his stomach…"

"In the *Ephemerides of the Curious* for the year 1675, it is related that a shoemaker, having for ten years been afflicted with violent pains in the abdomen, without finding any relief from medicines…stabbed himself in a moment of despair, below the stomach, and died of the wound. Preparations were made for the funeral…when a person wishing to examine the wound, removed the (coffin) lid, and found beside the body a serpent of the length of a man's arm, and as thick as two fingers. It had crept out of the wound, and lived for days afterwards." (Vol.3, p360.)

More typical of the multiple cases is the following, attended by the great Swedish doctor, Bertholin, of a 30yr-old woman who drank from a stagnant pond. "At the end of a few months she experienced singular movements in her stomach, as if something were crawling up and down; and alarmed by the sensation consulted a medical man… Shortly after (her medication) she vomited three toads and two young lizards, after which she became more at ease." But the following spring the stomach pains returned and she was caused to vomit up the irritants: "three female frogs, followed the next day by their numerous progeny." The following January she brought up five more living frogs, and over the next seven years ejected as many as eighty living frogs. It was during this period that Bertholin said he had listened to them croaking in her stomach. Well, whether creatures can survive in the human stomach, in a curious reversal of the Jonah story, is one thing; but can we really swallow the suggestion that they can live and maybe even breed in there for seven years? Plainly the old authorities believed they could, and there is at least one other case of regular vomitings of frogs and

toads, but over a period of six years. Though some sort of prize for variety should go to Marianne Fisher, 24, who was under the care of a Dr Heini, in the hospital at Friburgh, Germany, for the twelve months of 1811, during which time she discharged 1 frog, 3 small crayfishes, 52 leeches and 8 worms, caused, so Heini believed, by drinking marsh water the previous August. (Cited by Kriby; Vol.5, p50.)

A number of the instances cited by some authorities were recorded during witchcraft trials. Though, typically, the bewitched party would vomit forth all manner of small domestic items (nails, buttons, pins, etc), occasionally small insects were discovered too. In one 17th century case, cited in Lynn Thorndyke's huge *History of Magic & Experimental Science* (1923-1958), a spell-struck boy vomited frogs, toads, a lizard and a snake. (Vol.8, p531.)

Naturally, when one enters the fantastic genre of witchcraft stories, one can't help speculating about the tangible air of hysteria and compulsion displayed by the prodigious vomiters, and there is always the possibility that the person compulsively ate these disgusting meals, perhaps even without knowing it, in some kind of hysterical fugue. Some evidence for this comes from another of Kirby's cases (3, p360.) in which an 18yr-old girl became the talk of Paris in 1682. She frequently fell into violent convulsions followed by a period of lethergy lasting from 6–20 hours during which she lost all feeling, such that prodding with pins caused her no pain. After these fits she would cough up spiders, caterpillers, snails and other insects. Under medical interrogation she admitted that for eight months she had been swallowing these creatures by "an extraordinary inclination". For some time, she added, she even felt a longing to gulp down toads and frogs but couldn't

find any. The girl was convinced that they were able to nourish themselves inside her, and came out fatter or larger than when they went in. Almost as interesting is the fact that this case is devoid of the taint of witchcraft.

Interestingly, the story of Khadija's snake (above) drew the following reflection from one of our correspondents, Jean-Louis Brodu: "Have you heard of Aperception Test 9? I don't know who created it but it's been used in France to test trainee nurses for hidden sadistic impulses. They are given nine topics – a shelter, an animal, fire, a sword, a person, water, a fall or something falling, a cycle or something cyclical, and a devouring monster – and are asked to make a drawing using all nine elements, describe what's happening, and identify themselves in the drawing. I gave this test, last year (1981), to children between 11 and 15 in an English school where I was a French assistant. Some of the children drew a person with a snake turning forever in the stomach. That's what amazes me about the snake-in-the-stomach story – it is a common nightmare, an archetypal motif."

Many more cases could be cited, of course – including those of animals swallowed by other animals – but we have to stop somewhere. (Was that a shout of "Please!"?) And in all these instances I didn't find one case of regurgitated butterflies!

Credits: *Jean-Louis Brodu, Bob Skinner, Dwight Whalen.*
●
Bob Rickard

FROZEN FROG

A half-inch, three-legged frog, harvested with a pea plant, ended up in a packet of frozen peas, magistrates at Gosport, Hants. were told yesterday. Ross Foods were fined £150 for selling below standard goods.

Daily Telegraph 16 Sept 1983.

As if ball lightning (BL) wasn't weird enough, two instances of BLs emitting rays of light have come to our notice recently, and one of a chain or bead lightning strike. Corliss' definitive source on the subject (see 'Reviews' p56 last issue) gives other examples of both phenomena.

BEAD LIGHTNING

The first incident involved our friend Paul Devereux, editor of *The Ley Hunter*, who tells us that on Friday 22 April, this year, he was caught out in one of this spring's many freak hail and electrical storms. "The centre of the storm was extremely local and at approximately 2.45pm there was a great deal of fierce thunder and lightning. My office overlooks the Cain Valley near Llanfyllin, Powys, and I took the camera in case I should see any examples of ball lightning, as I know from the reaction to a photograph of purported ball lightning in my *Earth Lights* that genuine pictures of such phenomena are rare."

"While scanning the valley, which was regularly lit with lightning, I suddenly saw a bolt of forked lightning strike the corner of a field a bare quarter of a mile away. The bolt reached up out of my sight beyond the top of the window frame. It was so vivid and clear that it almost looked like a rigid structure fixed in the field, and maintained its coherence for about a second. Then it 'dissolved' rather than simply extinguished, and in its place was a series of balls of light, perhaps up to a dozen, each a foot or so in diameter, some slightly oval in shape, spaced out more or less vertically along the ragged discharge path of the lightning bolt.

These then went out. The colour of the light balls was the same as that of the lightning — a searing white."

"Shortly after this there was a fall of hail: the size of the hailstones was not exceptional but the rate of their fall was. Within a few minutes the whole valley was covered in ice up to two inches deep, and more in places. The scene looked like an instant snow-scape — but it wasn't snow, it was ice."

"I'm ashamed to admit I couldn't get the camera to my eye in time to photograph the lightning balls, the event being so swift and, to be frank, I was rooted to the spot. But having the camera to hand, I realize now why ball lightning pictures are so hard come by."

Although Paul talks in terms of "balls of light" he has in fact perfectly described so-called bead lightning, in which the bolt dissolves into 'beads', whose shape can vary, which linger for a while in the path taken by the parent bolt. There is possibly a connection between bead lightning and

The view from Paul Devereux's office showing the sudden hail cover, (not snow) and the position (marked) of the lightning strike. [Copyright: Paul Devereux.]

ball lightning, up to date no one had identified or suggested the mechanism.

RAYED BALL LIGHTNING

Our first BL incident occurred in North London, and was investigated for us by our columnist Mike Crowley. During a "freak rain storm" on 16th May, over South Harrow – see *Harrow Observer* 20 May 1983 – a "thunderbolt" struck and set fire to a bungalow in South Hill Avenue. After reading that Robert Tosler, aged ten, was crossing a railway bridge a few yards from the bungalow "when a bolt flashed past him," Mike decided to speak to him. The boy's mother told Mike that she had also seen what happened. She had looked out of her front room window because she was worried about her son being caught in the sudden downpour on his way home from school. As she sighted him on the bridge she noticed a "blue-grey spherical object" fly past him at great speed. The object travelled horizontally until it collided with the bungalow opposite her house. Upon impact the object sent out multi-coloured flashes of light, ("blue, green, red...oh, lots of colours"), across the road. All Robert Tosler could add was that the object had been about the size of a beachball, slightly ellipsoidal, ("rugby-ball shape"), and about the height of a double-decker bus off the ground. It was too bright for him to make out any colour, and he noticed none of the coloured rays or flashes that his mother had seen. Mike also spoke to Mr Tosler, who, although not witnessing the phenomenon in question, added by way of interest that the family had only learned of ball lightning from a recent TV programme about Nikola Tesla. When Mike commented on the similarity of the surnames (Tesla/Tosler), Mr Tosler said he did not know the origin of the name, and, as far as he knew his was the only one in England. To add to the

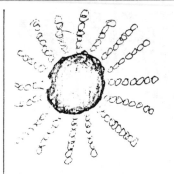

The BL object seen by Mrs Revell in 1924.

air of curiosity about the event, we note that just three days earlier another house in the same road caught fire, the origin of which the firemen could not determine.

The other, even more weird, BL datum, is much older, but came to light when Mike Rowe asked for cases in the *West Lancs. Evening Gazette*, and was written up in the April 1983 issue of the *Journal of*

Meteorology. The witness is a Mrs P.Revell, of Blackpool, who wrote two letters to Mike. "It happened in the afternoon (sometime) in 1924. There came a large ball of fire – or so it looked – but the thing was it had chains all the way round. It lasted about five minutes, then all the chains clashed together with a terrific bang; then we had a thunderstorm which lasted quite a long time." In the second letter she drew the object as a red ball with 16 rays composed of links like chains (see drawing), and continued: "You asked the size. From the ground it looked about four to five yards across, which would be larger than that in the sky. The chains opened from the top to the bottom..."

Credits: *Mike Crowley, Paul Devereux, Mike Rowe.*

●

Bob Rickard

One or two recent 'strange birth' cases sent us rummaging through our vast and gruesome files in search of more of the same. Relax, folks. Most of the kids were okay. But the mothers...

LIFE AFTER DEATH

Instant reincarnation, suggests one of our clipsters...

☐ **Stockholm, Sweden**, few details. An unnamed mother, dead of an unnamed disease. But doctors at the Children's Hospital, Huidsvall, kept the woman on a respirator for several days before delivering her baby by Caesarian section. The baby was several weeks premature, but apparently normal. The mother was

officially 'brain-dead' at the time of delivery. *Evening Standard* 14 Nov 79.

☐ **Naples, Italy:** Annunziata Morra, 18, dead of unspecified causes. Three hours after death she was put in a refrigerated cell; two hours after that an aunt lifted the covering sheet on the coffin, put a hand on the dead girl's stomach, and announced: "The baby's kicking!" A surgeon delivered a baby-girl by Caesarian section.

But although she breathed normally, she died a few hours later under intensive care. *D. Telegraph* 4 Dec 80.

☐ **Naples, again:** Mrs Pasqualina Chiacchio was in labour and being driven to a maternity clinic, with her husband, grand-mother and a family friend, when all four of them were killed in a high-speed crash. A baby girl was removed from the mother by surgeons, and apparently survived. *Guardian* (AP) + *Sun* 2 June 82.

☐ **Buffalo, New York:** an un-named woman, aged 24, died of an epileptic fit in June 82. She was 26 weeks pregnant at the time, and doctors at the Buffalo Children's Hospital decided to keep her vital func-tions going artificially, despite the fact that the woman was brain-dead. Over a week later, when they considered the baby had a chance of survival, they performed a Caesarian section. A healthy girl, who seems to have survived. Claimed to be the first operation of its kind, but see our first case. *D.Mail* 4 Sep 82, *Lab News* 1 Oct 82.

☐ **Southampton, Hampshire:** Mrs Susan Hickmott, 20, dead of a stroke and brain haemor-rhage. She was 6 months pregnant at the time and, after discussions with her husband Philip, 23, doctors kept her on a life-support machine for two days so that they could deliver her baby son, Michael Terry. Caesarian again. He was 13 weeks premature, and weighed a mere 2lbs 5oz. Doctors seemed to think there was a strong chance of the boy being handicapped, and offered no guarantees of survival. Sadly young Michael died of heart and brain failure just 22 days later. *Sun* 21 Jan + 9 Feb 83, *D. Telegraph* 22 Jan 83.

☐ **San Francisco, California:** an unnamed woman died of (either) a heart attack or massive brain damage when she was 22 weeks pregnant. She was kept alive artificially by doctors at SF's Moffitt hospital for a further nine weeks, despite diabetes, various infections and other complaints. The baby, a boy, was delivered by Caesarian section when it became clear he had stopped growing, and weighed in at 3lb 2oz. *Sun* 31 Mar, *D.Star* 2 Apr 83.

☐ **Stafford, Conn:** Diane Stager, 21 and 6 months pregnant, died an extremely rare death from herpes type 1 (that's the harmless type which causes cold sores; type 2 is sexually transmitted). She died of herpes simplex encephalitis, the disease inflaming her brain, and apparently only 8 other cases like it are in the medical records. Doctors delivered her son (by Caesarian) six days before she died, and when last we heard the baby was "strug-gling for survival". *Weekly World News* 3 May 83.

☐ **Dewsbury, Yorks:** Beverely Brooke, 19 and 8 months pregnant, collapsed and was rushed to hospital in Leeds with a fatal brain tumour. Doctors kept her on a life-support machine (for how long isn't clear) until her son could be delivered by Caesarian. *News of the World* 8 May 83.

☐ **America:** We end this section with a happier variant, even if the details are virtually non-existent. Sometime in 1980, somewhere in America. Some woman, with some name, died of something, aged something-or-other. Her baby, of some sex or the other, was delivered (by Caesarian) by some doctors, thirty minutes after her heart stopped beating. Sometime soon afterwards, the mother's heart started beating again, and apparently both mother and baby survived. A couple of years later, someone decided to report it to the press. Some concise reporting in the *Daily Star* 2 Sept 82, yes?

NOT DEAD BUT SLEEPING
☐ **Rochester, Minnesota:** a border-line case, Mary Stevens, 28, keeled over while on the phone, on 1 Nov 81. Confusing details: her heart stopped, there's no brain activity, she's on a respirator to keep her bodily functions normal, "to ensure the baby's well-being". But she's also said to be able to breathe without the respirator, and she's described as being in a coma. Anyway, after five months of this, her son, Adam, was delivered by Caesarian, weighing 5lb. And what happened after that, we have no idea. *Beaumont Enterprise & Journal* (Texas) (AP), 9 Jan 82.

☐ **Tel Aviv, Israel:** pregnant Mrs Ayala Gur, 34, was involved in a road accident along with her family. Her hus-band and two children were only slightly injured, but Mrs Gur seriously fractured her skull and arrived at the hospital (either at Kfar Saba, or Ramana; reports vary; both are near Tel Aviv) with a hole in her head. She wasn't expected to survive either that or the pneumonia she caught after-wards, but she did, though she remained in a coma. With medical assistance she continued to live, and after four months of unconscious-ness, doctors decided to deliver the baby (by Caesarian), using only local anaesthetics. The boy, born in the 35th week of pregnancy, weighed 5lb 3oz. One of the nurses swears that the mother smiled at the moment of delivery, but did not reawaken. Presumably the boy survived. Presumably the mother is still in a coma? *Guardian*, etc (UPI & AP des-patches) 9 Sep 82, *Sunday People* 14 Sep 82, *Midnight Globe* 14 Oct 82.

☐ **Tampa, Florida:** another variation. The mind awake, the body asleep. Mrs Nelda Helmbrecht, 23, had a bullet pierce her spine in a gun-clean-ing accident. She was 2 months pregnant at the time, and was paralysed from the neck down-wards. Doctors suggested an abortion, but she and her husband Wayne, 24, decided to persist. Unable to feel the labour contractions set in, she guessed she was due when she started to have headaches; was taken to hospital; and was delivered by Caesarian an hour later. Wayne Helmbrecht II weighed 5lb 14oz, and was apparently normal. We're glad to report that Mrs Helmbrecht can now lift her right arm and move her fingers; and she also claims to have felt all the kicking during the pregnancy. *Chicago Sun-Times* (AP) 13 June 82.

NOT DEAD, NOT SLEEPING, BUT...

But these ladies might just as well have been in a coma, by the sounds of things. At least, they were totally unconscious of the fact that they were pregnant, until...Oops!

☐ **Belle Glade, Florida:** 6ft 1in Mary West, 16, put on a little weight and didn't play as well as usual for her school basketball team. She was given a medical check-up which resulted in a clean bill of health, and included a negative result to a pregnancy test. Four weeks later she played in an important championship match. 31 hours after that, she gave birth to a 6lb 2oz baby girl, Cassandra. She gave birth at home, with only her 11 year old sister present, and though she felt pains before the birth, thought they were just 'ordinary cramps'. *Nigeria Falls Review* etc (AP) 10 March 80.

☐ **Fargo, Minnesota:** Bonnie Thompson, 24, who already had one son and ought to have known what it felt like, had another one by surprise fourteen months later, claiming that there had been no normal signs of pregnancy. She thought the baby's movements were just feelings caused by back trouble, it seems, and gave birth at 3:50 in the morning after lying awake all night. *The Forum* (Fargo-Moorhead) 4 Dec 80.

☐ **Battersea, London:** Margaret Porter, 35, thought too much Christmas food had given her stomach-ache. It got worse, so she went hospital, was put in an observation ward, and gave birth to a boy. Another total surprise, as she and her husband had been trying to have a baby for 14 years, and had given up hope. *D. Mirror* 6

Jan 81.

☐ **Portsmouth, Hants:** Evelyn Wallis, 39, thought her stomach pains were caused by a 'tummy-bug', and then gave birth to a son. She already had two daughters, 18 and 5, and her husband Reg, 62, said they had "given up hope of a son".

☐ **Trowbridge, Wilts:** tough bakery worker Mariette Hill, 21, recent completer of a self-defence course, was toting 70lb bags of flour into a lorry when she got a temperature. She thought she had flu and went home. Three days later she gave birth to a 5lb 4oz boy. Yet another surprise. *Sunday People* 25 Jan 81.

☐ **Chicago, Illinois:** Mrs Lucas 50, thought she was past menopause, and when she developed stomach pains and went to her doctor in spring 1980, he diagnosed a possible hernia. She was only discovered to be pregnant 11 days before the birth of her son on 22 December; 33 years after her first child. She has 3 grown sons, and her husband, Arthur, is 57, and a diabetic with a heart condition. Not surprisingly, Mrs Lucas "worries

about the future". Seems the little tykes have a habit of turning up by surprise after you've given up wanting them... *Omaha World Herald* (AP) 18 April 81.

☐ **Genoa, Italy:** Doctors operating on an unnamed pregant woman for an apparent tumour found her healthy baby had developed outside her womb, among the intenstines. The baby boy was delivered by Caesarian (again; maybe we should have called this section "Strange Caesarians!") and is apparently unaffected. *Guardian* 6 Apr 83.

☐ **Conisborough, Yorks:** 27 year old Kath Gwatkin spent months trying to shake off extra weight at slimming classes. Then she went into the bathroom complaining of stomach-ache, and gave birth to a baby boy. Seems she had no idea...*Sun* 26 May 83.

Credits: *B M Barter, Alan Cleaver, Peter Christie, Mike Dash, Tuuri Heporauta, Scott Parker, Nigel Pennick, Sam, Joe Swatek, Andy Townsend, Dwight Whalen, Howard Wolinsky.*

●

Steve Moore

Being a round-up of some recent religious and cultish curiosities.

RUSSIA

☐ From the odd news items which drift out of the Soviet block we gather that popular belief in mystics, healers, and virtually any of the subjects which we in the West call 'fringe', 'psychic' or alternative, is thriving as never before. But from the *Guardian* (13 April 1983) we learn that yoga and vegetarianism, at least, are now criminal abominations to the Communists. It seems that a

female "mystic", Mada Kolaya, who taught these subjects from her Moscow flat, has been jailed for slandering the State, calling on her students to "liberate their minds from the constraints of Soviet society. She also lectured on "the mystical powers of the earth and the universe", whatever they are? Probably the subversive activity of ley hunting!

☐ According to the paper

Selskaya Zhin, cited in the *Telegraph* (7 March 1983), an unusual chain-letter has a grip on some rural districts of Russia. Its message is that God has appeared to a 12-yr old boy with a prophecy about the Second Coming and the end of the world. Recipients are asked to make nine copies and send them to friends, with the usual dire threats (this time of "grief and suffering for ever after") to anyone who breaks the chain. The reward is salvation.

USA

☐ A weird new cult has come to light in New Mexico. According to shocked police, called in by social workers, the chief ritual involved spraying paint onto babies and young children. Members got high by sniffing the paint as the kids were passed around. I wouldn't be surprised to read, tomorrow, about a sock-eating society in Surinam! Anyway, the police rescued two children, aged eight months and 13 months. *Sun* 11 Feb 1983.

☐ How about a cult which has shunned food? That's right — there is one in California, called the Breatharian Institute. You'd be right about it not having many members too, but for a different reason. It seems that most of the leadership resigned following an outrage by Wiley Brooks, the 47-yr old leader who claims not to have eaten in 19 years, and who teaches them how to live on fresh air. He was caught sneaking into a hotel and ordering a chicken pie. *D.Mirror* 7 March 1983.

PHILIPPINES

☐ And at Easter this year, there was once more the bizarre sight of mass crucifixions. The *Sun* (2 April 1983) puts the figure at nine... but the *Guardian* (2 April 1983), mentions only three. In Manila, two men lasted five minutes after nails were driven through their hands; and in Bulacan province a crowd of 10,000 gathered to watch

24yr-old Luciana Reyes, a girl with seven previous crucifixions, nailed to a cross for a few seconds. What a way to spend Easter!

PAKISTAN

☐ On 24the Feb this year, police near Karachi, Pakistan, were called to a beach where they found 17 bedraggled people, survivors, it seemed, of a shipwreck. Their leader told an incredible story. They began as a band of 38, comprising two Shi'ite families, aged between six and 60, who had sold all their possessions in the town of Chakwal, in the Punjab, and they set out for the coast in two lorries. On the way they stopped to buy some large tin boxes, normally used for the storage of winter clothes, and in which they intended to sail to Iraq. A few members of the group changed their minds at the last minute, and watched in helpless horror as their relatives in their puny vessels were dashed against the rock of Hawkes Bay, about

25kms west of Karachi. Eight are still missing.

The origin of the trek is stranger still. The group were following a mission given by Allah to one of their number, a 16yr-old girl (some papers say she was 18) called Nasim Fatima, who was among the 13 dead. The girl had a reputation as a 'saint', having had dreams and visions since whe was two years old. The girl's father, Anwar Husain Shah, said she had dreamed about a "miraculous" pilgrimage to the town of Karbala, a Shi'a holy place in Iraq, in which Allah would cause them to float safely up the stormy waters of the Persian Gulf in their fragile boxes. *Guardian, Sun* 25 Feb; *Guardian*, UNI/ *Times of India* 26 Feb 1983.

Credits: *Claudia Boulton, Jean-Louis Brodu, Peter Christie, Peter Hope Evans, Sven Rosen, Anthony Smith, Ion Will.*

•

Bob Rickard

UNIDENTIFIEDS

We've fallen far behind with our coverage of monstrous doings. **Mike Dash** catches up with Chessie on USA's east coast.

BATTY

Chesapeake Bay, a jagged 150 mile long incision in the coasts of Maryland and Virginia, has been the reputed home of 'Chessie' since at least the 1930s. Mrs JE Hennaman of Richmond, Va., alleges she saw the local sea-serpent one evening in March 1980. While on her way to a restaurant she noticed an object in the Appotmattox river which she at first took to be a canoe. As it came down river towards her, she saw that it had a

turtle-like head, erect neck and two humps. The visible portion was at least 6ft. long and she watched it for five minutes before attempting to draw the attention of the clientele of the Harbor Light restaurant to the object. Unfortunately only a waitress, Betty Lipsey, took any notice. When asked later to substantiate Mrs Hennamann's account, she said, "I didn't have my glasses on and I'm as blind as a bat. I didn't see its head. I couldn't exactly tell what it was." *Times-Dispatch* (Richmond, VA) 27+30 Nov 1980.

APPARENTLY AN ANACONDA

On June 14 of the same year, a 59 year old farmer named Goodwin Muse watched a 10-14ft. long snakelike creature in the Potomac river. The animal was dark in colour, had a head no bigger than his hand, and no visible fins. Muse watched it with his wife and four friends. "I'd say it must have been as big around as a quart jar (5")", he said, The object was within 50 yards of them and they studied it through binoculars for 15 minutes.

Just over a week later, on June 22nd, a finance company manager and five others saw Chessie 15 miles downstream. GF Green III and his family were water-skiing when they noticed what they believed to be the monster about a quarter of a mile away. Green described it as about 25ft. long and 5-6" in diameter. It had three or four humps, which they felt might have been un-dulating, and a head which emerged occasionally. In some accounts Green is quoted as reporting the presence of a second, smaller creature of similar appearance some way from the first. They closed to within 15m. of the larger object, but it sank whenever they approached.

These and some other Chesapeake Bay reports seem to refer to remarkably thin animals. One explanation frequently advanced in the press was that the witnesses were meeting the third gener-ation of a clan of anacondas brought to the bay in the hulls of sailing ships half a century ago. These supposedly escaped when the vessels were left to rot in tributaries." *Times-Dispatch* (Richmond, VA) 20 June; UPI/*Houston Chronicle* (TX) + *Star* Washington DC) 21 June; *Star* (Indianapolis, IN) 23 June; AP/*Argus Leader* (Sioux Falls, SD) + UPI/

Middlesex News (Framingham, MA) 26 June; *D.Mail* 26 Nov 1980.

SEAL OF APPROVAL

A few months later three more sightings occurred in the space of one weekend. On September 13 1980 Coleman and Trudy Guthrie saw a 6-8ft object in Eastern Bay at 4.50pm. It was swimming at about the same speed as their boat — 4 knots — and was only 25ft away when first seen. The Guthries carefully checked for reports of missing persons, supposing they might have seen a corpse, before deciding to come forward. They described the object as having "skin like thin rubber, slick, shiny, perhaps even slimy." It was about 3ft. wide; no fins or flippers were visible andthe object itself was in sight for only a second or two before diving. The Guthries described its colour as beige with olive-drab shading, and this led WP Jenson, the director of tidal fisheries, to suppose that they could have encountered a seal. He had advanced the same theory in mid-August to account for a similar report by another couple, Charles and Susan Kepner. Mr Kepner himself felt that this explanation was probably correct in his case.

On the same day as the Guthrie sighting a crab fisher-man, Ray Ratajczak, felt something brush against his anchor as he hauled it in; he was in 40ft. of water at the time. There was a tremendous boil of water at the surface; for some unstated reason the fisherman felt that he had en-countered something more than 10ft. in diameter. And on either the 13th or 14th, Steve McKerrow — the boating correspondent for the Baltimore *Evening Sun* — watched an unidentified wake near the mouth of Middle river. *Bay Times* (Stevensville, MD) 17+24 Sept; *Evening Sun* (Baltimore, MD) 11 Oct 1980; *Journal* (Milwaukee, WI) 3 Jan 1981.

THE FREW TAPE

We first heard of Bob Frew, a computer salesman newly cast as a video pioneer, in July 1982 when news of his videotape, allegedly showing a 30-40ft sea serpent in the bay, reached the media. The tape was shot at about 7pm on May 31, 1982, but the headlines took a long time to catch up with Frew, who was unable to interest anyone in his film until the onset of the "silly season".

The four minutes long home movie shows an elongated snakelike animal which appeared off Love Point, Maryland, on Memorial Day. Frew, his wife, daughter and several dinner guests at first thought it was a log; but upon noticing that it was moving against the current the salesman grabbed his video equipment. The object, black or dark brown in colour, dived and resurfaced several times, showing more of itself on each occasion. It was about 10" in diameter and swam to within 200ft. of the shore, in water only 5ft deep. A group of children, further out in the bay, did not see it as it dived and apparently swam beneath them.

Frew would not attempt to identify the creature. "Our conclusions are: number one it's big; and number two it sure as hell doesn't belong here," he told the AP news agency. In an interview with CBS transmitted on BBC Radio 4's *P.M.* news programme on July 13th he elaborated, "We could definitely discern humps, several feet apart, a rounded head shaped something like a football, and no scales or visible means of swimming — it didn't have feet or anything we could see, and it looked like it was squirming through the water like a snake would." Elsewhere he added that the head seemed angular but with a blunted snout, and that the object appeared to undulate vertically rather than horizontally as snakes do.

Emory Kristof, an under-water photographer for the

National Geographic Magazine, felt the tape was a fake. "It looks like four kids swimming inside a plastic bag," he said, "It's so jerky and amateurish — you can't tell very much from it." Dr George Zug, Director of vertebrate zoology at the Smithsonian Museum, secured a copy of the tape for study. He commented "The usual explanations of a partially submerged log, a string of birds or marine mammals, or optical illusions, seem inappropriate for the dark, elongated animate object." Study of the film seemed to confirm that the creature undulated vertically, but Zug and his colleagues concluded that there was not enough visible evidence on the tape for a positive identification.

The Smithsonian also studied a series of pictures taken in May 1981 near the Choptank river on the lower Easter Shore. The photographer, Kathryn Pennington, had kept them secret until hearing of the Frew videotape. Robert Lazzara of the Enigma Project, a Baltimore-based investigation group which first gained possession of the Frew tape, said that the earlier pictures appeared to show "a marine mammal, perhaps an otter or a large muskrat." However the importance of Frew's home movie, perhaps the first film ever taken of a 'sea serpent', remains difficult to underestimate, even though the object is disappointingly indistinct considering the very short range. *Washington Post* 12+16 July; *Times* (Washington, DC) 13 July; *News World* (New York, NY) 17 July; AP/ *Houston Chronicle* (TX) 21 July; UPI/*Gazette* (Schenectady, NY) 1 Sept; *Ledger-Star* (Norfolk, VA) 27 Sept; UPI/ *Post* (Houston, TX) + *Star* (Indianapolis, IN) 24 Aug 1982.

Credits: *Loren Coleman, Mark A Hall, Kurt Lothmann, UFO Newsclipping Service, Howard Wolinsky.*

•

Mike Dash

Back in *FT*2 (Jan 1974) p14, we noted a secret Japanese invasion of Britain, which began the previous year, when an alien seaweed capable of growing an inch a day, was found in the Portsmouth area, and on the bottom of the Royal Yacht Brittania. **Nigel Pennick** tells the story of this insidious weed...

THE JAPWEED CHRONICLES

Despite their importance as generators of much of the atmospheric oxygen we breathe, marine algae are rarely considered newsworthy. Indeed many people, including shipowners, consider 'seaweed' as something harmful or distasteful. However, the ecological researchers into marine algae have been watching with interest the irrepressible advance of the large brown alga *Sargassum muticum*, or Japweed, which is taking over many coastal habitats. This alga was originally indigenous to Japan, but was accidentally introduced to the west coast of North America during the 1940s, probably as the result of post-war trans-Pacific shipping. Having established itself in British Columbia, it proceeded to spread northwards as far as Baja California by 1974, a distance of 3000km.

In 1973, growths of *Sargassum muticum* appeared 'spontaneously', on the coast of the Isle of Wight, causing quite a stir in the algological community. Desperate attempts were made to eradicate it, involving 'search and destroy' parties traipsing over the rocks pulling out every clump in sight. Of course this failed, and the population has extended, though it is still largely confined to the Solent region.

By 1976, Japweed had crossed the Channel and became established at several sites along the Normandy coastline, spreading from there along the southern coastline of the North Sea. Spring 1977 saw the first observations of loose (ie unattached) plants on the Dutch coast, and by 1979 such findings were commonplace. In 1980, attached plants had invaded non-tidal saline lakes in the Eastern Scheldt estuarine region of the Netherlands, threatening to alter the ecological make-up of the algae population.

Japweed is a prolific organism which can produce an entire new plant by vegetative growth from a small portion containing either a terminal or a lateral shoot apical meristem (growing tip). Dutch scientists believe that it is possible that in the relatively new lakes, created as part of the long-term land reclamation schemes in Holland, Japweed may form vast floating mats, as in the notorious Sargasso Sea, which will eliminate the native eel-grass upon which many seabirds and water fowl now subsist. And Japweed marches on!

REFERENCES

DRUEHL,L.D. 1973. 'Marine Transplantations.' *Science* 179:12.
FARNHAM,W.F., and JONES, E.B.G. 1974. 'The eradication of the seaweed *Sargassum muticum.' Britain.Biol.Conserv.* 6:57-58.
FARNHAM,W.F., FLETCHER,R.L, and IRVINE,L.M. 1973. 'Attached *Sargassum* found in Britain.' *Nature* 243:231-232.
GRUET,Y. 1976 'Presence de l'algue japonaise *Sargassum muticum* (Yendo) Fensholt sur la cote francaise de Normandie.' *Bull. Soc.Nat.Quest.France* 74: 101-104.
PROUD'HOMME van REINE,W.F. 1977. 'De reis van een bruinwier rond de wereld'. *Gorteria* 8:212-216.

•

Nigel Pennick

Editor's Note — *Even as we set Nigel's piece (above) we note an item in* D.Telegraph *(22 June 1983; credit Mike Crowley) that our algal aliens had lately established two beachheads in the Land's End area of Cornwall, at Sennen and Mousehole. Hmmm... Sennen has a fine Japanese ring to it too...*

Not since FT31 have I charted the antics of the great lexilink buffoon: so here are a few more cases where names seem to take on a daft significance, maybe beyond their station, (wherever that might be!)

☐ Mr Les Dymond of Bideford in Devon was rolling a cigarette when he found a diamond in his tin of Golden Virginia. (*Bideford Gazette* 5 Nov 1982.)

☐ The maiden name of the mother of Colonel Buzz Aldren, the second man on the moon, was Marion Gaddis Moon.

☐ The village of Frogmore in Hampshire was invaded by thousands of frogs, which were breeding on waterlogged building land. (*D.Mirror* 28 Mar 1969.)

BIRD GATHERINGS

☐ In 1969, John Bird moved into Old Gardens Close, Tun-bridge Wells, Kent. Over the next decade, several other birds became his immediate neighbours: David Nightingale, Roger Wren, Tim Sparrow and finally Bill and Pat Duck. Their local pub was the Swan. (*Sun, D. Express* 21 June 1980.)

☐ A duck farmer at Rothwell, Lincs, employs two people called Crow, four Robbins, a Sparrow, a Gosling and a Dickie Bird. And the latest recruit at Newport police station in Gwent, where there are already two policemen called Pidgeon, a Partridge, a Nightingale and a Bush, is P.c. Talbot Thrush. (*D.Telegraph* 3 June & 2 Sep 1982.)

☐ Kenneth Pigeon of Cleve-land (UK) was caught burgling a works club by security guard Reginald Peacock and arrested by Det. Cons. George Bird. (*D.Telegraph, D.Express* 31 Dec 1982.)

☐ Gorzo the performing parrot was stolen from a theatre in Morecambe, Lancs. The police had a clue – the thief's registration spelt PEK. Eventually they traced it – to Stanley Parrott, 31. He was fined £50 by the town's magistrates. (*D.Mirror* 5 Sep 1978.)

FISH CLUMPINGS

☐ In Haddenham, Cambs, Mr and Mrs Pike live next to the vet, Colin Fish. The Haddocks are up the road, and their neighbour is Mrs Salmon. Mr Guppy and Mr and Mrs Fish live and the other end of the village. (*News of the World*, 27 June; *D.Mail* 28 June 1982.)

☐ Three men were fined for stealing rainbow trout from Mr Herring's fish farm in Hampshire. The police who caught them were led by Chief Supt. Pike. (*D.Star, D.Mail, Sun* 16 Nov 1982.)

☐ A Dutch lorry overturned, spilling a ton and a half of eels near Stoneycross in the New Forest after hitting a car with the number plate EEL 293V. (*Scunthorpe Ev. Tel., Western Mail, D.Record* 24 Sep 1982.)

LEADER CLONES

☐ Richard Nixon arrested Jimmy Carter in Detroit in July 1980 for breaking and entering, after a stake-out at an advertising company's offices. On the same day that this item came over the wires, it was also learned that Jimmy Carter had been thrown out of the Moscow Olympics for being drunk and disorderly. This JC turned out to be a 23-year-old Olympic swimmer from Greenock in Scotland.

☐ Later that year, Reagan Carter, who owned a welding shop in Beaumont, Texas, was glad the election was over. Naturally, he had been bugged by indecision. Next door to his shop was the Nixon Ford Motor Company. (*Middlesex News* (USA) 30 July; *The Province,* Vancouver, 17 Aug; *Schenectady Gazette* NY 6 Dec 1980.)

☐ In September 1980, Prime Minister Mugabe of Zimbawe sent in Commander Hitler to restore order among a thousand Libyan-trained guerillas. One of his first actions was to detain a German TV crew who went to film the camp. (*D.Telegraph* 12 Sep 1980.)

IN THE NAME OF THE LAW
☐ Six bullocks escaped from a butcher's yard and stampeded along a street in Birmingham. They were halted and escorted back to the yard by police-woman Valerie Bull.
☐ The theft of 130 pigs from a farm near Saffron Walden in Essex was investigated by Constable Bacon and Constable Suckling.
☐ A couple were fined £500 for trying to smuggle a rabbit into Britain. They were caught at Dover by customs officers Warren and Fox. (*Weekly News* 14 Oct 1978; *D.Mirror* 16 Mar 1981; *S.Express* 2 Sep 1979.) Which brings us neatly to

FOXY TALES
☐ T.A. Shellswell wrote to *Reville* (20 Feb 1976) that a fox being chased by the local hunt once sought sanctuary in a neglected corner of his garden, later escaping safely. Every year since, wild fox-gloves have grown there, where nothing grew before.
☐ Also from *Reville* (9 June 1978) we learned of a young fox who lost his way in Thame, Oxfordshire, and took refuge in the cellar of a pub called The Fox.
☐ G.F. Tomlinson wrote to the *Sunday Express* (28 Aug 1981) that he was playing golf with a friend when they noticed a fox basking in the sunshine. His friend played a shot which landed near the animal, and it grabbed the ball and made off with it. Mr Tomlinson gave chase, and the fox dropped the ball. When examined, the ball had "R. Fox and Sons" written on it, with a red fox logo.

Thanks to: *B.M.Barter, Claudia Boulton, Peter Christie, Loren Coleman, Mike Dash, Peter Hope Evans, Brian Hain, Chris Hall, Chris Holtzhausen, J.Lang, David MacAdams, R.Maragna, Paul Screeton, Anthony Smith, P.M. Smith, Paul Thomas, Nigel Watson, Roland Watson, Heathcote Williams, Steve Wrathall, and Joe Zarzynski.*

•

Paul Sieveking

METEOROLOGICAL CURIOSITIES

Since 1980 the cornfields of Wiltshire and Hampshire have been the target of mystery 'holes'. Has their proximity to the notorious Warminster UFO window diverted attention from a novel meteorological manifestation? Read on.

ALIEN CORN
On Friday 8th July 1983 the *Wiltshire Times* published a story about five flattened circular areas which appeared mysteriously in a wheatfield (confusingly called a cornfield) near Westbury, Wilts, below the famous White Horse hill-figure. The journalist responsible, Paul Mellard, told me they had been found five days previously (3rd July). The field is adjacent to the B3093 Devizes to Westbury road, and overlooked by steep hills, which provide an excellent view for the photographers. The distinctive feature of these marks is their geometry: four small circles (apx 14ft dia) grouped roughly equi-distantly around a larger central circle (apx 50ft dia).

Mellard was quite restrained compared to the silliest of silly-season treatments which followed. He rightly pointed out that according to the belief of some ufologists the marks might have been made by fly-ing saucer landing gear. Other theories suggested were rutting deer, hoax, 'the weather', and even mating hedgehogs!

But on the other side of the weekend, Monday 11th July, the *Daily Express* had no doubts that ET had something to do with it. Over the week-end, they had chartered an air-craft and taken some aerial shots of the marks (see photo A), and gave nearly a whole page to their UFO theory, capitalizing on the proximity of Westbury to 'UFO haunted' Warminster. The next day (12th July) *Daily Star* and other papers were attempting to cock their collective snoots at the *Express*, claiming they had "solved" the riddle of the Westbury holes, and that, on the authority of the Met. Office, they were made by a whirlwind, (a theory proposed by Dr Meaden back in 1981 – see below).

By the time the story reached *Globe* and *Weekly World News*, both of 16 Aug 1983, it was one of "a gleam-ing silver starship" seen by "dozens of wide-eyed witnesses" who stared in astonishment as "two tiny... jaunty ET-like creatures" strolled around for a minute before blasting off again! There must be thousands of Americans, who read this, who now think Britain overrun by little green things...and it's no comfort to say they probably think the folks at Southfork are real too!

Photo A – *An* Express *photo of the five holes at Westbury, which appeared on 3rd July 1983. The wheat was not broken or crushed, but 'swept' in a clockwise spiral out from the center. The sharp cut-off at the circle edges does not seem characteristic of whirwind behaviour. Helicopter down-drafts could not create sharp cut-offs either; besides, they lack the force necessary. If there was any truth to the starship idea, then its landing gear would be quite literally eccentric, because none of the circles are exactly alike, equispaced or perfectly aligned.*

Every serious ufologist must have been embarrassed by such barefaced nonsense. Interestingly those ufologists asked for their views tended to be quite cautious — except for dear old Clancarty, who gets set up everytime by unscrupulous journalists wanting an impressive 'House of Lords' quote. Jenny Randles discusses the media treatment of this case in her editorial in *Northern UFO News* n103 (July 1983). She points out that no UFO sighting reports were logged in the Westbury area before or since the holes arrived. If there had been, the press was in a mood to ounce upon them. So, Jenny writes, "A media hype of the most extreme kind did *not* create masses of spurious sightings."

The fact is that ufologists have been aware of this phenomenon for years — though 'Ground Effects' or 'Landing Traces' are preferred over the old term 'Saucer Nests' — in the context of possible landing cases, but the link between flattened or burned areas in crop fields and UFOs has remained a hypothetical one. It was because of this historical association that the Wiltshire group SCUFORI and Ian Mrzyglod, editor of *The Probe Report*, got involved, and for Ian it wasn't the first time either.

Issues 2 and 3 of *Probe* (as it was called at first) detail the investigation by Ian and his colleagues into three holes at Westbury in 1980 very close to the present manifestation. They averaged 60ft in diameter, in oat and barley fields, two of which appeared on the 21st and 30th July 1980 and the other the prior May, since when it had been harvested. At that time the owners of the land said that they'd never seen the like in 40 years' farming the area. Issues 7 and 8 of *The Probe*

Report discusses three circles found in a cornfield at Cheese-foot Head, near Winchester, in August 1981, remarkable for their peculiar arrangement (see photo B). Curiously, the farmer said that "similar" circles had appeared on his land the previous year (1980).

Ian cooperated with Dr G.T. Meaden of the Tornado and Storm Research Organisation, of Trowbridge (TORRO), and included Dr Meaden's suggestions that 'fair weather' whirlwinds might be the cause. Certainly the weather and the topography of the area were right. Diagrams of two likely kinds of whirlwinds (a short-lived moving vortex, and a stationary one) appear in Dr Meaden's own account in *The Journal of Meteorology* (Feb 1982), which he edits, and in Ian's article for *The Unexplained* (pp2418-2420). The latter mentions earlier cases and explains the ufological context.

Which brings us to the present rash of holes, whose number and symmetry, Dr Meaden acknowledges, challenge his whirlwind hypothesis. Discussion with Ian brought more revelations. In May 1983, a large circular area was found flattened in a remote field near Warminster, visible only from the top of Cley Hill. A three hole pattern occurred near Cley hill the previous year (1982). Shortly after the latest ones at Westbury were found, a second five hole pattern was found at Cley Hill, and at Wantage in Oxfordshire. The loony fringe aside, clearly something strange was happening.

If the marks *were* made by alien spaceships, what in Fort's name are they doing pogoing about the West Country? Apologists for nuts and bolts ufology usually forget that Salisbury Plain is also riddled with military and MOD establishments; could the holes be the results of secret weapon testing? All highly unlikely (but not impossible) we think. While some kind of whirlwind effect sounds a lot more plausible, it is not without difficulties...Whirlwinds are messy things, so such neat handiwork would itself be anomalous. Why the repetitions in these places? It is difficult to explain the geometries by known meteorological processes. Why has it happened so frequently in the last few years, when prior records of the phenomenon are so rare? Etc.

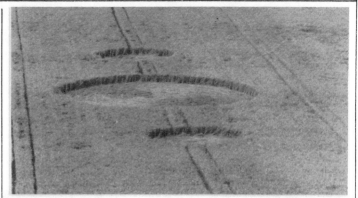

Photo B – *The circles at Cheesefoot Head, August 1981, photographed by Steven Broome. The flattened stalks radiate. in a clockwise spiral.*

When Daniel Goring, the editor of the Essex journal *Earthlink*, visited the Westbury White Horse site on the 19th they were astonished to discover that a second set of five circles had appeared alongside the original ones (see photo C) as reported in their journal for September 8th 1983. After writing a suitably mystified ending to this piece, Ian phoned me with some news. It seems that a team from the *Daily Mirror* had visited the area seeking someway to upstage the *Express* 'scoop'. Among others, they interviewed Francis Shephard, son of Alan Shephard, the landlord of the farmlands, who said he thought the whole thing had been a hoax anway. Having trained as a surveyor he thought such a design could be laid out quite simply. And so, on the 18th July, Francis and the *Mirror* men did just that

with the help of a long chain, while a camera snapped the men at work. We traced the pictures and learned they are to be used in a forthcoming article presumably to preempt any similar starship landing site stories. Not everything holey is sacred, it seems.

The new set of holes looks so like the others that it could not be told apart if its spurious nature had not been discovered. This raises the possibility, of course, that the others are man-made too. Or some of them are. (Look again at photo A and note the faint circular track in the standing wheat linking the four outer circles. This faint track goes through the centers of the small circles and is itself concentric with the larger one. It looks to me suspiciously like someone had spaced them out using a rope as a radius. It's just a thought.)

Photo C – *The original Westbury circles (on the left), photographed by Ian Mrzyglod on 6th August. The set on the right were created by Francis Shephard and a team from the Daily Mirror, ostensibly to demonstrate the possibility the others were man-made too. Note its different alignment. It was different inside too; the spiral of flattened stalks radiated anti-clockwise.*

If any of the cases mentioned are genuine, we are back to square one with a mystery phenomenon. In which case we look forward to next summer when the SCUFORI, Probe and TORRO teams will establish 24 hour CB watches in the favoured areas when the weather conditions seem right, hoping to catch a whirlwind in the act.

This story is still developing and we have to go to press. If you're interested in a fuller report I recommend you read Ian's own, to be published in the final issue of *Probe Report* later [Probe: 16 Marigold Walk, Ashton, Bristol, BS3 2DP. Try sending £1.]

Credits: *Ron Gauntlett, Dr G.T. Meaden, Ian Mrzyglod (who kindly lent us photos B & C), Anthony Smith, Joe Zarzynski.*

●

Bob Rickard

KURIOUS KIDNAPS
We think we've identified a bizarre new phenomenon — kidnapping descendants of the famous — which, to the fertile imagination suggests the visible tip of some vast and insidious conspiracy, which will doubtless get pinned on the Illuminati or their puppetmasters. There is something sinister, alone, in the fact that it was a descendant of Machiavelli, the Renaissance writer whose name is synonymous with conspiratorial politics, whom we first noted missing. According to the *Daily Telegraph* (11 May 1983) the beautiful young Marquise Ludovica Machiavelli, 24, had vanished on the way home from evening school, on 3rd May, in circumstances suggestive of kidnap, near the family castle at San Lazzaro, near Bologna, Italy.

Our interest sparked, and a quick look in our files found a note, also from the *Telegraph* (26 March 1983), to the effect that one Diego Prado y Colon de Caravajal, a direct descendant of Christopher Columbus, was snatched off the street on 25th March. The 53-yrs old banker and father of six was whisked away by four men outside his home in Madrid, Spain. On reading this, my thoughts turned to the Leif Ericson Society, who have maintained all along that the famed Christopher was a complete imposter. In fact we will have an article on this imposture, by LES president W.R. Anderson, in a few issues time.

Meanwhile, if you know of any more candidates for this new category of curious crime, please let us know.

CHINESE CRYPTO-CRAZIES
There is something strange going on in China on the cryptozoological front. The *Daily Telegraph* (9 March 1983), citing the *Tientsin Daily*, said that a hunter in Guangxi Province had found a strange "ape-man" in a trap, in 1980, but he let it go again. The creature — "It was more than 3ft tall, had a mouth like a monkey's, a nose like a dog's, and ears, hands and eyes like a human's. It's body was covered in hair." — had caught its hand in the trap in a forest. The hunter freed it, he said, after it had looked at him with tears in its eyes. Perhaps those cryptozoologists, who daily wail for want of a specimen, also wept a little at this news!

Then, as if to dramatise the opposite emotion, came the news that a peasant farmer, Leng Zhizhong, had been sentenced to two years on a chain gang for killing a panda, one of only about 1000 left in the wilds that are known. Leng had set wire traps all over the forest, and on finding the panda in one, strangled and skinned it and took the meat home for his family. But this was no anonymous crime; the panda's name was Han-Han, one of only six in the Wolong Reserve in Sichuan Province. Han-Han's fate was only discovered when the reserve's researchers noticed her radio-transmitter had not moved for several days and they went to investigate. Angry reserve officials are quoted as saying: "What this murderous fiend did to our beloved Han-Han is the most unforgiveable crime. Killing her was bad enough. But to chop her up like dog meat is more than the mind can comprehend." And: "Leng will pay for his savage deed on the chain gang. And there he will forfeit his worthless life. No one can survive more than six months on the gang of the doomed." *Sun* (citing *People's Daily*, Peking) 10 May; *World Weekly News* 14 June 1983.

FELINE FANTASIES
Back in my formative days, when I read voraciously and indiscriminately any book about anything out of the ordinary, the books by Brad Steiger served as my introduction to a variety of subjects, from the hostility of UFOs, some pre-Vallee ideas on the connexion between UFOs and fairies,

psychics and angels, to name a few. Then he joined his wife Francie, a professional psychic, in proclaiming the proposition that anyone who was the least bit psychic and more or less suffering from fairly common forms of alienation, was a "star person", someone who has been incarnated on this earth but who is really an ancient astronaut.

His latest Disneyesque nonsense, doubtless desinged to promote a forthcoming book, is that "millions" of domestic pets are really creatures from other planets. As cited in *National Enquirer* (3 May 1983) Steiger says: "One out of five dogs and cats are space pets – descendants of original alien creatures that were 'seeded' on Earth 50,000 years ago." How can you tell? Well, if your pet has a "charismatic personality", is "extremely protective", has "compelling eyes", "healing powers", and can predict disasters or can appear in your dreams, then you have an honest-to-Spock alien in your household. And how did it get inside the body of a cute kitten? It took it over, obviously...a bit like, you know, Steiger by his own computer, when he tried to analyse 20 years of research. Sounds like both master and machine have a few components loose.

THE COMET'S TALE

Well, Comet IRAS-Akari-Alcock 1983 whizzed past this earth in mid-May, the nearest pass by any comet for over 100 years, and just as in the heyday of omens and prodigies, all manner of calamities were being predicted as the after effects: Profs Hoyle and Wickramasinghe trotted out their three-book thesis, that viruses engendered in a comet's tail could rain down to create plague on earth, as, claim the profs, history shows that all the great plagues have followed brushes with a comet; and the *Shropshire Star* 10 May 1983) who pointed out that Maggie Thatcher could lose the coming

election, because throughout history comet's have spelled bad luck or worse for the great leaders of the day. So much for that!

More interesting is that the discovery of the comet marks another triumph for 70yr-old George Alcock, a retired teacher who lives in Peterborough. It makes the fifth comet he has spotted and had named after him since 1959, which equals the record of W.F. Denning, another British astronomer who found five comets between 1880 and 1894. Alcock is as modest as his equipment – a pair of WW2 German U-boat binoculars and a deck-chair. His latest discovery – found within two minutes as he stared at the sky from the landing window on 3rd May – is in the grand tradition, which interested

Fort and Thayer alike, of an amateur outdoing the hi-tech professionals at their own game. Alcock was awarded the MBE in 1979, for services to astronomy, and well deserved it is too. *D.Telegraph* 6 May 1983.

And yet...we did notice a few things that were buzzing near the comet's approach: at least one fall of ice, the Exmoor Beast, and one of our ball lightning incidents, all elsewhere in this issue. If our computer database was set up, this is the kind of correlation we would explore.

Credits: *Janet & Colin Bord, Peter Christie, Peter Hope Evans, Roy Gauntlett, Brian Hain, Ian Murray, Anthony Smith, Paul Thomas, Steve Wrathall.*

●

Bob Rickard

We know we promised a review of recent dust and stone falls for this issue, but the ice kept on coming down, you see...

MORE FALLING ICE

■ **22 July 1982 – Stuart, Florida.**

Our correspondent in the area, Michael Hoffman, found a brief account of the event in *St Petersburg Times* 23 July 1982, which updates the story we gave last issue [FT39p23]. The event, it seems, occurred on the 22nd, not the 23rd as previously cited. The new source adds an explanation we have not encountered before, and quotes Lee Guenther, a Federal Aviation Authority investigator, as being "concerned" the massive 100lb ice block "might have come from a missile which exploded after launching from Cape

Canaveral." Another source, the Lincoln, Nebraska, *Journal Star* 25 July 1982, attributes to the same gentleman the informative statement that "it could have been drinking water (from a plane) or it might not have been from an airplane."

■ **Early Dec 1982 – Arlington, Texas.**

The report doesn't give the date when Mrs Lucille Barthke was in her garden planting flowers when something made her look up. That something was a "shard" of blue ice about 10" in diameter. "For some reason I had looked up a few seconds before the thing hit, and I noticed it falling toward the house. When it crashed through my trees and into the roof I sort of ducked because I thought it might be a meteor." In their attempts to explain, the area FAA spokesman trots out the usual unproveable story of leaky plane toilets. AP/Green Bay, Wis, *Press-Gazette* 10 Dec 1982.

■ **26 Dec 1982 — Santa Monica, Calif.**
Clara Riddle and her family had come down from Seattle to visit her parents and they were sitting in the lounge, with the parents' neighbours, the Varadys, when, at 10.10pm, a loud explosion disrupted their get-together. Rushing outside they saw that something had smashed through a guestroom attached to the Varady's garage, on Pearl Street. On entering the apartment Dominic Varady said he saw a gaping hole in the ceiling with fragments of ice cascading through. The culprit was a massive block of ice "at least three feet thick and about 200 pounds," and it had snapped at least one wooden roof beam on its way through. Both families were reported to be keeping a souvenir of their unwelcome visitor in their fridges if only to celebrate the fact that the visiting Riddles, who usually stay in the apartment on their visits, were on this occasion staying with their parents, and thus escaped the ruination of their effects.

We note another curious detail which raises eerie echoes of similar synchronicities we have recorded elsewhere. It seems that one of the Varadys was in another room of their home at the time watching the movie *Meteor* on TV! *Los Angeles Times* 28 Dec; UPI/Albuquerque, NM, *Journal* 31 Dec 1982.

■ **2 Jan 1983 — North York, Ontario.**
Not much is known about this one, but the following outline is inferred from the source — Toronto, Ont., *Star* 5 Jan 1983 — which is a fairly general piece about the problem of 'blue ice' or frozen effluent leaked or dumped (illegally)

from planes. It seems a chunk of greenish-blue ice crashed through the roof of a house in Tobermory Drive, North York, belonging to Harry and Tilly Deeder. In this case the origin of the ice does not seem in doubt. "The smell was awful," said Mr Deeder. "Just like a toilet." Yet despite the whiff the Deeders have kept a piece of the missile in the vain hope that if the plane can be identified the owner can be sued. Interestingly, the report says that just such a case occurred in Mississauga in 1977, when investigators of Transport Canada found that ice which had wrecked a Cadillac had come from an Air Canada jet. In another case new to us , ice forming on the wing of a National Airlines 727, and found to have come from a leaking toilet outlet, actually caused an engine to fall off over Texas in 1974. Yet however much aviation officials would like it to, the leaky toilet hypothesis does not explain many of our ice falls for reasons we will restate another time.

■ **30 Jan 1983 — Vancouver, BC.**
The second strike in Canada within a month! This one fell through the roof of a house owned by Alan Carr, pictured looking out of a hole but too poor to reproduce. AP/Albuquerque, NM, *Journal* 1 Feb 1983.

■ **7 March 1983 — Birmingham.**
A block of ice, about one foot thick, crashed through the roof of a warehouse belonging to Alltransport International, on the Elmdon trading estate near Birmingham Airport, and insurers were keeping the ice-bomb in cold storage for analysis. Strangely, our report says this analysis "will not now be necessary", whatever they mean by that. One interpretation is that they have accepted the fact that despite the proximity of the fall to an airport the airport controllers have not been able to identify the aerial culprit. Wolverhampton *Express & Star*, *Sun*,

Western Mail 8 March 1983.

■ **11 April 1983 — Wuxi, Eastern China.**
At midday, a 50kg block of ice, nearly 20 inches across plummeted from the sky to smash on the pavement of Sheep's Skin Lane, in Wuxi, about ten minuutes before it began to rain. A traffic policeman on duty at the time said: "When it hit the ground it sounded like a car tyre blowing out, but louder, and it simultaneously gave off a layer of mist about 50cms high." Fragments were scattered as far as 20 metres. A five man scientific team spent eight days investigating the incident, and are thankful for an old lady who said she worshipped "everything from the heavens". She had taken some of the ice home and thus could provide them with a specimen. Witnesses said the block was nearly round in shape with an uneven surface, and milky white or greyish in colour. *China Features*, reprinted in *J.Meteorology* July/Aug 1983.

■ **9 May 1983 — Little Egg Harbour, NJ.**
Early in the morning a house in quaintly named Little Egg Harbour was visited upon by a little ice egg from on high. Well, not so little really...the 50lb chunk ripped a 12ft hole in the roof and landed in a pantry. The right place for eggs, one would think. AP/*D. Telegraph* 11 May 1983.

■ **??? 1983 -- Tuckerton, NJ.**
Could the Little Egg Harbour incident (above) be the same as this one? Our source gives no date, but says this 50lb ice block left a 14ft hole in the roof of the Cetrano home to shatter in the pantry (again). I've no New Jersey map to hand, but intuition suggests they are the same incident. If so we have the new datum — it happened at 2am. The FAA consoled the Cetrano family, who estimate the damage at $2,500, by assuring them that such events are of great "rarity". Oh yeah? *Weekly World News* 14 June 1983.

■ **???June 1983 — Archlid Green, Staffs.**

Daily Star 30 June 1983 — Farmer's wife, Gladys Evans, missed by a few feet by a block of ice which fell away.

POSTSCRIPT

As we go to press the parade of peltings keeps on Passing...

According to the (Nancy) *L'Est Republicain* 8 June 1983, a man strolling in a street in Belfort, in eastern France and not far from Basle, was shocked when a block of ice narrowly missed him to shatter at his feet. No other details. (Cr: JL Brodu.)

And back in England we had no less than three incidents within a week — our source is *D.Telegraph* 1 Sept 1983, but we'd welcome any local accounts...

27 Aug 1983 — a large chunk of ice fell into a garden in Highland Drive, Bushey, Herts, just missing a young girl playing there. A piece was saved by a boy neighbour.

27 Aug — a mere five hours after the incident above, and about 30 miles away, another young girl playing in her garden is missed by about two feet, at Ampthill, Beds. Also mentioned in *D.Mirror* 29 Aug 1983 (Cr: Cecilia Boggis).

30 Aug 1983 — Hitchin, Herts, an ice block demolished part of a steel garage roof.

The Civil Aviation Authority was said to be "scouring aircraft logs" to find the culprits, on the theory "that the defrosting device on a plane *or perhaps several,* could be faulty." Our emphasis. Even if they did find several planes with faulty equipment we'd be left with a coincidence and not an explanation!

ICE COMET

Astronomers at the University of Arizona, managed a prolonged observation of Comet Bowell, and discovered the first real evidence of the presence of ice in a comet. This will come as no great

Larry Cetrano, of Tuckerton, NJ, points to the icebomb hole in his pantry. [Weekly World News *14 June 1983.*]

surprise to those who have long believed in ice comets and that some of the many mysterious falls of ice that we chronicle may have such cometary origins. *S.Times* 6 Feb 1983.

FALL OF SHELLS

I can't recall one of these happening since Fort's day!

During a gale, which might also have been a light storm, there was a rain of tiny shells, supposed to have been swept up by the winds from the nearest seaside, on the Staffordshire village of Dilhorne, on 22 March 1983 — and that, in this wondrous age of hi-tech journalism, is all we know of this remarkable event. *D.Express, D.Telegraph,* 23 March 1983.

Perhaps one of our readers inthe Stoke area could look into this story for us. Perhaps the local paper had something? Our lack of information on this prompts me to say again that on coming upon an interesting story please do not assume we know of it already.

If everyone did that we'd never learn of most of the stories we print. So please send those clippings in — however trivial they may seem to you at the time, they may be a vital part of a larger jigsaw. *D.Express, Daily Telegraph* 23 March 1983.

Credits*: Jeremy Beadle, Mike Crowley, Mike Dash, Gene Duplantier, Philip Hope Evans, G. Fawcett, Brian Hain, Chris Hall, Michael Hoffman, F Hudson, Mick Malloret, Valerie Martin, Norman Oliver, Paul Screeton, Anthony Smith, S. R. Stebbing, Joe Swatek, P. R. Thomas, UFO Newsclipping Service, Roland Watson, Ion Will, Steve Wrathall.*
●
Bob Rickard

★ PLEASE ★
★ REMEMBER TO ★
★ RENEW QUICKLY ★
★ AND ★
★ NOTIFY ANY ★
★ CHANGE ★
★ OF ADDRESS ★

Fortean Extracts From
The Gentleman's Magazine:

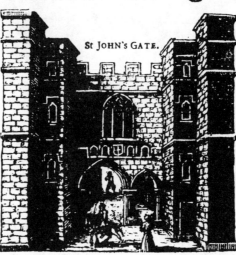

Lond Gazette
Londō Jour.
Fog''s Jouen.
Applebee's ::
Read'd :: ::
Craftsman ::
D. Spectator
Grubstreet ¶
W.ly Register
Free = Briton
Hyp = Doctor.
Daily Court.
Daily = Post
Dai. _ournal
Da. Post-boy
O. Advertiser
EveningPost
St James's Eb.
Whitehall Eb.
Lōdon Ebīg
_lying = Post
Weekly Mis-
cellany.

St JOHN's GATE.

York 2 News
Dublin 6 :::
Edinburgh 2
Bristol ::: ::
Norwich 2 ::
Exeter 2 :::
Worcester ::
Northanton
Gloucester ::
Stamford ::
Nottingham
Bury Journ.
Chester ditto
Derby ditto
Ipswich dit.
Reading dit.
Leeds Merc.
Newcastle C.
Canterbury
Manchester :
Boston ::: ¶
Jamaica, &c
Barbados :

Or, MONTHLY INTELLIGENCER.

...being the second installment from the pages of *The Gentleman's Magazine*, founded in 1731, and compiled chronologically for us by **Peter Christie**.

1743

• The year opened with an extraordinarily long and detailed account of one Margaret Cutting of Wickham Market in Suffolk who "speaks readily and intelligibly tho' she has lost her Tongue." This poor girl's tongue had dropped out due to cancer when she was 4 yet she was still able speak. The case was presented to the savants of the Royal Society who, true to form, thought it very interesting but couldn't suggest any working hypothesis. (page 48)

• On February 11th died in St Luke's Work-house in London,

"Mrs Agnes Milbourn, 106 years of age. She had 29 sons and a Daughter by one Husband, 20 of whom frequently follow'd her to Church, but outliv'd all her Children and Grand Children, except one Grandson." (page 107)

One wonders what the odds are against having 29 children of one sex and only one of the opposite gender.

• In May of this year a fascinating case was reported from Killmellford, Argyle in Scotland concerning John Ferguson.

"About 18 years ago he happened to over-heat himself on the Mountains, in pursuit of Cattle, and in that Condition drank excessively of cold Water from a Rivulet, near which he fell asleep; he awaked 24 Hours after in a high Fever: During the Paroxysm of the Fever, his Stomach loaths and can retain, no kind of Aliment, except Water, or clarified Whey, which last he uses but seldom, by reason of its Scarcity.

Archibold Campbell of Inerverliver, to whom this Man's Father is Tenant, carried him to his own House, and locked him up in a Chamber for 20 Days, and supplied him himself with fresh Water, to no greater Quantity in a Day, than an ordinary Man would use for common Drink; and at the same time took particular Care, that it should not be possible for his Guest to supply himself with any other Food; yet after that Space of Time, he found no Alteration in his Vigour or Visage. He is now about 36 Years of Age, middle Stature, a fair and fresh Complexion, with a healthy (though not seemingly robust) fresh Complexion; his Habit of Body is meagre, but in no remarkable Degree; his ordinary Employ is looking after Cattle by which means he needs must travel Four or Five Miles a Day in that mountainous Country...as to the grosser Excrements, it did not occur to me to inquire about them, but I conclude that he discharges none because the Country people, who strongly fancy him supported by supernatural Means, would not forget to object this to him..." (page 248)

We know that fasts till the death can last much longer than John's 20 days outlined here but surely he would have showed some signs of change after this period?

• On July 15th Enfield near London was battered by hailstones "as big as Nutmegs" and and 2 horses and a boy were killed by lightning. (page 388)

• On the same day in Ireland a rather hurried burial took place,

"Died (in Earnest) the Wife of one Kirkeen, who was twice at Dublin to be buried; but came to life to her Loving Husband's great Disappointment, who fearing the like Accident immediately put her into a Coffin, had it nailed up and buryed her the next Day." (page 389)

The thought of premature burial makes one's skin crawl but clearly it happened, if various writers are to be believed.

• In August a woman died at Louth in Lincolnshire and on being opened by a surgeon a foetus was found that had been there 13 years — a length of time during which she had given birth to 3 other children. (page 444)

1744

• The year opened spectacularly in Spain with a colourful and inexplicable aerial display,

"The 17th of last Month a surprising Phenomenon was observed at Carthagena in old Spain, about 5 in the Evening, on the side of Mount Orlando, some leagues West of that City. There first appeared a vast Stream of Light resembling a River of Fire falling in a Cascade, then it formed a Sheet of Flame, extending several Leagues to the East giving so bright a Light, as dazzled the Eyes of the Beholders. Afterwards appeared a great Globe of Fire beneath it, which in the Space of some Minutes broke into four lesser Balls, which flew off towards the four Cardinal Points. This explosion was attended with a Clap of Thunder so Loud, that it astonished the Inhabitants for several Leagues round. The four lesser Balls broke each, but with a Clap not so loud. It was remarkable, during the whole Time, the Sky was serene, and the Stars shone very Bright." (page 51)

If this was observed today what would we read about? — UFO mother ships and attendant scout vehicles? It would be interesting to find out if this area is on a fault line and thus fits in with Paul Devereux's theories concerning UFOs and strange lights as outlined in his recent book Earthlights.

• Some five months later on June 13 the inhabitants of Bristol were treated to a sight of something odd in the sky,

"At Bristol, was seen at Midnight in the West, a large Body of Light, resembling that of the late Comet, but much larger in its Body, and the Tail exceeding bright but broad and short." (page 333)

1745

• This year, when Bonnie Prince Charlie put the fear of God (or at least of mad Scots) into most Englishmen, there were only two notes of Fortean interest to appear in the Gentleman's Magazine crowded as it was with news of the rebellion. In June there was a review of the cumbrously titled "A dissertation of the uncertainty of the signs of death, and the folly of percipitant burials, and ambalments," Amongst many other cases cited were;

"...a gardener of Tronningholm in Sweden revived after lying 16 hours under water; a woman after lying 3 days; and that a man lived to be 77, who at the age of 17 was not taken out of the water till he had lain there seven weeks." (page 311)

The current debate on brain death and whether this constitutes actual death pales into insignificance against this 17 year old aquaman! It is a pity no other references are given — such anecdotal evidence isn't very convincing.

• The following month saw a tragedy with a strong element of black comedy in it,

"July 22. A young man at Lee in Essex, diverting himself with some flounders, put one alive in his mouth, which slipt down his throat, and tho' all endeavours were used to force it up again, he died soon after." (page 385)

I bet you thought loonies swallowing goldfish etc.was something new, didn't you?

1746

• In April of this year another example of the old belief in shocks affecting pregnant women and their unborn children was published.

"April 28. The wife of one Rich. Haynes of Chelsea, aged 35 and the mother of 16 fine children, was deliver'd of a monster, with nose and eyes like a lyon, no palate to the mouth, hair on the shoulders, claws like a lion instead of fingers, no breastbone, something surprising out of the navel as big as an egg, and onefoot longer than the other — She had been to see the Lions in the Tower, where she was much terrify'd with the old Lion's noise." (page 270)

As I mentioned in an earlier article this idea recently received a new airing in the film The Elephant Man.

To be continued
•
Peter Christie

PHENOMENOMIX

"I WAS IN DEEPEST AFRICA, APPROACHING THE MOUNTAINS OF THE MOON, WHEN THE TROUBLE STARTED...."

CLOSED

"I SAY, BWANA OLD CHAP — I'D STRONGLY ADVISE AGAINST PROCEEDING FURTHER!"

STOP

"...BUT NOTHING WOULD STOP ME, JACQUES LE FLACQUES — NOT WHEN I WAS THIS CLOSE."

"YEARS SPENT STUDYING SHOWERS OF FISH, FROGS AND SUNDRY ITEMS OF LADIES APPAREL HAD CONVINCED ME THAT ALL THESE MYSTERIOUS FALLS ORIGINATED AT THIS ONE SPOT...."

"I FOUND MYSELF AT THE GATEWAY TO A HUGE, SINISTER RUIN, OVER THE DOOR WAS AN INSCRIPTION, WHICH MY VAST KNOWLEDGE OF THE ANCIENT, ESOTERIC LANGUAGES OF THE WORLD IMMEDIATELY RECOGNISED AS ENGLISH!!"

SHIFTEM & DROPP SPACIAL DELIVERIES
·ANY STUFF·ANYWHERE·ORDERS TAKEN·

"HERE WAS THE HEART OF THE MYSTERY! FISH, FROGS, PERIWINKLES, CHUNKS OF ICE... ALL THE ODDS AND ENDS THAT DROP OUT OF THE SKY....."

STRAW HATS

PEAS

NEWTS

RED WORMS

BARLEY

OATS

RICE

SPARK PLUGS

WHEAT

TREACLE

SOCKS

COPIES OF F.T.

BLOOD

WINKLES

MICE

HAZEL NUTS

FROGS

"HERE TOO WERE THE SILENT FLYING MACHINES WITH THEIR CLOUD DISGUISES, SETTING OFF ON THEIR DELIVERY ROUNDS!"

"THE LOCALS SEEMED QUITE PLEASED TO SEE ME...THEY WERE SAYING SOMETHING ABOUT BEING ABLE TO FULFILL AN OUTSTANDING ORDER AT LAST, WHEN I FELL ASLEEP...."

DRUGS

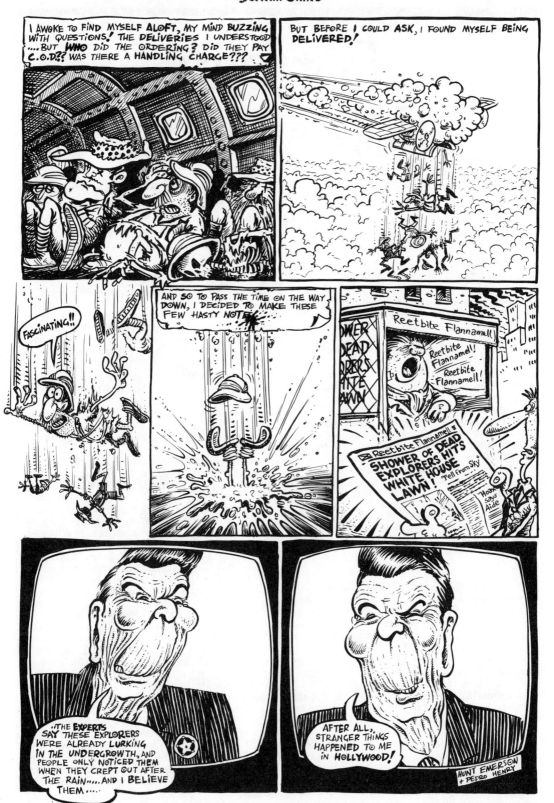

Fortean Follow-Ups.

The road to enlightenment is fraught not so much with danger as with frustration. **Paul Pinn** has tried to follow up some of the stories printed in earlier issues of FT and discovered new dimensions to the obstacles of apathy, obfuscation and unhelpfulness tinged in places with barely concealed contempt. Anyone who wishes to unearth a mystery the Establishment would prefer to remain buried must learn the lessons herein.

Everyone loves a mystery, but rarely does an unknowledgeable member of the public, like myself, attempt to follow-up a mysteriously sounding item that is published in a newspaper or periodical. I decided to enlighten myself on some that had mysterious connotations. The results were rather what I expected — disappointing. Bureaucrats seem to periodically suffer from some kind of inert apathy that manifests itself only when they are dealing with inquisitive members of the public on a subject that they think we should know nothing about. Bumbledom can be, and very probably is, a serious obstacle to Forteans. Now I know why people rarely bother pursuing mysteries; the results do not justify the time, effort and financial expenditure needed to make the attempt.

The following is a resumé of some of the cases I have tried to follow-up. Most remain as isolated mysteries — isolated by lack of knowledge and lack of helpfulness by official minions.

■ *Sunday Express* 3 July 1977 ■

Around February 1976 a student found a man lying on his back in a shallow crevice on Dartmoor, more than a mile from the nearest road and about 4 miles from Dartmoor Prison. The man was dead.

He was 5ft 7", weighed about 12 stone and was aged about 35. He wore a grey St.Michael's suit and shoes that were totally unsuitable for walking on the moor. His clothing was also unsuitable in view of the bitterly cold weather that prevailed at that time. Contained about his person were some rather odd items; 12 capsules of cyanide — enough to kill thirty people, a bottle of poisonous Laburnum seeds and a bottle of sweet and sour sauce. He also had an ordnance survey map and a wallet with a small amount of cash. There were no clues as to his identity. He had no keys, no drivers licence, no receipts and no bank card.

During a period of intensive investigation thousands of missing persons reports in the UK and overseas were checked — all to no avail. Dental records were also checked but with no results. Just to add to the mystery, extensive forensic tests failed to establish the cause of death, but doctors stated that no traces of cyanide were in his body and that there was no evidence to suggest that he had swallowed any of the Laburnum seeds. Detectives were also unable to determine where he obtained the cyanide.

A real mystery this one, I'm sure you will agree. Unfortunately, a mystery is exactly what it looks as though it will stay. The body was duly buried (I assume — unless it's in cold storage somewhere) without a cause of death being found, and to this day the police have no positive answers to the questions that are so abundant in this case. On the 10th March 1978, the Devon & Cornwall Constabulary confirmed to me that they had not succeeded in identifying the corpse.

■ *Sunday Express* 19 Feb 1978 ■

50-year-old Betty Wilson of 25 years residence at Cornwall Avenue, Peacehaven, Sussex, disappeared at the beginning of Feb 1978. She was a normal, happy housewife, married for at least 25 years with two sons and a daughter. She went shopping in Seaford and vanished. Police enquiries have led nowhere and Mr. Wilson's own search has been unfruitful. On the 26th July 1978, Eric Bailey, Deputy Public Relations Officer with the Sussex Police, confirmed to me that Mrs. Wilson was still missing and that Mr. Wilson had shifted the area of his private inquiry to the Cotswolds, otherwise no new developments on the case. I wish you luck Mr. Wilson.

■ *Sunday Express* 12 Mar 1978 ■
Claudette Souchon, 31, went riding with a spare horse and her dog. She was off on a two-day tour of the wild Camargue area in Southern France. Three days later she had still not returned. A search was instigated and thirty men followed her trail. On the second day of the search they found the horse she had been riding. It was dead and its body had been savagely and horrifically ripped open, but not by an animal. On the third day the spare horse was found. It bore no injuries but was very frightened and hardly able to walk. The police were called in and they patrolled the lonely trails of the area.

On the fifth day of the search, in a burned out glade, some of Claudette's clothing was found. Two days later she was found near Rodez, sitting on the ground, covered in mud, not moving, unable to speak and numb with shock. Her dog was lying exhausted beside her. She was examined at a hospital and doctors stated that there were no signs that she had been physically assaulted. Claudette had been turned into something approaching a zombie, and last heard of she still had not uttered one word.

A mystery with ufological undertones maybe. Unfortunately, the follow-ups shed no light on this bizarre series of events.

I sent a letter to the French Embassy in June and then a chaser in September. No reply has been forthcoming. A letter sent to Police Rodez, Aveyron, Commissioner Jean Dinard, who seemed to be handling the investigation, was returned by the GPO with unreadable French scribble all over the envelope. A letter was sent in July to the French branch of Contact International, a UFO organisation based in Oxford. As seems usual — no reply. I also wrote to Jacques Vallée care of his publishers, but this was returned by the GPO marked 'GONE AWAY'. Letters to the *Daily/Sunday Express* have always gone unanswered (on this case and others) so no luck there.

Is this not a classic example of further investigation being hampered by bad luck and official apathy?

■ *Sunday Express* 2 April 1978 ■
On the 12th March 1978 Mr. John Harrison, director of West Yorkshire Leathers Ltd., was found sitting on a clifftop apparently looking out to sea. He was dead. He had been missing for three days and was last seen in his blue Lancia. After searching for three weeks the police could find no trace of the car. One police spokesman said, "it looks as though the Lancia has vanished from the face of the earth." One wonders.

He had a happy home life and his company was in order. I obtained details on the company from Companies House in London, and its profit and loss a/c stood at £278,152 credit, year ended 31 Dec 1977. Also the company was not illiquid — so no money problems.

A post mortem was held and an inquest was resumed on the 21st April 1978. The results? I wrote to Bradford Central Division of the West Yorkshire Metropolitan Police and a reply came back from Inspector Richards. Unfortunately he couldn't, or wouldn't, tell me a damn thing! Only that I should write to the Telegraph & Argus in Bradford, which I did. They knew less than the Sunday Express.

I thank Inspector Richards for his co-operation. I suppose I could write to Mr. Harrison's wife, but somehow I feel that would be a little too imprudent — even for a Fortean.

■ *Sunday Times* 12 Mar 1978 ■
The *En Avant*, a 7-man British Antarctic expedition vessel, was supposed to have made a stop at the Falkland Islands in Jan 1978. In March a search was started to find it, but to no avail. In answer to my letter of 14th June 1978, Lloyds' Register of Shipping stated that the vessel was still missing. Is it missing now? I'm sure that if you write to the Corporation of Lloyds' at Colchester they will tell you.

■ *Sunday Express* 28 May 1978 ■
72-year-old Colonel John Halstead left his lodgings at 10am one Sunday in March '78. He was going to ramble through a wooded beauty spot called Fairlight Glen, two miles from Ore, Hastings.

He had lived at his lodgings for 14 years and was a precise and stable person. A regular churchgoer and probably the epitome of routine, the Colonel had nothing in his background that may have given an indication as to why he never returned from his walk. In August 1978, a Det. Chief Inspector of the Hastings Police wrote to me stating that the Colonel had not been found, dead or alive.

■ *The Guardian* 17 March 1976 ■
Briefly: two members of the Children of God sect were found dead in Belgium, the internal organs of both having been crushed "by amazing force." Jean-Paul Meurice was found at Dinant in Dec 1975 and Michel Piersette near Namur castle in Feb. 1976. Loyal readers of *Fortean Times* can refer to page 11 of FT21 for more background details on these two cultish deaths.

The Belgian Embassy chose to ignore my request for further information, as did the Police Commissioner of Namur. But the police at Dinant were polite enough to reply (in French) stating that they couldn't divulge the details of police cases — so tough luck Forteans!

■ *Fortean Times* 21p13 ■

The Case of the Superclean Boy. Peter Watts, 15, was found dying in an underpass near Euston Station around 1.30am on Monday 19 Jan 1976. His body was "impeccably clean" and his clothes were almost as clean. He had lots of injuries and needless to say he died. Forteans will have to dig out the back issue for more details, but a letter of mine sent to Albany Street P.S. in August 1978 went un-answered until mid-October. The Assistant Commissioner (Crime) at New Scotland Yard regrets that police are unable to assist me (yawn...).

■ *The News/Fortean Times* 13pp14—15 ■

This case is long and involved and is fully explained in The News(FT). It concerns the strange case of Frederick Merry who could have been a victim of an "invisible assailant" whilst in police custody! The whole affair begs many questions. My results were uninspiring and revealed a good example of "passing the buck". I dropped a line off to Hackney Police Station on 7th Aug 1978. They replied on 17 Aug stating that my inquiry had been passed to Bethnal Green P.S. Bethnal Green police replied on the same day, stating that they had passed it on to Bow Street police. Nearly two months went by without a word and then suddenly a letter came from Mrs. Cooper of the Publicity Branch of New Scotland Yard. Here is the essence of her reply:-

"I have read the police report on the death of Frederick Merry and there is nothing to suggest that he died in myserious circum-stances. On arrival at Mile End Hospital it was found that Mr. Merry's heart had stopped, and he was placed on a cardiac arrest machine; he died early on 13 June 1975."

He died of heart failure, but what caused his heart to fail? The questions go begging but the answers are scattered in the wind.

■ *The News/Fortean Times* 13p15 ■

Cause of death...unknown!

Three boys, aged between 16 and 20, were found dead in the living-room of a house in Arnold, Notts, in early Feb 1979. They had been playing acoustic guitars. The woman who owned the house and found the boys, said that the house was noticeably warm. A Det. Inspector said, "the case of death at this moment is a complete mystery."

A letter to Nottingham Constabularly prompted the usual reply: "...this is not the type of enquiry in which we furnish inform-ation." One wonders why.

The letter went on to suggest that I contact the *Nottingham Evening Post* for their report. This I attempted, but to no avail.

■ *The News/Fortean Times* 13p15 ■

In March 1975, George Hicks, 38, serving 6 months for motoring offences, was found dead in his Pentonville cell. Cause of death was given at the inquest as unknown. The letter from the Governor of the prison was sarcastic-ally brief, but in essence... "I cannot assist you in providing information on the case that you quote."

■ *Daily Mail* 30 June 1978 ■

Also *Daily Express* 10 July 1978. Professor George Kenner was working at Liverpool University on a project which would have led to a stunning breakthrough in the field of organic chemistry. He had almost produced the first pure laboratory-bred enzyme, the catalyst essential to all living processes. It could have helped to provide a cure to many diseases. Dr. Kenner often went walking in the Welsh hills to ponder on scientific problems, and this project was no exception. In June 1978 he left his car at Mold and disappeared. Thirteen days later his body was discovered near the top of a 600-feet ravine in Llangwyfan Forest. He was found "in a comfortable position" against a tree with no apparent injuries.

A post mortem was held on the 10th July 1978. On the 11 July I telephoned Holywell Police Station and spoke to the sergeant on the desk. Verbatim, he said... "We are unable to help you, because when the coroner has failed to find a cause of death, we automatically become the coroner's officers, and are, therefore, unable to discuss the case with the public. A few tests will have to be made and they will probably have an inquest in about a month's time."

The date of the adjourned hearing of the inquest was 2.30pm on the 5th October 1978 at County Hall, Ruthin, Clwyd.

Bryan Lewis, the Coroner, stated in a letter to me in September... "I am now in a position to inform you that I have been given a cause of death. You will appreciate that I cannot antici-pate the verdict, but from the present information that has been made available to me it will not be likely that this will be regarded as a mysterious death."

But the case begs questions which will be unanswered, probably forever. Why on this particular walk in the Welsh hills, when he was on the verge of a breakthrough, did Dr. Kenner die? Why was the cause of death so hard to find — if indeed it was found? The fact that he was found sitting up against a tree is odd, like John Harrison (above) sitting on a cliff-top looking out to sea. And the verdict of the inquest. Ring H.M. Coroner on Ruthin 2104 and find out!

●

Paul Pinn

END:TIMES BULLETIN

••Kevin McClure

The patterns we detect in Fortean events and occurrences are not restricted to physical and visual phenomena alone; they also exist in ideas, beliefs. For the umpteenth time in history, a consensus belief is developing and becoming established, despite its apparent illogicality and the frailty of its arguments. The belief is that the world is coming to an end — not quite immediately, but in the foreseeable future, and well before the year 2000.

Many religious movements of the past seem absurd in retrospect, just as do the principles and aims of many popular political movements: the only plausible arguments for their success seem to lie in the areas of psychological need and group delusion. From the Millerites to the Final Solution, from Pol Pot to Judge Rutherford, there is a record of multitudes of ordinary people believing in what is not only untenable, but generally harsh and heartless as well. Jim Jones and Charles Manson only had bit parts on a stage long-filled with crazies.

Of course, it is only later that the world at large even knows what has happened within such movements. At first, it throws up its hands in horror, but in the end explanations are found; by then, the

damage is done, both to the believers, and often to the society outside them.

You've probably heard the recurring joke about the optimists who set up premonitions bureaux in the hope of preventing disasters: the only way you can verify a premonition is if it comes true, if the disaster occurs. To date, I don't think anything was ever prevented. It is asking too much, I suspect, to hope that we can prevent much of the craziness. But we can have a fascinating time in the attempt.

Let's define the territory, and the sources of this new consensus, first pointing out that the central idea is, as yet, a little woolly. It isn't precisely "the end of the world", hunks of the planet drifting through space, etc, or even the holocaust and nothing left alive but radioactive cockroaches. It varies, but all falls loosely under "the end of the world *as we know it*". As with all the other movements I've mentioned, it appears to be the *change* that fascinates.

•

Initially, I can identify six directions from which the consensus is being fed:
•**1 Evangelical and associated fundamental groups.** Various forms of Millenialism, complex sequential scheme of 'the end' commencing, generally, with the Rapture, and moving

through a period of Tribulation, ending with the Second Coming. Always Biblically based, predominantly on *Revelation, Daniel,* and *Thessalonians.* Regards the end as always having been inevitable, but that world conditions mean it is now imminent. For an excellent presentation, approach your local Christian bookshop for Carol Balizet's ficitonalised *The Seven Last Years,* published in 1978.
•**2 Extreme Catholic and related sources.** Typified by those who have total faith in the twentieth-century visions of the BVM, particularly in the supposed Fatima Secrets, the messages at Garabandal, and the various communications to Veronica Leiken at Bayside, NY. A different approach to that of the fundamentalists, in that the BVM and other religious figures warn that the end *will come unless* mankind changes its moral and religious ways, the Church returns to traditional forms of worship, Russia is converted and so on. Of course, the full list of demands is so great that it clearly can never be met. A different form of inevitability and imminence, well-represented by the writings of Cyril Marystone, recently advertised in FT.
•**3 The Doomwatch syndrome** — anti-nuclear, anti-high technology generally. The spiritual aspect of the pessimistic side of the ecology/Green movements. The CND magazine, *Sanity* gives a good flavour of a desperation similar to #2 above — fighting to delay the apparently inevitable consequence of wrong and dangerous actions committed by humanity.
•**4 The New Age approach.** Not wholly disocciated from #3 in its adherents, but more optimistic, bearing much of the philosophy and attitudes of the late 1960's. Looks past the disaster and suffering — probably of nuclear conflict — to a new start, a decentralised society living a simple, low-tech life. See books by

Elizabeth van Buren, inter alia.

●**5 The Survivalist Movement.** Fortunately, mainly restricted to the gun-happy — and spacious — United States: somehow, it is hard to be holed-up in a valley near Rotherham, or Tunbridge Wells. Most closely related, oddly enough to #4 in that, though it sees the 'end of the world as we know it' more in terms of (race-inspired) social breakdown than divine intervention or nuclear doom, it sees the future in terms of small, enclosed, self-determining communities, albeit defended by guns and founded on brute-force. There often seems to be an element of Moral Majority-type Christianity involved. Vast amounts of relevant material in the US, but since the demise of *Protect and Survive*, very little available in Britain.

●**6 The Occult, Prophecy, Nostradamus & his kin**. You probably know this material better than the rest, because it's always brought out for special events, and in this context 2000A.D. certainly is special. The record of successful prophecy of world events is on a par with the battle honours of the Swiss Navy, but that point is continually overlooked. Right now, it is the recent book *Nostradamus: Countdown to Apocalypse* by Jean-Charles Fontbrune (Hutchinson, 1983) that provides the strongest impetus from the prophecy quarter and I'll look at that, and some of the religious source material, in the next installment of this column.

●

Any bits and pieces that you come across — pamphlets, articles, magazines and so on — particularly from the States — would be warmly welcomed, and thanks and credits issued in profusion. Please send to Kevin McClure at 56, Ring Road, Leicester. Thanks.

●

Kevin McClure

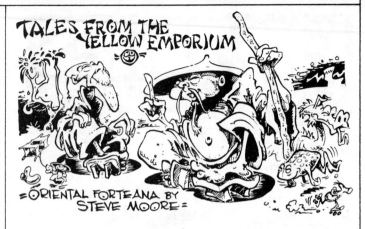

TALES FROM THE YELLOW EMPORIUM

= ORIENTAL FORTEANA BY STEVE MOORE =

One of the things I've always enjoyed about Chinese tales of the strange and supernatural is the air of modesty and matter-of-factness adopted by the authors, even when they're telling the most obvious and enormous whoppers. And it was in light-hearted tribute to the same that I added the tailpiece to last issue's item on hair-cutting panics; that it was only an afternoon's work and hardly exhausted the subject. Prophetic words, for no sooner did the issue see print than more material turned up. So here we go again.

First, more on the 1876 panic, which, according to Giles[1], "convulsed whole provinces". There are tales of harmless strangers being threatened with lynching upon giving the slightest grounds for suspicion, and the "Daoist Pope" (Zhang Tianshi, the Heavenly Master Zhang; probably the 60th of his line) went so far as to publish a charm to deal with the problem, translated as follows:

"Ye who urge filthy devils to spy out the people! The Master's spirits are at hand and will soon discover you. With this charm anyone may travel by sunlight, moonlight, or starlight all over the earth."

Paper men are again mentioned as being responsible for the hair-clipping, and Giles mentions that Daoist priests were generally credited with the power of cutting out human, animal or other figures from paper, infusing them immediately with vitality, and using them for either good or evil purposes... all of which seems a bit unfair to Daoists, as *everyone* was getting the blame for the panic: Buddhists, Daoists, non-denominational sorcerers, and expecially Christians.

And talking of Christians, we next come to the Rev. Henry Du Bose, fourteen years resident at Suzhou (Soochow) whose wonderfully preposterous book[2] not only completely fails to understand Chinese religion but is also written in the splendid "foaming maniac" style so beloved of Protestant missionaires at the time. Leaving aside such priceless allegations as that Buddhism and Roman Catholicism are only identical forms of idolatry, or that all Chinese gods are made of mud, he was actually present for an outbreak of the Tail-cutting mania. He dates this "widespread delusion" to two months of the summer of 1877; whether this is an error for 1876 or a separate incident, I have no idea.

Says Du Bose (or "Du Bozo" as I've come to think of him): that the wave passed down the Grand Canal (running roughly Shanghai to Beijing, though which direction it ran isn't stated), and that persons were allegedly being deprived of their pig-tails by flying paper-men. The peasants left their houses and slept in the fields or under trees, fifty or a hundred in a group. Gongs were imported and beaten, all night and every night, in every hamlet, while processing with lanterns, torches and raised voices passed from village to village (what Du Bozo fails to realise is that drums, gongs, loud noises and lights all have *yang* characteristics, and thus are powerful against the *yin* nocturnal spectres; the actions do have a certain internal logic). It was said that paper-men could enter a house through cracks in the roof, expand to the size of a cow, and crush the sleeping inhabitants. In Suzhou men kept to the streets all night long, afraid to enter their homes. Heat, fright, excitement, demoralisation and wild rumours made the city like a boiling cauldron, and eventually three Catholics (who Du Bozo does at least have the grace to pronounce innocent Chinese fishermen) were accused of sending the paper-men, and duly beheaded.

One night, we're informed, a rumour went round that two foreigners were on the roof of a temple, despatching paper-men. As he says he was absent from town at the time, we're not sure how much credence should be given to Du Bose's statement that the two were identified as himself and his friend. Anyway, "tens of thousands" assembled, beating gongs and yelling, in an attempt to drive away the two who were about to slay all in the city. Two companies of soldiers were marched a mile and a half into town to fire blank cartridges. Again, Du Bose fails to understand that the noise is the important thing, not the bullets, and attributes the use of blanks to fear that the "foreign devils" would unleash a massive shower of paper-men if physically attacked. After two hours, he says, the "foreigners" were discovered to be the shadows of trees, thrown on the roof by the moonlight; which sounds as unlikely as any explanation that the

Chinese might have offered.

In his concluding remarks, Du Bose changes the location of the panic to *Central* China, and mentions the sale by Daoist priests of "genii powder" in small packets, to be tied into the queue as a charm to frighten away the paper-men.

Lastly, we have what appears to be a folklore survival, in a collection of more modern ghosts[3]. This is the Barber's ghost, Gui Ti Tou (literally, the "Head-shaving demon") which is alleged to shave portions, but only portions, of a person's head while they're asleep. The hair never grows again on those spots, which remain bald and shining. It sounds like a

rationalisation of allopecia to me, but who can tell.

I'm tempted to say that that's all I have to say on the subject, but experience restrains me. You never know when some more *clippings* are likely to turn up...

•

Steve Moore

REFERENCES

1) Herbert A Giles, *Strange Stories from a Chinese Studio* (Dover, NY, 1969) p30.
2) Rev Henry Du Bose, *The Dragon, Image, and Demon* (Partridge, London, 1886) p370-371.
3) V R Burkhardt, *Chinese, Creeds & Customs,* (South China Morning Post, Hong Kong, 1958) Vol 3, p58.

CREATURES FROM THE BLACK LAGOON

Reading *Living Wonders* by John Michell and Robert Rickard certainly gives one the notion that a whole host of animals known and unknown, past and present, haunt the world. Indeed, the former inhabitants of this earth, according to Rickard and Michell, may be temporally teleporting, at will, into our own very personal twilight zones. A series of monsters may be jumbled in this catalogue or that category indicating just the point *Living Wonders* is attempting to demonstrate. The only problem is, of course, are these beasts from the past or the future? But more of that later, let's look at a collection of monsters giving clues to a deeper mystery.

In John A.Keel's *Strange Creatures from Time and Space*, Chapter Ten is devoted entirely to a hodgepodge of mostly American beasts Keel felt in some way were related to the Abominable Snowmen and Bigfeet. These ape-like monsters said to be roaming the "hollers and hills" of the eastern and southern United States were always a focus of my research efforts, and one third of Keel's cases for that chapter came from my files. I always wondered, however, what it was about Keel's grouping which made me feel uncomfortable. Finally, it dawned on me that Keel had labeled the chapter somewhat inappropriately. His title, 'Creatures from the Black Lagoon', was a very catchy Keelian way of noting something strange was slithering through the swamps, but the original movie monster he had used as the model was anything but ape-like. The eponymous *Creature from the Black Lagoon* was a reptilian "gill man", a bipedal, human-sized beast which looked more like a spiny skinned were-lizard than a hairy were-gorilla, or were-wolf. The thing was literally half-man, half amphibious reptile.

Now, as creatures go, these types of monsters are rare, but by no means nonexistent. In fact, a lot of monster lumping does occur by Forteans and cryptozoologists, so my task was to closely examine the accounts of existing swamp creatures be they termed Bigfoot, river monsters or whatever, to reveal the true

Creatures from the Black Lagoon.

One classic Bigfoot story — discussed in some detail in this column last issue — namely the Wetzel/Riverside, California sighting of November 8, 1958, clearly fits the reptilian mode better than the anthropoid one. Wetzel described, as you may recall, the fluorescent-eyed "thing" as having a protuberant mouth and a body covered with scales, looking like leaves. Wetzel's "thing" emerged from the Santa Ana River underbrush.

The connection to water is a strong theme in all of these accounts, so it is not so surprising that the next piece of the puzzle comes from the lake monster file. Trekking up the West Coast, the following

report concerns a monster which actually looks like it stepped out of the wardrobe room of the *Black Lagoon* movie.

Thetis Lake is near Colwood, British Columbia, not far from Victoria. Cadboro Bay off Victoria and Vancouver Island is well known for the perennial sea monster 'Cadborosaurus', so understandably a new creature in the neighborhood would be grouped under the same type of facade by the press. But the Thetis Lake Monster appears to be something else altogether.

On the 19th of August, 1972, Gordon Pile and Robin Flewellyn said a five foot tall animal appeared on the surface of Thetis Lake, and chased them from the beach. Flewellyn was cut on the hand by six razor-sharp points atop the monster's head. A Royal Canadian Mounted Police Officer was quoted at the time as saying: "The boys seem sincere, and until we determine otherwise we have no alternative but to continue our investigation."

The next Wednesday afternoon, 23 August, the Thetis Monster was encountered again. Mike Gold and Russell Van Nice said they saw "it" around 3:30pm, and on the other side of the lake, away from the recreation area of its first appearance. Mike Gold noted: "It came out of the water and looked around. Then it went back in the water. Then we ran!"

Gold described the creature as "shaped like an ordinary body, like a human being body but it had a monster face and it was all scaly...(with) a point sticking out its head... (and) great big ears." It was silver.

At last word, the RCMP were investigating the Thetis Monster "because it's been reported to us and we have to check these thing out."

The Thetis Monster account sound similar to one from Saginaw, Michigan, occuring in 1937. A man-like monster

The monster of Thetis Lake, British Columbia, seen on at least three occasions during August 1972.

climbed up a river bank, leaned against a tree, and then returned to the river. The fisherman who witnessed this appearance suffered a nervous breakdown.

This Saginaw tale, the reports of clawed and three-toed prints from Wisconsin to Missouri, and other supposedly "Bigfoot" or "manimal" encounters perhaps should be reexamined in light of the reptilian Creatures from the Black Lagoon.

The big Deltox Swamp, Wisconsin, flap, investigated by Ivan T. Sanderson in 1969, for example, has always been shelved with Bigfoot reports. But what is to be made of the tracks of the creature like footprints of "a good-sized man with swim fins."

In the annals of Midwestern monster hunters is a cryptic chapter few discuss as they talk about the fieldwork done at Louisiana, Missouri. In the early 1970's, many folks looked into the widespread reports of "Momo" (Missouri Monster). One investigator was traveling down a back road, and was surprised to see what *appeared* to be a grown man dressed in complete skin diving gear down to the swimfins, miles from a logical skindiving site. Does this report of a "frogman" have something to do with our inquiry?

The quest is pulling us to the Midwest USA, and is taking an even more unorthodox view of some already weird wonders. But before we get caught up in the focus of the accounts, let's deal with matters in New Jersey and New York.

In a continuous watery line down the Susquehanna River through the socalled Southern Tier of New York State, into the Tamarack swamps along the Delaware ending in the counties of Morris and Sussex, New Jersey, reports, tales and sightings of Creatures from the Black Lagoon are a matter of fact. In 1973, during the summer, residents of New Jersey's Newton-Layfayette

A scaled man-like creature is said to appear at dusk from the red, algae-ridden waters in the swamps of New York State's Southern Tier.

area described a giant man-like alligator they had seen locally. Newspapers commented that an old Indian tale from the region told of a giant man-sized fish which could never be caught. In 1977, New York State Conservation Naturalist Alfred Hulstruck reported that the state's Southern Tier had "a scaled, man-like creature (which) appears at dusk from the red, algae-ridden waters to forage among the fern and moss-covered uplands."

The New York-New Jersey record, however, cannot compare with the overwhelming series of narratives issuing from one place in the United States — the Ohio River Valley.

Over twenty years ago, by digging into the back issues of the Louisville, Kentucky, *Courier-Journal*, I discovered one of those gems which has kept me pondering its meaning for two decades. The interesting little item was in the 24th of October, 1878 issue. A "Wild Man of the Woods" was captured, supposedly, in Tennessee, and then placed on exhibit in Louisville. The creature was described as being six feet, five inches tall, and having eyes twice normal size.

His body was "covered with fish scales." This 1878 article now makes some sense.

And then almost a hundred years later, again near Louisville, there are more stories of reptilian entities. In October 1975, near Milton, Kentucky, Clarence Cable reported a "giant lizard" was roaming the forests near his automobile junkyard. Author Peter Guttilla described the creature Cable surprised as "about 15 feet long, had a foot long forked tongue, and big eyes that bulged something like a frog's. It was dull-white with black and white stripes across its body with quarter-size speckles over it."

On site field investigations by Mark A. Hall, however, indicated that this "giant lizard" ran bipedally, according to other Trimble County, Kentucky, witnesses. The Ohio River is Louisville's, Milton's and Trimble County's northern boundary.

On the 21st of August 1955, near Evansville, Indiana, Mrs. Darwin Johnson was almost pulled forever into the depths of the Ohio River. In what seems to have been a very close meeting with one of these creatures, Mrs Johnson of Dogtown, Indiana, was swimming with her friend Mrs Chris Lamble about 15 feet from shore when suddenly something grabbed her from under the surface. It felt like the "hand" had huge claws and "furry" (or scaly?) palms. It came up from behind her, grabbed her left leg, gripped her knee and pulled her under. She kicked and fought herself free. It pulled her under again. Although both women could not see the thing, they were screaming and yelling to scare it away. Finally, Mrs Johnson lunged for Mrs Lamble's innertube, and the loud "thump" apparently scared it away, and it released its grip.

Back on shore, Mrs Johnson received treatment for her scratches and marks on her leg. Fortean investigator Terry

Colvin passed on the information that Mrs Johnson had a palm print green stain below her knee which could not be removed, and remained for several days. (Interestingly, Colvin learned the Johnsons were visited by an individual who identified himself as an Air Force colonel who took voluminous notes and warned them not to talk further about the incident. (Of course, this sounds so similar to a Man-In-Black encounter that it goes almost without saying.)

For anyone who has seen *Creature from the Black Lagoon*, the Ohio River encounter of Mrs Darwin Johnson is already familiar, for her attack was foreshadowed in that movie.

John Baxter in his *Science Fiction in the Cinema*, recounts those moments: "A key scene of the film is when heroine (Julie Adams) enters the water for a swim, unaware that the creature is swimming just below her, admiring. Shots looking up towards the surface show the girl pentrating a Cocteau-like mirror, her white suit with its accentuated breasts, her choreographed leg movements all overtly sexual. Gliding beneath her, twisting lasciviously in a stylised representation of sexual intercourse, the creature, his movements brutally masculine and powerful, contemplates his ritual bride, though his passion does not reach its peak until the girl performs some underwater ballet movements, explicitly erotic poses that excite the Gill Man to reach out and clutch at her murmuring legs."

The Gill-Man, the first Creature of the Black Lagoon, is presented in the film, according to Baxter, "As a force of elemental power, not maliciously evil but 'other-directed', a fragment of a world where our ideas of morality have no relevance."

We can only speculate that the same may be true of the very "real" Creatures from the Black Lagoon.

From Evansville, Indiana's 1955 watery attack to Loveland, Ohio's 1955 case of the "trolls under the bridge", the story continues along the Ohio River Valley. Leonard H. Stringfield's enquiry into the "affair under the bridge" is perhaps well known to most readers of *Fortean Times*. In March 1955, after a guard had been placed at the bridge, and after the F.B.I. had investigated, Ted Bloecher started talking to the businessman who had seen the four little 3 foot tall creatures with frog's faces. The elements of the case have been well documented in the ufological literature, but there is one point I would like to make which may have mislead Forteans interested in such matters for years. The famous drawing of the "trolls under the bridge", with their lop-sided chests, was sketched by Stringfield based on his *impression* of what was seen, and not drawn under the direction of the witness. The exact description of the 1955 — Loveland "trolls" could more properly place them in Fortean creature chronicles than in ufo books. The frog-like nature of Loveland's 1955 beasts in reinforced by the sightings from near there for 1972. In March of that year, on two separate occasions, two Ohio policemen saw what has become known as the "Loveland Frogman". Investigated by Ron Schaffner and Richard Mackey, these researchers interviewed the officers involved but have not published their names, instead using the fictitious names, "Johnson" and "Williams".

The first incident took place at 1AM on 3 March 1972, on a clear, cold night. Officer Williams was on route to Loveland, via Riverside Road, when he thought he saw a dog beside the road. But then the "thing" stood up, its eyes illuminated by the car lights, then looked at him for an instant, turned, and leapt over a guard rail. Williams saw it go down an embankment into the Little Miami River, a mere fifteen or so miles from the Ohio River.

Williams described the thing as weighing about 60 pounds, about three to four feet tall, having a textured leathery skin, and a face like a frog or lizard.

Williams went on to the police station and returned with officer Johnson to look for evidence of the creature. They turned up scrapemarks leading down the side of the small hill near the river.

On approximately the 17th of March, 1972, Officer Johnson was driving outside of Loveland when he had a similar experience. Seeing an animal lying in the middle of the road, he stopped to remove what he thought was a dead critter. Instead, when the officer opened his squeaky car door, the animal got up into a crouched position like a football player. The creature hobbled over to the guardrail, lifted its leg over while constantly looking at Johnson. Perhaps it was the funny smirk on its face, but Johnson decided to shoot at it. He missed, he figured, since the thing didn't slow down.

Johnson later told how he felt it was more upright than the way Williams described it. One area farmer told investigators he saw a large frog-like or lizard-like creature during the same month of the officers' sightings.

And that is the end of the stories to date.

The evidence from the Ohio River Valley, therefore, is rather strong for these Creatures from the Black Lagoon being more reptile than man. Just exactly what these animals are, however, is anyone's guess, but the time teleportation theories expressed in *Living Wonders* could give us some crazy insights into what may be happening. What if these creatures were transporting themselves back in time from some future portal?

Dale Russell, a Canadian paleontologist, has of late promoted the idea that reptiles had/have as much a possibility to evolve an intelligent, bipedal form as did the mammals. His drawings of this animal look suspiciously like the composite picture we get from the sightings of the Ohio Valley/Black Lagoon creatures. Are these beasts future time travelers lost in some time/space warp? Or infrequent visitors?

Or do you feel more comfortable with the idea there is a breeding population of scaly, manlike, upright creatures lingering along the edges of some of America's swamps?

Something is out there. That's for sure.

●

Loren Coleman

- by Michael Hoffman -

UP ON THE CROSS (HAIRS)

Malachi was a 12th century Irish monk and "Prophet of the Popes" who has made accurate predictions about the Papacy. Malachi Martin is a 20th century Irish-American Jesuit, former Pontifical Biblical Institute Professor with a doctorate in archaeology and Semitic Languages from the Louvain Institute, personal secretary to the late Cardinal Bea, advisor to Pope John-23 and the author of *The Decline and Fall of the Roman Church* (Bantam), a history and prophecy of the Papacy.

Dr. Martin has suggested that Pope John Paul I was assassinated by: *"enemies... whose vital interests lay in completing the dismantling of Roman authority...(and by) those whose lives and fortunes were tied to Vatican material interests..."[1]*

The "dismantling of Roman authority" is the objective of Progressivist bishops and cardinals who wish to Protestantize the Papacy into a "first among equals" bishopric. The "material interests" are centered within the masonic Propaganda-2 (P-2) banking mafia.[2] Dr. Martin, who was and is in the good graces of Popes JP-1 and JP-2, has been instrumental in attacking/exposing the P-2 penetration of the Vatican on American television.[3]

According to Martin the forces of Freemasonry were beaten decisively in the Conclave that elevated Cardinal Albino Luciani to the Papacy. Dr Martin informed this writer that Cardinal Pironio, an Argentine–Italian, was the Papal candidate of the Marxist/ Masonic faction within the cardinalite during the August 1978 Conclave. But Pironio and all other "leftist" candidates were excluded from consideration for the Papal office by voice vote.[4]

"And that night when they closed the doors at the preliminary meeting, (Cardinal) Benelli stood up and said, 'We exclude, by voice vote, all leftist candidates'. And there was bloody murder at that."[5]

This power-move, on the part of the cardinals in favor of Luciani, came about according to Martin, as a result of black-mail:

"These men are utterly ruthless. You know clerics together. Oh, no holds barred. And there are no holds barred between these men...(Cardinals) Benelli and Ciappi, and Siri and Pappilardo and (the late) Ottaviani had (kept) a dossier on everyone of the Progressivist cardinals – their boys, their girls, their money and their masonic papers. And they said, 'Read those for bedtime and come back and talk'... They passed around the documents about the masonic affiliations. They passed around the photographs of cardinals "on beaches". It was a bloody meeting. a bloody meeting...So between the 7th and the 24th they battled this out. And Benelli and Ciappi and Wyszinski and Ratzinger... formed a new coalition of 60 or 70 cardinals – conservatives and traditionalists – and that's only 8 short of the Conclave majority (75)."[6]

Thirty-four days after his ascension, John Paul I was dead. His last words before retiring on the night of Sept. 23 were, "They are all starting to kill each other".[7] The prelate responsible for securing JP-1's corpse and investigating his death was Papal *camerlengo* (chamberlain) Jean Cardinal Villot who had taken such a drubbing at the hands of Luciani's allies at the last month's Conclave. Villot was also regarded as one of the foremost masonic agents with a notoriety shared only by Vatican Secretary of State Agostino Casaroli and *Novus Ordo* liturgical reformer Archbishop Annabala Bugnini.[8]

Civilita Cristiana, a conservative Italian lay group approached a Vatican prosecutor in autumn, 1978 urging the official to act on information they possessed about JP-1's alleged murder. The prosecutor did nothing but as a result of this and other pressure an autopsy was ordered by Villot under his jurisdiction. Verdict: natural causes, but with the credibility of Billot being what it was the mystery persists.

On May 13, 1917 in Fatima, Portugal a radiant woman who would later reveal Herself as the Blessed Virgin Mary (BVM) made the first of a series of appearances to three shepherd children which would culminate in the "Miracle of the Sun" and warnings against the spread of "errors" by Sovietized Russia if mankind did not pray and repent.

Exactly 64 years later, on May 13, 1981, Pope John Paul II, who presumably was elevated to the Papacy by factions and methods similar to the ones that brought JP-1 to power, was shot and seriously wounded in St. Peter's Square. Mehmet Ali Agca, a Turkish hit-man rumored to be in the employ of the Soviet KGB via the Bulgarian Intelligence-connected Stipam/Propaganda -2 narcotics & gunrunning front, was seized and charged with the crime.

He remains in jail where perhaps his thoughts have turned to contemplation of Fatima, the most beloved daughter of Mohammed; or even to the Lady Fatima Herself, who chose the former Moorish stronghold to make manifest what is widely regarded to be the most spectacular and enigmatic Marian apparition in recorded history.

In May of 1982, JP-2, the mystic-phenomenologist known to be immersed in end-time prophecy, journeyed to Fatima to give thanks for his recovery from the shooting. The mood among the thousands gathered was not unlike that experienced on a rainy October, 1917, on the same site that saw the sun "spin". For the "secret" of Fatima, entrusted to the child-seers by the BVM for opening by the Pope in 1960, had never been publically revealed, as purportedly intended by the BVM. Rumors about its doom-saying contents have circulated wildly eversince

John-23 (who took the name and number of a discredited 15th century anti-Pope and is alleged to have been a Rosicrucian[9]) read and suppressed it.

Now with Pope John Paul-II in Fatima on a personal pilgrimage of thanksgiving, the mood of the crowd was one of expectancy...of some great revelation. Sister Lucia, the sole survivor of the three children was on hand too. JP-2 told the crowd, "Do you want me to tell you a *secret?*"

The assembled multitude held its collective breath as the Pope responded to his own momentous question with "Pray...pray the rosary." If the crowd experienced an emotional let-down, it was well-concealed and, as events conspired, they were not to be denied a spectacle.

As JP-2 was heading for the altar at the Chapel of the Apparition, he was charged by Father Juan Fernandez Krohn who was wielding a bayonet and shouting imprecations against JP-2, Archbishop Casaroli, and accusing the Pope of betraying the Solidarity union in Poland. Interestingly, the conspiracy scenario for Ali Agca's attempt in 1981 has him shooting the Pope because the KGB wants to stop the Pontiff's encouragement of Solidarity.[10]

Father Krohn, who was recently sentenced to 6½ years in prison for his Papal attack, was ordained by French Archbishop Marcel Lefebvre and had been "helping out at one of (his)...priories right up to the time of the attempt."[11] Krohn is known to have clashed with Lefebvre over his (Krohn's) *Sedevacantist* ("Vacant See") convictions. This faction maintains that all the Popes beginning with John-23 are anti-Popes, i.e. self-excommunicated by virtue of the supposedly heretical reforms they've instituted and hence, no Popes at all.

The leader of the *Sedevacantists* is the former Archbishop of Hanoi, 85 year old

Pierre Martin Ngo Dinh-Thuc who was recently excommunicated for a second time (he has repented once) for giving episcopal consecration to dozens of "bishops" including Clemente Dominguez Gomez, the blind visionary of Palmar de Toya, Spain, who has since proclaimed himself Pope Gregory XVII.[12] Because the *Sedevacantists* are a sort of law unto themselves they regard even each other as potential heretics and it is likely that in the near future we shall see "several rival *sedevacantist* 'popes' anathematizing each other from different parts of the world, in addition to the 'pope' of Palmar de Troya, and another 'pope' reigning...in Canada." [13].

One church powerbroker opposed to many of JP-2's policies but unwilling to deny his status as legitimate Pontiff is Mgr. Marcel Lefebvre who has been meeting regularly with the Vatican's Cardinal Joseph Ratzinger (one of the Pope-makers of the 1978 conclaves). Lefebvre recently declared that a compromise is about to be struck. Externally, Lefebvre represents staunch opposition to Freemasonry and the "New Order" vernacular mass. But the *Sedevacantists* regard him as a sell-out and one has to wonder how Lefebvre is managing to be so intimate with the Vatican when a priest he ordained allegedly tried to kill the Pope.

In the brilliant *Holy Blood, Holy Grail,* authors Baigent, Leigh and Lincoln list Lefebvre lieutenant Mgr. Ducaud-Bourget as the Grandmaster of the *Prieuré de Sion,* a secret illuminist order of Europeans who believe themselves to be the blood descendants of Jesus Christ and Mary Magdalen. The *Blood Grail* writers say that Lefebvre's ability to avoid excommunication for his defiance of Vatican Council II and Paul-6 and his consistent cachet inside the Vatican is due to his knowledge as a "Sion" initiate. "It seems to have rendered the archbishop wholly immune to punitive action from Rome".[14] They go on to claim that Lefebvre may be an agent of the "More Catholic Than the Pope" aristocractic, hermetic, "Christian" 19th century Freemasonry known as the Hieron du Val d'or.

Was the Pope protected by some vestige of the Fatima Factor's occluded mass-mind-brain-power from 1917? Will this save him from the hate vibe generated by the traditional Biblical fundamentalist view of the Papacy as ever-present Antichrist incarnate? What of the new outlook of traditional *Sedevacante* Catholics who agree that JP-2 is an Antichrist type? Will masonic penetration of the Vatican proceed or can JP-2 reverse the trend? Are the fundamentalists and Zionists using "predictive programming" to launch a synthetic or forced Second Coming?[15] Is JP-2 attempting to halt or slow down the march toward the Apocalyptic scenario? Amid all the players, partisans and politicos manoeuvering for position, carving up the deals and stage-managing the future through manipulation of ancient archetypes like the BVM and pop ones as embodied in *Raiders of the Lost Ark* and Hal Lindsey's *Countdown to Armageddon*, who shall prevail? And who shall be the next to go up on the Cross (hairs)?

NOTES
1] Malachi Martin, *Decline and Fall of the Roman Church* (Bantam pb, Feb 1983) p 235.
2] Cf. 'America Mystica', *FT*39 pp50-51.
3] Cf. 'God's Banker.' *PBS Frontline* (Feb 1983); and 'St Peter's Banker.' *CBS 60 Minutes* (May 1983).
4] Statements by Malachi Martin from an interview in Rochester, NY, conducted 18 Sept 1978 with this writer and tape recorded. Besides Pironio, the exclusion targeted Cardinals Hume, Suenens and Villot.
5] Ibid.
6] Ibid.
7] Martin, op.cit.

8] Dominican Father R.McKenna, *Masonic Prelates in the Church* (ORCM Reprint No.6), gives masonic initiation dates for Casaroli (28 Sept 1957), Bugnini (23 April 1963), and Villot (6 Aug 1966; which can also be written 8/6/66).
9] Baigent, Leigh & Lincoln, *Holy Blood, Holy Grail* (Dell pb) pp159-161.
10] UPI, in a May 1982 wire story, reports that Father Krohn visited Solidarity unionists in Poland, introducing himself as "a monk and an anti-communist". The union's chaplain said he'd recognize the priest again "by his teeth"(1). Dr. Martin notes that the KOR Troskyite element within Solidarity wishes to "eviscerate" the Catholic Church in Poland.
11] Michael Davies, *The Remnant* (15 Dec 1982). Lefebvre was suspended "*a divinis*" in 1977 by Paul-6, which means that his episcopal functions, while illicit, nevertheless retain their validity. Lefebvre is listed in the current *Vatican Yearbook* compilation of prelates

officially recognized by the Church.
12] Cf. Bob Rickard, 'Clemente Dominguez: Pope, Heretic, Stigmatic.' *FT*30pp32-36.
13] Michael Davies, 'The Sedevacantists.' *The Angelus* (Feb 1983). An important Sedevacantist researcher is W.J.Strokie (41695 Clark-Smith Drive, Lebanon, Oregon 97355, USA). $1 for his catalogue.
14] Baigent, Leigh & Lincoln, op. cit. pp210-214.
15] M.S.Relfe, *When Your Money Fails...666*. On p232 she cites the film *The Final Conflict* and its prominent use of the 666 Beast/Antichrist numerical function as further testament to the growing power of 666. Relfe, a Biblical fundamentalist, neglected to mention that the film was produced in cooperation with Biblical fundamentalists.

•

Michael Anthony Hoffman II

First of all, an update on books already mentioned in this column. Loren Coleman's long-awaited book has changed its title to **MYSTERIOUS AMERICA**, and will be published on 31 October by Faber and Faber, Inc., of Winchester, Massachusetts, with either a UK edition or an import of the US edition to follow. The US price will be $6.95 for a 176-page paperback containing 'a mind-boggling harvest' of Forteana. **CLEAR INTENT**

by Larry Fawcett and Barry Greenwood (about the US government's role in UFO research) should be available in the spring of 1984 from Prentice-Hall.

This autumn sees a mixed bag of new books, with just about something for everyone. In September, Arrow paperbacks publish **THE BOOK OF CHINESE BELIEFS** (£1.75), which examines the Chinese world of the occult, a world of spirits, Earth magic, demons and ghost weddings (no author given in my source). I'm not quite sure what's in John Blashford-Snell's **MYSTERIES: Encounters with the Unexplained** (Bodley Head, £8.95, October), but it sounds possibly Fortean. For Atlantis freaks, September sees the publication of **IRELAND: Journey Into Lost Time** by P.A. O'Siochain (Turoe Press/Marion Boyars, hardback £10.95, paperback £3.95), which explains how Ireland and its western islands of Aran, along with some tiny islands further south in the Atlantic, are the last remnant of the Atlantean civilisation. UFO veteran John Magor has a new book with an odd title: **ALIENS ABOVE, ALWAYS** (CUFOR Books, Box 758, Duncan, B.C., V9L 3Y1, Canada, $11.50 in Canada and USA, $12.50 elsewhere). Floris Books of Edinburgh are publishing a new edition of **CASPER HAUSER: The Enigma of a Century** by Jacob Wasserman, first published in 1928. The 468-page paperback will cost £5.95.

Ghost-hunter Peter Underwood's autobiography **NO COMMON TASK** comes from Harrap in November (£7.95), covering 35 years of psychical research, including hitherto unpublished experiences from his casebook. In the same subject area, Brian Inglis' new book from Hodder & Stoughton promises to pull no punches, as he speaks out in **SCIENCE AND PARASCIENCE** (January £9.95) about the battles between psychical researchers and orthodox scientists. The quantity and quality of the original evidence for such phenomena as telepathy, clairvoyance, precognition, psychokinesis, poltergeist hauntings and dowsing is emphasised, and the unscrupulousness of some sceptics in their determination to destroy what they regard as occult superstition is made clear. A third title in this field is **THE OCCULT IN AMERICA: New Historical Perspectives**, edited by Howard Kerr and Charles L. Crow (University of Illinois Press, £14.45). The subject in America's 300-year experience with supernatural phenomena and esoteric wisdom.

'Truly iconoclastic, utterly convincing and highly controversial — a new book that challenges a century of scientific orthodoxy since Darwin' is the publisher's blurb for **THE INTELLIGENT UNIVERSE** by Sir Fred Hoyle, also noted on the cover as 'A New View of Creation and Evolution' (Michael Joseph, October, £12,95). The same publisher also has a new book by the ubiquitous Patrick Moore, **COUNTDOWN — Or How Nigh is the End** (£8.95, published in association with the Rainbird Publishing Group). He looks at end-of-the-world panics of the past and considers what will happen when the world really does end. I doubt it's a serious study, knowing PM's past record! Natural historian Stephen Jay Gould has a new selection of essays published by W.W. Norton, **HEN'S TEETH AND HORSE'S TOES** (September, £11.95/$18.75), discussing concepts central to science and in particular to an understanding of Darwin's theory of evolution, Gould's favourite theme. One to read immediately before or after Fred Hoyle's new book!

Paladin Books adds to its list of titles by Janet & Colin Bord in October when it publishes a paperback edition of **EARTH RITES: Fertility Practices in Pre-Industrial Britain** (£2.95). In January Penguin Books will publish a paperback edition of **ASTROLOGY: Science or Superstition?** by H.J. Eysenck and D.K.B. Nias. Yet another book on whale tumour stories, or urban legends, whichever description you prefer: **THE BOOK OF NASTY LEGENDS** edited by Paul Smith (Routledge & Kegan Paul, paperback, £4.95). It contains the usual 'friend of a friend' tales — hairy-handed hitch-hiker, granny on the roofrack, rat's leg in the restaurant, and so on. Much more edifying, not to say essential reading, will be the new series being launched by Aquarian Press/Thorsons Publishing in conjunction with ASSAP early in September, 'The Evidence' series. The first two titles are **THE EVIDENCE FOR UFOS** by Hilary Evans, and **THE EVIDENCE FOR VISIONS OF THE VIRGIN MARY** by Kevin McClure (both paperbacks, £2.50). Finally, **LEY LINES IN QUESTION** by Tom Williamson and Liz Bellamy, an argument against the existence of leys, is due soon from World's Work (£7.95).

I have details of five books in preparation, three of them UFO books, so let's start with a non-UFO title that is in the true Fortean tradition. Bob Skinner is researching what promises to be *the* book on toads-in-the-hole, provisionally entitled **ENTOMBED ALIVE: A Study of the 'Toad-in-the-Hole' Phenomenon**. He already has about 200 cases, but is anxious for more, and readers with · information should write to him at Squirrels, The Horseshoe, Banstead, Surrey, SM7 2BG. New UFO books on the way include another from Jenny Randles and Peter Warrington, provisionally entitled **SCIENCE AND THE UFOS**, which has developed from their 'New Scientist' article and will be published by Basil Blackwell. Jenny is also working on **THE FAMOUS FILES** for Robert Hale, a collection of strange happenings involving celebrities, for which she welcomes contributions and readers' information (9 Crosfield Road, Somerville, Wallasey, L44 9EH). Raymond Fowler, he of the two-books-already on the Betty Andreasson affair, is now working on a pictorial book on the case for Prentice-Hall, to include Betty's drawings with commentary. Another long-running US case is to appear in book form, the Cash-Landrum case in which the unfortunate witnesses were burned by a possible UFO. Authors are Bob Pratt and John Schuessler, and their intention in publishing **FIRE IN THE ROAD** is to help other people in a similar situation and to dispel rumours caused by fake events such as one in Venezuela when people were said to have been harmed by a UFO, this being a fabricated story based on the Cash-Landrum case.

After all this heavy fare, readers may be glad of a little light relief. They should look out for **THE OGOPOGO**, written and illustrated by Harry Horse (Macdonald Publishers, Edinburgh, October, 80-page hardback, £4.50): 'The Loch Ness Monster sets off for the North Pole in search of friends and meets the wonderful Ogopogo.' Nessie was probably tired of all the attention she's been getting in her golden anniversary year!

●

Janet Bord

Small Ads.

EDITORIAL
Cont from p

welcome. We are also looking into the possibility of becoming a limited company, perhaps even offering shares to existing subscribers.

Phase two would see the limited distribution of FT, perhaps to major cities at first.

Rest assured that, despite all this talk of expansion, we do not intend to lose sight of the fact that our subscribers are our first and best friends, and we hope that we will never become impersonal to you, or too complaisant. For Fort's sake tell us if we do. It is entirely possible that we'll turn our back on the normal distribution channels and simply devote our energies to increasing our subscriber base. It has a lot of advantages.

We are not under any illusion that we would be a best seller if we went on the open market; quite the contrary, we would be happy with a few thousand stable, faithful readers who enjoy their pursuit of our sort of subject range. The success of *The Unexplained*, with sales of several tens of thousands of copies each week has demonstrated the market potential admirably. *The Unexplained* will finish its run with issue 156, and in the full knowledge that we might never have such a chance again, we want to do all we can to catch as many as possible of those readers who will be left dangling. Conseqeuntly we took two whole page ads in TU itself (in issues 144 and 153), and we'll begin advertising elsewhere.

Our motives for this expansion are simple. It is not that we have dreams of empire, but that for too long our many projects have been hampered by the lack of funds, some of them never getting off the ground for this reason, others condemned to snail-like progress for lack of services or equipment. In the long run a profitable FT is the only stable way to generate some income,

which can be channelled into publishing books, funding research or the Fortean database, etc. Naturally it's jobs for the boys too, because we believe we all could accomplish so much more for Fortean studies if we were free of the additional burden of earning a living elsewhere. One of these projects, to be announced later, will be the formation of our associated academic arm, with a name like 'The Fortean Institute' or 'Center for Fortean Studies', whose main task will be archive and computer database work. Another will be... expanding our rudimentary book service into a full scale mail order shop for Fortean books.

●

Bob Rickard

The Exmoor Beast and Others.

The omens were all there — 1983 is to be another 'Year of the Cat', and by now you know I mean, not the cute kind, but those large, sinister lurkers which tantalize us with sightings and then are gone as suddenly as they came. One signal was the publication of *Cat Country*, by Di Francis (see last issue), in mid-January. Another, more celestial interpolation came in the episode of *The Archers* for 8 Feb, when this everyday story of countryfolk took an unexpected turn into said cat country and found itself peppered with mentions of "a mystery big cat", a "leopard", "tiger", or "puma", with references to the Scottish puma (see FT34p24), the Hackney bear (see FT37p45) and ewes found killed on farms around "the village".

Back in 'real life' the main circus has been on Exmoor, but as you'll see big cats were springing out of the bushes all over England, often simultaneously in different places from April to June. As you wander bemused through the sightings we've amassed for you below, perhaps you'll boggle, as we do, at the extent of the mystery, and its prevalence in May.

OTHER BEASTS, OTHER PLACES

Sightings of big cats have continued in Britain since our last roundup in FTs 34 and 35 in 1981. We simply had no room for them, but they are filed, and will undoubtedly be logged in the book currently being researched on the phenomenon by our own Chris Hall and Graham McEwan. Another big cat researcher who deserves mention for investigating local cases is Alan Gardiner. We file all reports and clippings, even if we can't acknowledge, look into or report them. For now, we begin our listing, arbitrarily, at Christmas 1982...

•

☐ **Brighton, Sussex** — Just after 10pm on the night of **23 Dec**, Douglas Owen thought he saw a cheetah. He was driving alone, at the junction of Mill Rd and Dyke Rd, when he saw the animal "lying down on its front paws" on a grassy bank. "After a short while it got up and loped off towards some houses." He reported it to the police. Brighton *Eve.Argus* 24 Dec 1982.

☐ **Ilkeston, Derbyshire** — Vincent Mizuro, of Drummond Rd, was feeding the ducks in his orchard when he saw what seemed to be "a large bundle of black fur or several cats together" curled up on a mound 100yds away. He whistled to rouse it "to see what it was" and to his amazement unfolded into a 3ft-long puma-like creature with long fur. It did not seem concerned at disturbance, but it had gone by the time Mizuro's wife arrived in answer to his call. He said he was prompted to tell the paper of the sighting after reading a review (that same week) of Di Francis' book. No date

is given for the encounter; we guess it was sometime before **2 Feb**, probably in the last week of January. Derby *Eve. Telegraph* 8 Feb 1983.

☐ **Withiel Turn, Roche, Cornwall** — At 9.30am, on **22nd Feb**, Mrs Beatrice Ould set out to walk her dog. As they passed her garage the dog dashed inside it to investigate a noise. A fearful fight ensued as, to her horrified gaze, she saw her dog battling two lion cubs. They were 7mths-old and "as big as Alsatians". The cubs had escaped from their owner, 200yds away across a field. Not a mysterious story, but in view of the predominance of 'lion' sightings, it has relevance. *Western Morning News* 24 Feb; *S.Express* 27 Feb 1983.

☐ **Buckinghamshire** — Dubbed 'The Chiltern Puma', there were two main sighting areas, Stokenchurch, and Wendover. At Stokenchurch, near High Wycombe, two people reported the date to be **15 April**). A police search on the **16th** found nothing. *News of the World, S.Mirror, S.Mercury* 17 April 1983.

Then after a short hiatus a puma-like animal was spotted on the RAF Halton housing estate, near Wendover, on **5th May**, by four women. Mrs Kim Griffin said: "I saw this big black cat. It was only eight feet away and moved off into the long grass. It had a tail as long as an Alsatian. But this was no dog. It was a puma." A plastercast of a five-inch diameter paw-print was sent to Oxford University for identification. A circus-owner reassured the public by stating that a puma is quite capable of "ripping a child to pieces." On the **8th**, police said the 'Chiltern Puma' had been seen at least six times in three weeks in a 13 mile radius, all by reliable witnesses, and that they acknowledge the fact that a large wild animal is in the area... but after that, no more news! *Eastern Daily Press, D.Telegraph, Sun, D.Star, D.Mirror* 7 May; *S.People* 8 May; *D.Star* 9 May 1983.

☐ **Didcot, Oxfordshire** — A 30-stone 5yr-old lioness escaped from an evening performance of Charlie Weight's mini-circus, and was at large for six hours before being cornered in a garage, on **12 May**. *D.Telegraph, Sun* 13 May; *D.Telegraph* 14 May 1983.

☐ **Adswood, Stockport,** Gtr Manchester — Granny Margaret O'Malley had noticed the large cat in her yard the previous night, and tried to shoo it away. As she left for work in the morning it was still there, lounging on the roof of the garden shed. "It looked hungry so I gave it a saucer of milk." Then, the even more unexpected happened: a cowgirl on horseback galloped up to her house. It's not said how the girl caught the cat, which was a young puma, but she then slung it over her saddle and rode off. The animal had escaped from a travelling circus. Minutes later dozens of police arrived to ring Margaret's home in the belief the puma was still there. No data given, but possibly between **9-14 May**. *News of the World* 15 May 1983.

☐ **Ysbyty Ystwth, near Tregaron, Gwent** — Seven ewes and five lambs dead; gaping holes in their sides, made by dog or fox, it is said. But three prints were "positively" identified as of cat family, though four times the size of a normal cat's. Casual reference to "Two previous sightings in two months," all within a 15-mile radius. That's a lot of territory, and if it applied to the Exmoor Beast, would take in Dartmoor as well! *Western Mail* 14 May 1983. Then, next day...

Rogerstone, Gwent — Milkman Robert Mitchum was delivering to Cefn Road at 4.45am on **14 May** when he saw a large cat-like animal in his headlights before it disappeared into an alley. It was "too big to be a dog" and he reported to the police that he thought it was a "puma or black panther." We have no further reports from this area, but see back to FT35p44 for our last Welsh sightings. *Western Mail* 16 May 1983.

☐ **Cuffley, Hertfordshire** — At 8am on **16 May** a "lion or lioness" was seen by several people in Sutherland Way, a road backing onto woodland. Cuffley is not a million miles away from the Bucks area sightings (above) and the report was taken seriously enough for public warnings and a helicopter search later that day...but as no further reports came in, the search was abandoned. Paw prints were found, but when these were identified as those of a large dog the case was closed as far as the press and police were concerned. From our experience we know this does not preclude the possibility there was a big cat there, because the same official reaction would occur if dog prints were simply found in the vicinity of where the animal was seen. The original sighting was made by a policeman who was with the other witnesses and therefore a reliable one, one would think. But following the popular verdict, the policeman refused to speak to the press. "He's taken a lot of stick from the lads," explained a colleague. However, one of the other witnesses, Mrs Gwen Shipman, said she had been making a bed when she looked out of a window to see the animal in her neighbour's back garden. She called it a lion. "There was no mistaking it. I could see it full in the face." Reading *Eve.Echo* 16 May; *D.Star, Sun, Yorkshire Eve.Post, Western Morning News, Western Mail* 17 May 1983.

☐ **Walton Heath, Surrey** — Laurie Perryman, 68, was driving towards Dorking, past Beecham's Pharmaceuticals when a 2ft high, 4ft long cat-like creature ran across the road in front of him, about 25-30yds ahead. No date. He did not stop and later reported it to the police because he thought it was a cheetah. "It was not a fox or a badger. It had spots like a cheetah." Part of Mr Perryman's certainty about the identity comes from the time he lived in South Africa, and having seen cheetahs run across roads in front of him. "I thought to myself, that looks remarkably like a cheetah." Mr Perryman was interviewed by Chris Hall, who comments: "Whatever he saw, I think we can say he had better observing conditions than many. Some sightings are up to 600yds away." This sighting has added interest in the light of the Cheetah sighting at Brighton, just before Christmas, about 30 miles to the south. I think we have a 'Southeast Cheetah' here. *Banstead Herald* 19 May 1983.

●

THE BLIND BEAST OF DARTMOOR

Before we plunge into the eight-month long saga of the Exmoor Beast, we'd like to give a curious mystery animal case from the south-western end of Dartmoor, almost exactly a year earlier (ie. in April 1982), and which may have some relationship to the doings at Exmoor, not far to the north.

●

Maurice Knowles' farm is hidden down old lanes through leafy woods, near Devon's Lydford Gorge beauty spot, near the southern edge of Dartmoor. On the 5th April 1982, Mr Knowles went out at 3 o'clock in the morning to tend a ewe about to lamb, in a field adjacent to the farmhouse. He had with him a powerful torch, and as he neared the top of the field its beam picked out "a black calf". That was his first impression; then he realized he had no calves in the field, and thought it must be a dog, but its behaviour puzzled him. Dogs usually run off when discovered, but this animal took no notice of the farmer or the powerful light shining on it. Seemingly oblivious, the creature snuffled its way along the top hedge, weaving from side to side, giving Mr Knowles the impression it was "looking for food".

Mr Knowles kept pace parallel but slightly behind with the animal about 20yds away [see map]. He could see it was no dog, but he now had no idea what it was. It was about 3ft high at the shoulder, and all black except for a couple of white spots near its left front leg. It passed close to some sheep and lambs but took no notice of them, as indeed they took no notice of the interloper.

The creature reached the corner of the field and turned, walking straight towards Mr Knowles. He had kept his beam on it all the time, studying it, and now the light shone full on its face. Its head was long, ears turned forward, one pricked and the other folded forward. It had a peculiar barrelled pig-like snout [see drawing]. About 10yds away it stopped and raised its head as if, for the first time it realized it was not alone. The light did not seem to bother it as it sniffed the air. It looked straight at Mr Knowles, and this disturbed him, because he could not see any eyes — only a thin black line where the eyes should be. The torch was shone full into the strange face, but there was none of the usual retinal reflection familiar from animal eyes at night. Mr Knowles became convinced, at this point, that the animal was blind. It stood there, sniffing — its nose round, wet and mobile, like a pig's.

They faced each other for serveral minutes, and then, because he didn't know what else to do, Mr Knowles shouted. The animal turned and "loped" towards the wall. "It seemed to bound in a flowing gait, rather like a foal cantering," he said. It tried to jump the wall and fell back. Thinking he had a chance to seize the creature — "Because no-one would believe me otherwise" — he ran forward. But the animal recovered, clambered to the top of the wall, and was gone. Mr Knowles remembers hearing the thump as it landed on the other side, and that the sheep in both fields were quite undisturbed by these events. The whole sighting had lasted ten minutes.

Mr Knowles was interviewed by Robert Boyd, who prepared a report on the event for the Plymouth UFO Research Group (PUFORG) from which we take our details. Bob Boyd continues: "Mr K. was amazed. How could an animal as large and as strange as this, and blind to boot, avoid being caught, or even seen? Where did it live during the day (though Lydford Gorge would make an ideal retreat)? How did this obviously mature animal grow up with no-one being aware of it?"

By the time Boyd visited the scene with Mr Knowles the footprints of the animal were long gone. Boyd jumped onto the wall, and

discovered some trace of the animal's struggles there — alas neither the photo of this, nor of the only trace of prints, came out. Boyd lifted Mr Knowles' sheepdog up to smell the stone, and it immediately bolted back to the farm. Mr Knowles said, with some puzzlement, that it had never done that before, and he now recalled that that night the dog had refused to come with him, another thing it had never done before.

According to Boyd, Mr Knowles came across as "an honest man simply reporting an event that happened to him." He is a hard-working farmer. His wife said that "if that is what he said, then that is what he saw." Boyd asked him if there had been any livestock losses recently, and Mr Knowles said that both before and since the sighting a lamb had been killed. At least one lamb — we cannot make out if this applies to both deaths — had been killed by a powerful single bite from a very large animal In his opinion a dog was not responsible, nor badger or fox. He had skinned the fleece to use as a coat for a motherless lamb, and found to his astonishment that the whole ribcage was "pulp". He could put one of his podgy fingers through the teethmarks in his skin. He was so impressed, that he later showed the skin to his wife, who confirmed it. He had never seen a killing like it — the whole ribcage being crushed with one bite. Interestingly, Mr Knowles did not link the killings with the strange creature, because, he said, the sheep in the fields had been quite unconcerned with the animal, which he felt would not be the case if the creature was out for blood.

Finally, another curious facet to this fascinating case. Boyd asked farmer Knowles if he thought the animal had been real or a phantom, like the old Black Dog legends of Dartmoor. "He disagreed, saying it was just an animal that had managed to keep itself well away from humans." Then he added: "When I got to bed that night I said to myself, 'I've just seen the devil', though he couldn't say just why he thought that. However, shortly after the event, Mr Knowles went to see his 89yr-old father, and told him of his experience. As he told Boyd, his father reacted unusually. "He wouldn't talk about it. Didn't want to know. He just said 'That's witchcraft...That's not an animal, that's witchcraft!'"

Folkloric footnote — The infamous Judge Jeffries, who held his bloody assizes at Lydford, is said to haunt Lydford Castle in the form of a huge black pig!

Fortean footnote — The Bords asked Heuvelmans' opinion of the case and the great cryptozoologist replied that he did "not see anything quite abnormal in the description of the animal. I could send you a photograph of myself with a great black Dane which looked very much like it, except that it had longer legs." Heuvelmans added that the light reflec-

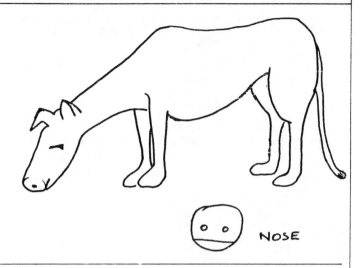

Mr Knowles' strange animal (right) as ambiguous as the Exmoor Beast. The following additional descriptions are culled from various statements by the witness: "Long legs, with hind legs more like a colt or a calf; hock fair high up. Long body with dropping stomach and long tail curving in between back legs...It resembled a colt in size and stance." Tail long, like a greyhound's, as was the coat. Short hair, not fur. Looked very strong and muscular, fit. Broad pad feet. A big animal; not at all nervous, even when witness shouted at it. Very strong upright front legs. Long neck.

NOSE

tion from the retina depends upon the angle of the lightbeam striking it...but "Of course, if Mr Knowles used his torch long enough he should have seen the eyes shining." In fact, Mr Knowles made a special point of the eyes not reflecting his torch!

Heuvelmans continues: "All the same the actual behaviour of the creature was very unusual. A blind dog *could* have behaved in a very strange way... The most intriguing part of this story is of course that the local people should not have heard of a rambling feral giant dog, blind or not.

Quite! This is Baskerville country after all. Can Mr Knowles' beast have anything to do with the puma-like creature, often said to be black, not infrequently sighted on Dartmoor? The moors make an ideal habitat for such an animal; the only question being whether it could find enough to eat. Does this explain Mr Knowles' dead livestock? And is this in turn related to the current sightings of the 'Exmoor Beast' [see elsewhere in this issue] not more than 30 miles to the north?

Sources: The PUFORG 'Sighting Report'; no date, but probably filed under 5 April 1982, Lydford. Sometime after the event it appeared briefly in the *Tavistock Times*, Devon 16 April 1982.

•

THE BEAST OF EXMOOR

The Beast's Saga did not take off until April, maintaining intensity until late June. By mid-July, as I write this, it is tailing off. It was even noised abroad: FT was asked to make a statement about it for Canadian Broadcasting System radio news programme. But let's go back to the beginning. We have a file on Devonshire mystery felines going back many years, and have mentioned them from time to time in FT, the last being sightings in June 1981, in

FT35p45. 1983 saw the public arrival of Di Francis, who has camped on Dartmoor and travelled widely interviewing witnesses in pursuit of the big cats. As she stated in the last FT (p34), and in her book *Cat Country*, she believes the mystery cats are not phantoms but a widespread and undiscovered species of native wild cat.

All we can say for sure is that a lot of people are convinced they've seen a large, distinctive cat-like creature not an obvious native of these isles. We also note the great differences in descriptions, but we'll come to that... Because our sources are newsclippings we are not unmindful of the social and psychological dimensions, but these we have to leave to another time and more detailed study. We find the best way to deal with such long-running stories, with all their intricacies, is to boil the verbiage down into a chronology of events.

•

☐ **Mid-Jan** — In the four weeks prior to our next sighting a large black panther-like cat was sighted four times in the Tedburn St Mary area, between Exeter and Dartmoor. No dates given. This same period saw the publication publicity surrounding Di Francis' book. *Western Morning News* 14 Feb 1983.

☐ **12 Feb** — Two 17yr-old boys, Ian Bowman and Michael Tewson, of Paignton, were taking a dog for a walk down a country lane at Woodland, near Ashburton, on the southeastern edge of Dartmoor, when a 2ft 6in high, black animal "frightened the living daylights out of them. It was late evening, and while shining a torch into a field, they unexpectedly saw a pair of eyes reflecting the beam. The animal moved behind a hedge. Further down the lane they came to a gate and again shone the light into the field. This time the animal came towards them and they got a clear view of it. "It cleared the gate and within seconds disappeared out of sight down the lane." Needless to say, boys and dog exited speedily back to their van. *Western Morning News* 14 Feb 1983.

☐ **Mid-April** — Whether the Exmoor beast is the same one as that of Dartmoor, about 30 miles to the south, or whether there is more than one mystery animal in the area, we cannot yet say. But the Exmoor story bursts upon the press scene almost fully formed, in *North Devon Journal-Herald* for 21 April 1983. The curiosity is that, in a large front page feature on a public hunt for something which was killing sheep on farms around South Molton, we learn that the local story goes back at least to 1982. In spring that year farmer Eric Ley, of Drewston Farm, lost 10 lambs and there were rumours of a large black animal in the area. This year, in a period from the time the first lambs were born up the latest attack on 15th April, Mr Ley lost "at least 30". The reason for his vagueness is that some "lambs were disappearing without trace" and others were found "stripped almost clean of flesh." Twice fully grown sheep have been attacked, and the nearby Bicknow, Limeslake and Pillavins farms have lost lambs in ones and twos. The publicized search, by 50 men, some mounted and most armed, supported by a police helicopter and the Torrington Foot Beagles, lasted all day on **19 April**, but found nothing. Yet, as if to cock a snook at the proceedings, the killer struck again in the midst of the hunt. All the national reports, of the 22nd, paraphrased the *Journal-Herald*.

The police view was that the animal was a dog, and they were looking for a large black one "with white feet". While farmer Ley had organized many all-night vigils over his flocks, and friends had even shot at "something", no one had actually seen the villain. In the midst of this a 16yr-old girl told police that she had seen a large cat-like black animal with white feet, "like a sheepdog...with a very long tail"(1) in a spinney near Drewsone farm just before the killing began. The police imagination seems to have fastened onto this flimsy description as that of the undoubted culprit, and as if to confirm it, lo! dogprints were found in the area.

We are also told that "a large black cat-like animal" was seen at Whitcott Farm, near Drewstone, *two years previously* by two building workers.

☐ **3rd week in April** — A school bus driver, John Franks, found himself following a dog, like no dog he ever saw before, down a lane (no date). This sighting did not surface for three weeks, and was not mentioned by any of the lcoal papers. Franks said: "It was broad in the beam, about two feet. Its jet black coat gleamed as, as though the thing had just stepped out of the hairdressers. It was about 2ft 6in to the shoulders and had powerful legs. I remember thinking, 'God, but you're ugly.' The head just didn't fit on the body. It was old

with grey streaks running back from its muzzle and a mass of whiskers. It didn't seem to have a neck, just this squat head stuck on the end of its body." *The Mail on Sunday* 8 May 1983.

☐ **27 April** — Farmer Ley continues his nightly watches over his sheep. Nevertheless, another lamb went early this morning, bringing his total losses up to about 40. And just three miles away, at Sheepwash, near Molland, farmer W.J.Hayes also lost a lamb, bringing the overall tally to about 60.

Enter former Ilfracombe zoo owner Charles Trevisick. He has a theory about a rogue bitch with a litter of puppies. "When the pups are about eight weeks old they will show themselves and reveal the hideout of the mother." We shall see! We are also told that during the saga so far a number of dogs, including a valuable black Labrador, had been shot in fields. It seems they simply could not get the right one! *North Devon Journal-Herald* 28 April 1983.

☐ **Last week of April** — no date. An unusual animal was sighted at North Molton by ambulance driver Richard Trehern. *The Mail on Sunday* 8 May 1983.

☐ I can hardly accept that the beast, however superbestial by reputation, can have accounted for 10-20 sheep in a few days, yet, according to the Exeter *Express & Echo* 30 April 1983, the current losses run at "70-80 lambs and sheep". It seems these figures originated with the police, for at a press conference the Assistant Chief Constable, Rupert Ormerod, confessed his force's bafflement at the epidemic, so much so that he was going to call in the Royal Marines from their training centre at Lympstone. By 1st May, AP bulletins on the hunt were appearing in US papers.

We are told the killing method — the skulls of the little lambs are crushed by powerful jaws and then they are devoured from the neck down. Sounds like classic Tasmanian Tiger MO to me, but then what do I know... Bristol *Eve. Post*, *Western Mail* 30 April 1983. Later, a different MO is described, or the old one revised: necks are broken at the base of the skull. A typical big cat MO, it is said.

After the press conference two more lambs die: one belonging to Mr Ley, and the other at Hilltown Farm, Molland. Exeter *Express & Echo* 2 May 1983.

☐ **1 May** — A senior policeman at Barnstable, said that a local man had come forward, saying a puma he once owned had now vanished — it's not said when — feared stolen and then released. *D.Mail* 2 May 1983. A farmer spotted a "large, black cat-like animal" at Brembridge Woods, near Filleigh.*Western Morning News* 5 May 1983.

☐ **2 May** — Monday, and the Marines move on South Molton. Great things are expected of the 12 men and their infra-red equipment. I don't

An eviscerated lamb – typical calling card of the Exmoor Beast. [Copyright: North Devon Journal-Herald Ltd.]

know why, because the farmers had been using night sights with little success. They are to base themselves at Mr Ley's farm and spend the whole week lying doggo in camouflaged trenches. Exeter *Express & Echo* 2 & 3 May 1983. Later, we learn that there had been a total of five killings over the preceeding three days, including one at Drewstone. *Western Morning News* 5 May 1983.

☐ **4 May** – At 5.35am, Marine sniper John Holden spotted what many subsequently believed was the 'Beast' a few miles from South Molton. He reported: "I was quite some way off but I could see it was very big, all black and looked very powerful. It was crossing a railway line, but there was a farmhouse in the background and it wasn't safe for me to shoot." *Western Morning News* 5 May 1983. Barnstaple Chief Inspector Roy Roberts wanted to reassure the public that the Marines' primary order was to bring it back alive if possible, and not as many feared to shoot on sight... One certainly gets an impression of the latter from Marine Holden's statement. *North Devon Journal-Herald* 5 May 1983.

☐ **6 May** – A Marine spokesman said their men heard a number of cat-like high pitched screams during the night vigils so far, yet they are convinced it's a dog. "We've found dog's hairs at the sight of sheep killings and we took plaster casts of paw prints from the same sites which experts siad belonged to a dog," said Maj. John Watkins, in charge of 'Operation Beastie'.

Interestingly, while advocating that a dog was responsible for the mayhem, a careful reading of the Major's words implies that there may also be a large cat in the area. He said: "There may well be two animals out there. I have heard rumours of a puma at large. I do not care what it is, we just want the one that killed all those sheep." The current total is given as 80, 40 of which were Mr Ley's losses. Exeter *Express & Echo* 7 May 1983.

☐ **7 May** – The *Daily Express* wades in with a front page reward of £1000 for any unpublished photos of the Exmoor Beast. The offer is dominated by a large picture of a black panther; suggesting, perhaps that a panther is what they'd like people to find. There is a sudden invasion of the South Molton area by numbers of would-be big game photographers.

Two daylight sightings were made, but by whom and of what, we have no details. *D.Express* 9 May 1983.

☐ **8 May** – As a direct consequence of the *Daily Express* offer the Marines publicly call off their hunt. The reward is slammed as being "irresponsible" by the police and Marines, and they are quoted with delight by most other newspapers. A picture is painted of the danger of trespassing on private land patrolled by nervous and angry famers ready to blast anything that moves. The *Daily Mail* demonstrated its responsibility by offering, according to the *News of the World*, to increase the reward by £200. *The Mail on Sunday, News of the World, Observer, S.Mail, S.Express* 8 May 1983.

Two more lambs are found partly eaten. Farmer Ley, whose lambs they were, was said to be bitter, blaming the Express. *D.Mail, D.Telegraph, D.Mirror, D.Express* 9 May 1983.

□ **9 May** –The *Express* is quite unrepentant about its reward, saying it had checked with the police and farmers beforehand, and are surprised to see them now vociferously against it. Local people and farmers are said to be furious: they want the Marines back, and they won't return while the reward may attract sightseers. The paper even rejected an appeal to stop the reward, from North Devon MP Tony Speller.

Meanwhile, South Molton farmers' chairman, Denys Smaldon, said he though the animal was a big cat of some kind. "It kills and eats lambs like no dog or fox ever did. This thing eats wool and all, and goes for the chops. It leaves the bone structure of the neck like you would leave a fishbone." And lion experts at Longleat concur. They suggest panther or leopard. Hmmm, I always thought a panther *was* a leopard. *D.Express, Western Morning News* 9 May 1983.

A creature, said to be the 'Beast', spotted late afternoon at Molland by a farmer. A posse of 30 farmers formed almost instantly, but they searched from Black Cock to Crimson Cross to no avail, giving up when it got dark. *Western Morning News* 10 May 1983.

The *Express* defensively maintains that the feared swarms of sightseers have simply not materialized, and that there is nothing to stop the Marines returning. *D.Express* 10 May 1983.

□ **10 May** – Di Francis joins the clamour to recall the *Express* reward. *D.Star, D.Record, Western Morning News* 11 May 1983.

Sometime in the previous two days, two more lambs were killed. *North Devon Journal-Herald* 12 May 1983.

□ **11 May** – during the night of 11/12th Mr Ley lost another lamb. The Marines say that had they been there – Drewstone Farm being the centre of their operations – "the animal would be dead and the farmers could sleep soundly once again." *North Devon Journal-Herald*, 12 May 1983.

Then...a straining at a leash, and the dangle of a lethal loop, as two more hunters beat their chests. Bernard Hogarth says his wire rope loop on a 10ft steel pole is a puma-beater. And Richard Blackmore extols the virtues of his 'lurcher' dog, a "killer" amalgam of collie, deerhound and greyhound; a breed favoured by gypsies. Blackmore regularly goes 'lamping'

with the dog, a canine equivalent of those missiles which home in one laser-lit targets. "We work at night with a spotlight," he explains. "Patch will kill anything if it is lit up. If I put my light on the beast, my dog would definitely go for him and tear its throat out." Exeter *Express & Echo* 12 May 1983.

□ **12 May** – Another of Mr Ley's lambs is killed during the night. And police say they are "plagued" with advice and offers of help from self-styled hunters, trackers and experts. One caller said the animal was none other than a monstrous African badger. Another caller, from Kansas City, Missouri, said the beast was being trained to kill humans, and even named the man resonsible. *Western Morning News* 13 May 1983.

On this same day, the cat theory goes back one square. Keith Mayhew, of the Animal Rescue Centre at Weare Giffard, took a cast of paw prints at a site designated by Eric Ley as the scene of one of his losses. After failing to identify it himself, Mayhew sent it to the mammal department of the British Museum (Nat.Hist.) and got back the answer – dog. "No-one has yet come up with any casts of footprints which might indicate that it is a cat," said Mayhew, who added that the 'Beast ' was obviously very intelligent and very dangerous. *Bideford Gazette* 13 May 1983.

□ **17 May** – The Marines take advantage of several quiet days to slip back into their trenches around Drewstone Farm, this day. The return was done with complete secrecy, and did not break until the next day. Exeter *Express & Echo, D.Mirror* 18 May 1983.

South Molton Farmers' Union organize people responsible for specific areas, who can call up posses within minutes in the event of a sighting or another depredation. They have also put up posters telling people what to look out for and where to report local sightings. *North Devon Journal-Herald* 19 May 1983.

And a Canadian Indian ex-tracker, now living at Redruth, says he thinks the animal is killing like a wolf. After seeing a film of some dead sheep, he added: "From the number of throat marks I believe there could be more than one dog responsible." *Western Morning News* 19 May 1983.

□ **20 May** – Afternoon, and the Beast, or one of his tulpas, was seen in broad daylight, by Mrs Doreen Lock, driving between Black Cock and Molland, a mere three miles from Drewstone. A search was in progress in the area at the time. She said: "I saw something in the road some distance from me. It was large, dark and had pricked ears. I only saw the front part. It then disappeared into the wood..." She insists it was like no animal she had seen before. *North Devon Journal-Herald* 26 May 1983.

☐ **22 May** — A lamb was killed in daylight at Higher Hunstone farm, Brayford, near North Molton. *North Devon Journal-Herald* 26 May 1983.

☐ **Fourth week of May** — No dates. Two sightings, by a girl on horseback, and a gamekeeper, add to the numbers of actual witnesses who describe the creature as "cat-like", in contradiction of the 'official' opinion of dog. However, a police spokesman said: "They both saw the animal at a distance and were unable to describe it accurately. Neither of them thought it was dog-like" *Western Morning News* 26 May 1983.

☐ **24 May** — The Beast is spotted prowling — not said where. *Western Morning News* 26 May 1983.

☐ **25 May** — About 50 miles due south of South Molton, on the other side of Dartmoor, Roger Dickinson, a sales executive watched a large cat-like creature through binoculars for five minutes before it vanished into hedges. He described it as at least 3ft long, 2ft high, and golden brown. "I thought it was a fox until I got the glasses on it. It sounds rather silly, but I thought it was a lion." Dickinson was in his back garden, about 8pm, when he saw the animal "stalking across the field from one clump of grass to the next". It would be a stupendous feat for the Exmoor beast to range so far and back in so short a time — not to mention the colour difference — so could we have *two* mystery felines in Devon at the same time? *Western Morning News* 26 May 1983.

☐ **29 May** — Two boys — Wayne Adams, 14, and Marcus White, 12 — spending the weekend at Wayne's uncle's farm — Willingford Farm, on Halfcombe Common, between Molland and Exford, right on the Devon/Somerset border as it runs through Exmoor — stumbled upon the Beast near a flock of sheep as they walked down a lane. Wayne said: "I looked over a gate and saw the animal about ten yards away. It stared straight at me with bulging greeny eyes just like a lion. It was jet black apart from white markings down its head and chest and had a head like an Alsatian dog, (but it was) bigger than any dog we've ever seen. I was dead scared and said to Marcus, 'There's the thing everyone is looking for,' and it lolloped away. It moved like a cat but I don't think it was a puma. It must have been heavy because of the deep impression it left in the ground. Marcus added: "It moved like a cat, but its face was like a dog's. I though it was a panther...I didn't know what to do. I just stared. There was no chance it was a dog, it was miles too big for that. It was standing still when we saw it, but then it heard a car and moved off." The boys later told the police it was four to five feet

Marcus White with his drawing of the Exmoor Beast. [Copyright: Exeter Express & Echo.]

tall, about 15ins wide across the back and powerfully built. Exeter *Express & Echo, D.Star, Sun, D.Mirror, D.Telegraph* 31 May 1983.

That same night a sheep was found savaged at Ash Mill. Police said the attacks were becoming more infrequent, and thought that the Beast was changing eating habits as wildlife, especially newborn red deer, became more plentiful. *Western Morning News* 2 June 1983. Also sometime that night, an animal, believed to be the Beast, was seen crossing the Mole valley between North and South Molton, by a North Molton man just mintues after he had talked to a Marine patrol. Exeter *Express & Echo* 1 June 1983.

☐ **End of May** — No date — David Mann, owner of a craft shop in Combe Martin, saw an animal on the edge of South Molton, just before another dead lamb was found there. *North Devon Journal-Herald* 2 June 1983. In the same paper for 30th June, Mr Mann says he was misquoted. What he saw was a "large dark-coloured animal" about 70yds away in a field, "with a feline gait...but casting like any hound with its nose to the ground, it came to within 30 feet. I was able to see that it was a large dog of lurcher type and the head resembled that of a wolfhound."

A theory told to the paper: the creature is a specially bred dog used, in illegal dogfights, which has escaped. Another theory, attributed to unnamed naturalists who have studied all the evidence so far: "an unknown species" — but an unknown species of what, we are not told, *North Devon Journal-Herald* 2 June 1983.

☐ **First week of June** — over several days of press briefings the police and Marines reiterate their belief in a dog. An officer of 42 Commando was more specific, describing it as "a large, totally wild, dark brown cross-bred dog", it having been seen a number of times by the men. Farmer Ley added darkly: "The Marines are keeping quiet about most of what they know of the beast." *S.Express* 5 June; *Times, Sun, D.Mirror* 7 June 1983.

☐ **4 June** — Two lambs found torn to pieces just across the Somerset border — not said where — but 12 miles from Drewstone. *S.Express* 5 June 1983. The death toll is given by various sources as between 90-100 sheep and lambs.

☐ **5 June** — South Molton taxi-driver Wayne Hyde (our second witness named Wayne) was driving down Silcombe Hill in the early hours, from Bishops Nympton, when he saw a large animal crouching in his headlights. He thought it was a big fox at first, then realized it was too big and had pricked ears, huge eyes and a large nose. "It had a cunning look in its eyes, and very powerful shoulders," he told police. He said it was gingery in colour. *North Devon Journal-Herald* 9 June; *North Devon Advertizer* 10 June 1983.

☐ **6 June** — The police say they believe the Beast is a mongrel greyhound lurcher with a bull mastiff's head, and show the hunters a specimen of both breeds. *Times* 6 June; *D.Mirror* 7 June 1983.

While the police were staging their line-up a fully grown ewe was found partly eaten across the moor, near Winsford. *North Devon Journal-Herald* 9 June 1983.

☐ **7 June** — The *Weekly World News* for this date gave a severely dubious summary, and curiously cited one farmer, who may or may not exist, saying that a cow of his had been killed, its skull crushed "by one incredible snap of (the Beast's) jaws".

☐ **12 June** — Sheep (not said how many) were killed on two farms near Dulverton, on the Somerset side of the border. *D.Telegraph* 13 June 1983.

☐ **13 June** — A large dog-like creature seen at

Pixton Park, near Dulverton; described as black or dark brown, 2ft 6ins high and with a large round head. The witness, working in a field, said he'd never seen anything run so fast. Exeter *Express & Echo* 13 June 1983. Marines at Drewstone decide to pack up and move camp to Dulverton, where all the action now is. *D.Mirror* 15 June; *North Devon Journal-Herald* 16 June 1983.

☐ **15th/16th June** — During the night, a lamb killed at Hillview, Exton. Exeter *Express & Echo* 17 June 1983.

☐ **19 June** — During the evening, Alison Healey, 13, was walking between the village of Bishops Nympton and the South Molton to Tiverton road when she noticed that sheep in a field were agitated. Then, a mere 80yds away, she saw a big, black panther-like beast. She watched it for so long that she was able to produce a sketch of it for the police — see sketch. *North Devon Journal-Herald* 23 June 1983.

☐ **20 June** — Two sheep found dead to the north of the main killing ground: a lamb at Coombeland Farm, Brompton Regis, to the north of Dulverton; and a ewe at Downescombe Farm, Exford, on Exmoor proper. And an enterprising clothing shop reports a complete sell-out of a special 'Beast of Exmoor' T-shirt. *North Devon Journal-Herald* 23 June 1983.

☐ **Fourth week of June** — No dates. A lamb killed at Simonsbath, in the heart of Exmoor, and a ewe dead at Dunster, the most northerly kill yet and on the coast; both in Somerset. *News of the World* 26 June 1983.

☐ **Between 26th and 29th June** — The Beast struck three times in three days; once at Timberscombe, near Dunster, and twice again near Simonsbath. We are not told the order of these, so we cannot tell if the Beast was doubling back or not. Devon police admitted "relief" that the Beast had left their territory, but were aware it could return. *North Devon Journal-Herald* 30 June 1983.

☐ **First week of July** — To the consternation of the hunters, the trail of the Beast has gone cold, and confused with more conventional sheep-worryings. One dog was brought down by a farmworker who rugby-tackled it as it menaced sheep. It was quickly dismissed as an imposter, and its owner reprimanded. *Times* 4 July; *North Devon Journal-Herald* 7 July 1983.

☐ **4 July** — Despite the elimination of several sheep-worriers, another sheep was killed at Simonsbath. *D.Telegraph* 5 July 1983. Also sighted this day at Emmett's Grange, near Simonsbath. Exeter *Express & Echo* 8 July 1983.

☐ **7 July** — Another sheep killed at Simonsbath. *D.Telegraph* 8 July 1983.

☐ **8 July** — Enter game park boss Capt. Philip

Lashbrook, who claims he can "outsmart" the Beast with his 9 years' experience of tracking animals in South Africa. Against the prevailing official opinion he believes "this animal could be a highly dangerous lynx or puma and not an overgrown cat." *D.Express* 9 July 1983.

☐ **15 July** — A lamb found partly devoured at Wellshead Farm, Exford. The Beast blamed, though by this stage almost any sheep death would be pinned on it. Bristol *Eve. Post D.Telegraph*, 16 July 1983.
☐ **Weekend 16/17 July** — Ewe killed at Holm Bush Farm, Withypool. Bristol *Eve.Post* 18 July 1983.
☐ **Second week in July** — The Beast lies low. A retrospective piece in the *Sunday Times* 10 July 1983, adds two notes of interest. 1) The Beast had been seen once jumping two hedges and the cart track between them. 2) One old farmer suggested it was a weird escapee from an experimental laboratory — shades of *The Plague Dogs* — an experiment that had gone wrong.
☐ **26 July** — Lamb killed at Warren Farm, Simonsbath, shortly after a large black "dog" was spotted. Bristol *Eve.Post* 27 July 1983. Various papers allude vaguely to other depredations in the last two weeks of July, but their idea of usefulness is to give no details.
☐ **29 July** — Police chiefs from the Devon, Cornwall, Avon and Somerset forces meet to discuss tactics. Surprisingly, they agree that the Beast — or dog, as they call it — is dead, having been shot by a farmer and crept off to die in secret. The Latest Dulverston area killings, they say, are the work of another dog, and the total number of killings is not much more than a year's losses. A barefaced attempt to play it all down, it seems, and some farmers have strongly disagreed with these statements. One farmer talked of "mysterious vans" and poaching dogs; and another of two huge black dogs seen being controlled by a man acting suspiciously. *S.Times* 31 July 1983.

That is the last clipping we have on the Exmoor Beast. It has been a classic Fortean story complete with false-endings, confusion, and petering out into a mystery. Where did it come from? What was it? And where did it go? Its adversaries, the farmers who suffered dreadful losses, are left with the impression of an uncatchable, unstopable and unearthly killer with remarkable skill and intelligence.

The area of depredations was in the midst of the legend of Black Dogs and that devil-hound of the Baskervilles, not so much created by Conan Doyle as recreated and publicized by him. Who can blame the old farmer, referred to above, for his half voiced fear that the Beast might be more than natural. "It sucks the blood you see. You tell me what other animal does that."

•

Alison Healey's sketch of the animal she saw at Bishops Nympton. [North Devon Journal-Herald 23 June 1983.]

Credits: *Peter Ann, Derek Banks, Janet & Colin Bord, Robert Boyd, Bruce Chatterton, Peter Christie, Mike Crowley, Peter Hope Evans, Ron Gauntlett, Brian Hain, Chris Hall, J Lang, Alexis Lykiard, Nick Malloret, Valerie Martin, John Michell, Ian Murray, Ray Nelke, I Simmons, Bob Skinner, Doc Shiels, Anthony Smith, David Sutton, Paul Thomas, UFO Newsclipping Service, Nigel Watson, Ion Will, Steve Wrathall.*

•

POSTSCRIPT

Predictably, just when it all seemed to be dying down, the Beast was heard from again. There were more (undetailed) killings during the week ending **1 Aug**, according to the *Times* of that date, and the police, with no trace of embarassment, say the idea that the Beast is dead is "wishful thinking."

2nd Aug: still warm sheep carcase — said to be the 100th victim, but I doubt if that'll make much difference to it — found partly eaten on farm of former Lord Mayor of London, Sir Bernard Waley-Cohen's farm at Simonsbath. *D.Star, D.Telegraph* 3 Aug 1983. We have to call a halt here...But there is bound to be more, then a winter hiatus, and a spring resumption — unless they catch the critter first.

Meanwhile... The Surrey Puma returned in mid-July. A four and a half feet long, large black cat was spotted at Hazeley Heath, near Hackfield. *Fleet News* 15 July 1983. It was seen again in Farnborough at midnight on 17th July, when it jumped a fence into a West Heath Rd garden. *Surrey/Hants Star* 21 July 1983. Shortly afterwards at the ranges near Caesors Camp, Aldershot. *Surrey/Hants Star* 28 July 1983.

And...another Scottish 'puma'. Called by police a "lioness or puma" it is said to be responsible for farm animal killings in the border hills area of Earlsdon (though I cannot find this on my map). Armed searches found nothing. *Times* 1 Aug 1983.

Bob Rickard

TORNADOS, DARK DAYS AND ANOMALOUS PRECIPITATION and
Related Weather Phenomena.
Compiled by William R. Corliss The Sourcebook Project, Box 107, Glen Arm, MD 21057, USA; 1983, $11.95hb, pp196, indexes, illos.

This is the second volume in Corliss' ambitious 'Catalog of Anomalies' project. Each of his efforts to date has been of such excellence and value that there is a great risk of my praise becoming repetitious. The series is essential for serious Forteans, but if it's beyond your pocket, pressure your local library to get it for their reference section. A listing of the contents is the best way to convey the scope of this volume.

White skies; cloud arches; polar bands; tiny thunderclouds; noisy clouds; noctilucent clouds; cloud rings; ionosphere effects of thunderclouds; holes in cloud decks; lines of clouds; clouds dispersed by the moon; morning glories; long hollow clouds; radiating cloud spokes; excess ice crystals; change in cloud brightness; anomalous haze layers; falls of ice, stone, sulphur, pollen, manna, hay & leaves, pwrde ser, webs, inorganic stuff, fish, frogs & toads, insects, birds, animals; large storm systems; rain from clear sky; giant snowflakes; conical flakes; coloured, luminous and point precipitation; odd hail shapes; giant hail; hail strew patterns; slow hail falls; explosive hail; unusual inclusions in hail; the 'cloudburst' effect of sudden torrential rain; temperature anomalies; firestorms; lunar phase correlations with thunderstorms; weather, ozone, temperature; solar activity correlations with thunderstorms and weather; effects of comets and meteors on weather; effects of planets on weather; dark days; pogonips (freezing fogs, now you know) and other ice fogs; mists and epidemics; dry fogs; dust fogs; electric effects in tornados; burning & dehydrating tornados; tornados & waterspouts with horizontal, thin, forked, knotted & multiwalled funnels; historical tornados; tornado pranks; reversal of funnel rotation; magnetic variation of tornados; waterspouts between clouds; squalls.

As before there is a comprehensive classification system, an anomaly rating, and discussion of the relevancy of cases to more orthodox knowledge, thorough referencing, and illustrations by John C. Holden.

RJMR

BEYOND THE SPECTRUM:
A Survey of Supernormal Photography.
by Cyril Permutt.
Patrick Stephens, Cambridge; 1983, £9.95, pp185, index, photos.

Although in this century the movie and advertising worlds have fed us with a plethora of visual fantasies, the idea that 'the camera cannot lie' persists. So far as a camera is a mechanical reproducing instrument, this is true, but the medium of photography can be used by liars and hoaxers and thus be made to record their lies and hoaxes which can then be presented as truth. There is also the matter of malfunctioning equipment producing apparently inexplicable results which in the eyes of the believer become incontrovertible evidence of paranormal forces at work. As Hollywood and Madison Avenue have shown us, there is no visual photographic result that cannot be achieved given the time and the money. So when judging the authenticity of a 'paranormal' photograph the skill of the photographer and the facilities available should also be known, which is not usually the case. Ultimately the investigation of paranormal evidence often becomes a question of witness reliability.

These are some of the pertinent questions which should be considered in a 'survey of supernormal photography', but regrettably the author of *Beyond the Spectrum* is not interested in such a dull approach. His first paragraph reads: 'The supernormal exists besides us, here and now! Only now in the 1980s we can at long last prove that the miracles, prophesying and magic that are found in the religious shows that the wonderful experience described by prophets and believers of all faiths are true.' Exuberant no doubt, but an unpromising start for what is presented as a serious factual look at supernormal photography. Mr Permutt is in fact a convinced spiritualist believer and his book is written from that point of view.

Chapter One is concerned with the spirit photographers who flourished in the late 19th century and early years of the 20th century. These 'mediums' took portraits in their studios which showed 'extra' of 'spirit' faces hovering above or besides the sitter, or as in one example shown in the middle of the sitter's stomach, peering out through his watch-chain. The better known practitioners of this phenomenon are all here, with such names as Mumler, Hudson, Buguet (misspelled as Baguet), Parkes, Hope, Boursnell and Duguid (misspelled as Daguid). All of these when competently investigated were found to be fraudulent. Some hardly needed investigation, as when Mumler who was producing spirit photographs in 1863 in Boston, USA, was shown to be using as extras, portraits of local people who were still living, which he had made himself a few weeks earlier. Buguet was sent to prison for fraud after he had confessed and his stock of draped dummies discovered, but even then many of his dupes clung to their illusions and refused to believe that the 'spirits' in their portraits were not genuine manifestations of their beloved deceased.

The tricks used covered the widest range that human ingenuity could devise, ranging from the simple use of the plate previously exposed with the spirit face (this method used only with the most gullible of sitters) through the substitution of marked plates or slides whilst loading them in the darkroom, to painting a face on the background in quinine sulphite which is invisible to the human eye but registered on the photographic emulsion.

William Hope was one of the best-known practitioners of spirit photography in Britain. He operated at Crewe from 1905 to 1933 and was thoroughly investigated by Society for Psychical Research members who were competent and knowledgeable photographers. His earlier results had 'extras' consisting of a veiled face which occupied a large part of the plate, a simple case of pre-exposure and plate switching, but when an unscrupulous investigator revealed this trick by bringing his own previously marked plates for use, Hope felt it wiser to change his methods. Subsequently he produced small faces within a 'glowing oval of light', this being achieved by using a small round flashlight apparatus which could be palmed in the hand and at a convenient moment pressed against the plate and a short exposure given by means of a battery in the pocket connected to it by wires. When Dr Higson from the British Photographic Research Association investigated Hope and his methods in 1920 he employed the same subterfuge as Hope so often used himself. A loaded plate-holder which had been in Hope's pocket for several minutes was adroitly switched by the investigators just before use and concealed and taken by Dr Higson when he left Hope's premises. The surprise expressed by Hope when no 'extra' appeared in the picture could only have been equalled by the satisfaction of Higson who, when the plate was later developed in his own darkroom, saw the 'extra' appear on an otherwise blank plate. Regrettably all such unfavourable reports are ignored by Mr Permutt whose presentation is completely uncritical.

Mr Permutt also chooses, wisely, to ignore the psychographs which Hope sometimes produced. These 'spirits' messages on photographic plates were in the recognisable handwriting of a dead person, but could only be produced from such spirits as had been in written communication with Hope during their lifetime. Apart from their general unconvincing appearance, with fuzzy retouching around the words to hide the cut edges, they also contained the spelling and grammatical mistakes of Hope himself, who was not a well-educated man.

If I have dwelt lengthily on spirit photography, it is only because the book is biased towards this aspect, and spirit photographs are dotted throughout the pages no matter what aspect of supernormal photography the text is dealing with. One might hope that other interesting questions relating to these spirit photographers would be discussed by the author, who runs what he calls the Bureau for the Investigation of Paranormal Photographs and so presumably has investigated and is prepared to vouch for the veracity of the pictures he has used. For example, why are the spirit faces so often lit from a different angle than the sitter's face? A prime example of this appears on page 116 where there are five spirit heads grouped around the sitter and each one is lit differently. Or again, why, when the spirit face is a recognisable likeness of the sitter's deceased relative, is it identical to an existing portrait? (The author innocently reproduces two examples of this on pages 13 and 26.) The obvious answer is fakery, but if Mr Permutt has investigated this phenomenon and has another explanation, he should tell us of it. This he fails to do.

He also fails to show us the results of his own 'experiments with supernormal photography', though he goes into detailed explanations on how to set up a session with a medium, giving the most suitable equipment and methods to use. He does not say he has produced any results, so perhaps all his efforts were fruitless. On one occasion he visited a medium who was reputed to be able to produce flashes of light, but although he made several hundred exposures, no phenomena were seen or recorded. Negative results are just as important to record as the positive, though obviously less encouraging to the experimenter.

Since its heyday spirit photography has fallen completely into disfavour. Why this should be is another interesting matter which the author makes no attempt to discuss. A large factor is the predominant use of rollfilm cameras in place of the traditional plate cameras, rollfilm being much more difficult to get at for adding 'extras'; and also there is the introduction of faster, more sensitive films which fog more easily when exposed to stray light. The success of such fakery relies upon the exponent being of a friendly, charming and apparently open nature which causes investigators to relax their vigilance for a brief time during which sleight of hand and distracting patter are used. Later the investigators will be positive that the plate-holder or whatever was never out of their sight and they could not possibly have been deceived, etc., etc. With the general public the spirit photographers relied on their will to believe and desire to recognise the features of their dead loved ones in any indistinct and blurry features that were presented to them.

Chapter Three deals with 'Modern Supernormal Photography' and the seven photographs reproduced lack the impact of the earlier 'spirit' pictures. Five 'extra' figures which have appeared on photographs taken in churches are shown and one of a country scene which has an outline of a praying figure superimposed, looking very much like a chemical stain on the original colour enlargement. As always, the authenticity of these photographs as depicting the paranormal relies on the veracity and technical knowledge of the photographers.

Other chapters refer to thoughtography, Kirlian photography, photographs of PK event and poltergeist activity,

and one of the many criticisms I have is that Mr Permutt does not differentiate between photographs recording psychic experiments such as Nina Kulagina suspending a ball in mid-air and photographs where the film is purported to have been spontaneously affected by a psychic energy. Judging by the predominance of the latter, in the form of 19th-century spirit photographs, and the scarcity of the former, Mr Permutt evidently considers the latter to be of greater evidential value. His accuracy is also suspect, for when he refers to an incident reported in D. Scott Rogo's *Phantoms* (p.90) where Michaela Kelly was reported to have produced a thoughtograph while hypnotised, he states that Scott Rogo was a witness to this event, but on referring to the book, *Phantoms*, we find that in fact Scott Rogo was not present but simply reports it, working from the original notes of Raymond Bayless, the principal witness. In such minor ways is the record blurred over the years and unwarranted authenticity bestowed on dubious events. Again, on page 76 he quotes an 'expert at Agfa' as saying 'There has been no trick photography used in taking this film, there has been no double exposure and there is no flaw in the actual film or fault in development.' The manufactures of photographic materials are not in the business of authenticating psychic photographs and in my experience will never do so. They can only comment on the physical state of the film emulsion and the evidence of processing faults. A real expert will know that it is impossible to categorically state that double exposure has not occurred, and in fact on studying the reproduced photograph, of a 'kneeling monk' in front of an alter (p.77), there is an appearance of double exposure as the altar steps can be seen through the figure. This is not proof that double exposure has occurred,

but it cannot be dismissed as impossible either. But this relevant and interesting observation is missed by the author.

Mr Permutt's closing statement that '...most people can and do produce psychic or supernormal photographs...' which 'are too often discarded' is extremely contentious and in my experience simply untrue. A professional photographer, who very possibly makes hundreds of exposure each week, depends on producing exactly what he wants on the film without any extraneous images appearing, and if unwanted images repeatedly appeared his job would obviously become impossible. What does happen is that too many people have cheap, malfunctioning cameras or expensive cameras that are too complex for them, and use cheap, low quality processing labs. With their ignorance of photography the resulting errors are then hailed as something inexplicable and mysterious, and are sent to experts such as Mr Permutt to be authenticated as images from the beyond.

So I find *Beyond the Spectrum* a biased, unsatisfactory book lacking in investigatory bite and discrimination with large parts of the text devoted to unreliable reports of mediums and seances at which there was no photography involved and which are therefore irrelevant to the theme of the book. The few genuinely puzzling pictures reproduced are overwhelmed by the mess of faked photography, all of which the author offers as veridical material. A far more comprehensive 'survey of supernormal photography' will be found in *Photographs of the Unknown* (this opinion *not* being influenced by the fact that one of the co-authors is FT's editor.)

The really definitive work on psychic photographs has yet to be written, and I suspect that if such a book were undertaken and a thorough and exhaustive investigation made of

the circumstances behind each picture, there would be little of substance remaining. As with so much in this area of study, the more the evidence is subjected to investigative analysis, the more ephemeral it appears. The obvious fakes are easy to weed out, the clever fakes more difficult, and a photograph of a genuine psychic occurrence is still only the visual equivalent of anecdotal evidence, i.e. based on observation but not verifiable as is a controlled experiment made under laboratory conditions. At best, photographs can provide anecdotal evidence in visual form, but can never provide conclusive proof.
Colin Bord

THE TERROR THAT COMES BY NIGHT
By David J. Hufford.
University of Pennsylvania Press, Philadelphia; 1982 $25.00 hb, pp278, index, bib.

The rather Lovecraftian title is qualified in lumbering academese 'An experience-centred study of supernatural assault traditions.' Hufford began his study of folk traditions about nightmares in 1971 expecting it to occupy a few months, but the subject revealed complexities and depths which absorbed his interest for the following ten years. The result is a remarkable book which has implications for ufology among other fields.

The nightmare, in its most vivid form, grips its victim with talons of terror; the strange paralysis, the cold sweat, the crushing oppression in the chest, the feeling of suffocation, the fear that one might never break free and not to wake will bring certain death. Above all there is a feeling that someone, or worse, something, is doing this to you. Hufford's primary material comes from his surveys and questionnaires of people from a variety of walks of life in Newfoundland. He then explores the folk and cultural traditions of the night-

mare, and finds that the phenomenology of the experience itself is remarkably consistent with traditions. Casting his net further afield he finds that the structure of the nightmare experience corresponds with both experiences of and legends (ie. things believed to be true) about hauntings, vampires, demons, out-of-the-body and near-death experiences "indicating that a single class of experience" lies behind these different cultural variations. He concludes that about one-sixth of the population has experienced an 'incubus', and that the experience itself has given to the variety of legends rather than itself being shaped by tradition.

Hufford's methodology, and his many explorations of related material from diverse sources makes this essential study for those seeking to understand visionary experiences of all kinds.
RJMR

THE REBIRTH OF PAN: Hidden Faces of the American Earth Spirit.
By Jim Brandon.
Firebird Press, Dunlap, Illinois; 1983, $7.95pb, pp301, refs, illos.

Having reviewed the rich variety of Forteana in North America geographically for his ealier book, *Weird America*, our old friend Jim Brandon returns to expound the thesis that this earth is a super-organism with an intelligence and powers of its own, is a an idea familiar through the revival of the 'Gaia' hypothesis. In this book grist to Brandon's mill is the variety of American curiosities, from falls to cattle mutilations, ufos to lake monsters, bigfoot to major accidents and technological disasters, mystery animals and ancient enigmatic ruins. Brandon has long pursued what he calls the "dark axiom" of journalism, the things not reported, and while some of these are explicitly Fortean,

like those above, there is another more covert and sinister genre to do with meaningful coincidences of names of people and places, and numbers and dates. There is a whole chapter given over to the quirks of 23 and 33, and the 'Fayette' naming syndrome. Brandon weaves both of these strands in and out of each other to create a complex and baffling tapestry of mystery which involves the role of the Freemasons in the founding of the USA, and the legacy of the mysterious peoples who built mounds and mines and littered the land with artifacts so challenging to modern conceptions of the history of the continent, and the pervasive reverence for terrestrial forces. Along the way he discusses the current "fad" for labelling every pre-Columbian ruin an ancient observatory, and finds more inspiration in understanding them in terms of the 'sacred geometry' synthesis of alchemy, myth and numerology. The organizing force, which, it seems, can create spontaneous images in nature, also influences the lives of the men who dwell on the land, and this force, argues Brandon, is none other than the being we call Earth itself. One disturbing aspect of this book is the growing realization that the distance modern man has placed between himself and the natural order is not without consequence for the planetary symbiosis. The Earth Spirit broods under our neglect and abuse. Some see in the crankiness of the weather and the increase in 'natural' disaster the final breakdown of an ancient contract, or perhaps even a growing malevolence.

All in all *The Rebirth of Pan* is as gripping as a novel, despite having no definite conclusion. Even if you disagree with Brandon's flights of imagination, which are in the Fortean tradition, his evocations of the controversies and quite unscholarly warfare arising from the discovery of archeological sites and objects are both amusing and thought provoking. It is a book every Fortean should read.

RJMR

UFO DYNAMICS (2 vols)
By Berthold E. Schwarz.
Rainbow Books. Box 1069, Moore Haven, FL33471, USA; 1983, $19.95 pb (2 vol set) + $2.50 P&P, pp561, index, refs, illos.

Any thoughtful person contemplating the mystery of UFOs must acknowledge the importance of the psychological dimensions of the problem, and there is virtual agreement among investigators that we simply do not have enough studies of the single most-important component of the phenomena, the witnesses. To some extent this can be put down to the fact that there are so few psychologists and psychiatrists working within ufology — I can only think of two, but there are probably more. There ought to be more. This is what makes the contribution of Dr Schwarz to the subject so valuable; apart from a very distinguished career in psychiatric medicine and counselling, he has regularly contributed his insights on cases, to FSR and other journals, for as long as anyone can remember.

The core of this two volume set is the collection of those studies of witnesses from UFO journals with supplementary material, asides, afterthoughts and even transcription of a panel debate, all illustrated with drawings and photos from Schwarz's own files. Even someone familiar with the original articles will agree that having them collected and added to in this way is of incalculable value.

To Schwarz the UFO experience is a nexus, a coming together of many influences from the physical and psychological worlds and the even stranger world of psychic phenomena. He pleads for a greater knowledge of psycho-pathology among investigators, or better yet a greater sharing of diversified skills and insights. In case after case we see how the competant psychiatrist can extract useful information from witnesses who may be exulted, frightened, exhausted or depressed, and ranging further, from interviewing relatives and friends. In this way Schwarz has found material which others, less observant, would have missed, like bizarre coincidences, previous UFO or psychic experiences, hidden tensions and anxieties, etc. Schwarz's invovlement with his cases is intense enough to exhaust the reader, and with no great surprise we find that the synchronicities, strange phone calls, accostings by mysterious strangers, and poltergeist-like activities begin to appear in his own life.

Almost every aspect of UFO phenomena is touched upon in this work, and we don't have the space to assess them all; suffice it to say that Schwarz is consistently original, vulnerably honest and very professional, and yet never stuffy, obscure or evasive. There is a compassionate quality to his investigations which never loses sight of the fact that the witness is in some way troubled by his experience. On the psychiatric side, he dispenses once and for all with the idea that the UFO experience is a form of psychosis, and shows, if anything, that it is similar to some neurotic phenomena. "Most of the contactees I have studied were excellent phypnotic subjects," he writes, "and perhaps this is a clue to their experiences." Further demonstrations of this succtibility comes in cases which involve whole families or groups of two or more friends in a kind of folie a deux symbiosis, or in cases in which odd compulsions, psychic and telekinetic phenomena take a major part. The latter connection is explored by several chapters on the highly thoughtographic movies of Stella Lansing and Schwarz's own experiments. Another chapter discusses Schwarz views on the necessary ethics for the hypnotic and psychological investigation of witnesses.

Without doubt this pioneering book set should be essential reading for concerned ufologists, and has our highest endorsement.

RJMR

UFOs: A HISTORY
By Loren E. Gross.
Arcutrus Book Service, 263 N. Ballston Ave, Scotia, NY 12302, USA.

Some of you may already know Loren Gross' previous booklets — *The Mystery of the Ghost Rockets, The UFO Wave of 1896* and *Charles Fort, The Fortean Society & UFOs* — the latter two of which began an ambitious project to chronicle the unfolding of the UFO phenomenon. If you do, you don't need me to tell of their excellences; if you don't, you have something to look forward to acquiring or reading. This has led on to the larger format UFOs: A History, Volume 1 covers the period July 1947 to December 1948 *(published 1982, $12.95 spiral bound, pp160)*, and volume 2 covers the whole of 1949 *(1983, $13.95 spiral bound, pp193)*.

With these volumes Gross' History moves into an important phase, because where previously he was dependent upon contemporary newspaper reports, this period saw the first wave of UFO books and the publication of more material in magazines. But even more importantly Projects Sign and Grudge, the first official attempts to whitewash the phenomenon while giving the appearance of doing something about it, were established at this time, many of the declassified records of which Gross has related to what was really going on. Essential for ufologists' libraries. *RJMR reviews*

MONSTERS

By George M. Eberhart.
*Garland Pub. Inc., NY;, 1983,
$25.00 hb, pp 344, indexes.*

Yet another bibliography labour of love from the amazing Eberhart. His prodigious *Geobibliography of Anomalies* is followed by this 'Guide to Information on Unaccounted-for Creatures'. Basically, each chapter begins with an outline of the subject, followed by an alphabetical listing of articles, authors, books and newsstories on that subject, with detailed references. The subjects chapters are: African dinosaurs; dragons; flying humanoids; freshwater monsters; giant birds, bats and moas; giant cephalopods; giant snakes; humanoids (6 geographical regions); land monsters; mammoths and mastodons; merfolk; phantom kangaroos; phantom panthers; phantom wolves and black dogs; sea monsters. The 4450 entries have been culled from classical literature right up to 1982 from both orthodox and Fortean sources, and cover the globe. There are author and periodical indexes, and a section on books for youngsters.

The book has been designed for reference librarians, but who's complaining? It will prove its value to the Fortean writer, especially those who want an index to most cryptozoological subjects. Once again, I say get your library to buy a copy.

RJMR

MU REVEALED

by Tony Earll.
Paperback Library, New York, 1970.

[*Editor's note — We don't usually run reviews of old books, but this one is of such obvious interest, that we gladly make the exception. As Hilary Evans pointed out to me, it is not only a 'sleeper', but represents an enigma about which we would like to know more*]

In 1959 an expedition, sponsored by the prestigious Marquina-Jolicoeur Institute of London, and led by the distinguished scholar Prof. Reesdon Hurdlop, set off in quest of evidence which might substantiate or lay to rest the late Col. Churchward's hypothesis of a lost continent in the Pacific. A member of the team was Tony Earll, who accompanied the expedition as architect but seems also to have appointed himself its chronicler so far as a popular account is concerned. There is as yet no sign of the definitive record of the expedition promised from the pen of Hurdlop himself, so that for the moment Earll's account is all we have.

Fortunately, Earll is both an accomplished and a knowledgeable writer: he cites many impressive sources, though his bibliography makes curious reading — one is surprised to find *A Pocket Guide to the Supernatural* juxtaposing Lévy-Bruhl and Tylor. Many of his sources are unknown to me — Dubois and Macé of the Institut Francais, Herbert of Clairvaux, Francois du Plongeon — but then I make no claim to be thoroughly versed in the lore of Mu, or, as Earll insists it should strictly be named, Muror.

It is no doubt for this reason that I confess I had not previously heard either of Hurdlop and his colleagues, or of their epoch-making discovery. This comprised 69 scrolls which turned out to be the diary of a priest of Mu, named Kland, from the age of 12 to 22, during which period he left Mu, which explains how his diaries escaped the cataclysm which overtook his homeland. Though incomplete and damaged, they provide a unique account of life on the doomed continent, 20,000 and more years ago. Tony Earll's easy-going translation brings vividly to life the daily affairs of a young man who could almost be our own contemporary.

One contributory reason for this may be that the names of his acquaintances are not so outlandish as is usual in ancient chronicles. His own name, Kland, could admittedly be from *Star Trek*, but his fellow-students at the Temple College — Jayen, Kered, Orbret, Narf, Leln — need only the letter-order changed to have first-names of our own day.

By a curious coincidence, the same is true of the explorers themselves. Maud. N. Robat could as easily be Maud Barton, while the Professor's splendid name, Reesdon Hurdlop, transposes readily to Rednose Rudolph. There may be some occult significance in this, akin to finding that the Pyramids spell the vicissitudes of 20th century politics, or it may be simply synchronicity. But only the most malicious of sceptics would go so far as to assert that the author is *not really* Tony Earll, or that Muror is nothing more than *rumor*.

• *Hilary Evans*

[**Ed's note** — the only M. Jolicoeur in the London phonebook is a private number, at which nothing is known of the 'Marquina-Jolicoeur Institute. Draw your own conclusion!]

THE POWERS OF EVIL

By Richard Cavendish.
Routledge & Kegan Paul, London; 1980, £4.95 pb, pp299, index, bib, notes.

ENEMIES OF GOD: The Witch-hunt in Scotland

By Christina Larner.
Chatto Windus, London, 1981; £12.95, pp244, index, bib, notes.

Richard Cavendish was responsible for editing the respected encyclopedia *Man, Myth and Magic*, which amply demonstrated his encyclopedic knowledge of the occult. He puts this to good use in this review of the supernatural concept of evil in Western religion, magic and folk belief, which falls into convenient categories: death and the dead, fate, darkness and night, chthonic entities, hell, the evil gods, the devil, satanism and witchcraft. and elemental forces. Cavendish attempts to discover the origins of the symbolic forms of evil in the beliefs of prehistory and antiquity. While refusing to believe in the objective existence of "evil non-human entities", he remains in no doubt of the psychological reality of demonic powers born of fear and anxiety "in the minds which give them credence."

Dr Larner's book concentrates on a particular manifestation of evil — the witchcraft persecutions in Scotland — with the skills of an academic sociologist. After a fairly penetrating assessment of the European witch craze Dr Larner plunges into the social minutae of the accused, the accusers, the trials and executions, and the belief systems of the Scottish phase of the phenomenon, with a detailed study of two horrible cases in Kirkcudbright in 1671. Despite the heavy subject matter, I found this book very easy to read and the arguments clear. A worthy reference for those interested in the witch-hunt phenomenon.

RJMR.

OTHER BOOKS RECEIVED

★ **ENGINEERING IN THE ANCIENT WORLD** by J.G. Landels. Reviews the principal Greek and Roman writers on technical subjects; with erudite descriptions and analysis of power sources, water engineering, cranes and hoists, catapults, ships and sea transport, land transport, and the extent of theoretical knowledge. A fascinating book in its own right and a useful companion to Sprague de Camp's 1970 classic *The Ancient Engineers, Chatto & Windus, London; 1980, £3.95 pb, index, bib, diags.*

★ **THE NEW VIEW OVER ATLANTIS** by John Michell. The old View Over Atlantis, in its many editions, has rightly been hailed as one of the major influences on the post-hippie generation of the early 1970s. It was certainly an eye-opener for me, making me aware of other subject areas beyond the scope of my *Complete Fort* — eg. leys, gematria, magical flight, the Glastonbury zodiac, and the mysterious megaliths — when I read the first edition, in 1969 by Sago Press. At that time the book was pioneer of the burgeoning fields of the so-called earth mysteries, and it has never been bettered for its scope, insight and erudition. The new edition has been reset, corrected and expanded with new material (eg. new work on ancient metrology) and illustrations (most noticeably the dramatic photos of the South American leys); and a striking cover painting by Una Woodruff. *Thames & Hudson, London; 1983, £8.95 hb, pp224, index, bib illos.*

★ **THE WOLFMAN: SIXTY YEARS LATER** by Karin Obholzer. Being conversations with one of Freuds most famous patients. Freud claimed a successful treatment of the Wolfman (named after a dream), upon which much of Freud's initial prestige was based. Ms Obholzer stumbled on the patient 60yrs later in Vienna, and these interviews with him are published posthumously. Significant, is the old man's statement that the whole episode of this vaunted treatment was a catastrophe. "I am in the same state as when I first came to Freud." Surely a re-evaluation of Freud's early work is due after this, and the revelation, last year, that "Anna O' the legendary first psychoanalytic patient was treated by Breuer and not Freud. *Routledge & Kegan Paul, Henley, Oxon; 1982, £12.50 hb, pp250.*

★ **A DIRECTORY OF DISCARDED IDEAS** by John Grant. A very amusing and opinionated romp through most varieties of crankery, in this case theories about life, man and the universe, ancient worlds, nature and evolution; though the flippancy with which he dismisses UFOs, the ancient astronaut idea, Velikovsky, etc do not do his wit justice, nor indicate the full complexities of these subjects. Grant has a keen eye for human idiocy, vide this opening quote from Ayatollah Khomeini himself: "If a person who is praying turns red in the face from suppressing an impulse to burst out laughing, that person must start the prayer over again." *Ashgrove Pess, Sevenoaks, Kent; 1981, £6.95 hb, pp249, index.*

BOOKLETS

★ **PETITE SELECTION DES SOURCES FRANCAISES DE CHARLES FORT** — transcriptions of a few of Fort's French sources, compiled by our colleague Jean-Louis Brodu. Crammed into 20 pages we have 31 original accounts, mainly pre-1900, coloured rains; falls of toads, leaves, ants, ice, fish, manna, etc; aerial lights & UFOs of the 19th century; luminous birds, toads in stone and Angelique Cottin, the 'Electric Girl'; and a few others Only 90 copies printed. Brodu says he might do another selection next year, if there's a demand. The price is 25FF; £2 or $3; money orders payable to: Pogonip (CCP Paris 1020753 V). Published by Brodu's La Foundation pour L'Analyse & La Diffusion des Anomalies; and available from the compiler at: *Pogonip, BP 195 — 75 665, Paris Cedex 14, France.*

★ **NIGHT SIEGE: The Northern Ohio UFO Creature Invasion** by Dennis Pilichis. In mid-1981 an isolated rural farm began to have frequent visits from large dark hairy humanoids with glowing red eyes, who seemed invulnerable to bullets and were strong enough to carry off a 100lb calf under one arm. They were also buzzed by large globes of light and flying dark box-like objects. When Pilichis and colleagues arrived, the main family of witnesses were in a highly disturbed state of mind. Feeling they were under seige by forces they could not understand, they would spend the night on roof blasting at anything that moved. The investigators stayed with the case for four months, and witnessed the creatures and other phenomena for themselves. The author then is hardly impartial and it is somewhat inevitable that the reader is presented with mainly anecdotal evidence and told that, like it or not, the story is true. The case for an objective series of events fails because the investigators became participants. That said, if half of what was described happening is true they could be forgiven their oversights. The author even joined in the indiscriminate frightened shooting, aiming flashlights for the gunmen, and later baiting rabbits with cyanide as a trap for the creatures, actions which most cryptozoologists would disapprove of...but no fatalities were found. No one seems to have asked why these creatures should have returned nightly to a place where they were regularly shot at. Grass was found crushed where dark bodies were seen to fall but none were found; strange cries were taped; and casts taken of some enigmatic three 'toed' prints, and yet one can't escape the conclusion that the psychological aspects are more important and at the same time neglected. We should all be indebted to Pilichis for this account of a bizarre episode of collective (there were 15 witnesses involved) paranormality, whatever its cause. *Published by the author at Box 5012, Rome, OH 44085, USA; Dec 1981, $6.00 (IMOs), pp40, illos.*

★ **PUZZLING QUESTIONS: Some Observations on the History of Prodigies** by John Nicholson. A gripping little book by one of England's few remaining pamphleteers, in which the social and political use and implications of prodigies, including Fortean phenomena, are interpreted against a background of radical traditional movements. John's erudition is a pointed stick which he pokes into every available crack in the edifice of orthodoxy. The suggestion is that so-called civilization has cost us the loss of an ancient symbolic language, one which, for all its faults, was more honest and natural than its 'rational' replacements. *Bozo, BM-Bozo, London WC1N 3XX, £1.80, pp52, bib, notes.*

★ **THE RUNNING WELL MYSTERY** by Andrew Collins. Andy Collins was fascinated by the strange Essex parish of Runwell, where he grew up, to investigate its reputation as one of the most haunted places in England. What developes is not the usual ghostly tour — although the church as a white lady, a corrupt priest and Old Nick himself as infrequent visitors — but an energetic and imaginative enquiry into the pre-Christian heritage of the site as a center for pagan worship, now evidenced only in place names, degenerated legend and a few historical clues. But by using psychometry and meditation techniques, as well as archival work in local libraries, Andy and his group not only located the long lost holy well but found that many references to a huge cross corresponded with geometrical configurations found on the surrounding landscape by map and fieldwork. A fascinating story, though incomplete; and an example of a new breed, the committed, imaginative earth mysteries researcher. *Published by The Supernaturalist, 19 St Davids Way, Wickford, Essex SS11 8EX; 1983, £2.00, pp82, bib, illos.*

★ **VELIKOVSKY'S SOURCES** by Bob Forrest. With the arrival of part six, Bob Forrest's rigorous examination of Velikovsky's citations (not his theories) is complete. Finally there is now an index volume containing a cross-reference index to *Worlds in Collision*, making the page total of the seven part work 575. Bob says that the complete set costs £10.50 (£20 overseas) inc. p&p but inquire about availability first because it's a limited edition. **Bob Forrest: 53 Bannerman Ave, Prestwich, Manchester, M25 5DR.** For the record: V doesn't come out of it too well.

★ **THE SUSSEX ELEPHANT** by Mike Collier. A description of the outline of an elephant found delineated in the Sussex landscape and footpaths, roads and parish boundaries. Just where you'd expect a tusk there is a tusk-shaped reservoir, and more astonishing, the tusk of a mammoth was found during the construction of the reservoir. The figure and tusk exist, but as to the purpose of it, who made it (if it isn't a simulacrum) and why here... 'your guesss is as good as anyone's. *This is a second edition, Jan 1983, by Institute of Geomantic Research, 142 Pheasant Rise, Cambridge, CB3 8SD; price on enquiry.*

★ Also from IGR (address above): **BRITISH GEOMANTIC PIONEERS 1570-1932** edited by Nigel Pennick (Dec 1982), price on enquiry; and a reprint of **VINTANA: GEOMANCY & ASTROLOGY IN MADAGASCAR** by Nigel Pennick, 85p.

★ Fenris World publications, available from IGR address above: **WE MUST TRADE IN TENTHS** by Alfred Watkins, being a plea for octaval coinage, a reprint from 1919 at 50p; **THE GEOMANCY OF GLASTONBURY ABBEY** by Nigel Pennick, at 40p; **THE 18TH RUNE** by Nigel Pennick; **SUNDIAL AND COMPASS ROSE** by Prudence Jones, on the old practice of eightfold times division; prices on application.

★ **TRAMS IN CAMBRIDGE** by Nigel Pennick, at 85p. Electric Traction Publications, March 1983, from IGR address above.

LETTERS

Cont from p3.

the main thrust of my books was against organized religion That if we are wrong about one apsect of the overall phenomenon, then we are undoubtedly wrong about all phenomena. This is hardly a 'Keelism'. It is a basic precept of the ancient philosophers. Scientific methodology can really only be applied to matters where our perceptions are deemed reliable. Science can play no role at all when the phenomena are beyond our perceptions, or are capable of altering our perceptions.

There is no such thing as a rainbow. Yet we have all seen rainbows. They are a visual phenomenon and can even be photographed. In a certain sense, UFOs are in the rainbow category. They exist to the percipient but they do not exist as an actual material object. As with a rainbow, you have to be in exactly the right place at exactly the right time to see them at all.

Practitioners of magick live in a dark world of hallucinations where reality is distorted by the power of their own minds and their will to believe. The wonders that they seemingly perform can rearely be perceived by outsiders.

Nigel quoted the Neil Armstrong statement which I deliberately used to close OTH. What he doesn't know, is that the editors censored that statement. Armstrong also said something about astrology, etc. which the editors—in their weird, twisted way—felt somehow discredited the rest of the statement! I was flabbergasted by their attitude. (They also banned any mention of FATE magazine in my text!)

As an intellectual exercise, read OTH and *Strange Creatures* at the same time (recognizing that the opening and closing chapters of *Creatures* were added, along with some other material about the animal world in general). Perhaps then it will all make more sense. The sense being

that there is no sense to any of it. Dinosaurs in Africa and huge sea serpents in shallow Irish lakes are part of this same twisted reality. There are not many types of phenomenas, as some Forteans would like to believe. There is only one... The Phenomenon. We are an integral part of it.

Incidently, after the disappearance of Andree's balloon in the late 1800's, there were many reports of mysterious spherical balloons from all parts of the world. Although dirigibles were not yet a practical reality in 1896-97, dirigibles were the subject of much speculation in the press and everyone was certainly aware that many inventors were hard at work on dirigibles. It was not so unusual that when a strange light appeared in the sky, the witness *assumed* it was attached to a dirigible. However, most of the 1896-97 dirigible reports were the work of mischievous newspapers (newspaper hoaxes were much in vogue in those days) and bored railroad telegraphers who concocted all kinds of jokes to amuse each other during the long dull nights. If you read the dirigible chapter of OTH very carefully you will note that my tongue is planted firmly in my cheek as I reviewed a handful of the hundreds of reports.

One reviewer in a prominent literary magazine here chose to devote his entire review to *the index of OTH*. OTH was the first UFO book to have an index, as you may recall. It took me two weeks of hard, boring, profitless work to prepare that index. My bibliography was another tiresome task and was originally much longer. The editors cut it in half. The final insult was that the book never earned a single pence in royalties and was later pirated and published as a paperback without my knowledge or consent. So it was a doomed project all round.

John A. Keel
New York

EYE, EYE!

Further to R.A. Wilson's article on Joyce (FT30p4-10). Not only are Freud and Joyce linked in virtue of their names (via their mutual derivation from 'joy'), but notice that their names have the same number of letters, namely 5. Five, as everyone knows, is a magical number, which denotes, among other things, the 'Pentacle' (star) and 'Pentagon'. The star is the symbol of the USA or at least it appears in disgusting profusion all over things Amurikan), and also of the US's putative enemies — the Commies (USSR in particular). The Pentagon is also of high significance (militarily) for the US. Bear this US link in mind, I will refer to it below.

The same magical-US-USSR-Freud-Joyce-synchronous link occurs in the colloquial forms of both Freud's and Joyce's forenames — Siggy and Jimmy respectively. *Both have 5 letters!* Notice further that both names have similar structures: Consonant-i-Double Consonant-y. Y is sometimes pronouced like an i, thus, reinforced by the 'double' occurring with the second consonant, we have 'double i' or two i's. It is noteworthy that both Freud and Joyce had two 'eyes'. (Freud also had a cigar). Furthermore 'eye' can be tortured into a reference to the 'eye-in-the-pyramid'; 'eye' has three letters (significantly one of them *isn't* an 'i') 3 is a magical number denoting 'triangle', which is a 2-dimensional [3+2=**5**] projection of a pyramid.) The eye-in-the-pyramid motif appears on some denominations of US currency, thus linking Freud and Joyce with the US again. Significantly, Joyce makes frequent references to the US, *and Freud went there once!* Moreover, RA Wilson has a noted affection for the e-i-t-p — see his jersey (US state and Channel Island) in pic (shovel) with article (p10). Thus RA Wilson *himself* is drawn *Cont on p72*

Cont on p72

Classified Exchanges.

FT welcomes an exchange of publications with those of mutual interest. This listing represents exchange publications received since last issue. Symbols: # = issue number; Pay = to whom cheques should be made if different from title, O = overseas rate; E = European rate; all rates inland or surface unless indicated; NFC = no Foreign cheques, many offer airmail rates, so inquire. Please mention FT when writing to listings.

FORTEAN

● **ASSAP News** N8 (Aug 1983) – Newsletter of the Association for the Scientific Study of Anomalous Phenomena. 6/yr. Free to ASSAP members, who also get reduced rates to *Common Ground*, below). *Inquiries to membership secretary Caroline Wise, 56 Telemann Sq., Kidbrook, London SE3.*
● **Common Ground** n7 – The ASSAP Journal of Record, ranges from comments on spiritualism, the 'Earth Lights' debate, Sai Baba, and Warminster. 4/yr. £3.75. E:5.50. O:$15 NFC *CG (new address): 56 Ring Rd, Leicester.*
● **Journal of Meteorology** v8 n76-80 – Frequently gives Fortean meteorology. 12/yr. £14.50. O:£17. *J.Met (new address): 54 Frome Rd. Bradford-on-Avon, Wilts BA15 1LD.*
● **Pogonip** N1 – Irregular journal of French Forteana, edited with style by Jean-Louis Brodu. 4/yr. Sample 12 Francs (by IMO), or for journal exchange. Pay: JL *Brodu, BP 195, 75667 Paris Cedex 14, France.*
● **Pursuit** v15 n4 – Journal of the Society for the Investigation of the Unexplained. 4/yr. Memb:$ 12. O:on application. *SITU, Box 265, Little Silver, NJ 07739, USA.*
● **The Shaman** n1-2 (incorp. AS&WR 18) – Wide ranging review journal, but still no sign of FT in its listings! 4/yr. £2. O:$6 ($13 air). Pay: *Paul Screeton, 5 Egton Drive, Seaton Carew, Hartlepool, Cleveland TS25 2AT.*
● **Skeptica** n1 – a journal discussing "Pseudo-science and off beat literature, published by an independent group of Danish librarians." For journal exchange. 2 or 3/yr. *Skeptica, Box 12, DK–9320 Hjallerup, Denmark.*
● **SIS Review** – A special issue (v6 n1-3) giving the papers read at an 'Ages in Chaos' conference held in Glasgow in April 1978, including two Velikovsky. 4/yr *Memb enqs to Bernard Prescott: 12 Dorset Rd, Merton Park, London SW19.*
● **SIS Workshop** v5 n2 – informal discussion journal of this Velikovskyan group, supplement to *SIS Review* (see above). Free to SIS members.

CRYPTOZOOLOGY

● **Champ Channels** v1 n1 (April 1983) – A newsletter from Joe Zarzynski about the hunt for and sightings of Champ, the denizen of Lake Champlain. 3/yr. $6. O:$7. Pay: *Lake Champlain Phenomena Investigation, Box 2134, Wilton, NY 12866, USA.*
● **Creature Chronicles** n6 (Spring 1983) – Reports from the Hominid Research Group division of the Ohio UFO Investigators League. 4/yr. $6. O:$8. Pay: *Ron Schaffner, Box 335, Loveland, OH 45140, USA.*
● **Cryptozoology** v1 (Winter 1982) – annual review of the International Society of Cryptozoology. 1/yr. $15. Free to ISC members (see *ISC Newsletter*, below).
● **ISC Newsletter** v1 n4 (Winter 1982), v2 n1 (Spring 1983) – Newsletter of the International Society of Cryptozoology. 4/yr. Memb:$25. *ISC, Box 43070, Tucson, AZ 85733, USA.*
● **Nessletter** n56-58 – News and views from Loch Ness, but takes in lake monsters generally. 12/yr. £2.50. O:$9. Pay: *Rip Hepple, Huntshieldford, St Johns Chapel, Bishop Auckland, Co Durham DL13 1RQ.*

PSI

● **New Frontiers Center Newsletter** n5-6 – edited by Mary Jo & Walter Uphoff. Intended to cover the whole field of psi research, but currently operating in an unexpected 'new frontier', the front line against James Randi and friends who have deliberately sought to undermine spoonbending research by planting tricksters in their midst who are later revealed to be magicians (as seen on recent QED documentary)' Randi has had much publicity from his 'expose' – here is the other side of the coin. ?/yr. $25 ($15 to students/sen citizens). *NFCN, Fellowship Farm, Rt 1, Oregon, WI 53575, USA.*

UFO

● **APRO Bulletin** v31 n3-6 – Aerial Phenomena Research Organization. 12/yr. Memb.$15. O:$18. *APRO, 3610 E. Kleindale Rd, Tuscon, AZ 85712, USA.*
● **BUFORA Bulletin** – Newsletter of the British UFO research Association. 4/yr. Memb: £12.50. Members also get JTAP and Probe (see below). *Membership secretary: Pam Kennedy, 30 Vermont Rd, London SE19 3SR.*
● **Centre Update** 3 – Newsletter and reviews, published by the Resources Centre of the Organisation for Scientific Evaluation of Aerial Phenomena (see *OSEAP* below). 3/yr.
● **Earthlink** n13 – 4/yr. £3. O:$9. NFC. *Earthlink, 16 Raydons Rd, Dagenham, Essex RM9 5JR.*
● **Journal of Transient Aerial Phenomena** v2 n4 – 2/yr. For journal exchange or free to BUFORA members (see *BUFORA* above).
● **Malaysian UFO Bulletin** n5-6 – Sadly ceased from the latest number.
● **Magonia** n12 – Essential reading. 4/yr. £2. O:$5. Pay: *John Rimmer, 64 Alric Ave, New Malden, Surrey KT3 4JW.*
● **Northern UFO News** n101 – 6/yr. £4.50. *NUFON NUFON, 9 Crosfield Rd, Somerville, Wallasey, Wirral L44 9EH.*
● **OSEAP Journal** V1 n2 – 3/yr. £5. O:$11. *OSEAP 170 Henry St, Crewe, Cheshire, CW1 4BQ.*
● **The Probe Report** v4 n1 – Soon to be replaced by *BUFORA Probe*, available only through exchange or membership of BUFORA but there's one issue of PR to go. Just send £1 to *Probe Report, 16 Marigold Walk, Ashton, Bristol BS3 2PD*
● **UFO Newsclipping Service** n166-168 – Clippings

from all over the world, with several pages of Forteana too. 12/yr. Apply for rates. *UFONS, Route 1, Box 200, Plumerville, AK 72127, USA.*

EARTH MYSTERIES

• **Caerdroia** n12 – Organ of the Caerdroia Project, researching & preserving Britain's mazes. apx 4/yr. £3.50. E:£4.50. O:$15. Pay: *Jeff Saward, 53 Thundersley Grove, Thundersley, Benfleet, Essex SS7 3EB.*
• **Earthlines** n1 – Welsh border each Mysteries. 4/yr. £4. *Earthlines, 7 Brookfield, Stirchley, Telford, Shrops TF3 1EB.*
• **Earthquest News** n6 – 4/yr. £3. E:£4. O:$7. Pay: *Andy Collins, 19 St Davids Way, Wickford, Essex SS11 8EX.*
• **Northern Earth Mysteries** n21-23 – 5/yr. £2. Pay *Philip Heselton, 170 Victoria Ave, Hull HU5 3DY.*
• **Stonehenge Viewpoint** n53 – 6/yr. £5. Canada $10. US$8. *SV. 2821 De La Vina St, Santa Barbara, CA 93105, USA.* UK orders to *SV, c/o 3rd Floor, 35 Gt Russell St, London WC1.*

• **The Templar** n4-5 – Now the main publication of the post-limbo institute of Geomantic Research. 4/yr. £3.25. *IGR, 142 Pheasant Rise, Bar Hill, Cambridge CB3 8SD.*
• **Terrestrial Zodiac News** v2 n3 – 4/yr. £2.50. Pay :. *Anthea Turner, 8 Eynsford Court, Hitchin, Herts SG4 9JS.*

OTHER

• **Walrus** n22 – Very 'Other'; official organ of the non-material world. Back from the brink. A fine ranting. Irregular schedule ("when the signs are right") but 50p will get you this or the next one. *Fenris-Wolf, Pheasant Rise, Bar Hill, Cambridge CB3 8SD.*
• **The Symbol** – a new magazine on symbolism in its widest context, from the irrepresible Nigel Pennick. Enqs to *Symbol: 142 Pheasant Rise, Bar Hill, Cambs, CB3 8SD.*

•

Small independent magazines need your support.
Please mention Fortean Times
if you respond to these listings

Help!

Any reader or researcher requiring help in research, questions answered, or contacts on Fortean topics may do so free in this column. Just send the details, on a separate sheet, keeping it brief.

O I am interested in correspondence/data on general **Fortean topics**; also hollow earth theory, Atlantis, UFOs and allied mysteries. **Peter Kells: Box 1670, Southport, Queensland 4215, Australia.**

O I would like to hear from anyone who has any knowledge of Albert McDonald or Guenther Rosenburg, and the publications they put out some 15yrs ago or longer dealing with legendary tales of the **inner earth and mysterious tunnels. Frank Brownley: 29 McCall Rd, Rochester, NY 14615, USA.** [We'd like to know too – Ed.]

O I would like to exchange information about unkown beasts; particularly about **giant octopi and 'hairy wildmen'. Michel Raynal: 22 Ave P. Semard, 11100 Narbonne, France.**

O I am trying to locate copies of a publication called **Pyramid Energy Magazine** (not the same as *Pyramid Guide*) seen in 1980. **Scott Parker: 5775 Kristin, Beaumont, TX 77706, USA.**

O I am looking for a copy of **Creatures of the Outer Edge** by Loren Coleman and Jerome Clark; and **Bigfoot Casebook** by Janet & Colin Bord. **Michel Meurger; 175 Rue de Javel, 75015 Paris, France.**

O Wanted – "the help of a very open minded and extremely inventive person" for Tesla-type experiments, including "the making of a sine wave oscillator with a DC input of 100 Kvolts, or preferably 750 Kvolts." No timewasters. *Cedric Vaughan-Spencer, 38 St Stephens Gardens, St Margarets, Middlesex TW1 2LS*

O Jenny Randles is researching a book about the **strange experiences** of **celebrities** (politicians, sports folk, entertainers, musicians, writers, scientists etc) to be called *The Famous Files.* She would welcome any information from FT readers, such as research outlets, anecdotes, and so on. **Jenny Randles: 9 Crosfield Rd, Somerville, Wallasey, L44 9EH.**

TRUSS FUND

Thanks to the following for their kind donations: *Larry Arnold, EM Carruthers, Steve Cohn, John Ellis, Michael Goss, Nick Malloret, and W Small.*

LETTERS
Cont from p70.

into the magical-US-USSR-Freud - Joyce - eye - pyramid-money-Jersey-shovel synchronous chain!

Furthermore, by using appropriate Chomskyan Deep Structure transformations it can be shown that each term in this chain may be converted into each other term. In fact, one may convert every word in Wilson's article into every other one in the article. Mind you that would be silly because the result would be gibberish.

My, what a funny synchronous world we live in.
PS: I suggest Wilson reads Jung's book to find out what synchronicity *really* is. It doesn't include the kind of *deliberate* punning relations that Joyce used. Nor the torturing of info. to fit an a priori model (as Wilson does).
Les Prince
Egbaston, Birmingham

FT Backissues.

- **FT31** – The Chinese Wildman; Gateways to Mystery; The Touch of Death; UFO muggers; mystery big cats; ball lightning; synchronous names; little people; fake doctors; Forteana from China; comix.
- **FT32** – The Mississauga Blob; Old Ives' Tales; Gateways (pt 2); occult murder; mystery big cats; fairy tales come true; Forteana from India and China; child sacrifice; mystery panthers in USA and Australia; comix.
- **FT33** – The Enfield Poltergeist; mythology of UFO abductions; Gateways (pt 3); mass hysteria at Nottingham; simulacra; coffin stories; Jeoff Watson's Nessie pix; UFOs; Forteana from China; giant snakes; comix.
- **FT34** – Congo dinosaur hunt; lake monster names; phantom hitch-hikers; interview with Dr Jean Bolen on synchronicity; the Welsh 'puma'; mystery big cats; beached whales; animal saboteurs; nature follows art; ice falls; inept crimes; Trashkashic records; odd Irish doings; giant squids; comix.

- **FT35** – The Myth of Darwinism; an SHC from 1744; The Runamo Runes; Forteana from Malaysia and China; spontaneous combustions; antiquities; strange trees; magic fuels; frog and stone falls; mystery big cats; bizarre bacteria; TV science; occult murder; Fortean travel in USA.
- **FT36** – Anomalistics; Photos of Jesus; Runamo Runes; Gent's Mag extracts; hermits and wildmen; strange tales; toads in holes; bleeding statues and visions; the Buddha's UFO; DIY surgery; coin, ice and sand falls; ASSAP and CSAR; jellyfish in the sky; Forteana from China; USA monitor lizards; Nessie; comix.
- **FT37** – Australia's Lizard Monsters; energy from space; encounters with Greek gods; interview with Dr Rupert Sheldrake on a New Science of Life; a female prophet; Irish oddities; mystery USA kangaroos; UFO hallucinations; falls of crabs, frogs, peas, fish; visions, stigmatics and fasting; plants in odd places; mystery UK bear scares; talking

polts; reflections; homing rings; locked-up by friends and relatives.
- **FT38** – Psychometry of cattle mutilations; Isotope myth; synchronicity of clowns and 22; Sieveking's Selection; two BVM visions; talking polts; recent discoveries of old and new species; objects penetrating brains; double image; strange fires; Rasta folklore; comix, columns, letters.
- **FT39** – Robert Anton Wilson on Synchronicity in Joyce's *Finnegans Wake*; SHC Survivors inc Jack Angel; The ET Law; Entombed Toads; Gentlemans Magazine Extracts Pt 2; Mystery Cats; Chinese Hair Clipping Panics; Homing Wallets, Snippers & Snatchers Etc; Death Tableaux; Ice Falls; Updates on Material in Previous Issues; + Columns, Letters, Comix.

ALL AT SINGLE ISSUE PRICE

• • •

JESUS CHRIST

is the *Sun* of God

AN INTRODUCTION TO THE GNOSTIC ORIGINS
OF THE CHRISTIAN MYTHOS

An Introduction to the Gnostic Origins of the Christian Mythos.
By David R. Fideler. 57pp, 49 illustrations, bibliography,
fold-out map, perfect bound with two-colour cover.
Published by Philosophical Book Service 1982
in a limited edition of 500 copies.

$6.00 + 80c postage. US funds/Int. Money Order.
Lindisfarne Press, RD No.2, West Stockbridge, MA 01266, USA.

Fortean Times

ISSUE No. 41 — The Foremost Journal of Strange Phenomena — PRICE £1·25 $3·00

10TH ANNIVERSARY ISSUE

BORDS/CHRISTIE/CLARK/COLEMAN/COSTELLO/EVANS/FIDELER
HEUVELMANS/HOFFMAN/JOHNSON/KEEL/MICHELL/MOORE/PENNICK
PERSINGER/RICKARD/SHEPARD/SHIELS/WESTRUM/and Mr X.

Fortean Book Club
&
Mail Order

Fortean Times

Cover art by
Hunt Emerson

The Journal of Strange Phenomena.

Winter 1983
ISSN 0308.5899

Contents.

Fortean Times

The Journal of Strange Phenomena

**96 Mansfield Road,
London NW3 2HX, UK.**

GANG OF FORT
Editor Robert J. M. Rickard
Mike Dash
Steve Moore
Paul R. A. deG Sieveking
Art Dir. Richard Adams
Comix Ed. Hunt Emerson

SPECIAL CORRESPONDENTS
Australia Greg Axford (Vic.)
Paul Cropper (N.S.W.)
Rex Gilroy (N.S.W.)
Tony Healy (A.C.T.)
Richard King (Vic.)
Belgium Henri Premont
Canada Dwight Whalen (Ont.)
Mister X (Ont.)
England Richard Cotton
Peter Christie
Peter Hope Evans
Alan Gardiner
Chris Hall
Valerie Martin
John Michell
Nigel Pennick
Paul Screeton
Bob Skinner
Anthony Smith
David Sutton
Paul R. Thomas
Finland Tuuri Heporauta
France Jean-Louis Brodu
Dr. Bernard Heuvelmans
Phil Ledger
Greece Anastasios D. Panos
Ireland Doc Shiels
Robert Anton Wilson
Japan Jun-Ichi Takanashi
Malaysia Ahmad Jamaludin
Roving Ion A. Will
Scotland Roland Watson
Jake Williams
S. Africa Chris J. Holtzhausen
Sweden Ake Franzen
Anders Liljegren
Sven Rosen
USA George Andrews (MO.)
Larry E. Arnold (PA.)
Tom Adams (TX.)
Loren Coleman (MA.)
Richard T. Crowe (IL.)
Ron Dobbins (AZ.)
David R. Fideler (PA.)
Mark A. Hall (MN.)
Steve Hicks (KS.)
Michael Hoffman (NY.)
Kurt Lothmann (TX.)
Gary S. Mangiacopra (CN.)
Joseph Swatck (NB.)
Paul Willis (MD.)
Joseph W. Zarzynski (NY.)
USSR Vladimir V. Rubtsov
Wales Janet & Colin Bord
Yugoslavia Milos Krmelj

Reprosetting Sally Gwynn-Seary
5 Woodside Terrace,
Ruscombe. Stroud. Glos.
Printing I.P.L. 'Old Convent'.
Stroud. Glos.
Overseas Overseas Postal Services Ltd.
Mailing 2-8 Hornsey St.
London N7 8HF
Label Anagram
Computing 316A Richmond Rd.
Twickenham TW1 2PD

Editorial

TICK TICKA TICKA TACK TOCK .TACKA

10 YEARS ON
Well, here we are at our long anticipated 10th anniversary issue. We tried to get it to you by Christmas — I won't say *which* Christmas. . . I know you'll be as impressed as we are at the range and quality of the articles in this special issue, and I thank all our contributors, on behalf of FT and its readers, for their support.

It was interesting to see how our different contributors viewed the state of our work and the future of it. Perhaps the single most consistent theme to emerge is the importance placed upon constructing functional hypotheses, against which to test our data. Only thus can we develop as a coherent discipline.

The Fortean's reticence to venture his opinions is quite understandable: the temptation to 'believe' in them as ends in themselves is too strong in most of us. They become entrenched and are hard to change or remove. But strictly speaking, a Fortean should have no strong committment to a hypothesis anyway. He should accept it, temporarily, until a better paradigm comes along, which can explain, account for or organize more than the old notion, and more simply. Fort himself is a good model — he fired off ideas and theories at every opportunity, some whimsical, some serious, knowing that in every fiction there is a little truth, and vice versa.

A number of contributors have referred to the 'final' exposure of the Cottingley Fairies case — a full summary of this, by Janet Bord, will appear in FT43.

NEW ADDRESS
Effective immediately, we have a new address. The old BM address will be kept on for a while to catch stragglers.

FORTEAN BOOKS
Our printer, **Richard Gwynn-Seary**, will be taking over our limited booklist. He intends to develop a specifically Fortean book service, and will retain strong links with FT. We will advise him on new and standard titles, and are negotiating a special discount for FT readers. **Please see inside front cover for details.** All orders received by FT will be passed on to the FBC&MO *(Fortean Book Club & Mail Order.)*

COVER BLOWN
A few readers, undoubtedly missing a few marbles, asked if photos of the staff could be printed. That would tempt the gods too much, but next best is our cover by Hunt Emerson, featuring the Gang of Fort (L to R): **Ion Will** (t), **Mike Dash** (b), **Steve Moore**, **Bob Rickard**, **Richard Adams**, **Paul Sieveking** (t) and **Hunt** (b).

Continued on p7.

The Ghost of Arthur Keith.

by Peter Costello.

The orthodox sciences tend to look down upon anecdotal evidence; yet the history of science shows that many a discipline began with reflection upon the words of witnesses. The emphasis upon physical evidence has formed the course of Western science and made it difficult for the orthodoxy to accept the existence of transient phenomena, for which, more often than not, the only evidence is anecdotal. Forteans argue that this is science's loss, caused by an unneccessarily restricted, exclusionist, attitude. As **John Michell** points out, elsewhere in this issue, Fort's dream of an inclusive science has quite a few ancient precedents, like those realized in China and Greece, described by **Steve Moore** and **David Fideler**, also in these pages. In its rejection of unidentified animals, phenomena or forces, for which the accumulated anecdotal evidence is both voluminous and strickingly consistent in its detail, scientists, says **Peter Costello**, are behaving unscientifically. In this examination of the problem, Peter shows not only that a tradition of an anomaly-oriented science has respectable foundation in English philosophy of science, but that there are extant sciences based upon, or incorporating, anecdotal evidence.

In January 1934, during the heyday of the Loch Ness Monster, Sir Arthur Keith, the eminent anatomist, was asked by the *Daily Mail* for an article giving the view of the scientific establishment on that elusive creature.

Sir Arthur was a rationalist — long associated with the Rationalist Press, which used to issue those quaint little volumes 'The Thinker's Library'. Naturally he had clear views on the mystery of the moment.

"I spent my boyhood on the banks of a river which flows into the Moray Firth. I knew many men and women who had seen kelpies in a certain dark pool, not once but many times. Like the Loch Ness monster, kelpies could be seen but not touched. I did not believe in them then, and nothing has happened since to alter my mind."

For his "evidence" about the Loch Ness Monster Keith himself drew upon the number of sensational articles about the creature which had been appearing in the national press since the autumn. The *Daily Mail* indeed had sent up a big game hunter who had found the "spoor" of the monster (later admitted to have been faked), and then came to the view that the "monster" was only a common seal. Sir Arthur thought otherwise.

"The only kind of being whose existence is testified to by scores of witnesses, and which never reaches the dissecting table, belongs to the world of spirits. . .

"I have come to the conclusion that the existence or non-existence of the Loch Ness Monster is not a problem for zoologists but for psychologists." (London *Daily Mail*, 3 January 1934)

It seems that if a carcass of Nessie could have been brought into his operating theatre in the Royal College of Surgeons, he could have dealt with it. Physical evidence, not anecdotes, was what he needed. Otherwise. . . Well, Nessie is still with us, but we are haunted daily by the ghost of Arthur Keith, for his inflexible view of what is evidence persists.

Two decades earlier in his career, in November 1912, Dr. Arthur Keith (as he then was) had gone down to the Natural History Museum in South Kensington to examine just such items of real physical evidence as he was later to demand from Loch Ness. Nothing could be more physical than bones.

Dr. Arthur Smith Woodward, who reluctantly welcomed Keith to the inner enclave of the Geological Department, produced from his safe the broken fragments of a braincase and half a jawbone. These, which Keith examined minutely, were the relics of the Piltdown Man.

In 1912 the bones were hailed as those of the true 'Missing Link'. In 1953 — while Keith was still alive — they were shown to be a complete fake.

The bones had been found at a site in rural Sussex, mostly by Charles Dawson, a local lawyer. Woodward, when he showed them to Keith that day, was putting the final touches to an elaborate reconstruction of the pieces into what he conceived to be their original form, combining human and simian characteristics. This unlovely creature – actually a speechless female some said – was to become the earliest Englishman. The find was unveiled with great excitment at a meeting of the Geological Society in December 1912.

At once Keith disputed Woodward's reconstruction, sparking off a row which ran on for several years and affected several old friendships. He claimed that Woodward had made a mistake about the median line of the skull, and had made it too small in his reconstruction. Keith made it larger, and more modern in appearance, which only made the ape-like jaw all the more curious. Abroad, the French, Germans and Americans were doubtful, derisory or merely highly critical of the whole business. But Woodward, Keith and their British partisans were not going to be lectured to by some Boche scientist. Piltdown Man was elevated into a leading position in British history where he stayed for over a generation.

Then in the Autumn of 1953, after a few days of clear thinking about the Piltdown problem, the Oxford don J. S. Weiner saw the whole thing must be a hoax. And so after further investigations, which lasted into the middle of 1954, it turned out to be. The Piltdown Man was revealed to be the most elaborate hoax in scientific history. The physical evidence which Keith had spent decades turning over in his lab, and around which he had largely built up his two-volume book *The Antiquity of Man* (1915), was a total fraud.

When Piltdown was known to be a fraud, the signs of fraud were clear to all. Pure reason, however, had not saved poor Arthur Keith from fatal error. If he had paid more attention to the circumstances of the find, he might have seen through it then, as some of the Germans did. But Piltdown, unlike Nessie, was acceptable because it fitted into what many anthropologists expected to find.

The evidence for Piltdown and against Nessie was not examined in that detached manner in which so many scientists (especially the second-rate careerists) imagine they function. Keith was proud enough of his *Daily Mail* article to preserve a copy of it among his papers still at the Royal College of Surgeons, but he was not humble enough to actually go up to Loch Ness and question the witnesses himself. (It was left to the amateur R.T. Gould to do that, travelling round Loch Ness on his motorcycle: he arrived eventually at a very different conclusion to Keith.) Nessie was a Monster, and as such had been beyond the pale of scientific consideration since the 17th century.

This need not have been so. Francis Bacon, Viscount St Albans, (doubtless better known to some readers of *Fortean Times* as the author of *Hamlet* and some other plays) in The *Advancement of Learning* (1605), the important book which inaugurated the beginings of modern science, distinguishes what he calls "the third vice or disease of learning, which concerneth deceit or untruth." He says that just as "an inquisitive man is a prattler, so upon like reason a credulous man is a deceiver." The credulity of an Arthur Keith may be more damaging than anything a mere Nessie enthusiast could achieve.

Bacon commends the method of Aristotle who set out his acute observations of animal life – simply expressed – in a series of books, putting "all prodigious narratives" into one volume, believing "that rarities and reports that seem incredible are not to be supressed or denied to the memory of man". (That might almost stand at the masthead of this journal.)

Later, Bacon returns to this point. "History of nature," he says, "is of three sorts," nature in course, nature erring or varying, and nature altered – the history of creatures, marvels and the arts.

Forteans are naturally concerned with the record of marvels. What Bacon says might stand, contrary to the Arthur Keiths of this world, as a Fortean charter.

"I find no sufficient or competent collection of the works of nature which have a digression or deflection from the ordinary course of generations, productions or motions; whether they be singularities of place or region, or the strange events of time and chance, of the effects of yet unknown properties, or the instances of exception to general kinds." (Everyman edition, p70) His demand for "a substantial and severe collection of the *heteroclites* or *irregulars of nature*" is surely being fulfilled by the Fortean tradition of free inquiry.

A rationalist like Keith lives in fear of fraud, and so is often hoaxed from unexpected sources. Charles Fort himself comments on this point. "Imposture pervades all things phenomenal. Everything is a mirage. Nevertheless, accepting that there is continuity, I cannot accept that anybody ever has been an absolute imposter. If he's a Tichborne Claimant, after a while he thinks that there may be some grounds for his claims. If good and evil are continuous, any crime can be linked with any virtue. Imposture merges away into self-deception so that only relatively has there ever been an imposter."

"Every scientist who has ever played a part in any developing science has, as can be shown, if he's been dead long enough, by comparing his views with more modern views, deceived himself. . .I can draw no line between imposture and self-deception. I can draw no line between anything phenomenal and anything else phenomenal, even though I accept that also there are lines. But there are scientists who have deceived others so rankly that it seems an excess of good manners to say that they also deceived themselves. If among scientists there have been instances of rank imposture, we shall expect to come upon much imposture in our data of irresponsible people." (*Lo!*, in collected edition, pp 669-70)

(One case which Fort mentions in this context, that of the Austrian biologist Dr. Paul Kammerer, who shot himself in 1926 after being 'exposed' was critically examined by the late Arthur Koestler in *The Case of the Midwife Toad* (1971), a book which every reader of *Fortean Times* should read, a *locus classicus* on the whole matter of scientific fraud.)

After Bacon, the development of modern science was away from any inquiring interest in monsters. The experimental tradition dislodged the older, anecdotal one of Aristotle. Arthur Keith with his call for a carcass to disect represents this tradition, which is now in turn dying away.

Once all biologists thought of was obtaining a specimen. The rarest animal in the world is the Tenrec (*Dasogale fontoynonti*), which is known only from the single type specimen in the Museum of Natural History in Paris. Other animals have become rare by being hunted to extinction just because they were very rare. That at least was what prevailed in the 19th century. But with the rise of Ethology – the study of animals as part of their living environment – all that has changed. Once such evidence as Niko Tinbergen has devoted his life to collecting and collating would have been dismissed as 'anecdotal'.

Unless behaviour could be controlled and repeated in a laboratory, unless the animal itself could be cut up in dissecting rooms, it was not science. But such conditions were not natural: as with Solly Zuckerman's studies of primate sexuality, more recent studies have shown his work with captive apes to be quite misleading, and dare one put it, 'unscientific'. Nowadays a whole new science has been raised on 'anecdotal' evidence.

The nature of what is thought to be evidence changes, despite the pretentions of people like Arthur Keith. The evidence for Nessie – or for ghosts – which Keith rejected, was anecdotal. The physical evidence which he accepted betrayed him. Forteans should ignore the beckonings of Keith's ghost. Pure rationalism is not the answer. We should not worry ourselves as he did about whether Nessie is a hoax or a ghost. (Those familiar with the evidence from Loch Ness will know how far this question is from a settlement, even after 50 years.) We can raise our studies to a science by following Bacon's advice to dilligently collect 'the *heteroclites* or *irregulars of nature*.' Anecdotal or not, fraudulent or not, the material will cumulatively be of great value. We should take the world as we find it. In doing so, we will be restoring an older, Baconian, non-experimental tradition, but one which seems to be in keeping with the latest trends of biolgical science. Which is more then can be said for Keith's rationalism.

•

Peter Costello

FORT-NOTE
by Pokkettz.

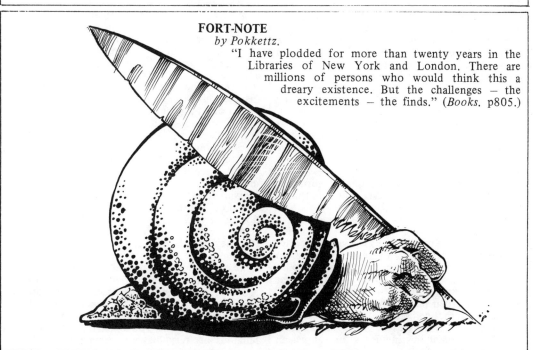

"I have plodded for more than twenty years in the Libraries of New York and London. There are millions of persons who would think this a dreary existence. But the challenges – the excitements – the finds." (*Books.* p805.)

The Exposure of A Philosopher.

by John Michell.

In adding his own appreciation of Fort to our celebration, **John Michell** unequivocally calls him the greatest philosophical genius to have come out of America. There are many who would disagree, citing the eccentricity of Fort's literary style, the impenetrability of his philosophy and his frivolity with profoundly disturbing ideas. Indeed, argues Michell, Fort's whole opus is constructed with such consummate skill that it reflects back its readers' own preconceptions, and thus will always remain as obstacle to the unthinking, dogmatic or bigoted mind. But for those who can see, Fort becomes a magnificent mirror upon which to reflect the mysteries of our existence.

Whenever I lose control of my tongue and babble about Charles Fort being the best modern philosopher and the greatest genius to come out of America, either people have no idea of what the hell I'm talking about, or they give the embarrassed smile which comes from not quite understanding the joke. Fort himself would probably add me to his collection of crank cultists. That man is absolutely foolproof. No idiot, bigot, dogmatist or true believer of any brand has ever been able to understand Charles Fort. That is why his writings have been so neglected and misunderstood, even among his followers. Some years ago, at a Fortean convention in Washington, I was struck by the number of delegates who honoured Fort as an early advocate of their own particular beliefs — in witchcraft, poltergeists, extra-terrestials, lake monsters, ancient civilizations or whatever — as if unaware that he no more absolutely believed in these than he believed in the 'laws' of science, or 'truths' of religion or the proposition that two plus two must inevitably, under every condition, make four. "I cannot accept", he wrote, "that the products of minds are subject-matter for belief."

Fort's use of 'data' was intended above all to demonstrate that every established faith and theory is based on 'exclusions'. "It is our expression that nothing can attempt to be, except by attempting to exclude something else." His way of undermining the grave theories of Newton and Darwin, by means of toads in stones, ancient artifacts in coal mines and piles of washing disappearing upwards into a clear sky, is shocking enough to pedants. But even worse, from their point of view, is his refusal to proclaim alternative beliefs in place of those he discredits. That is his greatest heresy, and that is the feature which distinguishes him above all

other philosophers of our times.

According to modern conventions, we may freely dissent from any of the received doctrines of science, religion or politics — provided we offer some other doctrines, thus perpetuating the existing structures. The real heretic, against whom every other school joins ranks, is the one who questions the very nature of belief. In a television discussion, for example, the participants are encouraged to express different opinions and state all sides of the question under debate, resulting in a dramatic clash of rival certainties; but the Fortean view, that this or any other question can never finally be resolved and is therefore meaningless, is the one view that may not be expressed. It breaks the rules of the game. The media demand clear-cut answers and attitudes, the very commodities that Fort most rigorously avoided. Thus he insured himself against ever becoming the object of a popular cult.

His other insurance against pompous idiots and cultists was, of course, his style of writing. It is outrageously original and hardly at all related to the type of English composition taught in college and practised by respectable men of letters. Yet, in terms of his own, highly individualistic code of grammar and punctuation, Fort hardly ever put a foot wrong. Nor does he ever fail in logic. His wisdom, however, is most effectively hidden from vulgar eyes by its packing of hilarity. There was never a funnier writer than Fort, certainly not in the field of speculative cosmology. He excelled at depicting the human comedy, and he faithfully reflected the absurd, paradoxical comedy of our universe. This has a disconcerting effect on those students of life who expect to see in it, not comedy, but a romance, tale of heroism, religious mystery play or noble tragedy. Even more it disconcerts the reverend, those who feel that subjects such as God, science and the nature of the universe should be treated with gravity and awe. Faithists, systematizers, theory-mongers and the single-minded of all persuasions thus exclude themselves from the circle of Fort's initiates. Of the many writers who have quoted or made use of his data, only a small minority deserve the honourable name of true Forteans.

One can aptly compare Fort's view of the world with that upheld by the Chinese, Greek and other ancient schools of philosophy, which were based on the Fortean notions of universe-as-organism and the transient, unreal nature, of all apparent phenomena. They recognized, like Fort, that there is nothing in this world worthy of being believed in. This hard, painfully realistic philosophy has always been the property of the few rather than the majority of people. We are by nature myth-making creatures, and the myths we dream up and adopt are those which structure our individual mentalities and collective societies. In conditions of civilization, where permanent institutions are required, myths are needed to create them. Thus we must have myths and settled beliefs if we are to live settled lives. The quality of our lives depends on the quality of our myths – as Socrates understood when he tried to reform the myths of ancient Athens and was executed for his pains. Fort also understood the need for myths, but the way he set about reforming the ideas of his time was far more subtle, and will probably prove more successful, than the attempt by Socrates. He reduced all the doctrines of the modern scientific high priests to the level of jokes, and then he added a few more jokes of his own, stirred them together and served up a stew of all conceivable notions, boiled in the same cauldron. Readers can either enjoy its flavour as a whole, or they can select the pieces that suit their taste, forming a personal cosmology from an even greater stock of material than was available to Einstein.

Fort treated all myths lightly, laughing at the concepts which he himself introduced – teleportation, poltergeist energy, man-eating fire demons, giant space-craft and so on – as heartily as he laughed at all the established theories. Yet behind the laughter one can glimpse a tendency, purposeful maybe, in his writings, which is apparent in their effect. After reading Fort, one's view of the world is inevitable changed. Certainties dissolve, while new ideas, previously unimagined, take root in the mind. That is the very process which has to take place for the rationalistic or nineteenth-century mind to adapt itself to the findings of, say, modern physics. The world we have inherited has been structured by the mental patterns of our forebears, which still dominate many of our institutions. To confront the problems of our own time, unforeseen by previous generations, a different world-view is obviously required. As Fort pointed out, there are many neglected aspects of reality, and any of them are potential ingredients in the world-view of the future.

My own feeling is that Fort's alternative concepts were not introduced entirely at random; that he was dropping hints; that he was drawing attention to certain powers and tendencies in the universe which, he thought, might usefully be recognized. How cunningly he went to work! Scorning the official robes of priest, scientist or teacher, he disguised himself in fool's motley, set his audience to laughing and left them, unknown to themselves, with changed mentalities, and new myths, better adapted to the circumstances of this delightfully varied universe.

Whatever Fort thought he was up to – and he was too clever for that ever to be known for certain – what he actually did was to provide a course of mental reconstruction, the most stimulating and enjoyable that can be imagined – designed to produce better-informed, more tolerant citizens of the universe. That is why I rate him among the greatest reformers and philosophers of all times. He is certainly far the most entertaining.

•

John Michell

EDITORIAL
Continued from p2.

NEW FORMAT & SHARES
To date about 10% of our readers have returned our query form in the positive – ie. they **would** be interested in taking up shares in FT – and more replies trickle in daily.

I would like to thank you for those responses, many of which included messages of confidence and encouragement, which mean a lot to us. Many of you also offered comments and advice, too numerous to reply to individually but all of which were sincerely appreciated and will be carefully concidered.

We are looking for a structure which will allow us to develop our activities on two fronts. We need to formalize our academic interests and are leaning towards the idea of an Institute for Fortean Studies. Whatever form this takes, it will form the nucleus of our archive and research programmes – for my initial thoughts on these activities, please turn to page 71.

We are certainly taking the idea of offering shares to readers further and will obtain professional advice in the New Year. It may take a little longer than I originally thought, but it is important to get it right, as you will appreciate. We hope to make some sort of progress report to you with FT42.

Continued on p30.

The Dialectic of Natural Science and Natural Philosophy:

Or Whatever Happened to Inclusive Cosmology?

by David R. Fideler.

Fort's technique was essentially dialectical: he opposed dogmatic seriousness with humorous heresies, smugness and certainty with shocking anomalies, and the cozy causal compartmentalized universe of science with an almost mystical view of organic interconnectedness. Philosophically, there is another dialogue rampant in Fort's writings, **David Fideler** points out here, representing the interplay between Aristotelian science and Platonic philosophy. The 'natural' artist and 'natural' scientist are in fact confronting a common ontological entity, and in their search for inclusive understanding the profound artist is scientifically creative and the scientist or technologist is at his best when creatively expressive. In his own way Fort is a good example of this union; he jocularly described himself as "a pioneer in a new kind of writing that instead of old-fashioned heroes and villains, will have floods and bugs and stars and earthquakes for its characters and motifs."

THE TIME BEFORE TIME
The Myth of the Golden Age

"We must then have, ourselves some part or share in Eternity. Still, how is this possible to us who exist in Time?" Plotinus.

According to the accounts of various creation myths and stories, the first men are said to have lived in a paradisial condition, having free communion with the eternal forces which bind and govern the cosmos, subsisting in perfect harmony with both the gods and their environment.

The Greeks conceived the beginning of time as a state of human and natural perfection, the Golden Age, when men lived without cares or labor, and where death was no more terrible than sleep.

In the Hebrew account of the Edenic Garden, paradise was maintained until the first man tasted the fruit of knowledge, after which he fell away from the primal unity into the temporal flux of generation, growth, and decay.

In the Greek version, even though the first men stood on the threshold of eternity, the Golden Age did not last forever. Speaking of the Golden Race in his *Greek Myths*, Robert Graves laments "... They are all gone now, but their spirits survive as genii of happy music retreats, givers of good fortune, and upholders of justice."

These stories of man's fall from a state of pre-conscious perfection express in symbolic terms humanity's relationship with the two manifestations of time, the temporal and the eternal. They also refer to certain stages in the evolution and development of consciousness.

It is interesting to note that the Greeks identified the ruler of the Golden Age as Kronos (the Roman *Saturnus*), who is the universal personification of time and form. Time has two obvious aspects, and these are admirably embodied in the figure of Kronos, who as the lord of the Golden Age symbolizes the part of nature which is eternal, perfect, and unchanging, and as the devourer of his own children in Greek myth allegorically represents the destructive influence of time on all that is born into the world of physical manifestation.

TWO MODES OF TIME:
Cyclical and Linear

In a certain sense, man could be considered as the bridge between time and eternity because he experiences both realms fully in terms of his psychological evolution.

Early man experienced time as a cyclical phenomenon, living within the unbroken circle of eternity. This state of consciousness corresponds to what the psychologist Erich Neumann refers to as the uroboric period of psychological development, named after the tail-biting serpent. Since there is no seperation between the observer and the outside world, at this stage of consciousness the concept of linear time is an alien one. Linear time is measured by the rational intellect which divides reality into segments, parts, and ratios for comparison and analysis. Hence, the concept of linear time is associated with the function of the ego or logical intellect which develops during the second stage of conscious development.

When one approaches to analyze what C.G. Jung calls the archetypes or the eternal images of the collective unconscious, one must be prepared to consider that which is psychologically much larger than our purely rational egos, because the elemental language of the unconscious transcends the boundaries of purely linear time, placing the mind in touch with its inner symbols and images which transcend the individual and suggest a universal or archetypal existence. This is especially reflected in the nature of the symbol, which unlike a static representation, bespeaks of a common level of living communication in some essential aspect of the human situation, for the images of myth, poetry, and religious experience all portray aspects of a timeless reality.

Jung in his studies has correctly recognized that these contents of the objective psyche or 'collective unconscious' possess a timeless quality, which becomes more pronounced at each successively deep layer. Jung's student Marie Louise von Franz in her book *Time: Rhythm and Repose*, presents a model of the various levels of experimental time. Her diagram and explanation is reproduced below.

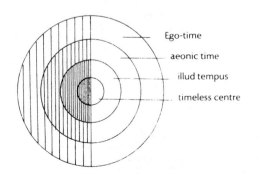

- Ego-time
- aeonic time
- illud tempus
- timeless centre

"One could compare time to a rotating wheel: our ordinary communal time, which we are aware of in our ego consciousness, would be the outermost ring which moves more quickly than the others. The next inner ring would represent aeonic time, moving origressively more slowly as the center is approached. This aeonic time is represented in the idea of the Platonic Year or the Aztec ages or Suns – a time which lasts infinitely longer than our ordinary time. The next and smallest would represent Eliade's illud tempus, which is right on the razor's edge between time and no-time, representing, as he says, as 'extratemporal moment of creation'. It is right between unutterable eternity and the beginnings of aeonic time, the latter being the slow-moving life of the archetypes. And finally there is the hole, the non-rotating empty center of the wheel, which remains permanently outside movement and time."

Regarding the reconciliation of the eternal and the temporal modes of human consciousness, Jill Purce makes the following cogent observation in her book *The Mystic Spiral*:

"There are within each of us three stages of knowledge. This is the spiral process by which not only individual man but the cosmos itself becomes realized; for it represents the course of evolution. Thus in the early days of humanity, as in childhood, there was no seperation between ourselves and the outside world, until we, individually or as a race, became self-conscious. As a result of successive windings, our individual and collective ego crystallized, and we could see ourselves as subject, and as distinct from the world, which became the object of our scrutiny. As we looked, the continuum differentiated into 'things'. Each branched into more things, which in turn branched into even more things, which in turn branched into even more, until the continuum had developed into a hierarchy; language, which once flowed in verbs and processes, broke up into nouns and connectives."

"The third stage for the individual is that of intuitive knowledge or enlightenment, in which subject and object again become one. In collective terms, this return to a continuum implies not only the need for a new language, like that which physicists are trying to develop, but that the analytic and quantitative world is winding itself into a new simplicity..."

In the third stage, through the mediation of what Jung calls the archetypal self, one is able to reconcile the temporal with the eternal. In this way, through the dialectic of self-conscious evolution, it is possible to realize the cyclical and universal rhythms of growth and creative process; a recognition which is only possible in the temporal world of particular manifestation.

NATURAL SCIENCE
AND NATURAL PHILOSOPHY:
Two Elements of an Inclusive Cosmology

Man is perhaps most happily at home in the universe as long as he can relate his experiences to both the universal and the particular, the eternal and the temporal, or the unmanifest and that which is easily seen. This understanding was recognized and followed by the cosmologists and philosophers of antiquity for many generations and was until recently embodied in the approach of the traditional scientist, whose method sought to encompass both the particular and universal characteristics of the world we inhabit.

Natural science takes an Aristotelian approach to the universe, delighting in the multiplicity of the phenomenal web. It is concerned with the individual parts as opposed to the whole, and its method is one of particularizing the universal. Natural science attempts to quantify the universal, through the reduction of living form and qualitative relations to mathematical and statistical formulations based on the classification of material artifacts.

By contrast, natural philosophy is primarily Platonic in that it is concerned with the whole as opposed to the part. Realizing that all things are essentially related to certain eternal forms and principles, the approach of the natural philosopher strives to understand the relation that the particular has with the universal. Through the language of natural philosophy it is possible to relate the temporal with the eternal and to know the organic relation between multiplicity and unity.

If the scientific spirit is seen as a desire to study the universe in its totality, it will be seen that both approaches are complimentary and necessary in scientific inquiry, for an inclusive cosmology must be equally at home when dealing with the part or the whole. The great scientists of Western civilization, for example Galileo, Copernicus, Kepler, Newton, and Einstein, each with their individual style, were able to combine both approaches in a valuable and fruitful way, as did Charles Fort, patron of this journal.

At this moment in time there is a greater amount of data and printed information available than at any previous moment in human history. But have we experienced an increase in true *knowledge* since the industrial revolution, or has there been a decline in appropriate knowledge since that time? Compare Plato's Academy with our modern campus; the latter has more facilities but at the former the instruction was undoubtedly more rigorous and satisfying. Today we have discovered the methods to construct the common TV, but more often than not have the greatest difficulty finding a program worthy of demanding our time and attention. From the standpoint of natural philosophy, a superfluous multiplicity of facts and compartmentalized data is useless in a higher sense unless one can determine their relation to the whole, or the universal patterns which underlie all creation.

Today there are millions of technologists, who are people that build artificial things, and by comparison, a much smaller group of thoughtful scientists in the traditional sense. In many circles, especially those of corporate industry, science has become confused with and subservient to technology, and from this perspective of an industrial culture it might be said that the ideal of a univeral or inclusive science has been lost. This is because the ideal scientist is also a natural philosopher who is interested in relating his discoveries to a larger universal framework, whereas the dull-minded technologist, if he has any interest in universal principles at all, limits that interest to their specific mechanistic applications, rather than their intrinsic worth of study.

Technology, in the modern sense of the word, is intimately connected with the industrial revolution and the conceptual mechanization of the natural order, which sou't to increase material profit at the expense oı the human spirit. This era, which gave rise to the nightmare of the modern factory — William Blake's "dark satanic mills" — gained its strength through the naive premise that the human spirit might be elevated and perfected through the agency of the machine. Failing to consider the implications, and the law of contraries, modern man has accomplished the opposite, for as recent experience has shown in nearly all fields of human endeavor, by constantly striving to increase the quantitative 'standard of living' we have reduced the quality and integrity of life. Instead of becoming masters of reality through the agency of the machine, we have become the depersonalized cogs of the *mechina*, valuable only to the extent that we worship at the altars of the materialistic 'vision'.

Charles Fort was expert at challenging the tyrants of the mind, and as long as such questioning souls exist all is not bleak. As an alchemist of the anomalous he fused together both the Aristotelian collection of significant data with a neoplatonic natural philosophy of Continuity. Furthermore, he fostered a unique dialectic between scientific paradigm and the 'damned army' of reported phenomena which do not conform to those sometimes narrow models. Thanks to those who would fend off the blind mechanization of the mind, such interchange continues within the pages of this and other journals.

The thrust of this somewhat rambling essay is not to point out the fallacies and dire results of a purely mechanistic paradigm, for these are readily obvious to the thoughtful reader. Nor is this writer's intent anti-technological. Technology is neither intrinsically good or evil; it all depends upon how it is applied. Rather, it is merely the author's intention to foster a dialectic between natural science and natural philosophy; to encourage the creative formulation of relevant questions; and above all to challenge all systems, whether mechanistic or academic, which threaten the freedom of thought, ongoing inquiry, and the development of an 'antropocosmic' perspective which incorporates and delights in a phenomonological approach to humanity's great achievements, scientific, philosophical, artistic, or otherwise.

With so many contemporary problems, and with so few firm solutions in sight, perhaps the most enlightened response is to keep asking questions. For example, having become aware of the mechanistic fallacy, based as it is on the premise of exploitation rather than true philosophical inquiry, is it possible to conceive of a higher conscious viewpoint as expressed in the third stage of psychological evolution? Through the dialectic of the temporal with the eternal man has always recognized, and sometimes achieved, a universal freedom through recognizing his primacy as the mediator between mind and matter, the universal and the particular, and indeed all perceivable opposites. The ability to conceive of an idea and make it real is uniquely human, and engaging in some creative process is perhaps the most liberating activity that man can know. Given this universal freedom, the only question remaining is what specifically we, as humans, choose to create: whether we will work with the dynamic harmony and equilibrium of nature as co-creators, or be trapped as slaves in a hell of our own making.

•

David R. Fideler

BIBLIOGRAPHY

- Eliade, M. *Cosmos and History: The Myth of the Eternal Return.* New York, Harper and Row, 1959.
- Neumann, E. *The Origins and History of Consciousness.* Princeton University Press, 1973.
- Priestly, J.B. *Man and Time.* NY, Dell Publishing, 1968.
- Purce, J. *The Mystic Spiral: Journey of the Soul.* London, Thames & Hudson, 1974.
- Riesner, D. *Art and Science.* London, Studio Vista, 1972.
- von Franz, M.L. *Number and Time: Reflections Leading Towards a Unification of Psychology and Physics.* London, Rider & Company, 1974. *Time: Rhythm and Respose.* London, Thames & Hudson, 1978.

FORT-NOTE
by Pokkettz.

"A squad of poltergeist girls. . .discussing their usual not very profound subjects. The alarm — the enemy is advancing. Command to the poltergeist girls to concentrate — and under their chairs they stick their wads of gum. A regiment bursts into flames, and the soldiers are torches. Horses snort smoke from the combustion of their entrails. Reinforcements are smashed under cliffs that are teleported from the Rocky Mountains. The snatch of Niagara Falls — it pours upon the battlefield. The little poltergeist girls reach for their wads of chewing gum." (*Books.* p1042.)

Heaven's Reprimands.

by Steve Moore.

A great many cultures have included a structure for monitoring anomalies, or changes from the 'natural' order, from Catholic priests in 15th century Scandinavia, and the College of Augurs attached to the Roman Senate, to the imperial court of China. These structures not only existed to collect data, but to interpret their relevance to the community. Modern society has lost the latter function with the rise of the division of the world into seperate realms of mind and matter. Archetypal psychology suggests that divination from portents has a valuable social cohesive function, forming a bridge between the collective unconscious and the phenomenal everyday world. **Steve Moore** takes a closer look at one such system in operation in China, long ago.

One of the interesting things about Charles Fort's work (perhaps even more so than his collecting of data, and scourging of 'explanations') is his underlying view of the universe. To him it was a single giant organism, the parts and forms of which are only different expressions of the same basic substances, all connected and of a primal oneness, even if the links aren't readily apparent to our eyes.

Having accepted the invitation to write a piece on parallel concepts in China, I then realised that the subject was far too vast for a short item for our anniversary issue. So what follows will concentrate on the period of the Han dynasty (206 BC – 220 AD); even so, it can be no more than an introductory glance, and the subject would be well worth a fuller treatment at a later date.

HISTORY AND HAN CONFUCIANISM

One thing we should perhaps make clear at the start is that, despite a common misconception that everything magical, organic or naturalistic in China must be Daoist, the philosophy with which we're dealing in this particular case is Confucian. But Han Confucianism is a peculiar and very different beast from the original moral and ethical teachings of Confucius (Kong Fu Zi), who lived c. 551 – 479 BC.

The centuries following his death were disturbed, to put it mildly. On the intellectual plane, numerous philosophical schools contended with one another, until the materialistic and totalitarian Legalist school carried the day. On a mundane level, there were more than two centuries of continual warfare between states, until the Legalistic Qin dynasty established the first empire in 221BC. Although the Qin empire lasted a mere fourteen years, the other philosophical schools suffered badly in this period, especially the Confucians, whose books and scholars were suppressed on a large scale.

The establishment of the Han dynasty marked a turning point, when attempts were made to recover the ancient literature and, more importantly, to interpret it in the light of the new and peaceful conditions then prevailing. And here's the crux. The Confucian Classics were the same (although being written in the 'New characters' introduced by the Qin dynasty there are grounds for suspecting they may have been tampered with in course of transmission), but their interpreters were radically different. Having simply been an ethical school from the small north-eastern state of Lu beforetimes, the Confucians now found themselves having to adapt their tenets to suit an empire which spanned the entire country. Not only had the political situation changed, but there were now a wide variety of rituals, philosophies, and occult beliefs to absorb, adapt or eradicate.

THE HAN WORLD-VIEW

Han 'Confucianism' should perhaps be renamed Han Electicism, for the world-view had changed by the second century BC. Particularly prevalent were the views of the Yin-Yang school, and the Five Elements school (originating with Zou Yen, 4th Century BC) which provided 'mechanical' explanations of how the universe worked, and both these were duly absorbed by the Confucians, who used the theories in the interpretation of their own classics.

Briefly, the Yin-Yang school posited two great cosmic principles. Yang is positive, masculine, light, dry, high, the sun, etc. Yin is negative, female, dark, wet, low, the moon, and so on. Universally, they're perfectly balanced; locally, one may preponderate. Thus men, summertime and mountains are preponderantly yang; women, winter and oceans are preponderantly yin, and so on. The Five Elements (or

Agents, Forces, Principles, etc) are Wood, Fire, Earth, Metal and Water, and these are seen as generating and destroying one another in endlessly repeated cycles.

Another part of the picture is classificatory and numerical thinking. The Five Elements were linked to the five visible planets (thus Mercury was known as the 'Water Star', Venus as the 'Metal Star', and so on); and also to the five emotions, five viscera, flavours, colours, directions, grains, etc. The end result of this thinking (applied to other numbers also, though 5 was by far the most popular) was a beautifully *patterned* conception of the universe, with everything in its place and a place for everything. And by that same patterning, everything was connected to everything else, either by direct correspondence (shared yin- or yang-ness, or a shared element) or cyclically through the generation or destruction of elements.

In a way, then, the Han philosophers went beyond Fort, not only attempting to show that the universe *is* continuous, but *how* it behaves in a continuous fashion. And we should perhaps emphasize that their view was not of a Newtonian mechanical cause-and-effect relationship; but rather one of patterns, correspondences and resonances. The Han Chinese would have no problems with the concept of action-at-a-distance or synchronicity.

DONG ZHONGSHU

Having pointed out the similarities of the Chinese system, we must now move on to the divergences, for in spite of everything else, Han Confucianism remained primarily concerned with politics and ethics, and its interest in natural phenomena was wholly related to this, rather than to any spirit of scientific enquiry.

We're dealing here with concepts originating with the philosopher Dong Zhongshu (c. 179 – 104 BC.) While working within the world-view outlined above, he and his fellows had an anthropocentric view of the universe. They saw the world as a trinity of Heaven, Earth and Man, and being mostly concerned with the actions of men, it was Man's relationships with Heaven and Earth which was the centre of their attention. Man being composed of the same Five Elements and Yin and Yang as the rest of the world, he was naturally connected to it; and his actions could have an effect on the universe, while the actions of the universe could equally have an effect on him.

Dong Zhongshu and his fellows used these notions to solve one of the major political problems of the day. Working on the assumption that a vast empire (the whole of the known civilised world) needs an absolute monarch to run it properly, how does the populace maintain some sort of control over the monarch, and prevent him becoming a tyrant? The answer

was to persuade him to work within the world-conception already described. As absolute monarch of all mankind, the emperor was also responsible for the actions of all mankind, and he became their representative in the Heaven, Earth and Man trinity. If there was violence, starvation or corruption, the Emperor was responsible as it was happening in *his* domain. And trouble in the human world, by causing an imbalance in the system, would draw a reaction from Heaven and Earth.

It's with these reactions that we start dealing with 'Fortean Phenomena'. Unusual events were taken as portents, and though their mechanics might be explained in terms of the Elements or Yang and Yin, their purpose was always moralistic. It was thought that the universe had a tendency towards peace and harmony. If the emperor's reign was peaceful and thriving, the portents would be good; if not, Heaven would first send warnings, and then reprimands. One way of maintaining this harmony was by the correct carrying out of court ritual; the carrying out of sacrifices at the appropriate times and places, wearing the correct coloured clothes, and so on. Not surprisingly, this mode of court life also provided work for a large number of Confucian scholars and experts in ritual! But even common men had their part to play in upholding this harmony: if the sun was eclipsed, that meant the Yang was being overpowered. Loud noises having Yang characteristics, it was thought that by beating large drums the Yang could be assisted in regaining its power. . .a solution which, of course, always worked before too long. . .

Interestingly, the evil portents are much more commonplace than the good ones. The major signs of Heaven's displeasure were earthquakes, fires, floods, famines etc. These were known as Reprimands or Catastrophes. Warnings, or Anomalies, were eclipses, comets, unusual movements of planets, women growing beards, and so on. Among the good portents, which were taken as signs of Heaven's blessing and satisfaction with the peaceful state of the empire, were the appearances of dragons, phoenixes, nine-tailed foxes, enormously over-productive grain and mythical trees which grew 15 leaves, one a day in the first half of the month, then lost them one a day in the second. Not among the most common of occurrences, so I suspect it was thought advisable to keep the emperor on his toes at every possible opportunity!

Dong Zhongshu was a specialist in the *Chun Qiu* ('Spring and Autumn Annals') a Confucian classic which, with its commentaries, records ths history of the state of Lu from 722 – 484 BC. His notion was that if, for example, there were two successive fires in the Ancestral Temples, the way to interpret the omen was to look back into the classics for the last such occurrence, and to judge it from the circumstances immediately preceding and following. This, of course, led to the collection of signs and potents on a large scale in the official histories and other writings, and this material includes Fortean phenomena such as rains of fish, strange lights, giant hail, etc, which would be well worth pursuing. There also developed a class of literature known as *Chan-Wei* ('Oracles and Apocrypha') which sought to continue interpreting the classics in the light of the Five Elements, portents, etc. . .none of which have been translated into English, to my knowledge.

THE FALL OF THE SYSTEM

What happened if the emperor performed all the rituals correctly, lived a good life and maintained the peace, and the evil portents still kept coming along anyway? That meant that his 'virtue' (in this context meaning more than mere moral rectitude) was deficient; or worse still that Heaven was withdrawing its mandate from the dynasty and seeking a replacement for the throne. And here was the great weakness of the political side of the scheme. It was open to manipulation; and indeed it was manipulated by Wang Mang, who usurped the throne for fourteen years in 9 AD, on the grounds that the omens were against the house of Han.

Apart from growing scepticism on this score, a purely scholarly dispute hastened the end. At the beginning of the Han, classical studies were based on the New Texts, written in Qin characters.

But by the middle of the second century BC, a number of 'Old Texts' written in the 'tadpole' characters of the state of Lu had appeared, apparently surviving from before the Qin suppression. Two schools of interpretation appeared: the New Text school using the Five Elements, the Chan-Wei, etc, and following Dong Zhongshu. . .and the Old Text school who used none of these to interpret their slightly differing versions of the classics. By the begining of the third century AD, the Old Text school had carried the day, and the New Text interpretations fell into dispute. Fell so far, in fact, that by the seventh century the Chan-Wei themselves were suppressed, and survive only in fragments today.

I think it would be fair to say that it was the political element in the system which finally killed it, for later Chinese dynasties were completely ruthless in suppressing anything that might provide a threat to the ruling house. Maybe we should remember that for the future; politics and Forteanism don't mix. . .!

•

Steve Moore

REFERENCES
See, amongst others, the following (much of the material overlaps, which is why this article hasn't been referenced point for point):

- Fung Yu-lan: *A History of Chinese Philosophy*, (trans: Derk Bodde). Princeton University Press, 1953. Vol 2, pp 55 – 58.
- Hu Shih: *The Establishment of Confucianism as a State Religion During the Han Dynasty*. Journal of the Royal Asiatic Society, North China Branch. Vol. 60, 1929, pp 20 – 41.
- Liu Wu-chi: *A Short History of Confucian Philosophy*. (1955) Delta Books, N.Y., 1964. pp 118 – 135.
- Joseph Needham: *Science and Civilisation in China*. Cambridge University Press, 1956. Vol. 2, pp 279 – 291, 299 – 303, 378 – 382.
- Tjan Tjoe Som: *Po Hu T'ung: Comprehensive Discussions in the White Tiger Hall*. E. J. Brill, Leiden, 1949, 1952. Vol. 1, pp 97 – 98, 112, 239 – 243; Vol. 2, pp 489 – 492.

FORT-NOTE
by Pokkettz.

"We shall pick up an existence by its frogs. Wise men have tried other ways. They have tried to understand our state of being, by grasping at its stars, or its arts, or its economics. But, if there is an underlying oneness of all things, it does not matter where we begin. . .One measures a circle, beginning anywhere." (*Books*. p544.)

The Chasing of Charlie.

by Doc Shiels.

The appeal of Fort's writings deserves a study in itself. While the narrow and literal-minded can find justification in Fort, as in anything else, for their beliefs, his greatest impact has been upon the genuinely creative and inquiring mind. It is significant that Fort's first champions — who discovered they were Forteans upon the publication of *The Book of the Damned* in 1919 — were among the leading journalists, and writers of the day. Part of this appeal must be because Fort's literary style was a unique creation, drawing his imagery from his data and expressing them as poetic or surreal dramas. In telling us how he found Fort **Doc Shiels** reveals his own grounding in surrealism, which helped him appreciate Fort all the more.

When I was eleven years old, back in 1949, being a keen sleight-of-handster, I subscribed to a fortnightly journal of prestidigitation known as the *Phoenix* [1]. It was published in New York and edited, in turn, by Walter Gibson and Bruce Elliott, two writers of 'pulp' fiction. Gibson, under the nom-de-pulp of Maxwell Grant, created 'The Shadow' [2]; and, in the golden age of the dime novel, turned out a full length book every ten days or so. Elliott, though rather less prolific, was, perhaps, the better writer. His short story, *Wolves Don't Cry* [3], is a minor classic in the literature of lycanthropy.

The *Phoenix* was their baby, written "by enthusiasts for enthusiasts", as they used to say. Its contributors included Martin Gardner, Clayton Rawson, William Gresham, Joe Dunninger, Cy Enfield and Orson Welles (all names with Fortean connections); but it was editor Elliott who first drew my attention to the works of Charles Hoy Fort. In the issue of July 29, 1949, he wrote: "Pick up, if you can, the *Book of the Damned* or *Lo!*. Skip through them, don't try to read them from cover to cover or you'll flip your wig."

Being the sort of lad I was. . . and probably still am. . . I decided right away that my wig needed flipping. For several weeks thereafter I searched public libraries and bookshops for the 'works', but without success. Nobody seemed to have heard of Charlie, and I could neither offer nor obtain information concerning the man himself or his publishers. Eventually, Fort was pushed back into the recesses of my mental filing cabinet. . . there were other fish to fry.

In 1956, I was living in Paris, painting pictures, not-quite-starving in a garret, and think-ing myself a wildly bohemian boyo. I made a kind of living, playing blues piano in a small all-night bistro, supplementing this by grabbing free food and drink offered at exhibition openings, which happened with useful regularity in many galleries around St Germain and Montparnasse. Invitation cards, the passports to these 'private views', were generously provided by the friend of so many young innocents abroad in that city, George Whitman. George, son of Walt, ran the Mistral Bookshop, and it was there that I eventually discovered *The Book of the Damned*.

Two weeks later, in Antibes, the book was lost on a drunken spree; but it had already worked its magic, from cover to cover, and, as promised, had flipped my wig. Synchronicty must have had something to do with the fact that I mislaid that particular book in Antibes. I was visiting the town in order to study the Picassos at the Grimaldi *Fort*, overlooking the azure sea. In 1946, Picasso had moved into the place, which he used as home and studios, from a house he had been renting in Golfe-Juan. . . a house owned by a man called *Fort*! [4]

It seemed appropriate, somehow, to find Charles Fort in France. Less snobbish, intellectually, than the British (& Irish!), French artists, writers and critics were always streets ahead in their genuine enthusiasm for outré individuals, such as Fort, and 'popular' art in the shape of horror and gangster movies, SF, strip cartoons, jazz, comic books and so on. The surrealist movement, with Paris as its headquarters, is largely responsible for this enlightened state of affairs, and Fort, with his anarchic humour, was a natural surrealist. He wrote: "My liveliest interest is not so much in things, as in the relations of things. I have spent much time thinking about the alleged pseudo-relations that are called coincidences. What if some of them should not be coincidences?"

Pointing up the relationship between, "Horses erect in a blizzard of frogs, and the patter of worms on umbrellas" he invokes the spirit of Lautréamont's "chance meeting on an operating table of a sewing-machine and an umbrella". Fort's vision was essentially poetic and his 'explanations' of phenomenal happenings and relationships remind me of Alfred Jarry's 'pataphysics', the science of imaginary solutions. Lautréamont and Jarry were major precursors of surrealism; so was Fort, it seems to me, and I'm delighted to have found his first phenomenal book sharing a shelf with some of the leading surrealists. . . and to have lost it in ancient Antipolis on the Picasso trail.

Years later, on the Irish monster trail, I discovered a massive star-shaped fortification which like Picasso's Mediterranean castle, overlooked a deep blue sea. Near Kinsale in County Cork, on the promontory of Rincurran, I found Charles Fort [5]. Ah. . . the relations of things.

NOTES

- 1 The *Phoenix* magazine links nicely with Dublin's *Phoenix* (Park) magazine, featured in Joyce's *Finnegan's Wake* and mentioned by Bob Wilson in FT39.
- 2 W. Gibson's creation, 'The Shadow', in tulpoid form, gets a nice plug in John Keel's *The Mothman Prophecies*, E.P. Dutton & Co, N.Y. 1975. Published in the UK, by Panther Books, as *Visitors From Space*.
- 3 Described in *Book of the Werewolf* by Brian J. Frost (Sphere Books, 1973) as "probably the first story to speculate on what would happen if a wolf was suddenly transformed into a man."
- 4 Louis Fort, master engraver, who printed so many of Picasso's finest plates. Another friend of Picasso's was Paul Fort, the theatrical symbolist.
- 5 In 1922, when C.H. Fort was spouting at Speaker's Corner and H.C. Earwicker was dreaming of the *Phoenix* magazine, Charles Fort (Co. Cork) burst into flames. Actually, it was set alight by a band of Republican Irregulars. Charlie may have read about the incident while he was working on *New Lands*.

●

Doc Shiels

FORT-NOTE
by Pokkettz.

"An unclothed man shocks a crowd — a moment later, if nobody is generous with an overcoat, somebody is collecting handkerchiefs to knot around him. A naked fact startles a meeting of a scientific society — and whatever it has for loins is soon diapered with conventional explanations." (*Books.* p541.)

The Untouchables.

by Michael A. Hoffman.

Some cultures make room for a Trickster, or Cosmic joker, to explain life's inconstancies, but Fort's cosmology had no place for a deity that wasn't sublimely unconscious, idiotic (in whom there is only reflex, not intelligence), and universal (besides whom there is no other). In one of his asides, Fort suggested there were two kinds of magic: one representing unknown laws, and the other lawlessness. For example: a man may fall and land unharmed through the operation of some undiscovered law of 'anti-gravity'; or he may land unharmed out of defiance of gravity, because there has to be an exception to everything. These "defiant fellows", as **Michael Hoffman** explains, were Fort's imps of "universal inconsistency".

"It is an uncatchable *again, a defiant fellow, operating openly, as if confident that he could not be caught." Charles Fort. [1]*

Fort didn't believe. He called the mass of humanity 'hypnotics' and said they were mesmerized throughout history by the 'proper authorities' [2]. It was out of his refusals that his shaman-like perceptions were honed and with them he drove a wedge of revolutionary reflection into the modern age with its newspeak, doublethink and memory holes.

There have been attempts to build a system of Deep-Thinking in Fort's name and to attach his vision to the 'ultimate new physics theorem of cosmic digital epistemological mechanics' (or some such). This as a means to the end variously depicted as space migration, Evolution, human potential enhancement or utopia; ie. the solution to the problems that face us in behaviour, philosophy and spirit. What the brilliant architects of this scene neglect to point out is that what we moderns regard as problems were once seen as solutions. But these geniuses (whether of the counter-culture or the Establishment) are latter-day Moses's, fascinated by their Deliverance Project(s) and unaware, as Fort put it that "every Moses leads his people out of Egypt into perhaps a damn sight worse. . ."[3]

The System-builders wish to capture Charles Fort nevertheless and place him in 'their' camp. But Fort's rediscovery of a thwarting, over-ride mechanism serves to illustrate that the phenomena he wrote about are hostile to every attempt at taming or shaping and that it cannot be accounted for by any theory or partisan viewpoint or discipline. Instead these partisan opinions exist to make money, promote secret police ideologies and entertain overstimulated consumers of weird notions.

The process of the uncatchable in the universe Fort personified as the 'mischievous' or 'defiant' fellow'. He also alludes to it as a 'universal inconsistency', the 'defiance of *everything'* (emphasis added).[4]

The professional 'improver' and 'problem solver' decrees that things have gone badly for humanity in the past because we have refused to recognize our god-like powers and have saddled ourselves with a negative and guilt-tripping conception of existence. This is primarily a Thelemic current, though not strictly so.

There is another school, that might be called traditional, which decrees that only when humankind recognizes certain sad truths about human nature can we best defend against illusion and manipulation.

Then there is the uncatchable.

In the fateful year of 1917, Elsie Wright and Frances Griffiths saw fairies in the garden and 'photographed' them. The 'Cottingley Photos' inspired several decades worth of analysis, of net weilding hunters trying to pin the wings of the People of Peace.[5]

"It was a joke", as Frances later said; a joke on Brain-Power and this pestiferous modern age. Because even though Frances now says that the pictures are a hoax, she also adds that the fairies that she played with in the garden are very real. By the mechanism of the uncatchable, they have become more real as a result of a fake. They have deceived the analyzers and solution-mongers from the beginning and they continue to do so by the very means employed to catch them and pin their wings.

Padre Pio was a 'mischievous fellow' who not only could 'do unaccountable things' (bilocate, read minds, emit fragrance and bear the stigmata) but took 'delight in mystifying' his 'victims'.[6]

This writer recently discovered that Padre Pio was once confronted by the sly and knowing hunter who supposedly had the capacity to pin Pio's wings. The hunter confronted the friar with hysterical conversion. That is to say, he explained to the peasant-monk-ignoramus from Pietrelcina that his bleeding stigmata were the result of a powerful faculty of Padre Pio's mind which, stimulated by his tremendous concentration on the iconography of Christ's Passion-wounds caused an imitation of these on the body of the friar. Padre Pio listened gravely to the learned occultist's diagnosis and after hearing him out, solemnly advised him to *"Go out to the fields and look very closely at a bull. Concentrate on him with all of your might. Do this and see if horns grow on your head."* [7]

To those who wish to place Charles Hoy Fort in the employ of the New Age or an old hat, to those searching fervently for the nuts and bolts of a crash-landed UFO, the corpse of a recently deceased Bigfoot or the photograph of a fairy, a caveat.

Even though your camera is infra-red and computer-enhanced and your knowledge so advanced, dare you find what you seek? The energy of your pursuit may furnish the fuel of the uncatchable. In the whirling of the circle, willed forgetfulness is the price of admission. Did you see them once, and then rested from the ordeal? What mystery is this? —

of mankind chasing after its tail?

"I think they are still around", said Frances Griffiths, "but with all the trouble, I don't want to see them anymore."[8]

●

Michael Anthony Hoffman II

NOTES

- ● 1 Charles Fort, *Wild Talents* (Ace Books paperback edition), p 37. The standard reference is *The Complete Books of Charles Fort* (referred to as *Books* below) p 874
- ● 2 Ibid., p221. (*Books* p1061).
- ● 3 Ibid., p110. (*Books* p949).
- ● 4 Ibid., p136. (*Books* p975).
- ● 5 This is the ancient title given to the fairy nation; another is 'the Good Neighbors'.

- ● 6 Fort, p29. (*Books* p866) [Fort's words here refer not to Pio, but to the exploits of the uncatchable burglar of Barberton, Ohio, 1927. — Ed.]

- ● 7 C. Bernard Ruffin, *Padre Pio: The True Story* (Huntington, Indiana: Our Sunday Visitor Press, 1982), p 150.

- ● 8 *Science*, March 1983.

FORT-NOTE
by Pokkettz.

"I think we're fished for."
(*Books*. p264.)

Phenomena and Philosophies.

by Leslie Shepard.

The practising Fortean must develop a 'professional detachment' from theories, beliefs and speculations, certainly; but as **Leslie Shepard** argues, he also has a duty to develop a "functional framework" for the anomalies he studies. If, as many Forteans suspect, our studies shed some light on the fundamental mysteries of reality and existence, then perhaps we ought to theorize or speculate more often and more boldly. Fort, as **John Michell** points out elsewhere this issue, did so in a manner which was deliberately provocative and comic, and therefore instructive.

Ever since the iconoclastic *Books* of Charles Fort were launched upon an astonished world, it has become fashionable to collect anomalous data to confound dogmatic scientists with incredible events that momentarily switch our consciousness back to a primitive wonder or fear of the unknown.

I have to declare my own anti-dogmatic bias in this direction, since I am particularly fascinated by such things as psychical phenomena, spiritual healing, fairies, astral projection, levitation and higher consciousness. However, I have too much awe of a science and technology that can put man on the moon or measure with the precision of a ten-thousandth of an inch to want to make scientists look like idiots. I simply think that there are many research areas which are unfashionable at a given time.

Although I am interested in certain anomalous phenomena in themselves, my overriding interest is in their relationship to some valid philosophy of life. I see little point in just collecting anomalies without reference to some functional framework. This is perhaps one of the basic problems of parapsychology. The attempt to validate the paranormal out of context in laboratory conditions often inhibits rare and sensitive phenomena or results in little more than ambiguous statistics and a new jargon.

Of course, some kind of scientific standard of evidence is needed if we are to avoid being deceived by conscious or unconscious fraud in paranormal areas. The staggering amount of deception is a formidable obstacle and it is not surprising that many investigators are hardened sceptics, seeking only to explain away claimed phenomena that they are already convinced are fraudulent. I suppose they balance up the over-trusting people who believe anything.

I see no harm in interim belief provided that one is prepared to modify or discard it when necessary. After all, it is standard scientific practice to postulate a theory and test it against new evidence. Hostile scepticism is just as psychopathological as crank beliefs and fanaticisms.

In my special interest in fairies, I have had to revise my former belief in the famous Cottingley fairy photographs taken by two girls between 1917 and 1920 in a Yorkshire village. These photographs were crucial to Sir Arthur Conan Doyle's book *The Coming of the Fairies* (1922; 1928) and their genuineness was never conclusively disproved until quite recently. James Randi's triumphant exposure in his book *Flim-Flam!* (1982) is typically aggressive and self-congratulatory but it is largely speculative and lacks any true understanding of the psychological factors involved. An article 'Cottingley: At Last the Truth' by Joe Cooper in *The Unexplained* (vol.10, issue 117) claims a confession by Elsie (one of the two girls in 1917), but the only detailed and sympathetic presentation of the story of these famous faked photographs is that of Geoffrey Crawley, editor of *British Journal of Photography* in a series of *BJ* articles between 24 December and 8 April, 1983. The earlier articles were submitted to Elsie and Frances, who specifically confirmed to Mr. Crawley that the photographs were fakes and not paranormal. The pictures were originally intended as a prank on grownups who refused to believe that the girls saw fairies, but themselves told tall stories about Santa Claus. The intention was to astonish the grownups with the photos and then reveal that they were fakes. Unfortunately the grownups thought the pictures a fake from the start!. By the time Sir Arthur Conan Doyle saw the pictures and published his book, the affair got out of hand and the girls were reluctant to make such a great man look foolish in public. Other understandable motives prevented disclosure at later dates.

What has been played down in the final demolition of the fairy photographs is that the girls have always insisted that they saw and played with fairies, even although the pictures were faked. I believe that this astonishing affair has great significance for the whole question of fraud in psychic phenomena. Many fake mediums also appear to have produced genuine phenomena. In short-circuiting the gap between the desire to believe and production of actual paranormal phenomena, it is probable that conscious or unconscious fraud sometimes assists genuine phenomena.

Do fairies exist? Many rational people have claimed to see them, and there are centuries of folk tradition. But nature spirits are said to be protean — capable of changing form to suit the convention of the viewer. In 1966 I suggested that some of the shining visitors from outer space in flying saucers might be a modern version of fairies appropriate to a technological society.

I think we have failed to understand the important part played by fantasy in human affairs. Why do civilizations need to spend such a large proportion of their time by nourishing the imagination with other-worldly stories of gods and goddesses, the larger than life nostalgia of ballad heroes, the ritualized mock battles of football and baseball fields, or the endless fictions of novels and television screens? Why should a factually based society support a massive industry of skilful and beautiful lies? After all, we already spend nearly half our lives in the world of dreams.

It seems that when we cannot have miracles we feel a need to invent them. Probably belief itself is a creative factor in the production of paranormal phenomena, possibly through a heightened condition of consciousness. Certainly hostility is destructive.

Psychic phenomena mainly interest me in relation to the claimed survival of consciousness after death. I am particularly interested in such phenomena as materialization and apports. If true, they hint at special anomalies in the laws of physics. However, metal-bending as popularised by Uri Geller, seems to me rather pointless. In fact, it has been a bad year for metal-bending, with the revelation that the ubiquitous Amazing Randi had organised fake metal-bending accomplices in an undercover operation to mislead investigators and make them look idiots. If there is anything of value in this particular field, I think it will be found by more sympathetic investigators like Prof. John Hasted.

Astral Projection (or out-of-the-body experience) is a strange phenomenon that bridges waking counciousness and supposed other dimentions of existance. It is essentially a very personal subjective phenomenon, although there is some objective evidence, notably with the late Eileen Garrett.

Sceptics have insisted that astral projection is an illusion or alternatively merely 'travelling clairvoyance' (whatever that is!). This seems to me merely playing with words on the part of people who do not have first-hand experience as evidence. Those who have actually experienced astral projection have usually been overcome by wonder at finding that individual consciousness can apparently exist outside the human body. My own personal experience is slight, but more convincing than sceptical arguments. The late Dr. Robert Crookall collected and collated hundreds of cases of astral projection, and suggested that if human beings could leave their physical bodies temporarily and continue to exist as a self-conscious being, this provided a strong presumption that when we leave the physical body permanently we may continue to exist after death.

Another intriguing area of psychic and spiritual phenomena is that of Psychic Dentistry. In the US, evangelist Willard Fuller has been praying for people with dental problems — cavities that need to be filled, crooked teeth that need straightening, gum disorders, spaces where teeth have been extracted and even denture problems. He has conducted healing sessions throughout the US, Canada, Mexico and elsewhere. It is claimed that every year some 1,500 dental miracles and healings occur as a result of his spiritual mission — supernormal gold or silver fillings, even rapid growth of new teeth.

It seems to me that this is one area where deception is virtually impossible. Nobody who has ever lost a tooth could doubt if a new one filled the gap miraculously, while the cost of gold and silver fillings (aside from the obvious impossibility of instances of instantaneous manipulation on the spot) would be prohibitive. In many instances, it seems that the paranormal gold fillings were of a finer quality than normally employed in dental work.

There is certainly a strong case for the reality of such amazing phenomena and the implications are staggering. It is feasible that in spiritual healing the normal processes of recovery take place but at an accelerated pace, possibly through a heightened level of psychic force stimulating the recuperative forces of the body. Paranormal dental fillings, however, suggest something like apport phenomena. Spiritual healing generally is one of those areas of the paranormal that suggests special modalities of the life force under conditions of heightened awareness.

Levitation is also a strange phenomena

associated with spiritual exaltation and frequently reported in the lives of Christian mystics like St Theresa of Avila or the monk Joseph Copertino. According to traditional yoga texts in India, levitation may be a side effect of spiritual development.

Ancient yoga treatises have described *kundalini,* a life force at the base of the spine which is converted into sexual energy for procreation or may rise up the spine with a serpentine motion to mystical centres in the body, culminating in a centre in the head which expands individual consciousness to cosmic consciousness. The accounts of the serpent, the tree, the divine garden and knowledge of sex in the sacred writings of many different religions reads like an allegory of the psycho-physical mechanism of kundalini.

Various *siddhis* or psychic powers are associated with the arousal of kundalini, including levitation. The Transcendental Meditation movement of Maharishi Mahesh Yogi, which successfully merchandised traditional forms of Hindu meditation, has also attempted to popularise siddhi programmes based on ancient yoga, in which levitation is said to be accomplished. So far, no convincing evidence for successful TM levitation has yet been produced, although the strong suggestive factors involved in such programmes could conceivably produce results. One remembers the great days of Animal Magnetism in the nineteenth century, when mesmerised subjects exhibited paranormal faculties.

Although the question of levitation intrigues me, I am more impressed by the phenomena of higher consciousness as demonstrated by Pandit Gopi Krishna, who has published a number of important books on kundalini, based on his personal experience. He is a humble man and has no desire to be a cult leader, unlike other individuals who have claimed kundalini arousal and permit their sycophantic followers to venerate them as 'The Master'. The Pandit believes that kundalini is an evolutionary force which will play an inceasingly important part in the development of the human race and its goals, indicating new directions for both science and religion. His books have already attracted the serious attention of scientists, and in 1974 an ambitious Kundalini Research Project was sponsored by the All-India Institute of Medical Science.

It seems to me that there are still forces in nature, and even inside every human being, that are not yet understood and that anomalous phenomena indicate such forces. Clearly paranormal phenomena may eventually be validated as part of the normal laws of the physical universe as yet another addition to the miracles of science that we already take for granted.

But the larger questions of meaning and purpose in life which are associated with spiritual development and higher consciousness, and of which miracles are only a side-effect, seem to me to be of greater importance. The great truths of existance tend to be veiled by the self-hypnosis of any given era and the limited awareness of individual consciousness, corrupted by petty desires, greed, egoism and power games. It may be that fantasy, day-dreaming, wishful thinking and the enormous outpouring of the imagination in art, novels, plays, films, radio and television, are a substitute or an interim stage in an evolutionary movement to a deeper understanding and a fuller life that may be lived within its own terms, to which the great religions of the past have been partial signposts.

•

Leslie Shepard

FORT-NOTE
by Pokkettz.

"I think we're property. I should say we belong to something. That once upon a time, this earth was No-man's Land, that other worlds explored and colonized here, and fought among themselves for possession, but that now it's owned by something. . .all others warned off." (*Books.* p163.)

Falling Into Place:

From Happening to Hypothesis in Anomaly Research.

by Hilary Evans.

While it would be wrong to court scientific acceptance out of a desire to become 'respectable', nevertheless, this will arise in its own time if we apply the appropriate rigour to our subjects out of respect for the material, and that includes developing useful hypotheses. The present state of our work resembles what the science historian, Thomas Kuhn, calls the "morass" of dissociated schools and data just prior to the emergence of an organizing paradigm. Fortean studies, or anomalistics as some call it, still awaits its Kepler or Newton, to be sure; but each one of us could pay more attention to theorizing from our data. Your editor is probably more guilty than most of sitting on fences, but not so **Hilary Evans**, who provides us with this exemplary piece.

A boy stands on the platform of a country railway station. As the trains come and go, he notes their numbers in his notebook, along with their times of arrival and departure. And one day, reviewing his notes, he discerns a pattern; there are recurrences, frequencies, periodicities. And gradually he senses, beyond the isolated events he has been noting, the larger process of which the individual visits of individual trains to his individual station are but components. Suppose, he asks himself, that somewhere someone has a plan. . .

Some of us have notebooks, some card indexes: once, the more ambitious of us punched holes in cards, today we programme our computers. But the data remain the same — so many frogs falling from the sky, so many deathbed visions, so many submarine objects moving at 200 km/h off the coast of Cuba. And then, every so often, one of us will stand up and murmur diffidently, "I say, chaps, eureka, I think. . ." and offer grounds for believing that UFOs can't tear themselves away from geological faults or that visions of the Virgin coincide with the lunar cycle more frequently than chance would suggest. . .

Some of these hypotheses are quickly shown to be erroneous — whatever happened to 'isocelie'? Others tantalise us with their arbitrariness — is there really a UFO-yeti tie-in? But no matter how insubstantial they turn out to be, all witness to man's instinctive desire to trace a meaning in the universe someone has dropped him into. If frogs fall from a clear blue sky, they damn well ought to fall into place — *any* place, but at any rate *some* place.

Pattern-making can be dangerous. It can tempt us to exaggerate some of our data and pretend that other items never happened; protagonists of the extraterrestial hypothesis for UFOs, for example, are guilty of both. And there are some who come to pattern-making with something less than an open mind, convinced ahead of time that poltergeists are evil spirits and ufonauts little better.

Nevertheless, the pattern-making instinct is a healthy one. A fact that tries to go it alone isn't going to get anywhere. It becomes of interest only when it socialises with others — when it is found to be like A but unlike B; when it is found to be larger than C but smaller than D, to be caused by E and to result in F; to coincide in time with G but to be repelled by H; when it cheerfully manifests in the presence of Mr I but obstinately refuses to replicate when Professor J is around. . .

The difficulty is knowing which of the data we should collect, out of the immensity available. If it was found that poltergeist phenomena never occur while bagpipe music is being performed but proliferate during harp performances, this would surely be significant — but what investigator has thought such information worth looking for? I have an index card which is a testimonial to man's patternising ingenuity; it is headed 'UFO PERIODICITY' and I can safely say that there isn't an item on it that has stood the test of time.

Yet we soldier on. Maybe it's So long, orthoteny, but it's Hail. Earth-lights! Farewell, rewards and fairies, but Welcome, birth-trauma-induced entity projections! For if there are going to be any breakthroughs, it's not going to be the data-collectors who will do it, but the data-jugglers — a Michell, a Keel, a Holiday, a Persinger.

All those four share another behaviour-trait; they don't just juggle the data, they also don't mind borrowing it from other acts. Each of them thumbs his nose at lines of demarcation, and derides the border guards who try to keep ufology for the ufologists and parapsychology for the professional parapsychologists.

I would have thought this lesson had been sufficiently well learnt; and yet only the other day a well-known authority on ghosts expressed to me his surprise that ASSAP was wasting its time devoting a whole book to something so insignificant as visions of the Virgin. Nor is that all; the author of said book on visions had to have his elbow jolted to remember to draw attention to the ufological correlations of his subject. . .

But this isn't intended to be a critical article: rather, it is exhortatory. But I think, too, you deserve a little practice with your preaching. So, in the second half of the article, I will stick my neck out and invite you to consider a hypothesis which spans just about every category of anomaly in the book. . .

THE PSI-SUBSTANCE HYPOTHESIS

In the summer of 1901 two English ladies, Miss Moberly and Miss Jourdain, had an experience in the grounds of the palace of Versailles which have become one of the classic anomalous cases of all time. [1,2] It has also been one of the most controversial; but there is good reason to think that the percipients were right in believing that they had somehow shared a vision of the gardens as they had been in the eighteenth century, possibly just at the time of the outbreak of the French Revolution. Not only did they see the grounds, not as they were in 1901, but as research showed them to have been at the earlier period, but they also encountered several figures whom it seemed possible to identify with persons of that time.

In short, despite some discrepancies (which confuse rather than contradict their interpretation), everything points to the likelihood that the two ladies had got involved in some kind of time-displacement. But who, or what, was displaced? Were the two ladies transported back to the 1780s, like time travellers in a science fiction story? Or was the past brought forward to 1901, as when the old news-reel is brought onto today's television screens?

Those who accept the ladies' account at all tend to go for some kind of explanation of the second kind. Time displacement is easier to imagine that way round; besides, there are analogies with ghosts and hauntings, and, more obviously, with normal memory. But even so, the implications are formidable.

For somehow, and (in the loosest possible sense) also some*where*, the 'memory' of the 1780s scene had to be preserved, and made available to whoever or whatever chose to repeat it in 1901. Whether we hypothesise, as the two percipients did, that they had 'entered into an act of memory' seeing the place and events as Marie Antoinette had seen them a century earlier, or whether we think of them as involved in a less subjective experience, the necessity remains for the record to have been preserved by some means.

For it is not enough to label such experiences 'psychic' and suppose that this absolves us from the necessity of establishing *what* is happening and *how*. A psychic experience is as 'real' as any other. Even if we suppose that the picture of 18th century Versailles was given to Miss Moberly and Miss Jourdain in the form of a mental communication, we have not dispensed with the necessity for determining the process by which that communication was effected. The brain is an electrical device, the senses are physical instruments. Beethoven's Choral Symphony was a series of electrical impulses even before it left the composer's mind, long before it was performed by the Vienna Philharmonic and returned to a further series of electrical impulses so that I can play it on my cassette player.

Unless we are prepared to duck out of the implications — and as inhabitants of a universe which is presented to us in physical terms, for which purpose we have been equipped with a range of physical senses, I don't think we have the right to duck out of them — we have to accept that what happened to the ladies of Versailles was at least partially a physical event. It may be that they picked up some kind of psychic signal, from Marie Antoinette or whoever — yet *it has to have been a signal*, like the one out there in the sky which our television sets catch hold of and convert into electrical impulses which are in turn translated into the latest happenings in Coronation Street. Alternatively, it may be that they unwittingly stepped inside the frame of a three-dimensional repeat performance of past events, in which case something like a hologram may be a closer analogy — but a hologram, too, has physical reality for all its insubstantiality.

Who arranged for these transmissions to take place, and why, and to what extent they were directed at the two ladies, are other questions which must be asked; but here and now we have to consider the question of how the information, given that it had been preserved in the files of some hypothetical 'image bank', is made available, what means exist, what process could be employed.

Back in the 1930s, some leading members of the *Society for Psychical Research,* in

London, were kicking ideas about on the subject of a psychic ether, a non-physical substance on which the events of the world were recorded. It was felt that some such process was demanded by the occurrence of apparitions and especially of hauntings. The Versailles case was one of those specifically mentioned as seeming to require some such hypothesis.

In the FWH Myers lecture given to the Society in 1937, CA Mace acknowledged the desirability of some such concept, but shied away from any expression of it as crude as a 'psychic ether'.

"Personally I am of the opinion that we can, with a good scientific conscience, postulate the existence of a medium which records impressions of all sorts of patterns of events, and which later or elsewhere may produce a corresponding pattern. We need not ask; what is the intrinsic constitution of this medium; we need not yet ask how it does it. But, however non-committal we may choose to be, we are bound to ask: Under what conditions do these events occur? Under what conditions does this medium receive impressions and under what conditions will these impressions be revived?"[3]

He recognised that there would have to be limits and controls:

"It may be entertaining to think of Nature as engaged in writing a very long book, not a single word of which will ever be read, but such a hypothesis, however entertaining, has no scientific function."

In other words, built into any such concept must be the notion of eventual use; our image bank, like any other, has no meaning unless we also presuppose customers who will make use of its services. And that use would need to be *specific*: total simultaneous playback on a continuous basis of all past events of world history would be total chaos. But the moment we start to think of limits and controls, we have also to ask, Control by *whom*? which leads to all kinds of splendid but not very helpful fantasies about cosmic librarians and infinitely accessible data banks whose credit cards are issued only to specially privileged persons. . .

In his Presidential Address to the same society two years later in 1939, the society's President, the philospher HH Price, took up Mace's tentative suggestions, and acknowledged the logical requirement for some such hypothesis. Price's thinking, however, ran towards a "psychic atmosphere" which would possess "some of the properties of matter — namely spatial extension and location in physical space — and some of the properties of mind". [4] He postulated an "ether of images" which he saw as "a special and limited form of the hypothesis of a Collective Unconscious".

But Price was at pains to demonstrate that his "ether of images" would possess not only the mental properties, which any component of the collective unconscious would have to have, but also material ones. "Naturally they will not be the same properties as we ascribe to ordinary matter, but they might be somewhat like them." By way of demonstration, he imagined a haunted room in which percipients had had experiences which suggested that somehow traces from the past were persisting there.

"If they are indeed physical traces, they must consist in some more or less permanent mode of arrangement of the molecules or atom or infra-atomic particles, of which the walls, furniture, etc. are composed. And in that case, it ought to be possible to varify their existence by the ordinary methods of Physical Science — by physical or chemical tests of some sort or other. But so far as we know, this cannot be done. It is therefore natural to suggest that the seat of these traces is something which is not material in the ordinary sense, but somehow interpenetrates the walls or furniture or whatever it may be: something which is like matter in being extended, and yet like mind in that it retains in itself the residua of past experiences. And this is just what the Psychic Ether is supposed to be. [4]

He then considered the implications of supposing that the images were derived from the mind of a former inhabitant of or visitor to the house:

"Let us suppose that the haunting is of a fairly complex sort. For instance, that the phantasm is seen in a number of different rooms in the house, and is seen to move from one room to another, so that the phenomena are 'cinematographic' rather than just 'photographic'. Here then is a group of persisting images, interrelated in a fairly complex way. Now since the original author of these images is dead, Anti-Survivalists will of course wish to maintain that his mind has ceased to exist. But can they quite maintain this, if our explanation is the correct one? For, to put it crudely, a bit of him does still survive, even though his body has long since disintegrated. This set of interrelated images is something like a very rudimentary secondary personality. It was split off from his main personality at the time when he lived in this room; it escaped from his control and aquired an independent existence of its own. And it has succeeded in 'surviving' the disintegration of his body, even if we say that his main personality has not. To be sure, it need not survive for ever. Eventually the images may lose their telepathic charge and fade away. The fact remains that a 'bit' of the deceased personality has succeded in surviving.

The notion of a 'psychic ether' is just one of the forms proposed for this material aspect. Some are ready to propose a more specific substance, the *astral body*. They suggest that we all have such a secondary body — some even hypothesise two or more — and claim that it is capable of seperation from our physical body, given the appropriate circumstances. This, they say, is the basis of out-of-the-body experiences, and also of voluntary projection. There have been some claims to have proved its physical existence [5, 6] but these have been ambiguous in replication, and cannot be said to be scientifically valid. There is also, however, a great deal of evidence at the anecdotal level of people — not necessarily declared 'psychics' — who 'see' an 'aura' surrounding people they meet, and which provides useful indications as to their character, state of health and so on.

Life would be a lot easier if some such scientifically testable constituent could be shown to exist: it would not answer all our problems, but it would give us a firm basis from which to start. Unfortunately the evidence remains uncertain, so that we have no choice but to stay with such vague concepts as 'psychic ether'.

The idea has been updated in the 'psi-substance' proposed by John Vyvyan [7]: I don't know that he has done more than give it a more acceptable name, but let us be grateful even for that. For if the idea of a substance, part-material and part-mental, is to gain any scrap of support, it needs all the help it can get.

But for those who study these questions, the issue is not whether we can support such a notion, for it is evident that the evidence *requires* the hypothesising of something as radical and scientifically unacceptable as this. If it isn't to be a psi-substance, then it will have to be something else equally way-out. For somehow we have to account for these entities which appear as a ball of light and slowly grow into full forms; for apparitions which gradually take shape in an empty room; for figures seen by two or more people simultaneously, or by one witness when it leaves the room and by another when it enters another; for entities who bring information, or carry it in the form of identifiable clothing and the like. None of these things can happen without some kind of material dimension; and for that dimension, 'psi-substance' is as good a working label as any other.

•

Hilary Evans

REFERENCES

- 1 Moberley & Jourdain, *An Adventure*, 1911.
- 2 Gibbons, A.O. (ed) *The Trianon adventure*, 1958.
- 3 Mace, C.A., *Supernormal faculties and the structure of the mind*, in PSPR XLIV, 1937.
- 4 Price, H.H., *Haunting and the psychic ether hypothesis*, in PSPR XLV, 1939.
- 5 Kilner, Walter J., *The human atmosphere*, 1920.
- 6 Bagnall, Oscar, *Origin & properties of the human aura*, 1937.
- 7 Vyvyan, John, *A case against Jones*, 1966.

FORT-NOTE
by Pokkettz.

"One of the greatest of secrets that have eventually been found out was for ages blabbed by all the pots and kettles of the world. . .A tree cannot find out, as it were, how to blossom, until comes blossom-time. A social growth cannot find out the use of steam-engines, until comes steam-engine-time." (*Books*. p530 & 557.)

Confessions of A Fortean Skeptic.

by Jerome Clark.

Fort showed by entertaining examples the advantages of not committing oneself to belief, but to a practice of temporary acceptance. Such 'detachment' — identical to that recommended by Buddhists — is no easy accomplishment in a world where the emphasis is on belief, but it is a skill the Fortean ignores at his peril, as **Jerome Clark** warns us from his own hard-won experience. Jerry is another member of that small band of committed Forteans who have contributed to almost every area of Fortean study, since their teens, over twenty years ago.

The nadir of my career as a Fortean was reached in 1973 when I was researching and writing an article which subsequently appeared in *Fate*. The article was later incorporated into the text of *The Unidentified*, a book coauthored by Loren Coleman, who is otherwise blameless in the horror story to follow.

Years before then, back when I was 11 or 12 years old, I was rummaging through the library of the small Minnesota town where I grew up. I came upon a book entitled *The Coming of the Fairies* by Sir Arthur Conan Doyle. It dealt with a series of photographs taken by two young English girls who claimed that they regularly encountered fairies in a wooded area near their Cottingley, Yorkshire, home. In due course they produced pictures of these beings. The pictures, which appear in Doyle's book, struck me as hilariously unconvincing. The 'fairies' resembled nothing so much as cardboard cutouts.

Many years later I read Jaques Vallee's *Passport to Magonia* and was taken with his attempt to link traditional fairylore to modern flying saucer lore. I began reading in the considerable scholarly literature on fairy beliefs. In one of these books, Katherine Briggs' *The Fairies in Tradition and Literature*, I came upon a brief account of the Cottingley episode, about which Dr. Briggs, one of Britain's leading folklorists, wrote, "As one looks at these photographs, every feeling revolts against believing them to be genuine." Yet, noting some of the unexplained aspects of the affair, she went on guardedly to suggest that the pictures might be psychic photographs.

She was troubled by a few odd items of evidence, such as the testimony of three photographic experts who said they didn't know how the pictures could have been faked.

Intrigued, I reread Doyle's book and two

others on the subject. I was impressed not so much by the testimony of the photographic experts as by the demonstrated inability of would-be debunkers to come up with plausible, nonextraordinary explanations. Typical of the blunders was Houdini's bold assertion that the models for the fairy figures came from a certain advertising poster. This allegation was widely published and uncritically accepted. But eventually, when investigators located copies of the poster in question, they found that the 'fairies' depicted on it looked not at all like those in the Cottingley pictures.

I was also interested to read that as late as the early 1970s, over 50 years after the events in question, the two photographers, both now elderly women, seemed to stand by their earlier testimony.

So, following Brigg's lead, I cast all caution to the wind. I was at least wise enough to concede that the Cottingley fairies didn't 'look' real but dismissed that as a subjective consideration. To me the absence of convincing negative evidence, coupled with the presence of positive evidence (however thin), added up to the conclusion that these might be authentic 'thoughtographs' much like those Ted Serios is said to produce.

To this day I can't believe how stupid and how credulous I was.

As we know beyond any reasonable doubt, the Cottingley pictures are clumsy and absurd fakes. In his 1978 book *Ghosts in Photographs* Fred Gettings reveals that the models for the figures came from a popular children's book of the period. Photoanalysis by William Spaulding's Ground Saucer Watch has shown that yes indeed, the figures are of cardboard, just as my 11-year-old eye had told me many years ago.

Robert Sheaffer, in his effort to debunk the story, contributed to the grand tradition of misleading nonsense by claiming, on the basis of the thinnest possible evidence, that Theosophical writer Edward Gardner was the mastermind behind the hoax — an assertion that quickly fell victim to Occam's Razor, but not before proving once again that the Cottingley affair could as easily make fools of disbelievers as of believers.

In their recent books nonadmirers of mine like Sheaffer and Martin Gardner have resurrected my foolish remarks on these nonfairy-nonthoughtograph pictures in an effort to discredit me. Sheaffer even claims that he, as the man who commissioned Spaulding to analyze the pictures in 1977, 'forced' me to relinquish my support. He doesn't mention that to the contrary, I accepted this first truly solid negative evidence with almost unseemly haste, in part because I like to think I am intellectually honest and in part because on some level — specifically the level of my psyche at which the embers of common sense still glowed, however faintly — I had long suspected that in taking the pictures seriously I was making a very, very dumb mistake.

Another mistake was in assuming the existence of 'thoughtographs', the evidence for which is shaky at best. In other words, I had attempted to explain a dubious claim with another dubious claim. Realizing belatedly that I was lost in a jungle of Fortean unreality, I decided that it was high time to cut and slash my way through the undergrowth and return to safety and skepticism. At the end of my harrowing adventure, my hair was whiter but my head was clearer.

The moral of the story is this:
(1) There is something to be said for common sense.
(2) Just because the debunkers are wrong, it doesn't necessarily follow that therefore the proponents are right.
(3) The time had come for this proponent to do some serious rethinking of his position.

* * *

There is a wonderful piece of verse by Spiritualist poet Ella Wheeler Wilcox. Its title is 'Credulity' and it goes:

If fallacies come knocking at my door
I'd rather feed and shelter full a score
Than hide behind the black portcullis
Doubt
And run the risk of barring one Truth out.

And if prevention for a time deceive
And prove me one too ready to believe
Far less my shame, than if by stubborn act
I brand as lie, some great collosal Fact.

That sounds to me like a prescription for the kind of 'open-mindedness' that permits the brains to fall out of one's head. But it is an apt description of a mentality we encounter all too frequently on this side of paranormal controversy. It's the Will to Believe coupled with the Refusal to Disbelieve. It is the mindset that is skeptical only of claims of fraud or error.

To achieve it, one starts with the love of mystery. There's nothing wrong with that in and of itself. The problem is that some of us, even after all this time, even after we have no excuse for not knowing better, seem more interested in pursuing mysteries than in securing answers. To some, mystification is the beginning and end of paranormal inquiry. Mysteries are to be preserved and defended at all costs. And that may be why, after all this time, all we have to show for our efforts are a seemingly unending number of unanswered questions and a certain grotesque satisfaction in declaring, in the words of the literature's enduring cliches, that such-and-such a mystery remains unsolved — proclaimed, incidentally, as an expression of triumph, not as an admission of defeat.

I suggest we take a fundamentally different view. If we are to make any progress in our inquiry, we would be better off celebrating the solutions of mysteries rather than the perpetuation of mysteries.

Charles Fort himself was less a lover of mysteries than an eccentric with a perverse taste for the kind of pompous humbug associated with authority figures who feel they must account for unaccountable phenomena about which they not only know little but apparently *prefer* to know little. The resulting 'explanations' are predictably preposterous and it is not hard to conclude that the explainers suffer from a case of anomaly-phobia sufficiently advanced to severely impair their reasoning facilities.

Anomaly-phobia, of course, continues to claim its victims. We all remember how the Air Force dealt with UFOs — identifying them, for example, as astronomical bodies not even visible at the time of the reported sighting. We have all seen the inept criticisms of psi, lake-monster reports and other anomalous claims. We have listened incredulously to self-appointed protectors of the public welfare who assert, apparently with straight faces, that acceptance of unexplained phenomena is not only wrong but dangerous, perhaps even conducive to the collapse of civilization. Some of us have exposed the errors and baseless claims of the debunkers, and recently we have seen scandalous revelations about the way these would-be defenders of science and reason deal with evidence that runs contrary to their beliefs.

Reading Fort and tracing all that has happened since his time, a number of paranormal proponents seem to have concluded that because some mundane explanations are bogus, *most* or *all* are bogus. In ufology, for instance, the standard line has it that 90 to 95 % of raw reports are potentially explainable; still, to some in the field, just about any scientific raw report of an object in the sky is of a UFO. Some enthusiasts still believe that Jimmy Carter saw a UFO, not the planet Venus, and that many of our astronauts encountered UFOs in space.

More Forteans than we might care to admit still consider the Bermuda Triangle a genuine mystery, despite Larry Kusche's masterful expose in *The Bermuda Triangle Mystery Solved*. In fact, the Triangle, along with its similarly fictitious counterparts, the 'vile vortices' of the world, still occupies a prominent place in the fertile imaginations of a few theorists. The alleged powers of Uri Geller and other metal-bending wonder-workers are blithely assumed to be real and incorporated into extraordinary explanation-schemes, even though the only thing about metal-bending that has ever been established with undeniable certainty is that fraud figures largely in the phenomenon. And our ranks are infested with guileless souls who still look to the novels of Carlos Castaneda as support for their metaphysical views. All things are possible in a seperate reality, we are told, but we are not warned that all things are possible as well in Cloud Cuckooland.

Those who wish to return to earth might consider some ways of getting back. Here are a few:

● *Don't assume that the experts are always fools.*

Scientists and other scholars are not infallible, it need hardly be said. They are human beings and they have human failings, prejudices and blindnesses. But at the same time we must always remember that as specialists who have devoted their professional careers to their special areas of interest that are likely to know far more than you do about these subjects. If you take issue with them, chances are they are right and you are wrong. It is even possible that you are a crank.

On the other hand, if a scientist pronounces on something *outside* his area of expertise, then he is an amateur and he has no greater claim on the truth then any other untrained commentator. When an eminent astronomer presumes to tell us what to think about UFOs, it is often immediately apparent to anyone who knows the literature that the man is talking through his hat. When, however, that same astronomer talks astronomy, you had better listen. And if you don't agree with him, proceed *very* cautiously.

● *Don't believe every story you hear.*

Some months ago my wife was babysitting for a married couple of our acquaintance. The man was an officer in the Army reserve, holding a high security clearance which rendered him privy to various military and intelligence secrets. He worked as a research scientist at a major university.

He regularly confided some of these secrets to his wife, who then confided them to my wife, who then told them to me. Beyond recalling that all these presumed secrets were sensational in nature, I have forgotten most of them. Of those I remember, one — related in the midst of the Iranian hostage crisis — was that our government knew the Iranian militants had excuted several of their American captives. My informant also said that on a particular date the United States would invade Iran. You get the idea.

I never believed any of this, needless to say, but I couldn't resist the temptation to ask him — tongue firmly embedded in cheek — if, as a man well-versed in hidden truths, he knew if there were any substance to those stories about crashed saucers and pickled aliens purported to be in the Pentagon's possession. He immediately assumed a stern, official-looking expression and declared that was something he couldn't talk about. Not long afterwards, however, he added that the truth, if he were to confide it, would shock me. On two or three subsequent occasions he brought up the subject and let it be known that if I pressed him at all, he would tell me the whole story. For obvious reasons I never bothered.

I mention this as a cautionary tale. Remember, the man has impeccable credentials. He *is* a military officer; he *does* have a high security clearance; and he *is* a research scientist at a major iniversity. And he is also, it is clear, a spinner of yarns. Next time you read a story about a crashed saucer told by a man with similarly impressive credentials, remember him.

In fact, there is a whole branch of modern folklore waiting to be seized upon and catalogued by scholars of popular culture. These are what I call 'Soldier's Tales; or, the Horrendous Secrets I Learned in the Service.' We ufologists hear them all the time. A few even purport to be first-hand accounts describing involvement in retrievals of crashed space-ships, the taking of spectacular UFO films, the witnessing of a fatal encounter between an airplane and a UFO, and so on. Such stories — or at least those with enough specific detail to permit follow-up investigation — seldom check out.

I can only speculate on the motives of the yarn-spinners, but it's not unreasonable to theorize that for many people the most important period in their lives was the time they spent in the military, when in fact some may well have been privy to secret information. All human institutions, including intelligence agencies, have rumor mills through which stories may circulate. The environment in which such fantasies are related may give them a false authority. Those individuals who pass into civilian life may repeat the rumors in good faith. Other persons, not acting in good faith, may simply place themselves inside the rumors

to impress girl friends, wives and acquaintances.
• *Don't get emotionally involved.*

I have always been amazed at the tenacity with which some people hold to favorite beliefs and the rationalizations to which they will resort when these beliefs are threatened.

I remember reading an exchange in a Fortean journal between a critic of the Bermuda Triangle and a prominent promoter of same. The critic outlined some quite specific reasons for disbelieving anything particularly mysterious is going on in the fabled region. The proponent responded by remarking that the critic didn't know what he was talking about because once, when the two were on a television show together, he had asked the proponent if the *New Yorker* were a newspaper!

Apparently this argument made sense to the proponent, but I can't imagine its making sense to anybody else. It is an extreme example of how emotional commitment to a position or to a specific claim can close us to rational argument and open us to irrational defensiveness. It can lead us — and this, by the way is as true of debunkers as of believers — to feel that the the truth is greater then the sum of its facts.

It is easy to say that facts are all that matter. It is not always easy, however, to act on that knowledge. This is especially true at a time when paranormal and other anomalous claims are under attack by professional debunkers who gleefully jump on any mistake proponents make (while of course refusing to acknowledge any of their own) and do their best to paint these proponents as fools who can't tell the difference between valid and invalid data. The effect is to force a proponent, if he isn't sensitive enough to know better, to assume a burden of infallibility.

Not long ago an ongoing controversy was settled when a certain item of information came to light. This new information proved that the claim in question was fallacious because it had been based on erroneous assumptions.

The controversy had gone on for several years, with debunkers on one side of the issue and a prominent proponent on the other. The proponent — let's call him X — and his allies skillfully refuted the debunker's arguments, most of which were demonstrably false or irrelevant. But finally an independent researcher, Y, who had no particular stake in the controversy, discovered disconfirming data which showed that while the debunker's arguments were mistaken, their conclusion — that the claim was unfounded — was correct. The critics, predictably passing over their own errors, equally predictably chortled about their 'victory' and had fun at X's expense.

X's response was to cast aspersions on Y's motives and to mount an emotional defense of the claim using post-hoc rationalizations

and shaky arguments. When I talked with him about the controversy, X talked less about facts than about face — his own in particular and all anomalists' in general — and about the use to which the debunkers were going to put Y's information. He made it appear that the fate of all anomaly investigation rested on the preservation of the claim. To him it seemed the finding of facts had become distinctly secondary to the scoring of points, just as it always had to those debunking opponents whom he had so long and so eloquently criticized.

Let's not be afraid to admit it when we're wrong. And let's not make the mistake of getting emotionally involved with — or staking our professional reputations on — a particular idea or a particular case. That doesn't mean that we aren't entitled to our opinions about the merits of various claims or that we should refrain from expressing these opinions and citing our reasons for holding them. It just means that we ought to understand clearly that what we believe and what we need does not necessarily bear a blood relationship.
• *Don't hesitate to criticize.*

Throughout this article I have referred to our critics the debunkers. They call themselves 'skeptics,' which they aren't, and I think we ought to stop calling them that, too. Marcello Truzzi defines the difference between the skeptic and the debunker as the difference between one who doubts and one who denies. In the paranormal field there is, Fort knows, plenty of room to doubt.

Unfortunately we hear too much from the deniers and too little from the doubters. We are not likely to get rational arguments from those who choose to define the controversy in apocalyptic terms. Anyone who believes, as some debunkers say they do, that civilisation will collapse if too many people believe that Bigfoot exists is not likely to concern himself with such small matters as reasonable arguments. That is too bad for the rest of us because it means we have to look elsewhere for the kind of good critical review that anomaly studies urgently require. This is not to say, I wish to emphasize, that the debunkers are always wrong or that they have made no contribution whatever to serious research. Some of their work does withstand critical scrutiny. So, however, does some of the work of extreme believers. My point is that debunkers' and believers' claims must be approached with caution, with judgement reserved until *all* sides have been heard from.

The true skeptics — at least those willing to put in the time to familiarize themselves with the literature, the issues and the personalities — are all too few in number. Most can be found in the pages of Truzzi's *Zetetic Scholar*, which I recommend highly to all serious anomalists.

But it appears that the major part of the policing of the field will have to be done by us. To our credit we have produced a surprising body of critical studies of various claims. But much, much more is needed.

The more we learn, the more we see the necessity for great care in assessing the data. Some stories hold up under the most searching scrutiny. Others, including some we hadn't expected (such as the 1897 UFO 'calfnapping' [exposed in *Fortean Times* 20 pp 5-8] and the Barbados 'restless coffins'), collapse and blow away. We can be certain that more of the old favorites will meet a like fate.

I urge each of you to pick a particular case — one that everybody 'knows' to be true but that has not been documented in our time — and follow it as far as it goes. If you are able to substantiate it, great; then we have a solid piece of evidence. If you dispose of it, that's great, too. Who needs a bogus mystery when we already have far more real ones than we can possibly deal with?

Let's not be afraid to criticize friends and colleagues — or even ourselves — when they or we stray from the paths of common sense and caution. Along the way some egos will get bruised, but if those you criticize — tactfully, I hope — are as concerned with fact-finding as you are, they'll get over it. We all make mistakes. The only unforgivable mistake is the knowing perpetuation of error.

• *Don't assume that all mysteries, even the genuine ones, have solutions.*

Once, reflecting on his involvement with the mystery of the Loch Ness monster, Roy Mackal remarked to me that he could never understand the resistance of so many scientists to the idea of Nessie. After all, he said, Nessie is a "rather mundane sort of idea. We already have other large freshwater animals such as the sturgeon. . . Sometimes I think it would almost be worth the game if the phenomenon at Loch Ness were all that earthshaking. But it's not. It violates no basic law of zoology to suggest that there are large animals in the loch."

Many of us have come to assume that we are dealing with phenomena that border on the miraculous, phenomena that if understood properly would shake the scientific establishment to its very foundations. That may be so in a limited number of cases, but in the great majority of cases I think it's wiser to conclude that the various mysteries will eventually yield to solutions that are not only un-extraordinary but also uninteresting.

The late F.W. Holiday once wrote a book in which he contended that Nessie is a strange phenomenal manifestation from another realm of being. In reality, as Mackal and other zoologically-trained investigators have shown, Nessie looks and acts precisely as any large animal would under the circumstances.

We read books that would have us believe fossilized footprints prove that *Homo sapiens* walked the earth millions of years ago. Yet a recent scientific investigation shows that the prints are neither of great age nor of human origin. They are almost certainly camel tracks and they may be only 8000 years old. 'Skyquakes', sometimes attributed to UFOs, are now being studied by Thomas Gold and Steven Soter of Cornell University. They have learned that such phenomena have a geophysical explanation. The fabled moving rocks of Racetrack Playa, California, are caused by the interaction of wind and rain.

And so on and on. We would do well to recall that before meteorites were understood they were considered so bizarre as to be utterly unbelievable. There was a time not so long ago when meteorites were Fortean phenomena.

* * *

It is high time that we get serious. And if we are going to be serious, then we are going to have to be cautious and careful. And if we are cautious and careful, we're going to look a lot more like skeptics than believers. Which is fine, and in the true Fortean spirit. Charles Fort was skeptical of establishment humbuggery and so are those of us who follow in his footsteps. That hasn't changed and I hope it never will. But now it's time that we train a skeptical eye on our own humbuggery as well.

•

Jerome Clark

•

This article is reprinted, by kind permission, from *Zetetic Scholar* 11 (1983). Zetetic Scholar: Dept of Sociology, Eastern Michigan University, Ypsilanti, MI 48197, USA.

EDITORIAL

Continued from p7.

In the meantime two definite conclusions have been drawn from the returned forms. The first was confirmation of something we have long suspected of our fellow Forteans: financial embarassment is almost endemic to our breed.

Secondly, a significant number have pleaded with us to remain the present format size. We had in fact made such a decision, but too late to alter last issue's editorial, for reasons too complex to give here. We still intend to make a few improvements, though, to our graphics and content, from FT42 onwards.

Here's to another ten years together.

•

Bob Rickard

The Piezo-electric Birth-trauma Syndrome.

by Janet and Colin Bord.

The range of enigmatic phenomena, mystery life-forms, objects and processes we bring under the Fortean umbrella may be short on grand unifying hypotheses, but within a number of relatively distinct areas controversy between hypotheses rages vigorously — a particularly quarrelsome field being ufology, here discussed by **Janet and Colin Bord.** In his writings Fort reveals himself to be one of the earliest advocates of human space-flight; and his imagination leaped to link mystery lights in the sky with what he called "vast superconstructions". Fort's whimsical suggestion of coal-burning UFOs was the forerunner of the hypothesis of extraterrestrial ufonauts. It was ventured for discussion, not veneration; it would have saddened him to have seen ufologists, each a slave to his pet theory, slugging it out like dogmatic scientists. And yet that would be balanced by his pleasure, I'm sure, at the arrival of two contentious new hypotheses. Let the Bords explain. . .

Students of Fortean events do not usually consider themselves to be followers of fashion. In fact Forteana was, at least until recent years, an obscure area of study pursued by a small coterie of dedicated souls whose principal joy was the amassing and ordering of Fortean facts and who in their more leisurely moments would exchange, discuss, or examine various bizarre theories evolved to explain these Fortean facts. Nothing was rejected and by the same token nothing could be easily or completely accepted. A theory advocated would be ingeniously defended against penetrative argument, but neither advocate nor prosecution were committed to their views and upon next meeting might equally reverse roles. This, dare we say, 'ideal' standpoint has, with the wider popular interest in Forteana and especially UFOs in recent years, been eroded. Conviction has entered into the matter of opinions held, and perhaps even passion.

Most Fortean events are of such an undisciplined nature that they refuse to be categorized, but the variety of events known collectively as UFOs are more easily marshalled, and this the lovers of 'explanations at all costs' have not been slow to do. The first very fashionable and widely accepted explanation was the ETH (extra-terrestrial hypothesis). In the earliest years of the UFO this was a reasonable hypothesis to consider. Ideas of space travel were in the air, 'we' were planning to go 'out there', so it was felt to be likely that 'they' should be able to 'come here'. But why not land on the White House lawn and introduce themselves to the President like any normal explorers would? In fact as more and more reports came in, it was apparent that normal behaviour was just about the last thing to be expected from the ufonauts. The only evidence anyone ever had to support the belief that UFOs were from other planets was that some people said they had met the pilots who told them so. Many of these witnesses and contactees did not understand the basic differences between the solar system, this galaxy and other galaxies, and their ideas on astronomical distances were rudimentary. Today there is still no more evidence for the ETH then in those early years. The arguments against have been well aired and appear sound, but they are confined by humanity's present understanding of physics. If we can concede that these present concepts need not be the last word, then physically spanning the vast interstellar distances is conceivable. But there is no proof, and the question remains open.

When the ufonauts stopped encouraging the contactees to proselytize they started to drag them into their laboratories for medical check-ups, and instead of contactees we had the abductees. This was more how an exploring race of star men were expected to behave, and the advocates of the ETH took heart. That is, until Professor Alvin Lawson gathered together a group of American college student volunteers who said they had no significant knowledge of UFOs, and by placing them under hypnosis and asking them to imagine that they were undergoing an abduction experience, extracted scenarios similar to those the genuine abductees were also producing under hypnosis, thus starting another fashionable theory. This was that all abductees were simply reliving the traumas experienced during birth and reproducing the imagery and emotions experienced at that time, but in a UFO context. However, Lawson's volunteers could never reproduce the stress and terror with which genuine abductees relived their experiences, and to believe that in 1977 one could find eight volunteers on an American college campus who had virtually no knowledge of UFO reports, either conscious or below the conscious level, reveals a degree of naivety hard to accept. Lawson and his co-workers acknowledge that their results do not show that genuine abductions have not occurred.

With its psychological implications and scientific appearance, this research has great appeal and has been eagerly and usually un-critically adopted by many as the definitive answer to the enigma. But the birth trauma hypothesis (BTH) does not even attempt to explain the experiences of those hundreds or thousands of UFO percipients who did not suffer a time loss, were not abducted, and have never been hypnotized, but have a fully conscious recall of an unnerving experience with physical entities who emerged from a strange vehicle, briefly interacted with them, and then re-entered the vehicle which then moved rapidly out of sight.

The third theory we are considering *does* attempt to explain these UFO percipients, as well as just about every other type of phenomenon sheltering under the UFO umbrella. This is the piezoelectric earth faults hypothesis (PEEFH), and it postulates that stresses in the earth's crust cause electrical fields which not only produce lights in the sky but also affect humanity's brainwave patterns so that people perceive or mentally bring into a physical reality spaceships, ufonauts, and probably Bigfoot, pumas, and the Loch Ness Monster too, though so far as we know the proponents of the PEEFH do not as yet claim the last three phenomena as their own. Nevertheless its proponents see this theory as all-embracing, and it has been eagerly adopted by those who feel the need to be riding the newest bandwagon.

The PEEFH in its latest incarnation relies to a large extent on the use of sighting reports collected by the British UFO Research Association (BUFORA), but it is evident to anyone who has been concerned with the organisation of a 'national' UFO research group that the lack of UFO reports for any given area may reveal nothing more than an inadequacy at one or more levels of the reporting/investigating chain; in fact it may simply be that in a given area such a chain does not even exist. Only those who have never been involved in the

BUFORA investigation 'network' would treat its report files as an accurate and comprehensive record of UFO activity over Britain. BUFORA is principally a UFO club like most other UFO groups. It is one of the joys of civilised life to have an absorbing interest and to meet with others who pursue the same interest, but let's not confuse that with scientific research. BUFORA are now reported to be making strong efforts to improve their scientific status, but it still remains a fact that their UFO records covering their first twenty years of existence are far from comprehensive, and this is inevitable when we consider the magnitude of their task which was and is tackled by volunteers who are self-financed and working part-time.

Let us now consider why these theories, each one useful within its limitations, should have such an eager but uncritical reception. The reasons are many, some evident and others obscure. There is of course the desire not to appear to be being left behind, unaware of current trends, stupid and dull witted. Although established scientific concepts do slowly change, the general trend is to resist new ideas until a younger generation who have grown up with them eventually occupy the seats of power. Ufology, being more of a popular and less of an acedemic area of study, embraces new ideas rapidly and discards the old more easily. Perhaps the greatest attraction of these latest theories (BTH and PEEFH) is that they do not involve any exterior intelligence, and are therefore non-threatening and safe. They emanate from and are contained within the human mind, even if not yet controlled by it. Any suggestion that humanity may have to contend with unearthly entities is reassuringly rejected and people are therefore free to continue undisturbed with their own mundane affairs.

We do not suggest that any theory be dismissed without consideration, although some are more likely to be productive than others. It must now be generally accepted that human knowledge is not stationary. The popular educationalist's view is of the relentless march of scientific light pushing back the black morass of superstitious ignorance. We see it more as an ebb and flow across the aeons of history, now uncovering one area, now another, while that which earlier was known and valued is once more lost. The arrival of physical beings from other planets, although it seems at present unlikely, cannot be completely dismissed and so we cannot totally reject the ETH. Equally birth traumas and piezo-electricity could be the causes behind other inexplicable events and reports, although the advocates of both hypotheses have not yet provided the evidence needed to prove that there is anything of substance to support their ideas.

No Fortean, when faced with incomprehensible data, will accept the stance which is taken by so many workers in established science, ie. it cannot be, therefore it is not, and that whatever the facts indicate, if they do not conform to accepted scientific belief then those facts *must* be inaccurate. It is true that far too many reports of the inexplicable have disintegrated when subjected to detailed examination by a dispassionate investigator, but there are many others which have withstood this test and remain inexplicable, and yet these are studiously ignored by the UFO researchers who desire to appear respectable and to be accepted by the scientific community.

Whether Fortean phenomena can always be usefully studied within the confines of the egocentric philosophy which dominates today's scientific work remains an open question. What must never be in doubt is that Forteans should continue to hold all hypotheses lightly and, observing but remaining uninfluenced by the rise and fall of fashion in such matters, should cultivate that broader viewpoint which will admit the possible existence of other intelligences which are able to interact with mankind.

•

Janet & Colin Bord

FORT-NOTE
by Pokkettz.

"Most likely my last utterance will be a platitude, if I've been dying long enough. If not, I shall probably laugh." (*Books.* p870.)

The Sociology of Hidden Events.

by Ron Westrum.

Back in 1970 **John Keel** drew attention to an aspect of ufology hitherto only considered by the few ufologists concerned with the UFO as a sociological phenomenon. Keel's *UFOs: Operation Trojan Horse* was the first public notice that the UFO myth was in part a product of, or certainly influenced by, the ways in which reports of sightings were treated (or even manipulated) in the reporting chain (witness, police, investigators, reporters, editors, etc) on the way to uncertain publication. The dramatic differences between a sighting and its published report give rise to quite different schools of study. **Ron Westrum** has specialized in what he calls "the dynamics of anomaly reporting". Having previously published studies of how UFO and lake-monster sightings are reported he recognizes that the "dynamics" involved apply to all forms of anomalies.

In 1966, when I was a college undergraduate, I remember trying to interest one of my professors, a brilliant sociologist, in the social relations of anomalous events. I suggested that one might discover some valuable insights by considering how society made decisions about the reality of UFOs. "Well," he said, "we could probably get some valuable insights by trying to figure out why this radiator makes noise." (He pointed at the radiator). "UFOs are only interesting if they have little green men in them, and anyone who thinks they have little green men in them is crazy." This nicely summarizes much of the scientific community's attitude toward anomalous events generally: if they are really there, they are terrifically important, but since they are not, why worry? (Or, looked at another way) If there was something that important, there is simply no way it could have been overlooked. One 18th century physicist put it very well:

"And here I venture to affirm, that after persuing all the accounts I could find of these phenomena, I have met with no well-vouched instance of such an event; nor is it to be imagined, but that, if these meteors had really fallen, there must have been long ago so strong evidence of the fact, as to leave no room to doubt of it at present" (James Pringle, 1759).

In the years since 1966 I have spent a considerable amount of time studying the generation, transmission, and evaluation of information about anomalies and my conclusions are very different. It is evident that all kinds of events can be witnessed and even reported without the scientific community knowing anything about it. Indeed, one of the results of my own researches has been to make me wonder, given the dynamics of these social processes, about the things even I don't know about. What are these dynamics?

First; what people see is affected by what they expect to see. This means that often people will interpret ambiguous aerial events as UFOs, if they believe in UFOs. It is no accident that most 'UFO sightings' turn out to be something ordinary. It is similarly true that many 'bigfoot' or 'monster' sightings are the product of overheated imaginations and social rumormongering. Yet this relationship also implies that when people see something that is genuinely unknown, it is going to boggle them. When people see something that nothing has prepared them to see, it will give their cognitive and emotional systems a serious shock. Anomalous events present the individual with a serious mental knot to untie.

Let me give an example. In a close-encounter case involving five persons on the Yakima Indian reservation in Washington state, two of the witnesses were married. After the sighting, the wife refused to discuss the events with her husband, a situation that contributed to their later divorce. Both the wife and another woman involved in the sighting later married other men. *Neither* told their new spouses about the experience, even though they discussed it with others. Meanwhile, the husband involved in the sighting also re-married, and he spent a large amount of time trying to figure out the UFO experience with his new wife. He continued to have nightmares and flashbacks involving the experience. His second wife said that sometimes when he was having the nightmares his heart beat so rapidly that she feared he was going to have a heart attack.

The individual's primary group is thus often important in helping the individual determine the nature of the puzzling experience, in untying the mental knot. But often even the person's own family and friends will not believe him or her, especially if the person was alone when the experience took place. The individual then must puzzle out the experience as best he or she can, with the aid of books, newspaper articles, or whatever else is at hand. This accounts for the immense relief of many witnesses when they finally get to talk with an anomaly investigator who can tell them, oh yes, lots of other people have had the same thing happen to them.

Reporting the anomaly is difficult. To whom is one supposed to report? Even for professionals the channels by which to report anomalous events are not clear. By the way, there is no evidence that highly-educated people are less likely to report anomalies than others; indeed there is evidence to the contrary. This does not mean, of course, that the reports will enter a proper data store. Society's mechanisms for accumulating and processing anomalous events are grossly inadequate. For this reason I have termed anomalies 'hidden events'. If they are seen they are typically not reported, if reported they are typically not recorded, if recorded they are typically not transmitted, and if transmitted they are typically not believed.

The role of the press has been misunderstood in regard to anomaly reporting. After a very considerable study of the matter, with data on UFOs and sea-serpents, I have now come to the conclusion that most national anomaly 'waves' are a press artifact. Furthermore, there is not a single 'silly season' (ie summer) which accounts for high anomaly coverage. There is instead a highly complex imitative process on the part of the press which determines what is currently 'news'. Some anomalists believe that the press more or less accurately reflects the ups and downs of anomaly sightings. I do not. The amount of coverage the press decides to devote to anomalous events is almost unconnected with the dynamics of the anomalies themselves, certainly at the national level. However, when anomalies *are* news, all kinds of junk is printed as long as the fashion holds and then, *zippo*: it's no longer news. Once the craze is off, almost nothing on anomalies can get printed. What researchers do not realize is that the press is essential for allowing them to find out about anomaly witnesses, and equally important for allowing anomaly witnesses to find out about them. Thus, the press is an important 'inter-

vening variable' in shaping researchers' perceptions and data files.

Some anomaly information reaches members of the scientific community. I have suggested that we call such information 'social intelligence,' analogous to military intelligence. As Charles Fort understood, the scientific community has potent intellectual resources for reducing the credibility of social intelligence and thus nullifying it as a source of information. The meteorite controversy (1772-1803 AD) is typical, and in many ways can be considered the model for later treatment of anomalies. Faced with repeated accounts of stone falls, scientists ridiculed the witnesses and discussed optical illusions, lack of education, and folk beliefs. Only after physicists Chladni and LaPlace had suggested theoretical mechanisms by which the events could happen were they taken seriously. Even so it took an immense stonefall within 70 miles of Paris to persuade French scientists. In the United States, Thomas Jefferson responded to the first news of the Weston meteorite fall in 1807 with the words "it is all a lie". Only later did he suggest that the American Philosophical Society might find it worthwhile to look into the matter.

In the series of papers I have written on social intelligence about anomalous events, I have shown that much of the 'rhetoric of disbelief' rests on *sociological* premises which are doubtful. Usually the efficiency of the social intelligence system and the resulting knowledge of potential anomalies by the scientific community are grossly overestimated. Furthermore, disproof of the physical possibility of certain anomalies often proceeds by methods which are, to say the least, doubtful. The most common of these is to assume that the phenomenon in question *must* have such a nature, then to show that such a thing is impossible.

Some of the arguments against the reality of UFOs show such a lack of logic and common sense that it is difficult to believe that their propounders are bright and even distinguished scientists. Many of them are reminiscent of attempts by 'experts' to demonstrate that Thomas Edison's electric power system was impossible even as Edison was working to develop it. The use of argument to reassure us that 'everything is under control' and that nothing unexpected can happen is a natural but dangerous tendency. Everything is not under control; we don't know everything; the unexpected does happen. To remain viable the human species must maintain a certain mental flexibility, *to allow it to sort out the genuine anomalies from the red herrings*.

The importance of anomalistics, as I see it, is that it forces us to keep open minds. This is

Continued on p70.

Nigel Pennick's Two Penn'orth.

by Nigel Pennick.

Fortean data, like everything else in this existence, is grist to many mills, and the way in which it is used, ignored or suppressed depends very much upon the views of the proponents. **Nigel Pennick** here fulminates against the curious modern attitude which trivializes anomalies by exploiting them as commercial spectacle. The Fortean approach is doomed to misunderstanding in this context because anomalies, by their nature, are outside the accepted explanation systems, and therefore constitute a disquieting reminder that the universe is not as cozy, or as orderly, as the main authorities would have us believe.

All research into the Damned, as Fort called it, is plagued by one fundamental metaphysical pitfall; that is the criteria for judgement. This applies to many areas of human knowledge, and is the root of belief. Perhaps one should take the line of the Greek negativist philosopher, Antisthenes, Diogenes' mentor, who asserted that nothing could be truly known. However, we cannot be allowed the luxury of ancient Greek philosophers, pampered by a society in which slaves saw to their every need. We are living in a harder era, supposedly one of political and scientific realities.

Since the late eighteenth century, scientific praxis has demonstrated by its technological products that it is indeed a reality. Everything from the steam engine to the typewriter upon which this article is being tacked out is the product of this world view. Incontestably, it works. But the viewpoint we take of its nature is very much dependent on our meta-physical approach to reality: if materialist, we can interpret it as the next step in evolution, away from the biological and towards the creation of artificial intelligence. If, on the other hand, we view it from the mystical or religious angle, we can see it as a perversion of God's law, or, from a related stance, to the working out of God's Purpose on Earth. Thus, in something as simple as technological praxis we can have varied and conflicting interpretation.

Science and the scientific method are relatively new arrivals in human history. Before the seventeenth century in Europe, and much later elsewhere, the concept of randomness did not exist. Indeed, many today see each and every event as a manifestation of God's Will, or conversely, the nefarious activities of a legion of demons or the demonic empire. The underlying antipathy of Christians towards 'games of chance' dates from this era, when all gaming was considered quite the opposite of chance — the consultation of the Gods. Dice, cards and chess were not just pastimes for an ill-spent youth, but actually seen as communication with unseen powers, who would favour some and spurn others. The Christians who banned such pastimes did so not out of a desire to prevent people from getting something for nothing, but to prevent access to the powers that they, too, believed in, and considered Satanic in origin. After the invention of randomness, all changed — except the religious opposition to gambling, which changed its reasons to the sinfulness of gaining something without working for it. Thus the scientific development of mathematics altered a fundamental world view, creating a science that worked and could be seen to work. Furthermore, within this framework emerged the scientific method, using hypothesis and experiment to test these hypotheses. Proof let us note, was never projected, for in science all is hypothesis and testable, and the mathematical notion of *probability* is all-important.

It is not commonly recognized that science is divided into two separate disciplines: exper-imental science and observational science, and it is in observational science that the Fortean finds her/himself. Rather, in observational commentary in most cases, for unless we view an event personally, we are reliant upon the means of communication for our informat-ion. And here we return to the vexed question of criteria for judgement, for the mass com-munications media are primarily concerned with spectacle.

We have all seen the exploitation books of 'Strange Phenomena' that parasitize others' original research — some readers no doubt have compiled or written them. These books, whilst disseminating the ideas of Fortean research, are primarily spectacle, created for the entertainment of the reader and the profit of the publisher. Now no-one begrudges an author or publisher an honest profit, but when motivation is solely profit-oriented, then we enter the field of spectacle. Of course, many Fortean events *are* spectacle — at least when witnessed. But their existance as spectacle is secondary to their existance as events — only the presence of a witness makes them spectacle. The reverse is true of exploitation books — if there were no consumers, the information would not be published. The studying of anomalous events — those which for various reasons do not fit in with the world view of orthodox pundits — is outside and beyond the area of spectacle, for it questions and challenges those areas of knowledge that are deemed the cornerstones of reality; those structures upon which are built the modern religions of science and politics.

Spectacle is, by its nature, trivializing. Just watch the news on TV, where a famine in Ethiopia is given equal prominence with a films star's award. The great events and places of the world are trivialized into 'news', 'history' or 'tourist attractions', packaged and pigeone-holed into manageable chunks of consumer product, neatly categorized and filed away. Forteana, too can be neatly filed away if it first is categorized, packaged and presented as spectacle, another *genre* like horror films or rock 'n' roll. And it is this process that has been going on over the last ten years and more, thanks to the unstinting efforts of the media in trivializing the unclassifiable.

Fortean events are a threat to many people's peace of mind. To survive at all in this mad world without being carted away to a place where we are out of sight and mind of Joe Public, we must create our own world picture and relate our own existence to that world picture. Many people do this by way of religion, society or even escapism, for all these activities help us to view the fundamentally inexplicable world in which we find ourselves as orderly, logical and sensible. To believe it otherwise is a dangerous thing. Like atheism or demon-ology, Forteanism challenges the assumption that the world and its structure are stable and comprehendable. On the contrary, it states that things are not what they seem even if they are things that seem to be nothing. A chaotic view paralleled only by the fantasies of the surrealists it may be, but where is the evidence for stable reality?

Now before I continue, let me stake my place in the matter. I am a practising scientist with numerous (descriptive) biological scientific papers to my name. But the production of publishable scientific work is in itself interest-ing, for the selectivity involved in observation is never brought into mind. Anomalies are, by their nature, oddities, and as such have no place in descriptive science. And this is why: scientists do not have the time, facilities or money to work upon projects to which there may be no conclusive end or result. Because of this, anomalies are filed away and forgotten; or, if not forgotten, passed on to the *Fortean Times*. The Fortean press, on the other hand, are doing the opposite. There, the anomalies are processed, and, by concentrating upon the anomalies, their place as part of the natural spectrum of reality is altered into spectacle, and they are categorized as something apart.

We have arrived, of course, in the area of *context*. Context is an important part of information, for it enables the observer to place the fact or observation within a framework of reference, something which a Fortean event usually cannot be. Anomalies are by their nature outside context, a fact that makes their dispassionate study so difficult. All knowledge, even Fortean knowledge, proceeds in an accumulative manner, and certain trends can be discerned. Some trends are caused by events, some by individuals, and some even by the structure of the subject as it evolves. In all cases, personalities and factions become involved at some time or another, and these can, in the worst circumstances, become destructive to dispassionate appraisals of information.

In the field of geomantic research, this has occurred, and for no good reason whatever. But now, the battle lines are drawn, and what could have been accepted as an orthodox part of archaeology has now become a *cause celebre* on both sides of the trenches. I refer, of course, to leys, those perfectly plausible alignments of ancient sites across the country. In the last century, several respected and orthodox arch-aeologists talked of alignments at respectable and orthodox meetings, and were written up in the official journals of learned societies. Later, their ideas having gained little interest, they were forgotten, and when Alfred Watkins revived the idea in a *popular* book, the archae-ologists of the day threw up their hands in horror and condemned the idea to a man. Since then, similar lines have been discovered in South America — ones that can be seen on the ground and which concur in every way with the earlier theories — but to no avail. To-day archaeologists dismiss the South American connexion by such persiflage as "a different cultural context". In other words, they will not accept it because dismissing it has become a cornerstone of their reality-system. And we may note that this is on the observational side of science, not the experimental. Similar problems arise in the out-of-place animal syndrome and other related discoveries of anomalous creatures, beings, structures and events.

Continued on p47.

....SAGAS OF THE BATHERS IN THE SUN...

...AND OF THE HERMIT WHO FLOATS ACROSS THE MOON

SAGAS OF HEROES, AND THE HAIRY MONSTERS OF THE SKY....

— EXTRA-GEOGRAPHIC SONGS OF BOILING LAKES AND FLOATING ISLANDS —

...BIOLOGIC EPICS OF THE CLOUDS OF MAMMOTHS AND HORSES AND ANTELOPES THAT ONCE UPON A TIME FELL FROM THE SKY UPON THE NORTHERN COAST OF SIBERIA—.....

...THE RHYTHMIC WALRUSES OF SPACE THAT HANG ON BY THEIR TUSKS TO THE EDGES OF SPACE-ISLANDS, SOMETIMES MAKING STARS VARIABLE AS THEY SWING IN COSMIC UNDULATIONS....

....FAIRY LANDS OF THE LITTLE MOON, AND THE TINY CIVILIZATIONS IN ROCKY CUPS THAT ARE SOMETIMES DRAINED TO THEIR SLUMS BY THE WIDE-MOUTHED OGRES!

Some Thoughts After Some Years On The Trail.

by Loren Coleman.

For more than twenty years, **Loren Coleman's** researches into mysterious animal sightings have led to his present authority as possibly the most widely experienced of the USA's growing band of cryptozoologists. At the same time he has been one of that rarer breed, an authentic investigating Fortean, with the added advantage of appreciating the Continuity of all phenomena. In 1962 he encouraged **Ivan Sanderson** to found an organization for Fortean research, and has been a frequent contributor to Fortean journals ever since. As he gives us the benefit of his considerable experience he emphasises, if not exemplifies, all the Fortean virtues.

Ten years ago, shortly before Ivan Sanderson's death, he and I exchanged some interesting letters on the various creature and phantom reports sweeping mysterious America. Sanderson, a well known investigator of the unexplained and successful Fortean author, had been corresponding with me for over a decade. Trained as a zoologist, as indeed I was, we shared a great deal of similar insights, intuitions and drollery with regard to the state of mysterious phenomena research of the time.

For example, in 1962, I suggested to Sanderson that an organisation be created to deal with an examination of the worldwide abominable snowmen reports, be they termed yeti, bigfeet, or North American ape. He thought that was a good idea, but jokingly said, "The only trouble is that it would probably be full of Russians". Five years later, the Ivan T. Sanderson Foundation was a reality, soon to be followed by his Society for the Investigation of the Unexplained. (S.I.T.U.) Sanderson seemed to have had built a formal organisation in response to the incredible numbers of creature reports flooding the countryside of America.

Ivan Sanderson, then of Columbia, New Jersey, and John Green of British Columbia, had been fed reams of case investigations of Eastern U.S.A. creatures accounts by me since the early 1960s, and they were beginning to wonder what was going on. In 1967, Sanderson finally wrote, "Yes . . .Please. . .any reports you have . . .Little Red men of the . . .or Giant Hairys in the suburbs. The whole bit is getting hotter and hairier by the month; and now we have the damned UFOs mixed up in it".

The lines between cryptozoology, parapsychology and ufology were merging again, after years of writers in the 1940s and 1950s had forced artifical boundaries between the creatures, UFOs and phantoms. As Charles Fort had noted after the turn of the century, there is a oneness to it all. During the 1970s this admixture seems to have been rediscovered by authors examining the mysterious. Personally, I am a product of this era. I wrote my first article of note in the March 1971 issue of *Fate*.

Living in Illinois at the time, I discussed in the *Fate* article my field investigations into local bipedal hairy creatures and black mystery feline reports. I invented the concept of phantom panthers, and began noting these beasts left some very unzoological clues behind.

After reading my article, Ivan Sanderson wrote a long letter to me detailing the dilemma such reports raised for him.

"Dammit. I don't like this sort of 'paraphysical' stuff, and I have kept strictly off it for 20 years now, despite ever increasing volumes of evidence (so called). But, in view of Jacque Vallée's ponderings on UFOs, and holograms, and solid (matter) projections-meaning , one can only assume, teleportation — I begin to wonder if the time has not come to take the proverbial ox by its frontal excrescences, and tackle the issue frontally also. However, it might do more harm than good, because it might put all of us serious minded and sane Forteans right back into the kook-klass in the eyes of both the genuine scientists and the newsmen. Quandary!"

Within two years, Ivan Sanderson was dead. It was left for others, Vallée, John Keel, Jerome Clark, D. Scott Rogo, myself and others to take the bull by its horns and attempt to answer some of the questions posed by the events breaking out all over mysterious America. Not coincidentially, when Ivan Sanderson died in 1973, part of the void he left was quickly filled by *Fortean Times* (first called *The News* way back then). Since then, the pages of *Fortean Times*, including a regular column by me, has served as the window on the theoretical mind of weird wonders investigators.

Now in 1983, looking back over the last ten years demonstrates an intriguing evolution in the thinking of those examining the accounts of strange creatures, foggy phantoms, and mysterious locations.

When Jerry Clark and I wrote our first two books in the mid-1970s, we suggested that UFOs and monsters were psychic projections of a collective unconscious, very literally thought forms which took on a solid state existence, be they clawed footprints where a phantom panther stepped, or knocking out of witnesses by a mad gasser.

As we observed, "Extraterrestrial spaceships could not be touring the earth in the massive numbers UFO sightings suggest. Neither could massive numbers of large unknown animals be roaming countryside and city streets without long ago having been officially recognized and catalogued (and probably driven into extinction as well).

"Moreover, they could not have done all this in such numbers without providing us with more conclusive physical evidence then they have given us so far. The 'physical evidence' is always just enough to suggest that the reported manifestation was not purely hallucinatory; it is never enough to prove that it was objectively real."

Through the 1970s, the idea that UFOs, monsters and poltergeist activity may be part of the same phenomenon, or as Janet and Colin Bord noted, at least triggered by the same stimulus, gained favor. For example, tales of creatures and phantoms with tattered, checkered shirts were compared to early occult literature by John Keel, Clark and myself. Such stories still pour in; the most recent being an accounrt of Nov. 1982 from Thomasville, North Carolina, where employees of the San-Mor furniture factory have seen a 6 foot ghost wearing khaki pants and a checked shirt. And such stories do have an impact. Twelve workers on the night shift quit after seeing the ghost.

The flesh and blood answers of cryptozoologists such as Bernard Heuvelmans and Ray Mackal, or the nuts and bolts solutions of ufologists such as Stan Friedman were eclipsed by the paranormal thoughts abounding in the 1970s. *Fortean Times'* Robert J. M. Rickard, and his colleague John Michell's interesting and intelligent notion that monsters might be time-travelers, that is animals teleported on a temporal plane, added a new twist to the parawhatever school in a novel attempt to account for the tangible intangibility of the creatures. In 1982, Rickard and Michell presented their 'theory of revivals' in *Living Wonders*, proposing that animals return from extinction. In 1983, Jim Brandon in *The Rebirth of Pan* detailed his belief that the pagan, earthy energy termed 'Pan' in folklore manifests itself from spook lights to sea serpents.

There is lots of enjoyment in hopping from one theory to another to explain phenomena as elusive as this. D. Scott Rogo and Jerome Clark's almost wholesale retreat from their earlier planetary poltergeist positions to embrace their 'intermediate reality' or parallel universe is another recent example.

After *Creatures of the Outer Edge* was published, I was aghast at the thought I was being labeled an occultist, a paranormalist, or somesuch. The paraphysical answer was articulated in an exercise in providing yet another possible explanation to the mysterious wonders surrounding us, but what became clearly apparent to me was the theorists were quickly pigeonholed.

This is unfortunate, as I and many other pursuers of the unknown, Forteans all, believe in nonbelief. An open minded attitude to the many unexplained situations is the stock and trade of the Fortean. Concrete answers, actual flesh and blood critters as the foundation to monster accounts can be accepted by myself, and the other membership of the International Society of Cryptozoology. But then again, a paranormal illusion may be at work here too with some of these beasts, and the rational conventional undiscovered animal answer may not be viable for all reports.

Lest we not lose our sense of humor about this business, I refer you to the words of Rickard and Michell, from their latest, where they note their theories should be taken 'with the customary Fortean promise that it will sit lightly on our shoulders, and that we will gladly give it up as soon as someone finds us something better to wear'.

Indeed, I feel some monsters in America are chimpanzee-like dryopithecines, that some mystery cats and maned lions are relic populations of *Felis atrox*, and some lake monsters are primitive whales. However, I also have room in my cosmic jokebox for teleporting 'gators, phantom clowns, Dover Demons, and phantom panthers which imitate UFOs in all respects but flight. Some spook lights in America, those ghostly globes of illumination which seem glued to specific locations, may be related to discharges of electric energy produced by geological fault stresses, to some kind of para-psychological disturbances akin to ghosts, or to a form of astronomical phenomena as yet not understood.

Simply stated then, I 'believe' in nothing and the possibility of everything. Ivan Sanderson once telegraphed me this message: 'Forteanism is not an organized anything'. Orderly chaos, an openness to the incomprehensible and unthinkable, and a jolly good sense of humor best describe how I have dealt with America's remarkable array of creatures, phantoms and strange events over the last twenty-five years.

Fortean reality has many levels of satisfaction, and these become more and more apparent to me everyday. The procession of the damned, those wonderful things excluded by science, schools and governments, continues daily. In some sense, in some ways, they exist, these things chased, and seen.

We are like viewers of a grand movie in some unknown foreign language. The pictures are forming images in our heads which are at once familiar, and yet uncomfortable and alien. We know it looks serious sometimes but at other times we feel we are witness to a great comedy with tragic overtones. All to often, however, the movie becomes three dimensional, and then there is no escaping the fact this experience is personal, and real or nearly so. Our mind curds up more rational explanations to make it all fit, but again we come away frustrated and unsatisfied. All the pieces—be they glowing red eyes, silvery balls of light, or rays of blue gas — don't fit the answers proposed. We try to sit back and grasp once again what is going on. Sometimes we succeed partially, more often than not we fail, and want to quickly agree with those around us saying this movie is an illusion, a false picture, a pseudoscientific fiction, or at worst, a hoax. It is a struggle, but we remain tied to the idea that the movie is something only mildly reflected and understandable in the context of *Homo sapiens* of the 1980s.

There is nothing wrong with not having all the answers at this stage of the game. Quandary, indeed.

•

Loren Coleman

FORT-NOTE
by Pokkettz.

"I now have a theory that, of themselves, men never did evolve from lower animals; but that, in early and plastic times, a human being from somewhere else appeared upon this earth, and that many kinds of animals took him for a model, and rudely and grotesquely imitated his appearance, so that, today, though the gorillas of the Congo, and of Chicago, are only caricatures, some of the rest of us are somewhat passable imitations of human beings." (*Books*. p966.)

On Monsters:

Or How Unknown Animals become Fabulous Animals.

by Bernard Heuvelmans.

Mystics and frontier physicists have been unanimous about the reflexive nature of our existence; that the kinds of answers we get are shaped by the forms of our questions, and these in turn are dictated by our world-view. **Bernard Heuvelmans** provides us with an illustration of this process from the field of cryptozoology. Monsters, it seems, are man-made: onto the unsuspecting forms of imperfectly known animals, man projects the images of his own fears and prejudices, each culture using its own iconography. This article was translated from the French for us by **Dr Mia Gerhardt**, to whom, our grateful thanks.

Charles Fort (*The Books of Charles Fort* (1974), p. 612) tells how Louis XVI, tired of being served lamb-chops, beef and bacon at every meal, one day sent up the prayer: "O Lord! Send me a new animal!"

Perhaps that's just a story, but there is no doubt that for centuries, it has also been the ardent prayer of every zoologist who wished to immortalize his name by discovering a hitherto unknown animal.

Of course, discovering "new" or "unknown" animals is only a way of speaking. It would be better to say "new to the Western world" or "unknown to our science". The only really *new* animals would be those belonging to species that, in the continuing course of evolution, appeared in recent times. (We talk about "prehistoric animals", but it would be very hard to name a single species—at least, among the Vertebrates— that is *not* prehistoric: a species evolved after the beginnings of History, that is to say, in the course of the last ten thousands years.)

Few animals are really *unknown* to Man: generally speaking, in any part of the world, the natives know the whole fauna that shares their environment. And in any culture, wise and learned men have always endeavoured to draw up the fullest possible inventory of the animals in the widest possible region.

The white-backed Tapir of India, described by Western Zoology only in 1816, under the scientific name *Tapirus indicus,* figured already two thousand years earlier in Chinese encyclopedias under the name *Mé,* and the giant Panda, discovered in Sechuan in 1869 by Father Armand David, is mentioned as early as 621 in a manuscript of the T'ang period, under the name of *Bei-shung* (white bear). The Gorilla, whose existence the Atlantic world admitted only in 1847, had names in all the languages of Central and West Africa, and had been carefully described in the early 17th century by the English adventurer Andrew Battell. When, in 1850, Brian H. Hodgson brought back from the Himalaya region skins and skulls of an ox-sized species of sheep, named by him *Budorcas taxicolor,* he merely introduced to the Western world the animal which the Mishmi of Assam called *Takin.* In 1878 the British Empire heard of the existence, in Kenya, of an amazing gazelle with a giraffe-like neck, subsequently named *Litocranius walleri;* but locally this animal had always been known as *Generuk,* and in Ancient Egypt it was even represented on rock-drawings five or six thousand years old, and on bas-reliefs dating from the 6th century B.C. In 1900, Sir Harry H. Johnston revealed to an astonished world the survival, in the Central African Ituri forest, of an ancester of the giraffe dating back to the Miocene (-15 to -35 million years), but the animal was familiar, as *Okapi,* to the Wa-Mbuti pygmies, who occasionally ate its meat. The Congo Peacock—two specimens of which were retrieved in 1936 from refuse collected from the Belgian Congo Museum at Tervuren and due to be burned the next day, to the general consternation of ornithologists—was the traditional game of the Bakumu called *Itundu* and the Wa-Bali, *Ngowé.* Even the most famous living fossil of our times, the Coelacanth, described in 1939 by Prof. J.L.B. Smith, was not new to the fishermen of the Comores, who sometimes caught it on their lines, and called it *Gombessa.* They even used the spiny scales of this four-legged fish, a species 300 million years old, to scrape the inner tubes of their bicycles when mending a puncture!

All this is to say that terrestrial animals, the easiest to observe, have always been known to the people living in their vicinity; not excepting the new species that keep being discovered. The big fossil peccary *Catagonus,* found alive and well in Paraguay in 1975, had been given the name *Tagua* by the Gran Chaco Indians, who hunted it for meat. When, in 1969, I personally offered proof of the survival into our time of Neanderthal population relics, based on the study of a frozen specimen recently killed and brought from Vietnam, the scientific name *Homo neanderthalensis pongoides* I proposed for them was really just another name after many others. My discovery came, in fact, at the end of a systematic investigation which had established that such men, hairy and wild, were known all over Asia—from the Caucasus to the Bering Straits and the Malay peninsula—and everywhere designated by a specific name among the local populations.

The only regions of the world where absolutely unknown animals could live are simply those where Man cannot live, which he cannot cross or enter; that is to say, some rare inhospitable expanses of ice, rocks, or sand, some unscaled mountain peaks, and of course the depths of the oceans.

On the other hand, no animal is perfectly known either. The habits of nocturnal and burrowing creatures, the hidden existence of desert and aquatic animals or those of the vast equatorial rain forest, make it impossible for us to know much about their way of life. And it must be said that there are blank spots and gaps in our knowledge of even the easiest observable animals. Even our very domestic pets keep some of their secrets: we still do not know exactly how a cat purrs!

The French philosopher of science Léon Brunschvicq used to say: "primitive man wants to explain everything, civilized man acknowledges gaps of ignorance". This distinction between "primitive" and "civilized" thought now stikes us as artificial. Whether we like it or not, the Unknown frightens us all. If, to push it away, primitive man invents explanatory myths, the modern scientist fills the gaps in his knowledge by constructing hypotheses. It amounts to the same thing.

Mythopoeic thought appears to me, more and more, to be an evolutionary adaptation enabling the members of our species to cope with traumatic new experiences, which cause all the more anguish since they were unknown before. It would seem that the information received from the outside world, when passing that part of the central nervous system sometimes called the "emotional brain", is stored in the same categories, submitted to the same stereotyped mental processes, and deformed in the same moulds of the mind as those that shape our mythologies, our heroic epics and our old wives' tales. It is customary to distinguish more or less clearly between **myth** (essentially religious), **legend** (or heroic saga), and **folklore** (the sum of popular beliefs, sayings and customs). Still, the three panels of the triptych one might designate as M.L.F. are shaped by the same essential laws, so that the awe-inspiring manifestations of the deified forces of nature, the high adventure of the lives of heroes, and the simple fairy tale, even the popular joke, can be shown to follow the same basic pattern.

The same mythicizing process is applied to sundry vicissitudes of our humble individual lives—the painful experience of birth, expulsion from the womb, cold hostility of the world outside, momentary deprivation of the first and deepest alimentary bliss, thwarted passion for the mother, rivalry with the father, that kill-joy; and, soon, competing brothers and sisters, feeling lost, first solitude; then, unsatisfied sexual desire, strife and defeat, disappointment and humiliation, tricks and treason, separation, death itself—all those daily tribulations seem to follow the eternal scenario of cosmic, historic and poetic tradition. That is what enables us to experience them as familiar; not terrifying and unforeseen, sprung out of the darkness to seize us by the throat; not a conspiracy of diabolic forces bent on destroying us.

If the imagination deserves to be called "the mad-woman of the household", as Malebranche proposed, its madness is of the paranoiac type, because it is severely systematized. The strict and compelling laws that govern the realm of the imaginary are closely connected with the structure and functioning of our brain. The same laws governed, among other things, the birth of language, the association—by no means fortuitous, but based on resemblances, analogies, parallelisms—of chosen phonemes with the various objects, sensations, sentiments and actions that constitute our Universe. These laws also help to complete our knowledge and understanding of the phenomena of nature, and particularly of all sorts of animals. The less we know about them, the more our description of their anatomy, their life and habits will be inspired by those thought-processes—associative rather than creative, and in any case pre-logical, irrational—and the more extravagant this description will therefore seem to science when it happens to take an interest in such animals.

When by fortunate circumstance we meet a quite unknown or a rare animal (to us, that is)—either because for some reason it has left its natural habitat, or because we were able to enter there—this meeting appears to us as such a marvel, because so exceptional, that we tend to regard it as a sign, perhaps an omen. This is why we took to calling such animals "monsters", because, as Cicero once put it, they "(de)monstrate" the future or whatever is hidden. (*Monstra appellantur quia monstrant.* Cicero meant this as a pun, because he knew quite well that the actual root of "monster" is *moneo,* "to admonish". Monsters were supposed to admonish people of some danger or of any unforeseeable event. All the same, this amounts to the same general meaning.) Not content with giving them this ambiguous name, we fashion, distort and adulterate their appearance as far as we have seen it, and extrapolate, with unconscious bias, the part we have not seen, in order to fit them all the more easily into the familiar structures of our mythical thought, those which C.G. Jung has called "archetypes".

If the strange animal, washed up on a beach where we can examine it at leisure, or barely glimpsed along a forest's edge, seems enormous, big enough to swallow us, and therefore terrifying, we will describe it as a sort of *dragon*. If we saw only one horn on its front or nose, even a tuft of hair, feathers or scales thus conspicuously placed, we will declare it a *unicorn*. If it has a human appearance without being quite human, or if it runs about with nothing on, or is hairy all over, we will call it a *wild man*. When it appears in the middle of the night, pale, lugubrious, a sort of phantom, we will take it for a *vampire* in search of a victim full of fresh, warm, regenerating blood. If the human-like animal appears gigantic, hungry and menacing, to us it will be an *ogre*. If, on the contrary, it is small and shy, we will see in it a member of the *goblin* or *fairy* tribes, humankind's diminutive poor relations, willing to give us help in exchange for small gifts, but so rarely seen that doubtless they are condemned to a subterranean existence. If the extraordinary animal emerges furtively from the dark waters of a lake, it must be, we will think, a guardian of underwater treasures, a special kind of dragon, a *lake monster*. If it appears like a huge bird, a frightening shape outlined for a moment against the twilight sky, we will suppose it to be an attacker, a kidnapper even, and identify it with the *Griffin* of classical Antiquity or the bird *Roc* of Arabian tradition. If, on the other hand, it is a splendid bird with many-hued, shining feathers, we will be reminded of the *Phoenix*, paragon of all winged creatures.

Of course the open sea and the sea-shore are particularly rich in "monsters", because an aquatic animal is most often seen indistinctly and for a brief moment only: imagination had to supply the lion's share. If the animal is long and slender—a shape the largest creatures tend to adopt for strictly mechanical reasons—it will be proclaimed that the *Great Sea-Serpent* has been sighted. If it appears to be surrounded by long, waving, grasping arms, it will evoke fearful memories of the *Kraken,* the tentacular colossus of ancient Nordic tales, or of the *Giant Octopus,* which can clutch at and drag down whole ships, terror of the conquering navigators of old. And if the aquatic creature shows even a fleeting or a partial resemblance to a human being, we will be forced to think in terms of a merman or, preferably, a *mermaid*. Our imagination will depict her as seductive, irresistible, and yet to be avoided, for we also credit her with man-eating propensities.

How can it be that all over the world, irrespective of race and culture, mankind has always invented the same fabulous animals, having similar attributes, surrounded by the same kind of reputation? It has long been supposed that such legends could have been transmitted through cultural exchanges, but as the possible period of their dissemination had to be pushed farther and farther back, until the dawn of humanity so to speak, it has finally become evident that their roots lie deep in all of us, in what Jung calls "the collective unconscious". The latter is most probably—as said earlier—a specific, genetically programmed adaption serving to protect us against the psychological disorders that might result from traumatic new experiences, just as the organism has natural defenses to cope with the various threats to it. "Monsters", as we call them, are in fact a reflection of our fundamental psychological problems.

The *Dragon* is a personification of evil, of all we must fight in order to survive with dignity. The *Unicorn,* phallic symbol, is the image of aggressive virility, male potency, but liable to be vanquished by defenceless woman at her most pure, most naïve, but at the same time most shy—her surest weapons. The *Mermaid,* on the other hand, represents the enveloping, devouring mother, the Belle Dame sans Merci, the vamp, to whom the male is but an eternal victim. The *Amazon* fills a similar niche on the social level: she does not seduce the male in order to eat him, but she rapes him and keeps him as a castrated slave once his reproductive duty is done. The *Wild Man,* the satyr, offers a double aspect: on the one hand, he enhances mankind's civilized state by representing its undeveloped, bestial, repulsive counterpart, on the other hand he evokes the idyllic, nostalgic image of a lost Eden: animality seen as freedom from the constraint of work and the harrowing consciousness of sin. The *Ogre* and the *Orgress,* man-eating giants, represent the adult and parental world as seen through the eyes of the terrified child. The *Little People,* gnomes, brownies and leprechauns, show the other side of the same myth, a transposition of the world lived in by children, set apart as they are by their small size: imperfectly understood, seen as belonging on an inferior level, and yet compelled to do the adults' bidding in order to merit their protection and win their favours. The greedy *Bogey-man,* the Beast which eats people, is as ambivalent as many other monsters; he embodies the fear of being devoured, suppressed, stamped out, but also the yearning, nostalgic in its way, for a return to the warm security of the womb. The *Lake Monster,* hidden under the surface of murkey waters, is the image of all the perverse, shameful, unspeakable thoughts we hide in the very depths of our heart. The *Sea-Serpent* is an eloquent symbol of the Devil, the Prince of Darkness, in this case of what was formerly called the "outer darkness", the vastness of the oceans beyond the horizon, imagined as the chosen domain of the powers of Evil. And just as the *Tentacular Monster,* surging up from the deep, represents the dangers that threaten us from below (from inside! our inner conflicts), the *Kidnapping Bird* represents those that may strike us from on high (the Demiurge, the moral authority that judges and, as the case may be, smites us). The *Phoenix,* messenger from a marvellous realm far away, and always reborn from its ashes, reminds us of the lost Eden, the country where death was not, and encourages us to believe in a possible return to that Golden Age. The *Vampire* also evokes dreams of immortality, but reminds us of its darker side, the malediction that follows it like a shadow.

To sum up, there are myths for every age, every sex, even for every singularity. That is why they attract, charm, trouble and captivate us, why they enlighten us, be it "as through a glass darkly", and on the whole, reassure and comfort us. No wonder we are so fond of monsters and imaginary beings, in films and in books!

Paradoxical as it may seem, fabulous monsters are surely the animals nearest to us, the most closely bound up with our inner life. The dog, the cat, the horse and some others live with us; the mythical beasts live *inside us.* Among the waves of our unconscious tumble mermaids, krakens and sea-serpents, the forests bordering them shelter unicorns and dragons, satyrs and amazons, ogres and pixies, werewolves and vampires. And across the sky of our dreams flies the giant Roc, clutching elephants in its talons, and the Phoenix, eternally returning to the paradise of its birth. Such myths concern us all.

That is the deeper reason why we are so eager, so impatient even, to shift the hide of our fabulous beasts onto the shoulders of ordinary, sometimes quite unglamorous, flesh and blood animals: an operation which is all the more easy if the latter are not well known, hardly known, or even, not yet quite known. . .

Since the Manatee has pectoral mammae, like its cousin the Elephant and also like the human female, and a body which tapers to a fish-like tail, it has always been identified, on both sides of the Atlantic, with the fascinating Mermaid— despite its, to our eyes, ungainly shape—and by the same token, considered as dangerous. Now can one imagine a more peaceable, inoffensive creature than this "sea-cow", which passes its days lazily browsing water hyacinths and other succulent plants?

In the past century, all over tropical Africa there were rumours about a hairy, fierce, lascivious giant, who bludgeoned elephants with a club and dragged women into the forest to rape them. This half-satyr, half-ogre turned out in the end to be the Gorilla, a large man-ape, which we know now to be a quite unaggressive and good-natured animal, practically vegetarian, and much less sex-obsessed than its cousin Man. But, now that we know him better, his bad reputation has had to be

passed on to another anthropoid, still incognito, from the Himalaya. Nowadays it is he who is reported to fell yaks with his fists before disembowelling them, and to abduct, preferably, young girls: the Abominable Snowman, to give him his name, complete misnomer as it may be.

When, just before the First World War, a small Indonesian island yielded the discovery of the biggest lizard yet known, a monitor lizard over 3 metres long, the name it received was, quite naturally, Komodo Dragon. It was, however, of modest proportions compared to the biggest crocodiles, which are at least twice as long, and weigh six times more, sometimes over a ton. Those truly monstrous · creatures are not, however, honoured with the impressive name of dragons, because they were too well known, and for too long, to be identified with some mythical beast.

Right now, people continue to apply the name of "sea-serpent" to all slender, apparently unknown, animals that are sighted now here, now there on the surface of the waters. Yet most of them swim, as only mammals do, by vertical undulations of the body, a movement of which reptiles are not generally capable, serpents least of all.

Particularly since 1933, unidentified animals of considerable size have been sighted with increasing frequency in the biggest lake of the British Isles. Clearly there must be a whole population of them to ensure their survival over many centuries; in fact, groups of several individuals swimming together have been observed more than once. Nevertheless, people keep speaking of *the* "Loch Ness monster", and it has been accused, without a shred of evidence, of killing sheep. The underlying intention is to pattern it upon the myth of the Lake Monster, guardian of treasures, which now and then claimed the sacrifice of a virgin.

In order to leave the discovery of unknown animals no longer entirely to chance, but to speed it up, as it were, by precisely aimed research—I have endeavoured over severel decennia—nearly 35 years now—to organise a new branch of Science, to which I gave the name of *Cryptozoology,* the Science of hidden animals. Its tasks are many and varied. Gathering, comparing and critically examining reports of sightings; eliminating hoaxes; analysing native information; studying possible representations in art, archeological or recent—all this may result in an identikit picture of the animal in question and the closest possible description of its habits. Another purpose is to decode and demystify the current rumours on sundry "monsters", continually reported from all over the world, and which might relate to as yet undescribed species.

But, let no one be alarmed! This enterprise does not spell the doom of monsters. When the animals of which they are an incarnation have been received into the fold of science and duly baptized, there will always be others to take their place and play their part. And if by any chance the animal world of our planet should ever come to be fully inventoried—a most improbable state of affairs, judging by actual zoological data—we should well be able to find food for our myths elsewhere.

Already the artificial Vamp, like the one in Fritz Lang's film *Metropolis,* is about to take the place of the irresistible Mermaid. In our "space operas", the Robot that kidnaps nymphets gradually replaces the nymph-pursuing Satyr of old. Flying saucers succeed the bird Roc as abductors of humans; little green men from other planets are our goblins and pixies, the fairy-folk of our times. And the Bermuda Triangle alone claims as many victims as that dread trio of the oceans, the Sea-Serpent, the Mermaid and the Giant Octopus.

Monsters are not about to die. Not that they are eternal: surely they were born with human thought and will vanish with it. Yet I wish a long survival to all the animals of flesh and blood that were successively embodied in them, that somehow fed them and kept them alive, all for the comfort of our souls. We owe them that at least.

●

Bernard Heuvelmans, D.Sc.

Nigel Pennick's Two Penn'orth.
Continued from p39.

Continued from p39.

But to worry about displeasing orthodoxy is to waste time in what some might see as a quest: like the knights of old seeking some (possibly) mythical Grail. And like the Grail, the achievement of it must by its nature be temporary: for the irony of Forteana is that to prove the existance of an anomaly is to pitch it from the status of anomaly to the status of fact; something that all of the orthodox lecturers will be teaching next term as though they'd known it all along.

Already many events that not long ago would have been considered Fortean (or in orthodox terms, non-existent), have been categorized and studied under the aegis of 'short-lived phenomena' or some such academic terminology. This, of course, is all to the good. Too many people are interested in phenomena primarily because they are mysterious, inexplicable, 'occult' in the true meaning of the word. Once 'explained', they feel cheated, as if another of the wonders of the world had been tamed by Blasphemous Man who Ought Not To Know Such Matters. It is as if to explain is to taint, to cheapen wonder. Not only anomalists feel this way. The orthodox scientist all too often crows that something unknown has been 'explained away', as if to determine the mechanism of an event is to deny that event's reality.

As Forteans, I feel that we should take the middle way — not to be dismissive of criticism that comes from informed opinion, but ready to determine whether indeed we are dealing with informed opinion, or merely bluster and rage from someone whose position is threatened by 'Damned Facts'. Someone who feels his position threatened by reality is in a pretty bad way already, and if many disciplines in knowledge feel that they cannot investigate anomalies without undermining their whole edifice, then that does not bode well for the continuation of those structures. We must take the middle way, too, in the battle between spectacle and exclusivity — a difficult task, yet one that is essential to both the standing of Fortean research as a discipline and to its continuance as a valid area of enquiry. In this, Forteans must not be afraid of exploding myths, both inside the subject and outside. But we must bear in mind that the explosion of myths is not to be done in a manner of creating spectacle. We see too much of that on the mass media — the recent debacle over the 'Cottingley Fairies' hoax comes to mind. There, the BBC Television did a complete U-turn, from naive acceptance of a 'wonder', to a 'told you so' sneer at Conan Doyle and his co-dupes.

The debunking of mythical events and mythical explanations can only do good when it is applied equally and across the board to all events which may require investigation. To do otherwise is dishonest, as in the creation of a certain world-picture by the media. One is forcibly reminded of the children's cartoon *Scooby Doo*, one of the lesser offerings from the Hanna and Barbera studios. There, each episode has a scary supernatural figure, that is equally unmasked as being a 'baddie' to be taken away for his crimes at the end by the local Police. In effect, it does not debunk the supernatural, but instead reduces its possibility to a limited spectacle for entertainment. On a similar scale, TV shows like that fronted by the professional debunkery of Arthur C. Clarke or his ilk, use the unexplained as a vehicle both for entertainment and a means of reinforcing the *status quo*. Like a ghost train, we are taken into the possibility of the unknown, scared a little by its implications, and then reassuringly brought again into the sunlit fairground, back to reality.

Despite this, there is a core of anomaly that cannot be dismissed so easily, and, even when made the material of spectacle, retains that quality that we call Fortean: a challenge to accepted modes of thinking about reality or what reality is. It is in these areas that the Fortean researcher can accumulate data; for to delineate and illuminate a hitherto-unexplained phenomenon is to add to the store of human knowledge and to demonstrate that all views of the world are primarily conditioned by the attitude of the observer rather then the nature of the event.

●

Nigel Pennick

Charles Fort and A Man Named Thayer.

by Robert Barbour Johnson.

Thanks to **Ray Nelke** who brought to our attention this old article which sheds some light on one of the darker episodes in the history of the old Fortean Society. It was published in the Oct/Nov 1951 issue of *Rhodomagnetic Digest*, a journal of criticism of SF and Fantasy, emanating from Berkeley, California, and published by a group who called themselves the Elves', Gnomes' and Little Men's Science Fiction, Chowder and Marching Society. The incident in question was the resignation *en masse* of the San Francisco chapter of the Fortean Society, which is only fleetingly mentioned in **Damon Knight's** biography *Charles Fort* (1970, p199f). Knight quotes a letter from **Robert Johnson**, a member of Chapter Two, as the group called themselves, which states that the "precise cause" of the rift was the publication in *Fate Magazine* (1949–1950), of the group's investigation of the collection of apports held by the Stanford Museum. (For more on these, by Johnson and **Loren Coleman**, see *INFO Journal* 12 & 13.) We thought this unknown history was worth reprinting for its illumination of the Fortean world of pre-1951, and for the bitter but salutory lesson therein of what can go wrong when personalities become more important than data.

On a certain January evening, back in the year 1931, a group of prominent gentlemen gathered in the New York flat of one Charles Hoy Fort, a resident of the Bronx. Present were Theodore Dreiser, Burton Rascoe, Harry Elmer Barnes, John Cowper Powys, Booth Tarkington, Harry Loen Wilson, Ben Hecht, Alexander Woolcott, Clarence Darrow, J. David Sterne, Aaron Sussman, the publisher, and several others, including H. Allen Smith, who later wrote an amusing though slightly inaccurate account of the proceedings. The purpose of the meeting was the establishment of a 'Fortean Society' to carry on the work of their host, and to spread his ideas.

As for Fort himself, he surely needs no introduction to devotees of fantasy and science fiction, since he may well be termed the 'spiritual father' of both fields of literature, especially in recent years. It was recently proposed to form a club that would be called 'Writers Who Have Stolen Plots from Charles Fort, Inc.' But the idea was dropped when it was realized that such a group would have to include virtually every modern author in the imaginative field, including many now deceased! At least a dozen full length novels, and more than a hundred short stories have been founded, directly or indirectly, on ideas set forth in his four books; *Lo!, The Book of the Damned, Wild Talents* and *New Lands*. And more are turning up all the time.

Nor is this surprising. For these books are a compilation, documented, indexed and classified, of strange, eerie, and inexplicable happenings on this supposedly mundane earth of ours within the last century — happenings far stranger than the most wild-eyed pulp fictioneer ever dreamed up! Through his pages stalk unknown animals, alien races, visitants from other planets, survivals of strange cults, rains of blood and living creatures, teleportations, and a whole host of people, living among us, yet seemingly possessed of powers and abilities that border on the supernatural. Men they could not catch. Men they could not see. Men they could not hang. The maddest menagerie and freak show ever assembled under one canvas! And all of them from fairly reputable sources; newspapers, records, police blotters, even scientific publications and textbooks. Yet somehow, they were ignored by a world that could not fit them into any definite category, and preferred to relegate them to oblivion; 'Damned facts', by orthodox science, yet well attested. Startling to read and nightmarish to speculate upon.

They may not all be true, of course. Indeed, there is strong evidence that Fort did not actually believe all of them himself, or the theories he drew from them. Many are unquestionably 'hoaxes' arising from the most gargantuan sense of humor in modern letters. Physically, the man was an almost exact 'double' for the screen comedian, Chester Conklin and he was also pure 'Mack Sennett' in mentality! His books were written with a slapstick instead of a pen and are one long guffaw from start to finish, interlarded with conceits and wisecracks to a degree that sometimes offends more serious readers.

Still, the fact that Fort himself invented nothing, but simply set down what had been previously recorded by thousands of observers all over the world — this seems to mitigate against hoaxing to a large degree. There is nothing obviously faked in the books. I have, of course, not been able to check all the innumerable references myself; it would take a lifetime. But I have checked a considerable number, and they are all correct. The things happened, or, at least, vast numbers of disinterested witnesses believed they saw them happen. Moreover, they have gone on happening, since Fort's death. The amount of 'Fortean occurrences' in recent years have been startling; certainly his books would have been colossally expanded had he lived a while longer. In one department alone, the famous 'flying saucers', more phenomena have accumulated in the last four years than in the century and a half previous! At the time he wrote *The Book of the Damned*, absolutely no one but himself believed in 'flying saucers'. Now, I think it is safe to say that a majority of thinking people do, though they may have variant theories to explain them.

So, at the very least, his theories deserve investigation. And it is highly unlikely that they will get it from orthodox scientists. Science has become a bit more broadminded since his day, what with Einstein and the atomic bomb! It's horizons have been enlarged somewhat, if by blasting! Still, the attitude remains pretty much that of a prominent physicist with whom I talked only the other day. He solemnly assured me that Fort was all wrong in his ideas about scientists; that while a certain dogmatism may have existed once, it was all gone now, and that present savants are wholly open-minded and ready to investigate anything, without preconceptions. "Do you mean," I pressed him, "that if I were to bring a werewolf into your laboratory, that you would investigate it without prejudice?" "Oh, well," he shrugged, "of course, there *are* no werewolves. . ."

Hence an organisation wholly dedicated to the collection and investigation of Fortean phenomena is not only desirable, but necessary, if anything is ever to be learned at all. It could be of tremendous benefit, in enlarging the knowledge of mankind. It is my painful duty to record, however, that the present Fortean Society is *not* that organisation, and shows no signs of ever becoming so.

The whole trouble seems to be that the group is in the hands of the wrong people; or rather the wrong person. Even that group of original Founders, though admittedly eminent, were none of them Fantasy writers, or even students of the subject. They constitute almost a 'Who's Who' of non-imaginative writing. Of the lot, only Woolcott and Hecht ever even dabbled in the field. Not a single famous *weird*, or science fiction writer is listed in that original roster. A few have joined it since: A. Merritt belonged until his death and Ivan T. Sanderson, the 'weird Naturalist', who has discovered evidence of so many strange creatures, is a present member. But such men are few and they have nothing whatever to do with running the Society. Indeed, they do not seem even to be welcomed.

The whole organisation has gravitated into the hands of one man, original secretary, Tiffany Thayer. Six of the Founders, beginning with Dreiser, edited one issue each of the Society's publication, *Doubt*, then gradually dropped out. Thayer has edited all subsequent issues of the magazine, collected the moneys, handles all the correspondence, and is very much a 'one man band'. To all practical purposes he IS the Society.

Nor, so far as can be learned, has Tiffany Thayer any qualifications whatever for that role, apart from having taken it over. He was a professional writer, but not in the least along Fortean lines. He is the author of such books as *The Old Goat, Call Her Savage*, and other works distinguished chiefly for a rather dull pornography, totally unrelieved by the imaginative touches of such as Thorne Smith. In recent years, Thayer seems to have devoted himself wholly to the running of the Society, which presumably also provides his income. He apparently uses it entirely as a vehicle for his own ideas and 'pet peeves,' with no check on his authority whatsoever.

The members of the San Francisco branch found that out to their sorrow, a couple of years ago! This Chapter, made up largely of writers, artists and students of bizarre subjects, all Fortean devotees, was not only the second largest in the country, but the first to hold regular meetings and investigate phenomena as a group. It was honored by the title "Chapter II", with New York as "Chapter I". Meeting in the 'Writers' Workshop' of Kenneth MacNickoll, on Lombard Street, its gatherings often numbered fifty or more. It gathered and forwarded tremendous quantities of data, none of which ever appeared in the Fortean magazine. Thayer was critical of the Chapter from the beginning, since it insisted on following straight Fortean lines and ignoring his innovations. "Most of the members," he complained in a letter, "are not so much concerned with two-headed calves as with other rebellions!"

Finding us adamant, he resorted to stronger measures. Using the pretext of some correspondence with *Fate* magazine, (of which he disapproves, possibly because it contains more actual Fortean matter than his own publication) he simply excommunicated the entire Chapter, forbade it to hold further meetings, or to use the Society's name in research. Seeking to appeal his decisions, we were horrified to discover that there is no one to appeal to! The original founders are all either dead or quiescent and Thayer rules alone; an absolute Fuhrer. Virtually all the local membership, myself included, resigned in a body, in protest. And none of us will ever again have anything to do with the organization, though of course we all retain an enthusiasm for Fort and his ideas.

And what, precisely, are these 'other rebellions' in which we fell short? It is possible to gain an idea of them by a glance at the magazine, *Doubt*. which is, in essence, the voice of the Society, since it has no formal organisation, no dues apart from the subscription price, and now holds no meetings. *Doubt*, a thin quarterly in microscopic print, is an unaesthetic affair, with some of the most hideous 'art-work' ever printed; daubs satirizing Religion, science, government, and almost everything else. Its advertising, apart from the Founder's works, blurbs chiefly two totally unknown (and completely un-Fortean) tomes called *America Needs Indians!* and *Raped Again!* The latter is described as a "blueprint for enslaving whole populations." So far as is known, Fort wasn't interested in enslaving populations. In an appended list of some twenty publications offered for sale by the Society, only one, a tiny pamphlet on an alleged sea-serpent off the New England coast, remotely borders on Fort. Its recent 'Holiday Issue' featured a sale of 'sacriligious Christmas cards'. The description is the magazine's, not mine. I didn't order any.

The editorial tone is distinctly juvenile; it reminds of nothing so much as the publication of the Louisville Male High School, which I attended at the age of 14! Much of its 'humour' is not even sophomoric. As one lone example, newspapers are always referred to as 'wypers'. This would be an exceedingly dull wheeze, even if used only once; when it occurs a dozen times in each issue, the effect is maddening. It is varied only by 'freeprez.' Irony is laid on with a trowel; Japanese are 'Yellow Bellies' and Russians, 'Those Damned Reds'. This is the intellectual tone of the whole publication. The childish pretense is consistently maintained that the foundation date of the Society was 'the Year One' and all items are double-dated from that, adding to the confusion. Thayer seems to write most of the material himself, signing himself 'YRS'. This also, presumably is supposed to be funny. An occasional short article sometimes creeps in, always by unknown authors, usually mathematical, and always unintelligible.

Extracts from the notes of Fort are published in a special section in the rear of each issue. This is the only really Fortean matter in the magazine, and it is largely meaningless, since the references are cryptic, in a sort of 'shorthand' and no attempt is made to translate or develop them. An occasional note on phenomena occurs now and then in the text, but it is usually coloured or slanted to make a political preachment. (Strange irony, since Fort himself utterly eschewed politics, and never wrote a line on it himself.) Thayer's own brand, wholly subversive, though so 'woozy' in content that it is difficult to say whether it is Communist or Fascist. It appears to be a blend of both. Thus, during World War II, *Doubt* sniped at the Allied side in every issue, attacked Civil Defence, and violently espoused the cause of Conscientious objectors. Its tone favored the Axis. More lately, however, it had taken a distinctly Red tinge, hailing the escape of Gerhardt Eisler as "the Most Fortean event" of its period. Garey Davis, the curiously deluded young man who renounced American citizenship and became a 'World Citizen', was made an Honorary Fellow of the Society for his action. Since Davis has since recanted his action and applied for reinstatement, he presumably is *non grata* now!

When the atom bomb first appeared, Thayer denounced it as an obvious hoax, a deception of the American government! For months he yammered at the 'palpable fraud' and denounced those silly enough to be taken in. He finally quieted down, under a deluge of protest by his members, but he has never officially retracted the absurd view.

He reacted likewise in the matter of the flying saucers, when they first appeared. These were perhaps Fort's greatest discovery, and the strongest verification of his theories. He was writing about such things, from records covering almost half a century, twenty years before Kenneth Arnold saw that historic first covey over Denver. Yet, incredibly, Thayer disbelieved in the saucers, too; they were another fraud of the villainous government, this time to stimulate recruiting of Air Raid wardens! Since there was no war going on in 1947 and '48, the great period of saucer activity, this appears to be crediting our officials with more foresight than they have shown in anything else. Likewise, if Fort's data is accepted, the government seems to have begun its campaign some years before the invention of airplanes! Yet, though his membership really howled this time, and deluged him with protests, Thayer again refused to retract. He still is reluctant to print any saucer data and continues to attribute it all to the Wicked Air Raid Wardens.

Wardens seem a fixation of Thayer's; presumably he was once spoken to disagreeably by one. At all events, he rails at the "pis mires in white helmets" continually; and is currently engaged in a program of rebellion against the whole Civil Defence set-up, urging the members to turn lights on during blackouts, refuse to cooperate, etc. He proposes to run advertisements in New York newspapers, seeking to persuade citizens to civil disobedience. "Let us all be blown up together, rather than submit to dictatorship by Wardens" appears to be his slogan. It is doubtful whether this will win many followers! Moreover, if he persists in it, he will undoubtedly wind up in the 'can', thereby paving the way for a successor who might put the organization back on the track from which it has so far strayed. So let it not be thought that I am trying to discourage him. . .

The whole thing would be amusing, were it not so serious, for Charles Fort deserves better of fate. His was the most original mind of our era; one that evolved some fascinating concepts, if they could be verified. And evidence for them continues to pile up, even after his death. The things he wrote about are still happening all about us. Strange objects in the skies. . .and a woman in a Southern hotel burns to a cinder, in a room showing scant traces of fire. . .Farmers near Sacramento comb irrigation ditches for an alligator seen by scores. . .and something walks on three-clawed feet, with an eight foot stride, across a Florida sandbar. . .and a chunk of ice, seen and handled by friends of mine, falls from a sunny sky in Oakland, with no airplanes overhead. It all goes on as before; but now no one is looking. The Society that was founded to carry on after Fort is off chasing the wicked Air Raid Wardens and following cheap and silly political ends. And all his work goes for nothing.

Yes, it is perhaps appropriate that Theodore Dreiser should have been among its founders. For the Fortean Society, as presently constituted, can only be called An American Tragedy!

•

Robert Barbour Johnson.

"It could be that, in reading what most people think are foolish little yarns of falling stones, we are, visionarily, in the presence of cosmic constructiveness — or that once upon a time this whole earth was built up by streams of rocks, teleported from other parts of an existence. The crash of falling islands — and then the cosmic humour of it all. . . the force that once heaped the peakes of the Rocky Mountains now slings pebbles at a couple of farmers, near Trenton, NJ." [*Books.* p571.]

FORT-NOTE
by Pokkettz.

The Man Who Invented Flying Saucers.

by John A. Keel.

To some extent **Robert Johnson's** jibe, in his article, that more Fortean material was appearing in *Fate Magazine* than in *Doubt* was very true. *Fate* was founded in 1948 and ever since has been the single most consistent professional press outlet for Fortean material, challenged only by private or society journals. *Fate* also took the lead, from the start, with frequent articles on the growing subject of UFOs, often with special issues on the subject. The modern myth and phenomenon is usually traced back to 1947 and the Kenneth Arnold sighting. In this slice of untold history, **John Keel** points to the pulp magazines of the late 1930s and early 1940s, and a man called **Ray Palmer**, who laid the goundwork for ufology and its enduring, if irrational, mythology.

North America's Bigfoot was nothing more than an Indian legend until zoologist Ivan T. Sanderson began collecting contemporary sightings of the creature in the early 1950's, publishing the reports in a series of popular magazine articles. He turned the tall, hairy biped into a subject for serious investigation, just as Rupert Gould rediscovered sea serpents in the 1930's and through his radio broadcasts, articles and books, brought Loch Ness to the attention of the world. Another writer named Vincent Gaddis correlated the many mysteries of the Atlantic in the 1960's and gave us the notorious Bermuda Triangle. Sanderson and Charles Berlitz later added to the Triangle lore and rewriting their books became a cottage industry among hack writers in the United States.

Charles Fort put bread on the tables of generations of science fiction writers when he assembled the many reports of objects and people strangely transposed in time and place, and coined the term 'teleportation'. Captain Kirk could never have been beamed up to the starship Enterprise if Fort had not first suggested that it could be, and is constantly being, done.

It took a politician named Ignatius Donnelly to revive lost Atlantis and turn it into a popular subject (again. . . and again) [1]. One Gray Barker gathered together a collection of stories about mystery men in the 1950's and launched the 'Men in Black' enigma [2].

However, the man who invented flying saucers by converting UFO reports from a Silly Season phenomenon to a *subject*, and then kept that subject alive in the United States during periods of total public disinterest has somehow been forgotten. He was a hunchback dwarf known as Raymond A. Palmer.

Born in 1911, Ray Palmer had a difficult childhood because of his infirmities and, like many isolated young men in those pre-television days, he sought escape in 'dime novels', cheap magazines printed on coarse paper and filled with lurid stories churned out by writers who were paid a penny a word. He became an avid science fiction fan and during the Great Depression of the 1930's he was active in the world of fandom. . . a world of mimeographed fanzines and heavy correspondence. (Science fiction fandom still exists and is very well organised with well-attended annual conventions and lavishly printed fanzines, some of which are even issued weekly.) In 1930, he sold his first science fiction story, and in 1933 he created the Jules Verne Prize Club which gave out annual awards for the best achievements in sci-fi. A facile writer with a robust imagination, Palmer was able to earn many pennies during the dark days of the Depression, undoubtedly buoyed by his mischievous sense of humour, a fortunate development motivated by his unfortunate physical problems. Pain was his constant companion.

In 1938, the Ziff-Davis Publishing Company in Chicago purchased a dying magazine titled *Amazing Stories*. It had been created in 1929 by the inestimable Hugo Gernsback, who is generally acknowledged as the father of modern science fiction. Gernsback, an electrical engineer, ran a small publishing empire of magazines dealing with radio and technical subjects. (He also founded *Sexology*, a magazine of soft-core pornography disguised as science, which enjoyed great success in a somewhat conservative era.) It was his practice to sell. . . or even give away. . . a magazine when its circulation began to slip. Although *Amazing Stories* was one of the first of its kind, its readership was down to a mere 25,000 when Gernsback unloaded it on Ziff-Davis. William B. Ziff decided to hand the editorial reins to the young science fiction buff from Milwaukee, Wisconsin. At the age of 28, Ray Palmer found his life's work.

Expanding the pulp magazine to two hundred pages (and as many as 250 pages in some issues), Palmer deliberately tailored it to the tastes of teenaged boys. He filled it with non-fiction features and filler items on science and pseudo-science in addition to the usual formula short stories of BEMs (Bug Eyed Monsters) and beautous maidens in distress. Many of the stories were written by Palmer himself under a variety of pseudonyms such as Festus Pragnell and Thorton Ayre, enabling him to supplement his meager salary by paying himself the usual penny-a-word. His old cronies from fandom also contributed stories to the magazine with a zeal that far surpassed their talents. In fact, of the dozen or so science fiction magazines then being sold on the newsstands, *Amazing Stories* easily ranks as the very worst of the lot. Its competitors, such as *Startling Stories, Thrilling Wonder Stories, Planet Stories* and the venerable *Astounding* (now renamed *Analog*) employed skilled, experienced professional writers like Ray Bradbury, Isaac Asimov and L. Ron Hubbard (who later created Dianetics and founded Scientology). *Amazing Stories* was garbage in comparison and hardcore sci-fi fans tended to sneer at it [3].

The magazine might have limped through the 1940's, largely ignored by everyone if not for a single incident. Howard Browne, a television writer who served as Palmer's associate editor in those days, recalls: "Early in the 1940's, a letter came to us from Dick Shaver purporting to reveal the 'truth' about a race of freaks, called 'Deros', living under the surface of the earth. Ray Palmer read it, handed it to me for comment. I read a third of it, tossed it in the waste basket. Ray, who loved to show his editors a trick or two about the business, fished it out of the basket, ran it in *Amazing*, and a flood of mail poured in from readers who insisted every word of it was true because *they'd* been plagued by Deros for years."[4]

Actually, Palmer had accidently tapped a huge, previously unrecognized audience. Nearly every community has at least one person who complains constantly to the local police that someone — usually a neighbor — is aiming a terrible ray gun at their house or apartment. This ray, they claim, is ruining their health, causing their plants to die, turning their bread mouldy, making their hair and teeth fall out, and broadcasting voices into their heads. Psychiatrists are very familiar with these 'ray' victims and relate the problem with paranoid-schizophrenia. For the most part, these para-noiacs are harmless and usually elderly. Occasionally, however, the voices they hear urge them to perform destructive acts, particularly arson. They are a distrustful lot, loners by nature, and very suspicious of everyone, including the government and all figures of authority. In earlier times, they thought they were hearing the voice of God and/or the Devil. Today they often blame the CIA or space beings for their woes. They naturally gravitate to eccentric causes and organizations which reflect their own fears and insecurities, advocating bizarre political philosophies and reinforcing their peculiar belief systems. Ray Palmer unintentionally gave thousands of these people focus to their lives.

Shaver's long, rambling letter claimed that while he was welding [5] he heard voices which explained to him how the underground Deros were controlling life on the surface of the earth through the use of fiendish rays. Palmer rewrote the letter, making a novelette out of it, and it was published in the March 1945 issue under the title: 'I Remember Lemuria. . . By Richard Shaver'.

The Shaver Mystery was born.

Somehow the news of Shaver's discovery quickly spread beyond science fiction circles and people who had never before bought a pulp magazine were rushing to their local newsstands. The demand for *Amazing Stories* far exceeded the supply and Ziff-Davis had to divert paper supplies (remember there were still wartime shortages) from other magazines so they could increase the press run of *AS*. "Palmer traveled to Pennsylvania to talk to Shaver," Howard Brown later recalled," found him sitting on reams of stuff he'd written about the Deros, bought every bit of it and contracted for more. I thought it was the sickest crap I'd run into. Palmer ran it and doubled the circulation of Amazing within four months." [4]

By the end of 1945, *Amazing Stories* was selling 250,000 copies per month. . .an amazing circulation for a science fiction pulp magazine. Palmer sat up late at night, rewriting Shaver's material and writing other short stories about the Deros under pseudonyms. Thousands of letters poured into the office. Many of them offered supporting 'evidence' for the Shaver stories, describing strange objects they had seen in the sky and strange encounters they had had with alien beings. It seemed that many thousands of people were aware of the exist-ence of some distinctly non-terrestrial group in our midst. Paranoid fantasies were mixed with tales that had the uncomfortable ring of truth. The Letters-to-the-editor section was the most interesting part of the publication. Here is a typical contribution from the issue for June 1946:

Sirs:

I flew my last combat mission on May 26 [1945] when I was shot up over Bassein and ditched my ship in Remaree Roads off Cheduba Island. I was missing five days. I requested leave at Kashmere (SIC). I and Capt. (deleted by request) left Srinagar and went to Rudok then through the Khese pass to the northern foothills of the Karakoram. We found what we were looking for. We knew what we were searching for.

For heaven's sake, drop the whole thing! You are playing with dynamite. My companion and I fought our way out of a cave with submachine guns. I have two 9" scars on my left arm that came from wounds given me in the cave when I was 50 feet from a moving object of any kind and in perfect silence. The muscles were nearly ripped out. How? I don't know. My friend has a hole the size of a dime in his right bicep. It was seared inside. How we don't know. But we both believe we know more about the Shaver Mystery than any other pair.

You can imagine my fright when I picked up my first copy of Amazing Stories *and see you splashing words about on the subject.*

The identity of the author of this letter was withheld by request. Later Palmer revealed his name: Fred Lee Crisman. He had inadvertantly described the effects of a laser beam. . . even though the laser wasn't invented until years later. Apparently Crisman was obsessed with Deros and death rays long before Kenneth Arnold sighted the 'first' ufo in June 1947.

In September 1946, *Amazing Stories* published a short article by W.C. Hefferlin, 'Circle-winged Plane', describing experiments with a circular craft in 1927 in San Francisco. Shaver's (Palmer's) contribution to that issue was a 30,000 word novelette, 'Earth Slaves to Space', dealing with spaceships that regularly visited the earth to kidnap humans and haul them away to some other planet. Other stories described amnesia, an important element in the UFO reports that still lay far in the future, and mysterious men who supposedly served as agents for those unfriendly Deros.

A letter from army lieutenant, Ellis L. Lyon, in the September 1946 issue expressed concern over the psychological impact of the Shaver Mystery.

What I am worried about is that there are a few, and perhaps quite a large number of readers who may accept this Shaver Mystery as being founded on fact, even as Orson Welles put across his invasion from Mars, via radio some years ago. It is, of course, impossible for the reader to sift out in your 'Discussions' and 'Reader Comment' features, which are actually letters from readers and which are credited to an Amazing Stories *staff writer, whipped up to keep alive interest in your fictional theories. However, if the letters are generally the work of the readers, it is distressing to see the reaction you have caused in their muddled brains. I refer to the letters from people who have 'seen' the exhaust trails of rocket ships or 'felt' the influence of radiations from underground sources.*

Palmer assigned artists to make sketches of objects described by readers and disc-shaped flying machines appeared on the covers of his magazine long before June 1947. So we can note that a considerable number of people. . . millions. . .were exposed to the flying saucer concept before the national news media was even aware of it. Anyone who glanced at the magazines on a newsstand and caught a glimpse of the sauces-adorned *Amazing Stories* cover had the image implanted in his subconscious. In the course of the two years between March 1945 and June 1947, *millions* of Americans had seen at least one issue of *Amazing Stories* and were aware of the Shaver Mystery with all of its bewildering implications. Many of these people were out studying the empty skies in the hopes that they, like other *Amazing Stories* readers, might glimpse something wondrous. World War II was over and some new excitement was needed. Raymond Palmer was supplying it. . .much to the alarm of Lt. Lyon and Fred Crisman.

Aside from Palmer's readers, two other groups were ready to serve as cadre for the believers. About 1,500 members of Tiffany Thayer's Fortean Society knew that weird aerial objects had been sighted throughout history and some of them were convinced that this planet was under surveillance by beings from another world. They would become instant experts, willing to educate the press and the public when the time came. The second group were spiritualists and students of the occult, headed by Dr. Meade Layne, who had been chatting with the space people at seances through trance mediums and Ouija boards. They knew the space ships were coming and were hardly surprised when 'ghost rockets' were reported over Europe in 1946. [6] Combined, these three groups represented a formidable segment of the population.

Tiffany Thayer was rigidly opposed to Franklin Roosevelt and loudly proclaimed that almost everything was a government conspiracy, so his Forteans were fully prepared to find new conspiracies hidden in the forthcoming UFO mystery. And indeed, the earliest cases seemed to indicate that some enormous conspiracy was actually underway.

On June 23, 1947, one Harold Dahl was

operating a small boat in the harbor at Tacoma, Washington. Suddenly there was a rain of slag-like pieces of metal. One struck Dahl's son and injured his arm. Another piece struck the boy's dog and killed it. Dahl rushed the boy to a hospital where his arm was treated. A few days later the boy vanished. Police found him a few weeks later, working in a restaurant in a distant state and suffering from total amnesia [7]. Meanwhile, Dahl had told a friend about the strange episode. The friend immediately wrote to Ray Palmer. His name was Fred Crisman and this was the beginning of the notorious Maury Island 'hoax'.

The following day, June 24th, Kenneth Arnold made his famous sightings of a group of 'flying saucers' over Mt. Ranier, and in Chicago, Ray Palmer watched in astonishment as the newspaper clippings poured in from every state. The things that he had been fabricating for his magazine were suddenly coming true!

For two weeks, the newspapers were filled with UFO reports. Then they tapered off and the Forteans howled "Censorship!" and "Conspiracy!" But dozens of magazine writers were busy compiling articles on this new subject and their pieces would appear steadily during the next year. One man, who had earned his living writing stories for the pulp magazines in the 1930s, saw the situation as a chance to break into the 'slicks' (better quality magazines printed on glossy or 'slick' paper). Although he was 44 years old at the time of Pearl Harbor, he served as a Captain in the Marines until he was in a plane accident. Discharged as Major (it was the practice to promote officers one grade when they retired), he was trying to resume his writing career. Ralph Daigh, an editor on *True* magazine, assigned him to investigate the flying saucer enigma [8]. Thus, at the age of 50, Donald E. Keyhoe entered Never-Never Land.

The Maury Island case turned into a nightmare after Palmer contacted Kenneth Arnold and asked him to fly to Tacoma and investigate. He sent him 200 dollars (about £40 at that time) for expenses. Arnold found himself involved in a mess that resulted, indirectly, in the death of two Air Force officers, two newspapermen and a frantic governmental effort to 'neutralize' Ray Palmer. The full story has never been told [9]. Fred Lee Crisman later became embroiled in the Kennedy assassination, and was hospitalized in 1969 after being shot during an attempt on his life only days before he was to testify before a Grand Jury in New Orleans investigating the Kennedy tragedy [10].

Shaken by Arnold's report from Tacoma, Palmer decided to put out an all-flying issue of *Amazing Stories*. Instead, the publisher demanded that he drop the whole subject after, according to Palmer, two men in Air Force uniforms visited him [11]. Palmer decided to publish a magazine of his own. Enlisting the aid of Curtis Fuller, editor of a flying magazine, and a few other friends, he put out the first issue of *Fate* in the spring of 1948. A digest-sized magazine printed on the cheapest paper, *Fate* was as poorly edited as *Amazing Stories* and had no impact on the reading public. But it was the only newsstand periodical that carried UFO reports in every issue. The *Amazing Stories* readership supported the early issues wholeheartedly.

In the fall of 1948, the first flying saucer convention was held at the Labor Temple on 14th Street in New York City. Attended by about thirty people, most of whom were clutching the latest issue of *Fate*, the meeting quickly dissolved into a shouting match [12]. Although the flying saucer mystery was only a year old, the side issues of government conspiracy and censorship already dominated the situation because of their strong emotional appeal. Arnold's report on Maury Island was then the major piece of evidence. The US Air Force had been sullenly silent throughout 1948 while, unbeknownst to the UFO advocates, the boys at Wright-Patterson were making a sincere effort to untangle the mystery.

When the Air Force investigation failed to turn up any tangible evidence (even though the investigators accepted the extraterrestrial theory) General Hoyt Vandenburg, Chief of the Air Force and former head of the CIA, ordered a negative report to release to the public. The result was Project Grudge, hundreds of pages of irrelevant nonsense that was unveiled around the time that *True* magazine printed Keyhoe's pro-UFO article [13]. Keyhoe took this personally, even though his article was largely a rehash of Fort's books, and Ralph Daigh had decided to go with the extraterrestrial hypothesis because it seemed to be the most commercially acceptable theory (that is, it would sell magazines).

Palmer's relationship with Ziff-Davis was strained now that he was publishing his own magazine. "When I took over from Palmer, in 1949," Howard Browne said, "I put an abrupt end to the Shaver Mystery — writing off over 7,000 dollars worth of scripts."[4]

Moving to Amherst, Wisconsin, Palmer set up his own printing plant and eventually he printed many of those Shaver stories in his Hidden World series. As it turned out, postwar inflation and the advent of television was killing the pulp magazine market anyway. In the fall of 1949, hundreds of pulps suddenly ceased publication, putting thousands of writers and editors out of work. Ziff-Davis and the other pulp publishers, like Street and Smith, slowly faded away. *Amazing Stories* has often changed hands since but is still being published, and is still paying its writers a penny a word [14].

For some reason known only to himself, Palmer chose to remove his name from *Fate*. Instead, a ficticious "Robert N. Webster" was listed as editor for many years. Palmer established another magazine, *Search*, to compete with *Fate. Search* became a catch-all for inane letters and occult articles that failed to meet *Fate's* low standards.

Although there was a brief revival of public and press interest in flying saucers following the great wave of the summer of 1952, the subject largely remained in the hands of cultists, cranks, teenagers and housewives who reproduced newspaper clippings in little mimeographed journals and looked up to Palmer as their fearless leader.

In June, 1956, a major four-day symposium on UFOs was held in Washington, DC. It was unquestionably the most important UFO affair of the 1950s and was attended by leading military men, government officials and industrialists. Men like William Lear, inventor of the Lear Jet, and assorted generals, admirals and former CIA heads, freely discussed the UFO 'problem' with the press. Notably absent were Ray Palmer, Donald Keyhoe, and Allen Hynek. One of the results of the meetings was the founding of the National Investigation Committee on Aerial Phenomena (NICAP) by a physicist named Townsend Brown. Although the symposium received extensive press coverage at the time, it was subsequently censored out of UFO history by the UFO cultists themselves...primarily because they had not participated in it [15].

The American public was aware of only two flying saucer personalities. Contactee George Adamski, a lovable rogue with a talent for obtaining publicity, and Donald Keyhoe, a zealot who howled "Coverup!" and was locked in mortal combat with Adamski for newspaper coverage. Since Adamski was the more colorful (he had ridden a saucer to the moon) he was usually awarded more attention. The press gave him the title of 'astronomer' (he lived in a house on Mount Palomar where a great telescope was in operation), while Keyhoe attacked him as 'the operator of a hamburger stand'. Ray Palmer tried to remain aloof of the warring factions so, naturally, some of them turned against him.

The year 1957 was marked by several significant developments. There was another major flying saucer wave. Townsend Brown's NICAP floundered and Keyhoe took it over. And Ray Palmer launched a new newsstand publication called *Flying Saucers From Other Worlds*. In the early issues he hinted that he knew some important 'secret'. After tantalizing his readers for months, he finally revealed that UFOs came from the center of the earth and the phrase *From Other Worlds* was dropped from the title. His readers were variously enthralled, appalled and galled by the revelation.

For seven years, from 1957 to 1964, ufology in the United States was in total limbo. This was the Dark Age. Keyhoe and NICAP were buried in Washington, vainly tilting at windmills and trying to initiate a congressional investigation into the UFO situation.

A few hundred UFO believers clustered around Coral Lorenzen's Aerial Phenomena Research Organisation (APRO). And about 2,000 teenagers bought *Flying Saucers* from a newsstand each month. Palmer devoted much space to UFO clubs, information exchanges and letters-to-the-editor. So it was Palmer, and Palmer alone, who kept the subject alive during the Dark Age and lured new youngsters (such as Jerome Clark, Allen Greenfield and Timothy Beckley) into ufology. He published his strange books about Deros, and ran a mail order business selling the UFO books that had been published after the various waves of the 1950s. His partners in the *Fate* venture bought him out, so he was able to devote his full time to his UFO enterprises. Ray Palmer had set up a system similar to sci-fi fandom, but with himself as the nucleus. He had come a long way since his early days and the Jules Verne Prize Club. He had been instrumental in inventing a whole system of belief...a frame of reference...the magical world of Shaverism and flying saucers...and he had set himself up as the King of that world. Once the belief system had been set up it became self-perpetuating. The people beleaguered by mysterious rays were joined by the wishful thinkers who hoped that living, compassionate beings existed out there beyond the stars. They didn't need any real evidence. The belief itself was enough to sustain them [16].

When a massive new UFO wave – the biggest one in U.S. history – struck in 1964 and continued unabated until 1968, APRO and NICAP were caught unawares and unprepared to deal with renewed public interest. Palmer increased the press run of *Flying Saucers* and reached out to a new audience. In the 1970s, a new Dark Age began. October 1973, produced a flurry of well-publicized reports and then the doldrums set in. NICAP strangled in its own confusion and dissolved in a puddle of apathy, along with scores of lesser UFO organisations. Donald Keyhoe, a very elder statesman, lives in seclusion in Virginia. Most of the hopeful contactees and UFO investigators of the 1940s and 50s have passed away. Palmer's *Flying Saucers* quietly self-destructed in 1975, but he continued with *Search* until his death in the summer of 1977. Richard Shaver is gone but the Shaver Mystery still has a few adherants. Yet the sad truth is that none of this might have come about if Howard Browne hadn't scoffed at that letter in that dingy editorial office in that far away city so long ago.

•

John A. Keel

NOTES

● 1 Donnelly's book, *Atlantis,* published in 1882, set off a fifty year wave of Atlantean hysteria around the world. Even the characters who materialised at seances during that period claimed to be Atlanteans.

● 2 Mr. Barker is at it again. In 1983, he published a new compilation of Men In Black stories titled: M. I. B. – *The Terror Among Us.*

● 3 The author was an active sci-fi fan in the 1940s and published a fanzine called *Lunarite.* Here's a quote from *Lunarite* dated October 26, 1946: "*Amazing Stories* is still trying to convince everyone that the BEMs in the caves run the world. And I was blaming it on the Democrats. "Great Gods and Little Termites" was the best tale in this ish [issue]. But Shaver, author of the "Land of Kui", ought to give up writing. He's lousy. And the editors at AS ought to join Sgt. Saturn on the wagon and quit drinking that Xeno or the BEMs in the caves will get them."

I clearly remember the controversy created by the Shaver Mystery and the great disdain with which the hardcore fans viewed it.

● 4 From *Cheap Thrills: An Informal History of the Pulp Magazines* by Ron Goulart, (published by Arlington House, New York, 1972).

● 5 It is interesting that so many victims of this type of phenomenon were welding, operating electrical equipment such as radios, radar, etc. when they began to hear voices.

● 6 The widespread 'ghostrockets' of 1946 received little notice in the US press. I remember carrying a tiny clipping around in my wallet describing mysterious rockets weaving through the mountains of Switzerland. But that was the only 'ghostrocket' report that reached me that year.

● 7 Revealed in the FBI file on the case, finally released in 1980.

● 8 Mr Daigh told the author the whole story of *True* magazine's UFO involvement in 1966.

● 9 I hope to publish a book on the Maury Island affair in the near future.

● 10 I corresponded extensively with Crisman in the 1970s, before his death in 1978. He was then living and working in the Tacoma area under the name of 'Jon Gold'.

● 11 See *The Real UFO Invasion* by Raymond A. Palmer, (Greenleaf Classics, San Diego, Cal., 1967).

● 12 I attended this meeting but my memory of it is vague after so many years. I can not recall who sponsored it.

● 13 See Ruppelt, Keyhoe and the thousands of books that were rehashed from those sources.

● 14 A few of the surviving science fiction magazines now pay (gasp!) three cents a word. But writing sci-fi still remains a sure way to starve to death.

● 15 When David Michael Jacobs wrote *The UFO Controversy in America*, a book generally regarded as the most complete history of the UFO maze, he chose to completely revise the history of the 1940s and 50s, carefully excising any mention of Palmer, the 1956 symposium, and many of the other important developments during that period.

● 16 A newsletter, *The Hollow Hassle*, is still published in the US.

FORT-NOTE
by Pokketz.

"Belief in God – in Nothing – in Einstein – a matter of fashion... Come unto me and maybe I'll make you stylish... I conceive of nothing, in religion, science, or philosophy, that is more than the proper thing to wear, for a while."
[*Books.* p993.]

Predicting Contemporary UFO Reports in Great Britain from Charles Fort's Data:

An Application of The Tectonic Strain Theory.

by Michael A. Persinger.

Fort said that he was not so much interested in the quantity of his data, or the datums themselves, but in the relations between them. Our methods of data-gathering today are very much the ones Fort used, but made easier by a few technological devices, like photocopiers. But although we have more data at our command than Fort had, we are not much more advanced in understanding our subject matter. Fort tossed us the vibrant notion of an organic universe, and if it has validity it is our task to try and demonstrate how that works. We need more studies of the relations between seemingly-related phenomena between which no causal connection exists in orthodox knowledge. One with the skills to show us the way in this kind of analysis is **Michael Persinger**, who presents a mechanism linking aerial lights and stress in rocks — the 'piezo-electric' theory referred to by several of our contributors.

Charles Fort's classic works [1] contain conspicuous references to the relationship between "luminosities", what many people now call UFOs (unidentified flying objects) and earthquakes [2, 3]. Unfortunately, Fort did not have access to the computer technology required to isolate the key factors that could be used to depict the relationship, if any, between these odd lights in the sky and later earthquake occurrences. The present paper describes the development of the tectonic strain theory for UFORs (UFO reports) and the use of Charles Fort's nineteenth century luminosity data to predict contemporary episodes of UFORs within Great Britain.

At its simplest, the theory states that most (but not necessarily all) UFORs, especially those most similar to Fort's classic luminosities, are associated with tectonic strain within the earth's crust. If the strain continues to accumulate to fracture levels, then earthquakes occur. Contrary to some popular interpretations, the theory does *not* state that luminosities are caused by earthquakes or occur only at the time of earthquakes. Instead tectonic strain is responsible for both luminosities and earthquakes.

There are several general predictions that follow from this theory. Firstly, most UFORs should occur weeks to months *before* earthquakes, although if strain continues after a fracture some luminosities could still be generated. Second, UFORs should follow the same, slow rise and fall of earthquake activity over decades within a region. Third, UFORs should cluster, historically, within areas prone to earthquake activity, including low intensity or tremor regions.

The latter prediction implicitly assumes that the optimal processes associated with the generation of luminosities are related to very specific strain conditions. They may last for a brief period and occur many years before a very intense earthquake. On the other hand, these processes could last for many months within an area prone to a very slow rise in these strain conditions. Great Britain is an excellent candidate.

Previous publications [4, 5] have demonstrated in fact, that most of the UFORs contained within the UFOCAT files from CUFOS (Center for UFO Studies, Illinois) are associated with processes during the six-month periods *before* increases in low intensity (Modified Mercalli V or less) earthquake numbers. (A V or less MM quake is felt by nearly everyone; some windows are broken and a few instances of cracked plaster are reported.) A similar relationship was found with a 20-year sample of UFORs published in *Fate* magazine [6].

The success of this theory to predict UFORs within the USA, especially the region within the New Madrid area, has reopened the enthusiasm of applying multivariate techniques, such as multiple regression, to the UFO problem. Indeed, by isolating the *optimal* cluster of tectonic and geomagnetic variables, UFOR flaps can be predicted [2, 5, 6].

Multivariate analyses should not be confused with multiple correlations. Multivariate analyses require a different mentality. The researcher realizes that different, perhaps even unrelated variables must occur together in a certain combination in order to produce the phenomenon. These variables must be considered simultaneously, hence the requirement for contempory computer software.

Multiple correlations, on the other hand, involve a simple extension of the bivariate (two variables) mentality, the one most frequently used by both scientists and nonscientists. Although there may be many variables in the problem, the bivariate mentality only considers two at a time. If a phenomenon has more than one variable controlling it, then the bivariate thinker would never find "the variable". The phenomenon would appear endlessly confusing and contradictory since all of the pieces of the puzzle are not considered together.

Reluctance to pursue the approach by most popular writers usually reflects the general misconception about correlations. Although few UFO researchers have competent skills in statistical software, most of them have learned the phrase "you can correlate anything with anything". This statement, usually evoked reflexively and punctuated by some absurd example, reflects the conceptual ignorance about correlational analysis.

Like any tool, correlational analysis can be misused. But there are many ways to determine the reliability of a result. Internal consistency of the correlation within the data and comparison of the correlation with other data sets are just two means to check for potential errors. The most rigorous evaluation for an equation is its capacity to accurately *predict* the occurence of events not involved in its generation.

Correlations do not necessarily dictate cause. Technically speaking, causal phenomena do not exist anyway. Two events that appear to involve a causal series are a special kind of correlation. If one divided the space and time occupied by the two "causal events" into small enough increments, the relationship would become statistical and correlational. It's a matter of perspective, as Fort clearly appreciated. Luminosities or UFORs are primary examples of this problem.

The original inspiration for the development of the tectonic strain theory must be traced to Charles Fort. When Lafrenière and I were writing *Space-Time Transients and Unusual Events* (1977), we did not realize the secret to the phenomena was already contained within Fort's monumental volume. Between the years 1968 and 1969, I had painstakingly classified each of his events within a temporal-spatial format. Like most Forteans, I experienced sensory overload.

With the availability of an IBM 360-40, about 4000 of Fort's data points were analyzed according to clusters in space. Since we had no idea which environmental variables might be associated with Fortean phenomena, although we suspected that the very energetic ones (like earthquakes, thunder-storms and intense geomagnetic disturbances) would be optimal candidates, we loaded a variety of routine geological and astronomical data files as well.

The first conspicuous relationship occurred between the numbers of reports in the luminosity categories and the earthquake history of the area. Typical correlation coefficients ranged between +0.45 and +0.80. This luminosity/earthquake coupling was very apparent in the USA, Great Britain, and western Europe. Other countries, less covered by Fort, demonstrated comparable "earthquake connections", but the numbers of observations were too small to be reliable.

In the first series of analyses, the major unit involved space. We divided the USA and Great Britain (our initial choice because of the long history of luminosities and tremors) into varying sized grids. As it turned out, the optimal grid size to maximize the luminosity-quake relationship was equal to about a quarter of the total area of Great Britain. Four cases are not very suitable for empirical analysis so we changed to the USA because of its larger area.

Unfortunately, space contains a persistent "confounding variable": population. Although the numbers of UFORs within an area may be correlated with the number of earthquakes, the numbers of UFORs are also correlated with the numbers of people living there. This

Figure 1.

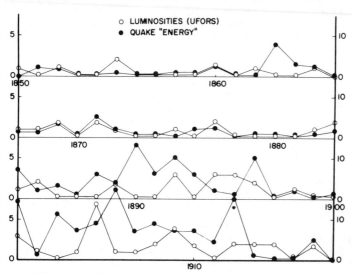

Numbers of luminosities (or UFORs) per year (open circles) according to Fort's publications and the quake 'energy' measure per year for Great Britain during the years 1850 to 1917. One value (asterisk) was off-scale.

"three-variable problem" is tricky but tractable. But even its solution did not allow the isolation of *dynamic* relationships between UFORs and tectonic strain as defined by earthquake activity.

Consequently, the analyses was shifted to temporal increments. Within the last few years, several important temporal parameters have been isolated [5, 6, 7]. For example, optimal increments of analysis peak at about 6 months or 1 year. In other words, the relationship between UFORs and earthquakes is best seen when the total numbers of reports per six-month period (e.g., January – June; July to December of each year) are compared to the number of earthtremors during these periods. Daily, monthly, 3-month, 2-year, or 4-year increments are less useful.

This temporal increment can be considered the optimal "window" by which to see the predisposing factor for the luminosities. Since large time reflects large space, it is not surprising that regional geological factors such as far-field stresses and the tectonic history of the area are involved. The effect can best be seen when one looks at the larger perspective rather than concentrating upon a few local cases. Fort, of course, would have been pleased.

"Trigger" events exist within time windows of a few days. Their effectiveness rides upon the existence of strain already present within the area. If the strain has not reached optimal conditions, then trigger variables would not be associated with UFORs. Classic trigger variables have been sudden geomagnetic storms (due, presumably, to injection of solar plasma into the upper atmosphere), the passage of air masses, and very unusual meteorological conditions.

The specific space in which the luminosity occurs will reflect the local history of the area and its geological architecture. Most UFORs should occur near old fault lines (which may be masked by streams, river beds or highways built near river beds) or other strain release areas. These areas should have copious historical references to "odd lights", which will be masked by the language each generation has used to describe odd phenomena.

In order to prepare this analysis for the *Fortean Times*, all of the major luminosity reports from Fort's data pool for Great Britain (England and Scotland combined) were sorted by computer according to one-year increments. Since Charlie could have referred to several incidents within what we would now call "a flap", the exaggerated contributions by many events within one flap were minimized by considering no more than one UFOR or luminosity report during a three-month period for either Scotland or England. As it turned out, this was a minor problem since Fort usually high-lighted only the most spectacular luminosity reports.

Earthquake references were also contained within the Fort data. Independent verification of his reports against the *Catalogue of British Earthquakes* indicates that Fort was accurate for major events in Great Britain; he did not leave out any of the major quakes throughout the 150-year period of his coverage. However for this analysis, numbers of different intensity quakes were used in order to determine the optimal seismic pattern that would discriminate UFOR or luminosity years. Such patterns are our simplest contemporary means to infer the optimal tectonic strain, theoretically, the true basis of luminosities.

For the major Fortean data period, the years 1850 to 1917, earthquake activity and intensity have been recorded systematically. The Davison

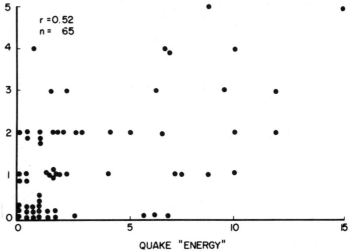

Figure 2.

r = 0.52
n = 65

QUAKE "ENERGY"

Scattergram between the luminosity measure (numbers of major UFORs per year) computed from Fort's data and the measure of quake 'energy' within England and Scotland during the Fortean era. The relationship is quantified by the Pearson product-moment correlation coefficient r; n refers to the number of cases (years).

scale, which is roughly equivalent to the Modified Mercalli scale at the lower levels, measures earthquake intensity (not magnitude like Richter) and is based upon estimates of local damage. A large earthquake for Britain usually involved an intensity of VII or VIII while intermediate rumbles ranged between V and VI; tremors involved intensities below V.

Many readers may not realize that Great Britain has had a long history of very noticeable earthquakes. Intensity VIII quakes struck Derbyshire on 18 November, 1796, Inverness on 6 August, 1816, Comrie on 23 October, 1839, Hereford on 6 October, 1863; Hereford on 17 December 1896; Inverness, 18 September, 1901; Swansea, 27 June, 1906. There were multiple instances of VII quakes. Since about 1920, the area has been relatively quiet, although a VIII intensity quake occurred in Derby on 11 February, 1957.

In order to weigh the appropriate intensity quakes as an indirect measure of earthquake 'energy', various weightings were given to VIII, VII, intermediate (V+VI) and low (IV or less) quakes. Computer analyses isolated the optimal weights for each earthquake type. They were determined by the maximum correlation between the seismic measure and the occurrence of luminous displays.

A final equation for the computation of earthquake "energy" per year (please note the quotation) was 6 times the numbers of VIII quakes, plus the number of intermediate quakes plus 1/6 times the number of low quakes. The addition of these measures produced the earthquake energy measure for the Fortean years.

As can be seen in Figure 1, which shows the number of major luminosity reports (open circles) and the earthquake energy measure (closed circles) per year for the years between

1850 and 1917, the two phenomena are clearly related. Luminous events tend to occur during the year or the year before increases in earthquake activity (as indicated by the energy measure). Similarly, the more intense the luminosity displays, the more intense the earthquake activity.

Since data streams can be seductive, quantitative analyses are imperative. In order to determine the strength of the relationship between Fort's luminosity measurements and the earthquake activity measures, the latter were correlated with the maximum luminosity measure during the same year or the previous year. This either/or selection was instituted since the accumulation of strain within Great Britain undergoes very slow drifts in rate of change. In other words, the same amount of change may require a year in some decades or more than a year in other periods.

The scattergram demonstrating the relationship between the luminosity measure and the quake index is shown in Figure 2. (Because of the technical aspects of time-lag analysis, the first few early years are not included in the scattergram.) As can be seen, there is a positive, moderately strong correlation (r = +0.52) between the luminosity measure derived from Fort's data and earthquake activity.

Split-half analysis, by which correlations were completed for the years 1850 to 1885 and 1885 to 1917 separately, indicated the same magnitude and direction for both coefficients. Consequently, we can conclude that the relationship between luminosities and earthquakes is internally consistent across decades. The results also suggest that Fort's sampling techniques were remarkably consistent and not prone to baseline drifts during this period.

This homogenity, however, could be misleading. Fort frequently juxtaposed luminosities with earthquakes, despite his clever semantic style. We may be being misled by Fort's bias for reporting only those luminosities reported during the year or the years before seismic events. Although this seems unlikely, especially in light of Corliss' stalwart verification of Fort's original references and the independent records of seismic history, there is a way to circumvent this possibility.

If Fort's observations are representative samples of the phenomenon, then an equation that demonstrates the relationship between luminosities and earthquakes during the nineteenth century should also *predict the relationship between earthquakes and UFORs* now. Assuming there has been no qualitative shift in the tectonokinetics of Great Britain, we should be able to predict UFORs within the area by knowing the appropriate seismic parameters!

Such prediction would be easier if the same type of earthquake information were available for the years after 1920; unfortunately there are many hiatuses in the seismic data streams and after 1975 most of the data available to me involved magnitude measures. Consequently, the earthquake energy index had to be modified to involve only the larger quakes (VII and VIII).

However, the introduction of a second source of variance (another factor) greatly enhanced the multiple regression correlation coefficient between luminosities and earthquake intensities. This variable involved a change in solar activity as defined by a sudden increase in sunspot numbers. It is weighed by an increase of 40 or more Zurich numbers between any two *successive* months during a year.

Traditionally, sunspot variables have been a source of derision, again because of the lack of understanding by critics about the nature of correlational analyses. Contemporary geophysical theory clearly integrates the relationship between changes in sunspot numbers and terrestrial events. In general, sudden shifts in sunspot numbers are correlated with increased 'solar storms'; these conditions contribute to flare emissions and alterations in solar wind that induce geomagnetic perturbations on the earth.

One compelling variable in the time lag, multiple regression analyses reported in recent years [5, 6] is the importance of geomagnetic variation during the contemporary interval, that is, during the same period as the luminous displays. It appears that processes associated with geomagnetic variation, characterized by sudden and intense storms with A_p index values over 80, are trigger events for luminosities if the tectonic strain exists already. These values are strongly correlated with the abrupt jumps in Zurich sunspot numbers.

The final multiple regression equation for the prediction of luminosities (now called UFORs) within Great Britain was composed of a weighted measure for VII and VIII intensity (Davison) quakes and the amount of solar activity change. Figure 3 shows the predicted flap score, on the basis of this equation, for the years 1850 to 1980. The multiple regression coefficient was 0.68.

If you compare the flap measures for the years 1850 to 1917 with the major clusters of luminous reports (from Fort) noted in Figure 1, you can see that the major luminous highs are predictable. According to the equations, the equivalent of a major flap (value 1 or greater) should have occurred around 1863, 1870-1871, 1884, 1901, 1903, 1906, and 1909. There were also periods of elevated baselines in luminous displays, that is consecutive years of not spectacular but maintained luminous displays.

Obviously there is no one-to-one overlap between the predicted flap scores and the data (Fort's work) from which the equation was generated. Since the equation accommodates no more than about 50% of the variance in luminosity report numbers, there should be disparaties between observed and expected values. Considering the nature of the data, only the larger excursions (what we now call flaps) and maintained elevations should be more or less reliable.

The source of the remaining variance in luminosity numbers has not been specified. Candidates include variable shifts in the rate of tectonic strain with different years or different parts of Great Britain. The measures used may be too crude. There is also the possibility that some as yet unspecified variable may be operating. It too must be isolated before the phenomenon can be predicted totally.

Even with these limitations, Figure 3 also indicates that major luminosity-type flaps should have continued, long after Fort's data collection days were over. Luminous events should have been reported between 1924 and 1926 and again around 1931, 1933, and 1939-1940. As emphasized by Keel [8], these years did not include references to UFORs, but reports of "odd airships", "ghost rockets", and "mysterious lights in the sky" abounded. The label changed, but the phenomena remained.

Certainly the most impressive results were the predicted large flaps starting in 1946 to 1949-1950, decreasing in magnitude between 1951 to 1956 and increasing again between 1957-1958. This period was predicted to be associated with an unprecedented series of UFOR flaps within Great Britain. Although the 1951 to 1956 hiatus was associated with elevated numbers of UFORs in other parts of the world with different tectonic strain conditions and seismic patterns, there should have been relatively fewer UFORs within Great Britain alone. Of course, the equation would not predict social sources of UFO reports such as media experiments or hoaxes.

Following a conspicuous decrease in relative earthquake activity and solar disruption during the 1960s, predicted UFO flap scores began to increase again. By far the most intense luminous displays should have occurred between 1973-1974 and 1977, followed by a gradual decrease in the events until 1980. In fact, the 1974-1975 to 1977 flap period should have been the largest protracted luminous series since the end of World War II or the infamous 1901 to 1906 interval.

Observations support these predictions. A resurgence of luminosities within several portions of Great Britain began during the latter part of the 1970s. Several field groups have documented the elevated baseline of UFOR numbers and the excessive, transient, excursions about this baseline. One excellent case study, *The Dyfed Enigma* [9] (by Pugh and Holiday) highlight the successive bouts of luminous displays reported in Wales between the years 1974 to 1977. As stated in the preface of their book "between 1974 and 1977, in the area of Wales around the St. Bride's Bay, a small community was shaken to its roots by an extraordinary spate of UFO visitations."

Although this and other predicted flap scores appear to overlap with the observed flaps of luminosities during this century, some caution must be applied. To really test the accuracy of the predictions, one must correlate the numerical values of predictions with the numbers of UFORs from an actual sample (preferably more than one). The sample, of course, must be controlled for changes in collection procedures, numbers of field observers and the social facilitation due to media coverage.

The increased incidence of large-scale luminosity sightings should have been associated with increases in tectonic strain. The major manifestation of this strain would have been enhanced seismic activity within the *region* of the sightings. Indeed there was a very clear increase in seismic events within the corridor between Swansea, Hereford and Derby, (all of which have been associated with very noticeable quakes in the past). Significant swarms of earthtremors began during the year 1975 near Stoke-on-Trent.

A second major line of activation occurred through central Wales. Seismic events within this region were apparently correlated with the strain field orientated along the corridor terminating near Stoke-on-Trent. These series of quakes culminated with a relatively large event in July 1980 near Chester.

According to the tectonic strain theory, the luminosities reported within the St. Brides

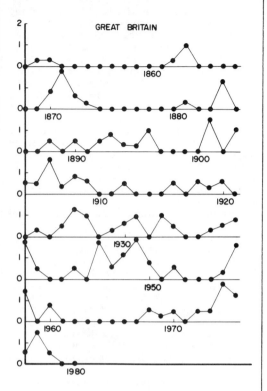

Figure 3.

Predicted flap scores (0 to 2 range) according to an equation containing the numbers of larger (noticeable) earthquakes within Great Britain and a measure of solar perturbations for the years 1850 to 1980. The years 1850 to 1917 involve the interval from which the equation was generated. Translated standard errors of the estimate indicate that predicted scores above 1.0 for a single year or sustained elevations above 0.5 for three successive years are most reliable.

Bay region in particular and western Wales in general should have been associated with the strain within these corridors. This means that the major thrust of the luminous phenomena was displaced about 150 km to the west of the epicenters, where the strain usually resulted in a fracture.

Spatial displacement of luminosities from the imminent epicenters is not unexpected. Indeed, the theory clearly predicts that major concentrations of UFORs should be some distance from the epicenter of detectable tremors. According to one third–order derivation of the theory, the more intense the imminent quake, the more distant the major cluster of luminous displays. For mid-magnitude quakes, such as those found within Great Britain or in the New Madrid region of the USA, an average distance of 100 to 200 km from the imminent epicenters are quite 'normal'.

The relationship can be demonstrated empirically by enclosing a flap area within a 50 km diameter circle (on a map). Next delineate the concentric circular areas between 50 km and 100 km from the region, between 100 km and 150 km from the center and so forth. If the numbers of UFORs (within the center circle) are then correlated successively with the numbers of earthquakes within more and more adjacent areas, there will be some distance where the maximum relationship between the luminous reports and the earthquake numbers peak. This is one way to approximate, crudely, the spatial displacement of the phenomena.

The maximum distance from which the local area could be influenced by far-field stresses is an important consideration. Coincident with the increased activity in Wales, earthquake intensity and numbers were increasing in Scotland. Historically, Scotland has been more prone to earthquakes (and to intense and varied Fortean events). While Wales was inundated with luminous displays, portions of Scotland were exposed to similar conditions. The strain within central Scotland culminated in December of 1979 near Glascow with a rare 4.5 Richter quake, the most intense event of the last 150 years.

Considering the relatively small area of England and Scotland (compared to larger geological contexts), one would expect that elevated seismic activity in one major area such as Wales should have weak temporal correlates in the more northern regions of the island. As a result, unlike the USA or Europe, major flaps of UFORs in Great Britain, could be pandemic. Depending upon the extent of the strain field, which could stretch from Wales to Glasgow, UFO-field groups could be inundated with bouts of luminous displays that shift from week to week throughout the island.

Clearly, such spatial displacement reaffirms the large scale at which the luminosities must be viewed. Although the individual events may be localised within a few meters, the actual strain fields responsible for them may be reacting to far-field stresses that are hundreds of kilometers away. As the strain field moves, in response to these complex combinations of stresses, the frequency of occurrence for the luminous events rise and fall.

Metaphorically, we could conceive the process leading to a series of luminosities as a strain field moving through a section of the earth's crust that may involve thousands of square kilometers. As the strain field moves and concentrates within a particular area, luminosities appear within the most probable strain release space within that area; they will be triggered by the small forces that influence those spaces.

Classic areas of strain release within a region involve old fault lines or imminent fracture zones (e.g. upwarps). These regions would display enhanced microseisms, if the equipment is present to measure them. Other signs of enhanced stress foci include the release of radon gas in regions containing felsic rocks (such as diorite) or increased incidences of electrical failures in nearby houses.

Once the strain field had achieved appropriate values, a small trigger event could precipitate a bout of luminous displays. Candidates include the passage of a severe wind storm, an unusually high or low pressure air mass and lunar tides (depending upon phase and declination). Sometimes, man-made triggers, such as the filling of a nearby reservoir or lake, may be sufficient to precipitate a small burst of UFORs.

The tectonic strain theory can also predict the probable areas where luminosities should be maintained. They should be more evident near sharp shapes (cliffs, towers, steeples) subject to electric charge collection and electric charge sources (radio towers, high tension powerlines). They would especially be attracted to insulated, charged conductors such as moving cars along a flat surface or ships at sea.

We can even predict the direction of the luminosity pattern from the strain theory. Luminosities should follow the directions of local fault lines. They should also follow the general strain field alignment of the local earth's crust. Since large areas share the same orientation of stress (due primarily to the last ice age), groups of luminosities should move in predictable directions. In North America, for example, the orientation is predominately from the southwest to the northeast. Obviously, there are local variations.

The specific movements and characteristics of *an individual* luminositity cannot be predicted by the large space-time application of the tectonic strain theory. Instead, *one must understand the physics of the luminosity itself.* Although both the physics of the event and the tectonic strain theory should be compatable, the precision required to accurately predict the luminosity's movement involves a different and methodology.

There is some evidence that the individual event is a fundamentally different kind of phenomenon that has not been described fully by modern science. The phenomenon appears to be an extraordinarily intense electromagnetic-like field containing a plasma-like condition. First order movements of the luminositity can be predicted when the local environment (the hills, the houses and even the people) is translated into the equivalents of electric conductors and dielectrics.

Laboratory experiments by Dr. Brian

Brady and his colleagues at the US Department of the Interior demonstrate that tractable episodes of miniature luminosities can be produced and measured. These miniature luminosities reflect all of the major characteristics of the field varieties, including spin (rotation), color changes, radiofrequency emission, splitting (into separate balls), fusion (into larger volumes), and the ejection of narrow beams of energy. Most of all, they are extraordinarily energetic events that display magnetic fields exceeding millions of gauss (calculated). The behaviours are predictable from a general field theory developed by Dr. Brady.

Characterization of individual events outside the laboratory is a particular hazardous procedure. Single cases are subject to the possibilities of fraud, misconception or confabulation despite the best recollection of witnesses and circumstances. Rejection of a single UFO event does not reject all UFO phenomena. Similarly, a very strong case of a particular UFO type does not demonstrate that all UFO reports are generated from the same source.

Once the reader leaves the large space-time scale of UFOR patterns and attempts to describe or explain the individual case, a change in methodology must occur. Now we require a model that can predict, on the basis of known or suspected mechanisms, the intensity of the magnetic fields associated with luminous events, the color, shape and spin. Now we must have a model by which the varied human perceptions associated with close proximity to luminosities can be accommodated. Such features cannot be derived directly from the tectonic strain theory applied to Fort's data.

•

Michael A. Persinger. Ph.D.

REFERENCES

• 1   Fort, C. *The Complete Books of Charles Fort.* New York: Dover, 1974.
• 2   Persinger, M.A. 'Geophysical variables and behaviour: VII. Prediction of recent European UFO report years by nineteenth century luminosity and solar-seismic measure'. *Perceptional and Motor Skills,* 1983, *56,* 91 – 95.
• 3   Persinger, M.A., & Lafreniere, G.F. *Space-time transients and unusual events.* Chicago: Nelson-Hall, 1977.
• 4   Persinger, M.A. 'Earthquake activity and antecedent UFO report numbers.' *Perceptual and Motor Skills,* 1980, *50, 791 – 797.*
• 5   Persinger, M.A. 'Geophysical variables and human behaviour: VIII. Specific prediction of UFO reports within the New Madrid states by solar-geomagnetic and seismic measures.' *Perceptual and Motor Skills,* 1983. *56.* 243 – 249.
• 6   Persinger, M.A. 'Geophysical variables and behaviour. III. Prediction of UFO reports by geomagnetic and seismic activity.' *Perceptual and Motor Skills,* 1981, *53, 115 – 122.*
• 7   Persinger, M.A. 'Odd luminosities (UFOs) and other Fortean events before earthquakes: The New Madrid Test.' *Pursuit,* 1981, *14*(2) 69 – 79.
• 8   A major portion of the file was derived from Davison, C.*A History of British Earthquakes,* Cambridge: Cambridge University Press, 1924.
• 9   Keel, J.A. *UFOs: Operation Trojan Horse.* New York: Putman, 1970.
•10   Pugh, R.J. and Holiday, F.W. *The Dyfed Enigma.* Coronet: Kent, 1981.

FORT-NOTE
by Pokkettz.

"If anybody can define the true characteristics of anything, or who can localize trueness anywhere, he makes the discovery for which cosmos is laboring. He will be instantly translated, like Elijah, into the Positive Absolute. My own notion is that, in a moment of super-concentration, Elijah became so nearly a real prophet that he was translated to heaven, or to the Positive Absolute, with such velocity that he left an incandescent train behind him." [*Books.* p70.]

Fortean Mysteries.

by Mr. X.

I know of no Fortean alive with the single-minded dedication of **Mr X**, which is his legal name. For nearly two decades he has been engaged upon a sweeping search for the sources of all Fort's citations and references. I (your editor) have been priviledged to be a part of this enterprise, which has the ultimate goal (at least several years away) of publishing a revised, annotated, verified, illustrated and fully-indexed edition of Fort's works. It is to some of Fort's unreferenced allusions that X addresses himself here, demonstrating both the extent of Fort's reading and X's own persistence in penetrating Fort's lapses into obscurity.

"I am a collector of notes upon subjects of diversity," states Fort as he begins his second chapter of *Wild Talents*.

What distinguished Charles Fort from other collectors of strange phenomena was his extensive use of highly respectable sources for his data. Few authors who wrote of ghosts, monsters, or showers of frogs sought out, with as much fervor, the indiscretions of *Nature, Comptes Rendus, Scientific American*, and scores of other scientific publications. In many cases, Fort expected his readers to seek out the details on their own with his many 'see' references, but few would have the opportunity to find those sources outside of the New York Public Library or the British Library.

Fort's writing was greatly affected by his use of notes scrawled onto small scraps of paper that were sorted into several boxes. When writing his books, Fort found it an easy task to select a group of notes for a chapter about one phenomenon, an extraordinary incident, or a chain of events over time. Sometimes examples of Fort's diversity would be rattled off without the benefit of any source citation. These Fortean mysteries deal with unusual phenomena, yet they remain obscure without Fort's having included them in his books.

In an effort to revise Fort's books, the search for sources goes beyond finding errors in spelling, quotations, and citations. Tracking down the sources of Fortean mysteries can involve a lengthy search for an incident known only from a fleeting passage or two. For example:

● ". . . At Seringapatam, India, about the year 1800 fell a hailstone —

"I fear me, I fear me: this is one of the profoundly damned. I blurt out something that should, perhaps, be withheld for several hundred pages — ·but the damned thing was the size of an elephant," (*Book of the Damned*, Holt/Dover ed., p.19).

Fort never again returns to Seringapatam, Karnataka, India, but he does provide other reports of giant hailstones in India at Bungalore in 1851, at Candeish in 1826, and at Poorhundur in 1854. In each of these instances, he is citing Dr. George Buist's article on the 'Remarkable Hailstones in India'. And here too one finds: "One near Seringapatam, in the end of the last century, said to have been the size of an elephant. It took three days to melt. We have no further particulars, but there is no reason whatever for our doubting the fact," *(Annual Report of the British Association for the Advancement of Science*, 1855, Transactions, p.34).

● "Mahogany logs on the coast of Greenland; bugs of a valley on the top of Mt. Blanc; atheists at a prayer meeting; ice in India," (*Book of the Damned*, Holt/Dover ed., p.24).

The 'bugs' on Mt. Blanc were actually moths identified as *Plusia gamma* of the family *Noctuidae*, and fortunately Fort provided the source without mentioning this incident. Albert Müller's article entitled 'On the dispersal of non-migratory Insects by atmospheric agencies' tabulates the following case:" 'Last year, one of my friends, Dr. Ordinaire, made an ascent of Mont Blanc. On arriving at the summit, the first object that attracted his attention, was a *Plusia gamma*, kicking in the snow.' (Bruand, *Catal. des Lepidopt. du Dept. du Doubs*, 1845, p. 83.) Ad. & Aug Speyer say in reference to this observation, 'so much is certain, that only an accident, an ascending current of air of rare steadiness and intensity, could have brought the creature into that inhospitable region. (*Die geograph. Verbeit. der Schmetterlinge Deutschlands und der Schweiz*.' 2nd part, 1862, p.29)" The lack of a specific date in the text may have been the reason why Fort excluded this item while citing others from the *Transactions of the Royal Entomological Society*, 1871, (May), pp.175-186.

● One of Fort's "deviations from concentricity" following upon the quote from *Wild Talents* was: a reported growth of hair on the bald head of a mummy". No reference is made to its source in his writings, but he does direct the reader in stories of the sudden blanching, or whitening, of hair to: "See the indexes of *Notes and Queries*, series 6, 7, 10," (*Wild Talents*, Holt/Dover ed., p.1016). Fort mentions the case of Marie Antoinette as being doubtful and neglects the blanching of the hair of Mary Queen of Scots or of Sir Thomas More in their last days, and he neglects the alleged growth of hair after death in the very same volume.

"One of the chief patron saints of Siena is St. Galgano, whose legend is one of the most romantic of the 'ages of faith.' The Sienese painters loved to depict him as a beautiful youth with a profusion of golden curls. He closed his poetical life of penance at the early age of thirty-three, in 1181, and the head was delivered, as the palladium of Siena, to the keeping of the convent of the maiden Polissena, who, when sent to win him back to the world, had instead been won by him to give herself to a life of religion. A magnificent reliquary of gold enamel was subsequently made for it, of such exquisite workmanship that it was long supposed to be Byzantine; but Count Pecci has traced it satisfactorily to the hand of Giovanni da Bartalo di Maestro Fredi, a brother of the painter, an orafo (goldsmith), who was much in Rome, but was working in his native Siena in 1373. It is still in a state of perfect preservation, as is the head of St. Galgano within it. The metal cover winds up and down with a key by a clever mechanism, which has kept in order for 500 years, and exposes the head to view in an inner case of glass. The face is little more than a skull, with the skin tightly dried, but the head is all covered with hair, and curls hang over the temples and brow. This hair is all said to grow (the curls more than the rest), and is regularly cut about every three years," Notes and Queries, 6th series, v.6, (October 28, 1882), p.344). The growth of hair after death is normally attributed to the contraction of the skin and exposure of sub-dermal hair. This was undoubtedly the explanation of the appearance of a bluish beard upon the clean-shaven Napolean Bonaparte upon his return from St. Helena; but, for hair to continue to grow after seven centuries, or eight centuries if the triennial haircut continues, would be miraculous. It is doubtful St. Galgano, (or St. Galganus), was bald as Fort suggests; but, this mystery might be further probed by inquiring of the Cistercians in Siena if hair does indeed grow on St. Galgano or the life-sized crucifix in the same city of which samples of both were given to R. H. Busk, whose letter gave this account to *Notes and Queries*.

The 'Mahogany logs on the coast of Greenland' was a more difficult mystery to trace, for the only clue given by Fort as to its source would be his claim; "Some years ago, I read five or six hundred pounds of literature upon the Arctic," (*New Lands*, Holt/Dover ed., p.493).

Aside from reading about the arguments as to whether Cook or Peary had been first to the North Pole or about the search for the Franklin expedition, Fort had undoubtedly read the arguments of those who sought the Northwest Passage and the unexplored Arctic regions. During this endeavor he read one of the books by William Scoresby Jr. which mentioned the absence of thunder when lightning had been seen, (as discussed in *Lo!*, Holt/Dover ed., p.733), and the 'mahogany logs'.

". . . In the Danish settlement at Disco, is a mahogany table made out of a plank which was drifted thither by the current, and is now in the possession of the governor. A tree of logwood was also picked up not far from this place. Another log of mahogany was picked up at sea by Admiral Lowenorn, when on his voyage attempting the re-discovery of Old Greenland. This piece of wood, which was so large that they were obliged to saw it in two before they could get it on board, they found within sight of the coast of Greenland, in latitude 65° 11'.longitude 35° 8' west of Paris. It was much perforated by worms, which circumstance the Admiral conceived might assist in giving it sufficient buoyancy to swim in the water.

"These logs of wood, the produce of the Isthmus which connects North and South America, could only reach the places where they were severally found, by floating up the west coast of America, towards the north, through Behring's Strait, and so along the northern face of Asia or America, or across the Northern Pole. Had they come by way of the Gulf of Mexico, they might have floated to the banks of Newfoundland, by the action of the Gulf Stream, and been carried from thence to any part of the western shore of Europe; but they could not possibly have passed northward from Newfoundland into Davis's Straits, or to the east coast of Greenland, in direct opposition to a current which perpetually flows towards the southwest," (Scoresby, William, Jr., An Account of the Arctic Regions, *Edinburgh: Archibald Constable and Co., 1820, v.1, pp.6-8*).

Further details of Lowenorn's discovery are provided by John Barrow at this location about the 3rd of July in 1786 as follows: "Every moment they became more and more surrounded with ice-burgs; and in this situation they discovered an enormous log of wood, which had been hewn square, and so large that it could not be taken on board until it had been cut in two with the saw. Several sea-gulls were perched on this log. The most remarkable circumstance was that of its being mahogany, which is generally too heavy to float in the water; but the wood was so worm-eaten, even to the very heart, that Mr. Lowenorn conjectured its specific gravity probably might have been diminished," *(A Chronological History of Voyages into the Artic Regions,* London: John Murray, 1818, p. 334).

Fort might have considered writing of this incident as one of extraordinary communications by persons unknown. In *Lo!,* (Holt/Dover ed., p. 592), he says: "When I go to think of what gets into the Houses of Congress, I expect to come upon data of mysterious distributions of cocoanuts in Greenland." And, he goes on to speak of the marked reindeer which had been discussed in Parliament when it was first found on Spitzbergen in 1852 up till 1921, (on p. 603). Yet, Scoresby Junior also made the remarkable find of a hewn log on which the letter 'G' had been carved; but, as this was found in 1817 on the Island of Jan Mayen, Greenland, its origins predated the excited search for communications from Sir John Franklin's lost expedition.

However, the mystery of the mahogany logs might still be pursued by discovering if the 'mahogany table' at Disco can yet be found. Even if 160 years have passed since related by Scoresby Junior, its possession by the governor and great value may have ensured its preservation to this very date. Fort may have sent one of his letters to find out for himself; for what other reason would he have discovered, as stated in *New Lands*, that: "Eskimos of Disco, Greenland, are publishing a newspaper," (Holt/Dover ed., p. 314).

One by one the Fortean mysteries are being traced. The obscurity of their origins need not distract from the careful research which has been cited in Fort's books. For too long a time, errors copied off Fort's notes and typographer's errors in the original printings have been allowed to persist. The marginalia inside Fort's own copies of his books attests to his own befuddlement by erroneous citations; and, some writers have plagarized his work by citing an erroneous source document unseen without mentioning its being found in one of his books. If a revised edition of Fort's books seems slow in its realization, one must consider the research being undertaken to establish the accuracy of all its source citations and the origins of several Fortean mysteries which have to be re-discovered.

●

X

FORT-NOTE
by Pokkettz.

"I have a story of a horse that appeared in what would, to any ordinary horse, be a closed room. It makes one nervous, maybe. One glances around, and would at least not be incredulous, seeing almost any damned thing, sitting in a chair, staring at one." (*Books.* p915.)

Some Suggestions for Improving Our Research Methods.

by Peter Christie.

It is the hope of quite a few Forteans that we are entering a new phase in our development — one of more consolidation of methodology, more cooperation over resources, more bold deductions, and a greater utilization of information technology. **Peter Christie** here outlines two simple steps which can be implemented immediately — that we compile indexes of the sources we search, and that he himself will act as a 'registry' of sources searched. The other subject Peter opens up is the welcome possibility of using government money to fund this, or projects like it.

Most of us would agree that FT is doing sterling work in advancing the 'cause' of Forteanism, especially in salvaging those stories that we class as Fortean from the daily tons of newsprint. As a contemporary record it is second to none — but where does it go from here?

I pose this question because from time to time FT prints articles on 'historical' Forteana which shows clearly the mass of material that is available if only we could get at it. At the same time it is clear that one magazine can never hope to publish all material concerning particular cases, whether they be contemporary or not — the recent 'Beast of Exmoor' is a good example. A precis of published reports is good but many specialists would like to see all the published items on the subject.

First and formost we need to know what newspapers and which journals exist and which have been searched already. Fort himself provides no list and we know that his four books were only artificial collections made up of his subjective choice of items. What is needed, therefore, daunting as it seems at first sight, is a total systematic search of all newspaper files. At this point you are probably muttering "mad, totally mad of course, Fortean loons etc". But is such a suggestion so bizarre?

Various listings of newspapers exist e.g. *Catalogue of the newspaper collections in the British Library*, P.E. Allen (London 1975) - 40,000 titles listed. Presumably similar listings exist for countries other than Britain. Access to newspapers listed presents few problems — most British Record Offices have original files or microfilm copies of their local papers whilst the national collection at Colindale (the British Library) is fairly complete.

Before beginning any search, however, we need to check whether a) an index exists, b) a Fortean researcher has been there before us. As to the first question — in Autumn 1981 the Colindale Newspaper Library *Newsletter* reported on the initial results of their survey of indexes to British newspapers. They said that "over 500 local newspaper titles have been fully or partially indexed". Clearly one needs to check whether an index to any newspaper you are interested in has already been prepared. A letter to Colindale will tell you this.

We also need a central holding of material, both past and present, accessible, indexed and available as print-outs/photocopies/microfiche to all interested parties. As to the mechanics of this I understand that a few people at FT are working on it. My interest comes in obtaining the original material to feed into such a system. Firstly and hopefully, the FT clipsters will maintain their usual steady flow of contemporary reports of unusual events. This would be supplemented by 'historical' material to make the collection useful and meaningful in the widest context of providing a study base for researchers.

What can be done now, even before the physical problems of information storage and retrieval are worked out, is to prepare an on-going list of topics being studied by Forteans, and a list of sources that have been searched. It would not be a list of actual cases. This research register would avoid duplication of effort and act as a clearing house for initial inquiries and information. An obvious core to this list is the series of mainstream scientific journals that have been searched by Corliss for his 'Sourcebook' project.

I have talked this suggestion over with Bob Rickard and have agreed to begin the register myself. If you are researching a specific topic or a specific source – e.g. your local newspaper/archaeological journal please let me know – my address is below.

To give you an idea of what can be done I might mention two of my own interests. The first is my reading through of the *Gentleman's Magazine* – the results of this are now appearing in FT's pages. The second is a more ambitious scheme which has now (July 1983) been going for 6 months. As a tutor in local history and a Fortean I was always aware of the riches in the back-files of the local newspaper – the *North Devon Journal*. Unfortunately the sight of over 150 massive volumes of close printed type tends to put one off searching!

I overcame the problem by contacting the Manpower Service Commission and asking for £12,000 to set up a job-creation scheme aimed at indexing all local news over the nineteenth century. After ploughing through the attendent paperwork etc. I soon became the 'employer' of three unemployed graduate students who now spend 5 days a week extracting, precising and indexing the *North Devon Journal* from 1850 on. The initial grant is for a year but this can be extended. Any Forteana found is, of course, a bonus – I don't think the MSC would have given me the money just to search for Fortean items!

As an indication of what we have come across I will quote the following SHC and 'Toad in the Hole' cases.

● *North Devon Journal* 15 April 1852 p5 column b.
INQUEST. Before the deputy coroner, John Toller Esq. – An inquest was held at Beaford on the 12th inst., on the body of William Vodden, aged about 60, whose death took place on Saturday the 10th under the following remarkable circumstances: – On that day the old man was at work with his wife in a field at Brinscombe-farm, picking up stones, William Gilbert, carpenter was also present, and about 10 o'clock in the forenoon, heard him go into the Mowstead. About two minutes later the deceased called to witness, who went to him, and he said he had set all the place on fire. His smock-frock was burning, but the fire from the other parts was all up over his head. Witness called for assistance, and the wife of the deceased, and one Roger Passmore came. Witness tried to put out the fire, but could not; he burnt his finger; went for a surgeon. Mary Vodden, wife of the deceased, on being called, looked towards the Mowstead, and saw the smoke rising up; she ran and wrapped her apron round the deseased; in about ten minutes the fire was put out. He died about eleven

o'clock on the same forenoon. He was a great smoker. No pipe was, however, found upon him or near him. The jury returned as their verdict, that the "Deceased was found burning, from the effects of which he died, but how the burning took place did not appear to the jury".

Lexilinkers will have noted the name of the farm – Brinscombe = Burnt valley. The classic SHC excuse of a smoker is again advanced but, as usual, quickly dismissed.

● *North Devon Journal* 19 January 1865 p5. *"Strange if True: It is stated that about three weeks ago, at Earl Fortescue's Stone Quarry, at Wear Dock, Wear Gifford; the quarrymen had taken out some immense stones, and, in order to ship them aboard Charles Hookway's barge for the use of the Bideford Improvements, at the West-end of the bridge, the gads were applied to split them. in the middle of the largest stone they found a large rat (supposed to be one of the Muscovy breed) of great length from tail to snout, with whiskers 6 inches long; supposed to have been hybernating since the flood. It is to be offered to the British Museum as an Antediluvian curiosity."*

If the idea of helping the unemployed and at the same time extending Fortean knowledge appeals to you then do write to me and I will let you know more about my own scheme and how to go about setting up your own. Also, please let me know about your research interests and sources being searched.

●

Peter Christie
30 Lime Grove, Bideford, Devon.

The Sociology of Anomalous Events.
Continued from p35.

important not only in dealing with anomalous events but also assists us in coping with the numerous social changes which advancing technology and evolving human consciousness bring about. A changing world requires people who can think.

And besides, anomalistics is fun!

●

Ron Westrum

REFERENCES
● 'Social Intelligence About Anomalies: The Case of UFOs,' *Social Studies of Science*, Vol.7 (1977), pp 271 – 302.
● 'Science and Social Intelligence About Anomalies: The Case of Meteorites,' *Social Studies of Science*, Vol.8 (1978), pp 461 – 493.
● 'Knowledge about Sea-Serpents,' *Sociological Review Monographs*, Vol. 27 (1979), p293-314.
● 'Witnesses of UFOs and Other Anomalies' and 'UFO Reporting Dynamics' in Richard Haines, Editor, *UFO Phenomena and the Behavioral Scientist* (Scarecrow Press, 1979)
● 'Social Intelligence About Hidden Events,' *Knowledge: Creation, Diffusion, Utilization*, Vol.3 (1982), pp 381 – 400.

The Reticulated Researcher:

A Vision of a Computer-aided Fortean.

by Bob Rickard.

For several years now I have corresponded with some of my closer Fortean friends on the subject of forming some kind of academic institution to further the methods and goals of Fortean research. This is an ideal moment to offer my thoughts on the subject, and outline what seems to me to be a practical solution, and invite discussion.

While the numbers of people interested in the wide range of strange phenomena we call Fortean are believed to be large, the actual numbers of dedicated Forteans, researchers, writers or clipsters are very few, and many of us are aware that we are a strange breed. The breadth of our subject matter, and its historical and geographical extent forces us to be philosophical about phenomena and their explanations.

The fount of Fortean philosophy, for me at least, lies in the necessity of a keen appreciation of what Fort called our "hyphenated existence" [1]. By this he meant that we are, ordinarily, incapable of perceiving or deducing anything about the world around us without recourse to pairs of extremes (eg: we think of orange as between red and yellow; warm between hot and cold; a mile between a point and infinity; up is relative to down, etc.) As an exercise it makes one aware of the arbitrary nature of our measuring and descriptive systems, particularly those upon which science is reliant. Another by-product is even more metaphysical, and that is an awareness of some of the primary tensions between states of existence (eg: positive — negative; stability — instability; or the local and the universal.) Not surprisingly most Forteans I know have leaned towards Oriental philosophies, in particular the Zen/Chan viewpoint, which, with its cultivation of humour, smoothly parallels and complements Fortean thought.

It is not my intention to expound on Fortean philosophy here, but this preamble was necessary to shed some light on another notable characteristic of Forteans — their valued independence of thought. In my experience the dedicated Fortean is a loner, a maverick; what Ed Saunders, in another context, called "a rogue element". Fort himself refused to join the (now defunct) Fortean Society, launched at a party in his honour in 1931, the year before his death, on the grounds that he feared it would institutionalize his philosophy, or worse, make a cult of him. Both of these fears were realized when people joined the Society out of admiration for Fort's writings only to find that it was dominated by a man who made it a vehicle for his own ego and cranky beliefs with disastrous results (see Robert Johnson's article on p48.)

The two other Fortean organizations — the International Fortean Organization (INFO) [2], and the Society for the Investigation of the Unexplained (SITU) [3] — have likewise been unable, despite their good intentions, to service the needs of the Fortean researcher and writer. Generally, the Fortean scholars are outnumbered by those who are content to simply pay their dues, bless 'em, without which there would be no publications. But although a society and its magazine are useful for deseminating news, opinions and discussion, they are not necessarily the best vehicle for Fortean research, which can often be dry and obscure to the uninterested. Our esteemed Canadian colleague, Mr X, tried publishing a journal for classic Fortean study, called *Chaos*, but could not find enough interested researchers to cover the costs. Our numbers are so few, and the tasks before us so great that any other policy than mutual aid is utter folly. It is to the problem of improving our research methodology and efficiency that I wish to address myself.

A key problem for the researcher is access to the files, data and publications held by the societies. There are very few places holding specialists collections, and these are mainly the archives of UFO or psychic research bodies. Of the Fortean archives SITU restricts access to members only, and although INFO has no stated policy, I suspect it is similarly restricted. Only the recently formed ASSAP [4] has taken a step in the right direction by starting to collect material for a national reference library covering the whole Fortean range, and which will be plugged into the interlibrary lending network. But it will be several years before its collection becomes functional and useful. So the researcher is still left to his own devices and the good offices of his colleagues.

Unofficially, the officers of SITU and INFO are quite helpful to fellow Forteans, but in practice research data requests usually fall prey to the old enemies, lack of time and facilities. This criticism also applies to the *Fortean Times* archives: we receive lots of requests for help and information, but we are not able to be as helpful as we would like. I regret this greatly, because I believe in a scholarly, gentlemanly ethos of mutual help, and I've tried to apply this to my work as editor. And yet another problem is a consequence of our need for individuality: because we share no common system so much of our work would be lost or indecipherable were any serious accident to happen to any one of us. Clearly we have to find new ways to improve our methodology and understanding if we wish to foster research and study of Fortean topics. Our unusual needs demand an unusual and innovative solution.

One thing a true Fortean values highly is his freedom to follow his own flag. How else are we to gain useful insights, investigate areas others avoid or haven't discovered, and have the affrontery to defy orthodoxy, or to choose *not* to challenge it, or even bypass it? One of the reasons my progress towards the 'institute' idea has been slow and erratic is that every form of institution I could think of would become stultifying as time went by; at worse becoming merely a social club. Factions could become entrenched; and the needs of administration could straddle it like a cancer, diverting valuable resources away from the intended purpose.

At this point the reasonable question is, why bother to organize Forteans anyway? I can't answer for anyone else, but I suspect any researcher will share the need to know who is studying what; and what sources have been scoured or checked for Fortean material, and by whom, in order to avoid duplication of effort. I need to have a system for filing or storing my books, clippings and other material in order to find what I want when I want. Even if we had no official organization, it is obvious that we would achieve a lot more, and faster, if we all spoke a common language; by which I mean sharing a common terminology, classification system, standards and methods. None of us would like to see these things

'imposed' — even if it were possible, which, thank Fort, it isn't — so any standardization or systematizing will have to be done by ourselves, by common agreement.

In pondering how we can learn from earlier attempts to organize Forteans, my correspondents impressed on me two criteria: firstly Forteans do not function well in heirarchical structures; and secondly, to avoid organizational dependence upon individuals our organization must arise out of the necessities of our work and be based on data, not personalities. The answer came to me halfway through a glorious mug of tea. . . we could set up an organization based upon data using the networking potential of the micro-computer. From my own experience I can say that the computer enhances my work because it can function as a word-processor and a database. There is already an unofficial (or 'invisible', as Vallée would have it) network largely based on correspondence with colleagues, and it is here that the computer, with its promise of the greater mobility of data, will have the most far-reaching and exciting revolution.

Instead of a massive centralized database, we could have many smaller ones as each individual pursued his own interests. Where two or more Forteans share an interest they simply duplicate that part of each others' databases, or the whole if needed. This could be accomplished in three ways: by sending data over the telephone (via a modem); by communicating through an 'electronic mail' network; or, simplest of all, by swapping 'floppy disks'. A Fortean network based on these facilities could include the following properties:

• It could be truely decentralised, having no fixed heirarchy or geographical location.

• It could allow unlimited scope for individual action and development. Autonomy would be preserved; and so would the sense of being a part of a movement. You're never alone with a network — unless you want to be.

• Individual projects and equipment would be individually funded and administered, eliminating the need for conventional financial or administratrative structure.

• The network would encourage trading in data and services, and hopefully foster a commonwealth of data.

• The network will always function well no matter how large or small.

• The more members, the more subject areas can be processed and put on-line. Quite naturally we'd begin with our own main interests, because these are the areas in which we have the most data and expertise.

• Members can specialize or generalize, as suits their interests, and still be a valuable part of the network.

• By ensuring a colleague has a duplicate of your database, you insure against the loss of data through accident, malfunctions, damage or theft etc.

- Databases can be quickly and easily updated by regular exchanges of disks, etc.
- Special messages, urgent requests and queries, and 'new case' alerts can be sent 'instantly' via an established electronic mail network.

There are drawbacks, of course. Swapping disks will only work if the computers share the same operating language; if your system runs CP/M or MSDOS (the two main contenders) you will have access to the widest variety of programmes and services. There are also differences between older 8 bit and the newer 16 bit machines, but I'm not sure yet how that affects speaking to one another. The latest computers have several central processors, allowing a choice between several operating systems, which should ease data transfer problems considerably. If all fails, programmes can be written to translate data from one system to another.

Data transfer, by modem or disk, could be obstructed further unless you share the same disk-formatting (how the data is put onto the magnetic disks) and the same file-design. Disk-formatting depends on your choice of hardware, so we need some kind of awareness of what each of us has or wishes to buy; and this goes for the operating system point too.

File design is something I've been working at sporadically for about four years. I hope I don't seem too arrogant if I say that a database design which can cope with the quantity and different types of data, and the complexities of cross-referencing, and compiling chronological or bibliographical lists, or statistical analyses, etc, as required by Forteans, should cope very well with specialist needs of ufology, parapsychology, or any other subgroup. If we set out from the beginning to acquire or develop systems which can support a network then there is no reason why the network should be restricted to Forteans – ufologists, folklorists, psi hunters, monster trackers, mysteriographers, anyone specializing in any aspect of the paranormal could function equally well.

That's what I'm aiming for, anyway, and a fuller exposition on the *Fortean Times* database will be published sometime next year (hopefully). One of the subproblems is to generate a grand index of every conceivable Fortean topic as a step towards a common subject coding system. Because Fortean research is open-ended the work of in-putting data will take many lifetimes. We are hoping that our database design will be powerful and flexible enough to become a standard through common usage, and to be in use for a long time to come.

Another obvious difficulty is the simple fact that most Fortean researchers can't afford a computer – or think they can't. Computer prices are stabilizing; they are about as far

down as they'll go, but the trend is to give you more for your money. The choice of hardware and software is formidable and deserves a special article, but hopefully the experience of luckier Forteans can be gathered to guide those about to buy a system. The amount of storage memory is also critical; it is coming down in cost all the time, and it pays to buy as much as you can afford. Do not overlook the possibility of second-hand or even ex-demonstration systems (as is my own).

But for most Forteans afflicted with that common Fortean complaint, poverty, a computer is simply out of the question; yet that needn't exclude them from the network. The great advantage of a standardized data format is that standard forms could be printed so that anyone anywhere would be able to put data onto a written record in the right codes and order. The forms could then be sent to anyone with a Fortean Database in-putting programme. An ideal situation would be for smaller networks, specializing in an area which interests them, to organize themselves around one or more computer-users. Forms and manuals, including guidelines to coding etc, could be made available to anyone wishing to join the network, with or without a computer.

Another subject for study and agreement would be the rights of the contributors to the data network; the problems of copyrighting work, and protection against piracy and unauthorized use or exploitation of another's work; and the commercial exploitation of publishable work arising out of database studies. These I leave to future consideration.

Each local database has the property of being a super-index to all the books, periodicals, clippings and case material in that part of the network. And if we can swap or compile these indexes we would have catalogues – perhaps even a grand union catalogue – to each other's libraries, which would be like having a central library without any of its physical problems. Naturally no-one is going to lend their valuable books to just anyone. Such decisions are best left to individual relationships anyway, and yet I hope for a high level of mutual help. After all, others might feel less inclined to help you if you are crabby or secretive about your own data.

I feel there will always be a need to store physical documents, and that involves special problems of its own. Personally, I see no need to store whole documents in the computer memory; it is wasteful of valuable time and expensive memory, and unnecessary if only the relevant details are needed in the electronic files. Because there will always be a need to consult the documents, or facsimilies of them, my own plan for FT's collection is to preserve them on microfilm or microfiche and incorporate the frame addresses into the database. The space saving is staggering, and the material better preserved. For access I'd use a printer/reader so that I can obtain a good xerox copy of the frame on view at the press of a button. Even microfilm could be exchanged between parts of the network, to duplicate holdings for completeness or safety's sake.

At this point I'll go back on what I said earlier with the realization that, perhaps after all, some kind of federation or association of the network members might be necessary, if only to act as a central clearinghouse for information to would-be members of the network. I can't make up my mind whether this should be formally constituted or not. There does seem to be a case for protection offered by a formal constitution, but only if it can be done with the minimum of fuss, expense and admin. Such a set-up could be the guardian of the grand amalgamated database.

One colleague, fearful of the dehumanizing spectre of 'automation', wrote to me: "The enjoyment of being a Fortean is in actually doing the research, chasing up elusive bits of data, contacting others who might be able to help. All this is lost if all one needs to do is press a button. Wouldn't that be depriving Fortean research of its guts?" To which I must respond with a resounding "No!" The heart of Fortean research did not die with the invention of the card index, the telephone and the xerox machine, because these, and other inventions, have made some aspects of our work easier. So it is with the computer which is simply a tool which allows us to store, retrieve and manipulate some kinds of data more quickly and in greater volume and detail. If you enjoyed chasing data before, working

with it, and trading data with colleagues, then a computer should help do it more efficiently. And if it can take some of the tedium out of our routine as well, it will surely increase our fun!

If there is any merit in these ideas, what is the next step? Peter Christie (see his article on p69.) has offered to begin a register of who is collecting data on what, and what sources they've checked out. The FT database project is underway and will proceed roughly as outlined, forming, I hope, a stimulus, if not a nucleus, to the network. These are good starts, but not enough. We need someone to hold a register of who has what computer system. We also need a simple newsletter — to be edited by someone other than myself, please — to keep interested parties informed of developments. But more urgently, I'd like to hear *your* views on these matters.

●

Bob Rickard

NOTES

- 1 "In Continuity it is impossible to distinguish phenomena at their merging-points, so we look for them at their extremes." *(Books* p 28.)
- 2 Founded in 1966. INFO: Box 367, Arlington, VA 22210, USA.
- 3 Founded in 1968, although a foundation of sorts existed from 1966. SITU: Box 265, Little Silver, NJ 07739, USA.
- 4 The Association for the Scientific Study of Anomalous Phenomena. Enquiries to Caroline Wise, ASSAP Membership Secretary, 56 Telemann Sq, Kidbroke, London SE3. Donations of books and publications are welcome for the ASSAP Library, c/o Purley Library, Banstead Rd, Purley, Surrey CR2 3YH.

Contributors in This Issue.

* **Janet & Colin Bord** venture into the Fortean landscape from their home in the mountains of mid-Wales. They have, jointly and severally, had long associations with ufology, earth mysteries, Forteana, and folklore, and their many books include *Mysterious Britain; The Secret Country; Earth Rites; Alien Animals;* and *The Bigfoot Casebook.* Janet has a regular book column in *Fortean Times.*

* **Peter Christie** is a teacher and genealogist who lives in Devon. He contributes extracts from *The Gentleman's Magazine* to *Fortean Times,* and has organized a local course in Fortean subjects.

* **Jerome Clark** is an associate editor of *Fate Magazine,* Highland Park, Illinois. He has contributed articles to most leading Fortean and ufological journals, and has co-authored three books, *The Unidentified* and *Creatures of the Outer Edge* with Loren Coleman,

and *Earth's Secret Inhabitants* with D. Scott Rogo.

* **Loren Coleman** somehow finds time from his professional work as a social counsellor to actively follow all his Fortean pursuits. He has contributed articles on his speciality, the mystery animals of North America, to all the leading Fortean journals, and is a regular columnist in *Fortean Times.* He co-authored *The Unidentified* and *Creatures from the Outer Edge* with Jerome Clark, and his first solo book, *Mysterious America,* has just been published.

* **Peter Costello** is a professional writer, living in Dublin, whose biographical writing ranges from James Joyce, Jules Verne and Bram Stoker to the Piltdown hoax. In Fortean circles he is chiefly known for his books, *In Search of Lake Monsters,* and *The Magic Zoo.*

* **Hunt Emerson** came into our lives with his 'Large Cow Comix', in 1973, for a Birmingham alternative paper. His headings first appeared in FT8 (Feb 1975) and have been making our eyeballs go funny ever since. Hunt's distinctive drawings appear in a wide variety of publications, and even animated for a TV ad. A special collection of some of his strips has recently been published as *The Big Book of Everything*, by Knockabout Comics.

* **Hilary Evans** is a frequent contributor of thought-provoking items to ufological and Fortean journals. In 1981, he was one of the founders of ASSAP (the Association for the Scientific Study of Anomalous Phenomena). His books include *Intrusions*, and *UFOs: The Greatest Mystery*. He runs the Mary Evans Picture Library with his eponymous wife.

* **David R. Fideler** used to run an outfit called Michigan Anomaly Research, in the late 1970s, as an outlet for his Fortean and ufological researches. Then he developed an interest in archetypal psychology and neo-Platonic philosophy, which he now pursues at the University of Pennsylvania, in Philadelphia.

* **Dr Bernard Heuvelmans** is Europe's most famous cryptozoologist and the acknowledged 'father' of the subject. A Belgian, he lives in France, where he founded the Centre de Cryptozoologists, at Verlhiac. The greater part of his work is still untranslated from the French, but for his two classics, *In the Wake of the Sea-serpents*, and *On the Trail of Unknown Animals*. In 1981 the newly formed International Society of Cryptozoology elected him their first President.

* **Michael A. Hoffman III** lives in New York State, and has a regular column in *Fortean Times* on the mystical and symbolic mysteries of American life.

* **John A. Keel** has been a professional writer since the mid-1940s, and a pioneer of some of the current hypotheses in Fortean, ufological and cryptozoological thinking. Of his twelve books, these ideas are expressed in *Jadoo; UFOs; Operation Trojan Horse; Strange Creatures from Time and Space; Our Haunted Planet; The Mothman Prophecies*; and *The Eighth Tower*.

* **John Michell** is widely known for *The View Over Atlantis* (recently revised), and *The City of Revelation*; two books which, more than any others, stimulated the current worldwide revival of interest in megalithic circles, leys and terrestial zodiacs and their interpretation as relics of ancient science. His Fortean books include *Simulacra*, and with Bob Rickard, *Phenomena* and *Living Wonders*.

* **Steve Moore** is an editor of *Fortean Times* with a watching brief on oriental Forteana. He writes comic strips and children's annuals and researches into Chinese divination; not a bad balance!

* **Nigel Pennick** studies algae in Cambridge, and is a prolific writer/researcher and publisher on geomancy, earth mysteries, paganism and symbolism. He is founder of the Institute of Geomantic Research; editor of the anarchist journal *Walrus*; and author of *Hitler's Secret Sciences; The Subterranean Kingdom; The Ancient Science of Geomancy*; and *Sacred Geometry*.

* **Dr Michael A. Persinger** is associate professor of psychology, and head of the Environmental Psycho-physiology Laboratory, at Laurentian University, Sudbury, Ontario. His "piezo-electric" or tectonic strain hypothesis of the origin of some UFOs was first proposed in his book *Space-Time Transients and Unusual Events* with Gyslaine Lafreniere. He is also author of *ELF and VLF Electromagnetic Field Effects*, and *The Weather Matrix and Human Events*. An interview with Dr Persinger will appear in the next issue of FT (FT42).

* **Pokkettz** lives in a Birmingham suburb (old Brummy joke) and modestly describes himself as "an unremarkable artisan". His embellishments have appeared in books and publications, like *Radio Times*.

* **Jenny Randles** is one of Britain's leading ufologists. She is a prolific writer/investigator/lecturer whose opinions, researches and letters have appeared in most British UFO publications. She was instrumental in founding both the Northern UFO Network (NUFON), editing its journal, and the UFO Investigator's Network (UFOIN) a more national structure. She also serves as director of investigations for both BUFORA and ASSAP (Association for the Scientific Study of Anomalous Phenomena). Among her published books are *UFOs: A British Viewpoint* with Peter Warrington, *Alien Contact*, and her latest *UFO Reality*.

* **Bob Rickard** is editor of *Fortean Times*. He has lots of ideas and if he could cut down on the tea-drinking and staring into space he just might get something moving. He has co-authored *Phenomena* and *Living Wonders* with John Michell, and *Photographs of the Unknown* with Richard Kelly.

* **Leslie Shepard** is another Fortean denizen of Dublin. He has advised several American imprints on reprinting classics of Fortean interest, most notably Rupert Gould's books for University Books. His largest project must be the *Encyclopedia of Occultism and Parapsychology*, for Gale Research, with over 5000 entries.

* **Anthony 'Doc' Shiels** is FT's resident shaman. Artist, writer, busker, playwrite, conjuror (by profession and by belief), and knowledgeable Fortean, he lives in Cornwall and periodically goes wandering in the ancient lands of southern Ireland, sharing "the crack" with its uncanny denizens. Doc has seen monsters. He is author of *Entertaining with ESP*, and has a regular column in *Fortean Times*.

* **Dr Ron Westrum** is an assistant professor of sociology at Eastern Michigan University in Ypsilanti, Michigan, where he specializes in the study of social reaction to unusual events and the sociology of science, and is associate editor of *Zetetic Scholar*.

* **Mr X** lives in Kingston, Ontario, and devotes all his time and resources to his Fortean work. He has contributed articles on his researches into Fort's topics to the leading Fortean journals, and is engaged in at least two other long-term studies: analysis of North American lake and sea monster sightings, and a protracted struggle with the Canadian authorities for the release of UFO-related material.

"I didn't *mean* to let my subscription lapse, honest!"

New FT Address. Effective Immediately.
96 Mansfield Rd, London NW3 2HX

F I N I S.